TD/B/1202

UNITED NATIONS CONFERENCE ON TRADE AND DEVELOPMENT

Geneva

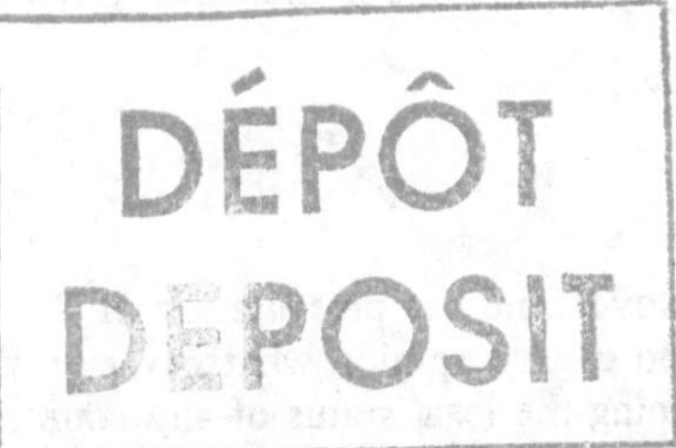

The least developed countries 1988 Report

Prepared by the UNCTAD secretariat

UNITED NATIONS

New York, 1989

NOTE

Symbols of United Nations documents are composed of capital letters combined with figures. Mention of such a symbol indicates a reference to a United Nations document.

*
* *

The designations employed and the presentation of the material in this publication do not imply the expression of any opinion whatsoever on the part of the Secretariat of the United Nations concerning the legal status of any country, territory, city or area, or of its authorities, or concerning the delimitation of its frontiers or boundaries.

*
* *

TD/B/1202

UNITED NATIONS PUBLICATION

Sales No. E.89.II.D.3

ISBN 92-1-112268-6
ISSN 0257-7550

06000P

Contents

Chapter II

INTERNATIONAL SUPPORT

Part Two

DEVELOPMENT OF THE ECONOMIES OF INDIVIDUAL LEAST DEVELOPED COUNTRIES

Annex

BASIC DATA ON THE LEAST DEVELOPED COUNTRIES

ABBREVIATIONS

FCDs	foreign currency deposits
FDI	foreign direct investment
MVA	manufacturing value added
MYRAs	multi-year rescheduling agreements
PFPs	policy framework papers
PSEs	public sector enterprises
UNDRO	Office of the United Nations Disaster Relief Co-ordinator
UNEP	United Nations Environment Programme
WMO	World Meteorological Organization

EXPLANATORY NOTES

The term "dollars" ($) refers to United States dollars unless otherwise stated. The term "billion" signifies 1,000 million.

Annual rates of growth and change refer to compound rates. Exports are valued f.o.b. and imports c.i.f. unless otherwise specified.

Use of a hyphen (-) between dates representing years, e.g. 1970-1979, signifies the full period involved, including the initial and final years.

An oblique stroke (/) between two years, e.g. 1980/81 signifies a fiscal or crop year.

The abbreviation LDC (or LDCs) refers, throughout this report, to a country (or countries) included in the United Nations list of least developed countries.

National currencies have been converted into United States dollars at the rates published by the IMF in *International Financial Statistics.* For flow figures (e.g. foreign trade, budgetary receipts and expenditures, debt service and aid statistics) the *average* exchange rate for the corresponding period was chosen. For stock figures (e.g. outstanding debt and exchange reserves) the exchange rate for the corresponding date was chosen.

In the tables:

Two dots (..) indicate that the data are not available, or are not separately reported.

One dot (.) indicates that the data are not applicable.

A dash (-) indicates that the amount is nil or negligible.

A plus (+) before a figure indicates an increase; a minus sign (-) before a figure indicates a decrease. Details and percentages do not necessarily add up to totals, because of rounding.

FOREWORD

(i) The group of least developed countries (LDCs), which currently comprises 41 countries[1] with a combined population of 380 million, are the weakest partners in the international community. They are particularly handicapped and ill-equipped to develop their domestic economies and to ensure adequate living standards for their population. Their average GDP per capita is slightly higher than $200, which is only about 2 per cent of that of the developed market-economy countries. Most of them suffer from one or more important geographical or climatic handicaps, such as land-lockedness (15 countries), remote insularity (8), drought and desertification (22) and high exposure to disasters such as cyclones, floods and earthquakes. Their economic and social development thus represents a major challenge for these countries as well as for their development partners.

(ii) To respond to this challenge, the international community unanimously adopted in 1981 the Substantial New Programme of Action for the 1980s for the Least Developed Countries (SNPA). The SNPA provides for action to be taken by the least developed countries at the national level, as well as for measures of international support. The SNPA also contains provisions for specific follow-up action at the country, regional and global levels.

(iii) UNCTAD, the institution in which consideration of the special problems of the LDCs started, is entrusted by the SNPA with the focal role of monitoring its implementation at the global level. UNCTAD's Intergovernmental Group on the Least Developed Countries met at a high level in 1985 to carry out the Mid-term Global Review of the SNPA and agreed on a set of conclusions and recommendations to speed up the implementation of the SNPA. Subsequently, the problems of the least developed countries constituted one of the four substantive items on the agenda for the seventh session of UNCTAD, which took place in Geneva in July 1987. The Conference adopted a Final Act which stresses the need for the full and expeditious implementation of the SNPA and of recommendations of the Mid-term Review, and sets out measures to attain this objective. The General Assembly of the United Nations, at its forty-second session in 1987, has decided to convene a Second United Nations Conference on the Least Developed Countries in September 1990, whose mandate is to review progress at the country level as well as in international support measures and to consider, formulate and adopt appropriate policies and measures for accelerating LDCs' development process in the 1990s.

(iv) As a contribution to the global monitoring exercise, the UNCTAD secretariat prepares annual reports on the least developed countries. The present report, which is the fifth in the series, reviews recent socio-economic developments in the least developed countries and progress in the implementation of support measures in the context of the present international economic environment, and identifies major challenges for the years ahead. The report also contains the Basic Data on the Least Developed Countries, which the UNCTAD secretariat has prepared periodically for several years.

(v) The UNCTAD secretariat would like to take this opportunity to express its appreciation to the Governments members of UNCTAD and to international organizations which, by replying to its questionnaire on the implementation of the SNPA, provided useful inputs to this report. It would also like to thank the organizations of the United Nations system for their co-operation, which has greatly facilitated the preparation of this volume.

1 The United Nations General Assembly at its forty-third session in December 1988 approved the inclusion of a 42nd country, Mozambique, which will be covered in the next issue of the Least Developed Countries Report.

FOREWORD

SURVEY OF THE QUALITY AND USEFULNESS OF UNCTAD PUBLICATIONS AND OF THEIR END-USERS

The UNCTAD secretariat, in the context of its programme evaluation activities and in response to intergovernmental requests, is seeking the opinions of end-users in order to have basic data for assessing the quality, usefulness and effectiveness of *inter alia* its research reports and publications. As the success of such an exercise is critically dependent on an adequate rate of response we should appreciate it if you would take time to answer the questions below and submit any other comments that you may have concerning the current document.

1. Title or symbol number of document ....

2. When did you receive the document? ....

3. How did you receive the document? *(tick one or more boxes)*

Through Permanent Mission to United Nations ( )
From ministry or government office ( )
Directly from UNCTAD secretariat ( )
By participating in an UN/UNCTAD intergovernmental meeting ( )
By participating in an UN/UNCTAD sponsored training course or seminar ( )
From UN bookshop ( )
From university libraries ( )
Own request ( )
UNCTAD initiative ( )
Other (please specify) ....
....
....

4. For what main purposes do you use the document? *(tick one or more boxes)*

Policy formulation ( )
Analysis and research ( )
Legislation ( )
Background information ( )
Education and training ( )
Management ( )
Other (please specify) ....
....

5. How do you rate the document as regards:

Its usefulness to your work *(tick one box)*

Extremely useful ( ); Very useful ( ); Useful ( ); Marginally useful ( ); Not at all ( ).

Its quality, in terms of the following aspects *(tick one box in each case)*:

	Outstanding	*Excellent*	*Good*	*Adequate*	*Poor*
Presentation and readability	( )	( )	( )	( )	( )
Originality of ideas	( )	( )	( )	( )	( )
Wealth of information	( )	( )	( )	( )	( )
Up-to-date information	( )	( )	( )	( )	( )
Technical accuracy	( )	( )	( )	( )	( )
Quality of analysis, including objectivity	( )	( )	( )	( )	( )
Validity of conclusions	( )	( )	( )	( )	( )
Clarity of recommendations	( )	( )	( )	( )	( )
Comprehensiveness of coverage	( )	( )	( )	( )	( )

6. Other observations *(if any)* ....

....

....

....

Finally, we would appreciate it if you could provide the following information about yourself:

Name ....Occupation/Functional title ....

Address ....

Your answers are for internal use and will be kept confidential. Thank you for your co-operation.

Please forward the questionnaire to : PROGRAMME CO-ORDINATION AND EVALUATION UNIT
EXECUTIVE DIRECTION AND MANAGEMENT
UNITED NATIONS CONFERENCE ON TRADE AND DEVELOPMENT
PALAIS DES NATIONS – CH-1211 GENEVA 10

Part One

TRENDS AND CHALLENGES

INTRODUCTION

Real GDP growth in the least developed countries reached 4.4 per cent in 1986 and provisional estimates for 1987 give a relatively favourable growth rate of 3.8 per cent. While this is in considerable contrast to the stagnant and, for some countries, often negative growth performance in the early 1980s, such rates are not high enough to make good the losses suffered earlier in the decade. Growth performance in the 1980s, at 2.2 per cent per year for 1980-1986, is still much lower than that achieved in the 1970s by the LDCs (an average of 3.6 per cent). For countries with populations growing at around 2.6 per cent, these rates are still too low. Furthermore, only a minority of 12 of the 41 LDCs registered positive per capita GDP growth over this period: this group includes consistently good performers such as Botswana (8.3 per cent), the Maldives (6.6 per cent) and the biggest LDC, Bangladesh (1.5 per cent). Nor should the slightly improved growth performance of the last two years be any cause for complacency. Seventeen LDCs in 1986 had rates of GDP growth below population growth and seven still recorded negative GDP growth (see annex tables 1 and 2).

The growth performance, which is clearly patchy and insufficient to redress past losses, also shows worrying signs of not being sustained. For instance, natural disasters as well as adverse economic trends in 1988 indicate that the recovery which was already showing signs of flagging in 1987 may not be sustained in 1988 despite national efforts and the emergence of stronger and more innovative international support measures. This phenomenon reflects once again the extreme vulnerablity of LDCs, the fragility of their economic recovery, and, on the human scale, how close they remain in terms of per capita income to levels which barely qualify as survival levels.

Nevertheless, the mere fact that such growth performance, albeit modest, has taken place in the midst of adverse external conditions (depressed commodity markets, insufficient aid flows, the collapse of commercial bank lending to developing countries, protectionist pressures), and against a background of severe natural disasters in many LDCs, constitutes in itself a clear demonstration of the capacity of these countries to overcome their secular handicaps, provided that a supportive response from the entire international community be accorded to them.

Agriculture is still by far the dominant production sector in the LDCs and its mediocre performance is a determining factor in their economic growth. Compared with the 1970s the average annual growth rate in this sector has improved to 2.3 per cent over 1980-1985 (it was 2.1 per cent in the 1970s). While these slightly improved rates may begin to reflect the increased attention paid to agricultural develoment in LDCs, and while the agricultural growth rate is marginally higher (by one tenth of one percentage point) than the GDP growth rates to which it is closely correlated, a rate of growth in agriculture of 2.3 per cent is still not enough to keep up with population growth.

Industry and manufacturing are a very small sector for LDCs, which is driven by the rest of the economy and by external demand conditions rather than being a driving force itself. Its rate of growth reflects that of the LDC economies overall (2.2 per cent over 1980-1985). Four of the six fast-growing LDCs in recent years have recorded high growth in the manufacturing sector. Conversely, some countries which have recorded poor or even declining agricultural performance actually belong to the group of fast growers overall - Botswana, Cape Verde and the Maldives are examples. These are also countries where investment has been expanding, contrary to the experience of LDCs as a whole (where investment fell by 2.4 per cent per annum over the period 1980-1985). Some of their strong growth is now coming from the services sector.

In addition to a few fast-growing small countries, Bangladesh has managed to expand investment and import volume in the 1980s, whereas for LDCs as a whole import cutbacks in the 1980s averaged 1 per cent per annum by volume and 3.5 per cent by value. This is a matter of concern: the capacity to import is crucial to sustaining economic growth. If growth performance of LDCs in the rest of the 1980s remains disappointing, it will have been in no small measure the result of constrained import capacity, often during the adjustment phase. Import levels are not determined solely by countries' merchandise export performance, as the references to the expanding services sector, even as export substitutes, show; they also depend fundamentally on the size of outgoings on foreign debt service and the support given to the balance of payments by donors and other external agents.

All such factors are considered in the rest of the survey highlighting the most notable recent national efforts and international support measures of the LDC group, of which a majority of countries are undergoing a formal programme of adjustment, while others are actively engaged in policy reforms of a similar nature. The ultimate aim of such reforms is to restore the conditions under which growth and economic and social development can flourish. LDCs however, being distinctly disadvantaged, are not in a good position to sacrifice growth in the short term in order to accomodate their economies to shocks largely determined by external conditions. Thus, although the growth record of LDCs in recent years is to a great extent country-specific, with some improvement in the overall performance, the common setbacks to growth identified throughout the decade indicate a range of requirements for a more growth-supportive framework specifically designed for the LDCs in the future.

Chapter I

NATIONAL EFFORTS

Throughout the 1980s, the LDCs have faced the formidable challenge both of carrying out the structural transformation of their domestic economies, consonant with the objectives of the SNPA, and of dealing with a mounting debt burden and growing payments difficulties. These objectives have been pursued against a background of shrinking foreign-exchange receipts due to a slackening world demand, depressed commodity markets, growing protectionist pressures, insufficient expansion of concessional flows, and the virtual collapse of commercial bank lending to developing countries. Major policy reforms have been launched in LDCs since the late 1970s and early 1980s with a view to meeting these two objectives. The reforms relate essentially to improving the efficiency of resource use and allocation, enhancing the contribution to GDP of the various sectors, strengthening the physical infrastructure, and improving institutional capabilities in the field of development planning and policy.

A. Improving the efficiency of resource use and allocation

Given the severe resource constraints under which LDCs operate and the need to overcome persistent external disequilibrium, the mobilization and efficient use of available resources constitutes a priority policy objective for these countries. The manner in which this objective has been pursued naturally varies among the LDCs according to individual characteristics and policy perceptions. The mix of policy reforms covers external sector adjustments, demand-management measures, mobilization of domestic savings and of human resources, promoting the role of the private sector, and improving the efficiency of public enterprises. A number of LDCs have carried out reforms in this regard in the context of adjustment programmes agreed upon with IMF, while other LDCs have pressed ahead with programmes of a similar nature but outside the framework of formal IMF agreements.

During the period running from mid-1981 to end 1987, 23 LDCs[2] have formulated and implemented adjustment programmes negotiated with IMF and, for that purpose, have received support through stand-by arrangements (typically of 12-24 months' duration) and/or the recently established Structural Adjustment Facility of IMF (see chapter II. A). Twelve of them have done so for more or less consecutive periods.[3] Such programmes have been increasingly supported by complementary long-term credits granted by the World Bank[4] and by regional development banks. The adjustment

2 Twenty-one LDCs have launched adjustment programmes supported by stand-by and/or extended arrangements entered into with IMF: Bangladesh, Burma, Burundi, Central African Republic, Ethiopia, Equatorial Guinea, Gambia, Guinea, Haiti, Malawi, Mali, Mauritania, Nepal, Niger, Samoa, Sierra Leone, Somalia, Sudan, Togo, Uganda, and the United Republic of Tanzania. Of these, 13 have also secured credits from the Structural Adjustment Facility of IMF. In addition, two LDCs (Chad and Guinea-Bissau) have secured credits from the latter Facility but have not entered into stand-by arrangements during the period in question.

3 Bangladesh, Central African Republic, Gambia, Haiti, Malawi, Mali, Niger, Sierra Leone, Somalia, Sudan, Togo and Uganda.

4 Sixteen of the 23 LDCs have received World Bank loans and credits. In addition, Sao Tome and Principe, while still negotiating a credit from IMF, embarked in June 1987 on a structural adjustment programme supported by World Bank credits (see section B.1).

packages typically contain measures which can be broadly classified into three categories: (i) measures directly aimed at improving the current account balance, in particular greater exchange-rate flexibility (currency depreciation); (ii) demand-management measures geared towards ensuring fiscal and monetary discipline; (iii) supply-oriented measures aimed at developing the productive base, which relate principally to improving the efficiency of public enterprises, expanding the role of the private sector in the domestic economy, and strengthening the directly productive sectors, especially agriculture, through price incentives (see table 1). The effectiveness of the programme is judged against performance criteria adopted by IMF, which take into account particularly the reductions achieved in the current-account and in the fiscal deficits as well as the containing of domestic inflation rates. LDCs which have pursued programmes of a similar nature but outside the IMF framework include Burkina Faso, Djibouti, Rwanda and Yemen.

1. *External sector policies*

Exchange rate devaluation has been carried out in LDCs as a means both of enhancing the international competitiveness of locally produced goods and of encouraging import substitution. Exchange rate devaluation has indeed been one of the key elements, if not a precondition, of the adjustment programmes negotiated with IMF. A persistent current-account deficit, it has been felt, constitutes in itself a symptom of overvaluation of the national currency, inasmuch as such overvaluation entails low local prices for both exportable and imported goods and, therefore, tends to both discourage the local production of such goods and encourage the demand for imported goods. Moreover, overvaluation is normally sustained by means of a multiple exchange rate system and/or of quantitative restrictions, which bring about distortions of the national price structure and thus cause a misallocation of national resources. It is with a view to overcoming these shortcomings that exchange rate devaluation has been carried out and that quantitative restrictions tend to be replaced by customs duties. Concomitantly, the marketing of exportable commodities has been liberalized so as to allow local producers to respond more directly to the stimulus of world market signals.

The number of LDCs whose currency depreciated in real terms with respect to the United States dollar increased from two in the period 1970-1975 to 31 in 1980-1985. Of these LDCs, nine are members of the CFA zone (Benin, Burkina Faso, Central African Republic, Chad, Comoros, Equatorial Guinea, Mali, Niger and Togo): the CFA franc is pegged to the French franc (one CFA franc = 0.02 French francs) and, therefore, has followed the same variations *vis-à-vis* other major currencies as the latter. Some of the devaluations recently carried out have been of a sweeping nature: Sierra Leone (floating of the Leone since 1986, entailing an 85 per cent depreciation); Sudan (44 per cent in 1987); the United Republic of Tanzania (68 per cent in 1986); Guinea-Bissau (60 per cent in 1987); the Gambia (53 per cent in 1986); and Sao Tome and Principe (55 per cent in 1987). In Guinea, the replacement of the Syli by the Guinean franc, undertaken in January 1986, was tantamount to a drastic 94 per cent devaluation. An auction system for the allocation of foreign exchange has been established in Guinea, Nepal, Sao Tome and Principe, Somalia and Uganda, which determines the foreign-exchange rate according to supply and demand conditions reigning in the market for foreign exchange at particular times.

To further promote exports, producer prices of major exported commodities have been raised or allowed to rise in a large majority of these countries; export taxes and duties have been reduced (Bangladesh, Haiti, Mali, United Republic of Tanzania), and rebates introduced (Nepal); and export monopolies eliminated (Guinea-Bissau) or limited to fewer goods (Sao Tome and Principe, to six goods only). In United Republic of Tanzania, exporters are allowed to retain 50 per cent of their foreign-exchange earnings, to be used for the importation of equipment and consumption goods they need.

As regards imports, measures have been taken in a number of LDCs with a view to eliminating distortions in the pricing of imported goods and thereby encouraging an efficient allocation of resources in import-competing activities. Such measures include: growing recourse to the secondary foreign-exchange market (as compared to the official exchange-rate market) to finance foreign trade transactions (Bangladesh); establishment of an auction system for the allocation of foreign exchange (see above); unification of multiple exchange rates (Guinea, Sudan); elimination or liberalization of quantitative restrictions or of import licenses (Bangladesh, Burundi, Guinea, Malawi, Nepal, Sao Tome and Principe); and simplification and rationalization of the import tariff structure (Bangladesh, Guinea, Guinea-Bissau, Niger, Sao Tome and Principe). Recourse has also been made to counter-trade agreements by, *inter alia*, Burma and Sudan, as a means of

Table 1

MAIN MEASURES TAKEN IN THE CONTEXT OF IMF-SUPPORTED ADJUSTMENT PROGRAMMES IN SELECTED LDCs [a]

Country	*Depreciation and/or exchange rate flexibility*	*Reducing govt. expen-diture*	*Improving tax collection /new revenue*	*Tightening monetary and credit policies*	*Introducing flexible interest rate policy*	*Expanding role of private sector (including privatization of parastatals)*	*Improving efficiency of public enterprises*	*Liberalizing pricing and marketing of goods*	*Stimulating agricultural production*	*Promoting export diversification*
Bangladesh	X	X	X	X	X (implied)	X	X	X		X
Central African Rep.	*b*	X	X (implied)				X		X	
Gambia	X	X	X	X	X	X	X	X	X	X
Haiti		X	X				X	X		X
Malawi	X	X	X	X				X		
Mali	*b*	X	X			X	X	X	X	
Niger	*b*	X	X	X		X	X	X	X (implied)	X (implied)
Sierra Leone	X	X		X	X		X	X	X	
Somalia	X	X		X	X	X	X	X	X	X
Sudan	X	X	X	X				X	X	
Togo	*b*	X	X	X		X	X	X	X	
Uganda	X	X	X		X (implied)		X	X	X	X

Source: IMF press releases and information available in the UNCTAD secretariat.

a LDCs having implemented IMF-supported adjustment programmes over consecutive periods since mid-1981.
b Member of the CFA zone: unilateral devaluation is thus not applicable.

promoting exports and of ensuring automatic financing of imports. The use of unconventional measures such as countertrade and dual exchange rates is illustrative of the awkward position in which many LDCs find themselves in attempting to stimulate their external sector.

2. *Demand-management measures*

Given unsustainable levels of external and fiscal imbalances as well as high rates of inflation, a large number of LDCs have had to implement demand-management measures aimed at reducing public expenditure, increasing public revenue and containing credit and monetary expansion.

(a) Reducing public expenditure.

Measures in this regard have taken the form of:

- *Cuts in public sector personnel and salaries.* In Benin, recruitment in central government offices has been suspended, and compulsory retirement has been instituted for government employees who have served for 25 years or are aged 50. In Chad, personnel in the cotton marketing board was reduced from 2,500 in 1985 to 1,200 in early 1988. In Djibouti, salaries of the public sector were frozen in 1987 for at least a one-year period. In Central African Republic, the civil service staff is being reduced from 25,000 in 1986 to 20,000 by the end of 1988. A decision was announced in Equatorial Guinea in 1987 to halve the 40,000 civil service staff. Guinea reached an agreement with IMF which provides,*inter alia*, for a 30,000 reduction in the civil service (whereas public salaries were increased by 80 per cent on 31 December 1987). In the United Republic of Tanzania, wage increases are being kept below the rate of inflation and the number of civil servants has been reduced. Civil servants with no real functions have been removed from the government pay-roll in Central African Republic, Guinea, Sierra Leone (estimated economy of Le 30 million per year) and Uganda. Similar cuts have been carried out in the Gambia, Guinea-Bissau, Mali, Mauritania, Niger, Togo, and Vanuatu. Financial incentives to leave the public sector are given to public employees in Guinea and Mali. In Gambia, an institution has been created (the Indigenous Business Advisory Services) to assist in the resettlement of dismissed public employees. Alternative employment opportunities are being created in Mauritania by using a fund, jointly managed with donors, from the proceeds of food aid sales.

- *Downward revision of planned expenditures involving in some cases public investment cuts*: Bangladesh, Burundi, Chad, Djibouti (10 per cent reduction of the allocations to all ministries in 1986 and reduction of public investment in 1987), Guinea-Bissau, Mauritania, Niger, Rwanda, Sao Tome and Principe (public investment programme for 1987 cut by more than half: $19 million compared to a planned $42 million), Uganda and the United Republic of Tanzania.

- *Reduction of public subsidies*: Afghanistan (petrol and diesel oil); Bangladesh (fertilizers); Benin (abolition of housing allowances to government employees, which represented around 10 per cent of government salaries); Chad (freezing of prices paid by the State-owned marketing board to cotton producers); Gambia (traditional exports); Guinea (gradual reduction of subsidies on a wide range of products and services); Guinea-Bissau (fuel, electricity); Kiribati (curtailing subsidies to public enterprises); Sao Tome and Principe (full cost recovery for imported fuels, electricity and water for 1988 onwards); Sierra Leone (rice and petrol); and Sudan (petrol, cement).

- *Restriction of purchases of goods and services by government departments*: Benin (reducing travel allowances and removing service vehicles), Chad (restricting government telephone calls, which had reached an annual average of CFA 400 million francs), Mali, Sao Tome and Principe (government travel cut by half), Uganda (elimination of unauthorized government spending), and Vanuatu.

- *Improving the efficiency of public enterprises and liquidating or privatizing public enterprises running at a loss* (a matter dealt with in sections (e) and (f) below).

(b) Increasing public revenue

Measures to improve tax collection rates have been taken in Bangladesh, Burma, Burundi, Central African Republic, Gambia, Haiti, Malawi, Mali, Mauritania, Nepal (where revenue collection increased by 28.4 per cent in 1986/87), Niger (where action has been taken to incorporate parallel market operations into the business, and hence taxable, sector, while providing for a reduction in value added tax and in other indirect taxes), Rwanda (efforts being made to recover tax arrears), Sierra

Leone (tax revenue increased by 45 per cent in 1987/88, and, as an incentive to increase tax collection, a bonus is being offered to customs officials equivalent to 10 per cent of collected amounts), Sudan, Togo, Uganda and the United Republic of Tanzania. Taxes have been introduced or increased in Bangladesh (on non-essential goods, on installed capacity in the soft drinks sector, on sugar), Chad (petrol and luxury goods), Guinea-Bissau, Rwanda, Sierra Leone (10 per cent export duty and increases in the vehicle registration fees, road licences, aircraft landing and parking, while reducing some import duties as well as income taxes), and the United Republic of Tanzania (import duties and sales taxes on several consumption goods, while income taxes have been reduced). A review of tax and duty exemption schemes was carried out in Sierra Leone and is under way in Guinea-Bissau and Mauritania. To reduce dependence on customs duties, a reform of the tax structure has been undertaken in Bangladesh. Consumption taxes were raised and the share of income tax in total government revenue has increased from 39 per cent in 1979/80 to 45 per cent in 1986/87.

(c) Containing credit and monetary expansion

Measures restricting credit have been taken in Bangladesh, Burundi, Gambia, Nepal (where the rate of growth of the money supply has been reduced from 26.7 per cent in 1985/86 to 11.7 per cent in 1986/87), Lao PDR (where the State bank and its branches are no longer obliged to provide the totality of funds requested by enterprises), Malawi, Niger, Samoa, Sao Tome and Principe (credit to central Government limited to Dobras 400 million, no credit to be granted to loss-making public enterprises), Sierra Leone, Somalia, Sudan, Togo, Uganda and the United Republic of Tanzania. Containing monetary expansion has in turn been pursued in two different manners: by setting a target ceiling to the inflation rate and fixing the expansion of money supply accordingly (Bangladesh, with an inflation rate ceiling of 10 per cent); by fixing the growth of the money supply (Guinea-Bissau, 25 per cent in 1987 *versus* an actual growth rate of 34 per cent in 1986; Sudan, 23 per cent annually). In Lao PDR, 10 per cent of public wages are paid in cash, the remainder being paid in tokens which may be used to purchase commodities in designated State shops, a measure which naturally tends to contain monetary expansion. As regards the nine LDCs which are members of the Franc zone, this mechanism strengthens monetary discipline and thus helps prevent excessive monetary expansion.

3. Mobilization of domestic savings

Thirteen LDCs out of 31 for which data are available experienced negative savings rates during an extended period in the 1980s (see table 2). Yet four LDCs - Botswana, Burma, Malawi and Togo - managed to achieve savings rates above 10 per cent annually during the same period. This indicates that even in LDCs there is scope for mobilizing domestic savings for development, provided that appropriate monetary and fiscal policies are pursued.

The poor savings performance in the majority of the LDCs is due to various factors, some of which may be beyond their control. The extremely low per capita income, averaging $222 in 1986, constitutes the principal constraint. Savings potential, however, has often been diminished by domestic factors which discourage or at least fail to encourage savings efforts. These include persistent pressures to increase recurrent expenditures, lack of institutions and instruments designed to mobilize small and scattered rural savings, and exchange-rate policies which spur capital flight. In addition, the combined effects of the fall in world prices and sluggish demand for many of the LDCs' export products, as well as natural and other disasters which have repeatedly occurred in a number of LDCs, have also impaired their capacity to save.

Some LDCs now appear to be able to cover a large share of their investment needs with domestic savings (see table 2). However, rather than reflecting success in increasing domestic savings, this development often masks the fact that a number of LDCs have seen their investment ratios fall either as the result of a deliberate policy decision[5] or as a consequence of growing or as a consequence of growing external disequilibria leading to sharp cuts in the imports of capital goods and, therefore, to a decrease in investment. The latter phenomenon has been much more common in LDCs, although investment has been sustained at the relatively high level of 20 per cent or more of GDP during 1980-1986 in Comoros, Djibouti, Guinea-Bissau, Mali, Mauritania, Rwanda, United Republic of Tanzania and Togo (see

5 This seems to be the case in Botswana. Rather than continue spending close to one half of the GDP on investment, primarily for new diamond mining facilities as in the 1970s, the country decreased its investment ratio from 41.5 per cent of GDP in 1980 to 20.8 per cent in 1985, but increased financial reserves by 3.5 times during 1980-1986.

Box 1

STABILIZATION AND ADJUSTMENT PROGRAMME: THE SUDANESE EXPERIENCE

In 1978 after experiencing high inflation, balance-of-payments difficulties and a sharp fall in GDP, the Sudanese Government sought the assistance of IMF and World Bank in carrying out a stabilization and adjustment programme. The main elements of this programme were: (i) maintaining GDP growth of 4 per cent per annum; (ii) reducing inflation from 26 per cent to 10 per cent; (iii) reducing the current account deficit; (iv) eliminating external payment arrears and improving debt management; (v) restoring output in the irrigated agriculture sub-sector and restructuring its cost recovery system; (vi) introducing an export action programme; (vii) increasing Government revenues to 18 per cent of GDP; and (viii) preparing a realistic three-year investment programme.

The Government implemented several important policy measures in support of the above targets. These included substantial devaluation, increases in nomimal interest rates, substantial price increases spread over the years of several consumer and intermediate goods (petrol, sugar, wheat, cotton seed, cement) and reform of the price structure in the irrigation subsector in 1981/82.

Despite the above measures, the economic situation continued to deteriorate. In 1981/82 gross domestic product (GDP) in real terms was slightly below the level in 1977/78. Domestic savings showed a sharp deterioration and the external resource gap continued to increase as a per centage of GDP. The budget deficit increased sharply due to poor performance on the taxation front and a continued high level of recurrent expenditure. The private sector also showed high demand for credit due to low real interest rates. The large increase in money supply contributed to high inflation rates which averaged 27 per cent between 1977/78 and 1981/82, in contrast with the target of 10 per cent prescribed under the agreement with IMF.

The substantial divergence between prgramme targets and actual performance led to a deadlock with IMF in 1981. It took almost a year before the new IMF standby agreement of February 1982 was put in place. Later in the year, the Government issued a comprehensive policy document: *Prospects, Programmes and Policies for Economic Development, 1982/83 - 1984/85* (PPPED I). This document formed the basis for discussion at the Consultative Group meeting in Paris in January 1983. The year 1982/83 can thus be considered as the beginning of the second phase of the adustment process. The PPPED was rolled over for a second year in 1983/84, though its third phase (1984/85) was not implemented.

Because of the drought conditions that prevailed in 1982/83 and 1983/84 and worsened in 1984/85, the GDP, instead of showing an increase, registered a continuous decline. The traditional rain-fed agricultural crops were most seriously affected. However, cotton production, grown on irrigated land, doubled during the three-year period, which more than fulfilled the target.

In the field of industry, the textile industry was given substantial assistance in the form of subsidized raw cotton and relief on its past debts. Yet capacity utilization remained as low as 25 per cent. In the sugar industry, except for the Kenana sugar factory - a joint venture - capacity utilization remained low. In the case of private industry, price controls, inadequate availability of foreign exchange and shortage of experienced management and trained labour remained major impediments to stimulating industrial production.

The new programme was successful in reducing private consumption. Government revenues, however, instead of increasing to 16 per cent as proposed in the programme, fell dramatically from 14.4 per cent in 1980/81 to 9.8 per cent in 1984/85. The money supply continued to increase rapidly and inflation remained far in excess of the target of 10 per cent.

The Government used the exchange rate policy to reduce the current account deficit. The Sudanese pound was successively devalued over the years. However, this measure did not achieve the intended objective of increasing exports and reducing imports, the main reasons being: the high inflation rate prevailing in the country; the low world prices of primary commodities; domestic constraints on output; and the increase in domestic demand.

statistical annex). Sao Tome and Principe also had very high investment rates during 1980-1985. However, only in the Comoros, Guinea-Bissau and Rwanda did this result in sizeable growth. In most of the other LDCs mentioned, growth either stagnated or was

Box 1 (continued)

Because of the continuing balance-of-payments pressure, the Government tightened imports in general and banned imports of several goods. As a result, imports showed a sharp decline and the trade deficit of the Sudan was reduced over the years. Yet, the current account balance did not improve because the interest payment liability on external debt increased rapidly from $190 million in 1981/82 to $559 million in 1985/86, while the fresh inflows of external resources were well below such repayment obligations. Consequently the arrears of interest and principal continued to mount, with no solution on the horizon.

In retrospect, the stabilization and adjustment programme of IMF and the World Bank during the period 1978 to 1985 did not succeed in any of its major objectives. The basic premise that devaluation would improve the current account balance was not realized. The Government also found it difficult to restrain expenditure in the face of lower revenue, and the resulting deficit financing contributed to the continued high rate of inflation. This led to a vicious cycle of inflation and devaluation. The balance of payments remained under severe strain and the Government could not pay most of the maturing loans and interest on its past debt. Debt relief was not forthcoming until new international initiatives on African debt were taken in 1988. The capitalization of unpaid repayment obligations and fresh borrowings led to the growing debt liability with the total debt amounting to $9.4 billion by the end of 1986 and an estimated $10.6 billion by October 1988.

In general, the production structure of the country did not undergo any material change, although rain-fed agricultural performance improved with the ending of the drought in 1985. The capacity of the country to finance future development from its own resources has not been enhanced. Just like the Government of Sudan, IMF and the World Bank had expected more positive and more rapid results from the years of adjustment. As further events in 1988 have shown, however, such adjustment policies have to be applied in perhaps the most hostile circumstances of any LDC, in respect of civil conflict and natural disasters. The particular vulnerablility of LDCs on this score argues in favour of much stronger international support measures (see chapter II.A.) to underpin national efforts at recovery.

negative, implying low rates of return, at least as regards the short and medium returns.

(a) Public savings

(i) *Government savings*

Most LDCs have been obliged to strike a balance between the need for coping with fiscal crises and attaining development goals. Although the mobilization of domestic resources through the government has improved in many LDCs, the disequilibrium between recurrent revenues and recurrent expenditures has remained high (see Chart I). Consequently, government savings available for development expenditures have therefore often been small or even negative.

(ii) *Savings from public enterprises*

Numerous public enterprises have been established in the LDCs with a view to accelerating economic growth. However, their contribution to public savings has often been disappointingly modest; and some public enterprises in LDCs are even dependent on government loans and subsidies to meet their losses. As an example, in Bangladesh, the combined rate of return on investment, defined as the ratio of net profit to net worth, of the 10 largest non-financial public enterprises dropped from 11 per cent in FY 1983/84 to a negative figure in FY 1985/86. In Samoa, the five major public enterprises incurred a cumulative total loss of $31.6 million between 1982 and 1986. In Nepal, the aggregate financial flows between the government and the public enterprises were negative for the period FY 1980/81 to FY 1986/87. The total loss incurred from public enterprises during this period was equal to about 11 per cent of Nepal's annual current expenditure on social services. Certainly, not all public enterprises in LDCs are inefficient or inappropriate, nor would the private sector necessarily do better in the national interest.

(b) Private savings

The savings problem in a number of LDCs relates not only to increasing the volume and the rate of private savings (objectives which are obviously constrained by LDCs income levels), but also to ensuring that a rising

Box 2

STABILIZATION AND ADJUSTMENT PROGRAMME: THE BANGLADESH EXPERIENCE

Soon after launching its second five year plan (1980-1985), Bangladesh, the largest of the LDCs, was forced to shift to adjustment for a number of reasons. The economy experienced a sharp decline in export earnings, a massive deterioration in the terms of trade (by over 30% in 1980/81 and 1981/82), and declining flows of external aid. To this was added a series of natural disasters - flood, drought and cyclones. Faced with unsustainable external and budget deficits, Bangladesh began a comprehensive adjustment programme in mid-1983 with the support of the World Bank and the IMF: this was aimed at achieving significant progress towards balance of payments viability by addressing structural and sectoral problems, and at the same time achieving and maintaining a satisfactory rate of economic growth.

The adjustment programme has been more successful in reducing external imbalances, fiscal dificits and monetary expansion than in assuring a transition to sustained growth with maintained provision of social welfare.

On the positive side, by 1986/87 the budget deficit, which had been around 9-11 per cent of GDP in the early 1980s, was down to about 8 per cent, and the current account deficit had fallen similarly from 10-12 per cent to barely 6 per cent of GDP. This was achieved through tough demand management measures, import compression, and the rapid growth of non-traditional exports (notably garments and shrimps) and workers' remittances. The inflation rate was brought down to 10 per cent. GDP growth averaged 4 per cent per year, a rate which, though higher than the rate of population increase, was well below the underlying potential of the economy, and also lower than the rates of growth achieved earlier.

But the adjustment programme which was earlier assumed to be temporary and transitional, and likely to be supported by adequate flows of external capital, jeopardized domestic poverty alleviation and human resource development targets. In addition to the adverse effects on households of the demand management measures, the programme has had untoward misallocation effects such as the rapid deterioration of physical facilities as a result of inadequate maintenance budgets, and declines in the offtake of fertilizer and use of irrigation equipment following price adjustments and the imposition of restrictions on agricultural credit. The Government now recognizes that the programme has imposed severe costs in terms of foregone economic growth and social welfare; the eocnomy's capacity for deflationary policies has been stirred to its limits and the setbacks to human resource development have diminished longer term growth prospects.

One reason for this disappointing result of an otherwise dynamic programme of adjustment was that financial resource inflows (especially concessional) were well below expectations. There is no evidence that the adjustment programme was supported by the transfer of additional resources overall. Moreover, the quality of development assistance deteriorated over the adjustment years. The share of grants in the total aid receipts fell from 53 per cent in 1979/80 to 41 per cent in 1986/87. Consequently, outflows increased substantially: debt service payments increased from \$85 million in 1980/81 to \$232 million in 1986/87 (or to \$384.5 million including short-term) [1], even though Bangladesh did not undertake major external borrowing like some developing countries. Moreover, after the IMF suspended its EFF in 1981, all the IMF balance of payments support has been short-term and at non-concessionary rates, until a three-year Structural Adjustment Facility was signed with the IMF in April 1987.

1 But excluding IMF repurchases (= repayments).

proportion of savings enter into the financial network. Policies aimed at expanding the monetized economy through commercialization, enlargement of the market economy, and establishment of financial intermediaton should thus constitute an integral part of national savings policies.

Although capital markets are still underdeveloped in most LDCs, some of these countries have ventured to make efforts towards the establishment of security markets. The Government of Vanuatu issued bonds worth \$4.6 million in 1987. In Nepal, a Security Exchange

Table 2

SAVINGS AND INVESTMENT RATIOS IN LDCs

(average 1980-1986)

Investment as percentage of GDP / *Savings as percentage of GDP*	*Negative*	*0-5*	*5.1-10*	*10.1-15*	*Above 15*
0-10	Burkina Faso Central African Rep. Chad				
10.1-20	Benin Somalia [a]	Bangladesh Burundi Ethiopia Haiti Mali Sudan	Equatorial Guinea Nepal Niger Rwanda Sierra Leone United Rep. of Tanzania	Burma Guinea Malawi	
Above 20	Cape Verde [a] Comoros Djibouti Gambia Guinea-Bissau Lesotho Samoa Sao Tome and Principe [a] Yemen		Maldives [b] Mauritania	Togo	Botswana Vanuatu [c]

Source: UNCTAD secretariat calculations based on data from the United Nations Statistical Office, the Economic Commission for Africa, the World Bank and other international and national sources.

a Average 1980-1985.
b Average 1981-1985.
c Average 1983-1985.

Center was set up as a first step towards an organized stock exchange. After initial problems, the activities of the Center have gradually expanded, including the listing of shares, sales-purchase operations, secondary and primary market activities. Alone in the primary issue market, the Center raised Rs. 230 million (about $10.5 million) from shares and debenture certificates of four corporations during the first nine month of FY 1987/88, thereby almost doubling the amount of FY 1986/87.

The widespread absence of an "insurance consciousness" is due to the often still intact family solidarity, which would take care of a family member who is in need of assistance. However, compulsory payroll deduction schemes, mainly in the form of a national provident fund, tend to promote the dissemination of the savings habit. These schemes focus primarily on civil servants and other salary-earners in the formal sector. In Niger, a savings-pension fund, established in 1978 for officials of the postal and telecommunications service, has been open since 1987 to all public and private employees.

Private remittances from labour force working abroad represent a considerable portion of national savings in Bangladesh, Cape Verde, Democratic Yemen, Haiti, Lesotho, Sudan, Yemen and in least developed Pacific island countries. Some of these LDCs, such as Sudan and Yemen, have made efforts to integrate private transfers into the economy through the promotion of foreign currency deposits (FCDs). In recent years, however, such remittances have been dropping in several LDCs.

Chart I
Current surplus or deficit as percentage of GDP: Selected LDCS 1982-1987

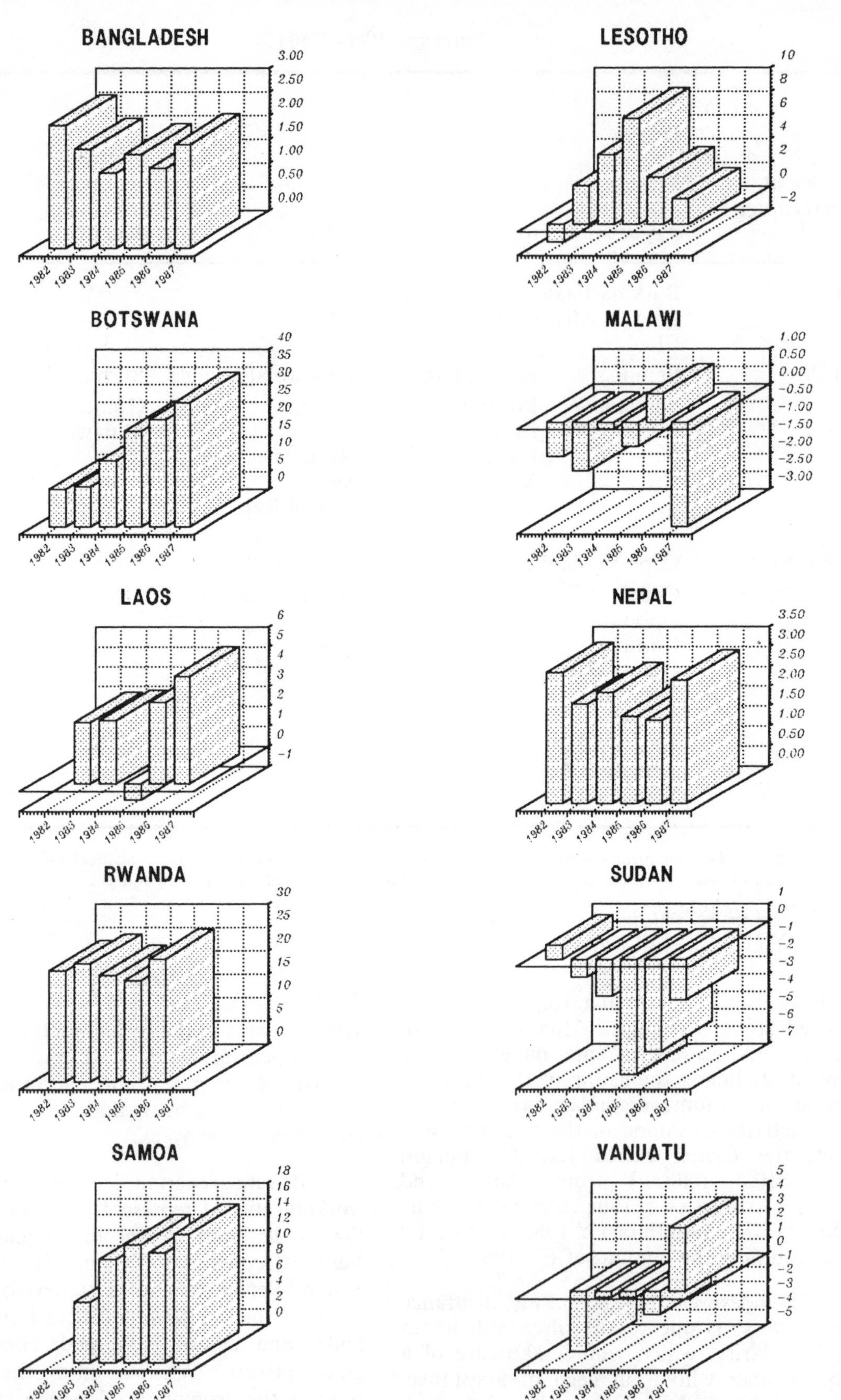

Source: Various national sources.

Box 3

PROBLEMS AND POLICY ISSUES IN MOBILIZING DOMESTIC RESOURCES IN AN ISLAND LEAST DEVELOPED COUNTRY - THE CASE OF MALDIVES

The Maldives constitute an island LDC consisting of over 1200 coral atolls scattered in the Indian Ocean and populated by about 200,000 people. The country faces numerous obstacles in its socio-economic development ranging from the small size of its population and poor resource endowment to high communication costs between the various parts of the country. Despite these handicaps, the Maldives have been able to achieve an average growth rate of 7 per cent per annum during the 1980s. Most of the resources that financed the investment necessary to sustain that growth came from abroad. Domestic resource mobilization has remained low. Private (household) savings were negative in 1981-82, turned positive in 1983, but remain insignificant. Government savings constitute the largest proportion of domestic savings in the Maldives.

Government and private savings, 1980-1986

	1980	*1981*	*1982*	*1983*	*1984*	*1985*	*1986*
Government savings in millions of rufiyaa	6.5	21.2	6.6	21.6	22.4	45.0	29.6
as % of GDP	2.0	5.2	1.5	4.4	4.2	7.7	4.7
Private savings in millions of rufiyaa	..	-22.2	-14.6	12.5	0.3	..	..
as % of GDP	..	-5.4	-3.3	2.6	0.1	..	..

Source: ESCAP, *Economic Bulletin for Asia and the Pacific*, vol. XXXVII, No. 1 June 1986. Ministry of Planning and Development, *Statistical Yearbook of Maldives, 1987.*

The composition of Government revenue is unusual but has shown some evolution. The preponderance of non-tax revenue, mainly profits of the State trading organization, public enterprises and from transport services as well as rents and leasing fees on Government property, that prevailed at the beginning of the 1980s, has been reduced. Due to a number of measures, tax revenue increased from about 35 per cent of total Government revenue in 1980 to about 53 per cent in 1986. Tax revenue is still raised almost entirely from indirect taxes, with import duties and tourist taxes being the major elements. Apart from a tax levied on bank profits, other potential sources for tax revenue, e.g. income and property, have remained untapped.

Efforts to increase domestic savings were confronted by a lack of adequate instruments and intermediaries, which are needed for pursuing a savings-encouraging monetary and fiscal policy and for channelling savings into productive investment. Foreign banks that opened branches in the Maldives as early as in the 1970s proved only partially suited to the mobilization of domestic resources as they largely preferred activities in international banking to an engagement at the national level. With a view to performing the function of a Central Bank, the Maldives Monetary Authority was established in 1981. A landmark in advancing the national banking system was the establishment of the Bank of Maldives in late 1982. For the first time savings efforts extended beyond the capital Male. Interest rates, which had not received enough attention previously, were increased. Discriminatory interest rates were offered to attract deposits from the outer islands. Furthermore, students were familiarized with the savings habit through the introduction of a school banking system. As a result, bank deposits rose considerably.

(c) *Institutions for mobilizing savings*

In Nepal, the Small Farmers Development Programme handles savings and credit operations for small-scale farmers. By early 1988, there were more than 8,000 savings and credit groups with a total membership of about 73,000. This scheme has contributed to strengthening the sense of self-reliance among the participants and helps the farmers to avoid turning to money-lenders in emergency situations. The Grameen Bank Project, started in Bangladesh in 1976, has addressed the financial needs of the rural poor. Apart from its savings mobilization function, it assists in creating economic activity and thus in generating income. In 1987, total membership reached almost 300,000.[6] In some African LDCs, such as Burundi, Rwanda and United Republic of Tanzania, various types of savings and credit co-operatives have been set up.

Although the traditional money-lending-cum-trading systems can hardly be expected to be a satisfactory substitute for the formal savings and credit facilities required for the modernization of rural areas, some customary savings and credit associations deserve to be revitalized. In Ethiopia, rotating savings and credit groups meet the needs of people that have otherwise no access to institutionalized credit. They are based on an agreement between the participants to contribute regularly to a fund that is given in whole or in part to each contributor in rotation.

It is not uncommon for informal financial groups to evolve over time and to grow into a formal institution. In Lesotho, small informal savings groups emerged in the 1960s and provided a good experience in managing small savings. Later on, they have transformed themselves into the Lesotho Credit Union Movement.

4. *Strengthening women's role in development*

(a) *The prevailing situation*

Throughout the 1980s, several LDCs have adopted measures to promote the status of women and their role in development as part of national development planning. However, there has not been a marked improvement in their economic and social situation as a profile of women in the LDCs based on some economic, social, demographic and health indicators shows (see table 3). Many of their problems stem from the precarious conditions which prevail in the LDCs' rural areas, where 80 per cent of the population (male and female) live. Women tend to be particularly affected as several tasks have to be performed by them in difficult conditions. For instance, it is women who have to go and fetch for water, often over long distances and in adverse conditions. Likewise, the dwindling forest reserves makes greater demands on women's time and effort as wood fuel collection is women's traditional task. The data available indicate that the average percentage of women who were attended during childbirth by trained personnel in 1984 was a mere 36 per cent, which is to a large extent due to the concentration of health services in the urban areas. Women's morbidity and mortality rates in LDCs are higher on account of repeated child bearing. In education, the overall illiteracy rate is almost twice as high for females as for males. Likewise, the percentage of females in the relevant age group attending schools is smaller than that for males at all levels, namely primary, secondary and university. The higher the educational level, the wider the gap. This in turn causes women to be concentrated in the low and middle level jobs when they are in salaried employment.

Women continue to face special constraints which impede their participation in development. Often they do not have the same access to funds, agricultural inputs, fertilizers and extension services as men have. Many still lack recognition of land rights. Even in countries where women have the legal right to own land, customary law, family traditions, inheritance systems and women's acceptance of subordination very often prevent them from exercising that right. The situation which emerges is often that women work on the land without having control over the labour process or the proceeds of their own labour.

In certain countries such as Lesotho and Botswana, where widespread male migration has caused women to become heads of households doing most of the work, women still have to wait until the return of their men to apply for credit, hire tractors, etc., and to take decisions on spending of remittances.[7] Although women assume the responsibilities of heads of households, they do not always acquire the status that would give them access to credit and other resources.

Cultural factors have a strong influence in obstructing women's access to education. Parents tend to give priority to sending sons to school; they believe that marriage renders a daughter's education useless. In some societies, girls can even be denied access to education because of the social requirements for sex segregation and female tuition.

In training, the stereotype image of male and female employment tends to limit vocational training for women to home economics, reserving technical studies for men. For cultural reasons and also for lack of understanding of women's economic role, extension services tend to be directed to men even though in many

---

6 See *The Least Developed Countries - 1987 Report*, box 2.

7 M.A. Savané, *Migration in rural development and women in Africa*, ILO, Geneva 1984.

activities it is the women who do the work. For example, in Lesotho, whereas women take a more active role in agricultural production, basic tasks such as pest control have to be done by women without the aid of insecticides as training in the use of insecticides was given primarily to men because of their contacts with male extension workers.

(b) *Overview and implications of policy measures and projects for women*

(i) *Policy orientation*

National mechanisms for the enhancement of women or special women's bureaux have been established in more than half the LDCs. These bodies are responsible for identifying, evaluating and monitoring projects on women and they could play a co-ordinating and catalytic role in influencing mainstream development policies and programmes. Some countries, such as Bangladesh, Burundi and Lesotho, have a fully-fledged Ministry of Women's Affairs while in several others the links of special women's bureaux to the President's or Prime's Minister office have recently been strengthened. In addition, some countries have set up special women's units within the Ministry of Education, Health and Social Affairs. Other LDCs, like Nepal and Bangladesh have made specific provisions such as fixing a quota (in Nepal's Seventh Plan) to enhance women's participation in training and programmes designed to raise agricultural production and productivity, and (in Bangladesh) setting up of a National Women's Training Academy.

(ii) *Impact of projects*

In a number of LDCs, programmes for the mobilizaton of the rural population increasingly contain elements which are geared to the special needs of women. In United Republic of Tanzania, Ethiopia and other LDCs, Government-sponsored activities have been launched with a view to enhancing rural women's knowledge of sanitary measures, cooking, combating diseases, child raising and other skills. Particular attention to the inclusion of girls and women in literacy campaigns has been given in some LDCs, such as Botswana, Cape Verde, Ethiopia and Lesotho. In Rwanda, women successfully manage rural credit companies. However, in many LDCs, the formidable contribution by women to the production of food and in some cases cash crops has not yet been fully acknowledged, although they often bear responsibility for the major part of the agricultural work, including retail trading. Their limited control over productive resources, including land, poses a prime obstacle to a better involvement of women in rural extension programmes, to easier access to rural credit and to a more active participation in the decision-making process on rural and village matters.

Past experience, however, has shown that, at the project level, benefits do not always reach women even when women were included as the target group. For projects to make a significant improvement in women's output and welfare, project design and delivery need to take into account women's specific needs and problems.

The increased recognition of the importance of women's income for meeting the family's essential needs has led to a proliferation of income-generating projects for women. However, many of these projects have neglected women's concerns in that they are designed as part-time activities to give women supplementary income while ignoring their main economic activities and their critical need for full-time employment and income to sustain themselves and their families. Supporting women in their main economic activities such as rice farming, cotton growing and vegetable gardening, and incorporating training, credit, marketing and infrastructural services can contribute effectively to improving women's economic position. An irrigated gardening project in Molepole, Botswana, is a successful example of a project focused on women's main economic activities.

The importance of considering the socio-economic and cultural factors in project design can be seen in the case of the introduction of solar reflective cookers in Sierra Leone. They were rejected by the women because they were introduced without taking into consideration women's time allocation and social habits. In fact, these cookers have to be used when the sun is at its zenith and the cooking has to be done outside the house; but in Sierra Leone women cook their main meal of the day after returning from the farm around sunset and, moreover, they cook inside the house. It is inconvenient in tropical countries to cook outdoors when the sun is at its strongest. An assessment made by the Agency for International Development on the degree of acceptance of cooking stove projects in three LDCs (Burundi, Lesotho and Nepal) found that the level of acceptance was high in Lesotho, where

Table 3

STATUS OF WOMEN IN THE LEAST DEVELOPED COUNTRIES

	Labour force participation rate (female/male)	*Growth of female labour force - (1960/1980)/(1980/2000)*	*Female life expectancy (1980-1985)*	*Per cent of adults literate, 1985 (female/male)*	*Enrolment in primary schools, 1985 (female/male), per cent*	*Enrolment in secondary schools, 1985 (female/male), per cent*	*Per cent of women employees in professional and technical positions (maj. group 0/1)*	*Per cent of women employees in admin. and managerial positions (maj. group 0/2)*	*Per cent of women employees in the service sector (maj. group 0/3)*	*Per cent of women attended during childbirth by trained personnel, 1984*	*Maternal mortality (per 10,000 live births, 1980*	*National machinery responsible for the advancement of women (G-governmental; NG-Non-governmental; SG-semi-governmental)*
Afghanistan	..	2.5/3.4	37	8/39	11/24	5/11				5	640	
Bangladesh	4/52	3.0/3.4	50	22/43	50/70	10/26	11	2	55	..	600	Ministry of Women's Affairs, G
Benin	38/49	1.9/2.2	52	16/37	48/37	12/29				34	1680	Organisation of the Revolutionary women of Benin, G-1983
Bhutan	38/59	1.8/2.3	45	../..	18/32	1/6				3		National Women's association, NG-1981
Botswana	24/46	1.7/2.1	62	69/73	109/98	31/27	61	36	70	..	250	Women's Affairs Unit, G
Burkina Faso	49/54	1.6/2.0	49	6/21	24/41	3/7				..		Ministry of Social Affairs Unit, G-1974
Burma	27/50	0.8/1.8	61	../..	../..	../..				97	135	
Burundi	41/52	1.3/2.0	50	26/43	44/61	3/5				12		Ministry of Women's Affairs, G-1982
Cape Verde	5/43	3.0/2.6	..	39/61	105/111	11/14				10		
Central African Rep.	50/56	1.5/1.8	51	29/53	../..	../..				..	600	
Chad	15/57	1.5/2.3	46	../..	21/55	2/11				..		Ministry of Labour, Special Women's Unit, G-1982
Comoros	23/44	1.4/2.0	..	../..	../..	../..	22	..	6	24		
Democratic Yemen	6/47	3.7/4.2	51	25/59	35/96	11/26				10	100	Yemen Women Union, 1968
Djibouti	../..	../..	..	../..	../..	../..				73		UNFD, SG-1977
Equatorial Guinea	34/52	2.6/2.4	..	../..	../..	../..				..		Ministry of Labour, Special Women's Unit, G-1980
Ethiopia	34/55	1.9/2.1	48	../..	28/44	9/14				58	2000	Revolutionary Ethiopia Women's Association, NG-1980
Gambia	39/57	1.3/1.6	..	../..	58/92	12/29	27	15	41	80		Women's Bureau, G-1981
Guinea	38/56	1.7/2.0	43	../..	19/42	6/18	22			..		
Guinea-Bissau	39/58	0.8/2.3	..	17/46	40/81	4/18	26	8	8	..		
Haiti	36/50	0.9/1.3	56	35/40	72/83	17/19	40	33	66	20	367	
Kiribati	48/89	../..	..	../..	../..	../..				..		
Lao People's Dem. Rep.	45/53	1.2/1.7	51	76/92	79/101	15/23				..		
Lesotho	41/55	1.2/1.8	57	../..	127/102	26/18	58	21	49	28		Ministry of Youth and Women Affairs, G-1986
Malawi	37/52	1.7/2.1	47	../..	53/71	2/6	25	6	18	59	250	National Commission on Women in Development, G
Maldives	../..	../..	..	../..	../..	../..	31	9	30	..		Women's Council, G-1986
Mali	11/55	1.8/2.3	48	11/23	17/29	4/10	20	7	27	..		National Union of Malian Women, (1974)
Mauritania	13/50	2.3/2.7	49	../..	29/45	6/19				23	119	
Nepal	29/53	1.9/2.2	47	12/39	../..	../..	11	5	12	10	850	Women Services Co-ordination Committee, NG-1977
Niger	49/56	3.0/3.3	46	../..	20/37	3/9				47	581	Women's Association, NG-1975
Rwanda	48/53	2.5/2.7	50	33/61	63/66	2/3	28	2	17	..	210	
Samoa	9/41	../..	..	../..	../..	../..	47	119	42	52		Women's Advisory Committee, Prime Minister's Department, G-1979
Sao Tome and Principe	../..	../..	..	../..	../..	../..	52	9	60	..		
Sierra Leone	25/51	1.5/2.1	42	../..	43/68	11/23				25	450	Ministry of Social Welfare and Rural Development, G-1957
Somalia	34/53	2.0/2.2	48	../..	18/32	12/23				2	1100	Somali Women's Democratic Organisation, 1977
Sudan	14/51	3.4/3.8	51	../..	41/58	17/22				2	607	Executive Bureau of the Sudan Feminist Union, SG-1971
Togo	31/53	2.4/2.2	54	28/54	73/118	10/33	21	8	37	..	476	Directeur Général de la Condition Féminine, G-1977
Tuvalu	../..	../..	..	../..	../..	../..				..		
Uganda	38/53	2.2/2.5	49	../..	50/66	5/11				..	300	National Council of Women, SG-1978
United Rep. of Tanzania	28/51	2.2/2.5	55	../..	../..	../..				74	370	Union of Women of Tanganyika (UWT)
Vanuatu	../..	../..	..	../..	../..	../..	32	8	62	72		
Yemen	6/45	3.3/3.8	47	../..	22/112	3/17				12	1	Women's Association, NG-1958
All LDCs	**20/52**	**1.9/2.4**	**54**	**21/43**	**48/68**	**10/19**				**44**		
All developing countries	**21/52**		**59**	**49/67**	**77/97**	**30/44**				**41**		

Source: Statistical Annex; World Bank, *Social Indicators of Development, 1987*; ILO, *Labour force estimates 1950-1970, projections 1975-2000*, Volumes I to III; ILO, *Yearbook of Labour Statistics*, 1977 to 1987, Table 2B; and replies to questionnaires sent to Governments by the World Conference to Review and Appraise the Achievements of the United Nations Decade for Women, August 1983, and to UNCTAD questionnaires on the implementation of the SNPA, 1986 to 1988.

village women were consulted about their preferences.[8] In the same vein, water supply and sanitation projects meet with more success when women and girls, who have the primary responsibility for collecting water and managing its domestic use, as well as for family hygiene and household sanitation, participate actively in the project and are supplied with follow-up health extension services.

Mechanisms have been established in several LDCs to help women to overcome the difficulties faced in their access to credits and loans. This is achieved by substituting pledges of group solidarity for standard collateral requirements, a feature of the operations of the above-mentioned Grameen Bank in Bangladesh. Women participate as a group, both as beneficiaries and as decision-makers. A similar operational approach was adopted by Burundi in its project "Femmes - Crédits-Production", which supports women's access to credit for revenue-generating activities.

(c) *Concluding remarks*

Women's access to credit schemes could be improved if the schemes designed could dispense with land title as collateral. Land reform can afford an opportunity to support the access of women to land rights. Reform schemes which require registration, individualization of land and other forms of changes in ownership of land should involve registration of land in the name of husbands and wives (and just women in the case of women-headed households). Another way to secure women's rights to the ownership of land is to ensure that title is granted to each individual, regardless of gender, or joint titles given to husbands and wives. But it is important that land improvement schemes ensure women's rights to the use and management of land and complementary inputs as well as equal access to returns from agricultural surplus. Cases have occurred where women farmers have had to fight in order not to be displaced from land once it has been improved.[9]

The attainment of the goal of wider and more equitable education of women can be better met if strong support is given at the national level to overcome cultural and attitudinal barriers. Training programmes can be made more relevant to women's role and the opportunities for gainful employment for women increased if they are broadened to include training in agriculture, animal husbandry, and management of co-operatives.

Long-term development planning should provide for a continuing assessment of women's technical needs in all sectors. Increased application of technology to women's tasks can raise their labour productivity and expand their productive employment opportunities. Extension services should be reoriented to assisting women farmers. Production or marketing co-operatives formed exclusively for and by women might in certain cases be appropriate.

5. *Expanded role for the private sector*

(a) *National policies*

In the course of the past two or three years, virtually all LDCs have promulgated policies favouring an expanded role for the private sector, and most of them have also taken measures towards implementing such policies. While these policies have normally constituted essential elements of structural adjustment or stabilization programmes negotiated with the World Bank and IMF, the scope of this policy trend is far broader, covering LDCs not currently beneficiaries of assistance from these institutions or from like-minded bilateral donors.

In many countries which had relied on State-administered fixed prices and State control of internal and external trade, these controls have been either lifted or liberalized. In part, this was done in recognition of the ineffectiveness of these measures in achieving their explicit or implicit goals, namely, making basic necessities readily available at prices affordable to the mass of the population; but in part the liberalization constitutes a way of removing impediments to the proper functioning of private-sector trade.

Perhaps the most important single boost given to the private sector comes from the gradual reduction of monopoly rights formerly accorded to public-sector enterprises (PSEs). This has often, but not invariably, been coupled with the offer made in many LDCs to sell selected PSEs to the private sector. Mali, United

8 Agency for International Development (AID). AID Program Evaluation Report No. 18, *Women in Development: AID's Experience, 1973-1985*, vol.1: Synthesis Paper.

9 See D. Bazin "Policy implications" in *Rural development and women in Africa*, ILO, 1984; and "The Gambia women win rights to land", in *Africa, Sowing the Seeds of Self-Sufficiency*, IFAD, 1986.

Republic of Tanzania and Bangladesh provide typical illustrations from different regions of LDCs that have pursued such policies. In Mali, a recent law provides for the privatization of 13 out of 40 PSEs, and reduced tax rates for commercial and industrial enterprises were announced in October 1987. In the United Republic of Tanzania the policy of quasi-total State control over prices and over domestic and foreign wholesale trade was relaxed in 1986, thereby providing renewed stimulus to the fledgling private sector. In Bangladesh, a ceiling on private-sector investment was lifted; a moratorium on nationalization was decreed; a large number of PSEs were privatized; and the share assigned to the private sector in the fulfilment of the current Third Five-Year Plan (35 per cent) is more than triple the corresponding share in the first Plan. In Sao Tome and Principe, the State has begun to redistribute land to the private sector after the sharp decline of cocoa yields wrought havoc with the country's main export crop.

The drive towards a more active private-sector involvement in the economy has often been accompanied by the promotion of foreign direct investment, either alone or in partnership with local entrepreneurs as joint ventures. To this end, several LDCs have revised and simplified their investment codes (e.g. Burundi, Guinea, Nepal) and/or provided more generous tax incentives (e.g. Chad, Niger, Kiribati, Vanuatu, Malawi and Lesotho).

In several cases Governments have reoriented the flow of investments by the national development finance institutions in favour of the private sector. In other cases they have set up new financial instruments or institutions to promote joint ventures or domestic private investments, usually with foreign assistance. Thus, Afghanistan received a Soviet credit worth Rb.50million (about $83million) earmarked for private or mixed - typically with private predominance - ventures. Nepal increased the flow of loans to the private sector through the National Industrial Development Corporation and provided guarantees to private-sector industrial investments. Guinea-Bissau set up a venture capital fund within the National Bank with United States and Portuguese support. The Lesotho National Development Corporation (LNDC) engages in equity participation in joint ventures with foreign investors as trustees for indigenous businessmen who might decide to take over the LNDC share later. Apart from joint-venture projects connected with the country's major Highland Water Scheme, LNDC has signed a joint venture agreement to process and thereby increase the value added component of the country's two principal export items, namely, mohair and wool.

Only a few LDCs still maintain single-channel export regimes, while many have encouraged the private sector to increase its involvement in the production and marketing of exportables, particularly of agricultural and fisheries products that were formerly closely controlled by Governmental monopolies. In Mali, the monopoly formerly held by the State-owned SOMIEX in the trade of tea, sugar and salt was abolished and the Government is actively promoting the creation of private cereals trading firms. In the United Republic of Tanzania the private sector was encouraged to invest in export agriculture, including investments directed at the purchase of Government-owned sisal estates, which once provided the country's leading export (when world demand for sisal was stronger). Other countries which have instituted similar policies include Comoros, Democratic Yemen, Guinea-Bissau, Malawi, Mauritania, Sao Tome and Principe and Uganda.

The balance-of-payments constraints have been so serious in most LDCs that little scope was left for increasing allocations of official foreign-exchange to the private sector.[10] Since these foreign-exchange shortages have often been accompanied by widening discrepancies between the official and the parallel exchange rates, the allocation of scarce foreign exchange to private-sector applicants became increasingly politicized. In these circumstances the importation of an increasing portion of manufactured goods was left to the private sector under essentially similar systems (although described by various different labels), under which licences are given relatively easily to private importers who do not request official foreign-exchange allocations. It must be recognized that this practice tends to encourage "unofficial" exports and other infractions of foreign-exchange surrender requirements, while diminishing the respective governments' ability to orient the composition of imports according to its development priorities. On the other hand, this private-sector role has enabled many LDCs not only to overcome severe shortages of consumer goods, but also to maintain a supply of spare parts and industrial inputs, in the absence of which industrial capacity utilization would have been even lower than it was.

Policy co-ordination towards the private sector - particularly *vis-à-vis* foreign direct investment - has sometimes been achieved by the establishment of central units capable of

[10] Malawi is one of the rare LDCs that deliberately and stringently reduced Government imports in 1986, so as to allow more scope for private-sector imports.

removing or diminishing the bureaucratic obstacles facing the potential investor. Thus, the Bangladesh Planning Commission established a "private-sector wing" to help improve the investment climate and explore the possibility of setting up a joint-venture bank. Tuvalu encourages private foreign investment through its Business Development Advisory Board, while Uganda has set up a Verification Committee to facilitate the repossession of private assets expropriated by previous regimes.

(b) *International policies*

Despite the more favourable policies adopted by LDCs to attract foreign direct investment (FDI), the actual recorded flows of foreign direct investment have been not only small, but also diminishing, both absolutely and relatively to similar flows to other developing countries. In terms of constant 1980 dollars, FDI flows to LDCs fell from an annual average of $145 million during the biennium 1981-1982 to a mere $34 million and $29 million during 1985 and 1986 respectively. This FDI flow accounted for only 0.3 per cent of all external financial flows going to LDCs in 1985 and 1986 (against 1.6 per cent during the 1981-1982 biennium), whereas it accounted for as much as 15.7 per cent of external financial flows going to developing countries as a whole. Looking at this discrepancy in a different way, it can be said that among all the identified types of financial flows to developing countries, FDI is the one within which LDCs attract the lowest share by far: 0.35 per cent during each year of the biennium 1985-1986, against a 1.6 per cent share of all non-concessional flows and a vastly higher share of concessional flows.

These negligible and highly unevenly distributed flows of FDI to LDCs[11] underline the need for facilitation measures on the part of multilateral and bilateral donors committed to the promotion of FDI and/or joint ventures in LDCs. The World Bank, which has begun to give direct assistance to the private enterprise sector, has also attracted private-sector resources into its own projects by way of joint financing. More recently it has strengthened its co-operation with the private sector by way of a series of information and training activities.

The International Finance Corporation (IFC), which is the World Bank Group's private-sector arm, can and does provide both loan and equity finance to private and mixed enterprises, but the IFC's preference for large-scale projects has in fact severely limited the actual scope of IFC intervention in LDCs.[12] Thus, in the fiscal year ending 30 June 1987, IFC participated in only seven LDC projects for a total of $12.6 million, corresponding to a mere 1.4 per cent of its total investments during that fiscal year. However, IFC is executing two project development facilities - one for Africa and one for the Caribbean - financed by the the United Nations Development Programme (UNDP) and several bilateral donors, which focus on projects costing between $0.5 million to $5 million (i.e. below the threshold at which IFC normally participates with its own resources) submitted by indigenous entrepreneurs. Once a project is adjudged technically and financially feasible, the project development facility concerned commits itself to mobilize the external capital required, for which purpose the IFC link proves particularly useful.

Several bilateral donors, such as the United States, the Federal Republic of Germany and France, have made private-sector development part of their aid policy package. Some donors even run programmes with a specific focus on stimulating small and medium-scale enterprises. Although LDC enterprises are eligible to draw both equity and loan finance from at least eight major national development finance institutions based in EEC countries, the minimum intervention thresholds, which vary from $150,000 to $450,000, normally exclude small-scale enterprises, and *ipso facto* most indigenous enterprises based in LDCs.

Private multilateral financing institutions established for Africa (or subregions thereof) limit their participation to projects of $1 million or more for reasons analogous to those motivating the official development institutions, namely, the high unit cost of evaluating and managing small projects. This, in turn, produces a bias against small enterprises and hence LDCs, where virtually all indigenous enterprises are small A challenge to be faced by LDC Governments and financing institutions alike consists in identifying more effective instruments for channelling investments into small and medium-sized enterprises in LDCs.

---

11 In 1984, two countries absorbed 72 per cent of net FDI flows to all LDCs; in 1985, two countries accounted for more than the total net flow; and in 1986 four countries accounted for over 78 per cent of the total net FDI flow to LDCs.

12 In principle, the IFC's intervention never exceeds 25 per cent of the total project cost and its minimum threshold for any single participation is $1 million, thereby excluding projects costing less than $4 million. The threshold rises to $1O million (implying projects costing at least $4O million) if IFC bears the promotional costs. However, in the case of LDCs even the $1 million threshold has been waived.

6. *Improving the efficiency of public sector enterprises*

The budgetary and economic impact of the losses suffered by public sector enterprises (PSEs) in many LDCs has impelled their Governments to undertake thorough reviews of these PSEs with a view to selecting one of the following options: (a) rendering their operations more efficient by way of management reforms and greater operational autonomy, including pricing policy; (b) privatization; and (c) liquidation.

The problems affecting the PSEs in LDCs, as in many other developing countries, were largely rooted in management structures and objectives which were both lax and lacking in productive orientation. Such inefficient management was often condoned by central governments in response to political and social pressures.

Firstly, the payroll was bloated by the hiring of excessive and frequently unqualified staff, a policy which was pursued as a way of overcoming unemployment pressures. Moreover, given the usual link between PSE and civil service salary scales, PSE staff tended to be underpaid in comparison with private-sector personnel engaged in similar activities, with evident consequences on motivation and efficiency. These shortcomings in the personnel policy were compounded by the selection procedures for top management posts, which were not always filled on the basis of competence and proven efficiency. Moreover, the absence of financial autonomy rendered management excessively accountable *vis à vis* the supervisory ministry of the central government in day-to-day decision-making, a feature which inevitably constrained the motivation of management to correct evident managerial shortcomings, and also lengthened the decision-taking process.

Secondly, under-pricing of the final output or service was often imposed on PSEs as a means of relieving inflationary pressures and avoiding consumer discontent.

Thirdly, to the extent that PSEs enjoyed single-channel importation or export marketing rights - coupled with privileged access to scarce foreign exchange, often at grossly overvalued exchange rates of the domestic currency - they were able to offset their losses. However, for most PSEs such offsets were not feasible.

Such factors have led to repeated and growing operational deficits in many LDCs' PSEs and to a lack of incentive for investment and modernization. The implications for the overall economies and for the governments' finances became serious with time, especially in the context of a deteriorating external economic environment. In the United Republic of Tanzania, for example, net transfers from the Government to non-financial PSEs rose from less than 1 per cent of GDP in the period 1978-1982 to over 2.5 per cent during the period 1983-1985. The drain on public finances caused by the current losses suffered by PSEs have not generally been compensated by higher growth impulses in that sector nor by relief on the balance-of-payments side. In four LDCs analysed by the World Bank[13] (Burma, United Republic of Tanzania, Bangladesh and Nepal), the share of value added by PSEs represents only a small fraction of their share of national investment, while PSEs have accounted for a growing share of all developing countries' external debt, a trend that is also likely to apply to the LDCs among them.

Some LDCs have set specific macroeconomic targets for reducing the budgetary impact of PSE losses, and almost all of these LDCs have announced policies going in that direction, usually as part of a policy framework paper worked out with IMF. The degree of policy implementation has varied greatly depending,*inter alia*, on: (i) the level of debt saddling the PSEs concerned; (ii) the priority attached by the central government to keeping a PSE under public control; (iii) the availability of private entrepreneurs able and willing to buy out the State; and (iv) the employment effects of any one of the three options mentioned above. To the extent that PSEs have accummulated large amounts of debt, these PSEs are unlikely to be privatized unless such debt is largely or wholly written off before privatization or transformation into joint ventures takes place. The write-offs would have budgetary implications which in the short-term contradict the deficit-reducing policies concurrently pursued by the same governments. The privatization by way of foreign-controlled enterprises - frequently the only viable bidders - presents obvious political problems when the PSE concerned is viewed as occupying a sensitive position in the national economy, either by virtue of the essential nature of the output provided or the service rendered or on account of the negative employment effect that a full or partial privatization usually implies. Furthermore, some of the early African privatizations involving purchases by foreign interests rapidly became a political embarrassment to the Governments concerned.

[13] *World Development Report*, 1988, figure 8.1.

(a) National policies[14]

Some countries have followed up their PSE policies by implementing institutional measures. For example, under an ordinance promulgated by Bangladesh in 1987, a system of performance contracts for the planning and control by PSEs was instituted, of which five were implemented in the fiscal year ending in June 1988. A system of reporting and evaluating autonomous bodies was expanded to cover 20 PSEs in the same fiscal year, while other PSEs were converted into public limited companies. These measures resulted in the sharp reductions of overhead costs and significant reductions of operational stoppages in productive enterprises caused by raw material shortages. For its part, Nepal has decided henceforth to itemize in the budget all subsidies paid to PSEs; moreover, all governmental guarantees of loans given to PSEs will be subject to an annual ceiling. Burma has so far been less successful in reducing the budgetary drain of PSE subsidies, despite the formal granting of autonomy in the mid-1970s and the introduction of a bonus scheme to reward manager and worker efficiency; in fact, prices continued to be controlled at levels covering only a fraction of the costs and PSE profit margins were guaranteed.

More common has been the recourse to privatization, usually involving, in the case of LDCs, sales of parastatals to foreign interests, rather than domestic institutional reform. In Africa, Togo is regarded as a pioneer in the policy of privatization of PSEs, instituted in 1985. Since then, the Government has offered various other parastatals for sale, lease or joint venture to foreign investors. Such divestiture has been achieved in the case of the country's only steel mill, its oil refinery, a dairy and two textile mills. In Guinea-Bissau, whose economy was once almost completely controlled by the public sector, almost 90 per cent of the outlets of two leading retail chains had been privatized by the end of 1986; since then, all foreign trade monopolies except for cereals have been abolished. In Malawi, a wide range of price and tariff adjustments were undertaken in 1987 alongside the decision to divest the Agricultural Development and Marketing Corporation of all its holdings in other companies and agricultural estates. Even the country's only nominally private dominated corporation, Press Holdings, has also been restructured under World Bank guidance. Similarly, Lesotho's National Development Corporation is pursuing a divestiture policy of viable PSEs. Burundi set up a national service in charge of overseeing the reform of the PSEs called for in the country's structural adjustment programme, which consist of the usual three-pronged approach (rehabilitation, privatization or liquidation). In Equatorial Guinea's reform programme, both foreign and local capital are buying out PSEs in the fields of air and sea transport, banking, agriculture and forestry. Guinea's commitment to the privatization of PSEs has already resulted in the sale of two agro-industrial units (quinine and tea), a printing shop and a soft-drink plant; further sales are planned of larger PSEs, such as a textile complex, a brewery and the national fuel board. Of its 54 PSEs, Niger has earmarked 5 for liquidation, 16 for privatization, 5 others for retention but under private management, and 10 for restructuring. In Chad, Cotontchad, the marketing board of the country's major export staple, began a major cost-cutting exercise in 1986, involving a salary freeze along with a 50 per cent personnel cut, a ceiling on the volume of purchases equal to the 1985 level, the removal of subsidies on cotton-growers' inputs, the closing of one half of the country's cotton gins and the introduction of stricter management procedures. In Mali, the restructuring has perhaps shown the most vivid quantifiable results: after 15 years of deficit, the PSEs yielded a CFAF 2 billion ($6.7 million) surplus in 1987. The liquidation in 1988 of the trading firm SOMIEX, the single largest deficit producer, should further improve the country's record in this regard. Conversely, joint ventures have been successful in attracting new financing, promoting exports, achieving higher productivity, and, it is claimed, maintaining employment.

In the Pacific LDCs, the improvement of PSEs' efficiency has also become a central objective of government policy. Thus, in Kiribati, where subsidies to PSEs absorbed as much as 6 per cent of GDP in 1986, the Government is imposing stricter controls on PSE budgets and has introduced more flexible pricing policies. In Samoa, the Government set profitability targets for PSEs as from 1988, to ensure termination of budgetary subsidies for current operations. Moreover, the Government is studying the possibility of establishing a holding company, which would assume responsibility for all PSEs with a view to streamlining their management or implementing the Government's divestment of its interests.

14 To the extent that the improvement of PSE performance is being sought by way of privatization, this section ought to be read in conjunction with the preceding section.

(b) International policies

The principal driving force on the international side for the reform of the PSEs have been the World Bank-sponsored structural adjustment programmes. In several LDCs these objectives have been translated into specific projects designed to aid the country concerned in the implementation thereof. In the Sudan, an IDA project is designed: (i) to submit 10 selected PSEs to one of the three above-mentioned rationalization processes (streamlining, privatization or liquidation); (ii) to strengthen internal planning and management of individual PSEs and the sector as a whole; and (iii) to propose legislative changes affecting PSEs. Some of the difficulties in implementing structural adjustment in Sudan are however outlined in Box 1.

In some LDCs, bilateral donors have assisted in the rationalization process. Thus, in the Comoros, a French-sponsored study found that some public utilities (water and electricity) were running reasonably well, while others (post and telegraph services) were deemed to be less efficient. In Benin, the reform effort has been jointly assisted by a $31.5 million project financed by IDA and the Swiss Government, which resulted in the liquidation of several publicly-owned loss-making industries in 1986 and the rehabilitation of other PSEs, for example a brewery and a textile mill, as well as a trading, a shipping and a forwarding company.

While it remains true that local private investment interests and entrepreneurs are often not available or ready to respond to privatization opportunities in LDCs (see the previous section) it is also true that the supporting finance made available internationally and/or bilaterally to LDC Governments endeavouring to reform and rehabilitate their PSEs has often been pitched at modest levels, compared with the task in hand and the political risks which Governments are likely to run in executing the reform process. Perhaps for this reason, participation and sales to foreign interests has tended to predominate over internal restructuring and reform in LDCs. The implications for these countries' future ownership and control over economic sectors have yet to be assessed.

7. Impact of the measures to improve the efficiency of resource use and allocation

It is difficult to ascertain on objective grounds the actual impact of the national measures described in this section, which have been taken with a view to improving the efficiency of resource use and allocation. This is particularly the case as regards the so-called adjustment programmes, both those negotiated with IMF and those carried out outside the IMF framework.

Indeed, against which framework should such programmes be evaluated? Against the performance of the adjusting countries in the previous period? On this score it can be argued that the programmes had to be adopted precisely because the economic conditions (internal and/or external) were no longer the same as in the previous period, that previous policies were no longer tenable: performance may therefore differ from one period to another, not so much because of differences in the effectiveness of policies but rather because of differences in economic conditions. Furthermore, any effects observed have to be attributed carefully to the recession or the adjustment process itself. Or again, should such programmes be evaluated against the performance of LDCs which have not adopted adjustment programmes? It can be argued that these LDCs have not had to implement such programmes precisely because they were facing less adverse conditions, or simply because their policies already contained the kind of measures which are embodied in the typical adjustment package: again, performance may therefore vary because of differences in economic conditions or because adjustment measures have been in operation for a longer time in these other LDCs than in those which have formulated adjustment programmes.

Empirical evidence indicates in fact that the performance of the 15 LDCs which have had consecutive adjustment programmes throughout most of the 1980s does not differ significantly from that of LDCs as a whole (table 4). Only four of them (Bangladesh, Malawi, Somalia and Yemen) registered a higher average annual rate of growth in 1980-1986 than that of the LDCs as a whole (2.1 per cent); and only two (Somalia and Uganda) improved their growth performance in 1980-1986 as compared to that in the 1970s. Moreover, in nine of these LDCs, the decline in the growth rate between 1970-1980 and 1980-1986 was more pronounced than for the group of LDCs as a whole (where annual growth fell from 3.6 per cent in the 1970s to 2.1 per cent in 1980-1986). As regards the current account deficit, its value as a proportion of the value of exports of goods decreased markedly or steadily only in 7 out of the 15 LDCs: Bangladesh, Gambia, Haiti, Malawi, Niger, Sierra Leone and Yemen. Inflation rates were in turn reduced significantly between the 1970s and 1980-1986 in six of these

LDCs: Bangladesh, Mali, Niger, Togo, Rwanda and Yemen; whereas they increased noticeably in four: Gambia, Sierra Leone, Somalia and Sudan (see table 4).

The lack of correlation between the existence of adjustment programmes on the one hand and economic performance in terms of growth rates and improvement in current account and in inflation rates on the other hand leaves open the question of the adequacy of these programmes for the LDCs. To the extent that the new measures ensure greater efficiency in the management of resources and correct price and inter-sectoral distortions, they are likely to have beneficial effects upon the level of output in LDCs and upon the capacity of these countries to overcome present external and fiscal disequilibria. Nevertheless, as the first generation of adjustment programmes reaches completion, it is becoming apparent that these programmes, as currently defined could bring about undesired effects, in particular in terms of high social costs and of weakening the LDCs' ability to achieve long-term economic development.

Unless adequate account is taken of the special characteristics of least developed countries, the effectiveness of adjustment programmes will be limited at best. These characteristics are: (i) a strong dependence on a few commodity exports; (ii) an extremely undeveloped manufacturing sector, which normally contributes less than 10 per cent of total GDP; (iii) major bottlenecks arising from inadequate physical and institutional infrastructure; (iv) a human resource base which has yet to be fully developed, and a particular lack of indigenous enterprise; (v) extremely low levels of per capita income, with poverty thresholds well below those defined in the industrialized world; and (vi) susceptibility to natural disasters. The problems encountered are discussed below.

(a) Depreciation and related external sector policies

The measures taken by LDCs concerning the external sector have started bearing results, and some examples can be given in this regard. Bangladesh has become a competitive exporter of textiles. Exports of manufactured goods from Burundi doubled in 1986, and these achievements were sustained in 1987. Merchandise exports of Guinea-Bissau increased in 1987 by 70 per cent in value terms and by 34 per cent in volume. In Mauritania, following the adoption of adjustment programmes, the current account deficit measured as a percentage of GDP fell from 24.3 per cent in 1984 to 12.8 per cent in 1985. Despite adverse environmental conditions, in particular drought, African LDCs have managed to maintain production levels of their principal exported commodities and, in some cases, even increased them. The current account deficit of Togo fell from 17.5 per cent of GDP in 1982 to 14.9 per cent in 1985, and domestic and external arrears were reduced considerably. As regards imports, depreciation and the growing use of tariffs, as opposed to quantitative restrictions, are likely to have encouraged the local production of import-competing goods, in particular food, and have stimulated a more efficient allocation of resources within the import-competing sectors. At the same time, however, the limitations of such measures in ensuring external account improvement can be seen from the information contained in table 4.

What is open to question, and has been subject to careful scrutiny both within the LDCs and in international forums, is the extent to which depreciation and related measures have actually contributed to such success cases and whether these measures have not brought about undue adverse effects on the standards of living in the LDCs.

It has been argued that the impact of currency depreciation and related measures is likely to be constrained by the supply rigidities which arise from the relatively undiversified structure of production of LDCs, as well as by the low price elasticities of their traditional exports. In addition, many of the commodities exported by LDCs are facing record international low prices, a trend which is largely determined by world over-supply in the face of flagging developed country demand. In such circumstances, the measures in question, rather than boosting export earnings, may lead to overstocking and to further national losses. This is particularly the case where several LDCs have been obliged to expand output simultaneously in the same export product: this is the reality of the "fallacy of composition" argument. Consequently, to be effective in boosting export earnings, devaluation needs to be accompanied by measures aimed at strengthening productive sectors and diversifying the export base (see section below), a policy issue which has not always received the priority it deserves.

As regards import policies, it should be noted that the share of essential goods in the total of imports is very high in the case of LDCs. Depreciation (and customs duties to the extent that they apply to essential goods), by raising the local prices of essential imports, is likely to have major adverse effects on the standards of living notably of low-income

Table 4

PERFORMANCE OF SELECTED LDCs HAVING IMPLEMENTED ADJUSTMENT PROGRAMMES OVER CONSECUTIVE PERIODS SINCE MID-1981

	Annual average growth rate of GDP (per cent)			*Current account deficit [a] as percentage of exports of goods*			*Average annual increase in consumer prices (per cent)*	
	1970-1980 [b]	*1980-1986 [b]*	*Difference*	*1981*	*1984*	*1986*	*1970-1980*	*1980-1986*
A. LDCs with adjustment programmes supported by IMF financing								
Bangladesh	3.7	3.7	0.0	196	137	139	20.7	11.7
Central African Rep.	2.2	1.5	-0.7	66	85	146	10.6	10.8
Gambia	5.4	1.1	-4.3	231	2	4	10.5	20.8
Haiti	4.4	-0.6	-5.0	160	95	76	10.9	8.1
Malawi	6.1	2.4	-3.7	70	17	36 [c]	9.5	13.3
Mali	3.8	1.4	-2.4	154	107	147	15.0	6.8
Niger	1.5	-2.2	-3.7	71	51	47	11.3	6.1
Sierra Leone	1.6	1.1	-0.5	109	36	8	11.5	57.2
Somalia	2.7	3.8	1.1	120	595	394	15.8	44.8
Sudan	5.3	-0.4	-5.7	83	[d]	80	17.5	31.1
Togo	4.1	-0.9	-5.0	30	17	66	10.3	6.5
Uganda	-1.5	1.3	2.8	54	[d]	18	..	93.7 [e]
B. Other (selected) LDCs with adjustment programmes outside IMF framework								
Burkina Faso	1.9	1.7	-0.2	140	115	..	9.1	6.2
Rwanda	8.8 [f]	1.8	-7.0	152	99	101	13.1	5.3
Yemen	9.7	4.3	-5.4	9494	5202	2011	22.4 [e]	6.5 [g]
C. All LDCs	**3.6**	**2.1**	**-1.5**	**107**	**79**	**95**	**..**	**..**

Source: UNCTAD secretariat calculations based on data from the United Nations Statistical Office, the Economic Commission for Africa, the World Bank and other international and national sources; IMF, *International Financial Statistics*: Yearbook 1987, and June 1988.

a Excluding official unrequited transfers.
b Exponential trend function.
c 1985.
d Surplus.
e 1981-1986; index numbers (April 1981 = 100).
f 1976-1980.
g 1972-1980.
h 1980-1984.

groups. Likewise, the measures in question tend to increase the local prices of imported inputs and capital equipment, which may have negative repercussions on the international competitiveness of local goods and on the levels of capacity utilization and industrial investment, or may further narrow the range of possibilities for product diversification.

(b) Demand-management measures

The adoption of demand-management measures is amply justified, and even inevitable, in countries facing unsustainable external and fiscal disequilibria and high rates of inflation. The measures taken by LDCs in this regard have had a measure of success: inflation rates have been kept below the 12 per cent level in 9 of the 15 LDCs pursuing adjustment programmes for which data are available in table 4, and budget deficits, though still a problem for all but 1 of the 13 LDCs surveyed in table 5, were showing some overall improvement in Malawi, Haiti, Bangladesh and even Yemen (where the 1986 budget deficit was still over 10 per cent of GDP). Some LDCs in table 5, like Burkina Faso (and based on 1985 data) have moved into budget surplus, and in Mauritania (a country not covered in table 5), restraints in personnel expenditure coupled with more efficient tax recovery have brought about budgetary savings in both 1986 and 1987. What must not be overlooked, however, is the danger that such demand-management measures may have undesirable side effects in terms of deterioration in the already low living standards of LDCs and of contraction of the level of domestic economic activity.

Contraction of public expenditure may adversely affect the provision of social services (health, drinking water, education) which, in the case of least developed countries, is already precarious. On the other hand, given the high social and political cost of compressing recurrent expenditure, LDCs have in many cases opted for sacrificing development expenditure when adopting demand-management measures, a phenomenon which has had a direct negative impact on long-term prospects.

Long-term development has been compromised further by the adverse impact that reductions in public expenditure have had on efforts aimed at environment preservation in LDCs. This is not a trivial issue for these countries, as environmental deterioration has assumed dramatic proportions in many of them (see section 8(e) below). Yet, faced with the need to compress development expenditure, LDCs have, more often than not, tended to procrastinate with regard to positive action on the environment. This should be a matter of serious concern for the international community as a whole, as environmental degradation may proliferate beyond the national boundaries and is likely to have spill-over effects on the world environment.

Lastly, austerity measures appear to contain a pro-cyclical bias. They are normally resorted to as a means of coping with external and fiscal disequilibria which arise to a large extent from shortfalls or a declining trend in export earnings and/or from unanticipated levels of debt service. The measures are thus adopted at times, as at present, when external demand remains depressed. Countercyclical measures in support are only rarely offered by the world community - some examples are considered in section I.B.2. Deflationary measures, therefore, reduce the ability of the domestic markets of LDCs to provide the stimulus to local production that world markets are failing to generate.

All these considerations point to the need to ascertain carefully the benefits, and costs, of demand-management measures. Benefits have certainly been derived from a more efficient allocation of public funds, from the stimulus given to individual entrepreneurship and from an improvement in tax collection rates. Costs, in turn, are largely related to the compression of the aggregate level of domestic demand and, in particular, of development expenditure. What is necessary is to pursue efforts to increase the former, and to adopt measures to minimize or avoid the latter.

(c) Measures to enhance the role of the private sector and the efficiency of the public sector

With an inchoate domestic private sector, and the vacuum created by the emigration of foreign entrepreneurs upon decolonization, it was only normal that, in previous decades, the public sector should be expected to play a leading role in the development efforts of LDCs. The performance of the public sector of LDCs, however, as in many other developing countries, has been undermined by the expansion of recurrent costs, notably in terms of personnel expenditure, as well as by a record of inefficient management of scarce financial resources and of State-owned enterprises. As a reaction to these shortcomings, recent attempts have been made, often on the advice of multilateral financial institutions and as part of the adjustment packages negotiated with them, to place stronger reliance on the private sector and to submit public sector management to more stringent efficiency criteria. The attempts have entailed, *inter alia*, the privatization, liquidation, and streamlining of public enterprises, as well as the adoption of measures aimed at attracting direct foreign investment.

The new policy trend will no doubt have positive repercussions to the extent that it will lead to greater rigour in the management of public resources as well as to a greater mobilization of the private sector for development tasks. But this sector (which is very limited and weak in most LDCs) can hardly grow overnight and assume the pivotal role that the public sector has hitherto been expected to play in certain key productive activities. This is not to say, of course, that the private sector cannot or should not assume a more important participatory role in the development efforts of LDCs; simply that LDCs, unlike many other developing countries, do not have widely developed and dynamic entrepreneurship. It will, therefore, take some time for the private sector in the LDCs to be in a position to respond fully to the incentives which are now being given to it. Moreover, for such a response to take place, it is necessary to expand public investment in development infrastructure, notably as regards manpower training, improvement of the transport and communications network, and cross-fertilizing research and development. Public investment in these fields, however, has been curtailed more than once in the context of the demand-management measures embodied in adjustment programmes, and a closer ordering of priorities for essential public services and investments to be maintained now needs to be asserted.

Table 5

CENTRAL GOVERNMENT DEFICIT/SURPLUS AS A PERCENTAGE OF GDP

(selected LDCs)

	1980	*1981*	*1982*	*1983*	*1984*	*1985*	*1986*	*1987*
A. LDCs with adjustment programmes supported by IMF financing								
Bangladesh	2.51	-3.17	1.18	3.12	0.82	-1.42	..	..
Central African Rep.	..	-3.08	..	..	..	..	..	..
Gambia	-4.31	-12.17	-7.50	-7.54	..	..	..	..
Haiti	-4.76	-5.05	-4.70	-6.68	-4.08	-1.13	-1.62	-3.24
Malawi	-15.55	-12.43	-7.63	-7.08	-5.17	-8.04	-6.97	-7.23
Mali	-6.31	-3.95	-7.82	-8.40	-7.55	-9.82	..	..
Niger	-4.98	..	..	..	..	..	..	..
Sierra Leone	-12.83	-7.52	-8.92	-9.94	-7.57	-9.88	..	..
Sudan	-3.19	..	-3.70	..	..	..	..	..
Togo	-1.97	-5.74	-1.78	-1.99	-2.69	..	..	..
Uganda	..	-7.15	-4.87	-2.82	-3.41	-4.83	-4.42	..
B. Other LDCs with adjustment programmes outside the IMF framework								
Burkina Faso	0.34	-1.44	-1.72	0.15	-0.86	1.69	..	..
Yemen	-19.58	-20.09	-32.10	-27.12	-24.30	-21.36	-10.78	..

Source: IMF, *International Financial Statistics*, Yearbook 1987 and September 1988.

8. *Challenges for the 1990s*

The analysis of the measures taken by LDCs to improve the efficiency of resource use and allocation confirms the need to ensure compatibility between structural adjustment and economic growth. The pressing need to overcome external and fiscal imbalances and contain inflation, and the mounting debt burden and inadequate external support, have obliged LDCs, as well as many other developing countries, to place the emphasis on adjustment, sometimes to the detriment of growth. It is now widely recognized, however, that adjustment needs to be made more compatible with the development efforts and potential of the LDCs concerned. This recognition has been translated by the multilateral financial institutions into the expansion or establishment of lending facilities which provide credits of a longer-term nature and which are suitable for the promotion of long-term development programmes. The view has been expressed in particular by the Group of 24 developing countries, which operates at IMF/World Bank meetings, that performance criteria (last reviewed in 1978-1979) need to be reappraised in the light of the current debt crisis and prevailing conditions in the international economic environment. Increased attention is also being paid to the need to protect the poor from hardships arising out of adjustment measures. This matter is crucial for the LDCs. The UNICEF study, *Adjustment with a human face*[15], stresses that there do exist adjustment strategies other than programmes involving a deterioration of the living conditions of the population. They require, *inter alia*, more expansionary macro-economic policies; the use of policies influencing directly the inter-sectoral allocation of resources ("meso policies"); restructuring of the productive sector; improving the equity and efficiency of the social sector; compensatory programmes (often of limited duration) to protect basic health and nutrition of the low-income groups; and monitoring of the human situation. Such measures have to be complemented by an adequate international economic environment and international support, in particular in regard to debt rescheduling or forgiveness, improved aid flows, increased lending and greater market access.

From past experience, it appears that the crucial policy aim cannot be to ensure growth compatible with immediate current-account and fiscal equilibrium. The aim should instead be to ensure *sustainable adjustment*, i.e. improvements in the current-account and in fiscal balances which are compatible with

15 *Giovanni Andrea Cornia*, Richard Jolly, Frances Stewart (ed.), Adjustment with a human face, vol. I (Oxford, Clarendon Press, 1987).

minimum long-term growth levels. This point is not a matter of mere semantics. It has implications in terms of priorities, strategies and policies regarding economic development and adjustment in the LDCs.

The effectiveness of adjustment programmes largely depends on four critical issues: (i) adaptation of policy prescriptions and performance criteria to the specific needs and possibilities of the LDCs; (ii) full utilization of the potential of economic co-operation among developing countries (ECDC); (iii) improvement of the international economic environment, in particular as it affects the LDCs' trade and foreign-exchange receipts; and (iv) arresting the deterioration of LDCs natural environment.

(a) Adaptation of policy prescriptions to match LDCs' development requirements

Sustainable adjustment in least developed countries will require both a sufficiently long adjustment span of perhaps a decade, and a proper output mix which takes into account the possibilities offered by the external and the local markets. To design short-term policies and targets can only lead to a self-defeating, frustrating exercise. Similarly, given the present disarray in world commodity markets, and the technological dynamism and fierce competition which prevail in the international markets for manufactured goods, LDCs will have to ascertain carefully where their competitive advantage lies and which productive sectors can be developed. Needless to say, policies aimed at influencing the output mix are selective by nature ("meso policies") and go beyond the across-the-board, macro-economic measures which constitute the bulk of current adjustment programmes. LDCs' development strategies would need to address the key issues discussed below.

(i) Appropriate degree of outward orientation

The degree of outward orientation that LDCs should aim at is largely determined by prevailing conditions in the international markets for the different commodities and manufactured goods. Whereas many world commodity markets are showing record lows, the situation and prospects vary as between individual commodities. A number of minerals and metals would seem to offer better prospects than the generality of agricultural commodities. It might thus be useful to identify the commodities whose production should be encouraged in LDCs. Measures to enhance the processing of traditional commodities in LDCs would need to be considered in this context. It is equally necessary to identify the non-traditional sectors which LDCs could seek to penetrate (notably agro-industries), with appropriate international support and market access, as well as the prospects and conditions for developing outward-oriented services (such as tourism, port facilities, financial services and satellite-tracking systems) in LDCs.

(ii) Development of the local and subregional markets

The need for LDCs to embark on outward-looking strategies, and to promote the expansion and diversification of exports, has largely been accepted without question the grounds that these countries possess extremely small local markets, whose size would justify the production of only a very few elementary goods. Nevertheless, given the present disarray in world commodity markets as well as growing protectionism, more attention should now be given to whether and how the local and subregional markets of the LDCs could be made to play a more dynamic role. This would require reactivating demand for locally produced goods as well as expanding the growth of the manufacturing sector, notably through use of excess capacity, rehabilitation and further investment. At the same time, it is essential to develop mechanisms to facilitate intra-regional trade (cf. subsection (c) below). Neither strategy need wait to be demand-led: local and regional demand should instead be stimulated, a device developed countries have regularly employed in order to end recession.

(iii) Mobilization of domestic savings

As regards savings from public enterprises, the experience gained points to some general considerations. Firstly, pricing policies aimed at providing essential goods and services at prices covering only a fraction of the real costs are incompatible with improving the profitability of public enterprises. Secondly, Government subsidies for operational and administrative costs should be available only for those public enterprises which, although they cannot be run profitably, are considered worth retaining for social reasons. Thirdly, in all other public enterprises, economic efficiency should be the yardstick for evaluating the management performance, and welfare-oriented objections can best be insured otherwise, with subsidies targeted on those most in need.

Whereas the expansion of the monetized economy will facilitate the mobilization of the savings potential in LDCs, this will not by itself lead to higher private savings in LDCs unless it is supplemented by adequate interest rate policies and appropriate savings and lending mechanisms. The establishment of various savings-*cum*-Credit institutions should become the basic approach in tackling institutional constraints affecting the mobilization of private savings in LDCs.

Inflationary trends need to be taken into account when designing interest-rate policies. Indeed, efforts to mobilize savings, including the prevention of capital flight and the repatriation of capital, are bound to fail if interest rates remain negative, as was the case in many LDCs during the first half of the 1980s (see table 6). Therefore, an interest-rate policy that properly reflects the scarcity of funds and the cost of money is a prerequisite for enhancing the volume of private monetary savings.[16]

The imbalanced distribution of resources between rural and urban regions can be perceived in LDCs as regards financial resources. Private savings generated in the rural sector often end up in the non-agricultural sector. In the absence of active policy measures, the tendency for rural savings to be directed towards urban investment is very likely to intensify, bringing about numerous effects which are detrimental to the overall socio-economic development of these countries. As a matter of policy, governments in LDCs should adopt measures that prompt financial institutions to seek productive credit outlets for their local savings deposits in the regions where they are collected. Differential interest rates for urban and rural areas can be introduced. In addition, banks may need to be directed to invest a substantial proportion of deposits derived from rural savings in rural areas.

(iv) Development of the technological base of LDCs

The gravity of the payments crisis of LDCs has obliged these countries to give priority attention to policies aimed at ensuring financial discipline rather than to the longer-term question of technological development. The development of technologies more suited to LDCs in future, such as flexible craft industries, would allow production to switch between different types of goods and would thus tend to minimize capacity under-utilization. There is an emerging trend in world technology towards more flexible, craft-like processes, as opposed to conventional assembly-line systems.[17] The fact that the industrial sector of LDCs is at an embryonic stage makes it particularly relevant for these countries to ascertain carefully the type of technology that they can and should promote.

Whereas private entrepreneurship will ultimately determine such patterns of development, the public sector has a useful role to play, in particular by disseminating information on options available and on the evolving world technology, by providing incentives to the acquisition or development of adequate technology, and by developing human resources and the physical and institutional infrastructure. These are precisely the policy objectives, among others, which tend to be neglected or sacrificed by current adjustment programmes.

(v) Enhancing the role of women in development

Without deliberate and concrete action, the marginalization of women is likely to be accentuated in the future as women will have to face up to new challenges. Women will have to compete in the formal wage sector, and they will have to do so against a background of difficult employment conditions. Technological development will probably continue to displace women from traditional, non-marketable activities while favouring men in newly-created employment opportunities, thereby forcing women more into the informal sector. Also, increased urban migration poses problems to the landless poor, among them the poor rural women who, with no training whatsoever, will invariably end up in low-level service jobs or be exploited for their labour.[18] The particular problems of drought and desertification to which African LDCs are vulnerable will, in turn, hamper women's role as food producers.

---

16 There is at least one LDC where the use of interest rate as an instrument to elicit savings is probihited owing to religious customs.

17 Cf. Michel J. Piore and Charles F. Sabel, The SE*cond Industrial Divide* - Possiblities for Prosperity (New York, Basic Books, 1984).

18 In a paper entitled "Women in urban labour markets of Africa: the case of Tanzania", in *World Bank Staff Working Paper No. 380*, Nwanganga Shields points out that cumulative discrimination over time in both the provision of and the demand for educational services has limited the participation of women in the urban labour force.

Table 6

AVERAGE RATES OF INFLATION AND INTEREST IN SELECTED LDCs, 1980-1987

(percentages)

Country	*Inflation rate* [a]	*Interest rate* [b]
Afghanistan	4.9 [c]	..
Bangladesh	11.4	12.0 [c]
Botswana	10.6	9.5
Burkina Faso	4.9	7.0 [d]
Burma	5.4 [d]	..
Burundi	7.6	4.8 [d]
Central African Republic	10.4	7.4
Ethiopia	3.8	..
Gambia	20.8 [d]	10.1 [d]
Haiti	5.3	..
Lesotho	14.1 [d]	9.7 [e]
Malawi	13.3 [d]	11.5
Mauritania	10.2 [d]	12.0 [d]
Nepal	10.8	5.4
Niger	4.2	7.0 [d]
Rwanda	5.1	6.2
Samoa	12.4	11.0
Sierra Leone	57.1 [d]	11.4 [d]
Somalia	44.8 [d]	9.9 [d]
Sudan	31.1 [d]	..
Togo	6.5 [d]	7.0 [d]
United Rep. of Tanzania	30.5	4.8 [d]
Vanuatu	7.8 [d]	8.4

Source: IMF, *International Financial Statistics* (various issues).
a Based on the consumer price index.
b Deposit rate.
c 1980-1985.
d 1980-1986.
e Excluding 1984.

In the 1990s, women may continue to bear to a large extent the brunt of the negative effects of adjustment programmes in LDCs. Increased prices and shortages of important consumption items will aggravate the situation of households. Given the disadvantaged position of women in traditional family settings, the erosion of consumption levels will probably hit them more than their family partners; and, taking into account poverty thresholds in LDCs, this may lead to a decrease in their food intake and quality of their diet. Cutbacks in public expenditure, especially in the social sectors, will limit still further women's access to such services.

The policy implications of the particular problems women have to meet in the years ahead point to the need for a systematic policy aimed at enhancing the role of women in the LDCs. National development plans could provide an important focus on women's development needs, making an assessment of their needs at all levels and in all sectors.

(b) Adaptation of performance criteria to LDCs' development requirements

Performance criteria applied to LDCs have so far been related to relatively rigid targets regarding external and fiscal balances as well as domestic inflation rates. The targets have often been set with scant regard for exogenous developments such as conditions in world commodity markets, magnitudes and terms of financial inflows, and adverse environmental conditions. It is not realistic to expect that economically vulnerable LDCs will be able to meet targets whether or not exogenous conditions are favourable.

It is possible to conceive of performance criteria as determined by three different sets of variables: (i) one set relating to the magnitude of external and fiscal balances and inflation rates to be aimed at; (ii) a second set relating to rates of national economic growth and investment; and (iii) a third set encompassing exogenous factors. The performance criteria would thus be a 3-variable function whose axes would be as depicted above. Targets regarding external and fiscal balances and inflation rates (i.e. the balances variables) would then be directly related to (positive) exogenous variables and inversely related to growth and investment rates. Targets regarding the balances variables would be higher the better the international economic environment; and lower the better the performance of the national economy in terms of overall growth and investment.

In the proposed approach, targets would be represented by a "performance plane" where achievements in the balances variables would be a function of conditions prevailing in the international economic environment as well as of the magnitudes attained in regard to national growth and investment. A further dimension, that of income distribution, could be added to what is essentially a crude macro-economic model. Although with concern for the balance of payments uppermost, the distributional consequences of adjustment have traditionally been assumed to be neutral, experience has shown that this is not the case, and even IMF, which itself remains policy-neutral in this regard, is prepared to countenance and support measures which protect and strengthen the poorer and more vulnerable groups during adjustment. It is above all for the LDC Governments to give priority to such concerns in their own programmes.

(c) Economic co-operation among developing countries (ECDC)

The enhancement of ECDC (at the global, regional and subregional levels) should be an important additional component of the adjustment policies of LDCs. This would aim at compensating for the limited size of LDCs' domestic markets and limited endowments in terms of installed capacity, input availability and skilled manpower. Action is already being taken with regard to the establishment or strengthening of trade preferences and multilateral payments arrangements as well as to the promotion of multinational enterprises involving LDCs, but this action has not yet been properly connected with the design and implementation of adjustment programmes.

(d) Improvement of the international economic environment as it affects LDCs' trade and foreign-exchange receipts

A crucial element of any effective adjustment strategy for the least developed countries is the recognition of the need to improve the international economic environment in which these countries operate. It must not be forgotten that the present payments crisis of the LDCs has been largely determined by an adverse international economic environment throughout the 1980s. It is now a commonplace observation that the means put at the disposal of developing countries in the form of aid, balance-of-payments support and structural adjustment loans were never adequate for the tasks involved - nor was a correct "scale of charges" ever devised to cope with emerging problems. The task, and burden, of adjustment need indeed to be shared by all partners of the community. Hence, the importance of adequate international support (cf. chapter II below).

(i) Compensation for export earnings shortfalls

The instability in commodity export earnings has a particularly negative effect on the economies of LDCs as their capacity to cope with fluctuations in export earnings is limited. Improvements in present schemes should be considered as an integral element of an adjustment strategy for the LDCs.

(ii) Market access

It is essential that open or preferential market access be guaranteed to LDCs. It would not be rational to advise LDCs to expand and diversify their export base - as current policy prescriptions do - if at the same time access to international markets of goods for which LDCs have an actual or potential comparative advantage is constrained by protectionist measures.

(iii) Financial assistance and debt relief

Well-tailored adjustment programmes in LDCs will require time and resources both to be carried out and to start producing results. Hence the importance for these countries to secure continuous and adequate financial sup-

Balances variables
(external and fiscal deficits, inflation rates)

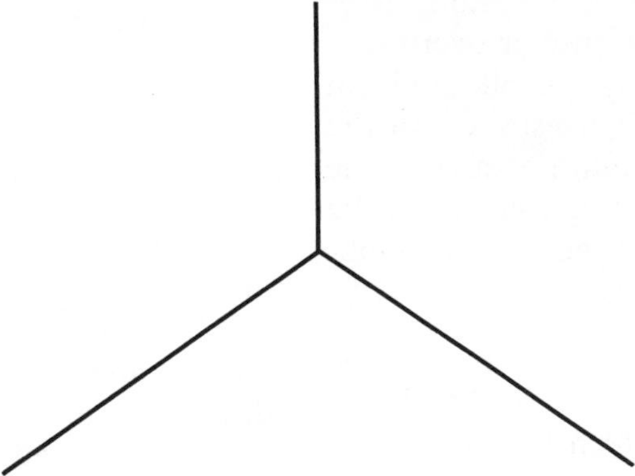

External environment variables
(terms of trade, level of world commodity demand, financial inflows)

Development variables
(growth and investment rates, diversification of supply capacity)

port throughout the period of adjustment, a matter which is dealt with at length in section A of chapter II below. The adequacy of support relates to its volume, form and sequencing. Reforms are belatedly being made in all three areas.

New longer-term facilities established by IMF and the World Bank can contribute to facilitating the adjustment efforts of the LDCs. Some of the new facilities are confined to low-income countries and, therefore, are of particular interest to the LDCs. Nevertheless, the establishment of such facilities does not eliminate the need to review and liberalize conditionality clauses and performance criteria embodied in the stabilization (stand-by) programmes: loans under the new facilities are usually (if not always) granted after the adjusting country has agreed to undertake a stabilization programme supported by an IMF stand-by credit. Such a link thus reveals a *de facto* obligation to accept the performance criteria embodied in the stand-by programmes or similar.

Further international support, notably from bilateral and other multilateral sources, has been expected to complement the adjustment efforts and the IMF/World Bank financing of adjustment programmes in LDCs. The adoption of adjustment programmes has by now become a *sine qua non* for mobilizing international support, particularly in the form of increased official development assistance and debt relief. What has happened in many cases is that IMF/World Bank financing has been substituted for sluggish or even declining trends in regard to other sources of finance, with the ensuing disadvantage for LDCs that there is not yet any mechanism for rescheduling or writing down multilateral debt. Action aimed at revitalizing such supplementary support becomes crucial for the LDCs, and the October 1988 decision by the World Bank effectively to fund the interest payments of countries now too poor to maintain their IBRD debt service points the way.

Debt rescheduling should be considered as an essential component of international support to the adjustment efforts of LDCs.

(e) Arresting the deterioration of the LDCs' natural environment

It is no exaggeration to say that halting environmental degradation is one of the most formidable, difficult yet inescapable challenges that least developed countries will face in the 1990s. Because of its ramifications and implications, environmental degradation in LDCs, should it continue, can in fact not only compromise and even nullify the LDCs' development efforts, but also affect the whole equilibrium of the earth's natural patrimony. This phenomenon has multiple manifestations which are related: steady deterioration of the natural environment, drought and its sequels, and other natural disasters. A further threat to the LDCs' natural environment which has arisen recently is the alarming use of poor countries such as the LDCs as the dumping ground for wastes generated in industrialized economies.

(i) *Steady deterioration of the natural environment*

Steady environmental degradation arises to a large extent from the misuse or overuse of arid and semi-arid land by people and, in pastoral economies, by their livestock. In the case of economically weak countries such as the LDCs, land misuse and overuse constitutes the inevitable response of a very poor rural population trying to cope with its subsistence needs.

A vicious circle operates in many LDCs: declining fertility and soil erosion lead to lower agricultural productivity, which forces a growing population to clear forest and to extend cultivation into marginal lands as a means of meeting food needs, which in turn reduces agricultural productivity, and so on. Deforestation is exacerbated further by heavy dependence on fuelwood in many LDCs: such dependence is reported to be as high as 90 per cent of total energy consumption in most African LDCs, and fuelwood demand is, for example, estimated to be 2.5 times the sustainable yield in Ethiopia and two times the yield in Sudan.[19] In addition, air and water pollution arising from rapid urbanization and/or uncontrolled industrialization is becoming an environmental problem in several LDCs, as it has been in more advanced developing countries for many years.

The relationship between poverty and environmental degradation has been highlighted in the report of the Brundtland Commission[20] , and the policy recommendations contained therein are highly relevant to the least developed countries.

Ecological degradation in LDCs is likely to have been aggravated by world-wide phenomena and climate changes such as the man-made greenhouse effect, which results from the release of increasing amounts of carbon dioxide into the atmosphere, principally in industrialized areas, as well as by large-scale atmosphere-ocean fluctuations occurring around the world.[21] Concerted international action in this regard would thus have positive repercussions on the LDCs′ environment and on the ability of these countries to surmount their structural shortcomings.

(ii) *Drought and its sequels*

Drought has been an environmental phenomenon of particular concern to many LDCs in recent years: it reportedly affects 20 LDCs in Africa and 3 in Asia. Intertwined with desertification, drought is a natural phenomenon due to various climatic and meteorological factors, although there is evidence that it may be induced by man-made devegetation.[22] A study commissioned by WMO and UNEP asserts that the inter-action of naturally-recurring drought with unwise land-use practices can result in desertification.[23] Surveys carried out in the West African region (including Burkina Faso, Mali and Niger) indicate that average rainfall has diminished considerably over the past 15 years as compared with the period 1934-1984.[24] Moreover, the fear has been expressed by environmental experts that drought episodes in Africa might in the future occur as often as every three years.[25] A solid anti-drought policy embodying both preventive and remedial measures is necessary for LDCs. Appropriate international support should be granted to these endeavours, and should be additional to that accorded to adjustment and strictly growth-oriented programmes.

Given a fragile environment, even improved rainfall in the aftermath of a drought episode may have adverse side effects. In Africa, good rains since late 1985 provided exceptionally favourable breeding conditions for the spread of grasshoppers and locusts. Control programmes currently implemented have had some success in reducing this threat, but it is not yet clear whether these programmes will be sufficient to prevent further increases in numbers.

---

19 Lester R. Brown *et al.*, State *of the World 1986 - A Worldwatch Institute* Report (New York, London, Norton, 1986), p.24.

20 "These links between poverty, inequality, and environmental degradation formed a major theme in our analysis and recommendations", in World Commission on Environment and Development, *Our Common Future* (Oxford University Press, 1987), p. xii.

21 World Meteorological Organization, *Report on drought and countries* affected by drought during 1974-1984 World Climate Programme (WCP-118), pp.5-6.

22 See *Countries stricken by desertification and drought,* report of the Secretary-General of the United Nations (A/41/346; E/1986/96), 9 June 1986, paras. 12-13.

23 Kenneth Hare, *Climate and desertification: a revised analysis, WorlD* Climate Programme (WCP-44), January 1983, pp.(ix) and 102.

24 *West Africa*, London, 3O May 1988, p.968.

25 *Marchés tropicaux et meditéranéens*, Paris, 28 August 1987, p.2289.

(iii) Other natural disasters

Environmental deterioration in least developed countries has been compounded by floods, cyclones, seismic disasters, civil strife and mass population movements. On the basis of long-term information (1960-1981) on the number of disasters and people killed, 15 LDCs have been identified by UNDRO among the vulnerable and disaster-prone countries.[26] Among them Bangladesh is by far the most disaster-prone, suffering 80 per cent of all the disaster-induced deaths recorded in the LDCs during 1960-1981. Disaster mortality tends to be higher the lower the income of the country affected.[27] It is for all these reasons that disaster preparedness will constitute a key policy priority for many LDCs in the 1990s.

(iv) The dumping of wastes in LDCs

An emerging serious problem concerning the LDCs' environment relates to the use of poor countries, such as the LDCs, as a dumping ground for wastes generated in developed countries. Developing countries in general, and LDCs in particular, are increasingly solicited for this type of transaction.[28] Unloading of wastes has been reported in eleven countries of Africa, five of which are LDCs (Benin, Equatorial Guinea, Guinea, Guinea-Bissau, and Sierra Leone). This practice is the result of a concourse of circumstances which include the pressing need for foreign exchange felt by poorer countries, the inherent institutional weaknesses of these countries in enforcing national legislation, the current lack of clear international instruments in this regard and, most importantly, the attempts by some big industrial enterprises (using in some cases affiliates/subsidiaries in LDCs) to reduce their waste disposal costs with little regard for the world environment. It should be noted that waste treatment costs in industrial countries are estimated to range between $160 and $1000 per tonne, whereas LDCs have reportedly been offered between $2.50 and $40 per tonne ($50 in the case of a joint venture). It should further be noted that, in some cases, shipments include radioactive wastes.

It is of the utmost importance that appropriate national and international legislation be formulated in this regard. Given the importance of this issue and the variety of approaches, international agreement on the action to be taken will need to be reached. This question is the subject of continuing consideration by the United Nations Environment Programme (UNEP) and by the United Nations General Assembly itself (cf. resolution 42/183 adopted in December 1987). A diplomatic conference is scheduled to be held in Basle, Switzerland, in 1989 for the purpose of adopting a global convention on control of transboundary movements of hazardous wastes, and preparatory technical work for the conference is being carried out by UNEP.[29] It is necessary that any future international action in this regard, *primo*, recognize the special difficulties encountered by LDCs, *secundo*, mobilize adequate international support for these countries to develop relevant physical and institutional infrastructures, and *tertio*, provide for mechanisms of compensation to LDCs having suffered damage from the traffic of wastes. The monitoring role that non-governmental organizations have played and can play in the future deserves to be clearly recognized.

---

26 UNDRO, *Disaster prevention and mitigation*, vol.12, 1986, table 3.

27 UNDRO asserts that certain patterns emerge from the analysis of the effects of natural disasters: "the amount of damage and lives lost usually bears a close relationship to the prevailing level of economic development. The smallest and the poorest countries are affected most severely by natural disasters, and the poorest and most disadvantaged members of a disaster affected community are likely to experience the most serious consequences" (*ibid.*, p.6).

28 For instance, the World Watch Institute reports that: "... shipments to the Third World represent a growing share of the total of the notifications of intent to export waste filed with the United States Environmental Protection Agency. The number of notifications for shipments to developing countries rose from 3 in 1984 to 22 in 1987. official figures probably represent just the tip of the iceberg, as many shipments are believed to take place illegally and therefore go undocumented" (*World Watch*, September/October 1988, p.6).

29 An *Ad hoc* Working Group of Legal and Technical Experts with a Mandate to Prepare a Global Convention on the Control of Transboundary Movements of Hazardous Wastes has been convened by the Executive Director of UNEP. The Ad hoc Working Group held three sessions in 1988 (in Geneva, Caracas and again in Geneva).

B. Policies regarding production sectors

1. *Food and agriculture*

In general, for the period 1980-1987, food and agricultural production growth rates (1.9 and 2 per cent, respectively) have not kept up with population growth (2.6 per cent) and remain below those for developing countries as a whole (see Statistical Annex). Within the LDCs category, some countries have performed particularly well: Benin, Bhutan, Burkina Faso, Burma, Gambia, Guinea-Bissau, Lao PDR, Uganda and Yemen have met the SNPA target of increasing agricultural production by "4 per cent or more" (SNPA, para. 13). These countries have also improved their performance with respect to the 1970s - the Gambia even reversing a 2.6 per cent decline in agricultural production in the 1970s to a 4.7 per cent average increase in 1980-1987. On the other hand, many others, including Afghanistan, Bangladesh, Central African Republic, Democratic Yemen, Ethiopia, Guinea, Lesotho, Malawi, Niger, Rwanda, Samoa, Sao Tome and Principe, Sierra Leone, United Republic of Tanzania and Vanuatu, have performed less well in the 1980s than in the 1970s, and their *per capita* food and agricultural production has declined. Among the types of production (see table 7) all cereals except maize have performed less well in the 1980s than in the 1970s, but for some primarily export crops (coffee, cocoa, cotton) the declines of the 1970s have been arrested or reversed.

(a) *Food self-sufficiency*

The SNPA included as one of its objectives the attainment of greater food self-sufficiency at the latest by 1990 (SNPA, para. 10) and called on "every least developed country to take important initiatives to reduce its dependence on food imports" (para. 12). Self-sufficiency ratios in cereals[30] (table 8) indicate that the situation has not greatly improved in the 1980s - the main exceptions being Lao PDR and Malawi. Of the 36 LDCs for which data are available (table 8), 16 had a self-sufficiency rate in cereals of 90 per cent or above in 1986, and another six of 80 per cent or above. Indeed, in almost all of them there have been local surpluses in certain regions, generally on a regular basis, and the main problem is often one of internal distribution, purchasing power, and competition with imports (often financed by aid programmes) rather than of production *per se*.[31]

A number of LDCs, although not fully self-sufficient, have had exportable surpluses in certain basic foodstuffs. Thus, in 1985/86, among the seven African countries which had exportable surpluses of coarse grain (of 2 million tons) four were LDCs (Benin: 30,000 tons; Malawi: 98,000 tons; Sudan: 780,000 tons, and Togo: 6,000 tons). These surpluses would have been sufficient to cover the total import requirement of the 16 African countries with deficits in these grains.[32] In 1986/87, the exportable surpluses of maize and sorghum of 9 African countries was estimated at 4.2 million tons (including Burkina Faso: 60,000 tons, Malawi: 100,000 tons, Mali: 100,000 tons, Niger: 500,000 tons, Sudan: 1,050,000 tons and Uganda: 20,000 tons), which represents more than twice the aggregate import requirements

30 Cereals tend to be the staple food in Asian LDCs and in the Sahel countries, but care should be taken not to analyse national food self-sufficiency in terms of cereals only. In several LDCs other types of food, such as root crops, pulses, plantains and coconuts, are an important part of the local diet. Cereals, and in particular wheat, should be considered as an exotic, even sometimes luxury, item in most island LDCs, and in Benin, Rwanda, Central African Republic and Equatorial Guinea the share of cereals in total calorie intake is 37, 25, 21, and 12 per cent, respectively, and there is considerable substitution between cereals and other foodcrops as relative prices change.

31 Local surpluses requiring external assistance for distribution are reported regularly by the Global Information and Early Warning System on Food and Agriculture of FAO. For example, in June, July and August 1988, such surpluses were noted in Burkina Faso, Chad, Mali, Mauritania, Niger, Sudan, United Republic of Tanzania and Uganda.

32 FAO, *Food Supply Situation and Crop Prospects in Sub-Saharan Africa*, 21 April 1986, p. 1.

Table 7

PRODUCTION OF MAJOR AGRICULTURAL PRODUCTS IN THE LDCs

Product	*Thousands of metric tons*	*Annual average growth rates (%)* [a]				
	1987	*1970-1980*	*1980-1987*	*1984-1985*	*1985-1986*	*1986-1987*
Total cereals	71818	2.9	1.2	10.3	3.6	-7.6
Wheat	6064	3.7	1.8	0.8	0.5	0.7
Rice, paddy	42477	3.1	1.2	2.0	1.9	-4.6
Sorghum	6123	3.5	-0.7	78.3	5.4	-27.2
Millet	5311	1.7	1.6	51.8	5.3	-12.5
Maize	9329	2.9	3.6	5.3	9.6	-5.4
Roots and tubers	27493	3.0	2.4	23.2	-1.5	-4.4
Cassavas	14422	2.8	2.3	28.4	-1.8	-6.3
Sweet potatoes	5701	2.9	3.3	31.0	-2.6	-1.1
Yam	2272	2.6	0.9	0.4	6.8	-1.9
Total pulses	4620	2.3	2.3	11.2	6.3	-5.5
Vegetables and melons	10766	2.0	2.4	2.5	2.5	1.5
Fruits excluding melons	23316	0.9	2.6	16.7	-0.1	1.3
Groundnuts in shell	2465	0.8	0.0	5.6	4.6	2.9
Oil crops	2161	0.0	2.3	5.3	5.0	4.0
Sugar, centrifugal raw	1468	2.8	6.1	-0.1	-4.2	10.6
Coffee	639	-0.8	2.4	9.5	2.8	4.0
Cocoa beans	46	-5.4	0.4	17.2	-3.4	-6.1
Tea	114	3.8	2.3	6.7	-5.9	5.9
Cotton lint	613	-3.5	7.4	5.7	-4.8	9.1
Jute and jute-like fibres	846	0.0	1.1	45.0	-10.1	-36.2
Tobacco	230	3.6	3.1	2.8	1.1	-6.1
Meat	4034	2.4	2.9	4.5	3.6	1.7

Source: UNCTAD secretariat calculations based on information provided by FAO.

a Exponential trend function.

of the 19 African countries with deficits in these grains.[33] In 1987/88, exportable surpluses had greatly diminished, but Burkina Faso, Chad, the Gambia, Mali, Mauritania, Niger, Somalia, Sudan, United Republic of Tanzania and Uganda had availabilities for export and/or local purchase. In that year, the United Republic of Tanzania exported 106,000 tons of cereals (104,000 tons commercially and 2,000 tons through triangular transactions), and had a small surplus left over. Following good harvests in 1988, FAO estimates that "several countries will again have exportable surpluses during 1988/89[34]."

(b) Policies adopted by LDCs

The agricultural performance of LDCs is determined to a large extent by exogenous factors (the weather[35], locust infestations, international prices of exported products and of competing food imports) on which national

33 *Ibid*, April 87, p. 3.

34 Ibid, June 1988, pp. 4, 11.

35 For instance, an in-depth econometric analysis of millet and sorghum production in Burkina Faso showed that by far the most important and significant factor affecting yields has been rainfall, accounting for more than 60 per cent of variations (Lecaillon, J., Morrisson, C., Schneider, H. and Thorbecke, E., *Economic Policies and Agricultural Performance in Low Income Countries*, Paris, OECD, 1987, p. 142.

Table 8

CEREALS : SELF-SUFFICIENCY RATES [a]

(Percentages)

	1970	*1980*	*1981*	*1982*	*1983*	*1984*	*1985*	*1986*
Afghanistan	97	100	98	98	98	100	99	97
Bangladesh	91	91	96	92	93	92	90	95
Benin	95	85	80	77	76	87	91	90
Bhutan	84	97	94	91	93	92	89	91
Botswana	14	39	51	23	11	4	12	12
Burkina Faso	97	93	96	93	94	88	89	96
Burma	108	105	105	105	106	105	103	103
Burundi	96	95	96	95	95	96	96	97
Cape Verde	4	12	5	7	4	4	2	15
Central African Rep.	90	89	86	88	87	87	87	79
Chad	99	97	93	87	90	81	87	90
Comoros	48	59	37	42	47	39	54	38
Democratic Yemen	31	36	34	29	35	28	26	33
Ethiopia	98	93	96	96	94	94	87	85
Gambia	84	64	70	75	61	55	63	66
Guinea	91	78	82	87	82	73	79	80
Guinea-Bissau	74	79	74	84	84	82	86	89
Haiti	91	68	69	66	67	69	67	69
Lao People's Dem.Rep.	93	90	95	97	96	96	97	98
Lesotho	83	64	63	53	41	50	56	48
Malawi	90	98	96	99	104	114	106	106
Maldives	4	0	1	1	1	1	1	1
Mali	97	91	93	90	89	75	86	91
Mauritania	58	24	37	28	17	15	19	37
Nepal	107	99	100	99	98	100	102	101
Niger	104	97	94	95	95	95	88	98
Rwanda	95	94	95	96	93	93	91	93
Sao Tome and Principe	7	7	6	8	7	6	8	8
Sierra Leone	84	87	87	83	92	91	80	82
Somalia	81	55	46	51	59	60	68	68
Sudan	90	102	99	100	90	75	78	86
Togo	94	88	83	85	78	84	84	85
Uganda	98	95	97	97	101	101	97	98
Un.Rep.of Tanzania	98	89	92	90	92	93	93	94
Vanuatu	8	9	12	9	8	7	6	7
Yemen	88	68	61	57	40	38	34	47
All LDCs	**96**	**93**	**95**	**94**	**94**	**92**	**90**	**93**

Source: FAO.

a Total production of cereals as percentage of total availabilities for domestic consumption (production *plus* imports *minus* exports) of cereals.

policies, however appropriate, cannot have significant impact.

Although serious malnutrition exists in almost all LDCs, on the whole arrangements, with the assistance of donors, to avoid famine and acute hunger have improved in the 1980s, even during the great African drought (1983-1985). Mechanisms such as the FAO Global Information and Early Warning System are now well established. Storage facilities on a national or regional basis have increased and donors have been generally quick to respond with food aid.[36] However, tragic local situations have existed and continue to exist, par-

[36] For instance, for 1988, the FAO had estimated the food aid requirements of Ethiopia (the most severely affected

ticularly in Ethiopia and Sudan. This is largely due to internal transport and logistical problems related to civil strife and displacement of populations. In Bangladesh food producers and consumers suffered particularly bad dislocations as a result of flooding again in 1988.

Although it is the stated objective of most of the LDCs to give the highest priority to food production and agricultural development, there have been many assertions in the past that some of the policies pursued were detrimental to agriculture.[37]

(i) Measures related to output

The main criticism is that food and agricultural prices had been kept artificially low and did not provide sufficient incentives to producers. The price of foodstuffs had in most cases been set by governments at relatively low levels, often much lower than international (or border) prices so as not to push up the price to consumers. As regards exported agricultural products, on which most governments had kept a close control, often through monopoly purchasing, the prices paid to producers had also in many cases been kept low. However, a general trend, particularly apparent in recent years, has been for a large number of LDCs to take steps to remedy these policy shortcomings. The extension of price incentives to food and agricultural producers has been an integral and major component of the adjustment measures taken by LDCs, as described in section A.1 above. In LDCs where governments intervene in the fixing of prices to food producers, the price levels have been regularly increased in a large number of LDCs. Even in Ethiopia, where the Agricultural Marketing Corporation (AMC) had long pursued a policy of unchanged grain prices to peasant farmers (which had hardly changed since 1979), prices were raised in early 1988, and the grain trade was partially liberalized. However, in LDCs official marketing organizations are hardly able to provide effective price support to food producers in times of surpluses, on a nation-wide basis. This is mostly due to inadequate commercial credit, storage capacity and transport networks. For instance, in Mali, as a result of bumper crops in 1985/86 and 1986/87, grains were being traded in 1987 at CFA 30 per kg, as compared to the official intervention price of CFA 55 per kg; and in late 1986, millet was traded at CFA 200 per "coro" (1.7 kg. unit) in N'Djamena (Chad) while sold at half that price at merely 30 km from the city.

Although in most LDCs the availability of food aid and cheap food imports[38] has tended to exert a downward pressure on food prices, a few LDCs have given incentives to local food producers by protective measures. Thus in 1987, in Gambia, subsidies were removed and a tariff was imposed on imported rice, whereas Niger started licensing rice imports. In Sierra Leone, subsidies on imported rice were terminated in 1986.

As for exported agricultural products, policies tending to favour higher producer prices have enabled farmers to sell their crops directly (outside the official marketing organs - e.g. for tea and sisal in United Republic of Tanzania). Elsewhere there have been reductions in export taxes (e.g. the export levy on rice in Nepal, the export tax on coffee in Haiti).

Among the most positive initiatives taken in the second half of the 1980s to encourage agricultural producers in sub-Saharan Africa is the arrangment for purchasing local surpluses for distribution to deficit areas within the same country or to a neighbouring country with financial assistance of donors. Information on such transactions involving LDCs in sub-Saharan Africa is provided in table 15. These transactions have allowed producers to dispose of their surplus against cash, and encouraged them to continue their successful production efforts. Another advantage is that the recipient area or country has received food supplies of the same or similar kind as produced domestically, thus avoiding the displacement effect and change of taste associated with exotic foods (such as soft wheat) imported from distant geographical areas. Finally, these transactions have helped to put in place or improve logistic arrangements that can be used or replicated for normal commercial transactions.

country in that year) at 1.3 million tons of cereals, and by April 1988 it was reported that 1,258 million tons had been pledged (while no commercial purchases had been made). FAO, *Food Crops and Shortages*, April 1988, pp. 11, 32.

37 For examples, see, for instance, World Bank, *World Development Report 1986*, chapters 4 and 5, and FAO, *African Agriculture: the next 25 years*, Annex V, *Inputs supply and incentive policieS*, Rome, 1986; UNCTAD, *The Least Developed Countries, 1986 Report*, paras. 45-46.

38 International food prices are artificially depressed by national support policies, leading to surpluses, particularly in OECD countries. This leads to "special measures to promote stock disposal", and the agricultural trade of OECD countries "suffers from substantial recourse to export subsidisation and the maintenance of import barriers, which is widening the gap between domestic and world prices", OECD, *Agricultural Policies, Markets and Trade*, 1988, p.8.

(ii) Measures relating to inputs

All LDC Governments have made efforts to support agricultural producers by making available direct or indirect inputs into the agricultural production process. The activities undertaken include the provision of extension services and agricultural credit, agricultural research (often on a regional basis), maintenance and extension of irrigation systems, provision of access to improved seeds and animal breeds, to assistance with pest control and animal vaccination,the distribution of inputs such as fertilizers or fishing vessels. These efforts have often fallen short of the needs and of the Governments' intentions owing to the lack of manpower and to budgetary constraints, and despite donors' support on a wide range of rural development initiatives. Lending institutions have been particularly active in encouraging liberalization of agricultural inputs too. Fertilizer policy is one particular area where many LDC Governments have agreed to switch to full-cost pricing and private supply, despite the obvious attraction for increased fertilizer uptake of government subsidies. Some input subsidies on fertilizers have been reduced for straight budgetary reasons (Bangladesh) or to prevent unofficial exports across the border (Nepal).

(iii) Supply and distribution of consumer goods in rural areas

Farmers in remote areas choose to limit production as they are unable to spend the monetary income they can obtain for their produce on consumer goods.[39] Thus, the availability of incentive goods can be considered as an indirect input into agriculture. In several LDCs, attempts have been made to supplement spontaneous private trading (which is often insufficiently operative in remote areas with low initial purchasing power), with the creation or promotion of additional distribution systems for consumer goods. Examples are the rural co-operative stores which have been set up in the 1980s with the assistance of NGOs in the pastoral areas of North-East Mali, and of the Iamesna in Niger, as well as in Rwanda and Burundi.

(iv) Farming systems

Most LDC Governments appreciate the crucial role of farming and land tenure systems in agriculture, and recognize that existing systems, either based on traditional patterns or inherited from colonial structures, often act as a constraint to the modernization of agriculture.[40]

Land ownership and farming patterns differ greatly among the LDCs, and indeed often within the same country. It is thus not surprising to find a great variety of policies pursued by LDC Governments in this area.

One common problem seems to have been the difficulty for States to influence or regulate actual practices as regards land tenure and farm organization. For instance, in Vanuatu, in spite of a number of regulations introduced since independence, a large number of land tenure disputes have continued to occur. Since 1984 Burkina Faso has attempted to deal with the mostly communal land ownership pattern, prevalent in most sub-Saharan African countries, by assigning the total land area of the country to the State (Ordinance 84-050-CNR PRES), a provision which is proving difficult to implement in practice. Mauritania, while dispensing with the traditional land tenure system in 1983 (Ordinance no. 83-127), has been more flexible since it also retained the principle of collective ownership (Articles 5 and 6), and provided for adaptation to the needs of individuals by encouraging private land ownership, provided the principles of the "sharia" are respected (Articles 1, 2 and 6). Nepal, which has pursued a land reform programme over a number of years, emphasizing protection of tenancy rights, rent fixation, termination of dual ownership, and selling excess land above ceilings, has asserted that it is making very little progress in this area, owing in part to "delay in preparing the legal basis" for carrying out land reform effectively.[41] In a number of LDCs with a socialist orientation, difficulties in implementing official policies have led in the 1980s to a more cautious and case-by-case approach to reforms in farm organization. Thus, in United Republic of Tanzania, the villagization (ujamaa) programme, which had been vigorously pursued since the late 1960s, has now been deemphasized. In the Lao PDR, the initial

---

39 This constraint is noted for instance in FAO, *African agriculture: the next 25 years*, annex V: *Inputs supply and incentive policies*, 1986, p. 88.

40 A typical assessment is in Sudan, where an FAO consultant (formerly Minister of Agriculture) noted: "The existing land tenure laws and regulations and production relations are out-moded and most of them have been out-paced by technological and socio-economic changes". Ali Eltom, *Towards a Long-term Agricultural Development Strategy*, paper presented at the Sudan Agricultural Sector Conference, Khartoum, 18-30 February 1986.

41 Nepal's National Planning Commission, *The Seventh Plan* (1985-1990), June 1985, pp. 460, 461.

attempt by the Government to establish co-operatives by decree in 1978-79, has been replaced in the 1980s by a long-term voluntary process providing incentives to form co-operatives (starting in the lowlands), so as to facilitate technology transfer, distribution of inputs and marketing of output. Similarly in Afghanistan, the first phase of the land reform whereby land was distributed to landless peasants from large and middle-size landlords took place in 1978-1979. However, in the 1980s the Government has asserted that land redistribution was carried out too hastily as it was not accompanied by tackling the problem of water distribution and technical assistance to peasants. Thus, since 1981, the Government has proceeded much more slowly, assessing land ownership patterns on a village-by-village basis and taking into account local religious beliefs and traditions, and registering new land rights in a more systematic manner.

In most LDCs, the mid-1980s have seen a contraction in the role of the State as a direct operator in agricultural production. Even in countries with an inclination towards State ownership (e.g. Afghanistan, Lao PDR), State farms occupy only a small fraction of the cultivated land, and have not been extended in the 1980s. In several LDCs, State or parastatal farms have either been discontinued or allowed to revert to the private sector. Thus, in Guinea, the Government has discontinued the state-run FAPAs (Fermes Agropastorales d'Arrondissement). United Republic of Tanzania has since the mid 1980s been encouraging private investment in export agriculture. Sisal farms have been privatized and a multinational corporation, which had withdrawn in the 1970s, has been expanding its activities in tea estates since 1987. In Sao Tome and Principe, since 1986, the management of several State agricultural entreprises have been handed over to foreign companies, and small farmers have been encouraged to own their own plot of land. In Malawi, a number of agricultural estates owned by the parastatal ADMARC are being sold off. In Ethiopia, on the other hand, an extension of the acreage of State farms has taken place in the 1980s. In Comoros, the formerly foreign-owned plantation company (Bambao-SAGC) was taken over by the State in 1987, but in 1988 negotiations were in progress for its acquisition by a multinational corporation in the perfume industry.

(v) Fisheries

Fisheries development often presents different problems from those encountered in crop or livestock production, whether the export or domestic market is dominant.

Total LDCs catches increased by 20 per cent between 1980 and 1986. Bangladesh, Burma and United Republic of Tanzania are the most prominent fishing countries among the LDCs, accounting for almost two thirds of the LDCs' total catch in 1986. Fish and fish products are among the main merchandise export products in Cape Verde, Guinea Bissau, Kiribati and Maldives. However, in terms of world fish catches, the share of the LDCs small, averaging a little over 3 per cent during the 1980s (see table 9).

Land-locked LDCs engage in fishing only in inland waters. Inland water fishing also yields most of the catch in a number of LDCs which have access to marine waters, such as Bangladesh, Benin, Ethiopia, Sudan and United Republic of Tanzania. This is due to the fact that inland water fishing is mainly an activity of the traditional sector. Traditional small-scale fishing also holds a strong position in the marine coastal fishing of LDCs. Conversely, modern deep-water fishing is capital-and energy-intensive and requires well equipped on-shore facilities and sophisticated technical skills, which restricts the participation of LDCs in this type of activity.

Under the United Nations Convention on the Law of the Sea, coastal and island LDCs have acquired national jurisdiction over greatly expanded Exclusive Economic Zones (EEZ). In view of the serious managerial, technological and technical problems which the LDCs concerned face in exploiting the living resources of these zones on a large scale, many of them have opted for the leasing of parts of their EEZ to fleets of developed countries or for the issuance of licences. The most comprehensive fishing agreement so far, to which LDCs are part, is the Tuna Fishing Agreement signed in April 1987 between the United States and the member states of the South Pacific Forum Fishery Agency, of which Kiribati, Samoa, Tuvalu and Vanuatu are members. Other instances of fishing agreements concerning LDCs are in the Comoros, Mauritania, and Sao Tome and Principe.

Marketing, storage and distribution of fish products in tropical countries poses more complex problems than in the case of crops or livestock, owing to the need for freezing/cooling throughout the distribution chain, or for accessible canning facilities for which only a few LDCs have the minimum concentrated catch. In the absence of adequate storage or processing facilities an increase in catches often leads to perishable surpluses which cannot find a market.

(c) Food aid

For no other group of countries is food aid as important as in the LDCs. They have received, in absolute terms and proportionally, an increasing amount of food aid in the 1980s, representing more than 40 per cent of total food aid to developing countries in the second half of the decade (table 10). On a per capita basis they receive about two and a half times the average for developing countries as a whole. In 1986, food aid was estimated to represent 5.7 per cent of the cereal production of LDCs (from 4 per cent in 1980) (see table 10). In view of the high level of subsistence or non-traded production, the impact of food aid is more important than these figures would indicate if compared to marketed food production. Thus, in Bangladesh, although in 1986 food aid was only about 5 per cent of total cereal production, food aid has represented in the 1980s between two and seven times the amount procured domestically by the Food Ministry.

Food and agricultural policies in LDCs thus cannot be discussed without addressing the question of food aid. There is an ongoing debate about the pros and cons of food aid in developing countries. Whereas there is unanimous agreement on the principle that food aid is vital in times of emergency to avoid acute food shortages, the definition of what constitutes an emergency is often very difficult in practice and there has been an understandable tendency among donors and recipients alike to feel that it is far more serious to err on the side of too little (or too late) than of too much emergency food aid.

As regards structural (i.e. non-emergency) food aid on a continuing basis and on an increasing level - which is what is happening in a majority of LDCs - its negative effects on domestic agriculture are well known. Briefly:

- It acts as a disincentive to domestic producers by lowering prices, by making it more difficult for procurement agencies to purchase and stock local surpluses (given the limited storage space), and by shifting tastes, particularly in urban areas, away from traditional locally produced foods (e.g. maize, millet, sorghum, cassava) to imported food (often wheat and rice);
- It reduces the priority that governments accord to agricultural and food production.

LDC Governments and donors are aware of these disadvantages, but the continued attraction of food aid, apart from the need thereof, is due to the combination of the following factors:

- From the recipient point of view, food aid - other than that distributed freely to specific target groups - generates counterpart resources which can be used flexibly by the recipient Governments. When food aid is sold at market - or near market - prices (which is recommended to lessen its negative impact on domestic producers), the budgetary impact of phasing out of food aid would be considerable.[42] In addition, food aid releases scarce foreign exchange to meet other crucial import needs if the alternative to food aid is imports on commercial terms and no alternative balance-of-payments support is available. In a sense, continued availability of food aid (and the non-availability of alternative programme aid or balance-of-payments support) means that many LDC Governments cannot afford food self-sufficiency, and have every interest in continuing to be classified as a "food-deficit" country.
- From the donors' point of view, surplus agricultural production in a number of OECD donor countries, makes this form of aid available at almost no opportunity cost.[43]

(d) Challenges for the 1990s

The development of appropriate food policies is one of the most complex challenges confronting LDCs. As the Executive Director of the World Food Council has pointed out, "decision-makers are confronted with a plethora of prescriptive pronouncements about the policy and programme reforms that are needed to reverse the present food situation. ... It has

42 In one East African LDC restoration of food self-sufficiency in maize in 1985 has been estimated as likely to lead to an increase of the recurrent budget deficit by $US 100 million or 30 per cent (R.H. Green, "Agricultural sector proposals, performance and potential in the SNPA context", paper prepared for the UNCTAD secretariat, 1985).

43 This point is well appreciated in many donor countries. Thus, the Minister of Overseas Development of the United Kingdom, Mr. Chris Patten, commented that "Food aid should now provide what recipients need rather than what we in Europe wish to get rid of" (speech to the Royal Institute of International Affairs, London, March 1987).

Table 9

FISHERY : NOMINAL CATCHES IN LDCs [a] (in 1000 mt)

Country	*1980*	*1981*	*1982*	*1983*	*1984*	*1985*	*1986*
Bangladesh	646	650	686	724	754	774	794
Burma	580	595	584	588	610	644	644
United Rep. of Tanzania	228	231	238	239	277	301	310
Uganda [b]	166	167	170	172	212	212	212
Chad [b]	115	115	115	110	110	115	110
Mauritania	22	59	54	82	100	109	104
Democratic Yemen	80	78	70	74	84	85	91
Malawi [b]	66	51	58	67	65	62	73
Mali [b]	88	76	74	61	54	60	61
Sierra Leone	49	51	53	51	53	53	53
Maldives	35	34	31	39	55	51	46
Kiribati	19	20	20	24	26	30	34
Guinea	20	22	24	26	28	30	30
Sudan	26	29	30	30	30	26	24
Benin	24	24	24	21	20	20	24
Yemen	17	16	14	17	18	21	22
Lao People's Dem.Rep. [b]	20	20	20	20	20	20	20
Somalia	14	10	9	11	20	17	17
Togo	9	10	15	15	15	16	15
Central African Rep. [b]	13	13	13	13	13	13	13
Gambia	13	14	9	12	12	11	11
Cape Verde	9	15	12	12	11	10	10
Other LDCs	64	64	66	64	67	70	68
LDCs [c]	2 323	2364	2379	2472	2654	2750	2786
LDCs [c] (as % of world)	3.2	3.2	3.1	3.2	3.2	3.2	3.0

Source: FAO : Fishery statistics, catches and lendings, vol. 62, Rome 1988.

a Ranked in descending order of volume of catches in 1986.
b Land-locked country.
c Excluding Lesotho.

often been assumed that all that is required to institutionalize these reforms is 'political will'. However, it is clear that political will for implementation is in part lacking because the inherent conflicts of interest which accompany these reforms are not being addressed. Many suggested reforms such as reducing subsidies, streamlining the public sector, devaluation, and increasing domestic food prices are classic recipes for political and economic instability[44]." Yet, in view of the importance of food as a basic need, and food production as one of the main economic activities in most LDCs, each LDC Government needs to formulate and implement a food policy. In spite of the diversity of the LDCs, some general principles are applicable to the great majority of them.

At this juncture, it is worth noting that the most advanced agricultural systems in the industrialized countries base their sustained success in terms of yields and security of supply - even surplus - on strong domestic policies in support of agriculture and, in particular, of farmers. It is surely neither desirable nor feasible for the LDCs to set up agricultural subsidy schemes of similar magnitude. However, the fixing by the Government of remunerative minimum prices for individual crops well in advance of the time at which the farmers have to decide on the kind and the quantity of the crop they will cultivate and the readiness on the part of an official agency to act as a buyer of last resort at these fixed prices, would protect the

44 "Effectiveness of aid in support of food strategies", *Report by the Executive Director, World Food Council,* WFC/1985/3, 25 February 1985, paras. 34-35.

Box 4

RECONCILING INCENTIVES TO FARMERS WITH FOOD SECURITY IN BANGLADESH

The Bangladesh Government's food and agricultural policy has been pursuing two objectives: to ensure food security to the population, at the same time as to provide incentives to producers so as to increase domestic production.

The Government's record in ensuring food security has improved greatly in the 1980s and, despite poor crops and natural disasters, acute food shortages have been avoided. This has been possible by arranging for adequate and timely imports, financed mainly by external aid and by improved management of the Public Food Distribution System (PFDS). The Food Ministry has to plan in advance for procurement quantities, including the amount to be purchased domestically and the (much larger) quantities which are needed as commercial food imports and made available under food aid. Any delaying of imports to ensure priority in procurement to domestic producers has tended to cause market nervousness and sharp increases in food prices.

At the same time, a key element in Bangladesh's agricultural policy in the 1980s has been to provide adequate incentives to producers by steadily increasing procurement (floor) prices for food grains. (However, this was accompanied by a reduction in input subsidies, particularly for fertilizers). Thus, the official procurement price of rice (including a transportation bonus) which was more than 45 per cent below the international (border) price in FY 1982 has been set above the border prices since 1985, and for wheat the gap which was over 20 per cent in 1982 had almost been closed by 1988. However, these higher procurement prices are not yet fully effective, in particular, since the procurement system often fails to buy up all the food grain offered to it at the announced price. Market prices often fall below the official floor price, when either crops are good and/or when the PFDS has sufficient access to imports and food aid. Procurement from domestic producers has often to be slowed down in order for the PFDS not to carry excessive stocks. This is done by such methods as tightening the quality criteria (e.g. moisture content) for purchasing food grains. It can lead to distress sales below floor prices, particularly by small farmers who need cash to meet their immediate commitments.

farmers against undesired effects of the operation of the market mechanism. In addition, such schemes could serve as an effective means for improving the quality of, as well as for attracting the farmers' attention to, crops which are at a premium either for domestic consumption or for export.

For price measures to become a mobilizing factor, effectively operating rural markets are a necessary precondition. Since localized surpluses of agricultural produce, however small they may be, exist even in drought-stricken African LDCs, improvements in the marketing systems, including the transport channels, can have a stimulating impact on the producers' willingness to extend production far above the mere subsistence level. A well functioning market system is not only crucial for draining local surpluses in agricultural products into deficit areas, but also for the reverse flow of agricultural inputs and consumer goods to the farmers. Action by the Governments of some LDCs aimed at replacing the traditional rural traders with State-owned wholesale and retail systems, on grounds of alleged monopoly positions and high profit takings by the former, have often proved a failure and adversely affected the production and the supply of export and food crops. The mobilizing effect of rural markets will certainly be enhanced if Governments help smooth the trade channels from and to rural areas by providing an appropriate physical infrastructure.

It should be noted that, given the importance of agriculture in the national output and production of LDCs and the high proportion of personal incomes spent on food in these countries, food and agricultural policies are intimately linked with macro-economic policies as a whole, as well as with policies in other sectors. Agricultural and food policies imply much more than the allocation of a given percentage of the national budget or of the National Investment Plan outlay to the agricultural sector. For instance, the correction of the overvaluation of exchange rates in a number of LDCs in the 1980s (see section A.1.(a) above) has had direct effects on encouraging agricultural output by improving the domestic prices of agricultural exports as well as by making local food production more competitive *vis-à-vis* food imports. Similarly, efforts made by LDCs to build or improve roads, particularly rural access roads, and to improve their transport system, are clearly one of the most powerful measures that can be taken to

Table 10

PRODUCTION AND SHIPMENT OF FOOD AID IN CEREALS

	Production in cereals (000 mt)		*Food aid in cereals* *Total (000 mt)*		*Per capita (kg)*		*Food aid as % of production*	
Recipient	*1980*	*1986*	*1979/1980*	*1985/1986*	*1979/1980*	*1985/1986*	*1979/1980*	*1985/1986*
Afghanistan	4370	4042	176	170	11.0	9.1	4.0	4.2
Bangladesh	21698	25333	1480	1287	16.7	12.8	6.8	5.1
Benin	346	504	5	11	1.4	2.6	1.4	2.2
Bhutan	105	182	1	3	0.6	2.0	1.0	1.6
Botswana	44	11	20	49	21.9	42.8	45.5	445.5
Burkina Faso	1036	1894	37	109	5.9	15.3	3.6	5.8
Burma	13393	15812	11	-	0.3	-	0.1	-
Burundi	297	464	8	6	2.0	1.1	2.7	1.3
Cape Verde	7	12	34	51	115.2	148.2	485.7	425.0
Central African Rep.	100	108	3	11	1.3	3.9	3.0	10.2
Chad	678	752	16	74	3.6	14.3	2.4	9.8
Comoros	19	23	3	8	6.7	15.8	15.8	34.8
Democratic Yemen	117	113	13	7	6.6	3.0	11.1	6.2
Djibouti	..	..	5	20	15.8	43.4	..	..
Equatorial Guinea	..	..	0	4	0.9	9.7	..	..
Ethiopia	5868	5720	112	793	3.0	17.7	1.9	13.9
Gambia	80	138	7	16	10.7	21.1	8.8	11.6
Guinea	481	604	24	55	4.5	8.8	5.0	9.1
Guinea-Bissau	37	211	18	16	21.8	17.9	48.6	7.6
Haiti	370	450	53	133	10.7	24.7	14.3	29.6
Kiribati	..	..	1	-	16.9	-	..	..
Lao People's Dem.Rep.	1081	1527	3	4	0.9	1.1	0.3	0.3
Lesotho	194	132	29	40	21.4	25.6	14.9	30.3
Malawi	1324	1564	5	5	0.8	0.7	0.4	0.3
Maldives	..	..	1	19	6.4	98.9	..	..
Mali	955	1775	22	83	3.1	9.9	2.3	4.7
Mauritania	29	112	26	137	16.1	70.0	89.7	122.3
Nepal	3792	3989	21	9	1.5	0.5	0.6	0.2
Niger	1777	1832	9	97	1.7	15.4	0.5	5.3
Rwanda	260	317	14	25	2.8	4.0	5.4	7.9
Samoa	..	..	2	-	10.3	-	..	..
Sao Tome and Principe	1	1	2	6	17.0	52.7	200.0	600.0
Sierra Leone	548	577	36	49	11.0	13.2	6.6	8.5
Somalia	253	639	137	126	29.3	22.7	54.2	19.7
Sudan	2933	4386	212	904	11.4	40.7	7.2	20.6
Togo	311	313	7	9	2.9	3.0	2.3	2.9
Tuvalu	..	..	..	..	..	..	..	..
Uganda	1078	1100	17	7	1.3	0.4	1.6	0.6
Un.Rep. of Tanzania	1416	3777	89	66	4.8	2.9	6.3	1.7
Vanuatu	1	1	..	..	..	..	..	..
Yemen	901	566	6	57	0.9	6.9	0.7	10.1
All LDCs	**65900**	**78981**	**2665**	**4466**	**8.1**	**11.7**	**4.0**	**5.7**
All developing countries	**465879**	**564934**	**8394**	**10484**	**3.7**	**4 .1**	**1.8**	**1.9**

Source: FAO, *Food Aid in Figures* No. 5, 1987, and *FAO, Production Yearbook*, vol. 36, 1982 and vol. 40, 1986.

promote agricultural development, although they are not usually termed "food and agricultural policies", nor do they fall within the purview of ministries of agriculture.

(i) Food security

A basic continuing objective of LDCs will be to ensure food security in order to avoid acute hunger and famines. The existing national, regional and international mechanisms to this effect, including advanced identification of risk populations, the pre-positioning of stocks and logistical arrangements for food distribution, particularly in emergency situations, need to be consolidated and improved. However, food security, in the sense of access by all people and at all times to enough food for an active, healthy life, is adversely affected mostly by a lack of purchasing power, and will only be attained with the eradication of poverty itself.[45]

In many LDCs, a major policy dilemma has been one of finding ways to balance the need for food security (which implies procuring and stocking food from the cheapest sources, including food aid and/or making cheap or free food available to poor sections of the population), with the provision of incentives to producers, which requires that they be offered or guaranteed renumerative prices (see Box on Bangladesh).

In order to reconcile more fully the incentives to farmers with food security, national authorities would need to announce the floor price well in advance of sowing, and be able to take up all the grain quantities offered without delay at that price. This would require additional finance and storage facilities to stock food, and in effect use imported food and food aid as procurement of the last resort; but without jeopardizing food security.

(ii) Food self-sufficiency

Continued or increased reliance on food imports and food aid is incompatible with the objective of food self-sufficiency. Apart from a few cases (e.g. Cape Verde, Maldives) where food self-sufficiency appears technically unrealistic, increased self-sufficiency in food is a declared and feasible objective for the great majority of LDCs, in line with the provisions of the SNPA and of other statements of goals such as the Lagos Plan of Action.

Given the availability of labour and land in most LDCs, and the fact that their agricultural production can be increased with relatively little recourse to scarce factors such as imported capital inputs and technology, food and agriculture are areas where LDCs have the least comparative disadvantage. There is in any case little alternative occupation available to the majority of their population. Thus, in most LDCs the achievement of self-sufficiency in food and the development of the agricultural sector, combined with processing of agricultural products, should be expected to remain a priority objective for the 1990s. Even in LDCs which do not enjoy favourable production conditions for agriculture, decisions could be taken on the level of self-sufficiency to be achieved (and on the ways to close the food gap). In most LDCs, where food self-sufficiency is feasible, there will be fluctuations based in particular on climatic conditions, and the aim should be to achieve trend self-sufficiency, exporting in years of good harvests, and storing and trading to offset annual fluctuations and ensure food security.

(iii) Agricultural and food support policies

Probably the most important principle that LDC Governments with the assistance of donors could attempt to follow in the long run is to provide adequate minimum intervention (or floor) prices to producers of basic food commodities, and to set up effective purchasing and storage arrangements to take up available production. This principle is well known and is the key component of the agricultural policies in most developed countries, where high guaranteed prices to producers have been successful - sometimes too successful - in producing large agricultural surpluses. More modest price support systems are working relatively well in India, and Bangladesh is also attempting to follow a similar policy (see Box 4 above). It is true that the agricultural pricing policies of developed countries have come under criticism, in particular since they imply a high level of protectionism, whereas the disposal of their surplus stocks on the world market is leading to low and unstable international food prices. These criticisms, however, would not be applicable to LDCs: it is out of the question for them to be able to sustain support prices ap-

---

[45] This point is made strongly in *Poverty and Hunger*, A World Bank Policy Study, World Bank, 1986.

proaching those prevailing in developed market economies[46] and, in any event, their eventual net food surpluses are likely to be insignificant by world standards in the foreseeable future.

The principle of support prices announced in advance is, admittedly, far easier to state than to implement. Even if the managerial and logistical arrangements to enable official institutions to act as buyer of the last resort are established, a major problem in LDCs is the fact that the higher prices paid to producers will be reflected in higher prices charged to consumers, including the urban population and the landless rural population, unless substantial financing for subsidies is available.

The setting up of support mechanisms would need to relate to the following policy objectives:

- Except in emergencies and for distribution to precisely defined target groups, food would not be sold at below "normal" prices, so as not to exert a downward pressure on prices obtained by domestic producers.
- The alternative of providing cash payments to target households to allow them to have access to food (e.g. as implemented under UNICEF projects in Ethiopia and Burkina Faso) could be further developed in appropriate cases.[47] These cash payments could replace food aid and not other forms of ODA.
- A priority for the use of aid funds and in particular of counterpart funds generated by food aid sales could be the stimulation of food production and increase in producers' incomes by providing price support (as was done for example in Mali with food aid provided by a number of donors including WFP[48]).
- Storage capacity would need to be expanded, so that in no case should stocking of security food aid pre-empt the purchase of locally available surpluses. Storage capacity for crops, and even more so for fish (cold stores) needs to be organized on a collective basis and cannot be efficiently handled at the individual small-producer level.
- Whenever supply of local foodstuffs is available, exotic food imports, such as canned fish, wheat or wheat flour in some LDCs, may have to be considered as luxury products and taxed accordingly.
- Competitive purchasing, marketing/distribution channels in the food and agricultural sector could be actively encouraged. This may require initial subsidies in remote rural areas.
- Efforts could be made to diminish and gradually replace the present level of structural (i.e. non-emergency) food aid by other forms of flexible programme aid. This is necessary so that those LDCs which increase their degree of food self-sufficiency are not penalized by a reduction of the level of ODA and counterpart resources available to them through food aid.
- Aid for local food purchases and triangular transactions within the region (see table 11) could be expanded.

LDC Governments could be assisted to implement appropriate price support policies, and provided with the resources so that the implementation of such policies does not lead to political and economic instability.

The "liberalization of prices" is an improved policy measure in cases where agricultural products - notably for export - are subject to monopoly purchasing arrangements leading to producers receiving prices below those prevailing in the market. But mere "liberalization", in the absence of effective price support and collection mechanisms, would continue to lead to unsold local surpluses, or to unpredictable or grossly sub-remunerative prices to producers in time (or areas) of surplus production. This would nullify the efforts made on the input side to increase productivity and production. This is one of the problems encountered for instance with the otherwise successful rural credit scheme in Mali described in the Box below.

(iv) Measures on the input side

Governments, with the help of donors, could continue to make available to producers direct and indirect inputs into food and agri-

46 In 1986, Producer Subsidy Equivalents as a percentage of the value of output of crops were 92, 60.4 and 47.2 in Japan, the EEC and the United States, respectively (OECD, *Agricultural Policies Markets and Trade*, 1988, p. 46).

47 As a World Bank study has remarked, "in (certain) situations cash transfers are more cost effective than the provision of food, are easier to administer, and reach the affected population more quickly". See *Poverty and Hunger, Issues and Options for Food Security in Developing Countries*, World Bank, 1986, p. 39.

48 The Mali project "has won the acclaim and support of the international community", *Monetization of WFP Food Aid*, World Food Programme Document WFP/CFA:24/5, 12 August 1987, p. 5.

Table 11

TRIANGULAR TRANSACTIONS (TT) AND LOCAL PURCHASES (LP) OF FOOD INVOLVING LDCS IN SUB-SAHARAN AFRICA, 1986-1988

Donor	*Type of operation*	*Source of supply*	*Recipient country*	*Tons*
1986/87 or 1987 [a]				
Australia	T.T.	Zimbabwe	Mozambique, Somalia	10,000
Canada	T.T.	Malawi	Mozambique	1,000
EEC	T.T.	Malawi, Zimbabwe, Sudan	Angola, Botswana, Ethiopia, Mozambique	72,000
	L.P.	Burkina Faso, Malawi, Mali	Burkina Faso, Malawi, Mali	21,000
France	T.T.	Mali	Mauritania	1,000
Germany, Fed. Rep. of	T.T.	Malawi, Kenya, Zimbabwe	Botswana, Cape Verde, Mozambique	18,000
	L.P.	Chad, Mali, Sudan	Chad, Mali, Sudan	32,500
New Zealand	T.T.	Zimbabwe	Botswana	1,750
Norway	T.T.	Malawi	Mozambique	1,100
	L.P.	Malawi, Mali	Malawi, Mali	1,625
Switzerland	T.T.	Sudan	Ethiopia	1,500
	L.P.	Mali	Mali	1,000
United Kingdom	T.T.	Kenya, Zimbabwe	Ethiopia, Mozambique	31,000
United States	T.T.	Malawi, Zimbabwe	Mozambique	23,400
WFP	T.T.	Kenya, Zimbabwe	Botswana, Mozambique, Sudan, Uganda	25,636
	L.P.	Malawi, Sudan, Zimbabwe	Malawi, Sudan, Zimbabwe	21,892
1987/88 or 1988 [b]				
Austria	T.T.	Kenya	Sudan	600
Belgium	T.T.	Zimbabwe	Botswana, Mozambique	6,000
EEC	L.P.	Sudan	Sudan	20,000
Germany, Fed. Rep. of	T.T.	Kenya, Un.Rep. of Tanzania Zimbabwe	Angola, Mozambique	16,800
	L.P.	Chad, Malawi, Mali, Niger, Sudan	Chad, Malawi, Mali, Niger Sudan	34,200
France	T.T.	Mali	Mauritania	3,000
	L.P.	Niger	Niger	5,000
Italy	T.T.	Zimbabwe	Botswana, Mozambique, Zambia	16,600
Luxembourg	L.P.	Niger	Niger	500
Netherlands	T.T.	Zimbabwe	Botswana, Mozambique	14,000
Switzerland	L.P.	Mali	Mali	1,500
United Kingdom	T.T.	Kenya, Zimbabwe	Ethiopia, Malawi, Mozambique	32,000
United States	T.T.	Kenya, Zimbabwe	Malawi, Mozambique	52,600
WFP	T.T.	Kenya, Zimbabwe	Angola, Botswana, Lesotho, Malawi, Mozambique, Swaziland	41,800
	L.P.	Cameroon, Sudan, Un.Rep. of Tanzania, Uganda, Zimbabwe	Cameroon, Sudan, Un.Rep. of Tanzania, Uganda, Zimbabwe	44,779

Source: FAO, *Food supply situation and crop prospects in Sub-Saharan Africa*, April 1987, February 1988.

a Based on information reported by donors as of early April 1987.

b Based on information reported by donors as of mid-February 1988.

cultural production. Efforts in this area include more applied agricultural research, improved extension, supply of improved seeds and animal breeds, vaccination facilities, maintenance and development of irrigation systems, the development of agricultural credit and the availability of fertilizers, machinery, or fuel and boats for fishing, at reasonable prices. In many LDCs there is also a need to promote the distribution of consumer goods in rural areas, this being an indirect input in and incentive to agricultural production.

Most of these direct and indirect support measures on the input side will, however, be severely constrained by the lack of skills, particularly for research and extension, as well as by insufficient budgetary resources. The subsidizing of specific direct inputs, such as fertilizers, will probably place an undue burden on most LDC Government budgets. In addition, contrary to price support to ensure minimum producer prices, subsidies would

Box 5

MALI : SUCCESS AND SHORTCOMINGS OF A RURAL CREDIT SCHEME

In 1985, an internationally-sponsored Village Development Fund Project (VDFP) was launched in Mali's Segou region with the view to, *inter alia*, providing credit to the peasants in that region. Since then, low interest loans have been extended to about 3000 farmers in 85 villages for the purchase of agricultural inputs as well as for the financing of diversification. On average, the loan sum credited to each of the individual beneficiaries amounted to about $350. The repayment performance has been remarkable and no credit defaults have been reported so far.

What is the recipe for the success of the VDFP in Segou/Mali, while failed lending schemes abound in LDCs? The key reason lies undoubtedly in the strict scrutinizing process, which a village has to undergo prior to its inclusion in the project, and, later, in the collective responsibility assumed by the village community for the accurate repayment of the credit. To be covered by the project, a village has to meet several economic, social and topographical criteria. First of all, the social organization of the village, its community spirit and social cohesion have to be sound. Secondly, the village must have a good record of tax payments to the Government. Finally, it must also have the potential for expanding the crop area.

Despite the excellent performance of the VDFP, serious problems have recently begun to threaten the project's future. Paradoxically, it is the success of the project that is putting its existence at risk. With the help of the loans extended under the VDFP, peasants have increased their output many times. The additional millet (the staple food of the area) was welcome as it improved the diet of the peasants and their families. In addition, this food could be easily sold in nearby urban settlements. However, for other crops, such as peanuts, groundnuts and cowpea, the situation was dramatically different. The peasants found that there was no market, at least not at remunerative prices, for the extra crops which were originally expected to produce a regular cash income for repaying the loans as well as for satisfying consumption needs.

Part of the increase in agricultural output, particularly peanuts and groundnuts, was assumed to be exportable. Indeed, Mali is a traditional exporter of oil seeds and nuts. However, the problem of collecting small amounts of these products from dispersed villages with a view to channelling them to exporters was not studied in advance. Nor was a fixed minimum price agreed on with a buyer of last resort so as to prevent prices from falling in a regional surplus situation. Therefore, a number of peasants are now in serious difficulty for loan repayments.

The surplus in crops would have certainly reached disastrous dimensions, if more villages in the Segou region had participated in the VDFP. Although the village communities act as a collective guarantor, failed loans would inevitably put a strain on their limited resources and adversely affect the social harmony in the villages, thus reversing the principal objectives of the project.

A number of lessons can be drawn from the VDFP in the Segou region of Mali. In the first place, the VDFP clearly demonstrates that within the framework of certain conditionality, rural credit schemes can be viable in LDCs [1]. Peasants are willing to take advantage of loans for productive purposes, boosting the agricultural output sizably. However, of equal importance is the experience that the effects of rural credit schemes have to be seen in a wider context of the economy. Their sustained success depends in the final analysis on the market price received by the producers. Therefore, collection and marketing channels for surpluses have to be identified before the peasants are encouraged to increase production. Remunerative minimum prices, set by a buyer of last resort, such as the Government, would act as a security against negative changes in the markets prices, and encourage the peasants to aim at high agricultural output.

Source: *International Agricultural Development*, No. 2, March/April 1988, pp. 8-12.

1 A similar illustration is provided by the case of the Grameen Bank project in Bangladesh. See UNCTAD, *The Least Developed Countries 1987 Report*, pp. 37, 38.

encourage non-economic use of the particular input which is subsidized.

The long-run development of agriculture necessarily implies the use of more inputs and the recourse to productivity-raising measures. These would be particularly effective in conditions where assured outlets for output are available. Conversely, higher producer prices will themselves stimulate higher commercial demand for inputs and increased eagerness by producers to improve agricultural practices.

(v) Farming and land tenure systems

The system of farming and land tenure constitutes an important area where constraints in LDCs have to be overcome. A generally agreed principle, which most LDCs could aim at implementing, is that land rights and land tenure systems should be clarified and made less precarious. Tenancy rights in particular have to be protected to the point that loans should be obtainable against tenancy certificates. The removal of uncertainty appears indeed to be a necessary condition to encourage farm operators to invest in property improvement, livestock and pasture management, irrigation or equipment, and to enable them to have access to credit. A second principle, applicable to landlord/tenant relations, is that the rents could be fixed in such a way that incremental production accrues mostly to the tenant. Past experience in land reform and farming re-organization, however, shows that this is bound to be a long-term process. Governments could set general guidelines, but actual implementation must be on a case-by-case basis, taking into account local traditions, with particular emphasis on the discouragement of fragmentation and the granting of equal access to women farmers. The imposition of too rapid changes would go against customary practices and is likely to be resisted and unnecessarily disruptive of important social values.

2. *Manufacturing*

Attempts made during the 1980s to accelerate industrialization in the LDCs have been beset by a number of exogenously-induced shocks. On the supply side, cuts in both imports and government spending in response to external payments crises have starved industries of vital materials, capital inputs and financing. On the demand side, shortfalls in rural incomes stemming from poor agricultural performance along with persistently weak export markets for agro-products have collectively compressed domestic - and often also regional - demand for industrial and consumer manufactures. As so many LDC industries are agro-based, natural disasters such as drought and floods to which many LDCs are highly prone, have dealt further blows, disrupting the flow of materials to industry. Moreover, technological advances are posing a two-way challenge to LDC industries: on the one hand, new input-saving techniques and the growing use of industrial substitutes are inhibiting expansion in the processing of traditional products[49]; on the other hand, changes in process technologies are compromising the prospects of industries relying on old technologies.[50]

Exogenous influences have not been the only deterrents to industrial progress: policy deficiencies, inappropriate investment choices, excessive regulatory controls, and distortions in pricing and incentive structures have imposed additional impediments on LDCs' industry. Contrary to expectations, industrialization has not played a dynamic role in leading the structural transformation of LDCs during the 1980s, and in several countries industrial decline appears to have reversed much of the progress achieved during the 1970s.

(a) Performance

The number of LDCs experiencing either negative industrial growth or industrial growth which has not kept pace with GDP growth increased from 12 in 1975-1980 to 18 in the period 1981-1986. Industrial trends in LDCs are heavily influenced by manufacturing which constitutes slightly over half of gross industrial output in 1985.

A breakdown of the composition of manufacturing output shows that LDCs remain at an early stage of the industrialization process. Primary industries comprising food, beverages, tobacco and textiles account for some 63 per cent of gross output; the contribution of metal-based and engineering industries is no more than 5 per cent (see table 12). Heavy industry involving the production of machinery and transport equipment is largely non-existent in the countries surveyed; where there is a semblance of such industries, activity is mostly restricted to final-stage assembly of

49 For example the jute industry, important to Bangladesh and Nepal, is facing competition from synthetics such as polypropylene fibres. Similarly, vanilla, which is the main source of livelihood for the Comoros, is facing intense competition from synthetic vanillin substitutes.

50 As an illustration, many African countries, among them LDCs, have not adapted to new recovery technologies in the leather industry. Reliance on traditional methods has resulted in end-products which are either useless or confined to local use, with the resultant loss of export potential.

Table 12

STRUCTURE OF MANUFACTURING IN SELECTED LDCs, 1985

(Values as a percentage of gross output)

Country	Gross output in $US million	Food, beverage and tobacco ISIC 31	Textiles and apparel ISIC 32	Chemicals and petro refinery ISIC 351-353	Metal products ISIC 381	Machinery and transport equipment ISIC 382-384	Other
Bangladesh	2024	22	30	29	10	6	3
Benin	178	57	17	4	6	0	16
Botswana	49	51	12	0	0	0	37
Burkina Faso	344	61	15	1	0	6	23
Burma	3662	71	7	0	4	3	15
Burundi	87	75	11	5	0	0	9
Central African Rep.	100	40	20	6	0	0	34
Ethiopia	1381	40	17	23	5	0	15
Gambia	44	70	2	2	2	0	24
Lesotho	28	29	11	0	0	0	60
Malawi	126	49	13	11	0	2	25
Rwanda	260	77	1	12	0	0	10
Somalia	132	30	14	15	2	0	39
Sierra Leone	71	37	4	38	0	0	21
Sudan	1052	35	12	33	3	0	17
Un.Rep. of Tanzania	1016	30	21	9	5	11	24
Total	**10,554**	**48**	**15**	**14**	**5**	**4**	**14**

Source: UNCTAD secretariat calculations based on data from UNIDO, World Bank and other national sources.

imported inputs such as vehicle parts, usually with very little domestic value added.

Whereas aggregate real manufacturing value added (MVA) per capita for the LDCs grew on average at 3.4 per cent per annum in the 1970s, the corresponding growth rate for the period 1981-1986 was negative since MVA increased at an average annual rate of 1.8 per cent as compared with a population growth of 2.6 per cent. Sixteen LDCs experienced negative growth in MVA per capita during the first half of the 1980s, while growth was static in another five countries. The low overall level and lack of progress in manufacturing is reflected in its share of the aggregate GDP of LDCs, namely 8 per cent in 1986, a figure roughly unchanged from the level in 1975. In the case of African LDCs, the share of MVA in GDP has progressively fallen from a peak of around 9 per cent in the mid-1970s to 6.7 per cent in the mid 1980s.

To the extent that agriculture supplies manufacturing with both inputs and markets, manufacturing performance has tended to move in tandem with agriculture. Thus the manufacturing performance of many drought-affected countries suffered along with the devastation of agriculture which occurred during the drought years (1983-1985), followed by recovery in 1986-1987. Partial data for 1986 indicate that for the first time since 1981, MVA for LDCs as a group recorded a marginal gain in per capita terms (see Statistical Annex). As with all previous years, the performance varies among the LDCs. Shortages of industrial inputs led to sharp MVA declines in Benin, Bhutan, Sierra Leone and Uganda. In direct contrast, the turn-around in agro-industries in Botswana and new investments in Lesotho and Mauritania resulted in significant MVA growth in all three countries, in excess of 14 per cent per annum.

During the period 1981-1986, the average MVA of five countries (Lesotho, Maldives, Mali, Samoa and Yemen) met or surpassed the SNPA target of an annual growth of 9 per cent in manufacturing output. Except for Lesotho, however, the contribution of manufacturing to GDP in the latter countries does not yet exceed 8 per cent. Particularly noteworthy are the exceptionally high growth rates recorded by Lesotho and Yemen, averaging 13 per cent and

15 per cent respectively. In Lesotho, foreign capital and managment has been a driving force behind sustained growth during the 1980s; in Yemen receipts of foreign remittances from Yemenis overseas helped the expansion of the agro- and building-materials industry during the early 1980s; but growth sharply slackened towards the mid 1980s along with the dwindling of overseas remittances. Burma, Burundi and Comoros are other examples of countries which, while not achieving the SNPA manufacturing growth target, have nevertheless accelerated the pace of manufacturing growth on a fairly sustained basis throughout the 1980s. Growth in the above countries has concentrated in agro-processing and textiles and has been achieved, especially in the case of Comoros, Maldives and Samoa, from a very small production base. The progress of this small group of countries, while encouraging, is none the less an exception to the widespread malaise which has come to characterize LDC industries in the 1980s.

Poor industrial performance is reflected in the incidence of excess capacity and the growing number of ailing industries across industrial sectors that are net users of foreign exchange and government subsidies. Fragmentary evidence indicates that capacity utilization in the African LDCs has shrunk from about 60 per cent in 1980-1981 to 20-30 per cent in the mid 1980s.[51] In Sudan a combination of foreign-exchange shortages and supply bottlenecks led to a drastic fall in capacity utilization and the closure of 74 firms, producing mostly consumer goods.[52] Results from a survey encompassing 24, predominantly least developed, African countries show that out of 343 industrial enterprises surveyed, 195 (57 per cent) were found to be operating with significant excess capacity, while another 79 (23 per cent) were driven out of business during the survey period. The sectors affected included wood-processing, cement, textiles as well as agro-based manufactures. The least developed countries worst affected by capacity underuse were Central African Republic, Guinea, and United Republic of Tanzania.[53]

To be sure, problems of capacity utilization have not affected all countries to the same degree: Afghanistan, Maldives and Nepal are among some of the better performers in this regard. Positive influences on industrial activity have ranged from factors such as a relatively unconstrained import capacity due to tourism receipts (Maldives), to access to external capital and technical assistance support (Afghanistan). Official efforts to ensure uninterrupted access to material and financial inputs have assisted the export industries in Nepal.

(b) Policy shortcomings

Perhaps the most predominant cause of industrial failures in the LDCs has been indiscriminate pursuit of import substitution strategies. Such strategies have often involved the shielding of domestic production under high protective barriers, frequently using inappropriate capital-intensive technologies where simpler labour-intensive technologies would have better addressed the employment demands of an expanding labour force. The Somalian experience is illustrative of this. The public sector began to embark on sophisticated capital-intensive strategies in the early 1980s which stretched its scarce managerial and technical capabilities. These industries performed badly but the State intervened, in order to protect employment, through pricing policies and by restricting imports to prevent competition. Finally these industries were driven to collapse, when the accumulation of balance-of-payments difficulties necessitated liberalization measures. Roughly 40 per cent of the 27 industrial enterprises surveyed were thus found to be producing at negative value added at world prices.[54] Rwanda, Sudan and United Republic of Tanzania are other examples of LDCs which have pursued similar strategies with similar results. Another feature of inappropriate strategies has been the tendency to opt for oversized industries whereas internal and external demand, supply and other efficiency considerations would have favoured smaller-sized industries. In Guinea-Bissau, for example, plant capacity for processing groundnuts is more than double the amount of groundnuts produced.

Overprotection, strengthened by overvaluation in exchange rates, has favoured import-intensive industrialization strategies while simultaneously discouraging exports. An examination of the structure of trade of selected LDC countries confirms this trend: the high import dependency of industries on the supply side has not been sustained on the demand side by a commensurately high propensity in gener-

---

51 See Economic Commission for Africa, "The extent of capacity underutilization and its impact on industrial development in the African least developed countries: issues for consideration", and "Survey of economic and social conditions in Africa, 1984-1985."

52 UNIDO, "Industrial Development Review Series, The Democratic Republic of Sudan," UNIDO/IS.541, July 1985.

53 G. Egnell " The rehabilitation of malfunctioning industrial units in the ACP States," European Commission, 1985.

54 World Bank, "Somalia, Industrial policies and Public Enterprise Reform", December 1987.

Table 13

SHARE OF INTERMEDIATE AND CAPITAL GOODS [a] IN TOTAL IMPORTS : SELECTED LDCs

Country	*Year*	*Share of intermediate and capital goods [a] to imports (%)*
Afghanistan	1983	56.2
Bangladesh	1986	44.9
Bhutan	1983	33.5
Botswana	1985	47.9
Burundi	1985	49.1
Burma	1984/85	70.0
Equatorial Guinea	1984	25.5
Ethiopia	1985	60.1
Gambia	1984/85	43.1
Haiti	1984/85	45.1
Mauritania	1983	50.8
Mali	1983	57.9
Nepal	1985	59.4
Rwanda	1983	54.4
Sierra Leone	1985	41.0
Sudan	1985	60.1
Togo	1984	31.4
Uganda	1985	68.0
Yemen	1985	47.3

Source: UNCTAD secretariat calculations based on national sources.

a SITC (5 + 6 + 7-67-68) including chemicals, machinery, transport equipment and spare parts & tools.

ating exports. Manufactures constitute, on average, more than half of the imports of LDCs but only about one fifth of their exports.[55] External dependence by industry on intermediate and capital goods is reflected in the very high share of such goods in imports (50 to 70 per cent in roughly half of the countries surveyed - see table 13). Tanzanian industry provides a highly illustrative case: in 1984, the sector generated $56 million in value added but consumed recurrent inputs worth $420 million, 70 per cent of which were sourced by imports.[56] Outside of food-processing, the modern manufacturing sector is highly import-intensive. Evidence from a UNIDO survey of industries in the African region, containing a majority of LDCs, reveals that in the brewing industry for instance, virtually all raw materials are imported with the exception of water. The same is true for practically all other branches of light and intermediate industries such as in soft drinks bottling, footwear, leather apparel and metals. Of the 100 manufactured products produced by 40 African countries covered in the survey, roughly 55 per cent of the product sample had an import content (of inputs) close to 100 per cent; only in agro-industries and textiles was the import content under 25 per cent.[57]

A closely related feature of import intensity is a conspicuous absence of intra- and inter-sectoral integration, a feature which limits considerably the direct and indirect effects of industrial expansion on overall economic growth.[58] In particular, the lack of appropriate linkages of industry with agriculture has meant that industry has not provided the impetus to the modernization of agriculture, and vice versa. Industry in most countries does not provide the implements needed to spur the modernization of agriculture; concomitantly, the lack of modernization of agriculture, with the ensuing consequence of low productivity,

55 See annex tables 13 and 14 in *The Least Developed Countries, 1987 Report*, TD/B/1153.

56 World Bank, "Tanzania, an agenda for industrial recovery," June 1987.

57 See UNIDO, Industrial Development Trends and Options, UNIDO ID/WG.439/2.

58 See, for example, the experience of the Central and West African States described respectively in "Revised Intergrated Industrial Promotion Programme for the Central African Subregion", UNIDO ID/WG.456/3/Rev.1 and "Revised Intergrated Industrial Promotion Programme for the West African Subregion", UNIDO ID/WG.455/3/Rev.1.

has inhibited domestic absorption of industrial outputs and the full exploitation of the export potential of agro-processing industries. The absence of strong backward and forward integration has consequently limited industry's contribution to the upgrading of indigenous resources and to the development of technological potential. High import dependence on the supply side is a stark contrast to the serious lack of export orientation of industry on the demand side. For roughly half of 29 LDCs for which data are available for the period 1982-1985, the share of manufactures in merchandise exports is well below 10 per cent; for 12 countries the ratio is about 5 per cent or less.[59] Export-led industrialization is prominent only in countries such as Bangladesh, Botswana, Lesotho[60] and Nepal; the share of manufactures in the export trade of the latter countries being about 70 per cent and above. In Botswana the very high share of manufactures in exports is largely attributable to diamonds.[61] In Lesotho a relatively wide range of manufacturing exports (e.g textiles, footwear, furniture and umbrellas) have gained ground from the stimulative effects of foreign participation in export-oriented industries. Textile industries in Bangladesh and Nepal, which have achieved strong comparative advantage, are particularly outstanding examples of successful export-led industrialization strategies.

Even where industrial sectors are export oriented, the lack of backward integration has limited the economic benefits from industrialization, as is vividly illustrated in a diagnosis of the Haitian experience[62]: the assembly industry is largely outside the Haitian economy; it provides employment but purchases few Haitian inputs and makes almost no fiscal contribution. Similar conclusions apply to Lesotho's export-oriented textile industry: it contributes to employment but, given its highly import-intensive nature and lack of economic linkages, is suspect of producing at very low or net negative value added after discounting for all appropriate costs in attracting such industries.[63]

The cumulative effects of policy distortions have served to heighten the vulnerability of LDC industries to external shocks. The consequent loss of economic efficiency was sharply accentuated when the shift to liberalization policies exposed industries to outside competition; problems of efficiency were magnified further when foreign-exchange shortages forced substantial cutbacks and interruptions in the flow of inputs to industry.

(c) Policy reassessment during the 1980s

In the wake of the flagging performance of their industries, policy-makers in many LDCs have reassessed their industrial strategies. LDC Governments have in the course of the 1980s re-oriented their industrial strategies so as to give emphasis to self-sufficient development, with priority attached to industries that are supportive of agriculture, food production and other essential needs. The use of indigenous labour and raw materials, and the diffusion of technological know-how, are similarly being encouraged.

Significantly, efforts to rehabilitate and increase the efficiency of existing plant capacity in several LDCs is taking precedence over new capacity creation. For instance, rehabilitation of rice mills in Burma has been under way since 1983/1984 and that of textiles, beverage and sugar industries in Uganda and Sudan since 1987. At the same time, the expansion of export capability is increasingly featuring in the policy shifts: creation of an export processing zone in Bangladesh in 1982; liberalization of export licensing in Nepal since 1986, establishment of an Export Development Council for export promotion in Sudan in 1988, Burmese efforts to upgrade rice milling for exports. Governments are attaching more and more importance to devising coherent strategies aimed at ensuring that all elements of the policy environment (such as trade regulations, prices, and access to credit) are supportive of industrial development.

As part of the policy reassessment, the relative role of the State and that of the private sector have similarly come under scrutiny. In the past, Governments have played a leading role in promoting industrialization not only through regulation but more directly in production activities through State enterprises. Contrary to expectations, growing State intervention in industries has not produced rapid growth. Instead, State monopoly has frequently nurtured inefficiencies as parastatals often had recourse to subsidies and excessive protective barriers. In many countries, expan-

59 See annex table 13 in *The Least Developed Countries, 1987 Report*, TD/B/1153.

60 It should be noted that the very high share of manufactures in Lesotho's export trade (71% in 1982) is somehwat overstated because of substantial re-export trade to the South African Custom's Union (SACU).

61 It must be mentioned that diamond exports from Botswana undergo very limited local processing.

62 See "A case for intensive treatment", in *South*, March 1988, page 24.

63 See UNIDO, "The potential for resource-based industrial development in the least developed countries, No 8, Lesotho," PPD.9, page 45.

sion of parastatals led to severe management problems. In other countries, State expansion through widespread nationalizations has often crowded out private initiative.[64]

Recent policies have encouraged greater participation from the private sector and greater foreign investment including through joint venture arrangements (e.g. Chinese-Malian joint management of textiles and sugar enterprises in operation since 1984, Belgian-Niger joint venture in salt extraction in 1987). Initiatives have been taken to encourage small and medium-sized industries(e.g through provision of integrated services in Nepal and Botswana) and to increase the efficiency of State enterprises remaining within the public domain (e.g. reducing subsidies to parastatals in the United Republic of Tanzania since 1984/1985, increasing parastatal autonomy in Lao PDR since 1985). The precise mix of policy elements varies from country to country, but the general direction of change is clear.

(d) Challenges for the 1990s

While it is recognised in most LDCs that agriculture must be the main engine of development, it is simultaneously acknowledged that opportunities should not be missed in exploiting the production and employment potential of industry if LDCs are to achieve more diversified production structures and self-sustained growth. While there is obviously no standard set of policy prescriptions which can be tailor-made to all countries, some policy concerns should be common to a large number of LDCs. In particular, the role of government in providing a regulatory and incentive framework that will stimulate the mobilization of risk capital, the rehabilitation of potentially viable industries, and the development of technological capabilities and entrepreneurship are factors of relevance to all LDCs in the decade ahead.

Over the longer term, the most challenging task will be the nurturing of a process of self-sustained industrialization. Such an effort will call, wherever possible, for the integration of industry with the domestic resource base. Where appropriate, developing dynamic linkages between agriculture and industry can have mutually stimulating effects. The potential for intensifying the agriculture/industry linkage is vast and is illustrated by the fact that, whereas developed countries process roughly 80 per cent of their agricultural produce, the comparable percentage for most least developed countries is in the range of 10 per cent to 20 per cent. Estimates indicate, moreover, that roughly 40 per cent of agricultural produce in many LDCs is currently lost for lack of sufficient storage, distribution and processing facilities. Development of industries can thus enhance the potential for achieving greater self-sufficiency in food production (through greater domestic processing), thereby reducing storage and marketing needs. Similarly, modernizing agriculture and increasing its productivity will have spin-off effects in increasing rural purchasing power for the absorption of industrial outputs.

Promoting small and medium-sized industries (SMIs) already constitutes priority in LDCs, as their domestic markets tend to be small if only in terms of purchasing power. This will require comprehensive service packages to potential entrepreneurs from start to finish, the provision of assistance in the identification of business opportunities and of partners, where necessary, and the provision of business training and infrastructural and credit facilities. The economic gains from such industries are by now well documented: apart from their employment-generating benefits, they are vehicles for fostering indigenous entrepreneurship, and their dispersion in rural areas helps to arrest urbanization pressures. SMIs, moreover, have a key role to play in strategies aimed at promoting self-sustained industrialization since they usually draw into the production process local raw materials, labour and savings.

Strong export orientation could be pursued in those LDCs able to develop comparative advantage in export sectors, as has recently been the case for a few of the relatively more industrially advanced members of the group. Preference must be given in this context to export industries with potential for backward linkages to the economy. Promoting exports is not inconsistent with small-sized industries which could well develop niches in export markets. Strengthening export capacities in industry need not preclude import substitution activities, which will remain valid for those industries able to perform at competitive prices, on a scale commensurate with domestic needs. Open and ideally preferential access to the markets of rich countries will need to be maintained if export-led strategies are to succeed.

For many LDCs, which are constrained by small population and poor resource endowment, a regional approach to industrialization may offer possibilities for outreaching domestic market size limitations in addition to opening up prospects for access to regional resources and possibilities for intra-regional spe-

---

64 See, W.F. Steel, "Adjusting industrial policy in Sub-Saharan Africa," *Finance and Development*, March 1988.

Box 6

IMPORT DEPENDENT INDUSTRIALIZATION IN UNITED REPUBLIC OF TANZANIA

An increase in import content in total manufacturing costs can sometimes signal a viable industrialization process, particularly when accompanied by a corresponding increase in industry's capacity to generate export earnings to meet import needs. This has not been the case in United Republic of Tanzania, where intensification of import dependance has been associated with an increasingly inefficient manufacturing sector whose export capacity has failed to meet even a small fraction of its import needs. By 1984, the average import content of Tanzanian manufacturing production was estimated to have reached about 70 per cent. In certain industrial subsectors such as the production of ball-point pens, galvanized and corrugated iron sheets and fertilizer, the import content approximates 100 per cent. Tanzanian industry's consumption of foreign exchange was some $365 million in 1984 for purchases of raw materials, spares and capital inputs, or roughly six times the level of manufacturing exports of $65 million for that same year. Moreover, the cost of recurrent inputs used by industry exceeded total manufacturing value added by a ratio of nearly 8:1 indicating that substantial savings would have accrued by shutting down the inefficient activities and redirecting resources to more productive activities.

Box 7

CLOTHING FROM BANGLADESH

LINKING MANUFACTURING TO THE DOMESTIC RESOURCE BASE IN BANGLADESH

Since the early 1980s, Bangladesh has made significant progress in reducing the import dependance of its manufacturing sector by turning to the use of indigenous resources. A principal feature of this effort has been the shift in industrial use from imported oil to domestically produced natural gas. Between fiscal 1980 - 1985, natural gas consumption in industry has grown by an equivalent of about 100,000 metric tons of oil [1]. Foreign exchange savings were simultaneousely realized in using indigenous natural gas for fertilizer production and in switching from imported inputs to the use of local scrap from ship-breaking in steel-using industries. Rough estimates indicate that the shift to indigenous resources in energy, fertilizers and steel saved the country some $400 million in foreign exchange in FY1985, equivalent to 15 per cent of exports in that fiscal year, without incurring inordinate change-over costs.

1 See section I.A.2.(b)(ii) for recent Bangladesh developments in gas output.

cialization of goods for both intra- and extra-regional markets. Regional co-operation is of particular significance in the development of heavy industries since such industries, to be viable, require large markets and huge investments which are normally beyond the scope of individual LDCs. Moreover, such a co-operative approach will allow for specialization at various stages of production, particularly relevant in the case of heavy industries.[65]

Given the determining role of import constraints on capacity underutilization in many LDCs, international support in strengthening import capacity through debt relief, complemented by additional programme assistance for rehabilitation of potentially efficient industries and by a resumption of trade credit flows for productive investments, will need to accompany initiatives to revive growth. International support would naturally be complementary to and not a substitute for LDCs' own efforts in mobilizing domestic and foreign risk capital into industry. The role of government in generating a confident and stable investment climate in which businesses can thrive will therefore be an important part of this effort.

65 For example, the South African Development Co-ordination Committee (SADCC) has mapped out an industrial development programme of action aimed at self-sufficiency for its nine member States, of which five are LDCs. The plan concentrates on three core industries: iron and steel, metallurgical and engineering, and petrochemical and natural gas. As an entity the SADCC, with a combined population of 60 million, offers a substantial market for projects which cannot be viably undertaken by individual countries.

3. *Energy*

Per capita total consumption of energy continues to be low in the majority of LDCs, with an average for the LDCs of 265 kg of coal equivalent as compared to 710 kg for the developing countries as a whole (1986). As for commercial energy the consumption of LDCs at 59 kg of coal equivalent is less than eight times that for developing countries as a whole (533 kg) (see Annex table 54H). The share of liquid fuel in total commercial energy consumption of LDCs declined from 90 and 80 per cent in 1970 and 1975 to 65 per cent in 1986[66], reflecting foreign-exchange constraints as well as a certain measure of development of domestic sources.

About 77 per cent of LDCs' energy consumption was provided by fuelwood, charcoal and bagasse as compared to 25 per cent for the developing countries as a whole in 1986 (see Statistical Annex). Electricity production and consumption are particularly low: per capita consumption being estimated at only 45 kilowatt hours, as compared to 542 kilowatt hours for all developing countries (1986) (table 14). The electric power sector is characterized by the small scale of operation, in terms of both the total installed power generation capacity and the geographical coverage of the power system.

Energy consumption in the least developed countries increased by an annual average rate of 3.5 per cent during the period 1981-1986. However, in per capita terms, energy consumption has increased by only 0.9 per cent during the same period, while that of developing countries increased by 1.1 per cent (see Statistical Annex).

(a) National efforts

Energy development and in particular the realization of hydroelectric potential and oil and gas exploration have been accorded high priority by the LDCs. Master plans have been formulated in the 1980s so as to ensure the development and improved management of the energy sector in a number of LDCs. Thus, in Bangladesh, an Energy Master Plan has been formulated for integrated energy planning up to the year 2000. The Energy Master Plan for Botswana, formulated in the context of the Sixth Development Plan (1985-1991), is regarded as the principal tool for improved management of the energy sector. A Ten-Year Master Plan for the exploitation of coal and a detailed National Energy Plan for Malawi were under formulation in 1988, and in Lao People's Democratic Republic, projects to increase production, domestic supply and export of energy are being implemented as parts of an Energy Master Plan.

The importance that many LDCs attach to energy development is reflected in the allocations to this sector in their development plans. For instance, in Bangladesh about 22.7 per cent of total public sector investment for the Third Five-Year Development Plan 1985-1990 has been earmarked for the energy sector; Ethiopia has allocated 12.3 per cent of development expenditure in the Public Investment Programme for 1985/86-1988/89 for the energy sector. Public investment in the power sector accounted for 10 per cent of development expenditure in 1986/87 in Burma.

(i) Fuelwood, charcoal and bagasse

The growth of energy demand in LDCs, coupled with the limited growth of non-traditional energy sources as well as with the adverse effects of drought and desertification, has resulted in an increasing scarcity of fuelwood supplies. In the rural areas people are spending more time collecting wood, which is becoming an expensive marketed commodity in urban centres. The formulation and implementation of practical programmes for the conservation and management of fuelwood in least developed countries has proved to be difficult. Efforts to increase the efficiency of the fuelwood consumption through the use of improved metal stoves and bread ovens have been neither highly successful nor widespread, while the depletion of forest resources for fuelwood, without suitable replanting programmes, has become a serious environmental issue.

(ii) Coal

LDCs with substantial coal deposits are Botswana (17 billion tons) Burma, Malawi (807 million tons) and United Republic of Tanzania (360 million tons). In these countries, significant progress has been made in substituting coal for imported oil in electricity generation and industrial use. In Botswana, two projects are planned for implementation under the Sixth

66 UNCTAD, *Handbook of international trade and development statistics, 1987 Supplement*, and United Nations, *Energy Statistics Yearbook, 1986*.

Table 14

PRODUCTION AND CONSUMPTION OF ELECTRICITY IN LDCS, 1986

Country	Consumption per capita (kilowatt hours)	Share of production in total consumption (percentage)	Share of electricity in total production (percentage)
Net exporters:			
Lao People's Dem.Rep.	84	337.6	4.8
Malawi	73	100.2	2.5
Uganda	34	120.1	1.4
Net importers:			
Benin	47	2.6	100.0
Bhutan	21	67.7	61.9
Burundi	15	2.7	100.0
Nepal	27	92.4	6.6
Niger	45	54.4	100.0
Rwanda	30	90.9	2.4
Togo	87	13.2	88.6
Other LDCs:			
Afghanistan	63	100.0	38.5
Bangladesh	51	100.0	91.2
Burkina Faso	17	100.0	100.0
Burma	59	100.0	51.6
Cape Verde	82	100.0	100.0
Central African Rep.	34	100.0	17.2
Chad	10	100.0	100.0
Comoros	25	100.0	100.0
Democratic Yemen	178	100.0	100.0
Djibouti	362	100.0	100.0
Equatorial Guinea	40	100.0	87.5
Ethiopia	18	100.0	19.3
Gambia	54	100.0	100.0
Guinea	80	100.0	66.8
Guinea-Bissau	15	100.0	100.0
Haiti	82	100.0	27.4
Kiribati	91	100.0	100.0
Maldives	69	100.0	100.0
Mali	21	100.0	24.4
Mauritania	47	100.0	100.0
Samoa	274	100.0	55.6
Sao Tome and Principe	109	100.0	58.3
Sierra Leone	50	100.0	100.0
Somalia	26	100.0	100.0
Sudan	47	100.0	50.9
Un.Rep. of Tanzania	38	100.0	29.5
Vanuatu	193	100.0	100.0
Yemen	38	100.0	100.0
All LDCs [a]	**45**	**101.0**	**56.5**
All developing countries	**542**	**99.5**	**56.6**

Source: UNCTAD secretariat estimates based on information from United Nations, *Energy Statistics Yearbook 1986.*

a Excluding Botswana, Lesotho and Tuvalu for which no data are available.

National Development Plan 1985-1991: the Expanded Coal Utilization Project and the Project for Detailed Investigations on the various Botswana coals. In Malawi, domestic coal production now provides about 30 per cent of local coal requirements. Further development of coal fields will be undertaken in the context of the Ten-Year Coal Master Plan. In Burma, coal production increased by 18 per cent in 1986/87, reaching 51,000 tons or more than twice the 1981/82 level of production.

(iii) Oil and gas

Several least developed countries have initiated geological and geophysical surveys and mapping of energy resources.[67] The least developed countries which have been producing oil throughout the 1980s are Afghanistan, Burma and Benin. They were joined by Yemen, which started exporting oil production in December 1987. Oil exploration and sharing agreements have been entered into by Democratic Yemen with foreign companies, and an agreement for joint oil exploration between Democratic Yemen and Yemen was signed in May 1988. Sudan has reached agreement with foreign companies to renew exploration activities which were interrupted since 1985 for security reasons. On the other hand, crude oil production in Burma declined by 8.5 per cent in 1985/86 by 1.5 per cent in 1986/87. These declines reflect the ageing of wells and the application of outdated extraction techniques.

Least developed countries with large natural gas potential are Afghanistan, Bangladesh, Burma and Sudan. Reserves of natural gas in Afghanistan are estimated at 150 billion cubic metres, and production has averaged about 2.5 billion cubic metres, most of which is exported. The output of natural gas in Bangladesh has increased by an annual average rate of 13.8 per cent during the period 1984/85 - 1987/88, reaching 4.2 billion cubic metres. To meet increasing demand for gas in Bangladesh a programme for drilling nine more wells is to be completed in 1988/89. Burma has abundant reserves of natural gas estimated at 10 trillion tons. After increasing by 34 per cent in 1984/85 and 1985/86, output of natural gas grew by 16 per cent in 1986/87. According to official estimates announced in February 1988, natural gas reserves in Sudan amount to 600 billion cubic metres, and agreement has been reached with a Swiss company for its development at a total cost of $190 million.

(iv) Hydroelectric power

Several least developed countries (including Bhutan, Burkina Faso, Burundi, Ethiopia, Guinea, Lao PDR, Lesotho, Malawi, Mali, Nepal, Rwanda, Samoa, Uganda and United Republic of Tanzania) have a substantial hydropower potential which is at different stages of development. About 74 per cent of the resources mobilized during the period 1980-1987 for the development of new and renewable sources of energy in developing countries were earmarked for large-scale hydropower projects.[68] The World Bank Consultative Group Meeting on Nepal held in May 1988 pledged about $600 million for the construction of a 402 MW hydropower project. However, it has been increasingly recognized that the development of small-scale hydropower projects, in particular in rural regions, would enable these countries to utilize fully their potential in an effective manner.[69] This is particularly important in order to reduce the dependence on imported fuel.

(v) Other sources

Given the limited availability of fossil fuel and hydroelectric power resources and the serious depletion in fuelwood resources, some least developed countries have initiated action to develop alternative sources of energy, including methane gas, ethanol and other renewable energy sources. Efforts to develop solar energy in Botswana, Malawi and Nepal have concentrated on small solar water heaters and the application of small-scale, photovoltaic systems to power a variety of equipment. The geothermal potential at Lake Asal in Djibouti is estimated at 20 MW. A United States company has provided about $17 million for drilling eight wells. The Italian Government has also agreed in principle to provide about $21 million over the next five years to finance two 5 MW geothermal power stations and install a 100 km high-tension power line to Djibouti. The 1988/89 Development Programme in Bangladesh aims in turn at achieving efficient

67 Derek Fee, *Oil and Gas DataBook for Developing Countries with special reference to the ACP countries*, London: Graham and Trotman, 1985. See also *Energy consumption and development trends in developing countries* - report of the Secretary-General of the United Nations (A/41/383-E/1986/101), 10 June 1986.

68 United Nations, *Promotion of the mobilization of financial resources required in the implementation of the Nairobi Programme of Action.* Report of the Secretary General of the United Nations, A/AC.218/16, February 1988.

69 UNCTAD "Technology issues in the energy sector of developing countries: small-scale hydropower projects in Nepal" (UNCTAD/TT/87) 1987.

utilization of existing biomass resources, harnessing new sources of energy, setting up of biogas plants and establishment of rural energy centres. In Nepal, 277 biogas stations were operating in different parts of the country by the end of 1987.

(b) Challenges for the 1990s

The structural transformation of the economies of the LDCs requires increased energy supplies. Substantial progress in agriculture, industry and transportation is critically dependent on the availability of energy. Furthermore, the urbanization process will continue to make new demands for energy, including for public and private transportation as well as for household consumption. At the same time, however, many LDCs, particularly those in Africa, are facing what has been called the second energy crisis, i.e. the serious depletion of fuelwood which is the most important source of traditional energy. The fuelwood crisis has serious economic, social and environmental consequences. Almost all LDCs are expected to face deficits in relation to demand by the year 2000, thus further aggravating deforestation and the degradation of the ecosystem (see section on environmental degradation, below). The development of alternative energy sources to fuelwood, particularly oil and gas, hydro, geothermal and solar energy projects, is highly capital-intensive. Donor countries and international financial institutions should expand their financial and technical assistance to the LDCs to help them choose wisely and realize their potential from these sources. The sectoral meetings on energy, being held as part of the UNDP round table and World Bank Consultative Group meetings, provide appropriate opportunities to examine, in detail, the requirements of individual countries.

(i) Increasing imports of commercial energy

In view of the difficulties and limited opportunities mentioned above, the LDCs will continue to resort to oil imports to meet their energy requirements. Although alternative forms of energy initially appear suited to LDCs, it must be remembered that costly investments can easily be threatened by abrupt falls or a long-term depression in world energy prices. In such cases, the declining trend in the share of liquid fuel in total energy consumption may need to be reversed.

(ii) Distribution and management of electric power

The LDCs should continue, with the assistance of their development partners, to create additional electric generation capacity and to expand transmission and distribution networks. They should intensify their efforts to implement technical and management measures to reduce system losses and improve the performance of these utilities, and to ensure cost recovery through higher prices, better bill collection procedures and improved administrative structures.

(iii) Shortage of skilled manpower

The acute shortage of skilled and technical manpower in the energy sector, particularly in cases where it is difficult to attract foreign investment, is a major constraint to efforts to discover, assess and exploit domestic energy resources. Financial and technical assistance should be provided to the LDCs to expand training programmes and to improve the efficiency of their energy departments.

4. *Services*[70]

One of the major differences between the role of services in developing countries (and particularly in LDCs) and that in developed countries is that in the developed countries services are often intermediate services rendered to enterprises, particularly industrial ones, whereas in the developing countries services have usually developed to absorb unemployed manpower and are usually final services. This is reflected in the pattern of exports of services from LDCs, dominated by tourism and the employment of nationals overseas.

(a) Tourism

In a number of LDCs (particularly Gambia, Haiti, Maldives, Nepal, Samoa, Vanuatu and Yemen) tourism makes a considerable gross contribution to foreign exchange earnings. Yet it has represented merely 7 per cent of merchandise exports in LDCs as a whole in the 1980s, with earnings from this source having stagnated between 1980 and 1986.[71] The income received by all LDCs from travel (including tourism) was only 2.3 per cent of the earnings of all developing countries from this source, so there is room in most LDCs for developing this sector further. Understandably, however, the required infrastructure for this purpose has not received a high priority compared to other sectors and more basic needs.

(b) Employment of nationals overseas

Of major economic importance are the services of LDC nationals working or residing overseas. An indication of the extent of this activity can be obtained from the remittances made to LDCs in the form of receipts from unrequited private transfers and labour income (table 15). Remittances are a dominant feature of the income of Democratic Yemen, Cape Verde, Lesotho, Samoa and Yemen. In a number of others (Bangladesh, Burkina Faso, Chad, Comoros, Ethiopia, Haiti, Kiribati, Mali, Nepal, Samoa, Sudan and Vanuatu)[72] remittances represent more than 20 per cent of merchandise exports. Although in some LDCs (e.g. Botswana, Burkina Faso, Mali) the relative and even absolute importance of remittances has declined in the 1980s, in others, including the two most populated LDCs (Bangladesh and Ethiopia), remittances are playing an increasingly important role.

In spite of the fact that it is often the most dynamic elements of society that emigrate, most LDC Governments have on balance a positive attitude towards employment of their nationals overseas and in some cases promote it (e.g. in Bangladesh through orientation and training schemes), as it eases unemployment and increases the availability of foreign exchange. Yet earnings from this source are particularly unstable and it is difficult for LDC Governments to exert a determining influence on the number of their nationals working overseas, since opportunities depend crucially on economic conditions and policies in host countries.

(c) Commerce and distribution

There is one traditional type of service which, although important to the development process, is not always, nor everywhere, duly recognized. This relates to commerce and distributive trade, including purchasing, transportation, warehousing order processing and after-sales service (wherever applicable). The procurement and efficient distribution of goods, whether produced domestically or imported, is vital to ensure the satisfying of basic needs of the population (e.g. food, pharmaceutical products), to provide inputs into production, and to permit domestic producers to sell their production and exchange it against consumer items.

---

70 This section considers a range of service industries in LDCs outside the social services, which are dealt with elsewhere. The analysis of the contribution of a services sector to economic performance poses numerous methodological and data problems which are far from solved, even in developed countries (cf. "*Services*") (TD/B/1162), 15 February 1988). As an illustration, the output of the main industry of Democratic Yemen, i.e. refining of petroleum products, was previously recorded under "merchandise exports" but, as from 1986, only the value added on the refining process is recorded as an "export of services". In fact, the complexity of the "services sector", particularly that of the new information-based services or "producer services", is such that very few countries, even among the developed ones, may be said to have designed a services development strategy. The LDCs cannot thus be criticized for failing to have developed a comprehensive policy on services.

71 In some LDCs other kinds of internationally traded services are important: international banking services (Vanuatu); aircraft refuelling and servicing (Cape Verde).

72 Tuvalu, on which no data are available, should be included here. As with Kiribati, earnings from seamen working on foreign vessels and from nationals working in phosphate extraction in Nauru, are important contributions to the economy.

Table 15

REMITTANCES OF NATIONALS ABROAD [a] : IN SELECTED LDCs

Country	*Remittances ($ millions)* 1980	1986	*Remittances as % of merchandise exports* 1980	1986
Bangladesh	301.4	617.7	38.0	70.3
Botswana	86.9	43.7	16.0	5.2
Burkina Faso	163.8	105.1 [c]	102.0	74.6 [c]
Cape Verde	38.0	22.0	422.2	666.7
Chad	0.5 [b]	18.2 [d]	0.5 [b]	29.4 [d]
Comoros	1.6	4.8	14.3	23.5
Democratic Yemen	352.3	283.4	591.1	932.2
Ethiopia	32.9	228.2 [d]	7.9	67.8 [d]
Haiti	106.1	109.2	49.1	57.2
Kiribati	2.0	2.0	66.7	40.0
Lesotho	265.4	275.0	443.1	1122.4
Malawi	32.1	27.3	11.3	11.3 [e]
Mali	59.3	45.0	28.9	23.5
Nepal	34.9	45.8	34.2	32.0
Rwanda	14.0	26.2	10.5	14.2
Samoa	18.7	28.6	108.7	272.4
Somalia	57.3	46.8	43.0	52.9
Sudan	262.5	115.0	38.1	35.1
United Rep. of Tanzania	48.0	26.1	9.4	7.2
Vanuatu	9.8 [e]	8.4	91.6 [e]	95.5
Yemen	1322.0	597.4	10492.1	3665.0

Source: UNCTAD, *Handbook of International Trade and Development Statistics, 1986 and 1987 Supplement*; IMF, *Balance of Payments Yearbook* tapes; and national sources.

a Includes unrequited private transfers and labour income receipts.
b 1978.
c 1984.
d 1985.
e 1982.

Such services are provided against a backdrop of complex logistical problems in almost all LDCs because of natural/geographical constraints coupled with underdeveloped physical infrastructure. Examples are the Sudan, which has one of the lowest road densities in the world (0.014 km/km^2), and archipelagic countries like Maldives, Vanuatu or Kiribati - the latter consisting of small coral atolls scattered over more than 5 million square kilometres of ocean. Furthermore, the low potential volume of trade for many remote locations does not encourage or permit the operation of viable trade channels, let alone of competitive structures.

Most trading and commerce activities in LDCs have traditionally been undertaken by the private sector - often combining them with money changing and lending operations - although many remote areas were entirely cutoff from the exchange economy. Under the severe resource constraints of the LDCs, consumers tend to find prices too high, particularly at times of currency adjustments, whereas producers often complain they do not get a fair price for their output. This naturally focuses attention on the agent linking the two - the "middleman" - a category whose activities are usually regarded as giving rise to income without being truly "productive". A number of rather perjorative expressions are often used to describe those performing these functions: "margin gatherers", "speculators", etc. Some LDC Governments have attempted to replace some of the trading activities of the private sector by State-owned structures, particularly where, given the small scale of operations, there is only room for one entreprise. Some of these State distribution systems are reported to be working well (EMPA in Cape Verde, STO in Maldives), but a general trend in the 1980s has been to disband such State trading monopolies and to return most trading and distribution activities to the private sector, sometimes keeping State structures as parallel circuits, e.g. in Bangladesh (irrigation equipment), Guinea, Nepal (fertilizers), Sao Tome and Principe.

Even when it is decided that the bulk of commerce and distribution activities are to be performed by the private sector, the State still needs to establish and regulate a framework under which the operators can legitimately carry out their functions, as is the case in developed countries, where legislation against restrictive business practices and against speculation normally exists. It has not been easy for several LDCs to formulate and implement policies in this respect, and in many of them there is an uneasy relationship between the State, the trading community and the consumers, leading to a range of attitudes from tolerance of a parallel market at higher prices to blaming traders for economic problems, sometimes accompanied by heavy punishment (or threats thereof).

In LDCs, as in other countries, the successful traders are those who are skilled in buying the right goods from the cheapest source at the right time, and in organizing the storage, transport and selling of the goods at a profit in response to demand. Operators who are not able to act in this manner are unlikely to be able to stay long in the business. A number of LDCs attempt to exert some kinds of price control or monitoring - often on a mark-up basis - at least for essential goods, but it is proving very difficult to formulate differential price schedules for various remote locations. It is also almost impossible in practice to verify transactions effectively, under conditions where many of them are unrecorded, where there may be almost no reliable invoices, and where unofficial border trade is significant. This lack of effectiveness has led many LDCs to greatly reduce their attempt to control prices and distribution margins. As an example, in the United Republic of Tanzania, it was announced in June 1987 that the National Price Commission would concentrate its activities on 12 essential items, as compared with some 100 that were officially controlled since the early 1970s.

Governments which try to ensure the maximum degree of competition among the operators engaged in distribution and trading (by encouraging new entrants, including government-backed structures and co-operatives), rather than attempting to enforce State monopolies or change the profit-seeking approach of commercial operators, are most likely to succeed in nurturing a healthy growth of their sector.

Liberalization of prices does have its own problems, however, as is illustrated by the case of Guinea, where most prices have been liberalized since the mid-1980s and petroleum distribution remains the only State monopoly. In this country, the sudden rise of prices of goods, taxi fares and rents in January 1988, following the announcement of increases of civil servants' salaries, led to popular protests in Conakry, necessitating the intervention of the President, who announced strict penalties and appealed to the civic and religious sense of traders.[73] Such indictments have been repeated in many developing countries, including LDCs.

Closely linked to commerce and distribution are the insurance and commercial banking activities. In the majority of LDCs, these sectors have been dominated by foreign firms, but there has been a tendency in recent years to encourage national participation - often through the State - with a view to retaining foreign exchange (see Box 8). Some LDCs (e.g. Nepal in banking) have also sought to diversify the number of foreign entreprises operating in the country, but in very small LDCs the existence of several competing entreprises can seldom be justified on economic grounds. Thus, in Comoros and Cape Verde, there is only commercial bank and in the latter country only one insurance company.

(d) Challenges for the 1990s

The provision of appropriate infrastructure and up-grading of human capital, including the mobilization of return migrants, may form part of a service sector strategy in LDCs. Apart from policies in health and education (discussed elsewhere), the national service policy could include:

- the encouragement of competitive structures in trade and distribution;
- a policy for the employment of nationals abroad, including for return migration of holders of specific skills;
- promoting the development of services that could have a stimulating effect on the rest of the economy, such as international subcontracting of certain operations or labour-intensive processes and tourism (while taking care that this does not divert resources from other priority areas);

The successful promotion of services in LDCs would require a corresponding up-

73 "Guinée: révolte contre la vie chère", *Jeune Afrique*, no. 1411, 20 January 1988, pp. 11-12.

Box 8

INSURANCE IN THE LDCs

Today, most LDCs have their own domestic insurance industry which is subject to local supervision. Some of these countries have gone further and established a State monopoly (see table below). However, there are still cases where risks "domiciled" in these countries get direct cover in other markets. Although local receipt of premium income is forgone, exposure on important risks is also limited in the national interest in such cases.

A strong insurance industry cannot thrive without an adequate volume of business. In LDCs the demand for insurance is often insufficient, and insurance companies have to face an unbalanced portofolio of risks. Hence the insurers in most LDCs have to rely heavily on international reinsurance services. This is, however, quite normal for a fledgling industry, and insurance even at its mature stage is in any case one of the most international of all service industries.

Gross premium written as a percentage of GNP in selected LDCs in 1983

Country	*Ratio*	*Market structure*
Afghanistan	0.15	State monopoly
Bangladesh	0.34	State monopoly
Bhutan	0.49	State monopoly
Botswana	1.34	Four (4) national companies
Burkina Faso	0.50	Three (3) national companies
Burundi	1.06	State monopoly
Cape Verde	2.34	State monopoly
Central African Rep.	0.40	Nine (9) companies: national and foreign controlled
Chad	0.25	State monopoly
Ethiopia	1.37	State monopoly
Gambia	0.99	Three (3) national companies
Lesotho	2.12	Six (6) national companies
Malawi	2.05	Nine (9) companies: national and foreign controlled
Mali	0.46	Four (4) companies: national and foreign-controlled
Rwanda	0.82	Single private company
Sudan	0.67	Twenty (20) national companies

Source: "Statistical survey on insurance and reinsurance operations in developing countries", (TD/B/C.3/220), Geneva, 1987.

grading of human resources, a matter dealt with in section A.4 above.

5. *Export expansion and diversification*

(a) *Recent performance and policy initiatives*

The LDCs' export structure continues to be highly concentrated on a few primary products, and the direction of their exports by major market groupings has remained virtually unchanged in the 1980s. Export volumes have mostly stagnated and prices are in general no more renumerative than before.

The value of LDC merchandise exports declined from $8.5 billion in 1980 to $7.3 billion in 1982, and recovered subsequently to attain $8.3 billion in 1986 (see table 16).[74] Provisional figures for 1987 suggest that the 1980 level has just been reached again. Within this total the value of agricultural products, including forestry and fishery products, remained almost constant at about $4.3 billion, with increased volumes offset by declines in prices. Coffee and cotton are the most important products for

74 The figures on total merchandise exports, non-factor services and factor services in this paragraph are derived from the balance of payments, those on commodity groups from the UNCTAD, Commodity Yearbook files.

Table 16

LDCs' EXPORTS OF GOODS AND SERVICES, 1980-1986

(Billions of dollars)

	1980	*1981*	*1982*	*1983*	*1984*	*1985*	*1986*
Merchandise	8.5	8.5	7.3	7.6	8.1	7.7	8.0
Non-factor services	2.5	2.7	2.7	2.4	2.3	2.5	2.4
Travel	0.5	0.6	0.6	0.6	0.6	0.6	0.5
Factor services	1.0	1.0	1.0	0.8	0.8	0.7	0.8
Interest income	0.6	0.6	0.6	0.4	0.4	0.4	0.4
Labour income	0.4	0.4	0.4	0.5	0.4	0.3	0.3
Total	**11.9**	**12.2**	**11.0**	**10.9**	**11.3**	**10.9**	**11.3**

Source: UNCTAD secretariat calculations based on balance-of-payments data from IMF; and UNCTAD, *Handbook of international trade and development statistics, 1987.*

Table 17

LDCs' EXPORTS OF PRIMARY COMMODITIES BY MAJOR GROUP

Commodity group	*1966*	*1970*	*1975*	*1980*	*1986*
			(In billions of dollars)		
Food	1.1	1.2	1.8	3.2	3.3
Agricultural raw materials	0.6	0.7	0.7	1.2	1.1
Minerals, ores and metals [a]	0.2	0.2	0.6	1.5	1.1
		(As a share of all developing countries' exports, in percentages)			
Food	8.9	7.6	5.3	5.0	4.9
Agricultural raw materials	13.0	12.7	13.4	6.6	8.1
Minerals, ores and metals [a]	3.9	3.0	5.0	5.8	5.5

Source: UNCTAD secretariat, based on information from FAO, and other international and national publications.
a Excluding non-industrial diamonds.

LDCs with a combined share of more than one third. The export value of minerals, ores and metals declined from $1.5 billion in 1980 to $1.1 billion in 1986 (see table 17). On the other hand, the value of other products, including non-industrial diamonds as well as manufactured products, increased.

Twenty of the 39 LDCs for which information is available recorded a negative growth rate in their merchandise exports in the period 1980-1986. However, 4 of the remaining 19 - Botswana, Burundi, Maldives and Mauritania - surpassed rates of 10 per cent annually.

The annual export value of the LDCs' non-factor services has remained close to $2.5 billion over the peroid 1980-1986. Travel services, including tourism, are the major item, representing about $0.6 billion. Earnings from factor services declined, particularly on account of interest receipts which fell from almost $0.7 billion in 1980 to $0.4 billion in 1986, in line with the running down of reserve holdings in the early 1980s and declining international interest rates.

In Chart II an idea is given of the extent to which LDC merchandise exports are still concentrated on a few primary commodities. The chart describes the concentration of exports on three products in two years, 1980 and 1986, for 20 LDCs. By comparing the situation in 1980 and 1986, the chart brings out a tendency towards a greater concentration in these countries.

Be that as it may, several individual LDCs have had a measure of success in the implementation of diversification strategies. The successful experiences of Bangladesh, Maldives and Mauritania, shown in boxes below, have some features in common. These cases (as well as that of Botswana for diamonds) show that the LDCs' small economic size is not always to their disadvantage; the successful penetration in a world market of one specific product can have a strong direct impact on the economy and the accelerated expansion of a small export base can also suddenly ease the foreign exchange constraint. The existence of a natural comparative advantage can be a basic element in the successful export expansion. The case of Bangladesh textiles shows how crucial access to the world markets is.

(b) Challenges for the 1990s

(i) Supply of raw materials and secondary inputs

A regular, reliable supply of the required primary commodity needs to be ensured for the success of a processing venture. In addition, a domestic sector of spare parts and machineries, which is capable of contributing to the construction, engineering and maintenance of a processing industry, needs to be developed.

(ii) Government support

Government support needs to be provided in areas such as personnel training, technology research, product research, market information gathering, and market promotion.

(iii) Transportation

The expansion of the transport network (discussed in section D below) is a prerequisite to the successful expansion and diversification of exports.

(iv) Technology and technological research

In the LDCs, the available technology is in general of a simple and outmoded character. The required technology and legal expertise to negotiate the purchase of missing technology is often not available or inadequate. The available technology is often not biased towards large-scale production.

A coherent policy aimed at technological adaptation and development needs to be formulated in LDCs. It should further be mentioned that the development of the LDCs, which in general is so much hampered by their small size, could benefit considerably both from economic integration and from the development of joint ventures.

(v) Support from LDCs' trade partners

In the past some developed countries have established insititutes in their countries that have the purpose of promoting the imports from developing countries. In this regard the Netherlands Centre for the Promotion of Imports from Developing Countries (CBI) and the Swedish Import Promotion Office for Products from Developing Countries (IMPOD) should be mentioned. The EEC as well as the International Trade Centre UNCTAD/GATT have set up special programmes for the LDCs as part of their overall trade promotion activity. Following their example, the developed countries that have not yet done so could incorporate special arrangements for the LDCs within the context of their import promotion from developing countries in general.

Chart II

CONCENTRATION OF MERCHANDISE EXPORTS IN SELECTED LDCs: Share of three major products, 1980 and 1986

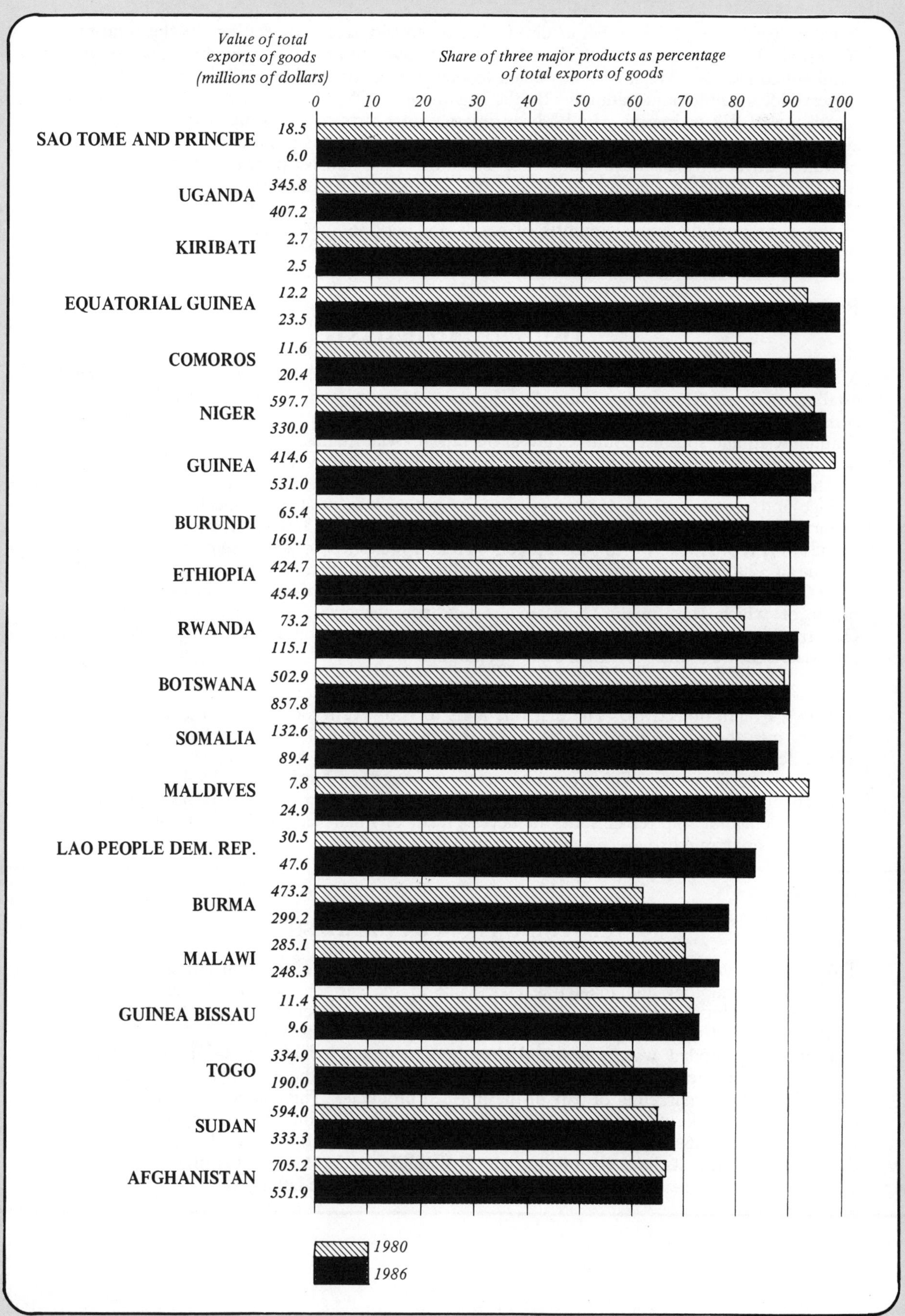

Source: UNCTAD secretariat, based on United Nations Statistical Office, FAO, IMF, and national sources.

Box 9

TOURIST SERVICES IN THE MALDIVES

Back in 1972, the Maldives began developing its tourist sector by setting up the semi-public "Crescent Tourist Agency", which established tourist resorts on individual and originally uninhabited islands. Much care was taken to preserve the original unspoilt island setting and to preserve local culture and tradition. By the beginning of 1980, 25 resorts were in operation with a capacity of 832 bedrooms. In 1981, an international airport was completed near the capital, allowing the operation of direct long-distance charter flights, thus minimizing the inconvenience of transit travel through nearby countries. Since then, the number of annual tourist arrivals has tripled, from 42,000 in 1980 to 122,000 in 1986. Gross foreign exchange earnings have risen from $9.4 million in 1980 to $40.7 million in 1986, the equivalent of 11 and 42 per cent, respectively, of the corresponding annual imports of goods and services. Most resorts obtain their clients through a few well-established foreign operators.

Box 10

FISH FROM MAURITANIA

Mauritania's fisheries policy, adopted in 1978 and modified slightly thereafter, has encouraged the establishment of Mauritanian-controlled joint ventures, which, *inter alia,* were required to construct an on-shore processing plant. At present, joint ventures with capital from Arab, Scandinavian and socialist countries are in operation. Mauritania's initial share in the capital has been provided by the foreign partner, to be paid out of future company profits. With new on-shore facilities in operation from 1982, fish catches have been offloaded in Mauritania for storage and processing. In 1984, a public corporation was created for the local purchase and export of high-value demersal fish and crustaceans. In 1986, this enterprise exported 60,000 tonnes of fish products, worth $153 million. Total fish exports, which in that year accounted for a value of $206 million, compared with $43 million in 1980, financed 29 per cent of imports of goods and services. These exports now represent the country's main earner of foreign exchange, much of which stays with Mauritania. The new fisheries policy has helped strengthen Government revenues, enabled diversification away from mineral export dependence, and has provided a secure market for small-scale operations.

More recently, in April 1987, the Government adopted a new long-term fishing sector strategy with two overall objectives. The first one aims to conserve resources and integrate the fishing industry into the rest of the economy. For this purpose, the Government has stopped issuing fishing licences for demersal fish to foreign vessels and has set out new fishing zones to restrict the catches in specific areas. The second objective of increasing local value added will be pursued through eight investment projects valued at up to $60 million. These projects include the establishment of a ship repair yard, the development of small-scale fishing and the organization of training programmes.

Box 11

CLOTHING FROM BANGLADESH

Towards the end of the 1970s, businessmen from the Republic of Korea transferred to Bangladesh production technology and marketing experience in the garment sector. Local entrepreneurs emulated such businessmen and adopted their techniques, a development which was stimulated in the early 1980s by the promotion of a free-trade environment by such businessmen, the institution of bonded warehouses and duty-free treatment of imported inputs, and by the provision of credit on favourable terms. The original link with the Republic of Korea has been maintained in the marketing of part of the finished products. This marketing was facilitated by the existence of underutilized quotas for Bangladesh within the Multifibre Arrangement. This has resulted in a rapid increase in garment production and exports. Foreign exchange earnings from the export of garments have risen from only $1.7 million in 1980 to a value of $235.9 million in 1986, financing 8 per cent of imports of goods and services in the latter year.

C. Social development

1. Education

The illiteracy rate of the population of 15 years and over has decreased between 1980 and 1985 in all the countries for which data are available, and of 27 of the present 41 LDCs for which data are available only 4 (Burkina Faso, Mali, Niger and Somalia) still fall below the 20 per cent literacy threshold, as against 18 in early 1970s (see Statistical Annex). The reduction of the illiteracy rates during the 1980s varied from one country to another, ranging from 1.8 per cent (Burkina Faso) to 27.4 per cent (Ethiopia, 1980-1983, including population of 10 years and over).

For 31 LDCs for which data are available, the number of illiterates aged 15 years and over was approximately 110 million in the early 1980s as compared to 95 million in the early 1970s.[75] Thus, the reduction of the illiteracy rate was not sufficient to reduce the absolute number of illiterates, and during the past two decades the campaign to eradicate illiteracy may be said to have been more successful in spreading literacy than in ending illiteracy[76] in the LDCs as in the developing world as a whole (see Chart III).

The SNPA recommended, in paragraph 25, that the LDCs "should aim at making primary education free and compulsory by 1990 at the latest". It is much clearer now than in 1981 that such an objective cannot be easily achieved, particularly during a period when for most countries the social costs of adjustment impose an additional burden. According to the most commonly used education indicator - i.e. the gross enrolment ratio - primary school enrolment in the LDCs is estimated to have risen by 19 percentage points between 1970 and 1985: from 39 to 58 per cent. However, appreciable disparities exist from country to country (cf. Statistical Annex).

The SNPA, in paragraph 26, stated that due attention should be given to the education needs of women to enable them to develop their full potential. As illustrated by chart 1 on adult literacy, the female illiteracy rate in the LDCs is significantly higher than the male illiteracy rate. Recent estimates on the distribution by sex of the gross school enrolment ratios show that female ratios increased 6 percentage points from 42 to 48 per cent during the period 1980-1985 in the primary school and by 3 percentage points from 7 to 10 per cent in the secondary school (cf. Statistical Annex and Chart IV).

These quantitative data conceal a serious situation as regards the quality of education. Studies carried out in Ethiopia, Guinea and United Republic of Tanzania[77], as well as evidence regarding other LDCs, show that the expansion of basic education, has been accompanied by a lowering of standards, owing to poor physical conditions, the low level of teacher training and the lack of books and stationery. Cutbacks in education and teacher training budgets have been extensive in LDCs in the 1980s. Table 18 gives an indication of the high repeater rates in the primary school system of many LDCs. In Bangladesh primary schools, only one in five students entering the system emerges literate. In Comoros, the educational reform to improve the quality of education carried out since 1985 has meant a reduction of enrolment in primary schools and a reduction in the number of teachers. In rural Mali, there are only six textbooks per hundred students, and seven out of twenty schools have no books at all. As illustrated by Mauritania's educational reform (see Box 12), the improvement of primary education is an urgent need in many LDCs.

Gross enrolment at the secondary level in the LDCs for which data are available registered an increase between the mid-1970s and early 1980s as shown in table 19. As can be seen therein, the progression varied appreciably from country to country. Secondary school enrolment in the LDCs is much lower than in other developing countries: in 1985 the enrolment ratios were less than half in the case of boys (19 against 44 per cent) and a third in the case of girls (10 against 30 per cent) (see chart IV).

75 UNESCO, *Development of Education in the LDCs since 1970: a statistical study* CSR-E-42, Paris, January 1983, p.5.

76 Coombs, P.H., *The world crisis in education: the view from the eighties*. Oxford University Press, New York, 1985. CH. 9, pp. 265-283.

77 UNESCO, *Educafrica*, no. 11, 1984.

Chart III
Adult literacy in LDCs and in all developing countries

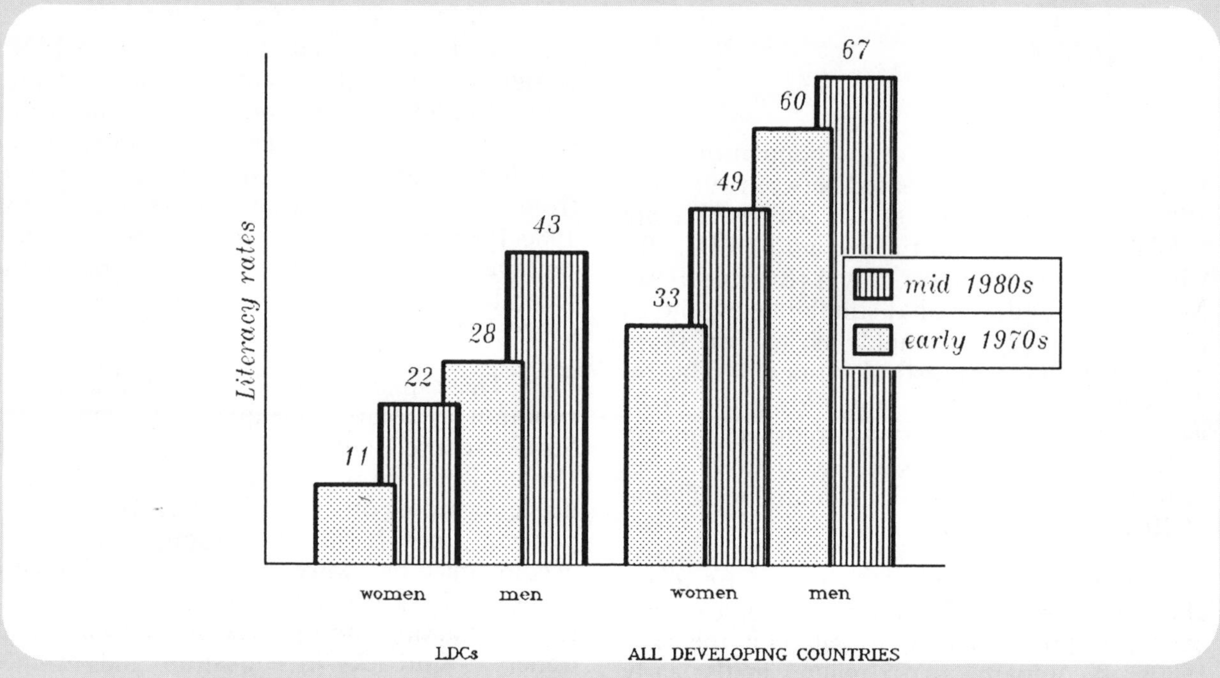

Source: Unesco and statistical annex table 54E.

Chart IV
LDCs: Gross school enrolments by sex (1985)

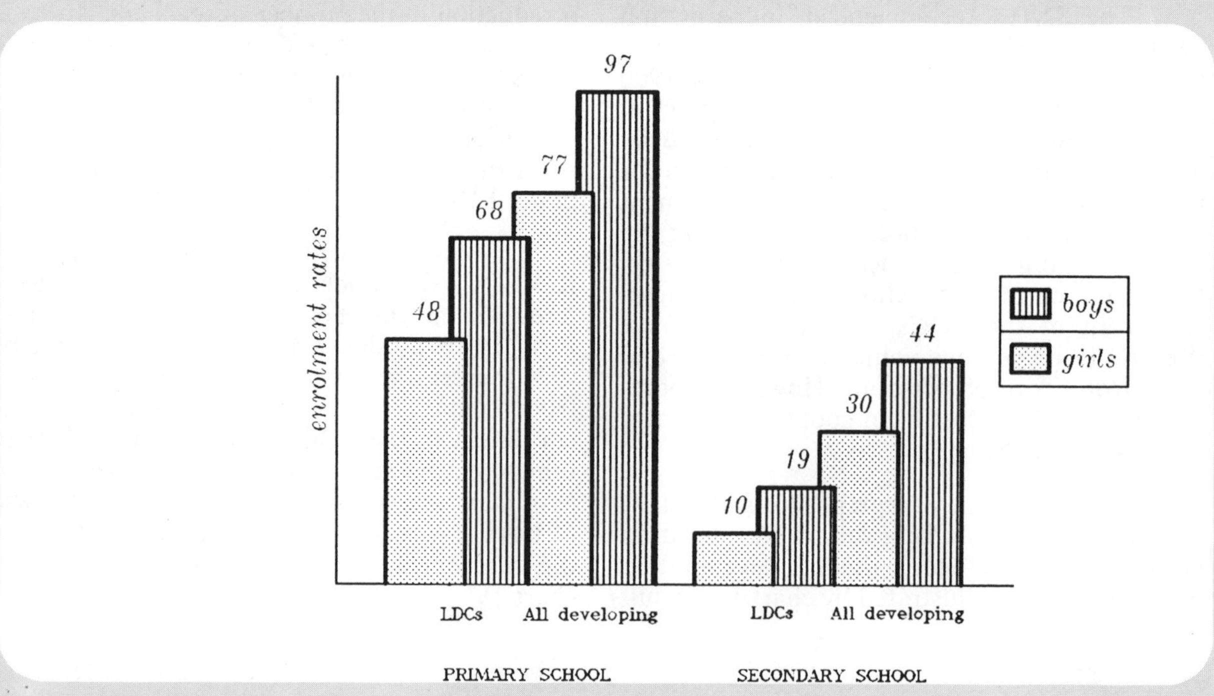

Source: Annex table 54E.

Table 18

PERCENTAGE OF PRIMARY SCHOOL REPEATERS IN SELECTED LDCs

(1982 or 1983)

Less than 5%	*5 - 9.9%*	*10 - 14.9%*	*15 - 19.9%*
Uganda (0,3) U.R. of Tanzania (1,2)	Botswana (5,9)	Bangladesh (10,0) Burkina Faso (14,1) Ethiopia (12,2) Gambia (12,2) Niger (14,3) Rwanda (11,9)	Burundi (15,5) Malawi (15,8) Mauritania (17,2)

20 - 24.9%	*25 - 29.9%*	*30% and over*
Comoros (24,6) Guinea (24,2) Sao Tome and Principe (20,9)	Benin (25,9) Cameroon (28,9) Cape Verde (29,5) Lesotho (24,5)	Central African Republic (35,3) Guinea-Bissau (30,0) Mali (31,0) Togo (36,6)

Source: UNESCO, *op. cit.*, 1987.

Box 12

MAURITANIA IMPROVES QUALITY OF EDUCATION AND EXPANDS ENROLMENT IN PRIMARY SCHOOL

Mauritania's educational system is characterized by a very low gross school enrolment rate (30.6 per cent in 1984), a low number of students enrolled in technical and vocational training programmes (4.5 per cent of the secondary enrolment) and a low productivity since only 35 per cent of the pupils complete primary education. In 1988, the Government adopted a reform programme aimed at: expanding primary school enrolment; improving the internal efficiency of education by means of reducing the number of students repeating classes and limiting the access to the different types of education; strengthening science programmes to help meet the growing demand for technical workers; and restructuring technical and vocational education towards short-term programmes that respond to training needs in rural areas and the informal sector, including economic activities such as home-based textile shops, street vendors and family-operated transport services. The reform programme will include measures aimed at improving the quality of education, such as the printing of 350,000 textbooks to be used in primary schools and 120,000 science textbooks for secondary schools, and the retraining of science teachers at the secondary level. The reform is supported by an IDA credit of SDR 13.2 million ($18.2 million); this supplements the already considerable budgetary resources which Mauritania is now devoting to education.

Table 19

RATES OF GROWTH OF GROSS SECONDARY SCHOOL ENROLMENT IN SELECTED LDCs

(Percentages)

Country	*Years*	*General*	*Teaching*	*Technical*
Benin	75-84	11.6	26.8	21.9
Botswana	75-84	9.4	2.0	8.3
Burkina Faso	75-84	12.9	-4.4	5.2
Burundi	75-83	9.6	4.9	15.8
Cape Verde	75-83	8.5	n.a.	0.6
Central African Republic	75-82	14.1	8.0	3.5
Chad	75-84	12.3	-10.6	14.2
Ethiopia	75-83	12.2	..	..
Gambia	75-84	10.0	12.6	13.4
Guinea	75-84	3.3	n.a.	19.8
Guinea-Bissau	75-83	22.6	26.1	-3.8
Lesotho	75-83	9.1	n.a.	10.2
Malawi	75-84	5.9	3.3	-0.6
Mali	75-82	4.1	n.a.	-11.4
Mauritania	75-82	21.5	30.4	n.a.
Niger	75-83	15.9	12.8	19.1
Rwanda	75-83	-5.6	16.9	10.0
Sao Tome Principe	75-83	6.4	n.a.	0.4
Sierra Leone	75-82	7.7	9.3	3.4
Somalia	75-83	9.1	-7.5	19.9
United Rep. Tanzania	79-83	6.9	-0.4	1.5
Togo	75-84	4.2	-8.0	0.1
Uganda	75-82	16.3	5.9	3.4

Source: UNESCO, *Les politiques de l'éducation et de la formation en Afrique sub-saharienne*, 1987.

2. *Health and nutrition*

The SNPA stressed the need to implement national policies, strategies and plans of action in the field of health based on the concept of primary health care. The first evaluation of the Global Strategy for Health for All by the Year 2000, carried out in 1985 and 1986, included 36 LDCs and found that all of them had formulated national health strategies and plans aimed at strengthening primary health care systems.[78]

Health indicators of most LDCs have improved to some extent during the 1980s. Average life expectancy at birth has changed very little, from 45 in 1980 to 47.9 in 1985. This last figure compares with 61.5 years for other developing countries and 72.4 years for developed countries (see table 20). The infant mortality rate declined from 160 per thousand live births in 1980 to 141.2 by 1985, as compared with the 78.9 and 12.8 rates for other developing and developed countries, respectively. With regard to the availability of treatment for common diseases and injuries and of essential drugs at the first level of contact - i.e. local health care - the coverage rates by the mid-1980s were as follows: 48.5 per cent of the population in the LDCs, and 72.8 per cent and 99.8 per cent in other developing and developed countries, respectively. LDCs are also less well endowed as regards the coverage rates of attendance during pregnancy and at childbirth.

Immunization coverage (against tuberculosis (BCG), DPT (triple vaccine), poliomyelitis, measles and tetanus (single vaccine) is also an important health indicator. Although the present immunization campaign in the LDCs represents a major public health gain, there is no room for complacency, since the immunization coverage is less than 15 per cent in 15 LDCs.[79] For example, as illustrated

78 WHO, World Health Statistics, Annual, 1986.

79 WHO, 1987, *Expanded programme on immunization: global status report*, Weekly Epidemiological Record 62(33):241.

Table 20

SELECTED HEALTH GLOBAL INDICATORS IN SELECTED LDCs AND OTHER COUNTRIES (1985)

Indicators	*LDCs*	*Other developing countries*	*Developed countries*
Infant mortality rate (per 1000)	141.2 [a]	78.9	12.8
Life expectancy at birth (years)	47.9	61.5	72.4
		(Coverage in per cent)	
Local health care	48.5	72.8	99.8
Sanitation	16.8	72.8	99.8
Safe water supply	34.7	57.2	95.8
Attendance at childbirth	36.7	44.5	99.4
Attendance during pregnancy	33.3	47.8	99.4
Population (Millions)	324	3.330	1.172
Number of countries	36	93	37

Source: WHO, *World Health Statistics 1986*, table XVII, p. 45.

a *Memo item* : The infant mortality rate in 1980 was 160 per thousand (*WHO, Global Strategy for HFA by the year 2000*, 1981, p.24).

Table 21

ESTIMATED IMMUNIZATION COVERAGE WITH BCG, DPT, POLIOMYELITIS, MEASLES AND TETANUS VACCINES IN THE FIVE LARGEST LDCS [a] AND IN ALL DEVELOPING COUNTRIES

			Immunization coverage (percentage)				
		Infants surviving to 1 year of age	*Children under one year*				*Pregnant women,*
Country	*Year*	*(millions)*	*BCG*	*DPT3*	*Polio 3*	*Measles*	*tetanus*
Bangladesh	1986	3.17	5	5	4	3	5
Burma	1986	1.02	32	20	4	3	21
Ethiopia	1984	1.92	12	7	6	13	3
Sudan	1986	0.91	23	14	14	11	6
Un. Rep. of Tanzania	1984	1.03	84	65	65	68	32
For reference:							
All developing countries [b]		103.01	49	50	51	39	18

Source: WHO, *Weekly Epidemiological Record No. 33*, 14 August 1987, table 1.

a LDCs with population exceeding 20 million.

b Including China.

in table 21, out of five LDCs for which information was available in 1987, only one is near to achieving the goal of universal childhood immunization by the year 1990. Thus, the likelihood of reaching the 1990 goals, even with extraordinary external support and special national efforts, seems to be remote. Programme acceleration requires two complementary actions: social mobilization and improved management of immunization services.

Environmental health, namely the supply of safe drinking water and sanitation services to under-served rural and fringe urban areas has been among the salient public health policies in many LDCs. Few public services have had as much popular appeal among both donors and national leaders, particularly since the inauguration in 1981 of the United Nations International Drinking Water Supply and Sanitation Decade. To some extent, advances were registered in the LDCs during the 1980s: between 1980 and 1985, urban water coverage increased from 49 to 53 per cent and sanitation from 40 to 46 per cent; whereas the coverage in rural areas increased from 27 to 33 per cent in the case of safe water, and from 8 to 15 per cent of the population with access to sanitation.[80] Despite this progress, widespread failures of new water supply systems, mainly from inadequate maintenance, have undercut the gains.

The primary health care approach led several LDCs Governments to re-orient drug policy and to adopt a list of essential drugs. Bangladesh provides an example of achievements in this domain. The 1982 Drug Control Ordinance provided legislative and administrative support for ensuring the quality and availability of essential drugs, reducing their price and the prices of raw materials, eliminating useless, non-essential and harmful drugs from the market, promoting local production, and developing a drug monitoring and information system. As a result, over 80 per cent of the country's requirement for drugs were produced locally by 1984, with the participation of the Government in the pharmaceutical industry.[81] The Bangladesh drug policy has in a few years permitted several steps forward to be taken in lowering prices, controlling transfer pricing, increasing essential drug production, stimulating local companies and removing dangerous drugs from the market. However, despite the remarkable progress in the production of essential drugs, 70 to 80 per cent of the population still have no access to basic essential drugs. In other LDCs, such as Afghanistan, Rwanda and Somalia, the list of a limited number of drugs that are available has recently been updated. Some other LDCs, such as Burma, Guinea, Mali, Nepal and Sudan, have embarked since 1986 on large essential drugs availability programmes.

Hunger and chronic malnutrition constitute a chronic plight for a large number of people in many LDCs. During the 1980s, population expansion was more rapid than food availability, particularly in sub-Saharan African LDCs, although poverty rather than food unavailability remains the main cause of hunger and malnutrition. Malnutrition in preschool children was particularly widespread (more than one third of the population) in Ethiopia, Haiti and the Sahel LDCs, and was increasing in Botswana, Lesotho and the Sudano-Sahelian LDCs.[82] According to a recent rural nutrition survey undertaken in Bangladesh, over 60 per cent of all children below the age of 5 were estimated to be moderately or severely malnourished. The greatest prevalence of chronic malnutrition was 75 per cent among children between 4 and 5 years.

3. *Population policies*

The population of the LDCs grew at an average annual rate of 2.7 per cent during the period 1965-1985, as compared to 2.2 per cent for developing countries as a whole. As shown in table 22, total fertility rates declined between 1965 and 1986 by more than one percentage point in Bangladesh, Burma and Haiti but increased or maintained their high level in several LDCs, notably Botswana, Central African Republic, Guinea, Malawi, Mali, Mauritania, Niger, Rwanda, Somalia and United Republic of Tanzania. These levels of fertility and population growth make the SNPA targets in health and education more difficult to attain.

The SNPA invited all LDCs to take appropriate measures for family planning and population control within the framework of national demographic policies. In many LDCs a constraint in developing population policies has been the unpredictable population movements due in particular to refugees, whether incoming or outgoing.

Table 23 presents the views of Governments of selected LDCs on their national population size and trends and shows that a number of them encourage family planning ac-

---

80 WHO, 1986, *op.cit.*.

81 WHO, *The World Drug Situation*, 1988, pp. 65-69.

82 See United Nations ACC/SCN, *First Report on the World Nutrition Situation*, November 1987.

Table 22

DEMOGRAPHY AND FERTILITY IN SELECTED LDCs

(Percentages)

Country	Growth rates of population (1965-1985)	Total fertility rates 1965	1986
Bangladesh	2.7	6.8	5.6
Benin	2.8	6.8	6.5
Botswana	4.0	6.9	6.6
Burkina Faso	2.2	6.4	6.5
Burma	2.2	5.8	4.4
Burundi	2.1	6.4	6.5
Central African Rep.	2.0	4.5	5.7
Chad	2.1	6.0	5.9
Democratic Yemen	2.2	7.0	6.6
Ethiopia	2.7	5.8	6.3
Guinea	2.0	5.9	6.0
Haiti	2.0	6.2	4.8
Lao PDR	1.6	6.2	5.9
Lesotho	2.4	5.8	5.8
Malawi	3.0	7.8	7.6
Mali	2.5	6.5	6.5
Mauritania	2.2	6.5	6.5
Nepal	2.4	6.0	5.9
Niger	2.8	6.8	7.0
Rwanda	3.3	7.5	8.0
Sierra Leone	2.6	6.4	6.5
Somalia	1.8	6.7	6.8
Sudan	2.9	6.7	6.6
Togo	3.1	6.5	6.5
Uganda	2.9	6.9	6.9
Un. Rep. of Tanzania	3.4	6.6	7.0
Yemen	2.7	6.8	6.8
Average LDCs	**2.7**	**6.6**	**6.0**
Average Developing Countries	**2.2**	**6.1**	**4.0**

Source: World Bank, *Social indicators of Development 1987* and World Bank, *World Development Report 1988*.

tivities as part of broader national and child care programmes.

In Bangladesh, population policies have been implemented over a number of years, and rapid population growth is officially recognized as the primary socio-economic problem. With the recent launching of an elaborate multi-sectoral population control programme, which involves eight ministries, Bangladesh is promoting a reorientation of strategy from the previous clinic-oriented, isolated birth control programme to an all-out multi-dimensional family welfare programme. Emphasis is now on domiciliary delivery of integrated maternal/child health and family planning services involving community participation, not only for the sake of health and welfare of the people, but also for improving the chances of child survival in order to make the concept of the small family norm widely acceptable. The Government expects a population of 115 million people by the year 2000 and 175 million by the middle of the twenty-first century. The Third Five-Year Plan (1985-1990) has set targets for sterilization of at least 3.4 million people and an increase of couples practising family planning from 4.5 million in 1984 to 10.5 million by the year 1990.

Table 23

POPULATION POLICIES IN SELECTED LEAST DEVELOPED COUNTRIES

	Government views on population	*Government policies*
Bangladesh	Population growth considered the major socio-economic problem	Elaborate multi-sectoral policy involving eight ministries
Ethiopia	Rate of population growth and fertility considered too high	Family planning supported
Gambia	Fertility and natural growth considered too high	Reduction in fertility aimed at
Haiti	Population growth considered too high	Reduction of fertility in 1981-1986 Plan
Kiribati	Population growth considered too high	Zero growth by year 2000
Lesotho	Population growth considered too high	Cautious control of fertility promoted
Nepal	Population control considered essential	A number of measures adopted to decrease fertility
Rwanda	Population growth considered too high	Reduction in fertility is one of the priorities
Samoa	Deeply concerned with high rates of natural increase and fertility	Firmly committed to promotion of family planning
Sudan	Rates of fertility and natural increase considered satis-factory	Efforts being made to formulate policy
Tuvalu	Population growth considered too high	Comprehensive family planning programme since 1978
Uganda	Population growth considered too high	Family planning supported
United Republic of Tanzania	Population growth considered too high	Family planning programmes supported
Yemen	Population growth considered satisfactory but fertility too high	Intends to reduce ferti-lity levels

Source: Based on United Nations Fund for Population Activities, *Inventory of population projects in developing countries and the world*, 1988.

4. *Challenges for the 1990s*

(a) Education

The future of LDCs will greatly depend on the education their youth will be receiving. Several key educational issues need to be addressed by them during the 1990s. Owing to population growth, a rapidly expanding education demand will have to be met, both in the formal and in the non-formal systems.

LDCs could, first of all, balance the long-term goal of a universal primary education with the immediate need for professional and technical skills. The improvement of educational curricula to make them relevant to current economic and social conditions will require to combine modern knowledge and attitudes with traditional customs and values, using local languages and introducing productive and practical work into general education. Likewise, infusing into the curriculum issues such as nutrition, hygiene and family planning would enhance its relevance.

Second, regarding non-formal education, the key issue is how to link formal and non-formal programmes in a coherent, cost-effective and mutually supportive way. Examples of initiatives in this respect are the use of regular teaching staff to provide non-formal training after school hours and the combining of literacy training for women with the development of pre-school education. In this respect, it seems that even if formal training is found to be socially and individually profitable, initial training in the context of the enterprise and apprenticeship in the informal sector could be more cost-effective than vocational or general education.

The mobilization of resources to face the increasing needs regarding adult literacy and child schooling will be an outstanding challenge for the majority of the LDCs during the 1990s. The LDCs could undertake and continue actions such as the local community participation in the construction and maintenance of educational facilities; the local production of learning materials with increasing use of domestic inputs; the encouragement to private sector participation in educational and training programmes. Such actions could be an important tool to improve resource use and availability.

However, increased international assistance in this area will be essential, since the basic needs far exceed the domestic resources likely to be available. The application of cost recovery principles in basic education in order to ease public budget constraints would restrict access to educational opportunities to those whose families are able to pay and would thus perpetuate internal disparities, which is not a desirable outcome.

(b) Health

Health strategies could increasingly take the form of preventive measures in areas such as health education, hygiene, drinking water supply and maternal and infant protection, as well as measures to support essential medical supplies and training schemes for health system managers and intermediary health workers. Efforts could be made for implementation at the grass-root level. Greater literacy and education would also contribute to improving health and nutrition.

Health policies, being a public responsibility, is likely to be assumed by governments at all levels. To expand health manpower as rapidly as possible, large numbers of health auxiliaries need to be trained to be front-line personnel for the delivery of primary health care.

Urban and rural areas need to receive an equitable distribution of health resources and health infrastructure could be organized to this end. The tendency towards a deployment of resources in favour of individuals and families of higher economic status, to the detriment of poor people, in cities and rural areas needs to be reversed. To this effect, the management of health services could be delegated to local communities and local health insurance schemes could be promoted. Non-governmental organizations, which are already playing an important role in this area, could be fully utilized.

The quality of primary health care depends to a large extent on the operation and maintenance of water supply and sanitation. In this area community participation, local supervision and leadership, appropriate training and sufficient recurrent funds and supplies are essential. The local people could thus be closely associated in determining what the community really wants and is able and willing to sustain with its own resources, particuarly in rural areas.

However, the availability of domestic resources for health care will continue to be strictly limited in LDCs. The need for international assistance in this area has again been reaffirmed recently by the international community. In particular, at the WHO meeting held in Riga, USSR, in April 1988, the statement entitled "Alma-Ata reaffirmed at Riga" included a recommendation aimed at setting up "a special international initiative focused on the tragic circumstances of the least developed countries, mostly on the continent of Africa, and especially those with markedly elevated infant, under-five-year-old and maternal mortality rates, which will address specific obstacles to progress and will set targets to be reached by the year 2000[83] ." This initiative could be followed up as a matter of urgency.

A new and severe challenge to be faced by LDCs in the 1990s concerns the spreading of AIDS. In many of the urban centres of such LDCs as Rwanda, United Republic of Tanzania and Uganda, from 5 to 20 per cent of the sexually active age-group has already been infected with HIV.[84] Since 10 to 25 per cent of the women of child-bearing age are currently infected with HIV, child mortality rates will be increased by 25 per cent, cancelling the gains achieved with difficulty by child-survival programmes over the past two decades. The social and economic impact of the AIDS

83 See document W.H.A., A41/19, 26 April 1988.

84 See *Scientific American*, October 1988, pp. 60-69.

expansion in many LDCs will be substantial and will have a selective impact on young and middle-aged adults, including business and government workers, as well as members of the social, economic and political elites.[85] To prevent the HIV spread, information and education programmes are needed in all countries. This will be a particularly difficult challenge in LDCs where education standards, including of health workers, are particularly inadeqate to deal with this new problem. To be effective, education programmes in this area must also be supplemented by appropriate health and social services.

(c) Population

The high level of population growth in most LDCs, should it continue in the 1990s, will affect negatively or nullify any improvement in incomes. It would in particular place unbearable burdens on the education and health systems and contribute to environmental degradation. Most LDCs Governments need to show more awareness of this issue and develop more purposeful policies to decelerate population growth, while respecting local cultural traditions. Prospects for international migration are not good, whereas death rates, and infant mortality in particular, can - it is hoped - be expected to continue to decline. Consequently, slowing down of population growth rates implies reduction in fertility rates, particularly in African LDCs where these rates are more than 50 per cent above those in developing countries as a whole.

D. Transport and communications

A major structural characteristic of the economies of the least developed countries is the exceedingly weak physical infrastructural base. The poor country-wide network of transport and communication linkages has helped to perpetuate an often stagnant dualistic economic structure. Development has tended to occur in a few monetized urban enclaves in relative isolation from the rural non-monetary sector, where the overwhelming part of the population and the natural development potential are located. The lack of access to transport and to an effective communications system extends beyond national borders so that any available opportunities for subregional cooperation in trade and development, from which least developed countries could benefit, have also been exploited only marginally. The following analysis provides insights into what the least developing countries have attempted to achieve in specific areas of the transport and communications sectors despite the harsh economic environment within which they have had to operate.

1. Transport

(a) Road transport

Road vehicles, not being tied to a specific route, provide greater flexibility than do railways. This is particularly vital for the least developed countries where one of the major tasks is to provide accessibility to isolated communities and to exploit natural resource potential. Several of the least developed countries have commendable investment programmes underway that are being supported by sizeable resource allocations to road development projects. For example, the pattern of the sectoral distribution of the public investment programme of Rwanda (1986-1988) indicates that the share allocated to infrastructure development is the largest (32 per cent), mainly owing to road-upgrading projects. Lesotho's capital expenditure on roads has, since the early 1980s, also continued to hold a dominant position and accounted for some 35 per cent of the total capital expenditure in 1985/86. A similar pattern of capital expenditure strongly oriented towards road infrastructure development is to

85 The Harvard Institute of International Development estimates that by 1995 the losses in economic terms due to the spreading of AIDS in sub-Saharan African countries will amount to $980 million. (*Ibid.*, p.68)

Box 13

LESOTHO'S EFFORTS IN ROAD TRANSPORT DEVELOPMENT

Lesotho is heavily dependent on road transport for both passengers and freight movements because of the absence of rail communications. The road transport development is, however, handicapped by the rugged terrain and the widely scattered population.

At independence there were no bitumen roads at all outside Maseru (the capital); the country was served by inadequate tracks and bridle paths. The first major road to provide access to the central mountains was begun only in 1976. The strategy of the Second Plan (1975/76-1979/80) was focused on the provision of adequate main and feeder roads in the lowlands and foothills and all-weather access roads in the mountains. The most important of this road network expansion programme was the reconstruction of the Mountain Road (St. Michael's - Thaba/Tseka) which provided access to the rural development project in the Thaba-Tseka area. When political problems with South Africa were exacerbated by the closure of the south-eastern border, top priority was given to the improvements in the rural areas. To accomplish this emergency programme, the total capital expenditures was raised by 15 million Emalangeni - well above the estimated cost in the Second Plan. Under the entire Plan period a road network covering 451 km was constructed.

During the Third Plan (1980-1985) a total of 177 km of bitumen roads and 543 km of gravel roads were completed. A significant innovation in Lesotho's strategy for rural road development was the widespread scheme of labour-intensive public works. The Labour-Intensive Construction Unit (LCU) complements the machine-intensive regravelling works and has proved cost-effective. Although the LCU has been involved in other activities such as soil conservation projects, housing programmes and the Highland Water Scheme, its main focus has been road construction and regravelling in the rural/mountain areas and in urban road infrastructure work. During this Plan period a number of initiatives were taken to promote training programmes both locally and abroad. The programme of road maintenance workshops was significantly expanded and decentralized to make services more readily available. The Government-funded Plant Pool Vehicle Pool Services (PVPS) was restocked particularly with heavy construction machines, such as dozers, graders, rollers and front-end loaders in order to meet rapidly increasing requirements.

There are still, however, acute road development and maintenance problems, not only because of the scarcity of resources but also due to the fact that the climate conditions and rugged mountainous terrain have rendered the maintenance effort a formidable task.

be observed in several other least developed countries such as Botswana (15 per cent in 1984/85), Democratic Yemen (9 per cent in 1981-1985) and Nepal (11 per cent in 1986/87). In the African region as a whole, where a large majority of the least developed countries are located, the second phase (1984-1988) of the United Nations Transport and Communications Decade has also given highest priority to the road transport sector. Out of the total programme of 1,040 projects, 236 (23 per cent) are road transport projects. In resource terms some 32 per cent of the total programme (US$15.9 million) has been earmarked for the road sector.

Road development programmes have, in most of the least developed countries, focused on the upgrading of existing networks of seasonal earth roads. Upgrading work has also involved the construction of asphalt roads to link up the main commercial centres and the extension of the road network of all-weather roads to selected population and production areas. The work in more remote areas has largely been limited to expanding the network of earth roads. This rural road development programme has been executed largely by labour-intensive methods under the management of local communities or public works departments. Such methods are particularly suitable in the least developed countries: they are lower in cost, have a lower dependence on imports, and their design can be better attuned to local conditions.

In spite of these efforts, however, the road sector development programmes in all the least developed countries still face formidable problems. Progress has been sluggish and the overall performance in the sector is still relatively poor. According to available data, 19 of the least developed countries have a road network density of less than 60 km per 1000 km^2 (see Annex table 54G). This is significantly lower than the level of many other developing countries.

Road maintenance is not given the high priority it deserves in many least developed countries. The relatively high allocation of capital development resources to the road sector by a number of least developed countries is not matched by an equally important share for the sector in the recurrent budgets. The World Bank has been particularly keen to see this imbalance redressed.

b) *Rail transport*

There are several LDCs with no rail infrastructures whatsoever. In general, the railway network in LDCs is sparse, with extremely low density. The insufficiency of rolling stock and poor track superstructure and alignments is widespread and the facilities for maintaining them are inadequate. The handling facilities for containers and the marshalling facilities are equally inappropriately equipped. Skilled manpower is scarce at certain technical and management levels. In many least developed countries the railway is subject to increasing competition, particularly from road transport. Although many other developing countries face similar problems, these are sharply reinforced in the least developed countries because of their overall vulnerability, extreme lack of financial resources and the very limited operational ability to cope with technological demands of modern railway management systems.

Available data for 18 least developed countries indicate that eight of them have a railway network density of less than 2 km per 1000 km^2 (see Annex table 54G). This is well below the average level for other developing countries. In view of the investments required, very few least developed countries have plans to build or expand the rail transport network.

(c) *Air transport*

Air transport has become increasingly important in many developing countries to strengthen in their efforts to promote tourism and the export of perishable produce to the major markets in the developed countries. Many LDCs have given priority to the establishment of a national airline. The impact of such efforts in the least developed countries, however, remains modest. Most least developed countries already have one international airport but the domestic aviation infrastructure is often lacking. Terminal facilities, including handling equipment, are also in many cases inadequate. The inadequate surface distribution systems, the low levels of traffic and the directional imbalance of freight flows imposes severe constraints on the LDCs' ability to expand air-cargo capacity at economic rates. Available traffic data on 21 least developed countries indicate that 14 of them recorded freight volumes of under 10,000 tonnes and seven above in 1986.

Efforts to expand passenger services in the least developed countries also remain subdued. Of the 24 least developed countries for which data are available, some nine recorded fewer than 100,000 passengers each on scheduled flights in 1986. Among the rest of them, none exceeded a passenger level of 1million in 1986, except Bangladesh which had 1.2 million passengers. The upward trend observed in the expansion of air traffic volumes in many developed and developing countries in recent years is applicable to only very few least developed countries. During the period 1982-1986 for several LDCs the growth of traffic volumes either stagnated or declined sharply.

Most technological improvements in air transport have been oriented towards the needs of the developed regions, although competition among manufacturers has produced a number of smaller aircraft suitable for LDC conditions and requiring minimal runways and other infrastructure. The tendency in several least developed countries has, however, been to over-invest in larger sophisticated aircraft which may require disproportionate investments in improved airport facilities.

2. *Communications*

(a) *Telecommunications*

Telecommunications facilities are at present largely concentrated in the main commercial centres which are often more effectively linked with centres in industrialized countries than with the rural hinterland. Available data indicate that the least developed countries as a group had only 2.7 telephones per thousand inhabitants in 1986 as compared to 29.4 in all the developing countries. With 38 telephones per thousand inhabitants, Sao Tome and Principe is the only least developed country which exceeds the average level for all developing countries.

Box 14

AIR TRANSPORT DEVELOPMENT IN NEPAL

Nepal's major efforts to support the development of the air transport industry have partly been in response to the particular challenge posed by the difficult terrain that traverses the greater part of the countryside, which has hampered the expansion of other modes of transport in the vastly isolated mountain areas. Air transport, therefore, not only helps to strengthen international relations but is also regarded as an important vehicle that can greatly contribute to domestic integration. Furthermore, Nepal's significant tourist potential depends heavily on a reliable and efficient network of air links between the much-admired mountain holiday resorts and the Kathmandu valley.

The Royal Nepal Airlines Corporation (RNAC) was founded in 1958 and has been at the helm of the country's major drive to promote air transport development. There are now some 43 airports in the country which continue to be upgraded to improve operational standards. The construction of the new terminal building at Tribhuvan International Airport is well underway and the 1988/89 budget allocation for air transport development as a whole has been significantly boosted to Rs.262.4 million($10.5 million), reflecting a 103.4 per cent rise.

The RNAC fleet currently consists of two 757 Boeings, which permitted the extension of international services - until recently restricted to the Asian region - to Europe. In addition there are three Boeing 727, 3 Auros, 10 Twin Otters and 2 Pilatus Porters. According to ICAO statistics the airline carried total cargo amounting to some 9,000 mt in 1986, the bulk of which was international. The number of passengers carried was 721.000, 73 per cent of whom were international.

The upsurge of air traffic operations, which has been partly fuelled by the thriving tourist industry, is large in comparison with many other least developed countries. Between 1982 and 1986 the number of passengers - the bulk of whose increase was on international routes on both scheduled and unscheduled flights - rose by about 24 per cent. International cargo tonnage nearly doubled but its level is still low and could be further increased in view of the expected increase of tourists to 1 million by the end of the decade (from about 275,000 at present). The national airline is expected to be able to expand.

(b) Broadcasting

Broadcasting services are an important form of information diffusion in countries where other forms of communication are inadequate. Available data for 1985 show that the least developed countries as a group had 88 radio receivers per thousand inhabitants. For comparison the average for all developing countries was 154 radio receivers.

(c) Postal services

Data on the post office networks in the least developed countries are scanty but what is available does reveal that more has been achieved recently in penetrating rural areas and providing a relatively wide spread of postal services. In 1986, 65 per cent of all the post offices in 27 least developed countries were in rural areas. The rate of growth in the total number of post offices has been about 2.2 per cent per annum during the period 1980-1986. The total number of post offices in the 27 least developed countries for which data are available was 4.6 per 100 thousand inhabitants in 1986 as compared to some 13 for 108 developing countries.

3. Challenges for the 1990s

Three objectives appear to constitutue the main challenges faced by least developed countries in the field of transport: expansion of the primary transport network, development of inter-urban links, and rehabilitation and maintenance of the existing national transport infrastructure.

The primary transport network encompasses the network of small feeder roads and tracks. It provides the basic link between the rural population and the overall economy. Its expansion is thus essential if the rural population is to play a more active role in national economic development. The development of

Box 15

UGANDA'S TRANSPORT RECOVERY PROGRAMME

The destruction of physical infrastructure during the 1970s has been a major impediment to rapid recovery in Uganda. Government initiatives supported by donor assistance in confronting the challenges have initially been focused on reversing the decline in the transport sector and putting in place viable transport core services.

By the end of 1983 some improvement was under way with the *railway rehabilitation* efforts supported by various donors who funded the purchase of additional rolling stock (420units), spare parts and locomotives. The settlement of the dispute among the former East African Community States regarding the redistribution of assets led to a further increase in the wagon availability. More recently, further arrangements with donors have been reached regarding the supply of 600 covered wagons, 100 tank wagons and 13medium main line locomotives. The Government now aims to make the URC the chief carrier of Uganda's international traffic along the Kampala-borderline to the port of Mombasa. Past experience has, however, shown that Uganda's heavy dependence on this Kenya route has often been rendered vulnerable by political conflict. The Government has therefore been making deliberate efforts to improve the alternative corridor via lake Victoria and the Tanzania rail system to the ports of Dar-es-Salaam and Tanga. The deficiencies of the Tanzania railway system, however, continue to be serious bottlenecks inhibiting full reliance on this route as permanent viable alternative to the sea.

As regards *road transport*, recovery began in 1984 with vehicle fleet replenishment and with the institutional rebuild of the Ministry of Works responsible for road construction. This was supported by the massive infusion of donor resources. Most of these resources were channelled to the rehabilitation of the main trunk roads, i.e. the Kampala-Masaka road, the Equator and lake Katwe road, the Lugazi-Jinja-Tororo road and the Northern Corridor major sections leading to Rwanda and Burundi. Further rehabilitation was supported by the Third Highway Project which focused heavily on road maintenance. By 1987/88, 430km of bitumen road and 2300 km of gravel roads were rehabilitated. Resources for the reconstruction of the entire Northern Corridor chain (Kabale-Malaba) have now been procured. The construction of the Mbarara-Ishaka and Ishaka-Katunguru sections in Western Uganda will be underway early in 1989. The progress of the maintenance programme under the Third Highway Project has been impressive. An urban road rehabilitation programme is also in progress as is the rehabilitation of the rural feeder road system.

Air transportation plays an important role in Uganda, as a land-locked country. The international airport at Entebbe has runways to handle wide-body jets. The terminal infrastructures, including navigational aids, meteological and fire-fighting equipmemt were, however, severely damaged during the civil strife in 1978/79. The 11 up-country airports have not been maintained and several of them are currently not fully operational. Resource constraints ruled out plans to purchase a new aircraft and the Government concluded lease arrangements with Zambia Airways and subsequently with Ghana Airways which enabled the airline to continue operating its long-haul flights to Europe. One of the old 707s which had undergone hush kitting repair work was put in operation again but was recently destroyed in a disastrous crash at Rome airport. Nevertheless, an increase in passenger and airfreight services had been recorded in 1986/87 following the expansion of routes to Europe and the Middle East and within the East African region.

inter-urban links in LDCs constitutes a major task for the future. As regards rehabilitation and maintenance, it is a well known fact that the financial difficulties which LDCs have encountered throughout the 1980s have imposed severe constraints on the achievement of these objectives. Considerable efforts will thus need to be made to redress the progressive decay which the existing infrastructure has undergone.

E. Measures to improve institutional capabilities in LDCs

Many LDCs have taken a variety of measures to improve institutional capabilities for macro-economic and sectoral management, for the development of their public and private sectors, and for the improvement of their financial system. In many LDCs, the measures have been in the context of adjustment policies supported by IMF and the World Bank.

1. *Institutional infrastructure for planning*

The maturity of development planning institutions varies greatly among the LDCs. In some LDCs like Cape Verde, Djibouti, Equatorial Guinea, Guinea-Bissau, Maldives, Sao Tome and Principe and Sierra Leone, the idea of planning has taken root only in the 1980s and these LDCs have been taking their first steps in the building up of planning institutions. Other LDCs where the foundations of a system of development planning were laid earlier (Nepal, Sudan in the 1950s, United Republic of Tanzania, Mali, Botswana in the 1960s, and Benin, Burundi, Democratic Yemen, Rwanda and Yemen in the 1970s) have tried to strengthen the planning institutions at national and sectoral levels through improvements in administrative and management practices.[86] These countries have also tried to establish and reinforce the network of co-ordination between central planning organizations and sectoral Ministries.

The development of planning institutions in each LDC has followed a more or less uniform pattern. The national agency is usually the Ministry of Planning, whose structure and authority are similar to those of other Ministries, and which generally reports directly to the head of the Government. Planning Ministries are responsible for the preparation of the medium-term plan and for ensuring the availability of funds for its implementation. Economic planning normally consists of a set of inter-related activities, which require the active participation of the finance ministry, the central bank and other ministries concerned.[87] Issues of economic policy - fiscal, exchange rate, and pricing questions - tend in turn to be mainly the domain of the Ministry of Finance, while monetary policy is usually the preserve of the Central Bank. Authority over the distribution of external resources may thus be vested in the Ministry of Planning, the Finance Ministry, the Economic Ministry or the Central Bank.[88] Some LDCs' Governments have created inter-ministerial committees so as to strengthen co-ordination of national plans and to ensure their implementation. During the 1980s, as stabilization and adjustment programmes are under way, the role and authority of finance ministries and central banks has increased significantly.

The process of strengthening institutional capacities is at different stages of development among the LDCs. Some LDCs (Bangladesh and Nepal) have developed fairly sophisticated systems of mid-term review and annual planning.[89] They have strengthened their capacity for the generation and analysis of data required for economic planning, research, and policy decision-making. They have also taken steps to improve development administration by establishing programme budgeting systems, granting greater authority to project managers, and creating units for the implementation of projects. Some other LDCs (Benin, Mali, and Sierra Leone) have been making efforts to improve or to create a monitoring system for development planning, but with limited success

86 Despite a history of multi-year planning dating back to independence, planning management is fragmented in many African LDCs. See, for example, the World Bank Report No. 7012-MAU.

87 In some LDCs (Botswana, Central African Republic, Mauritania, Sudan, United Republic of Tanzania), the functions of planning and financing are concentrated in one office.

88 See, for example, *Development Planning in the Arab States, an Evolution of UNDP Assistance*, by Ajit Mozoomdar, N.Y. August 1987, p.24.

89 *Bangladesh Adjustment in the Eighties*, World Bank, Report No. 7105-RD., p.XV; and *Report of the Nepal Country Evaluation Study*, UNDP, April, 1987.

so far due, to a large extent, to lack of qualified personnel.[90]

Moreover, attempts by many LDCs to develop comprehensive planning systems have been overtaken by political and economic crises. When plans are overtaken by changes in the economic environment, they are simply abandoned. In the 1980s, development planning has had to be put aside in many LDCs, especially in Africa, and replaced by rolling public investment and by economic stabilization and adjustment programmes.

2. *Improving public sector institutional capabilities*

In many LDCs stabilization and adjustment programmes have involved the strengthening of the institutional sector capabilities through measures such as:

- improvements in the macro-economic institutional framework;

- adoption of strict management and business principles in the operation of public sector companies;

- establishing criteria (by the government) for applying a system of rewards and penalties to public enterprise managers;

- establishing stricter management procedures at marketing boards;

- formal and on-the-job training for the staff of ministries and public enterprises and upgrading the administrative know-how of the institutions;

- economies in staff expenditure of central government institutions and in public enterprises;

- measures against corruption in the public sector;

- increasing remuneration of public servants;

- setting up or reinforcing institutions or cells within existing institutions for co-ordinating external aid and for the follow-up of structural adjustment programmes;

- delegation of more authority to project managers and other senior government officials;

- establishing trouble-shooting units to ensure smooth implementation of projects;

- establishing and developing monitoring and performance evaluation methods;

- promoting village associations in order to strengthen the regional administration and implementation of development projects based on a regional autonomy (cf. section A.5 above).

3. *Mechanisms to stimulate private industry*

The LDCs which are implementing structural adjustment reforms have introduced institutional changes to transfer public sector enterprises to the private sector, to encourage the private sector in the setting up of new enterprises and to promote joint ventures with foreign collaboration. Measures in this regard include:

- establishment of a legal framework aimed at stimulating private domestic and foreign business (commercial and banking laws, revised investment codes, mining codes, new tax rules, etc.);

- development of an institutional base to cater effectively to the needs of private investors (industrial promotion committees, industrial development corporations etc.)

- setting up of a private sector wing in the planning institution in order to further promote private savings and investment;

- introducing special fiscal and other incentives for the private sector;

- providing relevant infrastructure facilities;

- setting up venture capital funds to promote the involvement of private enterprises.

---

90 See *Government Monitoring and Evaluation Systems in Africa: What are the questions*? prepared by Simon Commander for UNDP, New York, April 1987, pp. 39, 40.

4. Improving sectoral institutions

(a) Agriculture

Public and private sector institutions in agriculture are being strengthened in different ways such as: the strengthening of seed corporations like the Agricultural Inputs Corporation and National Seed Board in Nepal, and the Seed Unit in the Gambia; institutional improvements in agricultural credit (Burundi, Mali, Burkina Faso, Lesotho, Gambia, and Guinea Bissau); and rationalization and restructuring measures and management reforms (Malawi, Niger, Uganda). The Governments of Bangladesh, Benin, and Uganda have introduced training programmes for strengthening agricultural and rural institutions. They have also taken measures to organize or to support co-operatives among the assetless and poorer smallholders.

(b) Industry

Some LDCs have undertaken a reform of the organizational structure of the ministry of industry and of parastatal enterprises. The restructuring of the industrial sector decided by the Guinean Government in December 1985 aims at associating private Guinean or foreign companies in the management of 45 State-owned industrial companies. Uganda is strengthening the planning unit of the Ministry of Industry and Technology, and is setting up a Public Industrial Enterprise Secretariat for analysing the portfolio of Government companies with a view to carrying out the necessary restructuring and reorganization of staff-owned firms.

(c) Banking[91]

In the 1980s many LDCs have restructured or strengthened their banking system so as to make it a more effective instrument for the mobilization of domestic savings, promotion of investment, credit control and debt management.

Several LDCs have reinforced financial institutions, often through: on-the-job training and external fellowships; implementing the computerization programme in the management information service; and streamlining the accounting, inspection and auditing systems and procedures. A State-owned agricultural promotion bank has been established in Mali (Banque nationale pour le développement agricole) . A rural development bank has been established in Nepal. Shilpa Bank and Shilpa Rin Sangstha now cater to the credit requirements of the industrial sector of Bangladesh. Uganda continues to strengthen its development and commercial bank.

Recognizing that monetization and the development of the financial network can play a significant role in mobilizing private savings for development, the monetary authorities in several LDCs have doubled their efforts towards the expansion of the branches of bank and non-bank financial institutions, both in rural and in urban areas. For example, between 1981 and 1986, the number of commercial bank branches in Bangladesh increased by 12 per cent, and in Nepal by almost 50 per cent. These countries have also expanded the network of other kinds of rural bank and non-bank financial institutions to mobilize savings (Krishi Bank and Jatiya Samabaya Bank in Bangladesh, Post Office Savings Banks, Agricultural Development Bank, Sajahs in Nepal).[92] In Mali the number of branches of the *Banque de développement* and of the *Banque Nationale pour le développement agricole* have recently been increased.

In Burundi and Rwanda, the network of savings and credit co-operatives specializing in the rural areas is being set up or strengthened. In Rwanda, the number of their members and the volume of their operations doubled between 1981 and 1985. In Burundi, the first co-operatives of this type were established at the beginning of 1985. The network was expected to cover the entire country within ten years, with at least one rural bank in each commune.

Side-by-side with the setting up and the strengthening of bank and non-bank financial institutions, the savings and credit institutions that originated as popular savings movements have been promoted. *Tontines* in Mali and Burkina Faso, credit unions in Lesotho, Murandimwe and Umuganda in Rwanda, are all examples of such forms of non-official banking institutions.[93]

---

91 For a more extensive treatment of the mobilization of savings in LDCs, see section I.A.1.(c).

92 UNCTAD/ST/LDC/3, 9 April 1985, pp.29-32.

93 See, for example, UNCTAD/ST/LDC/2.

(d) Institutions to stimulate export expansion

Several LDCs have made efforts to create and strengthen special export promotion bodies. Bangladesh, for example, has established a high-level committee for monitoring export credit and providing export credit guarantee schemes, and it has allowed private sector exporters to establish export houses abroad. Malawi has strengthened its Export Promotion Council and established an Export Revolving Fund providing credit facilities. Nepal has plans for an eventual export processing zone - a concept which could be attractive to several other LDCs. In January 1988, Sudan established an export promotion council.

Chapter II

INTERNATIONAL SUPPORT

A. Financial assistance

Shortcomings in the volume and quantity of financial resource transfers and the unexpectedly large return flows on debt service have been key factors hampering the growth and recovery of LDCs during the 1980s. Concern about insufficient flows to the LDCs is expressed in paragraph 109 of the Final Act of UNCTAD VII, and donors are "urged to enlarge substantially financial assistance to the LDCs in a volume and on terms which correspond to their immediate and long-term development needs. The volume and forms should be supportive of and commensurate with the growing requirements of the LDCs' adjustment programmes and broader development efforts" (*ibid.*, para. 116).[94] LDCs' requirements for increased external flows have grown during the second half of the 1980s as their debt situation worsened and rehabilitation and adjustment programmes gained momentum.

External resource transfers to LDCs have remained insufficient notwithstanding far-reaching commitments undertaken at the Paris Conference in 1981 and later on in other forums, and despite significant ensuing efforts made by both donor and LDC recipients, including strengthened co-ordination between them. A major task before the Second United Nations Conference on the Least Developed Countries will thus be to determine what can be done to redress this situation and ensure the proper financial support required by the LDCs in the years ahead.

This section of the report presents an analysis of the trends and salient features pertaining to financial flows and donors' policies. The more pressing issues affecting the LDCs are highlighted. Recent important international initiatives to improve the financial situation of the poorest countries and new proposals for action by the international community are reviewed. Finally, challenges for the 1990s, including some policy options, are presented.

1. *The dominant role of official development assistance*

(a) Recent trends in external resource flows

External flows to the LDCs have been disappointing overall since the Paris Conference in 1981: they remained below the 1980 level of $ 8.8 billion during the years 1981 to 1984; and while the levels reached in 1985 ($9.2 billion) and 1986 ($9.8 billion) were 4 per cent

[94] Statements along these lines concerning poor/low-income countries undertaking adjustment efforts are contained in the recent Communiqués of the IMF Interim Committee and World Bank Development Committee and of the DAC High-Level Meeting. The Economic Declaration of the Toronto Economic Summit held in June 1988, reiterates that "an increase in concessional resource flows is necessary to help the poorest developing countries to resume sustained growth"(para. 29).

Table 24

TOTAL EXTERNAL RESOURCE RECEIPTS OF LDCs

	Net disbursements in millions of dollars								Percentage distribution							
	Average 1976-1980	1980	1981	1982	1983	1984	1985	1986	Average 1976-1980	1980	1981	1982	1983	1984	1985	1986
I. CONCESSIONAL FLOWS	5261	7517	7184	7679	7661	7727	8767	9764	87.9	85.5	91.6	89.2	93.6	93.0	95.8	99.6
of which:																
DAC bilateral	2536	3722	3536	3767	3499	3627	4463	5278	42.4	42.3	45.1	43.8	42.8	43.7	48.8	53.8
DAC multilateral [a]	1502	2094	2107	2095	2222	2578	2889	3209	25.1	23.8	26.9	24.3	27.1	31.0	31.6	32.7
OPEC bilateral	807	955	742	963	863	698	480	480	13.5	10.9	9.5	11.2	10.5	8.4	5.2	4.9
OPEC multilateral [b]	114	140	221	190	164	105	82	94	1.9	1.6	2.8	2.2	2.0	1.3	0.9	1.0
II.NON-CONCESSIONAL FLOWS	722	1275	656	928	525	579	387	42	12.1	14.5	8.4	10.8	6.4	7.0	4.2	0.4
1. OFFICIAL FLOWS	201	429	356	247	373	355	264	67	3.4	4.9	4.5	2.9	4.6	4.3	2.9	0.7
of which:																
DAC bilateral	89	233	162	188	216	270	141	132	1.5	2.6	2.1	2.2	2.6	3.3	1.5	1.3
DAC multilateral [a]	63	89	88	103	116	65	147	-5	1.0	1.0	1.1	1.2	1.4	0.8	1.6	-0.0
2. PRIVATE FLOWS	553	903	375	714	151	224	121	-30	9.2	10.3	4.8	8.3	1.8	2.7	1.3	-0.3
of which:																
DAC guaranteed export credits	481	990	231	275	102	138	126	-72	8.0	11.3	2.9	3.2	1.2	1.7	1.4	-0.7
DAC direct investment	60	52	102	168	30	66	31	26	1.0	0.6	1.3	2.0	0.4	0.8	0.3	0.3
TOTAL EXTERNAL FLOWS	5983	8793	7840	8607	8185	8307	9154	9806	100.0	100.0	100.0	100.0	100.0	100.0	100.0	100.0
Memo items :																
In 1980 $ million [c] :																
Total ODA	6751	7517	7534	8330	8579	8769	9906	10864								
Total external flows	7652	8793	8222	9337	9166	9426	10344	10912								
In 1980 $ per capita [c] :																
Total ODA	21.7	23.0	22.5	24.2	24.3	24.2	26.7	28.5								
Total external flows	24.6	26.9	24.5	27.1	26.0	26.1	27.9	28.7								
As % of LDCs' GDP :																
Total ODA	9.4	10.7	9.5	10.4	10.5	10.1	11.0	11.7								
Total external flows	10.7	12.5	10.4	11.6	11.2	10.9	11.5	11.8								

Source: UNCTAD secretariat calculations based on data from the OECD secretariat, the World Bank and the UNCTAD secretariat.

a Flows from multilateral agencies mainly financed by DAC member countries.

b Flows from multilateral agencies mainly financed by OPEC member countries.

c External flows are expressed in terms of LDCs' command over imports at 1980 prices. Net disbursements were converted to 1980 prices using the import unit value index for LDCs as a group.

and 11 per cent, respectively, above the 1980 level, the latest increase was largely due to the appreciation of donors' currencies against the United States dollar. Measured in constant 1980 dollars, however, the LDCs' total external resource flows have increased in each of the last three years; ODA itself has increased, in constant dollar prices, every year since 1980 (see table 24). As a percentage of LDCs' GDP, however, total external flows declined from 12.5 per cent in 1980 to 11.5 per cent in 1986.

A major feature is now the overwhelming role played by ODA. During the 1980s, LDCs' traditional reliance on ODA increased to the extent that in 1986 ODA flows accounted for as much as 99.6 per cent of their total net external resource flows (as compared to 85.5 per cent in 1980). ODA flows to LDCs were relatively stable in nominal terms during the first years of the decade, but they grew by more than 10 per cent in 1985 and in 1986, to reach $9.8 billion in the latter year. Fuelling the increase the combined share of DAC countries and the multilateral agencies mainly financed by them in total LDCs' receipts rose to above 85 per cent in 1986. According to preliminary estimates, a further similar overall ODA increase may have taken place in 1987, when DAC bilateral and multilateral ODA reached some $9.8 billion. The increase in 1987, was, however, even more than in 1986, principally due to the fall of the United States dollar[95]; in terms of purchasing power, this increase must be assumed to have been much smaller. Nevertheless, LDCs have benefited as a group by the shift in DAC ODA towards sub-Saharan Africa, as against an estimated decline in real terms of 2 per cent[96] in DAC ODA to all developing countries in 1987.

Conversely, non-concessional flows to LDCs diminished sharply during the 1980s, from $1.3 billion in 1980 to $42 million in 1986, mainly reflecting a steep slump in export credits and a dwindling of the already very low levels of direct foreign investment. The curtailment of the extension of export credits to the LDCs was due, on the one hand, to more restrictive policies generally instituted by export credit agencies and banks and, on the other hand, to the erosion of LDCs' credit-worthiness. Moreover, chronic shortages of liquidity accompanied by severe problems of indebtedness led LDCs to institute adjustment policies aimed at cutting down imports and minimizing new borrowing, especially borrowing on commercial terms.

(b) Trends at the country level

At the individual country level, similar trends to those outlined for the LDCs as a group are discernible: the majority of LDCs increased their dependence on ODA, in particular on multilateral aid. ODA increases in 1985 and 1986 were relatively general, benefiting both those LDCs that have concluded arrangements with IMF and/or the World Bank and other LDCs; and almost all LDCs which had access to non-concessional lending suffered drastic decreases in such flows during the 1980s. In fact, in 1986, non-concessional flows were negative in more than 40 per cent of the LDCs (see Statistical Annex).

In the case of African LDCs, increased attention in response to the African crisis gave rise to a number of initiatives, including the establishment of the World Bank Special Facility for Sub-Saharan Africa in July 1985, and the adoption of the United Nations Programme of Action for African Recovery and Development 1986-1990 (UN-PAAERD) by the General Assembly in June 1986, which served as a further stimulus to aid increases. ODA to African LDCs thus grew at a relatively faster rate than ODA to LDCs as a group. In per capita terms African LDCs received on average larger amounts of ODA than LDCs as a group throughout the 1980s.

Despite similarities in trends, considerable differences can be perceived among LDCs as regards per capita levels of external resources and ODA, as well as ODA/GDP ratios and ODA/investment ratios. Information presented in the Statistical Annex shows that within the groups of LDCs with large and small population size[97], LDCs which experienced the lowest, even negative, growth (and thus the greatest difficulties) generally received larger amounts of aid in per capita terms than other LDCs. Round tables and consultative groups

95 Aggregates in nominal dollars are biased upwards during periods of dollar depreciation (March 1985 to end 1987) and downwards when the dollar appreciates (as was the case from 1980 to March 1985). According to OECD, the "valuation effect" was especially substantial in 1987 when the fall of the United States dollar inflated reported OECD ODA by 11 per cent. (See OECD, "Financial Resources for Developing Countries: 1987 and Recent Trends". PRESS/A (83) 32, Paris, 17 June 1988).

96 *Ibid.*, page 2.

97 In order to avoid a certain bias due to population size - countries with a small population tend to receive larger amounts of aid in per capita terms than countries with a large population - in Annex table 16, LDCs are classified into three groups, i.e., large-size LDCs with a population above 10 million, medium-size LDCs with a population below 10 million but above 1 million, and small-size LDCs with a population below 1 million.

may have been instrumental in securing these relatively higher flows.[98] The absence of a positive correlation between levels of financial flows and economic growth performance can be explained by lags, extraneous influences and technical factors, but it might also point to an inadequacy in the available aid volume directed to productive investment or the inappropriateness of the aid-mix provided.

(c) *Donors' policies: meeting the SNPA aid targets*

The adoption by donors of targets for ODA increases, such as those embodied in the SNPA, has stimulated higher ODA disbursements to LDCs, even though the "substantial increase" in ODA to LDCs called for in paragraph 63 of the SNPA, and the expected "doubling" of ODA flows "by 1985" did not take place.[99] Many donors have made additional efforts to honour their commitments undertaken at the Paris Conference. The share allocated to LDCs in DAC and in OPEC programmes has increased, showing that, despite the stringency in aid programmes arising from budgetary restraints in many donor countries, efforts are being made to spare the neediest countries.

As can be seen from Annex table 23, by 1986 the majority of DAC donors had at least in one year, if not in several, provided ODA amounts to LDCs which equalled or exceeded 0.15 per cent of their GNP or, alternatively, had more than doubled their ODA to these countries (as compared to average flows in 1976-1980). The Nordic countries (Norway, Denmark and Sweden) and the Netherlands, notably, continued to provide well above 0.15 per cent of the GNP to LDCs. By 1986, Italy and Ireland had increased their aid to LDCs more than nine-fold, and Finland more than four-fold, as compared to average flows in 1976-1980. If the DAC aid average remained throughout the 1980s at 0.08 per cent of DAC countries' combined GNP (except in 1982 when it reached 0.09 per cent), this was due to the relatively sluggish performance of a few major donors to LDCs. It is a matter of considerable concern that in 1986 six major DAC donors - United States, United Kingdom, Canada, Federal Republic of Germany, France and Belgium - as well as Denmark which already gives double the 0.15 per cent target, actually allowed their aid/GNP ratio to LDCs to fall.

As regards the socialist countries of Eastern Europe, two countries - namely the USSR and Czechoslovakia - reported that they have reached or exceeded the 0.15 per cent target. The USSR reported that it provided 1.5 billion roubles ($US 2.4 billion) or 0.2 per cent of its GNP, as net transfers to LDCs in 1987, as compared to 1.1 billion roubles ($1.5 billion) or 0.18 per cent of GNP in 1981, 1.7 billion roubles ($2.2 billion or 0.22 per cent of its GNP) in 1985 and 2 billion roubles ($3.2 billion) in 1986.

In the context of South-South co-operation, OPEC countries and other developing countries have been providing assistance to LDCs. Although OPEC aid to LDCs virtually halved in absolute terms between 1980 and 1986, and is expected to have decreased further in 1987, the share allocated to LDCs in OPEC aid programmes more than doubled during that period. OPEC aid as ratio to GNP fluctuated between 0.20 and 0.25 per cent from 1980 to 1984 and amounted to 0.14 per cent in 1985 and 0.15 in 1986, with Saudi Arabia and Kuwait as main contributors (providing respectively 0.61 per cent and 0.76 per cent of their GNP to LDCs in 1986). The United Arab Emirates and Qatar were also providing more than 0.15 of GNP to the LDCs in 1986 and in most other years.

China reported that its disbursements to the LDCs, in the form of grants and interest-free loans, increased from 294 million Yuan ($85 million) in 1986 to 409 million Yuan ($110 million) in 1987.

A lesson which may be drawn from the above-mentioned trends is the need for a more equitable burden-sharing among donors. ODA increases adequate to meet LDCs' external capital requirements can only be obtained when efforts are shared by all donors, including the major ones. This calls for an aid target for LDCs as a group linked to individual donors' capacities. The 0.15 per cent target set out in the SNPA which is related to donors' GNP is adequate in this respect. It may need to be revised, however, in view of LDCs' estimated capital requirements for the 1990s: not only are these capital requirements larger than in the 1980s because of the worsening of LDCs' situation and the additional adjustment efforts that they are undertaking; but also, the list of LDCs now comprises ten more countries than at the time of the adoption of the SNPA. Aid co-ordination mechanisms would ensure that the allocation of aid among LDCs responds to their

---

98 See also section (d) on "aid co-ordination" below.

99 ODA flows exceeded in 1985 and in 1986 the average 1976-1980 level by 67 per cent and 86 per cent in nominal terms (and 47 per cent and 61 per cent in terms of purchasing power).

Chart V

AID TARGETS

Net ODA from individual DAC members countries to LDCs as a group, compared to the SNPA targets, 1986

Per cent of GNP

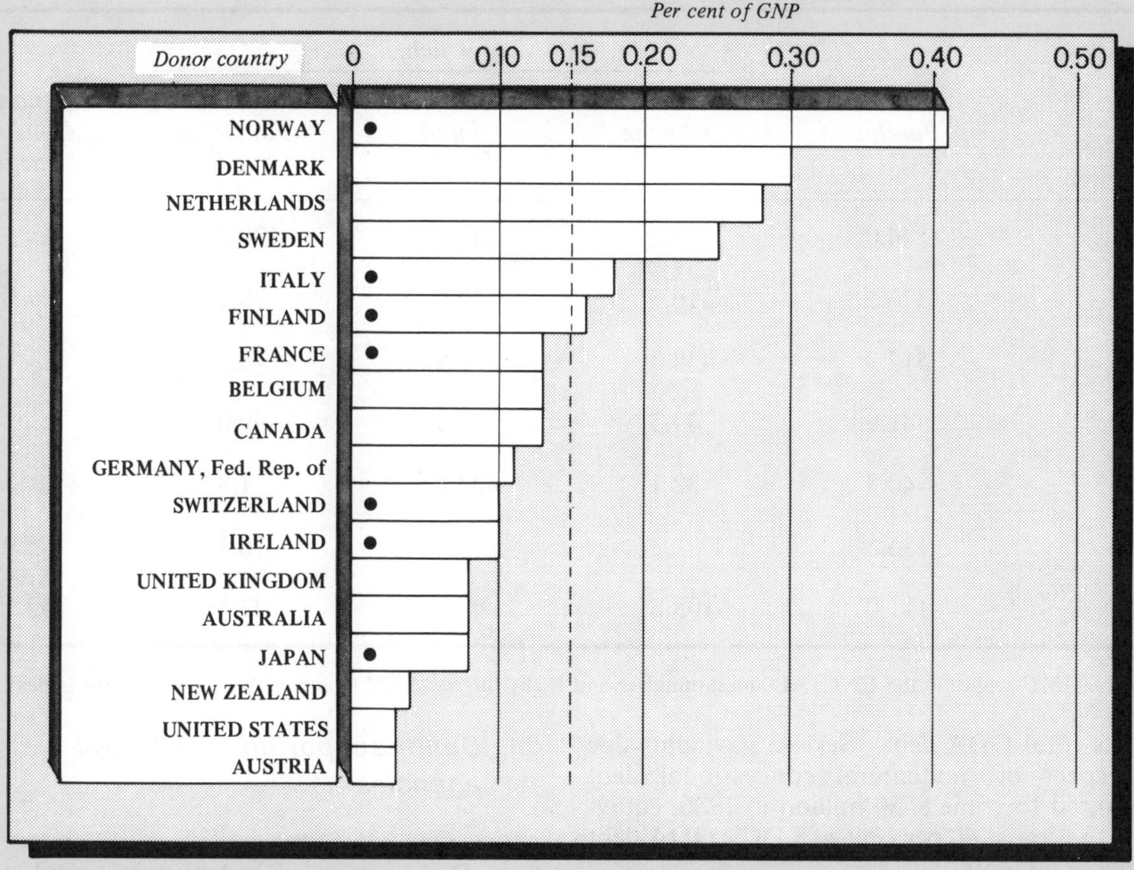

Source: Annex table 23.

● : aid to LDCs doubled since 1976-1980 average.

relative individual needs and that no LDCs be unduly deprived thereof (see page 188).

2. *The increased role of multilateral institutions*

(a) Volume trends

The changing pattern of ODA flows to LDCs was characterized by a continued increase in multilateral aid provided by agencies mainly financed by DAC countries. In the 1980s such aid increased by more than 50 per cent, from $2.1 billion in 1980 to $3.2 billion in 1986, and its share in LDCs' ODA rose from one fourth in 1980 to one third in 1986 (see table 24, above). Most of this increase was contributed by the development banks/funds, namely IDA, the African Development Fund and the Asian Development Bank, whose disbursements to LDCs almost doubled - in some cases more than doubled - between 1980 and 1986 (see table 25).

Multilateral agencies are by far the main providers of loans to LDCs. Even where concessional, these loans have serious, increasing, and up to now not negotiable, debt-service implications. Thus, LDCs' ODA debt owed to multilateral agencies (including those financed by OPEC countries) at the end of 1986 reached $14 billion, accounting for over 40 per cent of

Table 25

LDCs' NET PURCHASES FROM IMF 1981-1987, AND DRAWINGS UNDER THE STRUCTURAL ADJUSTMENT FACILITY

(in millions of SDRs)

		of which:			
Year	*Total net Purchases*	*Credit tranche*	*Extended Fund Facility*	*Compensatory Financing Facility*	*Structural Adjustment Facility*
1981	544.0	229.2	239.5	130.3	-
1982	376.5	316.7	-0.9	79.3	-
1983	512.9	438.3	2.8	-3.3	-
1984	-41.9	49.5	-8.9	-99.0	-
1985	-40.8	32.1	-22.5	1.8	-
1986	-135.5	-1.3	-59.2	-76.1	45.9
1987	-111.0	-108.8	-48.7	42.1	252.1

Source: IMF replies to the UNCTAD questionnaires and IMF, *International Financial Statistics* (various issues).

LDC's total ODA debt. Service payments due in respect of multilateral concessional debt amounted to some $450 million in 1986, equivalent to almost 40 per cent of LDC's ODA debt service payments.

Non-concessional flows from multilateral agencies, excluding net purchases from IMF, have always been small, however, as compared to multilateral concessional flows. After increasing from $90 million in 1980 to $147 million in 1985, they became negative in 1986.

Net purchases from IMF (excluding the Structural Adjustment Facility), which amounted to over $500 million in 1981 and 1983 and to some $380 million in 1982, have been negative from 1984 onwards (see table 25). In this perspective, the establishment of the IMF Structural Adjustment Facility, which provides credits on concessional terms, appears as one of the measures able to reverse a perverse trend in LDC flows.

LDCs' non-concessional multilateral debt has remained relatively small ($1.6 billion at end 1986) but service payments in respect of it are nevertheless significant ($240 million in 1986, equivalent to over half of LDCs' concessional multilateral debt service payments).

(b) Donor support to multilateral agencies

Donor countries have expressed their support to multilateral agencies not only through direct contributions but also through expanded co-financing. New mechanisms for concessional assistance, of special benefit to LDCs, have been created. Multilateral resources have thus recently been strengthened by the establishment of the World Bank Special Facility for Sub-Saharan Africa in 1985[100], the agreement on the IDA-8 replenishment (amounting to $12.4 billion) which became operational in September 1987, and the capital increase of the African Development Fund agreed also in 1987. Furthermore, the IMF Structural Adjustment Facility, designed to provide additional assistance on concessional terms to low-income countries facing protracted balance-of-payments problems, was established in March 1986; in late 1987 agreement was reached on an Enhanced Structural Adjustment Facility. SAF resources initially totalled SDR 2.7 billion. The Enhanced

100 Up to June 1988, 18 African LDCs had access to the Special Facility for Sub-Saharan Africa; the total commitments to LDCs, including special joint financing by bilateral donors reached $984 million, corresponding to 53 per cent of funds committed under the Facility.

Facility is to provide additional resources totalling SDR 6 billion.[101]

Of further interest to a number of African LDCs is the special action programme proposed by the World Bank to support low-income debt-distressed African countries pursuing economic policy reforms. In this connection, an agreement was reached in December 1987 to expand co-financing with bilateral and with other multilateral donors. This agreement involves $6.4 billion in concessional, quick-disbursing funding, of which an estimated $3 billion in additional aid flows to the countries concerned over the period 1988-1990.[102] The World Bank has established a reserve fund to pay a large proportion of the interest on past IBRD loans for those countries, including some LDCs which have since ceased to be appropriate borrowers from the Bank's non-concessional funds. (For details see section 5 (d)).

(c) Policy advice and conditionality

The role of multilateral institutions must not be viewed only in terms of the financial flows and technical assistance - including the additional bilateral flows that they are able to catalyse - directed to the LDCs: through their policy advice, multilateral institutions have come to exercise an important influence on the economic policies of the majority of these countries. IMF and the World Bank, in particular, have played a leading role in assisting countries to design and implement comprehensive structural adjustment programmes[103] and the adoption of such programmes has in many cases become a pre-condition for securing fresh donor funding or debt relief.[104] In the 1980s, twenty-three LDCs have undertaken adjustment efforts and policy reforms with the support of IMF and/or the World Bank (see chapter I and table 26 below).

An important issue affecting LDCs is the conditionality attached to policy-based lending: no softening is on the horizon.[105] and the use of resources under certain facilities appears to be subject to numerous and comprehensive prescriptions which may preclude some LDCs because of the difficulties in complying with the conditions. Difficulties may arise not only as a result of "excessive conditionalities" but also from "inconsistent requirements of different creditors and multilateral institutions[106]," in other words, onerous cross-conditionalities.[107]

The policy framework papers (PFPs) required for the use of SAF resources are an innovation which, among other features, provides for a co-ordinated approach to conditionality from the donors' side. These papers outline the borrowing country's medium-term economic objectives and priorities (i.e. over a period of three years) and set out the structural reform and economic policy measures to be implemented. They also contain an assessment of the social impact of the proposed policy measures and of the borrowing country's financing needs. Annual disbursements under the SAF are tied to the approval of annual arrangements by the Fund's executive board in the light of the progress made in the implementation of the programme. PFPs are designed to be of use also to other donors interested in supporting a country's adjustment programme and are expected to have a catalytic effect in mobilizing additional financial resources. In early 1987 Paris Club creditors decided to tie rescheduling

101 All LDCs except Botswana and Tuvalu (not a member of IMF) are eligible for SAF and ESAF resources.

102 According to the list of eligible countries agreed on at the World Bank-convened meeting of donors in March 1988, out of 17 African countries identified as currently eligible in this special action programme, 12 are LDCs, namely Burundi, Central African Republic, the Gambia, Guinea, Guinea-Bissau, Malawi, Mauritania, Niger, Sao Tome and Principe, Togo, Uganda and United Republic of Tanzania. The eligibility of another 8 LDCs (Benin, Chad, Comoros, Equatorial Guinea, Mali, Sierra Leone, Somalia and Sudan) is under review.

103 For a discussion of common prescriptions embodied in stabilization and structural adjustment programmes and their pros and cons for LDCs, see above chapter I.(a).

104 "Bilateral donors have relied on these institutions IMF and the World Bank for guidance as to the adequacy of such programmes and for management and advice in supporting financial programming through the consultative group process and in the context of Paris Club operations". There was now "a recognition of the central role of the World Bank and the IMF in the whole process of policy-based lending". See OECD, *Development co-operation, 1987 report*, (Paris 1988), p. 129.

105 The Executive Board of IMF completed a comprehensive review of conditionality in April 1988, including in-depth discussion of issues in the design of growth-oriented programmes and in the monitoring of structural adjustment, as well as of technical issues in programme monitoring, and left the 1979 guidelines on conditionality unchanged. The Interim Committee at its April 1988 meeting re-affirmed that "use of IMF resources must be linked closely to progress in the implementation of policies geared to the restoration of balance of payments viability and sustainable economic growth" (see Communiqué of 15 April 1988, Press Release No. 88/10, para. 8).

106 See Communiqué of the Intergovernmental Group of Twenty-Four to the Development Committee of the World Bank, of 24 September 1988, para. 13.

107 For examples within and between the Bretton Woods institutions and their supporting governments acting as donors, see Sidney Dell, "The question of cross-conditionality", *World Development*, vol.16 No.5. (1988).

Table 26

ARRANGEMENTS IN SUPPORT OF STRUCTURAL ADJUSTMENT IN THE 1980s
(As of June 1988)

Amounts in SDR millions (except otherwise indicated)

	IMF arrangements				World Bank loans and credits								
	Stand-by/Extended Facility		Structural Adjustment Facility		Structural adjustment				Sector and other adjustment				
						Amount				Amount			
Country	Period	Amount	Period	Amount	Date of Approval	IDA	African Facility [1]	Co-financing [2]	Date of Approval	IDA	African Facility [1]	Co-financing [2]	Purpose
Bangladesh	July 1979- July 1980	85											
	Dec.1980- Dec.1983 [3]	800 [4]											
	March 1983- Aug. 1983	68.4											
	Dec. 1985- June 1987	180	Feb. 1987- Feb. 1990	182.6					June 1987	147.8			Industrial Policy reform
Burkina Faso									Feb. 1985	13.8		France/CCCE (3.2); Netherlands (2.1) F.R.of Germany/GTZ (2); France/FAC (1.7)	Fertilizers
Burma	June 1981- June 1982	27											
Burundi	Aug. 1986- March 1988	21	Aug. 1986- Aug. 1989	27.1	May 1986	13.2	14.3	Japan (11); Switzerland (7.7);					
					June 1988	64.9		Japan (18.1); F.R.of Germany (6); Saudi Arabia (2.9)					
Central African Republic	Feb.1980- Feb.1981	4											
	April 1981- Dec. 1981	10.4 [5]											
	April 1983- April 1984	18 [6]											
	July 1984- July 1985	15											
	Sept.1985- March 1987	15 [7]			Sept.1986	12.3	14						
	June 1987- March 1988	8	June 1987- May 1990	19.3					July 1987	11.5		Saudi Arabia (2); Japan (6)	Cotton sector
					June 1988	28.9		ADF (25)					
Chad			Oct. 1987- Oct. 1990	19.4									

Table 26 (continued)

ARRANGEMENTS IN SUPPORT OF STRUCTURAL ADJUSTMENT IN THE 1980s
(As of June 1988)

Amounts in SDR millions (except otherwise indicated)

	IMF arrangements				World Bank loans and credits								
	Stand-by/Extended Facility		Structural Adjustment Facility		Structural adjustment				Sector and other adjustment				
						Amount				Amount			
Country	Period	Amount	Period	Amount	Date of Approval	IDA	African Facility [1]	Co-financing [2]	Date of Approval	IDA	African Facility [1]	Co-financing [2]	Purpose
Ethiopia	May 1981-June 1982	67.5											
Equatorial Guinea	July 1980-June 1981	5.5											
	June 1985-June 1986	9.2 [8]											
Gambia	Nov. 1979-Nov. 1980	1.6											
	Feb. 1982-Feb. 1983	16.9											
	April 1984-July 1985 [10]	12.8 [9]											
	Sept. 1986-Oct. 1987	5.1	Sept. 1986-Sept. 1989	10.9	Aug. 1986	4.3	9.9	United Kingdom (4.5); African Development Fund (9)					
Guinea	Dec. 1982-Nov. 1983	25 [11]											
	Feb. 1986-March 1987	33 [12]			Feb. 1986	22.9	15.6	F.R. of Germany (9.4); Japan (27.8); France (26.7); Switzerland (4.8)					
	July 1987-Aug. 1988	11.6	July 1987-July 1990	36.8									
					June 1988	47.0		ADF (12); Japan (11.2)					
Guinea-Bissau									Dec.1984	10.1		Switzerland (SW.F. 4.5 mn.)	Economic recovery programme [13]
			Oct. 1987-Oct. 1990	4.8	May 1987	8	4	Switzerland (5.2); Saudi Arabia (3.2); African Development Fund (11.3); IFAD (5.3)					

Table 26 (continued)

ARRANGEMENTS IN SUPPORT OF STRUCTURAL ADJUSTMENT IN THE 1980s
(As of June 1988)

Amounts in SDR millions (except otherwise indicated)

Country	IMF arrangements				World Bank loans and credits								
	Stand-by/Extended Facility		Structural Adjustment Facility		Structural adjustment				Sector and other adjustment				
						Amount				Amount			
	Period	Amount	Period	Amount	Date of Approval	IDA	African Facility [1]	Co-financing [2]	Date of Approval	IDA	African Facility [1]	Co-financing [2]	Purpose
Haiti	Oct. 1978-Oct. 1981 [15]	32.2 [14]											
	Aug. 1982-Sept.1983	34.5											
	Nov. 1983-Sept. 1985	60 [16]											
			Dec.1986-Dec.1989	28					Mar.1987	32.8			Economic recovery
Lao People's Dem.Rep.	Aug. 1980-Aug. 1981	14											
Malawi	Oct. 1979-Dec.1981 [17]	26.3											
	May 1980-March 1982	49.9 [18]			June 1981	36.7 [19]							
	Aug. 1982-Aug. 1983	22							Apr. 1983	4.6		IFAD (10.3)	Smallholder fertilizers
	Sept.1983-Sept.1986 [21]	81 [20]			Dec. 1983	51.9							
	March 1988-May 1989	13.0			Dec. 1985	28.0	37.3	F.R. of Germany/KfW (6.4); Japan/OECF (22.6) United States/AID (15)					
					Jan. 1987		8.4	Japan (17.7); United Kingdom (7.5); F.R. of Germany (5)	June 1988	50.6		OECF (30) USAID (25) ADF (19.5) EEC (16)	Industrial and trade policy adjustment
Mali	May 1982-May 1983	30.4							June 1988	29.4		Japan (38.7) Saudi Arabia (5.9) ADF (45)	Public enterprise sector
	Dec. 1983-May 1985	40.5											
	Nov. 1985-March 1987	22.9 [22]											
	Aug. 1988-Oct. 1989	12.7											

Table 26 (continued)

ARRANGEMENTS IN SUPPORT OF STRUCTURAL ADJUSTMENT IN THE 1980s
(As of June 1988)

Amounts in SDR millions (except otherwise indicated)

Country	IMF arrangements				World Bank loans and credits								
	Stand-by/Extended Facility		Structural Adjustment Facility		Structural adjustment				Sector and other adjustment				
						Amount				Amount			
	Period	Amount	Period	Amount	Date of Approval	IDA	African Facility [1]	Co-financing [2]	Date of Approval	IDA	African Facility [1]	Co-financing [2]	Purpose
Mauritania	July 1980-March 1982 [24]	29.7 [23]											
	June 1981-March 1982	25.8											
	April 1985-April 1986	12											
	April 1986-April 1987	12	Sept. 1986-Sept. 1989	21.5									
	May 1987-May 1988	10			June 1987	11.7	21.4	Saudi Arabia (4.8) F.R.of Germany (2.8)					
Nepal	Dec. 1985-April 1987	18.7											
			Oct. 1987-Oct. 1990	23.7	March 1987	40.9							
Niger	Oct. 1983-Dec. 1984	18											
	Dec. 1984-Dec. 1985	16											
	Dec. 1985-Dec. 1986	13.5	Nov. 1986-Nov. 1989	21.4	Feb. 1986	18.3	36.6						
	Dec. 1986-Dec. 1987	10.1							June 1987	46	15.4		Public enterprise sector
Rwanda	Oct. 1979-Oct. 1980	5 [25]											
Samoa	Aug. 1979-Aug. 1980	0.7 [25]											
	June 1983-June 1984	3.4											
	July 1984-July 1985	3.4											
Sao Tome and Principe					June 1987	3.1	2.3	African Development Fund (8.5)					

Table 26 (continued)

ARRANGEMENTS IN SUPPORT OF STRUCTURAL ADJUSTMENT IN THE 1980s (As of June 1988)

Amounts in SDR millions (except otherwise indicated)

	IMF arrangements				World Bank loans and credits								
	Stand-by/Extended Facility		Structural Adjustment Facility		Structural adjustment				Sector and other adjustment				
						Amount				Amount			
Country	Period	Amount	Period	Amount	Date of Approval	IDA	African Facility [1]	Co-financing [2]	Date of Approval	IDA	African Facility [1]	Co-financing [2]	Purpose
Sierra Leone	Nov. 1979-Nov. 1980	17											
	March 1981-Feb. 1984 [27]	186 [26]											
	Feb. 1984-Feb. 1985	50.2 [28]							June 1984	20.3		IFAD (5.4)	Agriculture
	Nov. 1986-Nov. 1987	23.2	Nov. 1986-Nov. 1989	36.8									
Somalia	Feb. 1980-Feb. 1981	11.5 [29]											
	July 1981-July 1982	43.1											
	July 1982-Jan. 1984	60											
	Feb. 1985-Sept. 1986	22.1											
	June 1987-Feb. 1989	33.2	June 1987-June 1990	28.1									
Sudan	May 1979-May 1982 [31]	427 [30]											
	Feb. 1982-Feb. 1983	198 [32]											
	Feb. 1983-March 1984	170							June 1983	46.4			Agriculture rehabilitation
	June 1984-June 1985	90 [33]											
Togo	June 1979-Dec. 1980	15 [34]											
	Feb. 1981-Feb. 1983	47.5 [35]											
	March 1983-April 1984	21.4			May 1983	36.9							
	May 1984-May 1985	19											
	May 1985-May 1986	15.4			May 1985 Aug. 1985	28.1	 9.7						
	June 1986-April 1988	23.0											
	March 1988-April 1989	13.0	March 1988-March 1991	24.4	Mar. 1988	33.0		ADF (17.3); Japan (20.8)					

Table 26 (concluded)

ARRANGEMENTS IN SUPPORT OF STRUCTURAL ADJUSTMENT IN THE 1980s
(As of June 1988)

Amounts in SDR millions (except otherwise indicated)

	IMF arrangements				*World Bank loans and credits*								
	Stand-by/Extended Facility		*Structural Adjustment Facility*		*Structural adjustment*				*Sector and other adjustment*				
						Amount				*Amount*			
Country	*Period*	*Amount*	*Period*	*Amount*	*Date of Approval*	*IDA*	*African Facility* [1]	*Co-financing* [2]	*Date of Approval*	*IDA*	*African Facility* [1]	*Co-financing* [2]	*Purpose*
Uganda	Jan. 1980- Dec. 1980	12.5											
	June 1981- June 1982	112.5											
	Aug. 1982- Aug. 1983	112.5											
	Sept. 1983- Sept. 1984	95 [36]							Feb. 1983	63.5		Italy/DCD (10)	Agriculture rehabilitation
									May 1984	47.2			Reconstruction
			June 1987- June 1990	63.2					Sept.1987	50.9	18.8	United Kingdom/ODA (16)	Economic recovery
Un.-Rep. of Tanzania	Sept.1980- June 1982	179.6 [37]											
	Aug. 1986- Feb. 1988	64.2							Nov. 1986	41.3	38.2	F.R. of Germany (17.3); Switzerland (9.2); United Kingdom (7.3)	Multi-sector rehabilitation
			Oct. 1987- Oct. 1990	67.9									
									Jan.1988	22.5	(26.0)	Saudi Arabia (4)	Multi-sector rehabilitation

Source: IMF *Annual Report* (various issues); IMF Survey (various issues); World Bank *Annual Report* (various issues); World Bank News (various issues).

1 Special Facility for Sub-Saharan Africa.
2 Including special joint financing and bilateral support; amounts in millions of dollar equivalents.
3 Extended Facility arrangement, cancelled as of June 1982.
4 SDR 580 mn. not purchased.
5 SDR 2.4 mn. not purchased.
6 SDR 13.5 mn. not purchased.
7 SDR 7.5 mn. not purchased.
8 SDR 3.8 mn. not purchased.
9 SDR 10.2 mn. not purchased.
10 Cancelled as of April 1985.
11 SDR 13.5 mn. not purchased.
12 SDR 6 mn. not purchased.
13 SDR Supported by IMF (SDR 1.88 mn. purchase in first credit tranche).
14 SDR 21.4 mn. not purchased.
15 Extended Facility arrangement.
16 SDR 39 mn. not purchased.
17 Cancelled as of May 1980; SDR 20.9 mn. not purchased.
18 SDR 9.9 mn. not purchased.
19 IBRD loan.
20 Original amount decreased from SDR 100 mn. SDR 24 mn. not purchased.
21 Extended Facility arrangement; cancelled as of August 1986.
22 SDR 6.6 mn. not purchased.
23 SDR 20.8 mn. not purchased.
24 Cancelled as of May 1981.
25 Not purchased.
26 Including an increase of SDR 22.3 mn. in June 1981. SDR 152 not purchased.
27 Extended Facility arrangement; cancelled as of April 1982.
28 SDR 31.2 mn. not purchased.
29 SDR 5.5 mn. not purchased.
30 SDR 5.5 mn. not purchased.
31 Extended Facility arrangement; cancelled as of February 1982; SDR 176 mn. not purchased.
32 SDR 128 mn. not purchased.
33 SDR 70 mn. not purchased.
34 SDR 1.75 mn. not purchased.
35 SDR 40.3 mn. not purchased.
36 SDR 30 mn. not purchased.
37 SDR 154.6 mn. not purchased.

to a SAF arrangement (instead of a stand-by arrangement), but on a case-by-case basis; only two LDCs (Guinea-Bissau and Uganda) have benefited in 1987 from such arrangements.

World Bank-supported structural adjustment programmes include the same macroeconomic elements as those embodied in IMF-supported programmes but the World Bank, in addition, is more deeply involved in sectoral policy issues through its sector adjustment lending. World Bank structural adjustment credits are normally provided in two tranches, with the second one released after a performance review.

LDCs' experience with internationally agreed adjustment programmes shows that their own structural handicaps and their extreme vulnerability to unforeseen exogeneous shocks may affect the implementation of these programmes. Conditionality requirements attached to the provision of policy-based lending to LDCs should, therefore, be more flexible and better adapted to the special situation and difficulties of these countries. The decision taken by the IMF Executive Board in August 1988, to set up the Compensatory and Contingency Financing Facility (CCFF), to help countries maintain the momentum of adjustment in the face of a broad range of unanticipated adverse external shocks, constitutes a step forward. However, LDCs may find it difficult to use a facility which, unlike SAF or ESAF, provides loans at non-concessional terms.[108]

Another area of financial support by multilateral agencies, which calls for improvement and action, relates to the debt accumulated by LDCs (see below section 5).

3. Adapting aid to the special needs of the LDCs

The worsening economic situation of the LDCs during the 1980s and the adoption of adjustment measures and programmes have brought about special aid requirements, in particular the need for substantially enlarged programme and sector assistance and for more flexibility in aid modalities. Increasing debt servicing difficulties, moreover, have rendered the provision of highly concessional financing more imperative than ever.

(a) The need for quickly-disbursable non-project aid

Non-project aid provided as quick disbursing balance-of-payments support is considered to be particularly appropriate assistance for adjustment programmes. Although project aid remains an essential support of these programmes, it is in respect of more non-project aid that the call to donors has been directed. In the Final Act of UNCTAD VII (para.130), "donors are recommended particularly to support domestic adjustment measures of LDCs, to provide aid in more flexible forms, in particular balance-of-payments support, and at a sectoral level for rehabilitation and improved maintenance, as well as for longer-term development objectives".

It is difficult to assess the extent to which donors have provided increased programme lending, especially structural adjustment assistance[109] geared to investment purposes (as opposed to food aid[110] and other emergency because of lack of uniform reporting, standard definitions and complete data. A number of donors have, however, reported setting up bilateral facilities for programme lending or shifting the orientation of their aid programmes to meet programme needs of LDCs. For example, among DAC countries, France has several facilities for extending this type of aid, notably loans and grants for economic and financial assistance and balance-of-payments loans. The Netherlands can extend balance-of-payments support from a special budgetary category for "macro-economic emergency assistance" as well as under regular country programmes, while balance-of-payments support is a long-standing feature of the Swiss aid programme. On the part of non-DAC donors, increased provision of import financing, e.g. oil grants and credits, to LDCs has also been reported. Recent policy initiatives include the structural assistance facility created in the 1987 aid budget of the Federal Republic of Germany, aimed at providing quickly disbursable commodity aid, and the facility for non-project aid in support of structural adjustment, created by Japan in the context of its

108 For the same reason, the number of LDCs using the former Compensatory Financing Facility (CFF) have been rather limited and in some years LDCs net drawings on the facility have been negative. The new facility preserves the essential features of the CFF in providing compensation to members experiencing temporary shortfalls in export earnings owing to circumstances largely beyond their control, or to those experiencing excess costs of cereals imports. The contingency financing element covers, in addition, key current account variables, particularly interest rates and import prices. For more details see section B.2.(a).

109 OECD, *Development co-operation, 1987 report* (Paris 1988), p. 75.

110 For a discussion of food aid in the context of food strategy, see chapter I, section B1(c).

policy to recycle its $20 billion surplus. Of special significance to the LDCs with regard to the latter, is the planned provision of $500 million in non-project grants over a period of three years to sub-Saharan and other LDCs.[111] Other examples are provided by Sweden, which has established a special allocation in its aid budget since 1985 for the low-income debt distressed countries - these funds are earmarked for debt relief measures and balance-of-payments support linked to economic reform programmes and adjustment operations - and the United States, which introduced its African Economic Policy Reform Programme in 1985[112], followed by the establishment of the "Development Fund for Africa" (DFA) in 1987; the DFA provides for much more flexibility in programming of funds, including non-project assistance in support of policy reform.

Among the multilateral agencies, as already indicated, the World Bank and IMF have been the lead agencies to support adjustment programmes in LDCs. The World Bank instituted its adjustment lending programme as early as 1979, but only since 1986 did a considerable expansion of structural adjustment lending to LDCs take place: during the period 1986 to mid-1988 nine LDCs undertook structural adjustment programmes supported by the Bank, compared to only two LDCs during the period 1980-1985. Meanwhile, policy-based lending to other developing countries shifted perceptibly from structural to sectoral adjustment World Bank loans. The Bank has in the 1980s provides adjustment- related financing to twelve LDCs in the form of sector adjustment and economic recovery and other programme loans. Thus, during the period 1980-1988 (up to end June 1988) $2.2 billion was provided from IDA resources as well as from the Special Facility for sub-Saharan Africa (including co-financing) in support of LDCs' structural and similar adjustment programmes.[113] (See table 26 above). In the next few years, LDCs should benefit from increased programme assistance from IDA.[114]

IMF support for LDCs up to 1986 has been provided mainly under stand-by and extended arrangements which, because of their short-term and non-concessional nature[115], have fallen short of the requirements connected with adjustment efforts. Altogether 23 LDCs received credit facilities from the IMF during the 1980s under stand-by arrangements and four of them also concluded extended arrangements (table 26). However, the net flow of resources under these arrangements has been negative since 1985 and by mid-1988 only 4 LDCs (Guinea, Malawi, Somalia and Togo) had stand-by arrangements in force. Nevertheless, the existence of an upper tranche IMF programme is normally an essential precondition for drawing on IMF, World Bank and some other donors' programme aid facilities nowadays. This has become a matter of some concern to LDCs although, as already indicated above, in 1987 two LDCs (Uganda and Guinea-Bissau)) negotiated debt relief on the basis of an IMF SAF instead of a stand-by arrangement for the first time.

The establishment of a mechanism providing assistance on concessional terms, namely the Structural Adjustment Facility in March 1986, as well as the agreement on the Enhanced Structural Adjustment Facility in late 1987, considerably strengthened IMF ability to support adjustment and policy reforms in LDCs. By 30 June 1988, sixteen LDCs had made arrangements for the use of the SAF, for a total of SDR 615.9 million, accounting for 45 per cent of the total value of SAF arrangements concluded up to then, and of this, SDR 318.5 million had been drawn. Potential access to Fund resources under the SAF was in 1987 increased to a maximum of 63.5 per cent (from 47 per cent initially) of a member's quota over a three-year period. Maximum access to ESAF has been raised to 250 per cent of quota (with provision for up to 350 per cent of quota in exceptional cases). Malawi was one of the first two countries having an arrangement approved under ESAF (in July 1988 for an amount of SDR 55.8 million).

Other multilateral agencies have also provided non-project lending to LDCs. For example, the African Development Fund has provided $83.1 million in co-financing for the structural adjustment programmes of six LDCs and $64.5 million for sector adjustment loans to two LDCs (see table 26). The African Development Bank group is a partner in the World Bank's expanded programme of co-financing mentioned above, and is to contribute also to the regional project facility, the SDA

111 United Republic of Tanzania was among the first three countries to benefit from funds under this programme.

112 Five African LDCs were among the countries which received funds under this programme during its first two years.

113 In addition, an IBRD structural adjustment loan of $45 million was provided to Malawi in 1981.

114 Under the eighth replenishment of IDA, the share of resources allocated to LDCs is expected to further increase, as it has been decided that a minimum of 45 per cent and up to 50 per cent would be available for Sub-Saharan Africa. Between $3 billion and $3.5 billion (out of $12.4 billion) should be available for lending in support of policy reform and economic adjustment.

115 In 1987, the charge by IMF for use of these resources was in the range of 6 to 7 per cent.

(Social Diversions of Adjustment), set up to assist African governments to plan and implement programmes to protect the poor during periods of economic adjustment.[116] .

A recent initiative has been taken by the Asian Development Bank whose Board finally approved in November 1987[117], a new quick-disbursing, sectoral adjustment programme lending instrument designed to support a sector development programme in its borrowing countries, which include some LDCs.

The recent introduction of the sectoral import support programmes under the Third Lomé Convention of the EEC is another example of multilateral non-project assistance. LDCs would also benefit from the Community's special debt programme - additional to that under Lomé III and given in the form of quick-disbursing aid - of providing ECU 300 million for highly indebted low-income countries in Sub-Saharan Africa.[118]

(b) Concessionality

In recent years a number of positive developments have taken place. All major groups of bilateral donors have provided a higher share of grants in their aid commitments to the LDCs. (Overall, the share of grants increased from 58 per cent in 1981 to 65 per cent in 1986). Moreover, the grant element of concessional commitments from both DAC and OPEC sources rose. Several DAC country donors, in particular, shifted to grant or increasingly grant-like terms in their aid programmes with LDCs. In 1986, all DAC countries with the exception of France and Japan met the DAC target norm for LDCs with respect to the period 1984-1986[119] (see Annex table 26).

Nevertheless, a substantial part of assistance to the LDCs continues to be provided in the form of loans. This continues to have serious debt service implications. In absolute terms, multilateral agencies are the main providers of such loans. Donors other than DAC or OPEC members also provide a high share of loans to LDCs. Moreover, some non-concessional loans are extended to LDCs by both bilateral and multilateral donors.

The terms of loans provided by multilateral agencies (mainly financed by DAC countries) have remained unchanged on the average during the 1980s. The decision under the IDA-8 agreement to shorten the final maturities of IDA credits - from 50 years to 40 years in the case of LDCs - will, however, somewhat lower the grant element in the coming years.[120] On the other hand, an important positive development for the LDCs in multilateral assistance is, as indicated earlier, the establishment of SAF and ESAF in IMF, the former using wholly and the latter partly Trust Fund reflows. The SAF provides assistance on concessional terms, with an interest rate of 0.5 per cent, a grace period of 5 1/2 years and a repayment period of ten years; the terms of the loans under ESAF are currently the same as those of SAF loans.

4. *Aid co-ordination and the role of country review meetings*

(a) Main trends since 1981

The institution of country review meetings as a mechanism for regular and periodic review and implementation at the national level was one of the innovative features of the SNPA, and the network of such consultative arrangements for LDCs which has been set up since 1981 must be seen as a major achievement

---

116 The African Development Bank group has reported diversifying its operations through such new lending instruments as sector and rehabilitation loans and other non-project lending. The Bank expects to channel one-fourth of the funds under its 1987-1991 lending programme to non-project lending, including support for structural adjustment programmes. The Fund will likewise support projects aimed at institutional and policy reform.

117 Such initiatives by the regional development banks were in response to concerns expressed that they might be undercutting the World Bank and IMF by continuing to lend only for projects when the Bretton Woods institutions themselves were seeking changes in the policies of the governments concerned as a condition of further lending.

118 Of the 17 "definite" beneficiaries, 12 are LDCs: Burundi, Central African Republic, Gambia, Guinea, Guinea-Bissau, Malawi, Mauritania, Niger, Sao Tome and Principe, Togo, Uganda, and United Republic of Tanzania. Another 8 ACP countries are under consideration including 7 LDCs (Benin, Comoros, Equatorial Guinea, Mali, Sierra Leone, Somalia, and Sudan). (See Telex Africa, No. 323 of 15 April 1988).

119 According to the target norm for LDCs set in the 1972 DAC Terms Recommendation, the grant element to each LDC should, on the average, be at least 90 per cent in one year, or alternatively 86 per cent over a period of three years. See also OECD, *Development Co-operation, 1987 report*, Paris 1988, table 3, p. 192.

120 This decision was taken with a view to accelerating reflows to IDA and making it possible in the future to redirect resources more quickly. The grace period has remained ten years long and a service fee of 0.75 per cent continues to be charged on disbursed amounts, but the commitment fee of 0.5 per cent on the undisbursed balance of IDA credits has been reduced to zero, with effect from 1 July 1988.

Box 16

SECTORAL FOLLOW-UP MECHANISMS IN THE LDCs

Effective sector strategies and programmes have increasingly come to be seen as a key element in improved development planning and strengthened aid co-ordination, and sectoral follow-up meetings have become an established feature of the country review process. These meetings provide an opportunity to discuss sector strategies in more detail than the focus on overall economic and development policy and the limited time available during round tables or consultative and aid group meetings allow. The LDC government can present its sectoral policies and supporting projects to its development partners, and the meetings can be a means to strengthen the co-ordination of the various activities carried out in the area selected for the consultations. Such meetings - which are most often held in the LDCs themselves - also provide a link between the review meetings held in Geneva or Paris, and local co-ordination mechanisms.

The detailed programme of follow-up drawn up at the round-table conference for Togo, held in Geneva in May 1988, illustrates the impulses given further work at sectoral and local level ensuing from the review process. The Togo follow-up programme envisages future sectoral consultations on energy, on transport and telecommunications, on water supply and on urban infrastructure. Moreover, three working groups were to be set up in Lomé to look into respectively the social dimensions of adjustment; technical assistance and training; and the possibilities to set up a project preparation fund.

Sectoral consultations on a variety of themes have already been held in the LDCs within the round table framework in particular. For example, such consultations had by mid-1988 been held on agriculture and/or rural development in Benin, Chad, Comoros, Gambia, Guinea-Bissau, Niger, Sao Tomé and Togo; on drought and desertification issues in Burkina Faso and Mali; on transport in Benin, Chad, Niger and Sao Tomé; on telecommunications in Benin and Rwanda; on water and sanitation in Lesotho and Rwanda; on economic and social infrasturcture in Togo; and on health in Burkina Faso, Gambia and Guinea-Bissau. Other meetings were planned for later in 1988 and early 1989, e.g. in the Central African Republic (on rural development, education, training and employment, small and medium size enterprises and transport), Chad (human resources, industry) and Djibouti (water resources, industrial promotion). Some countries with consultative groups are also arranging similar follow-up through meetings focused on specific sectors. Examples are Guinea and Mauritania; for instance the latter country was planning such consultations for the fisheries sector and on agriculture and rural water supply. Further consultations of this type were under active preparation or consideration in a number of other LDCs.

under the Programme. Up to mid-1988, 33 LDCs had convened one or several such country review meetings with their development partners.

UNDP and the World Bank have acted as lead agencies for these consultative arrangements. Eleven of the 41 LDCs have consultative or aid group arrangements with the World Bank. Four new such groups for LDCs have been set up since 1981 when the SNPA was adopted.[121] Burma, which was included in the list of the LDCs in 1987, has an Aid Group, established in 1976, which last met in 1986.

Twenty-three of the LDCs have since 1981 arranged round-table meetings with UNDP as lead agency.

In the course of the 1980s, both UNDP and the World Bank have attempted to adapt and improve the format for the country review process. The two institutions agreed on a set of guiding principles for aid co-ordination in sub-Saharan Africa, adopted in 1986. UNDP now consults regularly with the World Bank throughout the preparatory phases of round table meetings, while having been given the responsibility for presenting an assessment of human resources and technical assistance issues at consultative and aid group meetings. Other trends have been the fostering of in-country follow-up and supportive co-ordinative processes at the local level, an increased emphasis on sector programmes, the introduction of more streamlined investment programming and

121 For Guinea, Malawi, Mauritania and Somalia. The Consultative Group for Mauritania met for the first time in 1985. Mauritania was subsequently included in the list of LDCs in 1986. The Consultative Group for the United Republic of Tanzania, which had not met for nearly a decade, was reactivated in 1986.

efforts to strengthen economic and aid management capacity in the LDCs.

With the introduction of the new round-table format by the UNDP in 1985-1986, which has meant a major change in approach for these meetings, the round table process and the consultative and aid group format have become more like each other. The early round tables were often largely based on a sector-by-sector presentation of LDCs' development plans and programmes, eliciting pledges from donors against specific projects. Consultative and aid groups were, in comparison, more focused on policy issues. Under the new format, round tables are similarly focused, with the emphasis placed on economic strategies, structural adjustment and policy reforms, priority actions and related bilateral and financial support. The new round table process involves a succession of meetings to ensure a continuous process of dialogue and co-ordination. The main event in this cycle is now a round table conference normally held in Geneva under UNDP chairmanship and with participation restricted to the main donors. Proposed follow-up mechanisms are in-country review meetings with broader participation held in the LDC itself, and/or sector and special programme consultations. Follow-up and local co-ordination are discussed at the Geneva meetings, and follow-up arrangements specified. A large number of sectoral meetings had taken place by 1988, consecutive to both early and new-format round tables, and others were under preparation (see box 16). In contrast, follow-up in-country reviews with broader participation have so far been arranged only to a limited extent under the new format.[122] .

Consultative and aid group meetings are normally held in Paris, with the World Bank in the chair and limited membership. In-country joint monitoring committees have been set up for some of these countries. LDCs with consultative and aid groups have also introduced the modality of sectoral follow-up. (see box 16).

(b) *Periodicity of the review process*

The SNPA has thus given the impetus to a greatly expanded framework for co-ordination at various levels in the LDCs. However, while most of the LDCs have convened the type of country review meeting foreseen in the SNPA, this has not yet in all cases led to an on-going process of a "regular and periodic" character envisaged in the SNPA and emphasized also in the new round-table format. From this point of view, country coverage under the SNPA review process is not yet complete.

The consultative and aid groups sponsored by the World Bank are normally convened every one to two years. On the whole these groups have met fairly regularly to review the economic situation and resource needs of the LDCs concerned, although there have been notable breaks in activity in a few cases. Round-table reviews with UNDP as lead agency have likewise during the 1980s been established as a periodic activity. However, except for Asian LDCs which have been holding their meetings every two years, most of the African LDCs have so far held only one meeting. The new format is still in the course of being introduced in the African region. By early 1988, about half of the African LDCs concerned had requested assistance for the preparation of new-format round tables, although in a number of countries co-ordination activity has been upheld through sectoral meetings, as discussed above.

(c) *The mobilization of resources through the country review process*

Many factors other than a country's LDC status are likely to intervene in donors' decisions on aid allocations (such as historical links, political and commercial interests, humanitarian considerations, etc.). Results of the review process, especially as regards raising aid levels, are likely to be longer-run rather than direct and immediate. Available evidence (see table 27) would tend to confirm the view that round tables and consultative and aid groups are likely to have helped sustain the flow of concessional assistance to the LDCs, and may have been instrumental in securing increases in such assistance. The consultative process as such is not of course the single explanatory factor: some of the increases in resource flows to individual LDCs in 1984-86 reflect injections of multilateral or multilaterally-led support to countries which have embarked on structural adjustment and other reform progrmmes in which the consultative process is only one element (the increased role of the multilateral financial institutions in the transfer of resources to the LDCs was noted earlier in this chapter, see section above).

122 Of the five African LDCs which by mid-1988 had convened round-table meetings with their main donors under the new format, only Cape Verde arranged a follow-up meeting, held in Praia, for a greater number of donors and potential partners.

Table 27

TOTAL CONCESSIONAL FLOWS TO THE LDCs FROM ALL SOURCES 1981-83 AND 1984-86

	Dates of country review meetings [a]	*Total concessional flows $ million*	
		Average 1981-1983	*Average 1984-1986*
LDCs with consultative and aid group arrangements			
Bangladesh	Annually	1212.2	1305.5
Burma	1982, 1986	332.5	359.9
Guinea	1987	82.9	145.9
Haiti [b]	1981, 1982, 1984, 1985, 1987, 1988	122.7	154.3
Malawi [c]	1986, 1988	125.1	158.1
Mauritania	1985 1988/1989	177.2	208.5
Nepal	1981, 1983, 1986, 1987, 1988	195.5	245.4
Somalia	1983, 1985, 1987	391.5	433.0
Sudan	1983 (two meetings)	805.8	859.5
Uganda	1982, 1984, 1987, 1988	135.5	182.6
United Republic of Tanzania	1986, 1987, 1988	658.8	585.0
Subtotal		4239.7	4637.7
LDCs with round table arrangements			
Afghanistan	1983	276.4	253.3
Benin	1983	90.9	106.8
Bhutan	1983, 1986, 1988	11.3	27.4
Burundi	1984 (1989)	134.7	155.0
Cape Verde	1982, 1986	58.0	83.6
Central African Republic	1987	95.8	122.5
Chad	1982, 1985	72.5	154.2
Comoros	1984	41.2	45.3
Djibouti	1983	63.0	101.3
Equatorial Guinea	1982, 1988	12.9	22.9
Gambia	1984	53.1	67.7
Guinea-Bissau	1984, 1988	65.3	66.0
Lao People's Dem. Rep.	1983, 1986 (1989)	116.6	121.6
Lesotho	1984, 1988	101.8	94.7
Maldives	1983, 1986 (1989)	9.7	11.4
Mali	1982, 1985	224.8	368.3
Niger	1987	209.0	266.2
Rwanda	1982	152.9	186.4
Samoa	1983, 1986, 1988	25.5	21.7
Sao Tome and Principe	1985 (1989)	9.5	14.1
Togo	1985, 1988	83.4	133.1
Yemen	1982	388.3	317.4
Subtotal		2296.7	2740.9
No country review meetings in 1981-1987			
Botswana		100.5	102.6
Burkina Faso		204.4	223.4
Democratic Yemen		183.1	239.2
Ethiopia		360.7	692.9
Kiribati		15.7	12.5
Sierra Leone		73.8	75.4
Tuvalu		5.3	4.4
Vanuatu	1988	27.8	23.6
Subtotal		971.2	1373.9
All LDCs		**7507.9**	**8752.7**

Source: UNCTAD secretariat, based on information from UNDP, the World Bank, and the OECD/DAC secretariat.

a Meetings scheduled or tentatively scheduled for late half of 1988 or early 1989 are indicated within brackets.

b Member of the Caribbean Group for Co-operation in Economic Development.

c Malawi also arranged a UNDP-sponsored round-table meeting in 1984.

Of the LDCs with consultative or aid group arrangements, all but one received more assistance in current dollar terms in 1984-1986 as compared with the preceding three-year period, irrespective of the level of activity of the groups. In the case of the one exception, serious differences with donors on economic policy persisted throughout the first half of the 1980s, and the consultative group for this country was reactivated only in 1986. Most, although by no means all, of the LDCs which have engaged in the round table process also received more concessional aid in 1984-1986 than in 1981-1983. Whether this can be seen as a consequence of donor response to these meetings is not clear in all cases. Two of the LDCs in this group which registered notable aid increases in 1984-1986, convened their first round tables only in 1987.

As regards meetings held under the new round-table format, according to the lead agency's assessment, for the first three LDCs in the African region which used this format (Cape Verde, the Central African Republic and Niger), the Governments' estimates of financial requirements for the next few years should be more than adequately covered by the financing announced by the donors at the meetings.[123] Similar results have been reported from the round-table meetings held for Togo in May 1988 and for Guinea-Bissau in July 1988.

Of the eight LDCs which did not participate in the consultative group or round table process up to 1988, five registered a stagnation in aid receipts over the period 1981 to 1986. However, three of them received on average more concessional aid in 1984-1986 than in the preceding three-year period. Of these three, Ethiopia, which received massive emergency relief throughout the period, forms a special case.

With the strong emphasis on policy content in both the new-format round tables and consultative and aid groups, it is likely that the mobilization of resources through the country review process will become increasingly focused on the LDCs which have initiated reform programmes agreed with donors. The results of the round table meetings held under the new format appear to support such resource mobilization, although, as is the case with consultative and aid group meetings, the element of additionality in the funding secured is difficult to assess.

(d) Scope for further action

Areas where the country review process set in motion under the SNPA may need further strengthening, include the following:

Coverage and periodicity. Not all LDCs are currently fully engaged in the review process. A number of them have not yet or not recently had any review meeting at the central level. Attention needs to be given to the means to keep enough flexibility in the review process to ensure that the coverage of the LDCs remains as comprehensive as possible.

Resource mobilization and management. Improved investment programming and project preparation facilities, a clear setting out of the aid implications of LDCs' stabilization and structural adjustment programmes, measures to speed up disbursements, adequate provision of fast-disbursing support for policy reform, and the simplification and harmonization of aid terms and procedures are all elements which could contribute to increasing the flow of assistance to the LDCs and at which review meetings should aim. Longer-term aid commitments from the donors' side are also needed to match LDCs' commitment to structural adjustment and policy reform.

The strengthening of economic management in the LDCs is one area where further building up of LDC's aid management capacity remains one of the major tasks for a concerted programme for the LDCs for the next decade.

Monitoring systems. Weaknesses in monitoring systems at individual country level still exist in particular for countries which are less actively engaged in the country review process, e.g. which have not had any recent round table meetings. Monitoring should not be limited to the policy actions taken to implement adjustment programmes, but should extend to the monitoring of the country's evolving financial requirements and how they are met.

Systems have recently been put in place to monitor the implementation of policy reform in developing countries including LDCs, notably in the context of SAF and ESAF use and follow-up to the UNPAAERD. Steps have also been taken towards building up procedures for monitoring aid pledges and aid flows.[124] However, these various arrangements while covering a large number of LDCs, do not yet embrace them all. Moreover, operational conclusions at the country level need to be drawn from the information gathered through statistical and other reporting systems. Here, a strengthened country review process has an

[123] See DP/1988/24, para. 42.

[124] Following the April 1986 round table conferences for four Asian LDCs, a meeting was organized to assess the outcome of the round tables and to organize follow-up activities as well as the monitoring of donor intentions. A systematic procedure has been put in place to monitor aid flows and donor intentions in each of these four countries. Similar efforts are being made in African LDCs (see DP/1987/18, para. 13). The regional project to monitor economic data in the context of follow-up to UN-PAAERD covers aid flows as well. These monitoring arrangements are supplemented by in-country joint monitoring committees set up for some consultative groups.

important role to play. An area which also requires attention is the systematic monitoring of the impact of economic developments on living standards and social welfare in the LDCs. Of special interest in this respect would be the development and strengthening of early warning or forecasting systems, internationally and at the national level[125], which could alert the international community of emerging threats to the exposed population of the LDCs.

Broadening the scope of policy discussions. In addition to mobilizing the necessary financial and technical assistance support for LDCs' programmes, it would be desirable to include in the review meetings also an action-oriented discussion of issues hitherto dealt with mainly in other fora, such as debt and trade. LDCs' development partners are often also creditors of the LDCs as well as their trade partners. As the focus of country reviews has shifted from project financing to broader policy discussions, an analysis of external factors and their incidence on LDCs' reform efforts need to be put on the agenda of review meetings to give a full and fair assessment of the country's performance and prospects. Debt issues cannot be avoided in a discussion of financial prospects of the many debt-distressed LDCs and have already been raised in review meetings. However, scope remains for a more action-oriented discussion of debt, including the harmonization of aid and debt relief options and requirements. Moreover, although the SNPA recommended that a consideration of ways and means of assisting the LDCs to expand their trade in existing and new markets be included in the agenda of review meetings, specific trade issues have so far been dealt with only to a very limited extent.[126] .

Participation in the country review process. Under the new UNDP format, participation in the main round table conferences is restricted to main donor countries and funding organizations. While this also allows for the possibility of subsequent in-country review meetings for all interested aid partners, so far this type of follow-up seems not to have become the rule under the new format. Valuable information on individual LDCs' policies, priorities and support requirements is likely to be most useful for donors outside the restricted group participating in the main review meeting, and should be shared with them, perhaps through in-country review meetings with broader participation. Such broader-based meetings could also become an instrument for promoting economic co-operation among developing countries in favour of the LDCs.

5. *The question of debt*

(a) LDCs' debt overhang

With a total accumulated external debt representing over 60 per cent of their GDP and debt service payments absorbing over 30 per cent of their exports of goods and services (1986 estimates), the debt burden has become a major strain on the LDCs' economies. The roots of LDCs' debt problems can be traced back to the 1970s, when much of the LDCs albeit modest borrowing occurred (without resulting in a commensurate increase in productive capacity). During the 1980s, debt servicing difficulties were triggered by an unfavourable external environment. Declines in export earnings and high interest rates caused LDCs' debt situation to worsen considerably.[127]

Between the end of 1982 and the end of 1986, LDCs' total identified external debt (including short-term debt and use of IMF credit), rose by more than 50 per cent and debt service payments by over 75 per cent, to reach a level of $53.5 billion and $3.6 billion respectively (see Statistical Annex). A major and growing element of LDCs' debt is ODA debt (about two thirds of the total as at the end of 1986), over 40 per cent of which is owed to multilateral agencies. As a result, and also because renegotiations under the Paris and London Clubs had the effect of delaying non-concessional debt service payments (see section (c)), ODA debt service payments have been growing relatively faster as compared to other types. ODA debt service payments to multilateral agencies, which in principle can neither be cancelled nor rescheduled because of the revolving nature of resources of these agencies, grew the fastest, more than tripling during that period.

125 This issue and possibilities to improve inter-agency collaboration in this area was being taken up within the UN in 1988 by the Committee for Programme and Co-ordination and the Administrative Committee on Co-ordination.

126 The GATT Sub-Committee on Trade of Least-Developed Countries has a programme of *ad hoc* Consultations under which individual LDCs can consult their developed trading partners. However, not all LDCs are members of GATT. Such consultations have so far in the decade been arranged for only a few member LDCs.

127 See also UNCTAD, Least Developed Countries: *1987 Report*, pp. 63-64.

Chart VI

DEBT SERVICE AS A PERCENTAGE OF EXPORTS OF GOODS AND SERVICES[a]

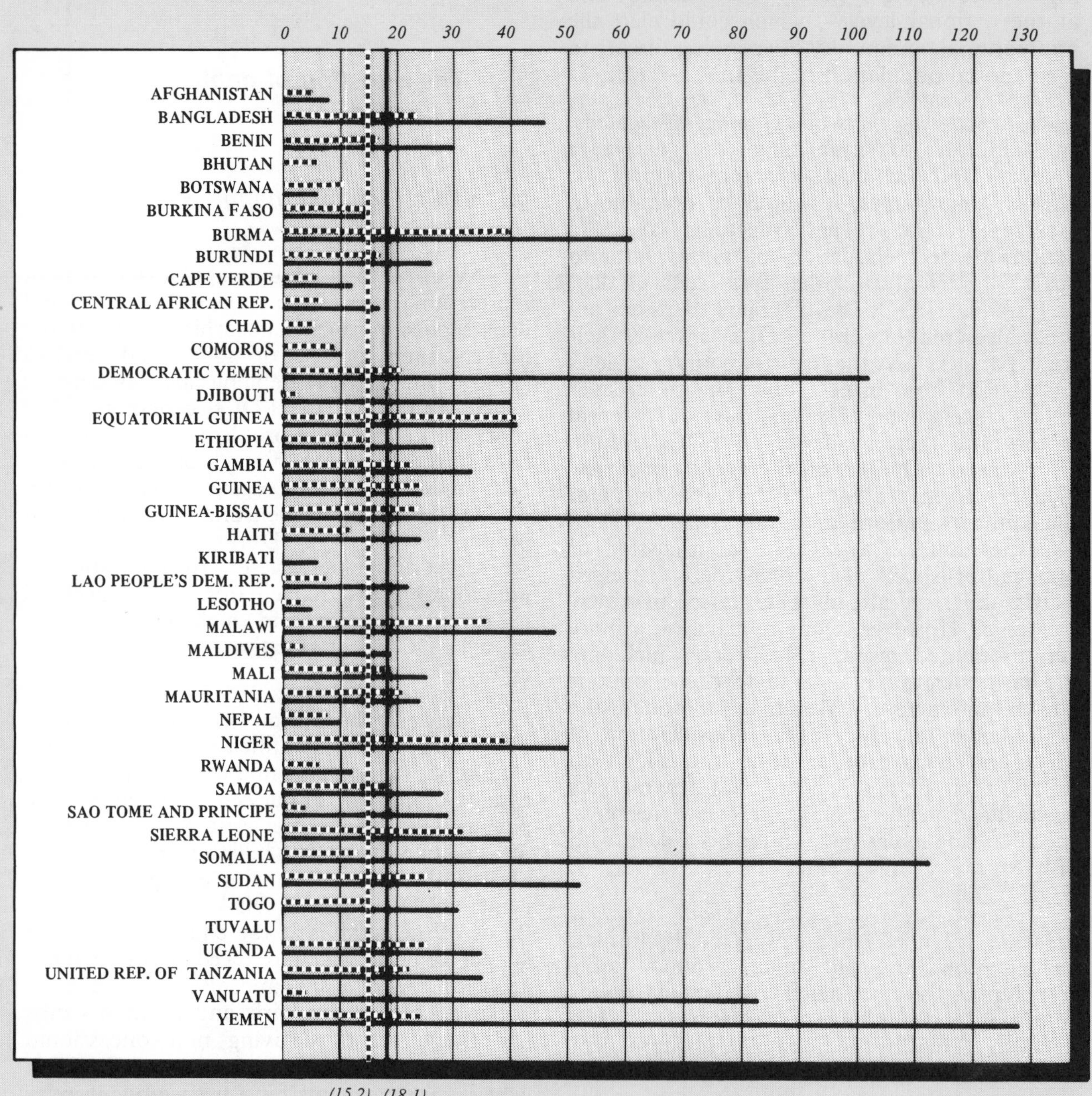

Source: Annex table 49C; UNCTAD Handbook of International Trade and Development Statistics, 1987 supplement, table 5.14.

[a] All services (factor non-factor)

Table 28

ACTION TAKEN UNDER SECTION A OF BOARD RESOLUTION 165 (S-IX) IN FAVOUR OF LDCs
A. Summary of debt cancellations

(millions of US dollars)

	Australia	*Canada*	*Denmark*	*Finland*	*France*	*Germany Fed.Rep.*	*Italy*	*Japan*	*Luxem-bourg*	*Nether-lands*	*New Zealand*	*Norway*	*Sweden*	*Switzer-land*	*U.K.*	*TOTAL*
Afghanistan		1.2						X							2.1	3.3
Bangladesh		16.8	40.2	6.7	14.4	472.5		X		43.1			10.0	7.7	33.3	644.7
Benin		14.1	23.6		4.0	20.4	0.8									62.9
Bhutan																-
Botswana		34.0	7.0			33.7							6.1		42.9	123.7
Burkina Faso		0.9	11.6		17.8	92.7				7.5						130.5
Burma								X								X
Burundi					0.3	30.1										30.4
Cape Verde																-
Central African Rep.					1.6	13.3										14.9
Chad			1.7		15.2	6.1										23.0
Comoros					5.0											5.0
Democratic Yemen			3.9													3.9
Djibouti					11.1	3.4										14.5
Equatorial Guinea																-
Ethiopia				1.8			9.8	X					10.9			22.5
Gambia						10.9									11.0	21.9
Guinea					2.8	23.6	6.4			1.0						33.8
Guinea-Bissau										9.8						9.8
Haiti						8.4										8.4
Kiribati	X															X
Lao P.D.R.		2.4						X								2.4
Lesotho			2.2			12.0									0.6	14.8
Malawi		36.8	38.9			49.1		X		7.2					64.3	196.3
Maldives																-
Mali		1.9			13.2	93.8	1.5									110.4
Mauritania			0.6													0.6
Nepal		2.4	2.8			43.1		X						5.8	4.6	58.7
Niger		37.7	7.9		·6.2	98.0										149.8
Rwanda						56.2		X	0.3		X					56.5
Samoa	X														0.4	0.4
Sao Tomé et Principe																-
Sierra Leone						47.5				5.5					18.2	71.2
Somalia						56.8	28.7									85.5
Sudan			7.6			237.0	7.4	X		16.9			10.2		20.4	299.5
Togo			9.3		3.7	101.0										114.0
Tuvalu	X															X
Uganda		2.2	7.2			27.7		X		3.6					25.2	65.7
U.R. of Tanzania		37.7	118.0	26.5		190.1	12.2	X		53.3		9.9	50.7		5.3	503.7
Vanuatu																-
Yemen						107.0		X		17.2						124.2
Total LDCs	..	**188.1**	**282.5**	**35.0**	**95.3**	**1834.4**	**66.8** [a]	**56.3** [a]	**0.3**	**165.1**	..	**9.9**	**87.9**	**13.5**	**228.3**	**3063.4**

For source and general notes, see Part B. of the table.

a Including interest payments.

Among LDCs, the major debtors are Bangladesh and Sudan, each with external debt in excess of $8 billion. Another 15 LDCs have accumulated debts exceeding $1 billion (see Statistical Annex).

(b) *The impact of retroactive terms adjustment measures*

Action in favour of LDCs to alleviate the burden arising from ODA debt has been taken mainly within the framework of UNCTAD Board resolution 165 (S-IX). Since its adoption in 1978, at least 36 LDCs have benefitted from retroactive terms adjustment (RTA) provided by 15 DAC countries, amounting to an overall nominal value estimated at $4.8 billion. Of this, $ 3 billion represent outright debt cancellation, $450 million were in the form of a waiver of interest payments and $1.3 billion correspond to the conversion (by the United States)[128] of payment of debt in local currency (see table 28). Similar efforts made by some socialist countries of Eastern Europe have benefited major LDC recipients. President Gorbachev stated that the USSR is prepared to institute a moratorium up to 100 years on the servicing of LDCs' bilateral debt to his own country and, in a number of cases, to write off such debt.[129] .

Notwithstanding action taken under Board resolution 165 (S-IX), LDCs' ODA debt grew and debt service continued to grow during the 1980s, and such growth took place at relatively high rates. There are several reasons for this: firstly, RTA measures taken from 1982 onwards were of a much narrower scope as compared to those taken in the first three years following the adoption of Board resolution 165 (S-IX) (when the bulk of debt relief action took place); secondly, Board resolution 165 (S-IX) is addressed to donor developed country governments only and does not cover other donors nor multilateral agencies to which LDCs owe a large share of their debts; thirdly, some major donors have taken measures of little impact and have continued to provide a relatively high share of loans to LDCs (see section 3 (b) above).

The scope for further relief under Board resolution 165 (S-IX) now covers over one fourth of the total debt of the LDCs but concerns mainly a few creditor countries only. As at the end of 1986, the United States, Japan and France accounted for over 85 per cent of LDCs' outstanding ODA debt to DAC countries. In the case of the socialist countries of Eastern Europe over 85 per cent of the LDCs' concessional debt is owed to the USSR. LDCs' total bilateral ODA debt-service payments currently due to the developed countries are estimated at $787 million per year for the remainder of the decade, of which $420 million is in respect of debt to DAC countries and $356 million in respect of debt to socialist countries of Eastern Europe. Bilateral ODA debt-service payments to developing countries which are not covered by Board resolution 165 (S-IX) would amount to an annual $566 million (see Statistical Annex).

Concrete measures continue to be taken. As regards debts owed to France and Japan, LDCs are expected to receive further relief following the adoption of new initiatives by these countries.[130] At the annual Economic Summit meeting of the seven major industrialized nations, held in Toronto in June 1988, France proposed a debt relief plan covering three options of which the first - which France is prepared to implement in respect of debt owed to it by low-income debt-distressed countries - involves the cancellation of one third of public and publicly guaranteed debts and the consolidation of the balance over a period of about ten years.[131] Japan's new medium-term target, encompassing the years 1988 to 1992, provides for an increasing share of grants in ODA to LDCs and debt relief of $ 1 billion in the form of cancellation of capital and interest payments on $5.5 billion loans to 17 LDCs extended between April 1978 and March 1988.[132] Japan has already been providing to LDCs cash grants to offset the debt service on ODA loans on which an exchange of notes was concluded before 31 March 1978.

Thus, the call for further action to support the adjustment efforts of the poorest countries, including the conversion of loans into grants and measures of a similar effect was

128 The United States has allowed, on a case-by-case basis, repayment in local currency of the dollar debt obligation arising from purchases of agricultural commodities.

129 President Gorbachev's address at the forty-third session of the General Assembly, 7 December 1988.

130 In its reply to the UNCTAD questionnaire on the implementation of the SNPA, the Federal Republic of Germany stated that further debt relief had been decided by the Federal Cabinet in June 1988.

131 The two other options proposed in a letter dated 7 June 1987, addressed by President Mitterrand to the six other Heads of State or Government of the major industrial countries are: longer debt maturity (with debt consolidation at market rates, but with a maximum duration of 25 years); and consolidation at lower interest rates (these should be reduced at least by half over a repayment period of some 15 years).

132 See *Herald Tribune* of 20 June 1988, and *Le Monde* Nr. 13488 of 10 June 1988.

Table 28 (concluded)

ACTION TAKEN UNDER SECTION A OF BOARD RESOLUTION 165 (S-IX) IN FAVOUR OF LDCs

B. Nominal value of other measures taken with respect to ODA debt

(millions of US dollars)

	Belgium		Canada	France	Germany Fed.Rep.of	Netherlands	Sweden	U.K.	USA	Total
	A	B	A	A	A	A	A	A	C	
Afghanistan			X							X
Bangladesh	1.9	0.05	X	4.6	X	13.7	2.0		575.8	598.1
Benin			X	2.0	X					2.0
Bhutan										-
Botswana			X		X		1.2	1.1		2.3
Burkina Faso			X	8.3	X	2.2				10.5
Burma										-
Burundi				0.2	X					0.2
Cape Verde										-
Central African Rep.				1.9	2.7					4.6
Chad				8.4	0.9					9.3
Comoros				3.0						3.0
Democratic Yemen										-
Djibouti				3.1	0.3					3.4
Equatorial Guinea										-
Ethiopia							2.0			2.0
Gambia					X					X
Guinea				0.8	X	0.2			47.0	48.0
Guinea-Bissau						0.7				0.7
Haiti					1.6				93.0	94.6
Kiribati										
Lao P.D.R.			X							X
Lesotho					X			0.2		0.2
Malawi			X		X	1.4		1.5	2.4	5.3
Maldives									2.7	2.7
Mali			X	5.6	X					5.6
Mauritania						-				
Nepal			X		X					X
Niger			X	3.2	X					3.2
Rwanda					X					X
Samoa						-				-
Sao Tome and Principe										-
Sierra Leone					9.2			4.0	30.1	43.3
Somalia					X				115.8	115.8
Sudan					X	5.9	1.8	0.8	351.2	359.7
Togo				0.9	21.1					22.0
Tuvalu										-
Uganda			X		5.0	0.6		3.7		9.3
U.Rep. of Tanzania	0.2		X		X	12.3	9.5	1.9	25.0	49.9
Vanuatu										-
Yemen					X	0.6			40.0	40.6
Total LDCs	**2.1**	**0.05**	**30.0**	**42.0**	**311.1**	**37.6**	**16.5**	**13.2**	**1283.0**	**1735.6**

Source: Information supplied by creditor countries to the UNCTAD secretariat as of 15 October 1988. Ireland and Norway have been providing their ODA to LDCs in the form of grants and are therefore not shown in this table.

Note: X indicates action taken by the creditor country in favour of the individual debtor country but amounts are not allocable by debtor country. The totals for LDCs include some unallocated amounts.

A = Waiving of interest payments.
B = Refinancing of debt interest.
C = Agreement to allow payment of debt in local currency.

reiterated at the Berlin (West) Meeting of the Development Committee of the World Bank in September 1988.[133]

(c) Developments in multilateral renegotiations with official creditors and new approaches to alleviate the burden of official debt

Over the past decade, 14 LDCs renegotiated their concessional as well as non-concessional debts owed to governments and their officially guaranteed export credits under the framework of the Paris Club. Between 1977 and 1987, the amount of the outstanding obligations of LDCs, rescheduled at the Paris Club, has totalled $4.1 billion. With the exception of Equatorial Guinea, the Gambia, Guinea, Guinea-Bissau and the United Republic of Tanzania, the remaining LDCs rescheduled their debts more than once: Togo rescheduled its debts at the Paris Club five times; Niger, Sierra Leone and Sudan four times; the Central African Republic, Mauritania and Uganda three times; Malawi[134] , and Somalia twice (see table 29).

The fact that reschedulings had to be repeated for most LDCs leaves the adequacy of the original rescheduling practice open to question. Experience has shown that reschedulings are at best only a temporary measure and have had relatively little effect in ameliorating LDCs' debt situation: frequent reschedulings have led to an increase in the stock of outstanding debt and higher debt servicing requirements. Moreover, even the temporary relief provided by the Paris Club reschedulings has proved to be of limited scope to LDCs, in so far as these negotiations do not include multilateral creditors to which LDCs owe a considerable part of their obligations, nor do they include the OPEC members and socialist countries of Eastern Europe, which are important bilateral creditors for a number of LDCs.

However, moves have been made recently towards providing, on a case-by-case basis, the poorest debtor countries with improved terms. Following the Economic Summit of the seven major industrialized nations held in Venice in June 1987, the Paris Club introduced significantly longer terms of repayment, from the previous limit of 10 years with five years grace, to 20 years as well as an extension of the grace period. Five LDCs had their debts rescheduled under the improved terms: in June 1987 the debts of Mauritania and Uganda were rescheduled at the Paris Club over 15 years with a 6-year grace period; in July 1987 Somalia obtained a 20-year rescheduling with a 10-year grace period; in April and May 1988 Niger and Malawi respectively obtained a 20-year rescheduling, including a grace period of 10-11 years. An equally important development is that reschedulings are now given for a higher proportion of debt service, as well as of previously rescheduled debts. The Paris Club has also relaxed the basis of conditionality to cover, on a case-by-case basis, those countries which have a structural adjustment facility in place with the IMF, rather than a conventional stand-by.[135]

At the Toronto Economic Summit, renewed efforts to ease the debt burden of the poorest countries led to a consensus by the Group of 7, which was later agreed upon by all Paris Club creditors, "on rescheduling official debt of those countries within a framework of comparability that allows official creditors to choose among concessional rates usually on shorter maturities, longer repayment periods at commercial rates, partial write-offs of debt service obligations during the consolidation period, or a combination of these three options[136]". Mali was the first country to benefit from the menu approach agreed at the Toronto summit, when it rescheduled its debt at the Paris Club in October 1988.[137]

Debt consolidation at concessional rates and partial write-offs of official debt service

133 "Developed donor countries in a position to do so were urged to convert ODA loans into grants for the poorest countries undertaking appropriate growth-oriented programs, or to adopt measures with a similar effect, such as increasing grants and the concessionality of ODA" (Press Communiqué of the World Bank Development Committee of 26 September 1988, para. 8).

134 In April 1988 Malawi rescheduled its debts at the Paris Club for the third time.

135 For a more detailed discussion of the evolution of Paris Club rescheduling terms and an evaluation of current practices, see also TD/B/1167.

136 Economic Declaration of the Toronto Economic Summit, para. 30.

137 Depending on the creditor country, the following options or combination of options were applied : (a) write-off one-third of debt service obligations to be consolidated, with a repayment period of 14 years (including an 8 year grace period) for the two-thirds remaining due; (b) consolidate at market rates, with a repayment period of 25 years (including a 14 year grace period); (c) consolidate at a preferential interest rate, which would be the market rate reduced by 3.5 percentage points or 50 per cent if 50 per cent is less than 3.5 points, with a repayment period of 14 years (including an 8-year grace period). As regards official development aid loans, it was agreed that the amounts to be rescheduled or refinanced should be reimbursed on a period of repayment of 25 years of which 14 year grace period and that the rates and the conditions of interest should be at least as favourable as the concessional rates applying to those loans.

Table 29

LDCs' MULTILATERAL DEBT RELIEF AGREEMENTS WITH OFFICIAL CREDITORS

(amounts rescheduled in millions of dollars)

Country	*1977-1979*	*1980*	*1981*	*1982*	*1983*	*1984*	*1985*	*1986*	*1987*	*1988* [a]
Central African Rep.			72	13		14				
Equatorial Guinea							38			
Gambia								17		
Guinea								196		
Guinea-Bissau									25	
Malawi				25	26					30
Mauritania							74	27	90	
Niger					36	26	38	34		30
Sierra Leone	39	37				25		86		
Somalia							127		153	
Sudan	487			203	518	249				
Togo	260		232		300	75	27			124
Uganda			30	19					170	
United Republic of Tanzania								1046		
All LDCs	**786**	**37**	**334**	**247**	**893**	**375**	**318**	**1406**	**438**	**184**

Source: IMF, *Multilateral official debt rescheduling : Recent experience*, by P.M. Keller with N.E. Weerasinghe, Washington, D.C., May 1988, and UNCTAD document TD/B/1167/Add. 1.

a January-August.

payments should undoubtedly provide substantial relief to the LDCs - especially when coupled with ODA debt cancellation in full - as the amount of service payments in respect of their official debts accounts for a large share of their total debt service.[138] On the other hand, the implementation of the third option under the approach agreed upon at the Toronto Economic Summit, namely longer repayment periods at commercial rates, will only provide very temporary relief to the LDCs and eventually increase their debt burden as reschedulings under current practices do. Moreover, not all LDCs may qualify for the debt relief plan agreed in Toronto as the eligibility of beneficiaries is subject to the undertaking of an internationally approved adjustment programme.

Of particular benefit to LDCs are bilateral initiatives for official debt relief such as that of Sweden. Between April 1986 and April 1988, Sweden has granted partial forgiveness on officially guaranteed export credits, amounting to a total of $43.5 million, to Guinea Bissau, the United Republic of Tanzania and Sudan. The recent French initiative (see section (b) above), which concerns not only concessional but all official and officially guaranteed bilateral debts owed to France, likewise constitutes a new departure.

(d) Coping with multilateral debt

The rising burden of LDCs' multilateral debt has been well recognized. The Final Act of UNCTAD VII, for instance, specifically refers (in its para. 134) to problems of LDCs' debt to the multilateral financial institutions. An increasing number of LDCs, unable to service their debts, have thus accumulated arrears with multilateral institutions, especially those providing non-concessional loans. As of May 1988, three LDCs (Sierra Leone, Somalia, and Sudan) were declared ineligible to use the general resources of IMF, owing to their overdue obligations to the Fund.[139]

The World Bank has recently set up a reserve fund (to be financed out of repayments on IDA credits) to help pay the interest on past (non-concessional) IBRD loans on the part of countries which are now eligible only for concessional IDA assistance. A condition is that

[138] At the end of 1986, service payments to OECD countries - mainly to the seven major industrial nations - in respect of official and officially supported loans accounted for $1.1 billion, i.e. almost one third of LDCs' total debt service payments, $ 855 million of which were due in respect of non-concessional loans (see table 9).

[139] In its Communiqué to the World Bank Development Committee (dated 24 September 1988), the Intergovernmental Group of Twenty Four stressed the need for a "cooperative, positive, and flexible approach" to the problem of overdue financial obligations to IMF (see paras. 15 to 18 of the Communiqué).

they should have recognized adjustment programmes. This fund will provide supplementary credits to these countries, which would equal to about 60 per cent of the interest they owe to the IBRD. In fiscal year 1989, about $100 million will be distributed for this purpose. Eligible countries include currently five LDCs (Bangladesh, Malawi, United Republic of Tanzania, Uganda and Togo).[140] This is a major departure in multilateral agency debt relief, since it allows the World Bank to refinance its loans, and effectively to reschedule IBRD loans which no longer seem appropriate to the countries concerned.

Although the IBRD is LDCs' main multilateral creditor of non-concessional finance - about one third of LDCs' non-concessional multilateral debt and debt service relates to IBRD[141] - scope for further action in respect of multilateral debt is called for. There are in addition to IMF and IBRD other important multilateral creditors providing non-concessional finance to LDCs, such as the African Development Bank (with an LDCs' debt estimated at $437 million at end 1986) and the Arab Monetary Fund (with an LDCs' debt amounting to $274 million at end 1986) (see Statistical Annex). Moreover, a number of multilateral institutions have been providing concessional loans to LDCs at terms much less favourable than IDA terms. A first step to alleviate LDCs' debt burden in this respect would be the creation of interest-subsidy schemes or refinancing schemes allowing the terms provided by multilateral institutions to be converted to terms which are as highly concessional as those of IDA.

(e) LDC commercial debt

Renegotiation of private debts to commercial banks (including export credits not covered by export credit insurance) are held within the steering group of banks known as the "London Club". As the debt is rescheduled at commercial interest rates, debt servicing requirements still remain highly unsustainable for the LDCs. Only a few LDCs (less than one fourth of them), however, have a share of private debt exceeding 20 per cent of their total debt. Up to end 1987, five of them, namely, Malawi, Niger, Sierra Leone, Sudan (5 times) and Togo (twice) had their debts renegotiated at the London Club (see Statistical Annex). The last restructuring took place in 1985 for Sudan. No LDC has been allowed to enter into a multi-year agreement.[142]

The search for long-term alleviation of the debt burden of developing countries has led to a large number of proposals, including a wide range of options open to commercial banks involved in rescheduling negotiations: some have indeed emanated from the commercial bankers themselves. Of particular interest to LDCs are the schemes aiming at a *reduction* of debt; indeed LDCs' debt problems are of a deep-seated nature and not mere liquidity problems: they cannot be eased or resolved by an increase in lending alone.

The "menu" approach proposed by United States Treasury Secretary James Baker at the 1987 annual meetings of the IMF and the World Bank includes, *inter alia*, the following instruments which could reduce the debt burden: (i) notes or bonds convertible into local equity which can facilitate debt-equity swaps; (ii) conversions of external claims into domestic currency denominated bonds and equity, or in some cases, into currency itself; and (iii) interest capitalization which reduces interest service directly. The scope of debt-equity swaps and other debt conversions has, however, been limited so far.[143]

The African Development Bank and the merchant bank S.G. Warburg have recently proposed a plan involving the securitization of debts to commercial banks together with official bilateral debts, in which medium-term claims would be converted into 20-year bonds carrying a below-market interest rate. Other proposals recently advanced range from schemes linking debt service to a fixed proportion of the debtor's export earnings to schemes

140 See *World Bank News* Of 13 October 1988, p. 3. An earlier proposal by the Nordic countries (introduced by Denmark, Finland, Iceland, the Netherlands and Sweden in late 1987) sought, through the establishment of a trust fund, to relieve the countries now eligible only for concessional IDA assistance, whose non-concessional IBRD loans represent a major burden. Nineteen countries had been identified as such, of which ten are LDCs (namely Bangladesh, Ethiopia, Guinea, Malawi, Mauritania, Sierra Leone, Sudan, Togo, Uganda and the United Republic of Tanzania).

141 Aside from IMF repurchase obligations which are the equivalent of short and medium term multilateral debt.

142 In 1984 multi-year rescheduling agreements (MYRAs) were introduced in commercial bank debt negotiations. These agreements were designed to help countries which have adopted strong policies to deal with their balance-of-payments difficulties. Debt is restructured over a minimum period of three years to remove the bunching of amortization payments and facilitate the debtor country return to capital market access over a multi-year period. The experience with MYRAs has not, however, been satisfactory because adverse external developments (falling commodity prices and natural disasters) have often impeded debtor countries from complying with the terms of the agreement.

143 See UNCTAD, Trade and Development Report, *1988*, chapter IV.

Table 30

LDCs' AGREEMENTS WITH COMMERCIAL BANKS: AMOUNTS RESCHEDULED ($m) [a]

Countries	*1980*	*1981*	*1982*	*1983*	*1984*	*1985*
Malawi	-	-	-	57	-	-
Niger	-	-	-	-	27	-
Sierra Leone	-	-	-	-	25	-
Sudan	-	498	55	790	838	920
Togo	69	-	-	84	-	-
Total	**69**	**498**	**55**	**931**	**885**	**920**

Source: World Bank, *World Debt Tables*, 1987-1988 edition.

a No renegotiation of LDCs' commercial debt took place in 1986 and 1987, nor prior to 1980.

including the creation of new international agencies. Many of these schemes require official support.[144] The example of Bolivia, which has benefited from contributions made by donors to buy back half of its commercial bank debt, could be easily applied to the case of LDCs.

For most LDCs, commercial debt is usually small: three quarters of the LDCs had a commercial debt estimated to be below $200 million at the end of 1986, with annual debt-service payments not exceeding $20 million. The financial commitments required to give guarantees where needed and to make funds available for such operations as buy-backs and securitization, are at levels which should, therefore, be politically acceptable.

6. *Challenges for the 1990s*

The review undertaken above shows that the volume of external finance was not sufficient to raise investment and stimulate growth in the LDCs during the 1980s. In particular the expected substantial increase in ODA flows to LDCs has not yet taken place. A new problem for the LDCs was the emergence of serious debt-servicing difficulties. The debt burden constitutes nowadays a major hindrance to their economic development.

The initiatives recently launched in favour of African countries are commendable and will no doubt benefit many LDCs, but not all of them. The SNPA thus remains today the only programme agreed by the international community specifically designed for the LDCs and covering all of them. After eight years of existence, its objectives remain entirely valid, but some adjustment regarding the measures designed to achieve these objectives are necessary, to take into account current trends, new problems and new approaches to problems.

In view of the overwhelming importance of ODA flows in LDCs' external resource availabilities, as a first step, all donors including the major ones should endeavour to attain the SNPA aid targets. For the 1990s, donors should aim at an *ODA target* for LDCs which can yield sufficient flows to meet the external capital requirements of all the LDCs in the list.

As regards the *use of aid*, this is an area where increased research is specially required and greater surveillance needed. Projects and programmes must be under continuous review as to their adequacy to foster economic growth without being detrimental to social welfare, and as to their effective implementation. The LDCs' institutional infrastructure needs to be further strengthened to enhance their aid implementation capability. Conditionality provisions would have to be made more flexible to take into account the LDCs' structural difficulties as well as unforeseen external developments beyond the donors' and recipients' control.

Terms of aid have to be highly concessional in view of the LDCs' debt overhang. In this respect there is wide scope for improvement in the aid provided by some donors and by some multilateral agencies.

---

[144] For more details on some of these schemes, see UNCTAD, *Trade and Development Report, 1988*, chapter IV, section B, and World Bank, *World Debt Tables, 1987-1988 Edition*, Vol. 1.

A viable solution to LDCs' debt problems is in the interest of both debtors and creditors. For the LDCs, *debt relief* has become an essential part of the assistance package. Measures aimed at the *reduction* of debt levels can help LDCs to improve their financial situation and restore credit-worthiness in the long-run. Retroactive terms adjustment measures have proved to be an appropriate instrument to deal with ODA debts. These measures would need to be applied by all concerned bilateral creditors of LDCs.

The options agreed at the Toronto Summit are an important step forward with respect to official debts in general, at least conceptually. The LDCs may not, however, derive sufficient relief under the option involving longer repayment periods. When write-offs are not feasible, reschedulings of LDCs' debts should always be at concessional rates. Consideration should be given to the negotiation of MYRAS linked to medium-term facilities of the World Bank and IMF. The situation of some of the LDCs might even warrant the refunding of the entire stock of official debt.

New instruments, including interest-subsidy schemes and refinancing mechanisms, could be set up to alleviate the burden of LDCs' debts to multilateral institutions and allow all LDCs' multilateral loans to be converted at terms as concessional as those of IDA. Officially supported buy-back schemes for LDCs' commercial debts could also be considered. In any event, debt relief should be additional to aid allocations to LDCs.

Mechanisms of aid co-ordination need to be strengthened. At the country level, review meetings such as UNDP round tables and World Bank consultative groups should be held at regular intervals for all LDCs, possibly every two years. These fora should be used to examine not only LDCs' programmes and aid requirements, but also LDCs' debt problems and debt relief needs. They should also serve as an effective mechanism to elicit pledges which meet LDCs' assistance needs. At the global level, a mechanism including all the LDCs and all their development partners, should be available to review, on a regular basis, aid flows, projects and programmes in LDCs as well as debt relief, and to make recommendations for action. The UNCTAD Intergovernmental Group on the Least Developed Countries could serve such a purpose.

B. Compensatory finance

1. *Recent developments*

LDCs remain highly dependent on the export of primary commodities, and given the volatility of the prices of these products, they are particularly vulnerable to earnings instability.[145]

For the period 1982-1986, the average annual export earnings shortfall for the primary commodity sector of the LDCs as a group is calculated to be $851 million on the basis of a 10-year exponential trend and measured in terms of dollars (see table 31). Part of these shortfalls was compensated by finance from the IMF's Compensatory Financing Facility (CFF) and from the EEC's STABEX scheme. An annual average of $81 million was provided by the CFF, while another $54 million was obtained through STABEX. Both figures are gross. This implies that the two schemes together covered only 16 per cent of the shortfall. Measured in terms of SDRs the export earnings instability is less pronounced and the coverage rate improves somewhat, to 19 per cent. In 1986, compensation was given to 4 non ACP LDCs by the EEC's newly established COMPEX

145 LDC exports of primary commodities, excluding fuels and non-industrial diamonds, amounted in 1985 to $5.2 billion, or 1.6 per cent of world exports and 5.4 per cent of developing countries exports in such commodities. This, however, represented more than 70 per cent of LDCs' total export earnings as compared to a share of 21 per cent for all developing countries (32 per cent if the major petroleum exporters are excluded). Including non-industrial diamonds, LDCs' share of primary commodities that year reached 79 per cent. Primary commodities in the UNCTAD, Commodity Yearbook files are defined as - section O, section 1, section 2 (less groups 233, 244, 266 and 267), section 4, division 68 and item 522.56, according to the SITC-Rev. 2.

146 In early 1987, the EEC established a compensatory scheme for LDCs that are not signatories of the Lomé agreement. This scheme was applied retroactively for the year 1986. See *Official Journal of the European Communities*, 13 February 1987, No. L43.

Table 31

ANNUAL AVERAGE SHORTFALL IN THE LDCS' NON-FUEL COMMODITY SECTOR EXPORT EARNINGS ON THE BASIS OF A 10-YEAR EXPONENTIAL TREND AND A 4-YEAR ARITHMETIC AVERAGE, AS WELL AS CORRESPONDING FINANCE PROVIDED UNDER THE IMF-CFF AND STABEX IN THE PERIOD 1982-1986 [a]

(In millions of dollars and (in millions of SDRs))

	Shortfall [b]				IMF/CFF drawings [c]		STABEX transfers [d]	
	4-year aritmetic average		10-year exponential trend					
Benin	3.5	(1.7)	1.2	(0.7)			0.9	(0.8)
Botswana	14.5	(6.1)	37.3	(28.1)				
Burkina Faso	7.7	(4.6)	9.7	(7.8)			1.1	(1.0)
Burundi	0.4		6.7	(3.2)			0.4	(0.4)
Cape Verde	0.1	(0.0)	0.8	(0.7)			0.0	(0.0)
Central African Rep.	3.3	(0.8)	9.7	(7.1)			0.8	(0.7)
Chad	5.0	(7.3)	14.6	(12.3)	1.4	(1.4)	3.3	(2.9)
Comoros	1.8	(1.7)	1.9	(1.7)			1.6	(1.5)
Djibouti	n.a.	(n.a.)	n.a.	(n.a.)				
Equatorial Guinea			0.2	(0.0)			0.2	(0.2)
Ethiopia	14.2	(6.5)	36.5	(15.9)	7.2	(7.1)	3.9	(3.6)
Gambia	3.8	(2.9)	1.6	(1.3)	1.1	(0.9)	2.6	(2.4)
Guinea	4.4	(14.1)	114.8	(87.0)				
Guinea-Bissau	1.8	(1.0)	2.7	(2.1)			0.9	(0.8)
Kiribati	3.0	(2.4)	0.4	(0.3)			0.5	(0.5)
Lesotho	n.a.	(n.a.)	n.a.	(n.a.)			0.1	(0.1)
Malawi	9.8	(7.9)	34.5	(27.4)	5.6	(5.2)	0.6	(0.9)
Mali	11.9	(12.0)	42.3	(31.5)			4.1	(3.6)
Mauritania	1.7	(2.1)	16.4	(16.0)				
Niger	99.8	(63.0)	191.8	(159.5)	5.2	(4.8)	1.1	(0.9)
Rwanda	5.2	(2.1)	11.6	(7.1)			1.0	(0.9)
Samoa	2.0	(1.6)	1.9	(1.7)	0.2	(0.2)	1.5	(1.3)
Sao Tome and Principe	5.5	(3.9)	3.4	(2.6)			1.2	(1.1)
Sierra Leone	3.4	(1.2)	2.1	(0.9)	4.6	(4.1)	2.1	(0.9)
Somalia	49.5	(40.4)	32.3	(28.3)	6.7	(6.5)	0.1	(0.1)
Sudan	65.5	(55.4)	46.9	(34.8)	8.6	(7.8)	12.4	(11.7)
Togo	21.3	(11.3)	19.2	(12.7)			6.3	(6.0)
Tuvalu	n.a.	(n.a.)	n.a.	(n.a.)			0.0	0.0
Uganda			0.4					
United Rep. of Tanzania	73.0	(47.3)	53.3	(32.2)			2.8	(2.7)
Vanuatu	5.2	(4.0)	4.3	(3.3)			3.2	(2.8)
ACP LDCs [e]	417.3	(301.3)	698.5	(526.2)	40.7	(38.1)	53.5	(49.1)
Afghanistan	37.8	(19.4)	47.6	(34.7)				
Bangladesh		(5.4)	15.7	(11.4)	28.4	(25.0)		
Bhutan	n.a.	(n.a.)	n.a.	(n.a.)				
Burma	24.0	(14.7)	71.6	(55.0)	11.4	(11.0)		
Democratic Yemen	2.7	(1.6)	2.9	(1.9)				
Haiti	10.5	(4.0)	11.0	(6.6)				
Lao People's Dem. Rep.			0.1					
Maldives			0.5	(0.3)				
Nepal	1.0	(2.0)	1.2	(2.3)				
Yemen	1.8	(1.0)	2.0	(1.3)				
Non ACP LDCs	77.8	(48.1)	152.6	(113.5)	39.8	(35.9)		
All LDCs	**495.2**	**(349.5)**	**851.3**	**(639.8)**	**80.5**	**(74.0)**	**53.5**	**(49.1)**
All developing Countries	**6205.8**	**(3909.7)**	**13917.9**	**(9926.4)**	**1639.9**	**(1496.1)**	**112.6**	**(101.5)**

Source: UNCTAD secretariat calculations on the basis of UNCTAD, Commodity Yearbook files and data from the United Nations Statistical Office, the EEC and the IMF.

a The commodity sector includes all food, agricultural raw materials and mineral and metal commodities, but excludes petroleum and precious stones and metals. Figures may not add up to totals exactly owing to rounding.

b The 10-year exponential trend formula has been recommended by the Group of Experts on the Compensatory Financing of Export Earnings. The 4-year arithmetic average formula corresponds to the one used in STABEX.

c Drawings by year of shortfall and not by year of drawing. Finance relates to shortfalls in total merchandise exports and exclude purchases of excesses in cereal imports under cereal decision EBD No. 6860 (81/81).

d Transfers by year of shortfall. Finance relates to the list of products covered by STABEX under the third ACP-EEC Convention.

e The third ACP-EEC Convention specifies as least developed countries 43 States, of which 31

scheme.[146] for an amount equivalent to $6.1 million, while some ACP LDCs can also draw on the SYSMIN scheme for mineral producers.[147]

Coverage of the CFF and StABEX has been very patchy, and LDCs have been particularly reluctant in recent years to draw on the CFF because of its onerous terms.[148] Taking both schemes together, over the four-year period studied, the LDCs' shortfall represented 6 per cent of the shortfall for all developing countries, and they received 8 per cent of the total compensation. It should be noted, however, that this refers to the commodity sector only. Considering the shortfall with respect to all export earnings, these shares are much lower for the LDCs. For other countries with less chronic commodity dependence, the instability of commodity earnings is partly cushioned by the less unstable earnings from other goods. Moreover, CFF drawings worldwide rose from SDR 593 million in 1986/87 to SDR 1.56 billion in 1987/88, but few LDCs did use the facility during that period.

There is, however, a growing awareness of the need to expand and improve compensation to developing countries for export earnings shortfalls. The Intergovernmental Group of 24 has called for major design changes to the IMF CFF, in order to make it less conditional and extend its coverage to all external causes of disturbances in the balance of payments. The Group has also requested an increase in the access limit for CFF drawings, using the shortfall as the basis for determining access, instead of quotas as at present, and has suggested giving relatively larger compensation to the poorer countries and easing the repayment periods for them.[149] At the second session of UNCTAD's Intergovernmental Group of Experts on the Compensatory Financing of Export Earnings Shortfalls, held in September 1987, it was agreed that there was a significant difference between the commodity export earnings shortfalls experienced by developing countries and the finance made available under existing financing facilities.[150] LDCs would share with other developing countries the benefits to be derived from less restrictive conditions and from increased compensatory finance under existing facilities, as well as from the establishment of STABEX-type schemes by developed countries which had not yet done so.

The IMF, which itself became concerned about the effect of its programmes on the poor and the lack of new CFF drawings by the LDCs, resolved that "program design should be improved to better protect the poor during the adjustment period[151]" and, having reviewed its current compensatory schemes, ecided to replace the CFF (in existence since 1963) and the cereals import fluctuation facility (in existence since 1981) with a new facility providing "broader protection against adverse changes in external economic conditions[152] " for countries pursuing IMF-supported adjustemnt programmes. At its meeting in April 1988, the Interim Committee of the Board of Governors of IMF agreed, INter *alia*, that "Fund assistance for export shortfalls and external contingencies should be combined into a single facility, with an overall access limit of 105 per cent of quota. Within that overall access, a limit of 40 per cent of quota would apply both to the compensatory element and to the contingency element, and an optional tranche of 25 per cent of quota would be available to supplement either element at the choice of the member. Use of the contingency element would be attached to a Fund-supported adjustment programme[153]."

The main feature of the new CCFF scheme, the Compensatory and Contingency Financing Facility, which was adopted experimentally by IMF in August 1988, is that it will in future cover fluctuations in such key variables as interest rates on external borrowing as well as import price changes and export earnings fluctuations. However, calculation of shortfalls in this three-tier scheme are to be made in different ways: export earnings shortfalls on the basis of five-year geometric averages, cereal cost excesses according to five-year arithmetic averages, as before, but

147 These two schemes have not the same semi-automatic compensation mechanisms as STABEX, and are not included in this analysis.

148 See the *1987 Report*, which showed that LDCs CFF drawings in 1986 were negative overall at SDR 60mn. That year, only one LDC had a positive CFF drawing, while thirteen were reimbursing the IMF on CFF account.

149 See *IMF Survey*, 10 August 1987.

150 UNCTAD's Intergovernmental Group of Experts indicated that it would make its recommendations once the current review by IMF has been completed. A resumed session of the Group is tentatively scheduled for April 1989.

151 *IMF Survey*, September 1988, p.2

152 *Ibid.*, p.10

153 In fact the scheme as agreed later by the IMF Executive Board extends to a maximum of 122 per cent of quota, comprising 40 per cent each for the export compensatory and contingency elements, a 25 per cent optional tranche for either, and additional access limit of 17 per cent for financing cereal import cost excesses. The quotation is taken from IMF, *Communiqué of the Interim Committee of the Board of Governors of International Monetary Fund*, Press Release No. 88/10, 15 April 1988.

contingency financing will be determined by deviations from baseline projections. The requirement for a drawing country to co-operate with the IMF to solve its balance-of-payments problems remains, and this again implies that only LDCs with current IMF-supported adjustment programmes will be eligible to draw on any part of the CCFF - although it has been asserted that Mexico (not an LDC) would be allowed to draw on the CCFF without submitting to an IMF or World Bank adjustment programme when agreement was reached bilaterally on a $3.5 billion bridging loan.[154] At this early stage in the scheme's history, it is not clear whether conditions can be relaxed and made more suitable to LDCs, although there remains a clear need for a more automatic compensatory mechanism addressing a wide range of shortfalls arising from exogenous shocks which are both temporary and beyond the control of LDCs, including not least on commodity export earnings.

2. *Challenges for the 1990s*

The IMF's new scheme, the CCFF, is now sensibly extending into areas such as interest rate fluctuations. But unless it is available to LDCs at affordable rates and drawings are provided automatically without associated conditionality, the scheme will continue to be shunned by LDCs and its stabilizing potential will be wasted. LDCs in any case can deserve special treatment in the new CCFF. As regards STABEX, where they are accorded softer financial terms, the financial endorsement of the scheme needs to be greatly extended in order to avoid the scale of shortfall which occurred again in 1988. The establishment of similar schemes by non-EEC developed countries could be considered to further help LDCs to minimize the effect of export earnings shortfalls.

C. Access to markets of developed countries

1. *The Uruguay Round*

The Ministerial Declaration adopted in September 1986 for the launch of the Uruguay Round on Multilateral Trade Negotiations (MTN) contains one paragraph dedicated specifically to the LDCs: "Special attention shall be given to the particular situation and problems of the least developed countries and to the need to encourage positive measures to facilitate expansion of their trading opportunities. Expeditious implementation of the relevant provisions of the 1982 Ministerial Declaration concerning the least developed countries shall also be given appropriate attention[155]."

In response to this mandate, the Sub-Committee on Trade of Least Developed Countries of the GATT Committee on Trade and Development was convened in February 1988, with the purpose of reviewing issues in the Uruguay Round of particular interest to LDCs, including, *inter alia*: duty-free treatment for all exports from LDCs; exemption from quotas and ceilings; use of simplified and flexible rules of origin; and establishment of import promoting offices by donor countries. In its turn, the UNCTAD Trade and Development Board adopted, at its thirty-fourth session, a decision to extend technical assistance activities in relation to the Uruguay Round, this being of particular interest to LDCs needing to strengthen their negotiating capacity.

2. *The generalized system of preferences*

The GSP was created to promote development by enhancing developing countries' exports and their industrialization. For this purpose, the GSP donor countries have given the beneficiary countries preferential and non-reciprocal access to their markets under a GATT waiver. During the last year, however, even the concept of special and differential treatment regarding trade access has been

154 See "Mexico able to draw on US loan ahead of approval from IMF", *Financial Times*, 19 October 1988.

155 This recommendation was endorsed at UNCTAD VII. See Final Act, paragraph 149.

Table 32

GSTP : NUMBER OF CUSTOMS ITEMS SUBJECT TO CONCESSIONS

Preference-granting country	*To non-LDC signatories*	*Additional items limited to LDC signatories*
Algeria	8	3
Argentina	4	1
Bangladesh	0	7
Cameroon	1	2
Egypt	20	4
India	32	*a*
Iran (Islamic Rep.)	10	3
Morocco	27	6
Pakistan	5	2
Rep. of Korea	26	11
Romania	221	44
Sudan	21	2
Tunisia	7	1

Source: Proceedings of the Ministerial Meeting on the Global System of Trade Preferences among Developing Countries (GSTP/MM/BELGRADE/12(vol. 1), Annex IV.

a More favourable margins are extended to LDCs on three items of special export interest to them.

questioned by a major trading partner.[156] Yet, at the same time, LDCs, especially those which are debt-distressed, are being pressed to adopt export-oriented strategies and so are increasingly relying on GSP preferential access to the markets of developed countries (and to other developing countries, see section D.2 below).

(a) Beneficiaries

The majority of the GSP-preference-giving countries recognize all least developed countries as beneficiaries of their schemes. However, several of them make exceptions to this general rule. Japan excludes Comoros and Djibouti, and the United States excludes Afghanistan, Democratic Yemen, Ethiopia and Lao People's Democratic Republic. Three out of the four socialist countries of Eastern Europe with GSP schemes[157] exclude Kiribati, Tuvalu and Vanuatu, while Bulgaria also excludes, in addition, Djibouti, Equatorial Guinea and Samoa. The USSR accords beneficiary status to those countries with which it has trade relations.[158] The German Democratic Republic has subscribed to a Joint Declaration on the GSP by the socialist preference-giving countries of Eastern Europe to introduce other economic and foreign trade measures of a preferential nature, designed to expand imports from developing countries.

Notwithstanding the above exceptions, the situation at the middle of 1988 represents an improvement on that at the beginning of the 1980s. The socialist countries of Eastern Europe have been increasing the number of beneficiaries in comparison with 1980. At that time, Czechoslovakia had not yet included Comoros, Djibouti, Kiribati, Lesotho, Malawi, Tuvalu and Vanuatu; Hungary had not yet included Bhutan, Cape Verde, Comoros, Djibouti, Equatorial Guinea, Guinea-Bissau, Samoa, Sao Tome and Principe, Sierra Leone and Togo; whereas Poland, had not included Cape Verde, Comoros, Djibouti, Sao Tome and Principe, and Samoa. Arguably the schemes of the socialist economies will become more effective under the present tendency towards decentralization.

(b) Special measures in favour of LDCs

In line with the provisions of the "enabling clause", adopted at the Tokyo Round of Multilateral Trade Negotiations (MTNs),

156 See "US attacks GATT special treatment", *Financial Times*, 15 September 1988.

157 Bulgaria, Hungary and Poland. The fourth country, Czechoslovakia, extended preferential treatment to Kiribati, Tuvalu and Vanuatu in 1982.

158 In the 1980s, the USSR was exporting to more than half the total number of LDCs, while more than one third of the LDCs were procuring imports from the USSR.

which recommends that the special economic situation of the LDCs should be taken into account, most of the GSP donor countries have extended special measures to the LDCs, usually within their schemes but sometimes also outside them.[159] In the 1970s five individual countries and the EEC had already done so. In 1976, Norway extended duty-free treatment to all imports from the LDCs, while in 1977/78, Bulgaria, Czechoslovakia and Hungary did the same with respect to imports from the LDCs which are beneficiaries of their respective schemes. The United States, in accordance with the Trade Agreements Act of 1979, gave the LDCs full tariff reductions without escalation for certain products which are not necessarily GSP eligible.[160] In the years 1977-1979 the EEC exempted the LDCs from tariffs levied on imports of industrial products up to maximum country amounts and ceilings, with the exception of sensitive textile products. In 1978, the EEC added to its scheme two agricultural products for the benefit of the LDCs only, and it extended duty-free treatment to these countries on the agricultural products in its scheme.[161] However, for those sensitive agricultural products subject to quotas, this exemption was granted only in the context of such tariff quotas.[162] In the 1980s, the other GSP donor countries, except Australia, followed suit and gave also special benefits to the LDCs.[163]

By mid-1988 the special relations between LDCs and developed market economies within the context of their GSP schemes can be summed up as follows. In Norway and Sweden, the LDCs have duty-free access for all their exports, while Japan, New Zealand and the EEC countries give almost completely free access for products covered. Coverage, especially of agricultural products, remains limited and tariff escalation remains a problem. Canada and, in principle, Switzerland limit free access to the products eligible under their schemes, Switzerland adding some products outside its scheme. Austria grants duty-free access to products within its scheme with some exceptions. The socialist countries of Eastern Europe accord preferential treatment to LDCs in the context of their GSP schemes. Although the United States in 1979 gave special treatment to the LDCs for a number of products, in the meantime these preferences have been phased out. The United States is exploring, in the framework of the Uruguay Round negotiations, the possibility of providing LDCs with duty-free access to the United States markets for all products up to the year 2000.

(c) *The impact of the GSP on LDCs' exports*

Although most of the GSP donor countries have adopted special measures in favour of the LDCs, the impact on these countries' exports has been small and its corresponding stimulus to their industrialization has been relatively modest. The weak effect on industrialization is partly a result of the fact that in the GSP schemes many products face reduced or no tariffs in their primary form, while the semi-processed or processed form of the product is subject to a considerably higher tariff. This tariff escalation has further hampered the efforts of the LDCs to make progress towards industrialization.

In a recent study by Karsenty and Laird, it is shown that the major benefits of the GSP have so far gone to a limited number of countries with a competitive industrial base, none of them LDCs.[164] The authors found that "The top three beneficiaries, Hongkong, the Republic of Korea, and Taiwan (Province of China) are estimated to receive 44.2 per cent of the total gains of the present system and each receives some three times the benefits of the next largest beneficiary, Brazil"(*op.ci*T., p. 271). For those developing countries which depend

159 See GATT, *Basic Instruments and Selected Documents*, Twenty-sixth Supplement, 1980, pp. 203-205. See paragraph 2d) and 8 of the decision on "Differential and more favourable treatment, reciprocity and fuller participation of developing countries", adopted by the GATT contracting parties on 28 November 1979 in the Tokyo Round of multilateral trade negotiations.

160 For full information on the products subject to the special treatment, see International Trade Commission," *Tariff Schedules of the United States Annotated*", Washington (TSUS 1980: General headnotes and rules of interpretation, 3(d)(i) and (ii), and within the schedules column "Rates of duty LDDC").

161 The two products are raw coffee (09.01AI) and dried grapes (08.04B). This latter product was to be deleted again in 1983 as a result of internal difficulties in the Commmunity. It should be noted that outside the scope of tariff preferences and in the context of the EEC's Common Agricultural Policy, some agricultural products are subject to import taxes or levies applied on the flour or sugar content of the products, even when originating in least developed countries.

162 Cocoa butter (ex. 18.04), preserved pineapples, etc. (ex 20.06), soluble coffee (ex 21.02) and raw or unmanufactured Virginia type tobacco (ex 24.01).

163 Within the context of SPARTECA, Australia together with New Zealand, gives preferential market access to four of the LDCs in the Pacific Ocean, (Kiribati, Samoa, Tuvalu and Vanuatu).

164 See Guy Karsenty and Sam Laird, "The GSP, policy options, and the New Round", Weltwirtschaftliches Archiv, Band 123, 1987, Heft 2.

mainly on exports of agricultural products and raw materials, particularly those from the tropical zone, the benefits of the system have been limited. Karsenty and Laird showed that among the 37 three digit SITC items with GSP benefits of more than $50 million, there were only three food products items: sugar and honey (SITC 061), dried fruit (SITC 052) animal feedstuffs (SITC 081).[165] This is because competing agricultural products which are produced in developed as well as developing countries, are usually excluded from GSP schemes. Tropical products are concentrated in general in developing countries only, and the system therefore cannot lead to shifts of trade flows from developed countries to developing ones. Moreover, consumption prices for tropical products have been kept relatively high in the GSP donor countries through the application of high internal taxes, thereby keeping demand for these products relatively low. The study by Karsenty and Laird estimated that, as a result of the GSP, the imports of GSP donors from all GSP receivers increased by slightly more than 2 per cent or $6.5 billion. They found that the exports of LDCs were only $242 million higher as a result of GSP. More than half of this amount was attributable to three countries only: Haiti ($68 million), Bangladesh ($38 million) and Uganda ($17 million).

One of the objectives of the special measures adopted in favour of the LDCs has been to improve the export performance of the LDCs. Global trade data available in the UNCTAD secretariat regarding food products and agricultural raw materials suggest that there has been no improvement for food products. The data for agricultural raw materials suggest that a turnaround of the declining trend took place in the 1980s. For minerals, ores and metals, the LDCs improved their participation until the 1980s, but have lost ground since. The GSP can, however, be at best a minor factor in such developments.[166]

To take the example of Norway, in 1976 Norway extended duty-free treatment to all imports from the LDCs. This decision, however, has had no significant positive impact on the imports of manufactured products from LDCs. In 1975 Norway's imports from the LDCs amounted to $2.9 million, in 1980 and 1985 they amounted to only $1.3 and $1.2 million respectively.

Another recent study by McQueen concluded that, "the mere provision of tariff preferences is not, however, a sufficient condition for the success of the scheme. Preference-giving countries must also adopt complementary measures through their *aid programmes* to increase the capacity of the less industrialized and least developed countries to design, produce and market products subject to preferences[167]".

Thus, the marginal preferences extended are not sufficient to compensate for the numerous protectionist obstacles and other handicaps facing LDCs. The EEC has now recognized that trade preferences should be complemented by other measures which address directly these countries' supply capacity and that more funds should be made available for this purpose. However, the biggest impediment to LDCs' access to markets is of course developed countries' market protection policies themselves, particularly in agriculture.

3. *Non-tariff measures faced by LDCs*

Imports originating in LDCs accounted for only 0.7 per cent of all non-fuel imports into developed market-economy countries in 1984. Despite this minor share in total imports, non-tariff measures (NTMs) affect nearly 15 per cent of the value of imports originating in LDCs: of total non-fuel imports from LDCs worth $4.5 billion (1984 figures), around $640 million were subject to NTMs, with about $300 corresponding to food items and the remainder to industrial products.

NTMs constitute a trade barrier against which LDCs receive no special favourable treatment. Most of the NTMs affecting imports from these countries are targeted against all suppliers. Clothing imported from LDCs constitutes a particularly affected export item.

There has hitherto been no noticeable progress in the reduction of NTMs affecting LDCs' exports, in spite of pledges made by LDCs' trade partners at the Uruguay Round and of the stronger than anticipated growth registered in the OECD area in recent years. The assessment of trade intervention based on UNCTAD's Trade Control Measures Information System shows in fact virtually no relaxa-

---

165 Melon and water-melon juice. (20.07 A III ex a) b) ex 1 ex 2).

166 To measure the impact of the GSP, a more detailed analysis would be required, considering the specific relevant products and particularly the dates on which the special measures were adopted and the dates on which the new LDCs have been included.

167 M. McQueen, "The EEC scheme of generalized preferences: the trade effects of quotas and ceilings", (UNCTAD/ST/MD/32), 16 May 1988, page 2.

tion of NTMs applied against imports from the LDCs. Consideration should be given, in the context of current trade negotiations, to across-the-board liberalization of NTMs affecting products of particular export interest to LDCs or to liberalization for LDCs on a preferential basis by exempting these countries from all quantitative restrictions and other measures having similar effects.

4. Challenges for the 1990s

If LDCs are to expand and diversify their export base, open or preferential market access needs to be guaranteed to them. Proposals to that effect were made by the spokesman for the LDCs at the seventh session of the GATT's Sub-Committee on Trade of the LDCs, held in February 1988. These proposals provide, *inter alia*, that: (i) action should be taken for advanced implementation in favour of the LDCs of all MFN concessions made by contracting parties in the Uruguay Round; (ii) the rules and disciplines to be elaborated in regard to textiles and clothing should provide for the fullest liberalization of trade in this sector for the LDCs in the context of differential and most favourable treatment; (iii) special and differential treatment in favour of LDCs should be ensured in the case of tropical products and other sectors of special interest to LDCs; and (iv) expeditious implementation should be ensured of the relevant provisions of the 1982 Ministerial Declaration, including improvement of GSP or MFN treatment for products of particular export interest to the LDCs and adoption of measures to promote a higher utilization rate of the GSP by LDCs. Furthermore, instead of curtailing GSP schemes, consideration could be given to granting GSP beneficiary status to all LDCs and to extending the GSP for a sufficiently long period, - for example, 20 years - to allow LDCs to embark on long-term investment programmes. LDCs would also benefit from specific exemption from any new safeguards clause which might be negotiated.

D. Economic co-operation among developing countries (ECDC)

1. Integration efforts

Within subregional integration groupings LDCs are the ones in greatest need of sharing the benefits of integration, since their small domestic markets (a) drastically limit the number of economically-viable national import substitution projects, and (b) cause them to be the ones least able to attract foreign investment.

Moreover, the smaller loads and the distances separating many LDCs from the major ports of entry raise their unit transport costs above the levels prevailing in the economically more-advanced countries of the same subregion. When such cost differentials occur within a single country, the less-advanced and more remote regions usually benefit from uniform rate structures, implying compensatory payments from the more advanced and more favourably located regions. Similar compensatory schemes, however, are seldom - if ever - achieved across national boundaries, but could be instituted if integrated railway, air and road transport systems were to be instituted.

Despite their intrinsic need to integrate, LDCs, being the weakest partners within integration groupings, are generally the ones least likely to benefit from formal integration efforts. This is partly due to economic factors, which favour the location of multi-national projects in the more advanced countries of a grouping (e.g., larger market, better physical and human infrastructure). In order for LDCs to take advantage of the benefits of integration, there is need for special measures to be introduced in their favour. In the case of LDCs that participate in customs unions, care needs to be taken to ensure that their participation does not result in subsidizing the protected subregional industries located in the more advanced partner countries, without corresponding benefits for the LDCs.

These problems are well known and have been formally addressed in many of the more recent integration groupings. The integration secretariats and the financial institutions attached to them are not always fully equipped to tackle these problems. Global and regional development finance institutions can play a crucial role by giving special support to the identification, promotion and financing of multi-country projects. This can be done by the earmarking of a given share of available funds (as is done by the European Development Fund), by setting up a pre-investment fund for integration projects and/or by appropriate internal project evaluation procedures that take into account possible link-ups between complementary or competing national projects.

2. *The global system of trade preferences among developing countries (GSTP)*

The first protocol of tariff concessions under the Global System of Trade Preferences (GSTP), adopted in Belgrade on 13 April 1988, confirmed the need for special treatment for LDCs, enshrined the principle of non-reciprocity for them, and adopted within its framework concrete preferential measures in their favour, particularly more liberal rules of origin and longer lists of eligible products benefiting from GSTP customs duties than the rules and lists applying to other signatories. Thus, products originating in LDCs can benefit from GSTP treatment with a value-added component that is 10 percentage points below the one required for the same products originating in other signatory countries. These more liberal rules also apply to cumulative origin requirements when the last operation occurs in an LDC.

Other measures foreseen in favour of the LDCs include: (i) the identification and establishment of industrial and agricultural projects in these countries; (ii) assistance in the formulation of export promotion policies and the creation of export training facilities; (iii) promotion of joint ventures with LDCs; and (iv) the provision of special transit facilities and freight rates for participating land-locked and island LDCs.

The six participating LDCs among the 48 signatories are: Bangladesh, Benin, Guinea, Haiti, Sudan and the United Republic of Tanzania. In addition to their ordinary rights as signatories, they have been given access to special technical assistance by a UNDP-financed project regarding their participation in the GSTP.

Thirteen signatories (including two LDCs - Bangladesh and Sudan) granted additional concessions on customs duties to participating LDCs. Twelve of them granted concessions on items other than those available to non-LDC signatories; India granted the LDCs supplementary margins of preference on three items contained in the general GSTP list (see table 32).

3. *Multilateral payments and monetary arrangements (MPAs)*

Although there are no special concessions for LDCs within existing MPAs, LDCs have drawn direct benefits from their membership in certain MPAs.

(a) The CFA Franc Zone

The CFA Franc Zone remains the most important functioning payments arrangement covering LDCs. Its 14 African member countries are divided as follows:

	BCEAO [a]	*BEAC* [b]	*Comores*	*Total*
LDCs	5	3	1	9
non-LDCs	2	3	-	5
Total	7	6	1	14

a BCEAO: Central Bank of West African States
b BEAC: Central Bank of Central African States

The net value of BCEAO's credits extended to LDC commercial banks and treasuries increased by 8.9 per cent to CFAF 207.6 billion ($777.5 million) in 1987 compared with the previous year; they represented less than 20 per cent of such BCEAO credits to all its member countries. The largest recipients were

Benin (CFAF 62.98 billion, equivalent to $235 million), followed by Mali (CFAF 53.49 billion, equivalent to $200.3 million).

BEAC's net credits to the commercial banks and treasuries of its LDC members (Chad, the Central African Republic and Equatorial Guinea) fell by 14.2 per cent to CFAF 70.4 billion ($264 million) in 1987 compared to 1986, accounting for only 10.2 per cent of such BEAC credits to all its member countries.

(b) The West African Clearing House

The West African Clearing House (WACH), established under the aegis of the Economic Community of West African States (ECOWAS) by the Central Bank of West African States (BCEAO), represents its seven member countries and the central banks of ECOWAS's nine other member countries. WACH counts 11 LDCs among its 16 members. Transactions channelled through WACH fell by 53 per cent to SDR 90.47 million in 1985/1986 compared to SDR 195.34 million in 1984/1985. Meanwhile, only Mauritanian transactions increased significantly (by 32 per cent) to SDR 33.44 million, making this country the largest user of WACH's facilities.

(c) The Arab Monetary Fund

The four LDCs which belong to the Arab Monetary Fund (AMF) - Mauritania, Somalia, Sudan and Yemen - have benefited from net receipts received from AMF. As of end-1986, the total of such receipts amounted to SDR 241.4 million, which represented a 5 per cent increase compared with end-1985. The largest net recipient was Sudan (SDR 92.69 million) followed by Yemen (SDR 64.29 million), with the remainder having been shared roughly equally by Mauritania and Somalia.

(d) The Asian Clearing Union

The Asian Clearing Union (ACU), comprising four LDCs (Bangladesh, Bhutan, Burma and Nepal) among its eight members, has been successful in channelling the overwhelming part of payments related to mutual trade through its accounts. As late as 1984, participating LDC central banks were net creditors to ACU by SDR 126.5 million, but two years later the net position of the LDC central banks towards the Union had been reversed, so that LDC debits exceeded LDC credits by SDR 23.4 million, representing a short-term credit extended by other members to their LDC partners. More than 75 per cent of LDC transactions with ACU were accounted for by the Bangladesh Central Bank. It must be noted, however, that payments between Nepal and Bhutan on the one hand and India - their largest trading partner by far - on the other hand, are not made through the Union, but are regulated by bilateral agreements.

Part Two

DEVELOPMENT OF THE ECONOMIES OF INDIVIDUAL LDCs

AFGHANISTAN

1. *Improving the efficiency of resource allocation*

The political difficulties which have now lasted nine years continued through FY 1987/88[168], and official reports suggest that the overall Afghan economy has suffered considerably. However, the Geneva accords signed on 14 April 1988 laid the foundation upon which peace and stability could be built and the country's economy rehabilitated.

(a) External sector policies

The external economic policy of the country has been formulated with a view to the expansion and diversification of exportable items and the substitution of imports.

(b) Demand-management measures

The Government has taken measures for improving the country's fiscal situation. This has involved policies designed to mobilise a maximum of governmental revenue, accompanied by a tightening of control over expenditures, increased revenue from public enterprises through improved management, and reduced price subsidies for petroleum products.

(c) Mobilization of domestic savings

Commercial bank savings accounts have been promoted with a scheme of prizes for holders of such accounts. In fact, savings and other forms of non-demand deposits with the commercial banks increased by more than one-half between end-1984 and mid-1987.

(d) Expanded role for the private sector

Official reports point to the role of the private sector both as a source of savings and as an instrument for utilizing such savings for capital formation contributing towards economic development. To extend and promote the private sector, 11 projects involving an investment of Af 220 million ($4.3 million) were approved on 31 December 1987 by the Council of Ministers. More recently, a new foreign and domestic investment law was promulgated to promote joint ventures and private domestic investments. Partly as a result of this, the private sector is expected to generate an estimated gross income of Af 39 billion ($770 million) during FY 1987/88, i.e. about 9 per cent above the level for FY 1986/87, corresponding to almost one-quarter of GNP.

(e) Improving the efficiency of public enterprises

Taking into account the important role played by public and mixed enterprises in the Afghan economy, a number of measures, including performance evaluations and reforms of these enterprises, have been taken with a view to securing efficiency, avoiding economic losses and upgrading the administrative capabilities of these institutions.

2. *Sectoral policies*

(a) Food and agriculture

Agriculture continues to be the mainstay of the Afghan economy, employing 85 per cent of the active population and accounting for more than 50 per cent of the GDP. Moreover,

168 The fiscal year (FY) ends on 21 March.

in addition to supplying raw materials for the local industries, agricultural products account for between one-third and one-half of the export earnings of the country.

The main policies and measures directed towards this sector include accelerated reforms of land tenure and water supply systems; promotion of the co-operative movement; provision of agricultural credit; intensification of agricultural research; extension of mechanized agriculture; provision of veterinary services; rehabilitation, improvement and construction of irrigation and drainage systems; scientifically planned diversification of agricultural production; and preparation of new land for cultivation.

(b) Industry and energy

Despite the destruction and damage to industrial facilities caused by the civil disturbances during the 1980s, government policies aim at an increased role for this sector. Measures taken in this direction include: heavy investment in and transfer of technology to the public-sector and mixed industries, rehabilitation of energy-generating plants and of mines, continuation of geological surveys for the purpose of mineral prospecting, and the rehabilitation and expansion of the power distribution networks.

Afghanistan's main energy resource is natural gas, reserves of which have been estimated at 150 billion m^3 and extraction of which has averaged around 2.5 billion m^3 annually. Drilling and exploration for gas and oil have been intensified in recent years, but oil reserves are officially estimated at only 100 million barrels.

(c) Social development

Official sources indicate that the Government has made streneous efforts in the literacy sector. In the last two years, the total number of general education schools has increased, while enrolment at the primary and post-primary levels is reported to have increased by 80 per cent and 60 per cent respectively.

Primary health care (PHC) has been recognized as the focal point for the dispensation of health services. Immunization of children, mother and child care, nutrition, safe drinking water, environmental health and health education are some elements of the planned PHC service centres, each of which is expected to care for 9,000-12,000 people within a 10 km radius.

3. *Measures to improve the physical infrastructure*

In the last two years, Government efforts have centred on the expansion and improvement of road vehicles both in the public and private sectors, the basic repair and asphalting of roads and highways, the completion of road building and the erection of service stations in the north, and the strengthening of the air transport infrastructure, for example through the repair and equipping of some airports. Improvement and extension of postal and other communication services at the national and international levels have also been reported.

4. *Measures to improve institutional capabilities in the field of development planning and policy*

According to official reports, a new five-year plan, covering the period 1986-1990, is being implemented. One of its main objectives is the centralized mobilization of all financial, economic and human resources of the State as the first step towards the rehabilitation and reconstruction of institutions and projects which have been damaged during the years of civil strife.

With the signing of the Geneva accords and the very considerable flow of external resources expected to follow thereafter, the Government has established an Emergency Preparation Department within the Prime Minister's Office to co-ordinate this international effort at the national level.

5. *International support measures*

Available information indicates that most economic assistance to Afghanistan comes from the CMEA countries. Of the total development budget of Af 22,753 million ($450.7 million) for FY 1987/88, Af 9,753 million ($192.7 million), or 43 per cent, was financed from external sources. Of this, 95.5 per cent was provided by CMEA countries (84 per cent from the USSR alone), while contributions from other bilateral and multilateral sources accounted for only 4.5 per cent. However, with the launching in 1988 of a United Nations Humanitarian and Economic Assistance Programme relating to Afghanistan under the guidance of a co-ordinator, it is foreseen that aid estimated at $1.16 billion will flow into the country over the next two years.

6. *Overall assessment of the impact of national policies and international support*

Official reports indicate that despite the acknowledged political difficulties resulting in the suspension of ODA and restrictions imposed on Afghan exports by Western donors, the economy was able to maintain growth. Thus, national income was reported to have grown by 2.3 per cent in FY 1987/88 with growth in agriculture at just under 1 per cent. However, a recent survey conducted in May 1988 by the Swedish Committee for Afghanistan based in Peshawar concluded that 55-70 per cent of the country's pre-1978 agricultural capacity had been lost or damaged.

BANGLADESH

1. *Improving the efficiency of resource use and allocation*

The mid-term review of the Third Five-Year Plan 1985-1990 (TFYP) undertaken by the Planning Commission in June 1988 reveals that despite relative success in macro-economic management, progress in the economy in many areas has lagged behind targets. However, even this sober assessment has been overtaken by the severe damage occasioned by the devastating floods that occurred during the third and fourth quarters of 1988.

(a) External sector policies

Bangladesh continues to pursue a flexible exchange-rate policy, keeping in view the need for strengthening the country's international competitiveness and improving the current-account position. Other external economic policies include the liberalization of imports, as well as incentives and facilities for the country's exporters. Recent estimates suggest that out of total exports of $835 million during FY 1988/89[169], ready-made garments are expected to contribute approximately $450 million (compared to $375 million during the preceding year), thereby far exceeding the raw jute and jute goods that dominated the country's export structure until 1985.

(b) Demand-management measures

Austerity has been the keynote of government expenditure policy. The Government is committed to gradually phasing out all types of subsidies. Strict monetary management has helped to contain inflationary pressure within the broad target foreseen by the Plan. The FY 1987/88 budget contained a public-sector development programme of Tk 50.46 billion ($1.6 billion), which was to be financed by Tk 7.42 billion ($237 million) of domestic resources and Tk 43.04 billion ($1.4 billion) of foreign resources. The FY 1988/89 budget provides for an 8.5 per cent expenditure cut on specified items.

(c) Mobilization of domestic savings

The main objective of fiscal policy has been to mobilize increased domestic resources. Tax policy has aimed at the broadening and deepening of the tax base. In the aftermath of the floods of 1987, the Government took several measures to mobilize an additional Tk 1,147 million ($37 million) from domestic sources. The FY 1988/89 budget introduced a new excise tax on luxury goods.

[169] The fiscal year (FY) ends on 30 June.

(d) Expanded role for the private sector

The scope of the private sector has been enlarged through the privatization of a large number of public-sector enterprises. The share of the private sector was raised to about 35 per cent of investments foreseen in the Third Five-Year Plan, compared with 11 per cent in the First Plan. A moratorium on nationalizations has been in effect since 1976.

(e) Improving the efficiency of public enterprises

Despite significant improvements in their operations, parastatal organizations continue to be a source of concern. The return on investment is still low or negative for many of these enterprises. With a view to developing a monitoring and performance evaluation system for public enterprises, the Monitoring Cell in the Ministry of Finance has developed a system called "Performance Contracts" for planning and controlling the performance of public enterprises. Moreover, with a view to broadening the base of ownership and improving management efficiency, shares of public enterprises are being offered for public subscription in phases.

2. Sectoral policies

(a) Food and agriculture

The focus of the agricultural programme has been on recovery of food-grain production from the losses suffered due to drought and floods, so that the target of attaining food self-sufficiency by the end of the TFYP can be achieved. In addition, efforts are also underway for diversification of agricultural activities, with greater emphasis on cash and other crops likely to serve as inputs for agro-industries for both internal and external markets. The forestry programme has emphasized the ecological balance and fuel needs of rural areas.

Food security in Bangladesh continues to be fragile, and the deficit remains a critical problem. Although prices of food-grains remained reasonably stable, food management continued to be difficult because of frequent fluctuations in production resulting mainly from the vagaries of nature. Accordingly, maintenance of adequate food-grain stocks has been recognized as an important tool for ensuring stability of food supplies. The focus of the public food-grain distribution system is being shifted towards the rural poor and other disavantaged groups through programmes such as Food for Work and Vulnerable Group Development.

(b) Industry and energy

The industrial programme has given priority to completion of major ongoing projects, modernization of existing units wherever necessary, establishment of new industries on a selective basis, and support services for the establishment of small and cottage industries, especially in rural areas. Under the New Industrial Policy of 1982 and 1986, the Government has continued to implement measures for industrial growth with an enhanced role for the private sector. Agro-industry and the promotion of labour-intensive export-oriented technology have also been emphasized.

Substitution of indigenous natural gas for imported fuel through expansion of the gas network, improvement in the reliability of the power supply and reduction in power system losses are the main elements of the energy sector programme for FY 1988/89. An Energy Master Plan has been formulated for integrated energy planning up to the year 2000 with emphasis on further expansion of the rural electrification programme.

(c) Social development

The family planning programme was further consolidated in FY 1988/89 on the basis of progress made and experience gained so far. Educational and motivational programmes for small family norms have been pursued. The policy of assigning a greater role to non-governmental organizations in family planning activities has continued. The development of a network of fixed health care centres and home services in rural areas is at the heart of the health programme for FY 1988/89. The education and manpower improvement programmes emphasize primary and mass education and reductions in drop-outs and course repetition. The mass education programme discontinued in 1982 has been revived, so as to step up the literacy rate.

3. *Measures to improve the physical infrastructure*

Major programmes in this sector include the provision of housing for low and middle-income groups, supply of safe drinking water, the improvement of sanitation in urban and rural areas and the implementation of physical and land-use master plans at the district and provincial levels. The transport and communications programme for FY 1988/89 has been geared to the improvement of the overall efficiency of the system, with emphasis on the operation and maintenance of existing equipment. The programme also provides for the expansion of the transport and communications networks, especially in rural areas, and the development of sea and inland ports.

4. *Measures to improve institutional capability in the field of development planning and policy*

Several important administrative reforms and improvements of national significance have been carried out in pursuance of the recommendations of the Committee on Administrative Reorganisation and Reforms of 1982. These policy reforms deal with the decentralization of decision-making responsibilities and the upgrading of the administrative capacity of local government in order to ensure effective participation of wider sections of the population in the development process. Moreover, implementation on schedule of development projects has been accorded high priority and is being closely monitored by the Government. In FY 1987/88 further steps were taken to deal with specific implementation problems, such as shortage of local currency, delays in project approval, recruitment of project personnel and land acquisition.

5. *International support measures*

Aid to Bangladesh continues to be coordinated under the World Bank's Consultative Group (CG) arrangement. During a meeting held in Paris in April 1988, pledges were announced in the order of $2 billion, which was roughly equal to the previous year's commitments. Moreover, an appeal was launched on 16 November 1988 at a meeting convened by the Secretary-General of the United Nations in New York in response to the emergency assistance needs of Bangladesh caused by the massive flooding of September 1988. During the course of the meeting, Governments and international organizations announced contributions totalling approximately $500 million. Similar appeals were addressed to donors by the UNCTAD Trade and Development Board at its September 1988 session.

6. *Impact of national policies and international support measures*

Despite the implicit praise the Government received from the traditional donors during the 1988 CG meeting for its macro-economic policies, for example its efforts to reduce the budget and current-account deficits, the maintenance of a realistic exchange rate, monetary restraint, liberalization policies and its handling of the 1987 floods, these measures had not yet produced a noticeable improvement in the lives of the people when Bangladesh became victim of yet another disastrous flood in late August-September and at the end of November 1988. Although no thorough assessment of the latest flood damage has been made, early United Nations estimates of the macro-economic impact point to a lowering of the rate of growth by one to two percentage points from an estimated 6 per cent. Widespread damage to the agricultural sector, factories and equipment has resulted in reduced production, scaled-down investments, lower government revenue and increased expenditure, reduced exports, an even more adverse balance-of-payments situation, and an increased rate of inflation further reducing the real level of consumption. This has added to the misery of those sections of the population which already suffer from endemic poverty.

BENIN

Benin, characterized by the predominance of its rural sector, has registered positive results in agriculture since 1985. In order to rehabilitate its economy, the Government has decided to strengthen the private sector and limit the investment budget to projects financed by international aid, with priority given to agriculture. Negotiations with the IMF with respect to a financial stabilization programme and with the World Bank concerning a structural adjustment programme have not yet been concluded.

1. *Improving the efficiency of resource use and allocation*

(a) Demand-management measures

Measures have been taken to rehabilitate public finances: (i) adoption of an austere 1988 budget with a $6.7 million deficit compared to one of $20 million in 1987; (ii) reduction of the public sector payroll by a freeze on new recruitment and the offer of early retirement for many serving staff members; (iii) blockage of housing allowances for civil servants; and (iv) provision of incentives to qualified public personnel to move to the private sector. A law foreseeing a provisional 10 per cent levy on civil service salaries as a contribution to the national economic effort, parallel to a similar deduction from the salaries of employees in semi-public and private companies, came into force in April 1988.

Benin has started to limit imports of goods, such as sugar and cement, that are produced locally. Distributors of such goods now have to source at least 50 per cent of their sales from local producers.

(b) Expanded role for the private sector and improving the efficiency of public enterprises

In December 1986, the World Bank approved a rehabilitation project of Beninese public enterprises with Swiss co-financing. The total cost of the project was estimated at $31.5 million, of which $15.0 million was provided by IDA, $8.4 million by the Swiss Government and $8.1 million by the Beninese Government, the latter to cover local costs.

In 1987, a review was initiated of 57 State-owned non-financial enterprises and banks. Of the former, six enterprises have been closed, while two others are expected to follow. A further 12 non-financial enterprises, including three whose operations had been suspended, have been selected for rehabilitation or privatization.

In order to improve the profit margins and productivity of public enterprises, the Government has delegated the decision-making powers in the areas of pricing, marketing and employment to enterprises' managers.

The banking system has been riddled with problems such as mismanagement, bad lending practices, particularly excessive lending to public enterprises which had performed very poorly in recent years, and severe liquidity problems. In order to solve these problems, restructuration and privatization of the existing banks have started. Thus, the Banque Commerciale du Benin (BCB) and the Banque Béninoise pour le Développement (BBD) have been privatized, while the Caisse Nationale de Crédit Agricole (CNCA) will be liquidated and replaced by a new institution.

2. Sectoral policies

(a) Food and agriculture

The agricultural sector acounts for about 47 per cent of GDP and 34 per cent of export earnings and employs 64 per cent of the active population. Along with rural development as a whole, it constitutes the priority sector within the Government's development strategy.

Measures adopted by the Government in support of this sector include provision of better-quality seeds, more agricultural tools, fertilizers and other inputs, the enlargement of extension services and better irrigation facilities. These measures have brought about increases in areas under cultivation and the diversification of agricultural production. The Government continues to import the bulk of the fertilizers and insecticides needed for agricultural production and has turned to its neighbours, particularly Côte d'Ivoire, for advice and co-operation.

An official food crop marketing agency (Office National des Céréales) was created in 1983 and its storage capacity developed in 1988 to avoid seasonal shortages in food crop supply and to solve storage and marketing problems. In April 1988, this agency took action to have the importation of potatoes temporarily banned by a ministerial decree due to a glut of the crop on the domestic market. Among the major cash crops produced (cotton, palm products, groundnuts, cocoa), cotton remains the most important in terms of marketed volume and value. It should further benefit in 1988 from a programme designed to improve marketing, harvesting and processing. This programme is co-financed by IDA, the French Caisse Centrale de Coopération Economique (CCCE), the International Fund for Agricultural Development (IFAD) and the West African Development Bank.

(b) Industry

Beninese industries are faced with problems of inadequate equipment, underutilization of installed capacity, limited market prospects and unfavourable cost/price ratios. The liquidation of some of the most unprofitable industries began in 1986.

(c) Energy

The Nangbeto dam, a joint venture between Benin and Togo with a 63 MW installed capacity, was completed in January 1988. It will reduce the country's reliance on imported energy by more than 30 per cent. Plans are being drawn up for a 40 MW dam at Adjarala, which is 100 km downstream from Nangbeto.

The United States-based Ashland Oil Company is negotiating to take over the Sémé oilfield. Selection of Ashland would reinvigorate production, which is now reported to be down to 6,000 b/d, as compared to 7,350 b/d in September 1986.

(d) Social development

A five-year plan (1988-1992) estimated to cost $4 million has been launched in co-operation with the United Nations Fund for Population Activities to implement a national policy on population.

3. Measures to improve the physical infrastructure

As part of the Government programme to increase the efficiency of the Port Autonome de Cotonou (PAC), the financial accounting system has been computerized, port statistics improved, and the basis for a training system established.

The Government has started to grant private firms access to the transportation sector and telephone network installations. In 1987 it undertook a $63 million project, financed by the World Bank and the European Development Fund, which aimed at improving the competitiveness of Benin's transit capacity towards its land-locked neighbours.

4. Measures to improve institutional capabilities in the field of development planning and policy

Early in 1988 the Government created a national commission entrusted with negotiations with the IMF and the World Bank. The work done so far by this commission, in agreement with the commission responsible for the preparation of the third development plan (1988-1992), has led to the drafting of a memorandum which, once it has been discussed with the IMF, should result in an authoritative Economic Policy Framework Paper.

5. *International support measures*

Foreign donors are awaiting an agreement between the Government and the IMF, before committing major new funding. In the meantime, they are confining their efforts to basic agricultural and infrastructural projects. The latter will receive a total of $70.5 million by 1992. Roads will receive the largest share ($55.6 million), followed by the Cotonou Free Port and two smaller ports ($13.3 million). Major donors of this programme are the African Development Fund, the West African Development Bank, the Islamic Development Bank and France.

In addition, France will provide $1.2 million for the road/rail link on which land-locked Niger depends for part of its imports and exports and which provides an important source of freight and service revenue for Benin.

Benin is now increasingly relying on multilateral aid sources as opposed to bilateral donors, which had almost exclusively financed the major investment projects of the late 1970s and early 1980s. It does not have any non-guaranteed private debt and has made only negligible drawings from the IMF.

6. *Overall assessment of the impact of national policies and international support*

Thanks to external help, improved results have been achieved in food and agriculture since 1985. Food crops registered a total production of 608,000 tons in 1986/87, which represents an 8.1 per cent increase compared to the previous season. Production in 1987/88 was expected to increase due to both favourable weather conditions and governmental action.

BHUTAN

1. *Improving the efficiency of resource allocation*

The fiscal year 1987/88[170] marks the first year of Bhutan's Sixth Five Year Development Plan (1987/88-1991/92). The Plan's overall strategy aims at achieving self-reliant growth through exploitation of Bhutan's hydro-electric, forestry and mineral resources.

(a) External sector policies

As a strategy to diversify export markets, the Government is encouraging the cultivation of non-traditional products (asparagus, mushrooms, herbal medicine) for markets other than India. Transit agreements have been concluded with India with a view to expanding trade with Bangladesh and Nepal. On the import side, stricter licensing has been enforced to curtail non-essential imports, particularly of luxury goods.

(b) Expanded role for the private sector

Private initiative is being encouraged through expanded access to credit facilities from the Bhutan Development Finance Corporation. The Government has launched a programme to train Bhutanese nationals for entrepreneurial and managerial jobs. State-controlled activities (e.g. retail trade in food) have been partially transferred to private hands.

170 The fiscal year (FY) ends on 31 March.

(c) *Improving the efficiency of the public sector*

The Government intends to consolidate its efforts begun during the Fifth Plan period to strengthen the public sector by a major reorganization of the bureaucracy through retrenchment exercises aimed at terminating unqualified personnel, eliminating unnecessary tasks and transferring other tasks to the private sector.

2. *Sectoral policies*

(a) *Agriculture and forestry*

The long-term objectives are to increase self-sufficiency in cereals, particularly rice, and to expand production of cash crops. Given the limited availability of arable land, emphasis is being placed on raising agricultural productivity through strengthening of extension services, increasing mechanization and improving financing facilities for farmers for the acquisition of inputs. Livestock breeding and the commercial production of dairy products are being encouraged by the expansion and upgrading of animal health services. Reforestation and salvage operations are underway to allow for exploitation of forest reserves on a sustained basis.

(b) *Industry and energy*

Industrial strategy aims at increased processing of indigenous raw materials, with emphasis on exportables. To this end, the share of manufacturing and mining in total Plan outlays will increase from 7 to 17 per cent under the Sixth Plan. Two-thirds of planned investments are earmarked for a cement plant intended to meet demand in India and Bangladesh. Industry will benefit from an assured and cheap supply of power from the Chukha hydro-electric project which was completed in early 1988. The Sixth Plan envisages further expansion of the hydro-electric generating capacity to meet the needs of households and local industries.

(c) *Social development*

The Government's medium-term priorities are to raise the availability of safe drinking water to 40 per cent of villages and otherwise improve sanitation for 30 per cent of villages. During the Sixth Plan period, the Government intends to develop packages of financial and technical assistance for villagers for home building and improvements in rural housing. The Sixth Plan envisages a doubling in nominal budgetary outlays for education, with emphasis on upgrading primary education and increasing secondary school enrolment.

3. *Measures to improve the physical infrastructure*

The completion in 1987 of a 600 km east-west highway, accessible to all types of vehicular traffic, marked a major milestone in Bhutan's development efforts. Economic activity in the less developed eastern and central regions will undoubtedly receive impetus from the improved road connections. The Sixth Plan envisages further extension of road linkages among major development sites. International traffic is expected to benefit from the recent purchase of a jet plane.

4. *Measure to improve institutional capabilities in the field of development planning and policy*

To enforce the tradition of self-help, the Government is gradually decentralizing development planning and entrusting implementation to the district levels and to rural communities. Government staff have been redeployed to rural areas to assist in strengthening local-management capabilities. The overriding constraint on development planning continues to be the lack of skilled personnel, a problem which is being addressed through extensive training and use of expatriate personnel.

5. *International support measures*

For the funding of its Sixth Plan outlays, Bhutan is seeking external support of about $450 million. Traditional budgetary support from India, the largest donor, is expected to accommodate roughly one-half of requirements. The balance is likely to come from other bilateral and multilateral donors, who were scheduled to convene in November 1988 within the framework of the UNDP round table meeting mechanism to address Bhutan's aid requirements.

6. *Impact of national policies and international support measures*

Aided by the generous support of the donor community, Bhutan continues to enjoy sustained growth with very modest inflation. From an average of about 6 per cent per annum in 1981-86, real GDP accelerated to an estimated 14 per cent in 1987 and a 10 per cent increase was projected for 1988. The main impetus for growth reflects the completion of the Chukha hydro-electric project and, to a lesser extent, increased output from the forestry sector. *Power generation* is expected to contribute some 10 per cent of GDP in 1988, up from under 4 per cent in 1986. Exports of electricity are expected to reduce the current account deficit with India - which accounts for 60 per cent of the global deficit - by some 40 per cent and boost government revenues by 50-60 per cent from the first to the final year of the Sixth Plan Period. Although statistical data are scarce, it is believed that the dominant *agricultural sector* has experienced moderate growth (about 5 per cent in each of the calendar years 1985 and 1986), attributable to expansion of cash crops such as potatoes and increased production of rice, oranges and apples. *Forestry* output, which had been declining through much of the early 1980s, resumed strong growth in 1986 and 1987 with the intensification of reforestation operations begun in the late 1970s.

Bhutan's high aid dependency is reflected in the very high ratio of aid disbursements to both GDP and imports, i.e. about 50 per cent in each case. Sustained external assistance has enabled the country to build up a comfortable level of hard-currency reserves - an estimated 11.8 months' import coverage as of end-March 1988 - despite the recent tripling of the chronic current-account deficit from about $10 million in fiscal year 1984/85 to an average level of about $30 million in the three subsequent fiscal years ending in 1987/88.

BOTSWANA

1. *Improving the efficiency of resource use and allocation*

(a) *External sector policies*

Since the introduction of the national currency, the pula, in 1976, Botswana has pursued flexible exchange-rate management and has also adopted a liberal exchange-control system, virtually free of restrictions on current international transactions. Government policy has been to build up foreign-exchange reserves as conditions on the world diamond market have improved following the slump in the early 1980s, and to minimize foreign borrowing. During the period 1982-1985, Botswana was not able to sell all its diamond output. The stockpile thus accumulated was disposed of in July 1987 against a share acquisition in De Beers Co. and a cash settlement. Since late 1986, a number of steps to further liberalize exchange-control regulations have been taken, including the relaxation of certain capital controls to give non-resident investors greater access to local financial resources. A new trade agreement with Zimbabwe was signed in September 1988.

(b) Demand-management measures

Since fiscal year 1983/84[171], Botswana has maintained an overall budget surplus and the Government has accumulated substantial cash balances. This has enabled the launching of some additional development programmes, such as the five-year P 500 million ($250 million) crash programme to speed up infrastructural improvements designed to provide serviced land for urban housing and for industrial and commercial development. However, government operations were being expanded relatively cautiously in view of the expected slow-down in revenue growth and the potential turn-around of the bugetary balance by the end of the current plan period in the early 1990s. In order to stimulate the demand for commercial bank credit and reduce the excess liquidity which had built up in the commercial banking system, the general level of interest rates was first reduced in September 1986. Further measures to reduce interest rates (e.g. a lowering of the prime rate) and move them towards a more market-oriented and flexible system were included in a comprehensive package of interest rate reform introduced at the beginning of 1988 and amended in July 1988.

(c) Mobilization of human resources

The shortage of skilled manpower is currently judged to be the single most significant constraint on Botswana's development. Increasing the supply of trained manpower, institution-building and localisation are priority objectives. Two basic training strategies have recently been developed, namely a training plan for the Botswana civil service and a proposed training programme for the private and parastatal sectors. Vocational and technical education is to be expanded and the apprenticeship and industrial training system developed.

(d) Role of the private sector and of public enterprises

The private sector is seen as the principal engine for future development and diversification of the economy and employment expansion. The Government is committed to creating an environment conducive to private initiative and investment and developing appropriate incentive structures. The Government's main direct incentive scheme is the Financial Assistance Policy (FAP), launched in 1982. Recent initiatives to deal with constraints on private-sector development include the reduction of interest rates, liberalization of exchange controls, and accelerated provision of serviced land, referred to above, and the creation of a mortgage scheme to facilitate access to funds for industrial and commercial property development by citizens. A national conference on strategies for private sector development, the first of its kind in Botswana, was held in July 1988.

Public enterprises are expected to be commercially oriented and financially self-supporting. A committee has been set up to review business regulations to see how the Government can remove the remaining obstacles to the efficient operation of the private and parastatal sectors.

2. Sectoral policies

(a) Food and agriculture

A National Food Strategy was adopted in late 1985, setting out four basic objectives: preparing post-drought recovery; achieving national self-sufficiency in main staples (maize and sorghum); ensuring a minimum diet; and building and maintaining a national capacity to deal with drought. A number of schemes, e.g. for arable land development and an accelerated rain-fed arable programme, have been set up to promote crop production. A small number of new commercial crop farms have been created in the Pandamatengo area in the north. The Government is also exploring the possibilities of irrigated agriculture in various parts of the country.

(b) Industry, energy and mining

An industrial development policy was adopted in 1984 and has the following main objectives: diversifying the economy and producing locally more of the goods and services consumed in Botswana; job creation; better regional distribution of income-earning opportunities; and increasing the participation of Batswana in business. A major evaluation

171 The fiscal year (FY) ends on 31 March.

of the FAP is being undertaken as part of efforts to strengthen the promotion of industrial development. Extension services for enterprise development have been integrated into one unit, the Integrated Field Services, which provides, *inter alia*, training to rural entrepreneurs. New initiatives under consideration are an expansion of labour-intensive diamond cutting, and a major new tannery. In the energy sector, the country's thermal power capacity (using coal from Morupule) is being expanded. A programme launched in 1987 aims to promote the use of coal by households as well as others. Expansion of the electricity network continues. A small gold mine near Francistown is under development and expected to start commercial production in FY 1988/89. Preparations for developing the Sua Pan soda-ash deposits were likewise under way. Other mineral exploration projects continue.

(c) *Social development*

Education received the third-largest allocation of development funds in the 1988/89 budget, to be used *inter alia* for the junior secondary education expansion programme and the renovation and improvement of existing schools. Secondary school fees were abolished as of the beginning of 1988. Primary education was already free. Extensive relief programmes were established to cope with the effect of drought on rural employment: in FY 1987/88, over 90,000 Batswana benefited from work and income-generating opportunities through such schemes.

3. *Measures to improve the physical infrastructure*

The provision of basic infrastructure is a high priority for the Government, which has continually allocated a high proportion of the annual development budgets to the development of transport and communications, including the improvement of links with the country's northern neighbours. A new all-weather airport is to be built near Kasane, and existing facilities at Gaborone and Maun airports are to be improved. Rehabilitation work has been undertaken in preparation for the take-over on the part of Botswana of the railway line running through the country. Telecommunications facilities are being further upgraded. A National Water Master Plan is under preparation. Ongoing projects include an emergency water relief programme for rural areas, as well as the improvement of the urban water supply.

4. *Measures to improve institutional capabilities in the field of development planning and policy*

Botswana's Sixth National Development Plan (1985-1991) came into operation in fiscal year 1985/86. Its two main objectives are rural development and employment creation. A mid-term review of the Plan's implementation was undertaken in 1988. Efforts have been made to decentralize the planning process, with planning units set up in the sectoral ministries and planning officers assigned to the local authorities.

5. *International support measures*

The net inflow of concessional aid to Botswana during the 1980s has remained relatively stable in nominal terms, fluctuating around a level of some $100 million annually. Other official flows such as bilateral and multilateral development financing on non-concessional terms have become increasingly important in recent years. Such inflows amounted to $70 million in 1986.

6. *Impact of national policies and international support measures*

Favourable economic trends continued in Botswana in 1986 and 1987. Real GDP was estimated to have grown by 14 per cent in NAY 1985/86[172] and by close to 15 per cent in NAY 1986/87. These results were largely due to the continued strong performance of the diamond sector. A particularly significant event was the sale of the diamond stockpile in July 1987, which contributed to a 66 per cent increase in total exports in pula terms during 1987 and to the large overall surplus recorded in the balance of payments and an increase in international reserves to new record levels. On a year-to-year basis, the rate of inflation decreased from 11 per cent in 1986 to 8 per cent in 1987. With revenue

172 The national accounts year (NAY) ends on 30 June.

growing at a faster rate than expenditure, again mainly due to the performance of the mineral sector, the overall surplus in the budget was much larger than originally anticipated in FY 1986/87. A similar budget outturn was expected for FY 1987/88. After six years of drought, there was good rainfall in the 1987/88 season.

Overall growth prospects for NAY 1987/88 were still favourable, with diamond markets remaining firm, expected improvements in agricultural output as the drought ended and a marked acceleration in construction activity. However, the impressive overall growth rates mask sectoral imbalances in growth, and longer-term prospects are more uncertain. During the 1980s, the performance of agriculture and manufacturing, the two key sectors on which the Government's objectives of economic diversification and employment creation are focused, has not been particularly encouraging. Agricultural growth has been negative due to the prolonged drought, and the rural economy has suffered severely. Despite the good rains in the 1987/88 season, the contribution of the livestock sector and crop output to national income might continue to decline; significant improvement in these sectors will require at least several seasons of good rains. The share of manufacturing in GDP actually halved from 6 per cent in NAY 1981/82 to only 3 per cent in NAY 1986/87. The expansion of diamond production has come to an end, and apart from the Sua Pan project, there are currently no plans for major new mining developments. Longer-term prospects are also affected by Botswana's continued vulnerability to drought and to changes in the international economic environment, as well as by a high population growth rate, which is expected to exert considerable pressure on the country's physical and social infrastructure and its fragile environment in the foreseeable future.

BURKINA FASO

Following the overthrow of the Government on 15 October 1987, a *programme de rectification* was launched, involving some policy changes in the socio-economic field, as mentioned below. However, the basic objectives of the national economic development strategy outlined in October 1983 remain unchanged, namely self-sustained development through the full mobilization of the national population, self-sufficiency in food, and strong reliance on economic planning.

1. *Improving the efficiency of resource use and allocation*

(a) External sector policies

A fruit import ban, introduced in April 1987, was lifted by the new Government in November of the same year.

(b) Demand-management measures

For the first time since 1982, the minimum wage of workers and salaries in the public sector have been raised (by 14.6 per cent and by around 6 per cent respectively). Public employees dismissed by the previous Government (mainly teachers) have been reinstated. The financial implications of these measures for the central Government have been estimated at CFAF 3.4 billion (around $11.5 million). The 1988 budget provides for a deficit of CFAF 5.99 billion (around $20 million), as compared to an actual deficit of CFAF 5.4 billion ($18 million) in 1987.

(c) Mobilization of domestic savings

Burkina Faso and the Libyan Arab Jamahiriya have established a joint venture bank with headquarters at Ouagadougou and an initial capital of CFAF 800 million ($2.7 million).

(d) Mobilization of human resources

The full mobilization of the national population continues to be considered the key instrument for achieving national socio-economic development. With a view to "organizing and mobilizing the masses", the new Government has established Revolutionary Committees (CRs), which replace the former Committees for the Defense of the Revolution (CDRs). The Committees encompass all major sectors of the population, e.g. youth, women, peasants, workers, civil servants and the military. Peasant co-operatives are to be promoted as well (cf. section 2(a) below).

(e) Role of the public and private sectors

The national development strategy stresses the importance of a strong public sector for securing socio-economic development. To this end, the strategy calls for the development of "state capitalism", namely the expansion and streamlining of parastatal enterprises and of joint ventures involving State participation. The private sector, both national and foreign, is invited to participate in national economic development "in conformity [...] with the areas of action which have been attributed to it". In June 1988, the Council of Ministers agreed to ratify the international convention for the creation of the World Bank-sponsored Multilateral Investment Guarantee Agency (MIGA).

2. Sectoral policies

(a) Food and agriculture

Food self-sufficiency is one of the key national policy objectives. The promotion of peasant co-operatives as well as public investment in agriculture and agro-industry are among the major instruments to be used towards this end. The new Government has furthermore expressed the intention of intensifying research in agriculture, and support for this endeavour has been received from IDA ($17.9 million).

Producer prices for cereals have been raised by the new Government (25 per cent for maize and millet), whereas those paid to cotton producers were reduced by around 5 per cent in response to depressed world market prices.

The Minister for Commerce has warned cereals traders that speculation and unauthorized exports of cereals would be sanctioned. To discourage speculation, 80,000 mt of cereals were to be thrown onto the market in 1988 (one-half thereof imported).

(b) Industry and energy

External financial support has been secured for the expansion of the national cotton-ginning capacity (from 120,750 mt to 180,000 mt per year, i.e. by 49 per cent), as well as for the construction of a packaging materials factory with a capacity of 4,000 mt of cartons per year, which covers most of the needs of exporters of fruits and vegetables.

(c) Social development

A family planning policy has been in operation since 1983, involving *inter alia* the legalization of contraceptives and the supply of relevant clinical services. During the first two years of the development plan period 1986-1990, the rate of execution of social development projects was as follows: 60 per cent of the 8,200 water points to be constructed in rural areas, the medium-term target on the way towards a supply of 20 litres of potable water per day and per person by the year 2000; 43 per cent of 3,343 projected classrooms; and 54 per cent of the projected health centres.

(d) Environment

The authorities are promoting the use of butane gas and of fuel-efficient stoves (*foyers améliorés*), so as to prevent deforestation. Between 50,000 and 150,000 ha of forest are destroyed annually for fuelwood consumption purposes. The consumption of butane gas has increased by more than 50 per cent since 1984, as more than 100,000 *foyers améliorés* were installed during 1985 and 1986.

3. Measures to improve the physical infrastructure

External support has been secured for the construction of a dam at Bagré, with an irrigation capacity of 7,500 ha. Construction was to start by the end of 1988 and was expected to last six years.

Due to financial difficulties, and at the request of Côte d'Ivoire, the jointly owned railway company which administered the 1,170 km railway linking the capitals of the two countries has been liquidated and replaced by two separate national companies. The construction of the 104 km railway linking Ouagadougou to Kaya and Tambao (CFAF 10 billion, or about $34 million) is under way, with 72 km having been laid as of mid-1988.

4. Measures to improve institutional capabilities in the field of development planning and policy

The recently established Revolutionary Committees (see section 1(d) above) are expected to play a major role in the implementation at the local level of national development policies.

5. International support measures

Bilateral ODA from DAC member countries reached $175 million in 1986, which is above the 1981 peak of $158 million and the annual average of $124 million recorded during the period 1983-1985. Likewise, concessional assistance from DAC-financed multilateral agencies reached $89 million in 1986, as compared to $69 million in 1985. OPEC countries have increased their concessional assistance to Burkina Faso more than tenfold since 1984 (from $1 million in 1984 to $11 million in 1986). Concessional assistance from all sources represented 101.6 per cent of imports in 1986.

A World Bank mission visited the country in June 1988 to negotiate the terms of a possible structural adjustment loan.

6. Impact of national policies and international support measures

The average annual rate of growth during the period 1980-1986 is estimated at merely 1.7 per cent, which is below the corresponding rate in the 1970s (1.9 per cent) and the current population growth rate (2.7 per cent). An improvement of the GDP growth rate was recorded both in 1985 and 1986, when it grew at 6.7 and 5.6 per cent respectively, after having declined in 1983 (-4.2 per cent) and 1984 (-0.9 per cent). Recovery has been made possible to a large extent by the relatively improved weather conditions since 1985; thus, agricultural production, which is a driving force in the national economy, recovered in 1985 and 1986 to annual growth rates of 22.3 and 12.6 per cent, respectively. Inflation rates were kept at an annual average of 6.2 per cent during the period 1980-1986, as compared to 9.1 per cent in the 1970s.

Total external debt rose to 53 per cent of GDP in 1986 from 41 per cent in 1985, whereas the debt service/export ratio was kept at 15 per cent between 1982 and 1986, with the exception of 1985 when it reached 19 per cent.

BURMA

1. Improving the efficiency of resource allocation

Burma's long-term development strategy is set out in its 20-year Development Plan (FY 1974/75 - FY 1993/94[173]), which is being carried out in a series of Four-Year Plans, the fifth of which (FY 1986/87 - FY 1989/90) is currently being implemented.[174] The broad objectives of the 20-year Plan are: the acceleration of economic growth within the context of a socialist

173 The fiscal year (FY) ends on March 31.

174 The 20-year Plan was first adopted in 1972, but implementation was delayed until the Second Plan, beginning in fiscal 1974/75.

system, reduction of unemployment and income disparities, and an increase in the country's economic self-sufficiency through a gradual transition from an agricultural to an agro-industrial economy.

(a) External sector policies

Export development efforts are geared to increasing the supply of exportable rice through expansion and upgrading of storage and milling facilities. In February 1988, the Government decontrolled rice exports, ending over 20 years of State monopoly in foreign trade. However, as of March 1988 the response from the private sector was limited, since domestic wholesale prices remained above the international price when converted at the overvalued official rate of exchange. Burma has increasingly resorted to countertrade in an effort to expand its external trade and to overcome import bottlenecks. A urea plant installed during 1987 by a firm based in the Federal Republic of Germany was financed through a buy-back arrangement; the installation of a liquified gas plant involved a similar arrangement.

(b) Demand-management measures

In response to growing foreign exchange shortages, the Government has maintained tight restrictions on capital expenditures, imports and non-concessional borrowing ever since FY 1983/84. Emphasis is being placed on completing ongoing projects, with priority being given to those with low capital-output ratios, short gestation periods and showing an export potential. In September 1987, about 58 per cent of the currency in circulation was demonetized, but despite an immediate price stabilization these measures failed to brake the underlying pressure of inflation and the parallel exchange market during the course of 1988.

(c) Mobilization of domestic savings

Mobilization of domestic savings has been a major problem ever since the country's independence. The most recent adjustment in interest rates occurred in 1977, when nominal savings bank deposit rates were raised from 6 to 8 per cent in a bid to mobilize savings. A three-year deposit continues to earn an additional 2 per cent, while the yields on 12-year savings certificates were raised from 7.6 to almost 11 per cent. Measures have been introduced since fiscal 1986/87 to strengthen the tax administration and increase non-tax fiscal income by raising water rates and tolls on highways and bridges.

(d) Expanded role of the private sector

Although Burma's economy is centrally controlled, private initiative predominates in small-holder agriculture, domestic trade (especially in the parallel market), transport and small-scale manufacturing. In September 1987, the Government liberalized prices and decontrolled domestic trade in rice and other staples, ending over 25 years of state monopoly. In early 1988 the authorities announced measures to allow private traders to pay their taxes in kind rather than in cash under a new system controlled by the Private Enterprises Rights Law.

(e) Improving the efficiency of public entreprises

Burma's last major initiative in rehabilitating State economic enterprises (SEE) dates back to the mid-1970s, when the SEEs were put on a quasi-commercial footing and given autonomy over administrative and financial matters. A system of incentives introduced in the late 1970s to increase managerial and worker efficiency through a bonus scheme continues to operate.

2. Sectoral measures

(a) Agriculture and forestry

Agricultural strategy is aimed at achieving regional self-sufficiency in food, enhancing the agricultural export potential and increasing the availability of agro-inputs to industry. This strategy has been sustained by the introduction of (a) high-yielding varieties of rice and other crops, (b) more efficient farm management, (c) improved technologies, (d) more intensive crop monitoring, and (e) greatly strengthened extension services. In the area of *forestry*, the strategy aims at increasing domestic value added by developing sawing capacity, plywood production and a furniture industry.

(b) Industry and energy

Government priorities in the industrial sector are geared towards the maximum utilization of domestic resources in promoting both import substitution and export industries. Short-term plans toward this end call for the rehabilitation of 120 rice mills to increase processing capacity. Over the medium term, investments in other processed foodstuffs (such as sugar), textiles and fertilizers are being emphasized. To encourage capacity utilization, the Government is giving foreign-exchange priority to imported industrial inputs. Moreover, advance payments are being made to farmers to stimulate the supply of agricultural inputs to industry. Recent policy initiatives in *mining* have been geared to the modernisation and expansion of a number of mines and smelting plants. A small gold mine is scheduled to begin operations in late 1989. *Energy* policy emphasizes self-reliance through effective utilization and development of indigenous energy resources, particularly by way of more intensive exploration of crude oil and natural gas. At the same time, the Government is vigorously encouraging the substitution of liquid fuels with natural gas, of which Burma has abundant reserves.

(c) Social development

Significant progress has been made in eradicating illiteracy. By 1986, illiteracy had been wiped out in 234 out of 255 townships covered by rural literacy programmes. Thus, an estimated 1.9 million formerly illiterate adults are now literate. Burma has endeavoured to gear the education system to the needs of the economy. In FY 1986/87, a new education curriculum was introduced with the aim of training technicians and skilled workers to accommodate the manpower needs of the manufacturing sector.

3. Measures to improve the physical infrastructure

Recent investments in the transportation infrastructure have included the upgrading of the main north-south trunk roads, which had last been improved before the Second World War. A major renovation of the Rangoon airport is also going on to accommodate an increasing number of visitors, as the country gradually opens up to tourism. To counter the shortage of rolling stock, buses and trucks have been converted for use on rails for short-haul passenger traffic.

4. Measures to improve institutional capabilities

Burma has emphasized the development of her indigenous research capacity in key areas. Internationally supported technical assistance for agricultural research, development and extension services has been a driving force in crop diversification and expansion of high-yielding varieties of paddy.

5. International support measures

During 1987, the Federal Republic of Germany committed the equivalent of approximately $23 million to finance inputs for ongoing projects; moreover, it cancelled previous loans amounting to $29 million. China committed itself to extending a $20 million loan to supplement earlier funding for the Rangoon-Syriam Bridge Project. Early in 1988, Japan agreed to provide $23 million worth of programme aid for general import support.

6. Impact of national policies and international support measures

Burma's economic performance has steadily deteriorated through much of the 1980s as adverse external disruptions have exacerbated the effects of economic management. After averaging 5 per cent over the Fourth Plan Period (FY 1982/83 - FY 1985/86), real GDP growth decelerated to 3.7 per cent in FY 1986/87 and is provisionally estimated at 2.2 per cent in FY 1987/88. Declining GDP growth is reflected in slower growth in *agriculture* (including livestock and fisheries) - around 1 per cent in FY 1987/88, down from a peak of 6.8 per cent in FY 1982/83 - stemming from a combination of adverse weather conditions, limited supplies of inputs and the erosion of the benefits from the paddy intensification programme instituted in the late 1970s. In FY 1987/88 output from *forestry*, the main foreign-exchange earner in recent years (replacing rice), remained stagnant because of constraints on logging and transportation due to power shortages; *mining* output declined marginally in real terms as the decline in oil production more than offset significant increases in the production of metals and coal and *manufacturing* remained stagnant as shortages of fuel and other inputs constrained capacity utilization.

Burma's external payments position has progressively deteriorated since 1982 with the exacerbation of the long-term structural decline in its terms of trade and rising debt-service payments. Import compression helped to narrow the current account deficit to 3.7 per cent of GDP in FY 1986/87 from 4.3 per cent in FY 1985/86. The sharp deterioration in its economic performance during the 1980s obliged Burma to apply for least-developed country status, which it obtained in December 1987 under General Assembly resolution 42/428. This event may open prospects for more relief for Burma's external debt, which was estimated to have reached $3.1 billion at the end of March 1988. Public debt service absorbed some 70 per cent and 75 per cent of export earnings in FY 1986/87 and FY 1987/88 respectively. The growing pressures on Burma's external liquidity were reflected in the emergence of arrears during FY 1987/88 and a vulnerable international reserve position. Even after a modest recovery, exchange reserves stood at less than $70 million at the end of June 1988, corresponding to little more than three months of the drastically reduced import level registered in 1987.

BURUNDI

1. Improving the efficiency of resource use and allocation

Burundi initiated an economic adjustment programme in 1986, aiming to redress economic and financial imbalances and to promote a medium and long-term restructuring of the economy by stimulating the productive sectors and private investment. The programme entered its second phase in 1988 with the adoption of a new package of policy reforms supported, like the first phase, by funding from the World Bank and the IMF.

(a) External sector policies

Among the first measures of implementation of Burundi's adjustment programme was the adoption of a flexible exchange-rate policy starting with a devaluation of the Burundi franc in July 1986. Between that date and March 1987, the Burundi franc was devalued by 24 per cent against the SDR to which it is pegged. It was again devalued by a cumulative total of 20 per cent during the first nine months of 1988. Most import and price controls have been removed and a major tariff reform initiated. New emphasis is being given to strengthening regional co-operation and developing regional trade opportunities. Duties on manufacturing exports have been abolished. Producer prices for Burundi's two main export commodities, coffee and tea, were raised in real terms for the 1986/87 crop year. Among the measures taken to strengthen debt management, an interministerial committee has been set up to monitor Burundi's external debt and advise on new borrowing.

(b) Demand-management measures

Interest rates have been adjusted and raised to provide incentives to private savings and improve credit allocation. An important aim of the economic adjustment programme adopted in 1986 was to reduce credit expansion, in particular net credit to the Government. Steps were taken to improve tax collection, restrain Government expenditure growth and eliminate domestic payments arrears. Restrictive public expenditure policies will be pursued during the second phase of the adjustment programme, the aim being to reduce the budget deficit as a share of GNP from some 12 per cent in 1987 to 5 per cent in 1991. Public expenditure programming and budget management are being strengthened to this end. Further steps are also being taken to develop the tax system, particularly revenue sources other than coffee. The second phase of the adjustment programme foresees a further liberalization of financial markets.

(c) Mobilization of domestic savings and human resources

The co-operative movement is of some importance in Burundi generally and in the country's rural development efforts in particular. The first of a new type of savings and credit co-operatives operating in rural areas was set up in 1985, and the network of such institutions is being expanded. The pilot stage of a new project aiming to give rural women access to credit for revenue-generating activities was to be launched in 1988.

(d) Expanded role for the private sector and improving the efficiency of public enterprises

An expanded role for the private sector is envisaged, e.g. in industry. Limits on outward foreign remittances have been raised and the country's investment code has been revised to promote private investment. A Guarantee Fund has been created to facilitate access of small and medium-scale enterprises to bank credit. The Chamber of Commerce and Industry is to be strengthened. Reform of the public enterprise sector also forms an important part of the economic adjustment programme. Four loss-making public enterprises have been closed, and rehabilitation programmes formulated for a number of others. An administrative service in charge of public enterprises was set up in 1987 to oversee this reform.

2. Sectoral policies

Burundi's Fifth Five-Year Plan, covering the years 1988-1992, was being finalized in the course of 1988. Under the new Plan, special efforts will be made to develop the directly productive sectors, i.e. agriculture, industry, energy and mining. These sectors are to be allocated over one-half of planned investments of FBu 159 billion (about $1 billion) under the Fifth Plan. Priority will be given to agriculture, the conservation and rehabilitation of the country's physical infrastructure and natural resources, the diversification and promotion of exports, the promotion of small and medium-scale enterprises and the redistribution of incremental output among sectors directly affecting the population, such as health, education, etc.

(a) Food and agriculture

The maintenance of food self-sufficiency will remain the primary objective under the Fifth Plan, together with improving nutritional levels and raising the output and quality of the export crops (coffee, tea and cotton.) Agriculture is to receive over 30 per cent of planned investment under the new Plan.

(b) Industry, energy and mining

Industrial policy under the Fifth Plan will aim at promoting export production, with emphasis on local raw materials, as well as at import substitution. Objectives in the energy sector are to develop domestic energy resources and improve the supply of energy to rural areas and for industrial and artisanal activities. Mineral exploration will continue.

(c) Social development and infrastructure

Among social development objectives are universal primary school enrolment and "health for all", emphasizing social and preventive medicine. Family planning is one element of the maternal and child health programme. Efforts will also be made to provide an adequate supply of drinking water to all households by the year 2000, and to develop social housing and secondary urban centres. Special attention is being paid to the social dimensions of adjustment: the Government has sought external financing to prepare social action programmes in this context and will set up a special unit to co-ordinate the preparation and implementation of such programmes.

3. Measures to improve the physical infrastructure

A major part of public investment during the 1980s has been allocated to transport infrastructure and road-building. As a landlocked country, Burundi depends on long transit routes to the nearest seaports on the Indian Ocean. A master plan has been elaborated for the port of Bujumbura, which serves the central transit corridor. Priorities during the current Plan period will be to maintain and extend the road network, to further improve transit transport links and to develop air transport. The postal and communications infrastructure is also to be improved.

4. *Measures to improve institutional capabilities in the field of development planning and policy*

A monitoring committee at ministerial level has been set up to co-ordinate and follow up the implementation of the structural adjustment programme. A three-year rolling public investment programme has been introduced, and a budget reform aiming to establish a consolidated budget and a comprehensive public expenditure programme are under preparation. As part of the effort to strengthen overall economic management and the planning and programming of human resources, a national seminar on technical assistance was held in September 1988.

5. *International support measures*

The first phase of Burundi's economic adjustment programme was supported by a structural adjustment credit of $31 million from IDA and its Special Facility for sub-Saharan Africa, accompanied by joint financing of $19 million from bilateral donors; a stand-by arrangement with the IMF running from August 1986 to March 1988 (no drawings were made under this arrangement); and a loan of SDR 27 million under IMF's Structural Adjustment Facility (SAF). The second tranche of the SAF loan, equivalent to almost one-half of the total loan, was drawn in May 1988. In June 1988, a second structural adjustment credit was extended by IDA in support of the programme; the IDA credit itself amounted to $90 million, and an additional $27 million was anticipated as co-financing from bilateral donors. IDA project lending to Burundi has also been stepped up, with four credits for agriculture and rural development, population and health, education and enterprise promotion totalling $63.5 million extended in 1987 and 1988. Burundi is one of the countries identified as eligible for assistance under the World Bank's special action programme for low-income debt-distressed countries in sub-Saharan Africa.

A Round Table Meeting with Burundi's development partners, to be held in Bujumbura, to present development policies and planned projects throughout the Fifth Plan period was scheduled for 1989. A preparatory meeting for the Round Table Meeting was held with the main donors in Geneva in July 1988, presenting the main outline of the Fifth Plan and examining the policy measures undertaken or proposed in the context of the short-term adjustment programme.

6. *Impact of national policies and international support measures*

Burundi's policy performance under the first phase of its adjustment programme was lauded by donors at the July 1988 preparatory meeting, which also expressed its strong support for the recently adopted policy measures intended to extend the programme and introduce further reforms. However, while policy performance has been largely in line with the programme, objectives were not fully met. Real GDP at market terms is estimated to have grown by close to 5 per cent in 1986, above the average growth rate of Burundi's GDP previously in the decade. Inflation remained low in 1986 and both the budget and the balance-of-payments deficits decreased slightly as a share of GDP. The growth in manufacturing exports, albeit from a small base, has been particularly encouraging. However, the overall redressment expected under the adjustment programme has largely been obliterated by the sharp drop in world coffee prices, the impact of which began to be felt as early as 1986 and came to dominate the evolution of Burundi's economy in 1987. The terms of trade deteriorated by about 40 per cent in 1987. With the volume of coffee exports dropping by about one-third from the 1986 level, coffee export earnings in FBu decreased by 65 per cent in 1987. Consequently, the budgetary and balance-of-payments situation again deteriorated. External debt service payments jumped to well over 40 per cent of export earnings in 1987. Targets for the second phase of the adjustment programme have been revised, taking into account the worsened economic prospects. Additional financing needs identified at the July 1988 donors' meeting amounted to $148 million for the period 1988-1990.

CAPE VERDE

1. *Improving the efficiency of resource allocation*

Because of its limited resources, Cape Verde has been unable to generate a level of production of goods and services capable of sustaining domestic demand. The level of consumption and investment, which is much higher than GDP, is sustained to a large extent by proportionately large amounts of external assistance and emigrants' remittances. The bulk of the investment programme under the Second National Development Plan (1986-1990) comes from external sources, mostly as grants and soft loans, with counterpart resources being generated by the sale of food aid. Cape Verde is acknowledged to be managing the use of resources at its disposal with wisdom and integrity. However, it is proving difficult to identify projects which provide an adequate economic rate of return.

One illustration of the lack of local productive investment opportunities is provided by the purchase by Cape Verde in 1987 of 10,700 hectares of prime land in Paraguay (for $1.12 million), which is intended for maize cultivation, forestry and livestock production under the management of Cape Verdian agronomists. This area is equivalent to one-quarter of total cultivated land in Cape Verde and more than five times that under irrigation.

The Cape Verde escudo is pegged to a basket of currencies. With respect to the US dollar, the escudo has appreciated over the past few years from nearly 90 escudos to the dollar in 1985 to 77 escudos in September 1988.

2. *Sectoral policies*

(a) Agriculture

Agriculture has a very limited potential in Cape Verde. The Government, with the help of many aid partners and FAO, has a large number of projects to support the agricultural sector and rural development more generally, but output is much more dependent on the pattern of rainfall than on Government policies. This is clearly apparent in the performance of the main crops following the good rainfalls in 1986 and 1987, as contrasted with the earlier part of the decade, which was marked by drought or erratic rainfall. Thus, production of the main cereal (maize), which was slightly over 2,000 tons on average in 1983-1985, exceeded 12,000 tons in 1986 and 21,000 tons in 1987. However, even this record crop represents less than one-third of cereal consumption needs. The livestock population, whose level is critically dependent on the availability of fodder, also increased in 1986 and 1987, although to a lesser extent than the output of fodder, of which there was an excess supply by 1987. The major part of the scarce irrigated land is used for sugar cane, intended to produce local rum. The Government has imposed a tax on the acreage under sugar cane in order to incite farmers to diversify into other crops.

(b) Fishing

Fisheries, particularly tuna, are one of the main resources of Cape Verde. This sector has been receiving increasing attention. For instance, allocations in the Second National Development Plan (1986-1990) have been increased to over 6 per cent of total investment, as compared to only 2 per cent in the First Plan. One of the factors that constrain catches is the lack of small fish (as bait) during the main fishing season. The Secretariat of State for Fisheries has been undertaking efforts since 1987 to keep and raise bait fish in captivity. Lobsters also offer a good potential. In this area, improvements are being sought in the nets utilized and in conservation methods after capture.

(c) Industry

Cape Verde, with its small and fragmented market, seems to have approached the limit for import substitution industries. For instance, the major industrial project - a cement factory on the island of Maio, which was to cost $29 million and for which a loan from the African Development Bank had been secured - had to be suspended in February 1988 as it was not considered to be economically viable. Although a number of industrial projects aimed at the domestic market were presented (e.g. ceramic, soap, oxygen and acetylene plants) at a Solidarity Ministerial Meeting for Co-operation in Industrial Development organized by UNIDO in Cape Verde in December 1987, the Second National Development Plan has clearly indicated that for the longer-term future Cape Verde plans to develop outward-oriented industries and activities, so that the country can fully participate in the international division of labour. Some manufacturing entreprises have had some success in exporting, notably in pharmaceuticals and in garments, where large repeat orders for military uniforms have been received from Angola. The Cabnave Shipyard, a major investment undertaken in the early 1980s, is reported to be working at a higher capacity in 1988 than in early years. It is acknowledged, however, that the transformation of Cape Verde into an internationally competitive economy will take a number of years.

(d) Transport

The loss of earnings from the drastic diminution of South African Airways traffic due to the ban on landing rights of that company in the United States since 1986 has been estimated by the Ministry of Foreign Affairs to amount to $6 million per annum. The Government is seeking to attract other airlines to Sal airport, and facilities have been improved since 1987 to make this more attractive. In order to maintain the link with Boston, where a large Cape Verdian community resides, the national airline (TACV) has leased an aircraft from the Mozambican airlines since April 1987.

(e) Education

The level of illiteracy, estimated at 45 per cent among the population aged 15 years or above in 1986, remains a major development bottleneck. Reform of the education system to improve its efficiency and to meet the country's needs is one of the objectives of the Second National Development Plan. Part of this reform is being carried out by means of a primary education project financed by the World Bank ($5.3 million). This project, which started in 1988, will help to replace the present two-cycle primary school system with a single six-year cycle and aim at reducing the large number of drop-outs.

CENTRAL AFRICAN REPUBLIC

The Five-Year Development Plan 1986-1990 outlined policies on agricultural development, the most important ones being the restructuring of cotton production, the reorganization of the public sector, comprising both the Government itself and the parastatals, and the creation of an environment to stimulate private investment. The Government's structural adjustment programme supported by the World Bank and the IMF is embedded in this Development Plan. The broad objective of the programme is to achieve positive real per capita income growth over the period up to 1990, while reducing the current-account deficit to a sustainable level.

1. Improving the efficiency of resource use and allocation

(a) External sector policies

The liberalization of the trade regime was a parallel process through which import quotas and licenses were abolished and the export authorization system was replaced by an export declaration system. The reform of the price and trade regimes is a far-reaching component of the adjustment programme. These measures, together with the liberalization of food-crop pricing and marketing, created a favourable environment for efficient resource allocation and for the development of agricultural and private investment.

(b) Demand-management measures

A new tax regime came into force on 1 January 1988. Controls have been relaxed and most goods are now sold at market prices. Food prices are estimated to have fallen by 6 per cent in 1987. Wages have been restrained and real salaries have fallen by 40 per cent over the four-year period 1983-1987. A plan to reduce the number of civil servants has started to be applied, and a programme of voluntary redundancies for 2,000 civil servants is currently under way. The 1988 budget estimated revenues at CFAF 45 billion ($152 million) and expenditures at CFAF 53 billion ($179 million), of which 45 per cent was earmarked for civil servants' salaries and 30 per cent for debt servicing.

(c) Mobilization of domestic savings

Domestic savings, which had improved in 1984 and 1985 (4.5 and 4.7 per cent of GDP), reversed to a negative position the following years due to increasing deficits of the Government and major public enterprises' accounts. To finance domestic investment, equivalent to 14.6 per cent of GDP, larger foreign capital resources are necessary during the present Development Plan than in the previous one.

(d) Expanded role for the private sector

During the last few years, the Government's endeavours to find private partners to manage some of the 25 mixed enterprises have been successful in the case of the petroleum-importing and the textile companies, while domestic private participation is under negotiation in two other parastatal companies. Urban and inter-urban passenger transport is provided by private transporters.

(e) Improving the efficiency of public enterprises

The Government has embarked on a comprehensive reform programme with a view to improving productivity and efficiency in the public enterprise sector, reducing the financial burden on the central Government budget and liberalizing the economic environment, especially pricing policy. The ultimate goal of the Government is to withdraw from non-strategic and productive sectors, either by privatizing or liquidating the parastatals concerned.

2. *Sectoral policies*

(a) Food and agriculture

The poor performance of agriculture in the last two years was mainly due to the situation in respect of crops, where falling world prices, particularly for coffee, cotton and timber, depressed production. To encourage the development of cash crops, the Government has pursued a policy of guaranteed producer prices (except for tobacco) maintained largely through the operations of the Caisse de Stabilisation et de Péréquation des Produits Agricoles (CAISTAB). Current development projects in the coffee and the cotton sectors reinforce the policy of encouragement. Food crop production in 1987 was enough to sustain self-sufficiency, following timely action to promote local food crops.

(b) Industry and energy

Government policy is aimed at promoting small and medium-scale manufacturing enterprises.

(c) Export development and diversification

Government policy is encouraging the small miners of diamonds to use official export channels, *inter alia* by reducing export taxes from 18 per cent to 10 per cent.

3. *Measures to improve the physical infrastructure*

Because of the country's land-locked position, road and river transport are of vital importance to economic development. The rehabilitation of the road network has progressed significantly during recent years through the implementation of various projects.

4. Measures to improve institutional capabilities in the field of development planning and policies

The High Commission for Planning, the Co-ordinating Committee for Economic and Financial Policy, and the Ministry of Economy and Finance are becoming the Government's key institutions for preparing the national investment programme and reform policies.

5. International support measures

Credits from IDA and the Special Facility for sub-Saharan Africa, totalling $30 million, as well as a Structural Adjustment Facility (SAF) arrangement for SDR 19.3 million with the IMF, supported the implementation of the country's structural adjustment programme. The Central African Republic is to appeal to the Paris Club for a rescheduling of its public debt and it is eligible to draw up to SDR 76 million under the enhanced structural adjustment facility (ESAF). Budgetary support from France amounted to FF 92 million ($15.3 million) in 1987, and backing on a similar scale was anticipated for 1988.

6. Impact of national policies and international support measures

GDP grew by only 1.5 per cent in 1987, as against a target of 3.3 per cent foreseen in the structural adjustment programme. The 7 per cent reduction of the consumer price level rate in 1987 was mainly due to the slowdown in general economic activity. Attempts at diversifying the agricultural sector have not yet contributed significantly to overall performance.

CHAD

1. Improving the efficiency of resource use and allocation

Chad continues to implement policy measures aimed at improved resource use which were set forth in the Interim Development Plan for 1986-1988, presented at the UNDP-sponsored Round Table Conference held in December 1985, and for which international support has been granted (see section 5 below). The cessation of military strife will undoubtedly permit the Government to concentrate efforts on reconstruction and economic recovery.

(a) External sector policies

Measures having implications for the external sector relate to the streamlining of the cotton marketing board, the termination of the meat and cattle export monopoly, and the expected resumption of import-competing oil drilling, all described in greater detail below.

(b) Demand-management measures

The measures recently taken to contain public expenditure include:

(i) Reduction in personnel and salary cuts in the central government and in parastatal enterprises, notably in the case of the cotton marketing board; and

(ii) Measures to limit operational costs in the public sector, such as the decree adopted in March 1988 restricting telephone calls by government officials, whose cost had reached an annual average of CFAF 400 million (about $1.3 million).

(c) Mobilization of domestic savings and human resources

A number of professional associations (labour unions and a trade association called Union nationale des commerçants du Tchad) have recently seen the light of day. Rural development projects are being implemented with international support, including one which foresees the settlement of around 1,100 families in the Lake Chad region.

(d) Expanded role for the private sector

Private initiative is welcome. Substantial tax incentives are offered to foreign investors, the length of the incentive period varying with the amount of the investment (e.g. up to 25 years for investments amounting to $25 million or more). The export monopoly held by the State-owned Sotera in cattle and meat exports (the main export item after cotton) was terminated in April 1988.

(e) Improving the efficiency of public enterprises

The salient feature in this regard relates to the streamlining of Cotontchad, the 75-per-cent State-owned cotton marketing board, through measures initiated in 1986 with a view to reducing operating costs. These measures include:

(i) Freezing producers' prices at CFAF 100 per kg;

(ii) Setting a raw cotton purchase ceiling of 100,000 tonnes per year, which corresponds to the 1985 purchase level;

(iii) Removing subsidies granted to producers for the purchase of technical inputs;

(iv) Personnel cuts (from 2,500 in 1985 to 1,200 at present) and a salary freeze;

(v) Closing more than one-half of the 26 cotton gins; and

(vi) Establishing stricter management procedures at the marketing board.

2. Sectoral policies

(a) Food and agriculture.

The policy aimed at the liberalization of the marketing and prices of agricultural commodities has been pursued. Cereal imports (including food aid, which is sold at concessionary rates) have tended to depress local food prices and have thus had discouraging effects on local production. On the other hand, despite interventions of the marketing board, sharp price fluctuations have been recorded both between the pre-harvest and the post-harvest periods and between regions. Thus, in late 1986 the "coro" (1.7-kg unit) of millet was traded at CFAF 200 at Ndjamena and at only CFAF 100 about 30 km away. The wide fluctuations are explained to a large extent by the limited storage facilities and transportation network.

A priority programme relates to livestock development, which provides for the training of breeders, the reorganization of extension services, and the improvement of veterinary services and of water resource management.

(b) Industry and energy

The local manufacturing sector has been adversely affected both by the depressive effects of demand-management measures and by competitive supplies from neighbouring countries. Local manufacturing costs are magnified by electricity tariffs, which were three to nine times as high as in neighbouring countries in 1987, as well as by oil prices, which are higher than in the coastal countries because of transport costs.

Chad possesses oil reserves estimated at 70 million tonnes. Oil drilling had been affected by military unrest and by low world prices, but it is expected to resume soon.

(c) Social development

A project for the rehabilitation of the educational sector, estimated at around $24.3 million, is to be carried out with World Bank support. The project aims at improving the educational infrastructure, as well as the working and living conditions of teachers.

(d) Environment

The first week of August 1988 was consecrated as Tree Week (*semaine de l'arbre*), when reforestation was to be enhanced through the mobilization of the local population.

3. Measures to improve the physical infrastructure

The rehabilitation of 2,000 km of priority roads began in 1985 and is to be completed in the near future. A four-year plan for road development, amounting to CFAF 50 billion ($167 million) is to be launched with international financial support. Currently the country's paved roads do not exceed 253 km. A number of micro-irrigation projects are being implemented in the eastern region, the majority of which are being carried out by non-governmental organizations.

4. Measures to improve institutional capabilities in the field of development planning and policies

Technical assistance is being provided by IDA for the training of government officials in the assessment of the social impact of adjustment programmes.

5. International support measures

Bilateral ODA from DAC countries in nominal terms tripled from $31 million in 1981 to $96 million in 1985 and reached $102 million in 1986. Concessional assistance from DAC-financed multilateral agencies rose from $29 million in 1981 to $85 million in 1985 but fell to $61 million in 1986. Concessional assistance from all sources accounted for 87.2 per cent of imports in 1986.

Policy reforms outlined in the Interim Development Plan for 1986-1988 are supported by the IMF (through a three-year SAF loan of SDR 19.4 million approved on 30 October 1987), the World Bank Group (SDR 32.4 million), the African Development Bank and bilateral donors.

6. Impact of national policies and international support measures

After four consecutive years of decline, real GDP grew in both 1985 and 1986 by 6.9 and 5.2 per cent respectively. Recovery has been due to a large extent to improved weather conditions, which allowed agricultural production to recover by 23.2 per cent in 1985. However, the small (1.4 per cent) increase in 1986, followed by a 2.1 per cent decline of agricultural production in 1987, suggests that economic recovery may not be sustained.

COMOROS

There were no major changes of economic policy in the Comoros in 1986-1988. However, the deteriorating economic and financial situation (fall in export earnings leading to an increase in the current-account deficit, arrears on foreign debt) in 1987 and 1988 points to the need for adjustments in the near future. Negotiations for a structural adjustment loan have been in progress for some time. A World Bank/IMF/African Development Bank mission visited the country in November 1987 for this purpose, but by late-1988 no agreement had been reached. France, the major donor, has encouraged the Comoros to conclude such an agreement and embark on a structural adjustment programme (SAP). The structural reforms envisaged are likely to be supported by a World Bank structural adjustment loan of slightly over $7 million, together with an African Development Bank loan of an equivalent amount.

1. *Resource use and allocation*

(a) External sector policies

The Comoros is a member of the Franc Zone and the Comoro franc is equivalent to the CFA franc used in a number of Francophone African countries. No change is envisaged in exchange rates. A 16 per cent increase in the domestic price of rice (which represents 14 per cent of the import bill) was announced in November 1987. In order to limit the inflationary impact of this measure, as well as to save foreign exchange, the purchase of lower-quality rice was envisaged. Other increases in the domestic price of imported foods, including sugar, are expected to be part of the SAP package. The marketing of the main export product - vanilla - continues to be done through three trading houses. Direct sales by producers have been suggested, but there has been no change in current practice so far.

(b) Monetary and fiscal measures

There has been no alteration in the tax system, although revenue collection is acknowledged to be lax. The 1988 budget is virtually the same as that of 1987. In spite of the budgetary assistance from France, there is a global budget deficit. There are considerable government arrears, and in 1988 France agreed to pay off the Government's domestic debt amounting to $ 8.8 million.

(c) Role of the private sector

In 1987, the Government took over the foreign-owned plantation company Bambao for a token payment of one franc, as well as its commercial subsidiary (SAGC). However, in 1988, negotiations were reported with SANOFI, a transnational corporation in the perfume business, to buy the plantation, which would provide the company with a source of raw materials - vanilla and ylang-ylang - and assure the country of a dependable market for its principal export items. The meat-importing monopoly (SOCOVIA) was nationalized in 1987.

(d) Efficiency of public enterprises

A number of parastatals, including the post office and the power and water utility (Electricité et Eau des Comores), are reported to be working inefficiently. They would probably be the subject of restructuring under the proposed SAP. Given the difficult budgetary situation, the agricultural marketing board (Caisse de Stabilisation des Prix des Produits Agricoles) has had to use STABEX compensation payments to finance general government expenditures.

2. *Sectoral policies*

(a) Fisheries

In October 1987, a fisheries agreement was signed with the EEC, entitling 40 EEC tuna-fishing vessels to operate in Comorian waters.

(b) Agricultural exports - the vanilla crisis

Total exports (all agriculture-based) in 1987 were estimated at $11.5 million, corresponding to a reduction of 50 per cent in relation to the 1986 level ($20.37 million). This was largely due to the crisis in the vanilla market, inasmuch as vanilla represented 77 per cent of exports in 1986. The Comoros has been caught in a price war between the largest producer - Madagascar - and Indonesia, which has emerged as the world's second largest producer, although the vanillin content of the Indonesian product is not as high as that of its Indian Ocean counterpart. Indonesia has been selling its vanilla at about one-half the price agreed in the 25th Annual Vanilla Agreement (AVA) of March 1987, to which the Comoros, Madagascar and Reunion are parties. Madagascar in turn is also reported to have given large discounts on the AVA prices. Consequently, much of the Comoros vanilla production of 1987 has remained unsold. Traders could not afford to give discounts to overseas buyers in view of the high Government-fixed producer prices. The latter had been increased in March 1987, but were substantially reduced in 1988. The 26th AVA (April 1988) increased the annual export quota of the Comoros by 20 per cent to 180 tons, while that of Madagascar was reduced. A longer-term threat is the development of synthetic vanillin.

(c) Services: tourism

The largest hotel (190 rooms) of the Orchid Hotels Group was to open in the second half of 1988. This would double the room capacity in the islands and make a direct air link with Johannesburg viable. Air France is the only airline currently linking the country with Europe.

(d) Social development

Reforms in education have been taking place since 1986, but stricter control of standards is leading to decreases in pupil enrolment and in the number of teachers as the result of the dismissal of the unqualified ones.

All 11 health centres in the Archipelago and the hospital on one of the islands (Mohéli) have depended entirely on the presence of United Nations Volunteers in the 1980s. UNDP has decided to continue to finance this programme until 1991 by providing the services of 43 UNVs, some of whom will also work in education. Anti-malaria campaigns are continuing, supported mostly by WHO.

3. Measures to improve the physical infrastructure

In 1986, the first deep-water port of the country was completed at Mutsamudu (Anjouan). In 1988, the European Development Fund allocated funds for the construction of a jetty and the rehabilitation of the port of Moroni, the capital, but difficulties have been reported in the allocation of the contract.

4. International support measures

The Comoros receives a relatively high level of aid per capita ($98 in 1986). France, the main donor, has included budgetary aid of FF 29.5 million (about $6 million) in its 1988 aid package. However, there is some doubt whether this will continue at the same level in the future. Japan emerged as the second most important donor in 1987, while assistance from OPEC countries has declined in the 1980s.

5. Impact of national policies and international support measures

The sectoral composition of GDP has not changed in the 1980s. In most years gross national product has grown at rates below that of population (estimated at over 3 per cent). In 1987, GNP probably fell due to the problems in the vanilla sector.

DEMOCRATIC YEMEN

1. Improving the efficiency of resource allocation

The Third Five-Year Development Plan (1986-1990) was revised and approved in September 1987. The delay in the launching of the Plan was caused by the rehabilitation and construction requirements resulting from the damage caused to productive units and infrastructure during the events of January 1986. Development expenditure in the Plan is set at about $1.7 billion, of which the largest share - about 46 per cent - is directed to the industrial sector. The share of agriculture was maintained at the same level as in the Second Plan. The share of geological and mineral surveys was increased from 7 to 17 per cent, reflecting increased requirements for further oil exploration. External resources are to finance about 65 per cent, as compared to 50 per cent of actual outlays during the Second Plan Period.

(a) External sector policies

There has been no significant change in the tight control which the Government imposes on all current payments, covering both transfers and foreign trade. The exchange rate against the US dollar has remained unchanged since 1973. The domestic prices of export and import commodities are determined by the Government on the basis of cost and prescribed profit margins. The differences between international and domestic prices are financed through the Price Stabilization Fund. Several measures have been initiated recently to increase exports. These include: increasing producer prices of cotton by about 57 per cent and subsidization of salt, tobacco and fish exports. The quality and marketing of other export commodities are being improved.

(b) Demand-management measures

Public sector wages have been increased moderately since 1980, mainly through job reclassification. In 1987 the average wage increase was estimated at two per cent only. The prices of virtually all goods and services are set by the Government, thereby limiting official inflation. However, the Government has increasingly relied on domestic bank financing of the budget deficit, thus contributing to the excess liquidity and exacerbating underlying inflationary pressures.

(c) Mobilization of domestic savings

In 1987 domestic budget revenues are estimated to have increased by 11 per cent, due to the payment of arrears by public enterprises and the sharp increase in excise duties on cigarettes and beer. The contribution of public sector enterprises to the domestic budget revenue was estimated at 35 per cent in 1987.

(d) Expanded role for the private sector

While maintaining the leading role of the public sector, the Government has been encouraging the private sector to participate in the production and marketing of agricultural and fishery products through improved pricing and marketing policies.

2. Sectoral policies

(a) Agriculture and fishing

The agricultural sector is divided among state farms, co-operatives and peasant freeholdings accounting for 10,70 and 20 per cent respectively of agricultural output. Livestock-raising remains largely in private hands. The expansion of agricultural production is constrained by limited arable land and irrigation facilities. In order to increase productivity, some State farms have been converted into co-operatives or merged into larger units, incentive schemes have been introduced and the prices of some crops have been raised. The fisheries sector is being developed with the help of the USSR. A study for the development of the sector up to the year 2000 is under way.

(b) Industry and energy

The Third Five-Year Development Plan projects a sharp increase in industrial exports, which currently consist mainly of light consumer goods, thus reversing the past trend of consuming the bulk of output domestically. To improve the performance of manufacturing enterprises, wage incentive schemes are being introduced. Small-scale industrial enterprises are being established, mainly by expatriate capital. A biscuit and candy factory, with a production capacity of 4,000 tons of biscuit and 3,000 tons of candy, was launched in January 1988. Aden Refinery is the major industrial complex. A rehabilitation programme for containers and berths is under way. The refinery is receiving about 10,000 b/d from the domestic Shabwa oilfields. Production from these fields is expected to increase to 70,000 b/d by early 1989. Joint oil exploration is being undertaken with Yemen in the area between Marib-Jowf in Yemen and Shabwa in Democratic Yemen. The expected oil revenue will have profound effects on the economy of Democratic Yemen and will substantially boost the meagre merchandise export proceeds, estimated at $71 million in 1987.

(c) Mining

A three-year contract was signed with the USSR for the survey, evaluation and production of gold in a 40 km^2 area in Abyan Governate.

(d) Social development

The share of social services in the Third Five-Year Development Plan in total investment outlay was reduced to 19 per cent (as compared to 27 per cent in the Second Plan) in favour of the productive sectors. This will adversely affect the development of health and educational services. Several water supply schemes, mainly foreign-financed, are at different stages of implementation. These include the Mukalla scheme ($35 million) and the Laboos scheme ($23 million).

3. Measures to improve the physical infrastructure

Efforts are concentrated on rehabilitating the damaged infrastructure, continuing ongoing projects and embarking on new projects only if foreign-financed. Aden Port is being expanded at a cost of $60 million through the construction of reinforced concrete berths and unloading bays. Asphalt roads have increased from 1,475 km in 1980 to 2,102 km in 1987. Two roads in the eastern part of the country measuring 150 km and 44 km respectively are under construction.

4. Measures to improve institutional capabilities in the field of development planning and policy

The second population census was carried out during the period 30 March - 4 April 1988.

5. International support measures

Official transfers were estimated at $55 million in 1987, representing a 75 per cent increase over the average for the previous three years. Net capital inflows are also estimated to have increased to $146 million in 1987, compared to $127 million in 1986. However, these positive developments were more than offset by the decline in workers' remittances, which have accounted for about three-quarters of current account receipts in recent years. International reserves have consistently declined from their 1982 level of almost $300 million to less than $80 million in July 1988.

6. Impact of national policies and international support measures

The economy of Democratic Yemen, which suffers from domestic constraints, has been adversely affected by the deterioration in the external economic environment since 1984. Private transfers, mainly workers' remittances, declined by over 40 per cent between 1984 and 1986, while official transfers were stagnant during the same period. The extensive damage to production facilities and infrastructure caused by the disturbances in 1986 has exacerbated the adverse effects of these developments. A sharp reduction in imports occurred and the Public Investment Programme was affected. Imports stabilized at a level only two-thirds as high as the 1981-1985 average. Thus, real GDP, which had registered an average annual increase of about 6 per cent between 1980 and 1984, was stagnant in 1985 and declined by 9.7 per cent in 1986. A modest recovery about 3 per cent was registered in 1987. Agricultural and industrial output have increased, while the construction and services sectors have continued their decline due to the low level of investments and reduction of imports. The 1988 development budget projects a growth rate of 10.4 per cent in GDP as a result of growth rates of 20 and 15 per cent in the construction and manufacturing sectors respectively and an increase of 13 per cent in imports.

DJIBOUTI

1. *Improving the efficiency of resource allocation*

(a) Demand-management measures

Budget expenditures increased by 7 per cent in 1986, largely due to a 13 per cent increase in current expenditures. The increase was limited to less than 2 per cent in 1987 as a result of a freeze of salaries, which constitute the major item in current outlays. The 1988 budget projected a 4.8 per cent expenditure increase, but this estimate was revised downwards in April, due mainly to a decline in tax revenues.

(b) Mobilization of domestic savings

The following new taxes were imposed in January 1988 to support the projected increase in expenditure: a profit tax on industrial and commercial companies; a surtax and sales tax on qat, alcohol and tobacco; duties on sales of new land plots; and a new real estate tax. However, the increase in revenue from these taxes fell short of expectations, leading the Government to revise its expenditure estimates.

(c) Expanded role for the private sector

Private-sector investment is to be promoted by assisting enterpreneurs to identify sources of technical assistance, making available, free of charge, feasibility studies and finding sources of finance. In 1988, four companies were granted tax concessions under the 1984 Investment Code, which promotes investment in manufacturing.

2. *Sectoral policies*

(a) Agriculture and forestry

The objective is to increase food self-sufficiency. About 11 per cent of funds committed under the Public Investment Programme 1983-1989 were devoted to this sector. Efforts are concentrated on developing small, labour-intensive agricultural projects, promoting diversification of agricultural production and improving the marketing network for fresh products. IFAD is considering the financing of two projects: (a) a project in the south-west, aimed at removing structural handicaps for smallholder agriculture, such as the lack of credit facilities, water and flood protection, and (b) a project to develop Djibouti's only remaining forest area through a short-term protection plan and a long-term investment plan.

(b) Industry and energy

The aim of industrial policy is to promote medium-sized enterprises based on the processing of local resources and to promote private-sector development. An animal feed factory, with an annual production capacity of 20,000 tons, was inaugurated in June 1988. It represents the third industrial unit in the country, the other two being the milk and mineral water factories. Djibouti depends almost entirely on imported petroleum products for its energy requirements. To reduce this dependence on imported oil, the Government is exploring new sources of energy, particularly solar and geothermal energy. The second stage of the development of geothermal energy at Lake Asal, where substantial flows were found, is projected to cost $30 million. The finance is to be provided by the World Bank and bilateral donors.

(c) Social development

The urban development plan, launched in 1985, is designed to reduce pollution and improve water supplies. The EEC, UNDP and UNICEF are providing financial assistance for projects aimed at the extension of health service coverage in remote rural areas, provision of fresh water supplies, elimination of malnutrition and the promotion of vaccination campaigns.

3. Measures to improve the physical infrastructure

The Kuwait Fund for Economic Development and the Saudi Fund for Development are providing concessional loans amounting to $19.2 million for the rehabilitation of Djibouti's port. The project aims at increasing the port's capacity and efficiency by repairing marine berths and improving handling facilities in the container section and the free-trade zone. The scheme for the modernization of Ambouli International Airport, at a cost of $14 million provided by various Arab development funds, aims at reinforcing the runway and aprons, improving telecommunications and rehabilitating the terminal.

4. Measures to improve institutional capabilities in the field of development planning and policy

A technical assistance project in the area of economic planning (1988-1990) is being implemented by UNDP. The project aims at establishing the mechanisms and planning structures needed for improved management and better utilization of the country's human and financial resources in the development process.

5. International support measures

Net disbursements of ODA, which had declined by 33 per cent between 1984 and 1985, almost recovered this loss in 1986, to reach a level of $110 million. The efforts of the Government to stabilize the economy are being supported by financial assistance from France - Djibouti's major donor - averaging $52 million in 1987 and 1988. Djibouti's heavy dependence on external flows is highlighted by the fact that 44 per cent of the budgetary deficits during the period 1985-1987 were financed by external grants.

6. Impact of national policies and international support measures

After two years of decline, real GDP is estimated to have increased by 3.0 per cent in 1987. The recovery was due mainly to the high growth rates in agriculture (7.2 per cent) and construction and public works (6.2 per cent). In the key transport and communications sector, the declining trend, which started in 1985, continued. The weak economic activity in neighbouring countries and the competition from the ports of Aseb in Ethiopia and Berbera in Somalia have affected the utilization rate and hence the profitability of the port of Djibouti.

EQUATORIAL GUINEA

1. Improving the efficiency of resource use and allocation

The development strategy for 1987-1991 sets out global and sectoral priorities with policy guidelines and identification of projects that will have to be implemented. The assumption of the strategy is that the economy of Equatorial Guinea should grow considerably faster than in the previous five years, since otherwise the imbalances in the public finances and in the external sector will become more accentuated, with the risk of further deterioration in the standard of living. The minimum goal for the next five years is an average annual

GDP growth rate of 5 per cent, based mainly on the expansion of export-oriented agricultural production (cocoa, timber, coffee) and on food production for domestic consumption.

(a) External sector policies

Equatorial Guinea's membership of the Central African Customs and Economic Union (UDEAC) and of the Bank of Central African States (BEAC) since 1985 has had a decisive influence on its economic development. At the beginning of 1985, external payments problems were eased and capital movements were appreciably facilitated by the introduction of a freely convertible currency, the CFA franc. Membership of UDEAC opened up the economy and a large trade flow with Cameroon ensued, which in turn led to an improvement of telecommunications, as well as air and sea transport links, between the two countries. Import and export licences are issued freely by the Ministry of Commerce and Industry. The authorities are in the process of drafting legislation aimed at stimulating foreign investment in the agriculture, forestry, fishing, construction, public works, mining and industrial equipment maintenance sectors. Export tax reductions on cocoa exports aim at maintaining remunerative prices for the producers and reasonable profit margins for the exporters in spite of falling world prices. The removal of import taxes on agricultural and industrial inputs was designed to make local production more competitive with the more freely available competing imports.

(b) Demand-management measures

The preparation of a national budget was resumed in 1984. In spite of sharp reductions in current and capital expenditures, major deficits were unavoidable, owing mainly to the reduction of receipts from cocoa export duties. Foreign debt obligations constitute an important constraint on fiscal policy. Real incomes of civil servants declined sharply; at present the average monthly wage is about CFAF 15,000 ($50). The Government has also decided to lay off one-half of the 40,000 civil servants. The 1988 budget provides for a current deficit of CFAF 747 million ($2.5 million). On the domestic revenue side, the objective of CFAF 7,147 million ($24 million) seems possible. As for expenditures, which are budgeted at CFAF 7,894 million ($26.3 million), civil servants' salaries account for 22 per cent, other administrative costs for 23 per cent, and interest on external debt absorbs 22.8 per cent. Anticipated investment, which is outside the regular budget, is CFAF 900 million ($3 million). Apart from the current budget, Equatorial Guinea must also pay CFAF 2,975 million ($10 million) in 1988 for amortization on the external debt, which was estimated at CFAF 47 billion ($157 million) at the end of 1987. Thus, the Government has to set aside 66.9 per cent of its current revenue for servicing the external debt.

(c) Mobilization of domestic savings

A two-year crisis of the banking system culminated in 1987 in an almost total lack of liquidity, resulting from an external drain of already scarce domestic savings and investment funds.

(d) Mobilization of human resources

The country is small and underpopulated. Village councils set up recently have the responsibility of strengthening national unity. The Government is encouraging women to play a greater role in economic development. A Department for the Promotion of Women was created within the Ministry of Labour, and women active in their communities have been delegated in the provinces "as agents of social change responsible for the co-ordination and execution of socio-economic projects leading to an improvement in the population's living standards". ILO is supporting the national efforts through the creation of small enterprises for women and the training of women advisors in villages to improve daily life, organization and management.

(e) Expanded role for the private sector

The State's role in production has been strictly defined to create the best conditions for private sector participation. Recent governmental measures provided for the restructuring and privatization of public-sector companies. Thus, private domestic and foreign capital is replacing state companies in air and maritime transport, banking, agriculture and forestry.

2. *Sectoral policies*

(a) Food and agriculture

Food self-sufficiency and agricultural development are the top priorities of the 1987-1991 development strategy. Producers' co-operatives will be formed, and the State will supply technical assistance to enable the farmers to achieve high yields, thereby stimulating development in rural areas.

(b) Export development and diversification

The government policies are oriented towards the rehabilitation of production of cocoa, which used to be the most important export crop, and the development of fisheries and forestry resources.

(c) Social development

Achieving substantial progress in the fields of education and health, particularly primary education and primary health care, is a basic objective of the development strategy for 1987-1991. A substantial increase in the training of human resources, including in-service training, is also expected.

3. *Measures to improve institutional capabilities in the field of development planning and policy*

The Government is promoting the consolidation of the national system for planning, economic policy and projects through the creation of planning and project units in the principal technical ministries and through the establishment of co-ordination machinery for planning, government budgeting and monetary policy-making. Efforts are also being made to strengthen the national statistical system, including the elaboration of national accounts.

4. *International support measures*

If the economy was able to grow over the period 1984-1987, that was mainly due to external support (grants and loans), which are estimated at some CFAF 12 billions ($40 million) per year, or 168 per cent of domestic budgetary revenue. Spain and France provide the bulk of budgetary aid to Equatorial Guinea. Credits from IDA and the African Special Facility amounted to $34.8 million.

5. *Impact of national policies and international support measures*

Policy measures favouring agricultural development have yielded encouraging results. Wood production has recently recovered, reaching the same level as in the last pre-independence years, with 127,487 tonnes exported in 1987. This sector accounted for 56.5 per cent of the value of exports. Exports of cocoa reached nearly 8,000 tonnes (42.1 per cent of exports, worth CFAF 3.52 billion or about $12 million) in 1987, i.e. twice as much as in recent years. Finally, only 163 tonnes of coffee were exported, with production of some 600 tonnes. Altogether exports amounted to CFAF 8.4 billion ($28 million) in 1987, against CFAF 18 billion ($60 million) worth of imports, leaving a trade deficit of CFAF 9.6 billion ($32 million), which is more than offset by external support.

ETHIOPIA

1. Improving the efficiency of resource use and allocation

With the Ethiopian economy recovering from the disastrous drought of 1984-1985, the Government launched the second phase of its Ten-Year Perspective Plan in July 1986, covering the three year period 1986/87-1988/89.[175] This Three-Year Development Plan (TYDP) aims at boosting food production and expanding foreign-exchange earnings.

(a) External sector policies

In an effort to increase external borrowing and to improve the structure of new borrowing, the Government recently established a new institution at the ministerial level for co-ordination of foreign borrowing activities. The recently announced measure to resume issuance of export licences to private firms is intended to stimulate the country's trade performance.

(b) Demand-management measures

Ethiopia's monetary policy has been traditionally very conservative, avoiding too much deficit spending and corresponding inflation. In fact, the official consumer price index declined both in 1986 and 1987, although most of this decline had been reversed by mid-1988.

(c) Mobilization of human resources

The policy of villagization, which aims at improving the availability of health and social services and marketing facilities is continuing. By the middle of 1987, almost 16,000 new villages had been established, involving more than 8 million people. The aim is to reach around 12 million people, or 31 per cent of the rural population, by 1988. The settlers are entitled to two hectares of land for individual exploitation, in addition to having the option to join production co-operatives, which enjoy incentives such as priority access to production inputs, consumer goods and extension services.

(d) Expanded role for the private sector

Government policy, as enunciated in the Ten-Year Perspective Plan and reiterated in the TYDP, foresees a diminishing role for the private sector, in particular restricted access of this sector to domestic credit and foreign exchange. However, recent reforms have relaxed controls on farmers' private grain sales, and the Government's resumption of the issuance of export licences to some private firms should help stimulate the fledgling private sector.

2. Sectoral policies

(a) Food and agriculture

The Agricultural Marketing Corporation has been fixing the price of grain at virtually unchanged levels since 1979; moreover, these prices do not take regional differences in transportation costs into account. Producer prices for the principal export crops and cereals have been kept virtually constant in spite of price increases in agricultural inputs. The ever-shrinking or negative producer margins may have inhibited agricultural growth and export diversification. Private trading of grain has been restricted and so has the movement of grain from one region to another. Agricultural land is owned by the State. State farmers have been paid better prices than private farmers for the same crop. However, policy changes announced in early 1988, such as partial liberalization of the grain market and adjustment of

[175] The fiscal year (FY) ends on 7 July.

prices in general, are expected to bring about significant improvements.

(b) Industry and energy

Ethiopia's manufacturing, which stagnated for several years following nationalizations in 1975, is now the fastest growing sector of the economy. It is reported to have increased by 6 percent between FY 1986/87 and FY 1987/88, to over Br 2 billion (about $965 million at the official exchange rate). Manufacturing caters largely to the home market, although exports of some processed products such as sugar, semi-processed hides and oil-seed products have increased. Soviet experts have been prospecting for oil, largely in the Ogaden region. Ethiopia's hydroelectric potential, estimated at over 60 billion kwh per year, is barely tapped. Under a 20-year energy development programme started in 1982, the Government intends to increase installed capacity from 300 MW to 1,000 MW.

3. Measures to improve the physical infrastructure

The Ten-Year Perspective Plan contains a substantial investment programme for the transport sector. Thus, the master plan for Assab Port includes the construction of a 74-meter tug berth and two new deep-water berths and installation of cargo-handling equipment. Both Assab and Massawa ports will be substantially improved by the end of the Ten-Year Plan.

Repairs to the Addis Ababa-Djibouti rail line are being carried out under an EC-funded programme, which includes the purchase of wagons and maintenance equipment. An 860 km rail link from Addis Ababa to Assab, estimated to cost $1.4 billion, is to be constructed with multilateral financial assistance from the Council for Mutual Economic Assistance.

A key project in the area of transportation infrastructure is the improvement of the vital Assab-Addis Ababa road link, which is being co-financed by the African Development Bank, the World Bank, Norway, the EC and China.

4. International support measures

While foreign Governments and international organizations have generally been quick to offer relief assistance, Western donors have made their development aid conditional on economic policy changes. The policy changes announced by the Ethiopian Government in December 1987 to increase agricultural producer prices induced the EC to resume payments of part of the $275 million development aid package promised under the Lomé III Convention. The World Bank also started to release funds that had been frozen since 1986.

5. Impact of national policies and international support measures

The period immediately following the revolution of 1974 was marked by slow economic growth owing to disruption caused by the rapid change of management in many enterprises. Although the gradual adaptation to the new social environment, stable domestic conditions and vigorous development campaigns helped to turn the tide, economic performance encountered renewed setbacks from the recurrent droughts of the 1980s. Nevertheless, some sectors, notably manufacturing, have made significant progress. Export receipts from industry in 1987 amounted to $60 million, having risen from less than $30million in 1979. However, inasmuch as agriculture accounts for 85 per cent of export revenues, its development remains crucial.

The increasing strains on Ethiopia's external payments in 1987 were due to a combination of deteriorating terms of trade (sharp decline in international coffee prices and increase in import prices in terms of dollars), a drop in gross disbursements (resulting partly from a decrease in new commitments and partly from a lengthening aid "pipeline"), and a considerable deterioration of loan terms, with suppliers' credits accounting for more than 60 per cent of total new commitments in mid-1987 as against 12-13 per cent at the beginning of the 1980s. Ethiopia's urgent needs for international support include debt relief inasmuch as external debt rose by one-half in the four-year period ending in July 1987 to a level equivalent to 38.9per cent of GDP, while the debt-service-to-exports ratio almost doubled to reach 31.2 percent in FY 1986/87.

THE GAMBIA

1. *Improving the efficiency of resource use and allocation*

(a) External sector policies and demand-management measures

The Gambia's development policy in the mid-1980s is largely governed by the Economic Recovery Programme (ERP) launched in August 1985 under a World Bank Structural Adjustment Programme covering FY 1985/86 to FY 1988/89[176], which was further supported by the IMF Structural Adjustment Facility in October 1987. The adjustment policies are essentially aimed at achieving external and internal equilibrium through the adoption of appropriate monetary and fiscal measures on the one hand, and improving the productive capacity of the economy through the elimination of exchange-rate and price distortions and the introduction of selective production incentives on the other hand.

(b) Mobilization of domestic resources

Efforts to mobilize resources are being made by way of: (a) fiscal cutbacks, notably reduced salary bills and subsidies; (b) savings by parastatals through an ongoing rehabilitation programme; (c) implementation of revenue enhancement measures; and (d) promotion of private sector savings. The interest rate was made flexible, and in July 1986 the Government introduced a tender system for treasury bills, according to which the levels of other administratively determined interest rates are adjusted.

(c) Improving public entreprise efficiency

Steps taken include reducing of the scope of the activities of the parastatal sector and improving the performance of enterprises remaining within the public sector through the use of performance contracts, technical assistance, adjustments of public utility rates, settlement of interlocking arrears, etc. With effect from 1 January 1986 a moratorium was placed on the creation of new public enterprises and on joint ventures with a government equity participation of more than 10 per cent. The Government has divested its holdings in some fishing enterprises and hotels.

2. *Sectoral policies*

(a) Food, agriculture and fishing

The agriculture sector will remain the mainstay of the economy in the foreseeable future. The Government's strategy is to encourage the expansion of food crops, some recovery of groundnut production (which accounts for over 85-90 per cent of domestic exports) and diversification into other cash crops, horticulture and livestock. Measures adopted include the provision of adequate price incentives; significant institutional improvements, particularly in the areas of agricultural extension; seed multiplication; agricultural credit; distribution of inputs and fertilizers; and marketing services. The implementation of the Jahally Pacharr Smallholder Rice Project increased the area under cultivation from 931 hectares in FY 1985/86 to 1,100 hectares in FY 1986/87.

(b) Industry and expansion of the private sector's role

The Gambia's manufacturing sector (about 9.1 per cent of GDP in 1985) is limited to local- resource-based and export-oriented industries which operate on a small scale. Priority is placed on diversifying the Gambia's narrow productive base, and efforts are directed at attracting foreign private investment, *inter alia*, by allowing free repatriation of capital. The Development Act enacted in February 1988 incorporates investment incentives by way of income tax. The Government has intensified efforts to promote new industrial ventures and to assist the established enterprises with technical and economic advice. The assistance

[176] The fiscal year (FY) ends on 30 June.

of the World Bank to the "Private Enterprise Development Project" will enhance resources for small and medium enterprises.

(c) Services - tourism

The tourist sector is one of the fastest-growing sectors of the economy, which the Government is promoting under the export diversification drive, but the sector contributed only about 20 per cent of the country's net foreign exchange earnings in FY 1986/87. Following the ERP measures to expand output of fish, livestock and horticultural industries, the hotel industry reduced the importation of goods and services and turned to local supplies.

(d) Energy

The Government accords high priority to energy development, as the cost of importing petroleum products is a strain on the balance of payments. A technical and legal framework now exists to attract international oil companies to carry out exploration and production activities in the Gambia. Attempts are also being made to exploit other potential sources of energy, such as solar power, wind and biogas. An effort is further being made to restore the depleted forest cover by discouraging the use of fuelwood for domestic consumption. Groundnut shell briquettes have also been introduced as a substitute.

(e) Social development

In the light of the current economic conditions, expenditure in the social service sectors is oriented towards rehabilitation and meeting the non-salary recurrent costs of these sectors. A proposed population, health and nutrition project financed by the International Development Association with co-financing by several other donors will assist in meeting short-term recurrent cost problems and will support selected long-term investments in manpower development, communications, infrastructure and analytical capacity. The project will also help strengthen family planning services in the Gambia and assist in the development of a comprehensive family planning policy.

3. Measures to improve the physical infrastructure

Major investments have been undertaken to improve the road network. The road on the north side of the river will be upgraded, linking it to the Senegalese road network. Progress has been made on the highway project linking Banjul and Serrekunda. An EC-financed feeder road project in the outlying districts is completed.

4. Measures to improve institutional capabilities in the field of development planning policy

As from FY 1986/87 the Government has adopted a three-year "rolling" investment programme with strengthened links to the annual recurrent budget in order to raise the overall productivity of public investments. Stringent criteria for investment selection have been established. Priority is given to projects with high rates of return and significant net foreign-exchange- generating or saving capacity, as well as to the rehabilitation and maintenance of existing capital assets.

An economic monitoring unit has been established in the Ministry of Finance and Trade. Technical assistance from UNDP is given in the areas of project analysis, recurrent cost forecasting and sectoral planning. To ensure successful implementation and co-ordination of the ERP at the ministerial level, two committees were established: the Steering Committee on the National Economic Recovery Programme monitors the implementation of the recovery measures, prepares quarterly progress reports for the Cabinet and the donor community and advises on impediments to implementation; and the Working Group on Civil Service Reforms monitors the implementation of the reforms and structural changes in the civil service.

5. International support measures

With its reform measures in place, the Government is assured of continuing balance-of-payments support. The second tranche from the IMF Structural Adjustment Facility worth SDR 5.1 million was disbursed late in 1987. In addition, the Gambia's eligibility for the Enhanced Structural Adjustment Facility (ESAF) could make available up to SDR 42.75 million, or 250 per cent of the Gambia's quota. Several multilateral and bilateral donors have given assistance amounting to $28.0 million for developing a water supply and electricity project.

A rescheduling agreement reached with the London Club in January 1988 amounting to $19.5 million also helped to ease the country's debt burden during the year.

6. *Impact of national policies and international measures*

The Government's adjustment efforts aimed at addressing the economy's external imbalance, helped by the good weather and substantial external financing, have resulted in considerable economic and financial gains. Real GDP, which grew by 5.3 per cent in FY 1986/87, was sustained in FY 1987/88, when it grew by 5.4 per cent. Growth during FY 1987/88 was spread across all sectors, although not evenly. The agricultural sector grew by about 1.9 per cent, industry by 7.2 per cent and the service sector by 6.3 per cent. The increase in consumer prices, which had reached 46 per cent in FY 1986/87, declined to 13.2 per cent in FY 1987/88, the lowest rate for five years. The liberalization of exchange and interest-rate policies has helped to revive private-sector confidence, and foreign-exchange reserves have improved to eight weeks' import cover from less than one week at the commencement of the ERP.

GUINEA

1. *Improving the efficiency of resource use and allocation*

An Economic Recovery Programme (ERP) was introduced in December 1985 covering every area of Guinea's economic activity. Far-reaching reforms were decided upon, *inter alia* the privatization of commercial, industrial and agro-pastoral undertakings and the state's withdrawal from the domestic trading network, and priority was given to the achievement of self-sufficiency in food. In January 1986, a monetary reform introduced a new currency, the Guinean franc, in replacement of the syli, accompanied by a drastic devaluation of the currency. Since June 1986 the exchange rate has been determined through weekly auctions. The rate had fallen to GF 495 per dollar by August 1988, implying a cumulative devaluation of only about 22 per cent vis-a-vis the parallel rate prevailing before the major devaluation of January 1986. Prospects for economic recovery will also depend on how the country copes will declining revenues from projected decreases in bauxite exports. The predicted drop in revenues comes at a time when the country's institutions need strengthening and its infrastructure, including power, water, telecommunications and transportation networks, will need to be built up.

(a) External sector policies

The trade regime has been progressively liberalized. Import licenses were abolished. Foreign exchange for imports was made available through auctions and the Central Bank ensures that importers' foreign exchange receipts are surrendered. The structure of import tariffs has been simplified, as follows: rice is duty-free; a 5 per cent tariff is levied on certain primary foodstuffs, including edible oils, wheat flour, sugar, meat, and fowl; all other imports are subject to a 10 per cent tariff. In addition, a surtax of 20 per cent to 30 per cent is imposed on all luxury goods. The import tariff payable by two mixed enterprises in the mining sector is subject to special agreements. In January 1988, foreign-exchange payments among residents were banned, excluding payments for port and airport services.

(b) Demand-management measures

In January 1986 the Government decided to cut subsidies on a large number of products and services, resulting in substantial price increases. These were only very partially offset by the wage adjustments decided on at the same time. In January 1988 the Government announced that all consumer prices would be frozen for the interim to halt the huge price rises following civil servants' year-end salary increases of 80 per cent. Consequently, the prices of essential foodstuffs, such as rice, bread, meat and milk, which had tripled, returned to their original levels. Longer-term measures are to be taken to control retail prices, inasmuch as retail trade is now almost entirely in private hands.

(c) Mobilization of domestic savings

Treasury bonds, bearing a nominal rate of interest of 35 per cent compared to a consumer price inflation rate of 33 per cent during 1987, were issued in 1986 as a new savings instrument. At the beginning of 1987, the Government announced major changes in the interest-rate policy to strengthen incentives for investment and saving. A minimum annual interest rate of 15 per cent for bank deposits and a maximum rate of 20 per cent on bank credits were introduced.

(d) Mobilization of human resources

The restoration of freedom to rural activities was the basis for the Government's efforts aimed at mobilizing the rural population, which represents more than 80 per cent of the total population. A reduction of about 30,000 civil servants is currently under way, but it has fallen behind the timetable agreed with the IMF in 1986.

(e) Expanded role for the private sector

The Government is committed to the privatization of public companies. Two agro-industrial units (producing tea and quinine), a printing works, and a fruit-juice and a soft-drink factory have been sold to Guinean and foreign investors. Other concerns to be privatized include bigger firms, such as a textile complex, a brewery and ONAH, the national fuel board. The legal infrastructure aimed at stimulating private domestic and foreign business includes the 1986 commercial and banking laws, the 1987 codes for investment and mining, and a simpler tax system.

(f) Improving the efficiency of public enterprises

Due to the standstill in personnel cuts and in the transfer of public companies to domestic or foreign investors, no improvement in the efficiency of public enterprises has been registered.

2. Sectoral policies

(a) Food and agriculture

Agriculture is the top priority set out in the nation's ERP. Food output, particularly rice, is expanding fast as a result of the adjustment of agricultural prices and price liberalization. Incentives to rural producers included: liberalization of prices, abolition of the tax-in-kind which farmers and herdsmen were obliged to pay, removal of internal barriers and forced marketing. Food self-sufficiency is still a distant target, since rice imports continued to grow during the 1985-1987 period. An IDA-supported project was approved in December 1987 aimed at facilitating the production and marketing of better cereal and groundnut seeds.

(b) Industry and energy

The restructuring of the industrial sector decided by the Government in December 1985 aimed at the association of private Guinean or foreign partners to replace 45 state industrial companies. With the support of the EC Sysmin financial facility, a rehabilitation investment programme of the Friguia alumina plant was to be implemented from 1988 onwards. Other rehabilitation operations in 1987 included the Sanoyah textile plant, the Soguiplast plastics and the Entag tobacco companies.

(c) Services

Public utilities supplying water, electricity and telecommunications have had financial and managerial autonomy since 1986.

(d) Social development

The performance of the Guinean health system has been constrained by a lack of financial resources, weak planning and management, inadequately trained personnel, and the absence of an adequate drug programme. As a consequence, facilities and equipment have deteriorated, drugs are scarce, the quality of health services is limited, and the population lacks confidence in the system. The Government has begun to implement a health care policy that emphasizes health promotion, disease prevention, and the provision of basic health care services to mothers and children and to the rural population.

3. Measures to improve the physical infrastructure

Re-establishing reasonably dependable transport and communications among the main production, consumption and export centres and opening up Guinea's rich hinterland will be essential for the success of the recently launched structural adjustment programme. This job will take at least 10 years. In approaching this problem, the Government has accorded the highest priority to the formulation and implementation of policy reforms aimed at introducing a market-oriented environment in the transport sector and to the re-establishment of essential transport services. In support of this strategy, the Government's investment programme focuses on the elimination of four major bottlenecks: (a) the heavily deteriorated basic trunk-road system; (b) the serious congestion in the commercial port of Conakry; (c) the unreliable and unsafe air transport system; and (d) the inefficient management of the transport industry on the part of the parastatals. Rehabilitation and extension operations in the port of Conakry started in 1987 with financial assistance from the African Development Bank. A four-year project (1988-1992) for the development of hydraulic systems at village level was approved in 1987. The aim is to supply, daily, 10 litres per capita of drinking water by 1995. The project will be supported by France's CCCE.

4. Measures to improve institutional capabilities in the field of development planning and policy

In December 1985 the Government announced the reorganization of the agencies responsible for planning and management of the state's finances. Formal and on-the-job training has been undertaken for the staff of the Ministries for Planning and International Co-operation, National Resources, Economy and Finances and the Central Bank. This state development programme is integrated into the agencies' work programmes.

5. International support measures

Guinea's Economic Recovery Programme has been strongly endorsed by the international community. At the World Bank-sponsored Consultative Group meeting held in March 1987, indicative pledges were made by aid donors for $670 million to support the three-year public investment programme. During the three years ending 30 June 1988, IDA and the Special Facility for Africa approved credits totalling $344 million, of which $228.8 million were for structural and sectoral adjustment while $116 million were earmarked for projects, mostly in transportation and agriculture.

6. Impact of national policies and international support measures

The first phase of Guinea's Economic Adjustment Programme has yielded encouraging results. The economy grew by 6 per cent in real terms in 1987, inflation fell from 78 per cent in 1986 to 33 per cent a year later, and private sector participation in the economy has grown. The full impact of government actions to put the country on a sound financial footing and establish an incentive framework needed to revitalize the economy will be felt only in the medium term.

GUINEA-BISSAU

1. *Improving the efficiency of resource use and allocation*

Measures undertaken in 1987 within the framework of the three-year Structural Adjustment Programme (SAP) 1987-1989 included a substantial devaluation of the official exchange rate followed by frequent adjustments thereafter; the full repercussion of the devaluation on controlled prices; a major liberalization of the exchange and trade system; the adoption of a tight Government budget, including a number of tax measures; and a restrained wage policy. The broad thrust of policies within the framework of the second Development Plan for 1989-1992 will involve the continued promotion of sustainable economic growth, the containment of inflationary pressures and the reduction of external and internal financial imbalances. The Government will pursue appropriate incentive policies to enhance private-sector economic activity, to improve the programming and monitoring of public investment, to promote revenue mobilization and to render financial resource management more efficient.

(a) External sector policies

In August 1986, the export monopolies for the three main export products (groundnuts, palm nuts and cashew nuts) were abolished. The present exchange regime grants automatic import licenses for a list of goods other than petroleum products accounting for 75 per cent of total commercial imports. On the other hand, exporters still have to surrender to the National Bank all their foreign-currency receipts.

(b) Demand-management measures

A monetary programme covering the period July 1987-June 1988 was agreed with the IMF aimed at decelerating the rate of inflation. The interest rate policy is to be pursued with flexibility and to be adapted to market conditions. The Government's budget for 1988 confirms the structural insufficiency of budgetary revenue to cover current and capital expenditure of the public sector. It is estimated that the overall deficit in 1988 will amount to 17.3 per cent of the GDP.

(c) Mobilization of domestic savings

Interest rates were raised from a range of 4.5-8 per cent in 1986 to 21-30 per cent in 1987 in order to direct savings into domestic financial institutions. Since even the higher range fell short of the rate of inflation, this implies the continuation of negative real interest rates. Neither the Government nor the public enterprises have funded their investments from domestic savings. Budget deficits have been financed by unsustainable levels of domestic and foreign borrowing. The pace of money-supply growth engendered by the budget deficit feeds inflation and more than offsets the effects of frequent devaluations.

(d) Mobilization of human resources

As from the first four-year plan (1983-1986), a major policy objective related to mobilization of human resources has been the organization of the rural population into village associations based on co-operative principles in order to strengthen the regional administration and implementation of development projects based on a regional autonomy criterion, as well as to limit rural migration. The mobilization of human resources will also include the lay-off of about one-third of the more than 16,000 civil servants over the three-year period 1987-1989. With regard to the role of women in development, the UDEMU (Uniao Democrática de Mulheres) is pledged to advance women's issues at the governmental level and to work to overcome the prejudices in society that impede the access of women to education and job opportunities. The forthcoming Development Plan for 1989-1992 includes as a main objective the optimization of human resources through an integrated policy involving education, training, employment and technical assistance, as well as support for the most vulnerable groups.

(e) Expanded role for the private sector

Retail stores operated by two state-owned chains - Armazens do Povo and Socomin - were transfered to the private sector. By end-1986, at least 186 out of 210 retail stores owned by these state enterprises had been sold to the private sector. Private traders have become completely free to engage in any aspect of foreign trade, with the exception of cereal imports. At the end of 1987, a venture capital fund to promote private enterprise was set up in the National Bank, with Portuguese and United States support.

(f) Improving the efficiency of public enterprises

The restructuring of the public enterprise sector aims at reducing its weight within the economy through the privatization of some units as well as improving the organization, management and profitability of the enterprises. Concurrent with the privatization of retail activities described above, Armazens do Povo is to be limited to wholesale trading, while Socomin will take over state import/export operations.

2. *Sectoral policies*

(a) Agriculture and fishing

Since agriculture represents more than 50 per cent of GDP, the performance of this sector has an enormous impact on overall growth, income and exports. The Government will therefore focus on food production for the domestic market, the expansion and diversification of agricultural export crops, the promotion of agricultural research and extension services, rural transport and agricultural credit. The Government stresses the importance of the fisheries sector, which should comprise both small-scale traditional fishing as well as industrial high-technology fishing in association with foreign capital and know-how. Agriculture and fishing will be the top-priority sectors of the Second Development Plan 1989-1992.

(b) Industry and energy

In the energy sector the most urgent need relates to the rehabilitation programme of the insolvent government utility (EAGB), so as to remove a major bottleneck in overall economic growth. Due to the small size of the domestic market, the force of international competition and limited raw materials, capital and skilled manpower availability, the Government decided to reduce investment expenditures on industrial projects. During the Second Development Plan, the objective regarding the manufacturing sector is to improve the utilization of existing capacities, as well as the management and the training of personnel. Small private construction firms are to be encouraged, along with the setting up of housing co-operatives.

(c) Social development

The alleviation of the social costs of adjustment should be partly effected through the provision of health and educational services, especially for the urban poor, whose real incomes have declined, in contrast to those of the rural population. In this connexion, a major World Bank study was expected to be issued by December 1988.

3. *Measures to improve the physical infrastructure*

One of the public investment priorities is the expansion of physical infrastructure which supports the growth of exports and overall economic activity. Water transport may be the key to solving the country's internal transport difficulties, especially those encountered in moving agricultural produce to the coast for export. Thus, port improvement projects are under way with a view to rehabilitating and expanding the port of Bissau and four up-river ports.

4. Measures to improve institutional capabilities in the field of development planning and policy

The National Commission for Economic Co-ordination and Control, created in July 1986 and chaired by the President of the Council of State, includes the Ministers of Finance, Planning, Commerce and Tourism, the Governor of the National Bank and the Secretary of State of the Presidency for Economic Affairs and International Co-operation. This Commission is responsible for co-ordinating and assuring the implementation of the measures which make up the Government's economic programmes in the areas of fiscal, monetary, trade, price and wage policy. At the same time, the Commission is entrusted with controlling the execution of the SAP.

5. International support measures

The cumulative external financial gap for the period 1988 to 1992 was estimated by the World Bank and the IMF at about $380 - $400 million. Thus, donor support of the order of $100 million per year will be required if Guinea-Bissau is to maintain the momentum of adjustment and to continue to grow. According to indications provided by donor countries at the Round Table Conference held in July 1988, Guinea-Bissau's financing needs for the next two years should be covered. In the past, the SAP attracted balance-of-payments support from the Netherlands, the Saudi Fund, Switzerland and, more recently, Sweden, the African Development Bank, IFAD, IDA and the IMF. Guinea-Bissau is one of the 17 so-called LIDD (low-income debt-distressed) countries that meet the three criteria for eligibility for debt relief, namely, low per capita income, high debt-service-to-export ratio and an ongoing World Bank and IMF-supported adjustment programme.

6. Impact of national policies and international support measures

The adjustment measures resulted in a positive supply response, particularly in agricultural production and exports. Domestic rice production increased by 12 per cent and the volume of exports rose by 34 per cent in 1987, while the growth of real GDP was estimated to range between 5 and 7 per cent.

HAITI

1. Improving the efficiency of resource allocation

Following the change in regime in February 1986, the provisional National Government Council (CNG) took a number of macro-economic and fiscal measures supported by a three-year structural adjustment loan of SDR 28.0 million under the IMF Structural Adjustment Facility in December 1986 and a World Bank/IDA Economic Recovery Credit of $40 million. However, since June 1987, there have been several serious constitutional crises and Government changes, accompanied by civil stife, as a result of which economic policy reforms have lost their momentum. None of the four Governments that were in office between January and September 1988 had sufficient time to determine or implement a coherent set of economic policies.

(a) External sector policies

The gourde is still officially pegged to the US dollar at the rate of five gourdes per dollar, but the discount of the gourde in the parallel market has widened, reaching more than 6 gourdes to the dollar in January 1988.

Substantial import liberalization was initiated in 1986. By December of that year quantitative restrictions were lifted on all but nine products. In March 1987, a new tariff structure was introduced, replacing the former specific tariffs by *ad valorem* ones. With the exception of five products (rice, maize, millet, flour and gasoline), the tariff rates range from zero to 40 per cent. However, smuggling is reported to have been taking place on an increasing scale since 1987. The export tax on coffee, the main commodity export, was reduced from 22 to 10 per cent in October 1986 and eliminated in October 1987.

(b) Fiscal policies

In the fiscal year 1985/86[177], the overall public sector deficit was reduced, due to cuts in expenditure and improved revenue collection, as well as increased grants-in-aid. This improvement continued until the middle of 1987, at which time the disruption of economic activity, including the collection of taxes, reversed the situation. In 1988 the suspension of economic aid by several donors in the wake of the political events led to sharp cuts in public expenditure.

(c) Improving the efficiency of public enterprises

The public entreprise sector had expanded significantly prior to 1986, in particular through the acquisition of a number of manufacturing entreprises. Since then, several important reforms of this sector have taken place. Thus, two of these entreprises - an edible-oil refinery and a sugar mill - were closed in 1986. The flour mill had been able to generate large operating surpluses in the past, in spite of its high production costs, because of its monopoly situation. However, since 1986, the mill has had to compete with imports, including illegal ones, causing its production to fall. Moreover, it has had to reduce prices considerably and to institute a number of cost-cutting measures. It is expected to break even in FY 1987/88. Surpluses of the electricity company were adversely affected in FY 1986/87 by lower rainfalls, which reduced the relatively cheap hydro-power generation, and by difficulties in ensuring payment of bills in the wake of political disturbances.

2. Sectoral policies

(a) Agriculture

Since 1983, the production and export of coffee, the main export crop, has declined steadily. This is believed to be due to the ageing of trees, and their replacement by food crops, a practice which also worsens the already serious erosion on hillsides. In an effort to increase incentives to producers, the coffee export tax was reduced and then eliminated in 1987 (see above). The production of food crops for domestic consumption increased in the 1985/86 and 1986/87 seasons. However, production of sugar cane and rice was adversely affected by the increase in unofficial imports. The price of sugar was kept artificially high, but the contraband imports led to unsold stocks at factories. In September 1987, price controls on sugar were lifted. The Haitian and Dominican Governments have come to an agreement to construct a $2 million dam for irrigation on the Massacre River dividing the two countries. Work is due to start in 1989.

(b) Industry

Since 1986, the lack of investor confidence and civil disturbances have led to the relocation of several export assembly plants, many of them to the free zones in Santo Domingo. Employment in the assembly industry, which had reached 60,000 in 1984, is estimated to have declined to 40,000 by the end of 1987. Several import-substitution entreprises were reported to be in difficulty due to competition from contraband imports during FY 1987/88.

(c) Tourism

This sector continues to suffer from image problems. Annual receipts from this source stagnated in 1986 and 1987 at around $60 million, which was less than the figure during the early 1980s.

---

177 The fiscal year (FY) ends on 30 September.

(d) Exports

The value of coffee exports dropped sharply between FY 1986 and FY 1987. The volume exported (212,000 bags) was the lowest in recent history, while the unit price obtained fell from $208 per 60 kg bag in FY 1986 to $165 in FY 1987.

(e) Dumping of waste

In January 1988, 20,000 tons of fertilizer ash from the United States were unloaded near Gonaives. After local protests about the dumping of waste, the Government ordered the ash to be removed, but it is believed that this decision has not been enforced.

3. International support measures

Considerable donor support was made available for the policy reforms undertaken in FY 1986/87. However, since the cancellation of elections in November 1987 and the subsequent controversies, several major donors have suspended or frozen their economic aid to Haiti. Venezuela continued to supply oil at concessional rates in the first part of 1988, but this is also reported to have been suspended since the June 1988 military coup.

Haiti is eligible to benefit from preferential trade access under the United States Caribbean Basin Initiative (CBI) and the Canadian CARIBCAN scheme (effective June 1986). There are preliminary indications that the successor to the present Lomé III Convention (1985-1990) between the European Economic Community and the associated African, Caribbean and Pacific (ACP) States might include Haiti among the associated States.

4. Impact of national policies and international support measures

GDP growth, which stood at 0.6 per cent and 0.5 per cent in 1986 and 1987, respectively, continue to be below population growth (1.5 per cent), and 1987 consumption levels are estimated to have been substantially below those of 1980.

KIRIBATI

1. Improving the efficiency of resource use and allocation

Kiribati's National Development Plan (1987-1991) is an expression of the Government's determination to overcome the almost insurmountable obstacles confronting the country's socio-economic development and to secure a higher degree of national economic self-reliance.

(a) External sector policy

Kiribati continues to maintain a liberal foreign-trade regime. Apart from imports prohibited for health, safety or environmental reasons, imports are not restricted. Likewise exports are not impeded by taxes or quantitative barriers, with the sole exception of copra, that can only be exported through the national marketing company. Australian currency remains legal tender in Kiribati. Plans to establish a central bank and to issue a national currency were shelved as being premature, due to the smallness of the country's economy.

(b) Demand-management measures

The Government has pursued cautious fiscal policies aimed at avoiding a large budget deficit. Current expenditure was contained by imposing restraints on salaries in the public sector, as well as by curtailing subsidies to public enterprises. Despite constant budgetary pressure, the Government confined itself to the use of the interest from the Phosphate Reserve Fund to help finance budgetary expenditures, leaving the capital of the Fund intact. As Kiribati does not have a central bank or a national currency, the Government is not in a position to conduct an active monetary policy.

(c) *Mobilization of domestic savings*

The National Provident Fund, to which all public and private sector employees are obliged to contribute, has functioned well. Its assets amounted to more than $8 million at the end of 1985, corresponding to about one-third of GDP, with about two-thirds invested abroad. The tax system underwent repeated modifications, such as the replacing of a flat 25 per cent corporate tax by a two-tier corporate tax system in 1986.

(d) *Expanded role for the private sector*

Private investment, including foreign direct investment, is welcome. However, indigenous private-sector activity outside the subsistence economy is very limited. Export-promoting or import-substituting investments are preferred by the Foreign Investment Commission, which must approve all investments. The Foreign Investment Act provides for duty-free imports of capital goods and raw materials and tax holidays of up to five years. Repatriation of profits and capital is normally unrestricted.

(e) *Improving the efficiency of public enterprises*

Subsidies for public enterprises were estimated at 6 per cent of GDP in 1986. The Government has undertaken efforts to curtail subsidy payments through stricter controls of these enterprises' budget and finance plans, as well as by way of more flexible pricing policies. The possible privatization of a number of enterprises, such as hotels and retail services, is being studied.

2. *Sectoral policies*

(a) *Agriculture and fisheries*

Copra production is increasingly affected by the superannuation of coconut trees. Replantation targets have remained unfulfilled, partly due to the shortage of planting material and partly due to the reluctance of growers to forego current income. Fruit and vegetable farms have been set up with the objective of replacing imports and improving the diet of the population. After the failure to come to terms with the Soviet Union on the renewal of a fishing agreement, the Government has continued its policy of granting fishing rights to foreign fleets. In early 1988, an agreement was concluded with a fishing company based in the Republic of Korea which will pay an annual fee of $420,000 for the right to fish in Kiribati's vast economic zone of 3.5 million km^2. Four new vessels were expected under the EEC's 1987/88 assistance programme designed to strengthen the technical capacity of the domestic fishing fleet.

(b) *Industry and energy*

The Government undertook initiatives to launch small-scale industries with assistance from Australia and China.

(c) *Export development and diversification*

Within the limited options available to the country, the Government has undertaken various efforts to promote the expansion and diversification of exports, but copra and fish continue to be the main export products. Salt has emerged as a new export item, but the Government is facing serious problems in finding outlets for this product. In another development, foreign companies were encouraged to study the feasibility of resuming phospate mining on Banaba (Ocean) Island.

(d) *Social development*

The employment situation is rapidly deteriorating. The increasing number of school-leavers cannot be matched by adequate growth in job opportunities. In addition, employment abroad, particularly in the phosphate mines of Nauru, has become very uncertain due to the fast depletion of resources, while labour demand by foreign merchant ships is stagnating. In 1988 the Government approved a plan to resettle several thousand people from overcrowded atolls, and particularly from the capital, to sparsely populated islands.

3. *Measures to improve the physical infrastructure*

A number of infrastructural projects, almost exclusively financed by external sources, have been implemented. Investment has concentrated on water supply, sewerage and telecommunications.

4. *International support measures*

Since 1986 the country has no longer requested budgetary cash grants from the United Kingdom, but external aid finances the entire development budget, which is of the order of $A 20 million ($16 million).

5. *Impact of national policies and international support measures*

The limited range and uncertain quality of available data make the interpretation of recent economic developments difficult. However, provisional data indicate that real GDP growth was negligible during the first half of the 1980s. In 1986, economic activity picked up, as several public investment projects were started, resulting in an estimated GDP growth rate of 3 per cent.

LAO PEOPLE'S DEMOCRATIC REPUBLIC

1. *Improving the efficiency of resource use and allocation*

The second Five-Year Plan (1986-90) places stress on the need for national industries to make greater use of locally available raw materials, to use wage incentives to raise productivity and to improve the quality of output. The Government has relaxed restrictions on private trading, in the hope that non-regulated industries would respond efficiently to demands for improved supplies of consumer and producer goods.

(a) External sector policies

Several measures have been taken to stimulate exports, such as the simplication of the procedure for allocating foreign exchange and import licenses by allowing public enterprises to retain up to 100 per cent of their export earnings for importing inputs and spare parts; the authorization granted to public enterprises and provincial authorities to export their own products directly; and a greater decentralization of decision-making power to the enterprise level. Preliminary reports show a substantial growth of forestry exports in the period 1985-1987, the sector where the changes were first introduced.

(b) Demand-management measures

The Government has laid down important policy guidelines as part of the 1988 budget exercise and has taken measures to rehabilitate public finance. These measures include: deficit financing through external resources, introduction of financial incentives for civil servants, expenditure control through reduction in civil service employment and consolidation of ministries and Government agencies, overhauling of the tax system, and limiting and postponing projects which require substantial capital investment financed by domestic bank borrowing. The Government is of the view that financial planning requires supplementing the development plan based on constant prices with projections of output, expenditures and the balance of payments at current prices.

(c) Mobilization of domestic savings

A major objective of the Government has been the mobilization of resources at the central government level. In contrast to its past position, the Government now considers it advantageous to finance the 1986-1990 invesment plan through a combination of external assistance and domestic savings. This increased reliance on savings stands in contrast to past practice of transferring nearly all operating income and depreciation allowances of public enterprises to the Government and relying on taxation of the agricultural sector for financing of investment. Moreover, recent reports suggest that increased lending rates have been accompanied by an increase in deposit rates designed to encourage household savings.

(d) Expanded role for the private sector

The available information suggests that the private sector (excluding co-operatives) still plays a large role in production, inasmuch as private agricultural output still accounts for about 20 per cent of the GDP. Moreover, the existence of a parallel market, where a wide variety of commodities are traded, suggests that the private sector is playing a crucial role in commerce. Recent developments in this sector include increased cross-border trade with Thailand, a proposed new investment code which will allow foreign firms to invest either in wholly owned enterprises or to participate in joint ventures, and major reforms in the state-controlled banking system, creating a type of commercial bank which will eventually facilitate private-sector transactions.

(e) Improving the efficiency of public enterprises

Since 1985, the process of improvement in the management system of public enterprises has undergone a significant change, with a considerable adjustment in most official prices and the start of the gradual introduction of a New System of Economic Management (NSEM). Accordingly, the Government has pursued the following policies: (a) placing all public enterprises under a decentralized system of economic management; (b) limiting the degree to which public enterprises are centrally managed, eliminating administrative controls whenever possible; and (c) increasing productivity, volume and quality of production.

2. Sectoral policies

(a) Food and agriculture

Agricultural policies aim at crop diversification, the promotion of cash crops for export, and the resolution of the problem of food shortages and inadequate nutrition. Moreover, government policy would make co-operatives the dominant form of organization for agricultural production in the future. The initial target is to organize all paddy ricelands into co-operatives before the end of the 1986-1990 Plan period. Reports indicate that in 1986 a total of 3,976 farming units, accounting for 42 per cent of the total cultivated area, were operated as co-operatives. Another important aspect of government policy has been to improve farmers' incentives and increase the number of state and co-operative stores from 532 in 1980 to 1,641 in 1985. To the extent that these stores offered manufactured goods at prices far below those in the parallel market, the value to farmers of selling paddy to State shops was increased.

(b) Industry and energy

Industry is largely confined to the processing of agricultural or forestry products, mining and energy generation. Under the NSEM, firms have been granted autonomy. Local managers, in consultation with authorities, devise plans for their enterprises, determine wages and prices on the basis of production costs and anticipated profits, arrange purchases of materials from public or private supplies and are responsible for paying debts, borrowing capital (from the banking sector) and making capital investments. The Council of Ministers has stressed that inefficient, uncompetitive companies unable to make profits or to secure credit from banks will be allowed to go bankrupt and will not be rescued by the State, as was the case previously.

In the energy sector, planned investment has been relatively large. The two main projects currently identified would involve the construction of a hydro-electric power station at Xeset and rural electrification in three southern provinces. The latter is planned to result in additional exports of electricity to Thailand worth about $5 to $6 million per year after 1990.

(c) Social development

The Government has promoted rural health care and has adopted the following policies in the health sector: (a) at the base, a village health clinic, staffed by a health worker, plus one or more nurses; (b) at the district level, a 20- to 30-bed district hospital, staffed by a doctor; (c) at the provincial level, a 100- to 250-bed provincial hospital, with at least four specialized departments. A notable improvement has been reported in this sector. In the field of education the Plan provides for a reform of general education and training institutions to make these correspond more closely to the country's human resource requirements.

3. Measures to improve the physical infrastructure

Priority in the first Five-Year Plan was given to the reconstruction and asphalting of Route 9 (246 km long) from Savannakhet City to Vietnam, which is scheduled for completion by the end of 1988. This road links surplus areas of southern Laos to the Vietnamese seaport of Da Nang. Similarly, river transport has been reported to have improved in recent years, alongside other infrastructural development favouring expanded trade with Viet Nam and with rural regions. In addition, the high cost of road building and its slow progress in recent years have encouraged the Government to proceed with the construction of a 396 km oil pipeline, linking Vientiane to the Vietnamese border near the seaport of Vinh. The Government plans to allocate about 30 per cent of State investment to the transport sector during the 1986-1990 period. Moreover, increased emphasis has also been given to strengthening provincial construction companies.

4. Measures to improve institutional capabilities in the field of development planning and policy

The measures to be implemented in this regard during the 1986-1990 Plan period include: (i) reform and strengthening of economic management, including public-enterprise management, in order to increase investment efficiency; and (ii) the promotion of small and medium-scale projects on the basis of an appropriate economic analysis.

5. International support measures

The Lao People's Democratic Republic continues to receive assistance both from CMEA and Western countries. Recent estimates of official transfers have reported an increasing trend, involving $30 million both in 1986 and 1987, the major part of which came from the convertible-currency area. Similarly, in response to a national subsistence shortfall, an estimated 40,000 tons of rice aid were donated in 1988 by Western Governments, international agencies and NGOs. Moreover, it has been reported that the EC granted agricultural aid worth of ECU 5.5 million in 1988, while Sweden pledged Skr 140 million ($22 million) for 1989-1990.

6. Overall assessment of the impact of the national policies and international support

The economy is reported to have grown by an estimated 7 per cent in 1986, roughly equal to the rate obtaining during the first Plan period (1981-1985). However, due to drought and the consequent set-back in agriculture and hydro-electric production, the GDP growth rate for 1987 has been estimated at only 3 per cent. In spite of some difficulties encountered in 1988 in implementing the economic reforms, as confirmed by official pronouncements, continuation of economic growth has been reported.

LESOTHO

1. *Improving the efficiency of resource use and allocation*

In 1988 Lesotho adopted a new economic programme for the three-year period up to March 1991, supported by a structural adjustment facility (SAF) arrangement with the IMF. The principal objectives are to achieve an average GDP growth rate of 4 per cent during this period and a substantial reduction of the budget deficit. The programme also aims at reducing the debt service ratio, increasing the level of net official reserves, and moderating the rate of inflation. The Government has adopted a number of production and demand-management policies in order to achieve these objectives.

(a) External sector policies

In Lesotho, external sector and monetary policies continue to be largely circumscribed by the country's membership in the Southern African Customs Union (SACU) and the Common Monetary Area (the former Rand Monetary Area). The recently adopted economic programme envisages measures to promote export-oriented and import-substitution industries, to discourage capital outflows, and to limit foreign non-concessional borrowing. The Government has decided to set up an export financing scheme to support exporters with credits at preferential terms. This scheme was expected to become operational in 1988. A new exchange control order was promulgated in 1987 in order to provide for more efficient administration of exchange controls.

(b) Demand-management measures

Since 1985, the budgetary situation has been characterized by stagnating revenues from SACU, an increasing overall deficit and recourse to domestic bank borrowing. There has been a slow-down in spending on development. In FY 1987/88[178], certain foodstuffs and other basic commodities were exempted from sales tax in order to reduce the burden of taxation on the poor. The Government has taken steps to convert part of its short-term domestic debt into longer-term debt. Under the new economic programme, the overall budget deficit is to be reduced through a combination of revenue-raising measures and expenditure restraint, especially of recurrent outlays. A major objective under the programme is also to diminish the constraints on financial intermediation and encourage the expansion of credit by the commercial banks to the private sector. Following increases in South African interest rates, Lesotho also increased its rates in the first half of 1988.

(c) Mobilization of domestic savings and human resources

Funding was arranged in early 1988 to provide for expanding the rural branch network of the Lesotho Agricultural Development Bank, the apex organization for mobilizing rural savings. The co-operative movement continues to be an important vehicle for mobilizing the rural population. New manpower development programmes have been set up, in part to strengthen the pool of technical and managerial skills required for the Lesotho Highlands Water Project.

(d) Role of the private sector and of public enterprises

The Government encourages the development of private enterprise, both local and foreign, and welcomes foreign investment. The tax holiday offered to investors in Lesotho has been increased from 6 to 10-15 years. The parastatal Lesotho National Development Corporation (LNDC) continues to follow a divestiture policy of transferring viable companies to the private sector. Under a new policy

[178] The fiscal year (FY) ends on 31 March.

initiative, LNDC will provide equity participation in joint ventures with foreign investors, holding shares in trust for indigenous businessmen for future participation. Local participation is encouraged, *inter alia*, in projects linked to the Highlands Water Project. However, the strengthening of public enterprise operations is also foreseen under the new economic programme.

2. Sectoral policies

(a) Food and agriculture

The Government's agricultural strategy aims at expanding and diversifying agricultural production, as well as raising productivity. A review of land-tenure legislation has been undertaken with a view to promoting more efficient land utilization. Other policy initiatives taken or envisaged include improvement of livestock management, watershed management programmes, the setting of crop production targets and development of contract farming, improvement of distribution and marketing facilities, and the promotion of high-value horticultural crops. Restructuring of some agricultural support institutions is also foreseen, including the marketing parastatal Co-op Lesotho.

(b) Industry

Industrial policies will focus on the provision of incentives for private investment through tax relief, the establishment of industrial estates and promotional support, particularly for export-oriented industries. The LNDC has already intensified its investment promotion efforts and embarked on a stepped-up capital investment programme. A number of new manufacturing enterprises have been set up, and others (e.g. clothing, pharmaceutical products) have been expanded. The advance-factory-shell programme of LNDC has been expanded (six new factory buildings were inaugurated in August1987), and a fourth industrial estate is planned. Some 40 projects have been identified for possible implementation by Lesotho-based companies to service the Lesotho Highlands Water Project. Among the first ventures on this list to be realized were a crushed stone project and two steel fabrication projects. A joint venture agreement on the establishment of a wool and mohair scouring plant and a wool-tops-making mill was signed at the end of 1987. The corporation will eventually carry out the scouring and combing of the entire Lesotho clip (wool and mohair being Lesotho's major traditional exports).

(c) Energy

The Lesotho Highlands Water Project includes a hydropower component. Some alternative hydro-electric schemes were also under study (Oxbow project) or under way (a series of mini-projects).

3. Measures to improve the physical infrastructure

Road building and rehabilitation has received a sizeable share of capital expenditure in recent years (see part I, box 13). Among other spin-off benefits, the Highlands Water Project will improve the rural infrastructure, e.g. roads in the project area. An urban development project was to be launched, providing for housing and land development.

4. Measures to improve institutional capabilities in the field of development planning and policy

The Fourth Five-year Development Plan of Lesotho, covering the period FY 1986/87-1990/91, was published at the beginning of 1988. The Plan provides the general framework for the country's development over the medium term, and is supplemented by the economic programme adopted in mid-1988, which focuses on adjustment measures and the improvement of economic management. The Ministry of Planning and Economic Affairs has been restructured to carry out its functions more effectively. The formal establishment in 1986 of Development Councils at three levels - village, ward and district - aims to strengthen development planning machinery, with the focus on popular participation.

5. *International support measures*

The net inflow of concessional resources to Lesotho steadily decreased from the peak of $108 million reached in 1983 to only $88 million in 1986. Other official flows fell back to $4 million in 1986 after an upsurge to $25million in 1985, when substantial inflows of multilateral development financing on non-concessional terms and of private export credits were recorded. However, an increase in new aid commitments in 1986 point to a possible recovery in the aid inflow in the near future. The SAF arrangement concluded with the IMF in July 1988 provides for a loan totalling SDR 9.6 million in support of Lesotho's new economic programme.

6. *Impact of national policies and international support measures*

Real GDP increased by 5.8 per cent in 1986, mainly due to a strong recovery in manufacturing, construction and domestic trade. Growth in 1987 was somewhat lower, at 4.7 per cent. However, agriculture, which had experienced a decline in 1986 owing to unfavourable weather conditions, performed better in 1987, mainly due to a recovery in crop production. Manufacturing also continued to expand, and its share in GDP is estimated to have doubled to over ten per cent between 1980 and 1987. These developments did not offset the effects of the uneven and low growth in real GDP in the first half of the 1980s, which was lower than the population growth rate. Thus, while real per capita GDP recovered appreciably in 1986 and 1987, it did not recover the level attained in 1980. Real GNP, almost one-half of which is accounted for by workers' remittances, grew only marginally in 1986 and 1987. GNP per capita is also estimated to have declined in real terms since 1980.

Both the budget and balance of payments remained under pressure in 1986 and 1987. The overall budget deficit widened significantly in FY 1987/88, as total receipts grew only marginally, while both recurrent and development spending expanded. According to balance-of-payments projections for 1987, a further deterioration in both the current account and the overall balance was projected, despite the remarkable performance of merchandise exports. These increased by over 60 per cent, albeit over a modest base, mainly as a result of the rapid expansion of exports of manufactured goods. Workers' remittances constitute the preponderant part of external receipts, and a fall in these in 1987 was thought to explain in large part the overall balance-of-payments developments. There was a slowdown of inflation in 1987, reflecting both a lower rate of increase in import prices and the application of measures taken by the Government to lower the tax burden on low-income households.

The construction phase of the Lesotho Highlands Water Project to exploit the vast water resources of the country, the largest development scheme ever undertaken in Lesotho, has started with the construction of access roads to the dam site. The impact of these project activities and continued expansion in trade and industry were expected to sustain the growth momentum in 1988.

MALAWI

Malawi continues to pursue the stabilization and structural adjustment efforts which have been undertaken with IMF and World Bank support since the early 1980s. In July 1988 Malawi became the first country to use the resources of the Fund's enhanced structural adjustment facility (ESAF).

1. *Improving the efficiency of resource use and allocation*

(a) External sector policies

The exchange rate of the Malawi kwacha is periodically adjusted. A devaluation of 15 per cent in terms of the currencies of Malawi's principal trading partners took place in January 1988. Import controls had been introduced in 1986 as the foreign-exchange constraint was tightening. At the beginning of 1988, the liberalization of the importation of key raw materials and spare parts needed by industry was announced. Foreign-exchange allocations for these can now be dealt with by commercial banks without prior approval from the Reserve Bank. Further import liberalization will involve the phased elimination of foreign-exchange controls for other imports and the lifting of certain licensing requirements. The Government has launched an export incentive programme to provide fiscal and non-fiscal incentives to exporters (e.g. ensuring access to foreign exchange through an export revolving fund).

(b) Demand-management measures

The current stabilization and adjustment programme aims at restraining aggregate demand through strict monetary and credit policies and reduction of the budget deficit. Price liberalization was a key element in the earlier phases of the structural adjustment programme. A programme of fiscal action to mobilize revenue and contain expenditure was initiated in 1987. A comprehensive tax reform programme is being implemented over a period of several years, *inter alia* By way of an enhanced revenue-raising capacity based on more efficient tax structures and administration. Controls on the interest-rate structure of commercial banks have been removed to facilitate the emergence of market-determined rates.

(c) Mobilization of human resources

Community development programmes aim to help rural people to raise their standards of living and develop their communities through local participation, initiative and various self-help projects. A pilot programme launched in 1987 for income-generating activities for women in selected rural growth centres has proved successful, and such activities are being expanded. A National Commission on Women in Development has been formed. A comprehensive human resources study has been undertaken to assess the need for high and middle-level manpower in both the public and private sectors.

(d) Role of the private sector and of public enterprises

Government policy in relation to the expansion of production capacity is to create a general climate which encourages private enterprise and investment, both domestic and foreign. The recently adopted economic policy initiatives particularly aim to stimulate private industrial activity. For instance, measures instituted in 1986 to limit Government imports have been further strengthened in order to reduce any "crowding out" effect on private-sector imports.

Action has been taken to improve the performance of the parastatal sector, in particular the Agricultural Development and Marketing Corporation (ADMARC). A number of cost-cutting, rationalization and restructuring measures, as well as management reform, were implemented in 1987 with respect to the Corporation. ADMARC is to relinquish its shareholdings in a number of companies, and a number of agricultural estates owned by it will be sold off. Other parastatals are also implementing programmes aimed at restructuring and cost control, as well as strengthening of their management. At the same time, action has been taken to encourage private-sector participation in the marketing of smallholder produce. A wide range of tariff and price adjustments were implemented during 1987.

2. Sectoral policies

In 1988 Malawi published a Statement of Development Policies 1987-1996 (DEVPOL), setting out the country's longer-term development strategy. In the Statement, emphasis was placed on four key sectors: agriculture, industry, trade and tourism; mining; and the social sector. However, the strengthening of the transport sector was also foreseen.

(a) Agriculture

Smallholder producer prices are being periodically reviewed. At the beginning of the 1987/88 crop year, producer prices for a number of smallholder crops were increased, e.g. for maize by 36 per cent. A nation-wide credit fund has been set up to assist smallholders to purchase necessary inputs. Fertilizer subsidies are to be gradually removed over a period of time, in conjunction with increasing producer prices. Policy focus in this sector remains on food self-sufficiency, improving productivity and reform of agricultural marketing.

(b) Industry

Recent measures to increase investment and production in industry include: an intensified dialogue between Government and industry through a series of consultations; general policy measures to create a climate conducive to industrial activity, in particular the liberalization of imports and the tax reform programme mentioned above; and special export incentives. A major feature of future industrial policy will be the promotion of small-scale manufacture enterprises. A number of industrial priority projects are being promoted by the Government in collaboration with the national development financing institutions and private entrepreneurs. These include projects for a tannery, a refrigeration assembly plant, and pesticide and fertilizer-producing plants. Studies have also been conducted on the prospects for developing agro-industries.

(c) Social development

The new Statement on Development Policies places high priority on improving social infrastructure, particularly in primary health care and education. Special attention is being paid under the current economic adjustment programme to safeguarding the provision of social services. A nation-wide functional literacy programme launched in 1986 aims at covering two million Malawians by 1995.

3. Measures to improve the physical infrastructure

The new Northern Transport Corridor, which is being developed to seaports in the neighbouring United Republic of Tanzania, is expected to reduce transport costs and to stimulate trade, including trade with neighbouring countries. It should ultimately have the capacity to handle one-third of Malawi's external traffic. Work on the Corridor also involves upgrading and rehabilitating the road network within Malawi. Work is also going on to reopen the traditional rail link to Nacala (Mozambique).

4. International support measures

Bilateral concessional aid to Malawi showed a declining trend in the first half of the 1980s but picked up in 1986 both in terms of disbursements ($90 million in 1986, as compared to $53 million in 1985) and commitments. Multilateral institutions have been instrumental both in providing finance from their own resources and in mobilizing stronger bilateral support for Malawi's economic adjustment. Earlier in the 980s, the World Bank and IDA provided three structural adjustment loans to Malawi, while several stand-by agreements and an extended arrangement were concluded with the IMF. A new 15-month stand-by arrangement with the IMF for SDR 13 million was concluded in March 1988. This was followed by an ESAF arrangement in July 1988, under which Malawi will have the right to draw up to SDR 56 million from the Fund. Moreover, Malawi obtained an industrial and trade policy adjustment credit of $70 million from IDA in June 1988. Co-financing for an additional $90.5million from bilateral and other sources was expected in conjunction with the IDA credit. Malawi is one of the countries eligible for support under the special programme of assistance for low-income debt-distressed countries in sub-Saharan Africa, sponsored by the World Bank.

Following the latest IMF stand-by arrangement, Malawi reached agreement with its Paris Club and London Club creditors in April 1988 on rescheduling its external debt. In the Paris Club, official and officially guaranteed debt was rescheduled over a 20-year period, including a grace period of 10 years.

The Consultative Group for Malawi met for the second time in Paris in June 1988. The Group commended the Government's medium-term strategy and expressed its strong endorsement of the ongoing adjustment programme. According to estimates presented at the meeting, external resource flows of $555 million over the next two years were needed to implement this programme successfully. Commitments made or indicated at the meeting suggested that these financing requirements would be met. It was agreed that a large proportion of the funds would have to be in the form of balance-of-payments and budget support. Additional financial requirements arise from the need to care for the large number of displaced persons who have entered Malawi.

5. *Impact of national policies and international support measures*

Recent economic developments in Malawi have been affected by worsening terms of trade, an increased external debt burden (debt service payments averaged over 50 per cent of exports of goods and non-factor services in the biennium 1986-1987) and regional instability, causing the country's traditional transport routes to the sea through Mozambique to remain closed and a major influx of displaced persons to move into Malawi. While there had been some recovery in the economy after the introduction of the stabilization and adjustment programme in the early 1980s, with GDP increasing at an annual rate of 4.1 per cent in real terms in the period 1982-1985, real GDP contracted by 1.1 per cent in 1986 and by 0.2 per cent in 1987. Manufacturing has stagnated for several years, and there was only small growth in smallholder agriculture in 1987. While Malawi had previously produced regular food surpluses, a food deficit appeared in the 1986/87 growing season, as parts of the country were affected by drought and crop pests. Inflation, as measured by the retail price index, increased to 27 per cent in 1987 from 15 per cent in 1986. Both the budget and the current account have come under heavy pressure. However, the overall balance of payments turned around from a deficit in 1986 to show a surplus in 1987, due *inter alia* to continued import contraction and to the structural adjustment assistance received from multilateral and bilateral donors.

The inflow of displaced persons from Mozambique has significantly added to budgetary pressure and put a strain on social services, as well as land resources. The number of such persons rose from an estimated 80,000 in December 1986 to more than half a million by mid-1988 and was still increasing thereafter.

MALDIVES

1. *Improving the efficiency of resource allocation*

The end of 1987 marked the culmination of the Maldives' first National Development Plan (1985-1987), which had three major objectives; improvement in general living standards; reduction of population and economic imbalances between Male and the outer atolls; and the attainment of greater self-reliance for future growth.

(a) *External sector policies*

The Government's strategy aims to maximize net foreign exchange receipts through expansion of traditional sectors - fisheries and tourism - and diversification into non-traditional products and markets. In recent years, major investments directed at the upgrading of processing, canning and other infrastructural facilities have significantly enhanced the export capacity of fisheries. Improved processing, in addition to increasing value added, will allow for maximum conversion of fish waste into exportable products. At the same time, domestic production of tin cans and block ice is being encouraged as a foreign-exchange savings measure. The recent conclusion of marketing arrangements with the Federal Republic of Germany and Switzerland for fish, and with Canada for textiles, is designed to reduce dependence on traditional markets. The export drive is expected to receive additional impetus from the establishment in Gan Island of an export processing zone backed with port, airport and electricity services.

(b) *Demand-management measures*

In response to growing foreign exchange shortages, deliberate measures have been taken to dampen import demand through the imposition of strict credit ceilings on banks for both domestic and foreign-currency loans. Guidelines have also been established to channel credit to priority sectors. Also in force is an import licensing system, which gives priority to foreign-exchange allocations geared to activities with foreign-exchange saving or earning potential. Measures of import restraint have been complemented by the rationalization of the tariff structure, with the aim of promoting essential imports and discouraging low-priority imports.

(c) *Mobilization of domestic savings*

Plans are being considered to expand commercial banking facilities in the outer atolls to mobilize domestic savings. An increase in the coverage of dutiable imports and an upward revision of tariff rates have helped to accelerate domestic resource mobilization.

2. *Sectoral policies*

(a) *Fishing and agriculture*

Substantial investments have been made in recent years to stimulate the key *fisheries* industry, through increased mechanization of vessels, improvements in fuel distribution, and an increase in procurement prices paid to fishermen. Several projects are under way to expand and upgrade fish catching, processing and related infrastructural facilities. In *agriculture*, the government strategy aims to reduce dependence on imported food staples by encouraging production of vegetables, fruit and poultry through distribution of improved varieties of seeds and extension services. A major rehabilitation of coconut plantations is under way through substantial replanting programmes, pest control and the free distribution of seedlings.

(b) *Services*

Promotional activities in the tourism sector have focused on attracting visitors from Australia, Hong Kong, and the United Kingdom, the development of new resorts and the upgrading of existing hotel facilities. The establishment of a second tourist resort at Ari is expected to give additional stimulus to the industry. Plans are under way to start a hotel school in Male to upgrade the quality of tourist services. In the area of shipping, rationalization measures have consisted of a drastic reduction in the fleet size to counter problems of overcapacity and the replacement of old vessels with more fuel-efficient substitutes.

(c) *Industry*

Industrial strategy is geared primarily to export promotion and diversification away from traditional sectors. Incentives are given to encourage substantial investments in export-oriented industries by the waiving of import duties on capital goods and on recurrent imported inputs for a prolonged period after commencement of operations. Textile production is being encouraged through improved incentives for workers. The authorities are also promoting collaboration with foreign capital through joint ventures in primarily export-oriented activities (e.g. a Maldivian-Hong Kong joint venture in textiles).

(d) *Social development*

The authorities' main preoccupation is to promote decentralization to alleviate congestion in Male. Consistent with this objective, the Government is planning to convert two tourist resorts in Male into residential areas. Several areas in outlying islands have moreover been designated as development centres. The strategy for development of the outer atolls will focus on the implementation of fisheries and agricultural development programmes supported by a full range of educational, health and training facilities. In the educational sector, the authorities are planning to expand secondary schools in the outer atolls through acceleration of teacher training programmes.

3. *Measures to improve the physical infrastructure*

A project to expand and upgrade the airport to accommodate larger planes has been under construction for the last several years. New and more efficient commercial harbor facilities have recently been completed in the north-western part of Male, while the expansion of inter-island air and sea linkages is being planned. In the area of urban development, a land reclamation project is in progress in Male Island, the aim being to add some 30 per cent to the existing land area for housing purposes. Male is highly congested with an estimated population density of 33,000 inhabitants per square kilometre in 1985; the comparable figures for the entire Maldives archipelago and for the Comoros are 576 and 176 respectively.

4. Measures to improve institutional capabilities in the field of development planning and policy

A Ministry of Planning and Development was created in 1982 with the intention of strengthening the planning and administration machinery of the country. The Ministry has so far developed its first National Development Plan (1985-1987), and efforts are under way to lay the groundwork for medium and longer-term development planning.

The authorities have relied to a large extent on multilateral assistance to assist in the conceptualization of broad national as well sectoral development strategies and the presentation of projects for the mobilization of donor assistance.

5. International support measures

Donor funding was mobilised in 1987 for four major projects: (a) a $22 million project for the expansion of Hulule International Airport, to be funded by a consortium of OPEC donors; (b) a $16.1 million Asian Development Bank-funded electricity project; (c) a project for combined water and road development supported by Danish grants (about $6.4 million); and (d) a project for coastal protection in Male financed by Japanese grants in the region of $6-7 million.

6. Impact of national policies and international support measures

After experiencing an annual average growth of 14 per cent for 1984 and 1985, real GDP growth moderated to 7 per cent in 1986, as unfavorable weather dampened fisheries, while civil disturbances in Sri Lanka adversely affected tourism. Preliminary indications point to a recovery in GDP growth in 1987, aided mainly by a recovery in tourism. In the *fisheries* sector, the decline in production by some 3.9 per cent from 1986 levels was somewhat cushioned by higher international prices for tuna prevailing in the latter part of 1987 and an increase in the value-added component of tuna exports with the coming into operation of new processing facilities. *Tourism* recovered with a 17 per cent increase over 1986 levels in the number of arrivals. *Construction* activity was similarly buoyant due to significant infrastructural development. Rationalization measures in the *shipping* industry enabled the sector to report a modest profit for the second year in succession. *Manufacturing* developed positively, with the main growth impetus coming from the garments sector.

Maldives' extensive reliance on external financing for its investment programmes is reflected in its very high debt-to-GDP ratio, averaging 98 per cent in the 1985-1986 biennium. The debt-service-to-exports ratio, which averaged only some 16 per cent during the same period, has been limited by the concessional nature of the debt. Pressures on external liquidity during 1986 obliged the authorities to seek rescheduling from the Islamic Development Bank of a $7 million loan to finance a lease purchase agreement for two ships.

MALI

1. Improving the efficiency of resource use and allocation

Mali continues to implement policy measures aimed at improved resource use which were recommended by the IMF during the negotiations on several successive stand-by agreements (see section 5 below).

(a) External sector policies

The 1986 revision of the investment code provides for measures to encourage export business, such as reduced taxes and duties for a period of 2-5 years. Import tariffs on 54 raw materials and intermediate goods were reduced in early 1988.

(b) Demand-management measures

Great emphasis is being placed on containing public expenditure. Measures taken recently in this regard include:

(i) Reducing personnel in the central Government and in parastatal enterprises. As of April 1988, personnel cuts in the parastatal sector had reached 3,688, with facilities being offered for the recycling of dismissed personnel in the private sector. Personnel cuts in the parastatal sector are planned to total 10,000.

(ii) A campaign against corruption in the public sector, with severe sentences pronounced in 1987.

Despite these measures, the 1988 budget provides for a deficit of CFAF 34 billion (about $115 million and equivalent to about 6 per cent of GDP). This compares with balanced *ex-ante* budgets in the previous two years, which nevertheless produced realized deficits estimated at around CFAF 20 billion ($57.8 million) and CFAF 30 billion ($100 million) respectively.

(c) Mobilization of domestic savings and human resources

Village associations (*tons villageois*) continue to be promoted, serving *inter alia* to mobilize and channel financial resources and human resources in rural areas. The Government intends to provide assistance for the retraining of employees affected by personnel cuts in privatised enterprises.

(d) Expanded role for the private sector

The private sector is expected to play the key role in the marketing of grains; to this effect, the Government is promoting the organization of cereals trading firms. A law enacted in December 1987 provides for the privatization of 13 out of 40 State-owned companies. In seven of them, the Government is to retain a controlling share. The decision to liquidate SOMIEX, the State-owned import-export company, was reported in July 1988 to be definitive, notwithstanding the large number of jobs (4,500) at stake. The company's monopoly privileges had already been abolished twice before.

Reductions in tax rates for industrial and commercial enterprises were announced in October 1987.

There exists a clear tendency favouring joint ventures, probably in view of the limited response so far of the local private sector to the incentives described above. This has become particularly evident in the mining sector (see 2(b) below).

(e) Improving the efficiency of public enterprises

Measures have been taken with a view to improving the effiency of public enterprises, and external support for this purpose has been secured, in particular from IDA, the African Development Fund and bilateral donors. The measures relate to:

(i) Personnel cuts;

(ii) The restructuring or divestiture of State-owned enterprises, including the reform of the Banque de développement du Mali, the privatization of 13 State-owned enterprises and the liquidation of 15 other enterprises;

(iii) Agreements entered into with foreign companies and Governments joint management of state-owned concerns.

The Government announced that as a result of these measures the parastatal sector registered a global surplus in 1987, for the first time in 15 years, which amounted to more than CFAF 2 billion ($6.8 million) and that some of the parastatal enterprises had become exporters.

2. Sectoral policies

(a) Food and agriculture

Mali's current food policy is based essentially on three elements:

(i) Rehabilitating the Office du Niger, the State-owned concern responsible for the management and irrigation of the Niger River region, which supplies most of the local production of rice and one-third of that of sugar. Financial support for this purpose has been secured from IDA, the Federal Republic of Germany, France, the Netherlands and the USSR.

(ii) Liberalizing the marketing of foodstuffs. As announced in December 1987,

OPAM, the State-owned marketing board, is to withdraw from the marketing of cereals and will concentrate on the management of food security stocks and on the distribution of grain in food-deficit areas.

(iii) Restricting imports of low-priced rice, so as to facilitate the sale of local rice, stocks of which had accumulated in the 1986-1987 season, and thereby encourage future local production. With international prices for rice reaching a 17-year low in 1986/87, imports of rice were restricted in 1986 and suspended from April 1987 to June 1988. As a result, local paddy rice was being traded at CFAF 90 per kg in July 1988, as compared to the official intervention price of CFAF 70, and rice importers have been investing in local rice production, e.g. through the purchase of a husking plant. The rice import ban was lifted on 29 June 1988, as Mali is not self-sufficient in rice, but consideration is being given to the imposition of a variable import levy on this item, which would offset fluctuations of world prices.

(b) Mining, industry and services

The policy favouring joint ventures has yielded the following concrete achievements:

(i) A joint venture for the mining of gold in the western region was set up between the Malian Government and a French company. Commercial exploitation is expected to start in early 1989, for a period of nine years, at an annual exploitation rate of 400 kg during the first half of that period and 800 kg during the latter part. In addition, a three-year gold prospection agreement was entered into in July 1988 between the Malian Government and the Canadian-Mali Gold Corporation.

(ii) Joint Chinese-Malian management of several textile, tanning and sugar enterprises, as well as of a pharmacy, has been going on since 1984.

(iii) A joint venture with a French company was established in 1987 for the production of cottonseed oil.

(iv) A joint Belgian-British-Malian venture was created in 1988 for the exploitation of marble deposits (estimated at 30 million tonnes).

(c) Energy

In view of continuing low water levels in the River Niger and of the ensuing adverse effects on hydro-electric power generation, several thermal power stations had to resume operations in 1987. A 150 km high-tension line, allowing for a greater utilization of hydro-electric power, is to be built with external financial support, principally from Canada. Efforts aimed at energy diversification are under way, including trial solar power units and plans to develop ethanol (ethyl alcohol) production from sugar cane.

(d) Environment

A programme of action to combat desertification was adopted as a follow-up to the Round Table Meeting held in Bamako in December 1985. A sectoral follow-up meeting with donors was held in Bamako in June 1987. Anti-locust brigades have been set up in hundreds of villages, with the aim of training and preparing the local population for the prevention of and fight against locust upsurges.

3. Measures to improve the physical infrastructure

A major dam involving irrigation and hydroelectric power generation is being built at Manatali within the framework of the Organization for the Development of the Senegal River (OMVS), membership of which comprises Mali, Mauritania and Senegal. A second bridge across the River Niger at Bamako, expected to substantially reduce urban congestion, is to be constructed with external support.

4. Measures to improve institutional capabilities in the field of development planning and policy

Mali is currently engaged in fundamental policy reforms, an endeavour which has led to a delay in the elaboration of the 1987-1991 development plan to succeed the previous one which ended in 1985.

5. *International support measures*

Bilateral ODA from DAC countries and DAC-financed multilateral agencies increased from $210 million in 1981 to $331 million in 1986. Concessional assistance from all sources represented 80.3 per cent of imports in 1986.

The latest agreement with the IMF was finalized in August 1988, involving a support package which includes SDR 12.7 million under a 14-month stand-by arrrangement and SDR 32.3 million under a three-year SAF loan. Support for this programme is further granted by France (FF 160 million, or about $27 million), whereas the Federal Republic of Germany has extended a DM 1O million ($5.7 million) credit for the purchase of goods. Mali was the first country to benefit from the menu approach agreed at the Toronto Summit, when it rescheduled an unspecified portion of its external debt at the Paris Club in October 1988.

6. *Impact of national policies and international support measures*

After three years of stagnation or decline, real GDP grew by 10.8 per cent in 1986 reflecting two years of good rainfall which led to agricultural production growth of 5.0 and 5.8 per cent in 1985 and 1986 respectively. Agricultural production, however, is estimated to have slightly declined in 1987 (-0.3 per cent).

MAURITANIA

1. *Improving the efficiency of resource use and allocation*

Mauritania's efforts to cope with structural economic disequilibria, are being implemented within the framework of the Economic Recovery Programme 1985-1988 (ERP).

(a) External sector policies

The Government continued to implement policies involving a progressive liberalization of pricing and marketing. Within the framework of its 1988 budget, Mauritania reduced import tariffs on about 700 items, such as publications, which are now tariff-exempt, and motor vehicles, tariffs on which were reduced by 10 per cent.

(b) Demand-management measures

The Public Investment Programme has been scaled down, placing emphasis on rural development, and strict limits have been placed on personnel expenditure.

(c) Mobilization of domestic savings

The 1987 and 1988 budgets introduced major reforms in the field of tax revenue, *inter alia* adoption of improved collection methods to avoid tax evasion, better co-ordination within the Ministry of Finance to strengthen the means of distraint for unpaid taxes, widening the tax base by stricter controls on potential taxpayers, and re-examination of tax and duty exemption schemes. These measures generated central government budgetary surpluses in the years 1986 and 1987. As a result of low income levels, private savings play a negligible role in the development of the economy, although they have increased substantially since 1985.

(d) Mobilization of human resources

Although no official record of the number of unemployed exists, the Government acknowledges that the total is significant and on the increase. Migration from rural areas have contributed to the rise. The restructuring of public enterprises involving personnel cuts is under way. Alternative employment opportunities are being created by using a fund, jointly managed with donors, from the proceeds of food sales.

(e) Expanded role for the private sector

Among the measures taken within the framework of the ERP are the restructuring and privatizing of selected state companies and the promotion of private sector activities.

2. Sectoral policies

(a) Food and agriculture

Government policies related to rural development and agriculture are geared towards two main objectives: increased food production, in order to reduce dependence on imports, and incentives for the rural population to remain in its present location.

(b) Industry and energy

Government policy is aimed at promoting private initiative as the main driving force for the growth of the industrial sector. In manufacturing, the policy is to promote both national and foreign private investment and to create small and medium-size enterprises. In the field of energy the first priority has been assigned to energy savings and the second priority to conserving and reconstituting the vegetation cover through a reforestation programme.

(c) Mining activities

Despite the recovery in output and production during the period 1985-1987, medium- and long-term prospects for iron-ore marketing are weak. The mining of other mineral resources, such as copper, gypsum and phosphates, has been affected by limited demand and low world prices.

(d) Export development and diversification

Since 1983 fishing has surpassed mining as a source of foreign exchange. In April 1987, the Government adopted a new long-term strategy for the fishing sector containing two overall aims: to conserve resources and integrate the fishing industry into the rest of the economy. In this respect, the Government stopped issuing licenses to foreign vessels for demersal fishing. New fishing zones have been set out to restrict the catches in specific areas. The second objective of increasing local added value will be pursued through eight investment projects costing up to $60 million. They include a ship repair yard, the development of small-scale fishing and training programmes.

(e) Social development

In 1986 the Government launched a five-year literacy campaign. The Secretary of State for the Elimination of Illiteracy, a new post, is responsible for the campaign. In 1988 an educational reform was launched, aimed at expanding primary school enrolment.

3. Measures on physical infrastructure

The Manantali Dam, the largest civil engineering project in the Sahel region, was completed on 31 March 1988, as scheduled. The dam took over six years to be built, and the cost of $575 million remained within the budget. This construction is central to the scheme of large-scale irrigation, water transport and electricity for the three partner countries (Mali, Mauritania and Senegal) grouped in the Organization for the Development of the Senegal River (OMVS).

4. Measures to improve institutional capabilities in the field of development planning and policy

Since 1985 the Government instituted significant changes to establish firmer control over economic and financial management. The Ministries of Plan and Finance were merged into a single Ministry of Economy and Finance (MEF). For the first time, external debt commitments and aid agreements were subjected to prior authorization by the Ministry. The investment budgeting framework was broadened to cover not only domestic but also external resources, including counterpart funds from the sale of food aid. A task force was constituted to prepare the consolidated investment budgets for 1987 and 1988. An Interministerial Committee has been created, consisting of the Minister of Economy and Finance, the Governor of the Central Bank and the Secretary-General of the Government, to strengthen co-ordination of ERP implementation. Finally, in order to help the MEF to meet the increasing management challenges of the ERP implementation, the Minister requested a comprehensive internal assessment of the Ministry's organization and performance, department by department, with emphasis on those functions most critical for the accomplishment of the ERP objectives.

5. *International support measures*

The implementation of the ERP has been supported by three stand-by agreements with the IMF, two debt reschedulings under the auspices of the Paris Club, and a three-year Structural Adjustment Facility (SAF) loan of SDR 21.5 million approved in September 1986.

6. *Impact of national policy and international support measures*

Real GDP during the period 1981-1985 grew at an average annual rate of 3 per cent a year, or about the same as population growth. During the ERP period, the average GDP growth rate rose to 3.6 per cent. Financial stringency has allowed public savings to accrue and to offset at least in part the budgetary effects of servicing the country's external debt. Substantial real gains were achieved in agriculture, fishing and mineral production. Food remained the largest single import item in 1986 and 1987, reflecting Mauritania's persistent inability to achieve self-sufficiency in food. This situation could be aggravated due to the catastrophic proportions reached by the locust invasion.

NEPAL

1. *Improving the efficiency of resources use and allocation*

Late in 1985 Nepal embarked upon a medium-term Structural Adjustment Programme (SAP) for sustained economic growth. The objectives of this SAP included macro-economic stabilization, improved resource mobilization, increased investment efficiency, improvement in the working of the public sector enterprises and greater participation of the private sector in areas such as agriculture, forestry, trade and industry. More recently, in October 1987, the International Monetary Fund (IMF) approved a loan of SDR 23.69 million over the subsequent three years under the Structural Adjustment Facility (SAF) to support a new phase of the SAP extending until 1990.

(a) *External sector policies*

Several external trade policy measures were implemented in 1988. These have aimed at facilitating the supply of imported inputs for exportable commodities and import substitution. The measures have included the introduction of an open general licensing (OGL) policy, a duty drawback system, the construction of bonded warehouse facilities and improved incentives for both exports and efficient import-substitution activities. With a view to identifying current problems in the export sector, a high-level Export Promotion and Monitoring Committee was constituted in 1988. Similarly, a flexible exchange-rate policy has been maintained since 1985 which takes into account the differential between Nepal's rate of inflation and that of its main trading partners. Provisions to encourage foreign private investment either in fully owned foreign enterprises or in joint ventures have led to such investments in the fields of textiles, cold-storage facilities, transport, pump-sets, television and ready-made garments.

(b) *Demand-management measures*

The Structural Adjustment Programme

requires an increase in development expenditure from 12 per cent of GDP in FY 1985/86[179] to 16 per cent of GDP in 1990/91. The increase is to be achieved by way of a larger allocation of resources to selected investment programmes and to the operation and maintenance of completed projects. Despite this increase of planned expenditures, fiscal policy aims to reduce the budgetary deficit by maximizing revenue mobilization (see section (c) below). The figures for the first nine months of FY 1987/88 indicate that revenue collection in fact increased by more than 22 per cent over the comparable period of the preceding year. The objective of monetary policy is to control the growth of the money supply within the stipulated limits, notably by limiting expansion of credit to the Government.

(c) *Mobilization of domestic savings*

In FY 1987/88 revenue collection as a share of GDP increased by 1.2 percentage points from the preceding year to reach 10.2 per cent. However, the target for FY 1990/91 is set at 12 per cent of GDP, compared to about 9 per cent in FY 1985/86. Measures taken in this sense as from FY 1986/87 include a rationalization of sales tax rates and the introduction of sales taxes on services. Moreover, a package of fiscal reforms introduced during FY 1987/88 includes the reform of customs, excise, sales and income taxes.

(d) *Expanded role for the private sector*

The Government has adopted policies which call for the gradual transfer of public-sector industry to the private sector; accord the private sector guarantees in the setting up of new industries (except defence plants) and commercial banks; encourage the private sector in the promotion of joint ventures with foreign partners; review credit, tax and import procedures so as to attract private investment; develop a one-stop investment centre in the capital, which will provide the multitude of offical services which investors require before starting operations; and extend such centres gradually to other regions. To this end, it has been decided to float shares of some publicly owned industrial units to the private sector though the Security Exchange Centre, and to activate and strengthen the Industrial Promotion Committees, so that they can facilitate the obtention of permits, credits and promotional and other facilities required by investors.

(e) *Improving the efficiency of public enterprises*

Nepal's public enterprises represent a very mixed group of undertakings, but they have generally performed poorly. The Government's measures have focused on improving the operating efficiency and strengthening the financial position of public enterprises (PEs). With a view to limiting the budgetary effects of PE deficits, the Government recently adopted a policy of limiting the issuance of government guarantees for PE borrowings from the banking system. The Government has established criteria of awards and penalties for PE managers on the basis of their performance, so as to enhance the management efficiency of the PEs. In addition, the Government is also providing some autonomy to PE's in fixing the prices of their products.

2. *Sectoral policies*

(a) *Food and agriculture*

The Seventh Plan (FY 1985/86-1989/90) has accorded high priority to the agricultural sector, which accounts for 58 per cent of GDP, provides 91 per cent of employment and supplies 80 per cent of all industrial inputs. The Government has introduced agricultural policy measures that promote private initiative, with the public sector's role limited to providing essential support functions within the sector. The initial measures have concentrated on the improved supply of fertilizers and seeds, foodgrain marketing, agricultural research and a more rational exploitation of private and communal forests.

A newly-functioning foodgrain price stabilization programme, in which the Nepal Food Corporation (NFC) undertakes open-market operations, is operating in the Kathmandu Valley. Excessive and poorly focused foodgrain subsidies have been phased out, and the authorities are mounting a programme to identify groups that are vulnerable to food shortages. Logistical arrangements for distributing food to them, when required, are being implemented. Moreover, the procurement of the required supplies will be at prices providing incentives to farmers.

179 The fiscal year (FY) ends on 15 July.

(b) Industry and energy

The principal elements of the industrial policy have been the liberalization in industrial licensing, rationalization in the level of protection, encouragement of industries based on domestic raw materials or producing essential goods (such as construction materials), and the promotion of export-oriented industries. Moreover, the industrial policy has taken into account the facilities required by foreign investors. Nevertheless this sector's contribution to GDP growth, generation of employment opportunities and improvement in the external sector is reported to be rather modest.

Due to the high pressure on forests as a source of energy supply, as well as the continuous increase in the import of commercial sources of energy, efforts have been undertaken to develop alternative domestic energy sources, such as establishment of bio-gas plants and the use of solar power. Also, small electricity projects and mills with a capacity of 5-30 kw have been established in rural areas with the participation of the private sector.

(c) Social development

In line with the objective of meeting basic needs, the Government is currently rendering primary-level education free to all citizens of the country. Reports indicate that in 1987 the number of schools had increased by 3 per cent. A new university - "Mahendra Sanskrit University" - was established recently. Moreover, the Government continued to implement policies outlined in the Seventh Plan to enhance average life expectancy, control the population explosion and curb the problem of malnutrition. Health services have been revitalized with a view to enhancing general health standards and making preventive health services available to the rural masses.

3. Measures to improve physical infrastructure

Policies and measures have been adopted to emphasize the complementary nature of rural development and urbanization, transform regional centres into modern towns, and gradually improve major population centres into semi-urban townships. Moreover, Government has committed itself to creating adequate transportation and communication facilities for the economic and social development of the country. The areas of concentration in FY 1987/88 included the development of road transport, a trolley-bus system, bridges, rail, ropeway and air transport and adequate communication facilities, including increased telephone capacity, rural communications, television and increased post office services.

4. Measures to improve institutional capabilities in the field of development planning and policy

Policies have been implemented to improve the management of individual projects and to strengthen control structures. Steps to improve the development planning administration have included the introduction of programme budgeting in the Ministry of Finance and the delegation of more authority to project managers and other senior government officials. More recently, a trouble-shooting unit was established in the Cabinet Secretariat to ensure smooth implementation of projects.

5. International support measures

Nepal continues to receive foreign aid under the World Bank Consultative Group (CG) arrangement. During its last meeting held in Paris in November 1988, the members of the CG commended efforts made by the Government in its Structural Adjustment Programme and reaffirmed their support for Nepal's development priorities by announcing their pledges. Moreover, in March 1987, an IDA structural adjustment credit of $50 million was approved. Funds were also pledged during the May 1988 CG meeting held in Paris for the Arun III hydro-power project. Japan became the largest contributor ($160 million out of an estimated cost of $657 million). For its part, the IFC pledged $12.33 million to assist private-sector development in Nepal.

6. Impact of national policies and international support measures

The trend of the country's main economic indicators shows that the economic adjustment programme has had a positive impact on Nepal's economy. For FY 1987/88 it is estimated that the real GDP increased by 7.1 per cent, up from 2.4 per cent in the previous fiscal year. Similary, the balance of payments has been favourable, even though the trade deficit increased. Moreover, the consumer price index rose by only 10.7 per cent during 1987, which is just over one-half of the increase in 1986.

NIGER

1. *Improving the efficiency of resource use and allocation*

Niger has been implementing policy measures aimed at improving resource utilization, promoting the role of the private sector and strengthening the agricultural sector. The measures were supported by four stand-by arrangements with the IMF during the period 1983-1987. Thereafter, a full-fledged structural adjustment programme for 1986-1988 was launched with IMF/World Bank support involving, *inter alia*, an SAF loan of SDR 21.4 million for the period November 1986-November 1989. Policy measures towards similar ends are embodied in the Five-Year Development Plan for 1987-1991.

(a) External sector policies

Import duties have been reduced in the context of ongoing fiscal changes. In view of depressed cotton prices in world markets and in neighbouring countries, producer prices for this commodity were reduced in the 1987/88 season by 15 per cent as compared to the previous year.

(b) Demand-management measures

Measures taken to contain public expenditure include cuts in public personnel and in investment expenditure and measures to improve the efficiency of parastatals. Tax rates were reduced in 1987 through cuts in customs duties, value-added tax and consumption taxes (3,000 mass-consumption items were to have benefited from such cuts). Concomitantly, action was taken to improve tax collection and to incorporate parallel market operations into the formal (and hence, taxable) business sector; such action involves better business monitoring and limitation of customs fraud, which reportedly amounts to an annual average of CFAF 12 billion ($40 million). Partly as a result of these measures, the fiscal deficit declined from 7 per cent of GDP in 1982 to 3.6 per cent in 1987.

(c) Mobilization of domestic savings

A savings-pension fund established in 1978 for officals of the postal and telecommunications service (PTT) was enlarged in 1987 to all public and private employees. Membership had attained 4,000 by the end of 1987, involving gross annual receipts of CFAF 200 million ($0.7 million).

(d) Mobilization of human resources

Campaigns for the mobilization of local population groups have been launched for a number of activities, such as removal of encroached sand in the River Niger, construction of a dam near Niamey, small-scale gardening, tree planting, development of dry-season crops, and promotion of rural initiatives. Preference is being given to the employment of qualified nationals in the mining sector (*nigérienisation des postes*). A Round Table Meeting on rural development was held in Niamey in March 1988 under the auspices of UNDP.

(e) Expanded role for the private sector

This is one of the key objectives of current policies. A programme of support for private initiative was launched in October 1987. In addition to privatization of public enterprises (see below), measures in this regard include: (i) establishment of a bonus system to encourage qualified civil servants to move to the private sector; nearly CFAF 3 billion ($10 million) have been allocated for this purpose, with individual bonuses ranging between CFAF 3.5 million ($11,700) and CFAF 7.5 million

($25,000); (ii) tax reductions for enterprises engaging in capital expansion; (iii) price liberalization; (iv) privatization of veterinary services; and (v) support for herder co-operatives. A Round Table Meeting on the promotion of the private sector was held in Niamey in June 1988, with the participation of national and foreign experts.

(f) Improving the efficiency of public enterprises

A wide-ranging reform of the parastatal sector is under way: out of 54 State-owned enterprises, 5 are to be liquidated, 16 privatized, 5 will be kept in the public sector but under private management, and 10 will be restructured. The management boards of parastatal enterprises have been granted larger autonomy. The Government announced in July 1988 that candidates for management posts in public enterprises will be selected strictly on the basis of competence, without taking into account regional or ethnic origins.

2. Sectoral policies

(a) Agriculture and fishing

Producer prices for sorghum and millet were raised in 1987, while rice production is being encouraged through protectionist licensing of rice imports and expansion of irrigation. Priority is being given to dry-season crops in the supply of inputs and credits. Measures to support the livestock sector provided for in the Plan relate to improved veterinary and livestock marketing services. The Plan also provides for the promotion of inland fish farming and the development of fish hatcheries and weirs.

(b) Mining

The Plan provides for the expansion of non-uranium mining operations (tin ore, coal, salt, gold and phosphates). A joint venture (with Belgium) has been established to carry out salt extraction. Gold deposits, recently discovered, will be exploited in 1988 with financial assitance from Canada. The mining code and licensing policies are to be reviewed with the purpose of encouraging the participation of domestic firms in the mining sector.

(c) Energy and environment

With a view to reducing the consumption of fuelwood, which accounts for 85 per cent of total energy consumption, the Plan provides for the establishment of solar and wind generators and for the development of hydroelectric power. To discourage deforestation, the wood-cutting fee is to be raised sixfold from CFAF 350 per m^3 in 1987 to CFAF 2,000 per m^3 in 1991, and the use of fuel-efficient stoves (*foyers améliorés*) is to be promoted through the distribution of 150,000 such stoves by 1991 (annual consumption of firewood is estimated to amount to nearly two million tonnes). Some of the campaigns of mobilization of human resources relate to environmental improvement. A national centre to fight grasshoppers was inaugurated in August 1988. The Government has announced its intention of applying the resolution adopted at the meeting of Heads of State of ECOWAS, held in June 1988, calling for a refusal to accept toxic wastes coming from industrialized countries.

(d) Export expansion and diversification

Export expansion and diversification is being pursued through the development of non-uranium mining and the promotion of livestock and cereals exports. A campaign has been launched to identify prospective livestock buyers in neighbouring countries and the Middle East.

(e) Social development

In early 1988, the Government authorised contraception in cases of frequent pregnancies.

3. Measures to improve the physical infrastructure

The maintenance and expansion (by 100 km) of the road network is being carried out with donors' support. An air terminal is being constructed at Niamey.

4. Measures to improve institutional capabilities in the field of development planning and policy

Niger has an elaborate network of overlapping social and economic plans and programmes: (i) a Five-Year Plan for Economic and Social Development for 1987-1991; (ii) a three-year rolling investment programme (*Programme triennal glissant*); (iii) a structural adjustment programme for 1986-1988, supported by the IMF/World Bank and complemented by a programme for the streamlining of public enterprises (PASEP); (iv) a programme of support for private initiative and for the creation of employment (PAIPCE); and (v) an annual recovery programme (*Programme significatif de relance*), which sets up annual objectives and provides for incentives to the private sector.

5. International support measures

Bilateral ODA from DAC countries and DAC-financed multilateral institutions reached $300 million in both 1985 and 1986, as compared to an annual level of $150-170 million during the preceding four years. Concessional assistance from all sources represented 85.5 per cent of imports. Between 1977 and 1987, Niger rescheduled its external debt four times at the Paris Club and secured a further 20-year rescheduling in April 1988, including a 10-year grace period.

6. Impact of national policies and international support measures

After three consecutive years of decline, due principally to drought conditions affecting agricultural production, real GDP grew by 5.9 and 6.5 per cent in 1985 and 1986 respectively. An estimated 9.0 per cent decline in agricultural production in 1987, however, suggests that economic recovery may not be sustained.

Total external debt doubled from $703 million in 1981 to $1,493 million in 1986, during which year debt service rose to absorb one-half of exports of goods and services.

RWANDA

1. Improving the efficiency of resource use and allocation

Rwanda is one of the LDCs implementing a national adjustment and policy reform programme (without formal agreement with the World Bank or IMF), centring on prudent fiscal and external policies and on measures to develop the rural economy. Initially, a number of austerity measures were adopted in late 1982, and a comprehensive economic recovery programme (*Programme d'assainissement et de relance de l'économie rwandaise*) was launched in 1985. Additional policy measures to contain government expenditure and raise revenue were adopted in 1987 as the external environment again deteriorated.

(a) External sector policies

The Rwanda franc was delinked from the US dollar and pegged to the SDR in September 1983. Thereafter, external economic policies largely focused on import control through strict licensing and an advance deposit requirement. Some of these requirements were later eliminated as the economic situation improved. There was a small rise in the producer price for coffee (Rwanda's major export commodity) in 1986, the first since the doubling of this price in 1977. In the period 1981-1986, the producer price represented an average of about 63 per cent of the export price for coffee. Debt management is being strengthened with a view to exercising stricter control over external borrowing.

(b) Demand-management measures

Budgetary policy under the austerity programme has aimed at containing recurrent expenditure, particularly the payroll. A general sales tax was introduced in May 1986. Following the fall in world coffee prices and export receipts during 1987, expenditure budgets were revised downwards, *inter alia* by way of the suspension of a planned increase in civil service pay and of certain development projects, while a number of tax-rate increases were implemented. The 1988 budget foresaw no increase in recurrent expenditure. Efforts to recover tax arrears were to be intensified. Interest rates were revised in July 1987 with a view to making their structure more flexible and competitive.

(c) Role of the private sector and public enterprises

Government policy assigns an important role to private enterprise, particularly to small and medium-scale enterprises, as a means of promoting employment creation. Recent policy measures designed to promote private-sector activity include the revision of the investment code and credit and interest rate policy. The new investment code adopted in August 1987 aims, *inter alia,* to provide incentives for small and medium-scale enterprises and for the establishment of enterprises outside the Kigali area. The Rwanda Development Bank already has a special programme for promoting small and medium-scale enterprises. The current adjustment and recovery programme also lays stress on the rationalization and improved management of public sector enterprises. The previously State-owned match factory has been privatized and is being rehabilitated. The Government also planned to divest itself of its equity holdings in some other enterprises.

2. Sectoral policies

(a) Food and agriculture

Securing food self-sufficiency remains the first development priority of Rwanda, on which successive development plans have been focused. The Government pursues its established policies for this sector with emphasis, *inter alia*, on extension services and anti-erosion programmes, including reforestation. A comprehensive food strategy has been drawn up. There are a number of parastatals both for cash crops and food crops which aim to regulate markets, e.g. through improving the marketing infrastructure, for example with storage and transportation facilities.

(b) Industry, mining and energy

After the liquidation in 1985 of the mining company SOMIRWA, which operated the country's only tin-smelting plant, the Government has been considering how to restructure the production and processing of cassiterite. The creation of a co-operative for artisanal mining was expected to relaunch small-scale production. In addition, in May 1988, the Government decided to set up a new enterprise to handle the concessions left by SOMIRWA. Methane gas is extracted from Lake Kivu, and an agreement has been signed with Zaire on the development of this resource.

(c) Social development

The National Population Office continues its awareness-raising campaign on population issues and has extended its network of information, training and education with respect to family planning. The immunization programme for children was intensified with the aim of covering all children under one year of age by the year 1992. A large-scale five-year literacy campaign was also to be launched.

3. Measures to improve the physical infrastructure

Increasing water supply has been one of the priorities of the Government, and the urban and rural water distribution network has been significantly expanded in recent years. The transport and communications network has also been expanded. A Road Fund with responsibility for road maintenance was set up in 1986. Transit transport facilities will be improved, with the planned road link to be built to the road and rail transshipment station at Isaka in the United Republic of Tanzania. A round-table meeting with donors for the communications sector was arranged in February 1988. Projects included in the second phase of the master plan for this sector, for which financing was sought, concern rural telephones, an extension of urban telephone networks, an extension of the earth station, improvements in the postal service in rural areas and the rehabilitation of Kigali Post Office.

4. *Measures to improve institutional capabilities in the field of development planning and policy*

Rwanda's Third Economic, Social and Cultural Development Plan covered the years 1982-1986. As worsening economic conditions affected the Plan's implementation, the Government adopted the 1985 recovery programme to adjust the economy and prepare the launching of the fourth development plan, which will cover the period up to 1991. Internal policy co-ordination has been strengthened through the setting up of interministerial co-ordination committees in key policy areas. Sectoral planning and project preparation capacities are also being strengthened under an IDA-financed technical assistance project.

5. *International support measures*

While the net inflow of concessional resources to Rwanda stagnated in nominal terms at a level of around $150-155 million annually in the period 1980-1983, aid disbursements started increasing in 1984 and reached a level of $213 million in 1986. Rwanda received financing totalling $25 million for a highway project under the World Bank's Special Facility for sub-Saharan Africa, as well as special joint financing for this purpose and other adjustment-related assistance from bilateral donors. The food strategy is being implemented with support from the EEC.

6. *Impact of national policies and international support measures*

After the drought year 1984, Rwanda's economy recovered in 1985 and 1986 with real GDP growth estimated at 7.5 per cent and 4.9 per cent respectively. Good weather conditions contributed to a continued expansion of food crop production and coffee output in 1986, although tea output decreased. The rate of inflation in consumer prices moderated in 1985, but after actually turning negative in 1986 regained some momentum in 1987 to reach a level of 4 per cent. With a major increase in coffee exports, a significant narrowing of the trade deficit and higher capital inflows, the overall balance-of-payments deficit turned around to show a surplus in 1986. The ratio of external debt service to exports of goods and services remained below 15 per cent. However, in 1987 the economic situation deteriorated under the effect of falling coffee prices and the depreciation of the dollar, leading to a fall in coffee receipts, and GDP growth was arrested.

SAMOA

1. *Improving the efficiency of resource use and allocation*

The Sixth Development Plan (1988-1990) establishes the increase in production and the maintenance of internal and external financial stability as prime objectives for the country's medium-term development. More dynamic growth is to be achieved without overburdening the financing framework. The budgetary deficit is not allowed to increase, and the need for external assistance is expected to be only slightly higher than at present. The major concern will be the efficient utilization of domestic resources and foreign assistance within the agreed strategic framework.

(a) *External sector policies*

The external sector is affected by a number of regulations and restrictions concerning the export and import of goods and capital. Thus, the import of several products, mainly consumer goods competing with locally produced goods, is restricted. In addition, there are also restrictions on the importation of vehicles and capital goods of a value exceeding $WS 10,000 (about $5,000 in 1987). The export of capital has to be approved by the Central Bank. All exports of goods require licenses. The currency continued to be pegged to a basket of currencies of the country's major trading partners, resulting in an appreciation of the tala *vis-à-vis* the US dollar of about 9 per cent during 1987.

(b) Demand-management measures

Recurrent expenditure was allowed to increase by 3 per cent in 1987, following a 5 per cent increase in the previous year. The Government abandoned the salary freeze in the public sector with a view to containing the drain of qualified labour by offering remunerative salaries to public-sector employees. The officially fixed minimum wage rate, which had been raised by 13.6 per cent in 1986, was further increased by 5 per cent in 1988. In 1987, the Central Bank announced new credit control measures aimed at curbing excess liquidity. However, policies aimed at reorienting the lending activity of the commercial banks to productive investment, export growth, import substitution, tourism and construction have failed so far. About 60 per cent of commercial bank lending is still directed towards import-related business. In order to reorient the banks' activities towards sectors that contribute to economic growth and structural transformation, the Central Bank issued a guideline in early 1988, requiring the banks to reduce the share of loans to the retail sector by at least 5 percentage points by the end of 1988.

(c) Mobilization of domestic savings

In 1987, the Government undertook some modifications in the taxation system, such as an income-tax rebate for low-income groups and income-tax relief for pensioners. Furthermore, excise duties levied on domestic products based on local raw materials have been eliminated. The clergy has been exempted from income tax on donations. Interest-rate policy continues to maintain positive real rates for savings accounts to mobilize private savings and appreciably higher rates on loans to contain credit demand.

(d) Expanded role of private sector

The Government has continued its selective privatization policy. A number of public enterprises which were unable to fulfill their economic objectives have been offered for sale to private investors. Furthermore, the Government is wedded to the policy of non-participation in the promotion and setting up of new industries. Given the problems of nascent local entrepreneurship and inadequate access of the domestic private sector to technology and markets, the Government welcomes private foreign investment.

(e) Improving the efficiency of public enterprises

In 1988, the Government set targets for the profitability of public enterprises so as to ensure no further recourse to the budget for recurrent finance. The possibility of amalgamating all government investments under one organization with a view to facilitating efficient management and expediting the divestment programme is under consideration.

2. Sectoral policies

(a) Food and agriculture

The income tax holiday for primary producers granted since 1975, which was to end in 1987, has been extended for another year. Furthermore, the Government started an Agricultural Bonus Scheme in 1988 aimed at encouraging the replanting of coconut and cocoa trees. In addition, the cocoa suspensory loan scheme started in 1984 will be continued. Under this scheme part of the loan to a farmer is converted into a grant if he meets certain targets. The system of administering the Stabilization Fund for copra and cocoa is being reviewed with a view to making it approach a producers' price support system. However, the major obstacle to increased agricultural productivity is considered to be the traditional land tenure system. To improve the efficiency of land use, the Government undertook efforts to introduce commercial plantation norms and practices in village land and to implant freeholders by bringing virgin land into cultivation.

(b) *Industry and energy*

The incentive provisions in the Enterprise Incentive Act of 1984 are being reviewed. A Small Industrial Centre will be set up, providing factory space and utilities to local entrepreneurs.

(c) *Services*

Guidelines for tourism policy have been issued and measures to promote tourism, including the enlargement of hotel-room capacity and the improvement of transportation, have been approved. An autonomous official tourism organization has been established. The opening of an offshore banking centre was announced for 1988.

(d) *Social development*

The Government remains committed to improving social services. About 9.5 per cent of development expenditures under the Sixth Development Plan are allocated for this purpose. Emphasis is given to the maintenance and expansion of medical-care facilities. Education and training programmes will be better geared to meet the country's requirements for skilled labour.

3. *Measures to improve the physical infrastructure*

Measures were undertaken to improve infrastructural facilities related to tourism. The Feleleolo Airport has been completed. The Chief Post Office, which had been destroyed by fire in 1986, was rebuilt in 1987.

4. *Measures to improve institutional capabilities in the field of development planning and policy*

A Department of Industries and Trade will be established with the mandate of assisting the Government in planning and policy formulation for industrial development and in monitoring the effective utilization of incentives.

5. *International support measures*

External development assistance has played a crucial role in the development of virtually all major economic and social sectors of Samoa. ODA covers about three-fourths of the country's development expenditure. At the third Round Table Meeting for Samoa held on 26 October 1988, donors identified priority areas for future external assistance, such as agriculture, manpower development, strengthening of public services and improvement of the institutional infrastructure. Furthermore, it was agreed that regular on-the-spot consultations between donors and the Government should take place on development issues, aid modalities and aid implementation.

6. *Impact of national policies and international support measures*

In 1987 the economy continued its sluggish and lack-luster growth. Real growth of GDP is estimated at 1 per cent, as compared to 0.5 per cent in 1986. For 1988 a growth rate of 2.5 per cent is provisionally forcast as producers were expected to respond to higher international prices for coconut products and to the policy measures undertaken by the Government. Overall government deficits during the first half of the 1980s may have turned into surpluses in 1986 and 1987. Inflation slowed down steadily from 16.7 per cent in 1983 to 4.5 per cent in 1987, but foreign debt rose again to 63.8 per cent of GDP in 1987 after having declined from 66.8 per cent of GDP in 1984 to 58.9 per cent in 1986.

SAO TOME AND PRINCIPE

1. *Improving the efficiency of resource allocation*

Since June 1987, Sao Tome and Principe has embarked on a Structural Adjustment Programme (SAP) supported by an IDA credit of SDR 3.1 million, (about $4 million), a World Bank African Facility credit of SDR. 2.3 million (about $3 million) and an African Development Fund credit of $8.5 million. The programme aims at implementing a series of important economic reforms (discussed below). However, negotiations with the IMF for a proposed Structural Adjustment Facility loan of SDR 1.9 million ($2.4 million) continued in 1988 and are unlikely to be concluded before 1989.

(a) External sector policies

In May 1987, the dobra was devalued from 45.25 dobra per SDR to 100 dobra per SDR. (The SDR/Dobra parity had remained unchanged since 1977, causing the effective exchange rate of the dobra to increase by about 80 per cent between 1977 and 1985). Further currency adjustments were contemplated in 1988, so as to eliminate the gap between the official rate and the parallel market, which remains substantial.

Since 1984, the Government has pursued a policy of trade liberalization by allowing private traders to compete with the state trading corporation ECOMEX for certain internationally traded goods. Trade was further liberalized in 1987, as a result of which import licenses are now issued through an auction system. The change of the import tariff to *ad valorem* rates was undertaken in 1988, together with the removal of all quantitative import restrictions. Import duties were increased by a minimum of 30 per cent in May 1988. In 1987, subsidies on 10 basic import items were reduced by one-half, but their complete abolition had not yet taken place by mid-1988.

(b) Demand-management measures

Under the structural adjustment programme (SAP), the Government has agreed to cut the recurrent fiscal deficits substantially, but this is proving difficult to implement. Civil servants' salaries were moderately increased (by 10 per cent) following the devaluation, and Government travel expenditure in foreign currency was halved. A hiring freeze on public sector personnel was imposed, but the retrenchment of government employees which would normally be needed under the budgetary stringency programme has not yet taken place. The planned public-sector investment programme for 1987 was cut by more than one-half, namely to $19 million compared to a planned $42 million.

A restrictive monetary policy is also being implemented. Under the SAP, new Central Bank credit to the central Government is limited to Db 400 million. No credit is being extended to loss-making public enterprises.

(c) Expanded role of the private sector

The Government is accelerating the liberalization of commercial activities started in 1984. Since 1987, the private sector has been allowed to compete with the former trade monopoly ECOMEX in all goods, except six on the strategic list. Land distribution from the State to private individuals and co-operatives has been initiated outside the 15 large Government-owned estates. Three of these estates have been handed over to foreign management, and negotiations have been completed for a similar arrangement concerning a fourth. In May 1988, the state fishing entreprise was dissolved and its operations taken over by a joint venture with a Greek partner.

(d) *Improving the efficiency of public enterprises*

In 1987 a study of public enterprises was undertaken as part of the SAP. A number of them are to be restructured, privatized or closed. For instance, the state shipping company, Transcolmar, will be transformed into a joint venture, and the parastatal company Enco placed the domestic distribution of petroleum under tender in January 1988.

2. *Sectoral policies*

(a) *Agriculture*

The rehabilitation of cocoa plantations is continuing, but this has yet to be translated into increased production and exports. All price controls on domestically produced food crops and fish were abolished in 1987.

(b) *Energy*

The Government has increased the price of energy in line with the 1987 devaluation. Full-cost recovery for imported fuels, electricity and water is planned for 1988. The proposal to build a large hydroelectric station in the south of Sao Tome has been postponed.

(c) *Export development*

In the 1980s, cocoa has accounted for about 90 per cent of exports. However, due to the overvalued currency, as well as insufficient incentives for both management and workers of state enterprises (lack of access to foreign exchange for inputs, arrears in payment of wages), cocoa exports declined steadily from 6,000 tons in 1980 to 4,000 tons in 1986 and an estimated 3,500 tons in 1987. Exports of coffee and palm oil ceased entirely in the second half of the 1980s.

(d) *Social development*

Education has expanded considerably since independence in 1975. The number of secondary school pupils is estimated to have quadrupled over the past decade, and about 300 nationals have returned from training abroad since independence. About 100 trainees will be sent abroad during the biennium 1987-1988, mainly to the USSR, Cuba, Portugal and France. In 1986 a severe malaria epidemic occurred, and this is believed to have increased the infant mortality rate significantly. No case of AIDs has been diagnosed in the islands.

3. *Measures to improve physical infrastructure*

The road network has deteriorated since independence. Combined with the lack of spare parts and tyres, this means that most transportation beyond the immediate outskirts of Sao Tome City is problematic. The African Development Bank has allocated $6.5 million for a major road improvement programme, but its implementation scheduled for 1988 is being delayed for administrative reasons.

4. *Institutional capability*

The Government's administrative capability is particularly weak, and the SAP is being supported by a number of international technical experts. In January 1987 and in January 1988, there were some important ministerial changes. An unsuccessful coup attempt took place in March 1988.

5. *International support measures*

Sao Tome and Principe has attracted external assistance from a wide variety of sources. The main OECD donors are Portugal and France. Other sources providing assistance to the country include China, the OPEC Fund, the German Democratic Republic and Angola, which supplies petroleum products on concessional terms. ODA disbursements increased from $9.9 million in 1982 to $17.2 million in 1986, but in 1988 some donors were reported to be withholding disbursements, pending an agreement with the IMF.

6. *Impact of national policies and international support measures*

It is estimated that in 1984, GDP per capita ($328) was almost a third lower than in 1980. There are no official figures to evaluate the impact of the economic reforms initiated in 1985, but output data for the main economic sectors (cocoa, food crops, fishing) do not yet reflect a recovery, while in 1988 cocoa prices fell to their lowest level in 15 years.

SIERRA LEONE

1. *Improving the efficiency of resource use and allocation*

(a) *External sector policies and demand-management measures*

In fulfilment of the demands of the IMF in respect of a one-year stand-by agreement and a structural adjustment facility in November 1986, Sierra Leone floated its currency in June 1986, liberalized its trade and payments system, decontrolled consumer prices, removed subsidies on rice and petroleum products, and tightened its fiscal and monetary policies. In addition, foreign-exchange retention privileges accorded to exporters of various goods and services were abolished in June 1986. These measures were supplemented in November 1987 by "emergency economic regulations" under which private gold and diamond export licences were cancelled in favour of the State-owned Government Gold and Diamond Office. In an effort to boost flagging Government revenues, the emergency measures also included the imposition of a 15 per cent import surcharge, a reduction of the public sector wage bill and an increase in the export tax on rutile and bauxite.

A new Fishing Management and Development Act was passed in January 1988, giving the Government exclusive management control over the country's fishing zones. The Act provides, *inter alia*, for extension of the fishing-zone limit, environmental and other protective measures to preserve the country's fishing resources, and increased fees, licences and royalties.

(b) *Mobilization of domestic savings*

Two new rural banks were established to mobilize savings in the rural areas and to provide quick-disbursing credit facilities to farmers.

2. *Sectoral policies*

(a) *Food, agriculture and fishing*

The Government drafted a blue-print on a "green revolution" in December 1986 aimed at attaining food self-sufficiency. Under this programme the country is divided into seven regions, each of which has its own development programme. The scheme envisaged a total planned investment of $200 million over three years, the bulk of which is expected to be financed by foreign sources. The first project to be launched under the scheme is the Gbondapi rice development project, which aims at accelerating food production by way of mechanization. Japan provided an initial contribution of $1.6 million in vehicles, machinery and chemicals. On the whole, the Government's policies to promote agricultural production through increases in producers' prices have suffered a setback in the face of rampant inflation and chronic foreign-exchange shortages, which have restricted imports of inputs and machinery.

(b) *Industry*

The major industrial activities, especially mining, are in the hands of a few powerful business interests, who have had control over their export proceeds for many years, in so far as they were not subjected to foreign-exchange surrender requirements. Specific measures have been instituted on several occasions to ensure that the foreign-exchange proceeds from these exports enter official channels, but so far the results have been limited. In March 1988, the President stated that diamond smuggling had continued despite the stiff penalties announced under the emergency regulations. On the whole, industrial production has been severely hampered by foreign-exchange shortages. However, repeated efforts to develop diamond production at the Kimberlite Mines appear to be bearing fruit, inasmuch as operations were expected to commence by January 1989.

(c) Energy

Sierra Leone is in dire need of new energy sources, as its power supply suffers constantly from breakdowns due to machinery obsolescence and shortages of fuel. Italy has agreed to fund a hydroelectric scheme at Bumbuna. The country may also receive assistance from France to develop its solar energy potential, and from the United Kingdom to construct a thermal power station.

3. *Measures to improve the physical infrastructure*

There are presently about 7,900 km of roads, but even those with all-weather surfaces are mostly in a very poor state of repair. A number of major road development projects are under way, including a new 140 km road linking the country with Liberia. Financing has been obtained from the EC to construct a 35 km road linking Fadugu to Kabala. The work was scheduled to start in the first half of 1988 and is expected to take 30 months to complete. Completion of the road will facilitate rural development in the Northern Province.

British Teleconsult is to provide $2.3 million worth of consultancy services under a $16.9 million project funded by the EC to supply telecommunications equipment. The British firm is also to rehabilitate the national trunk system and to install solar power at remote microwave relay sites.

4. *International support measures*

There have been no transactions between Sierra Leone and the IMF since November 1986, when the first instalments of both the stand-by and the structural adjustment facilities were drawn. In April 1988 the country became ineligible to use IMF resources, because it had accumulated arrears of SDR 40 million to the Fund. The World Bank has also stopped new disbursements, because of arrears of $4 million. This has also had a detrimental impact upon the willingness of other donors to support the country.

5. *Impact of national policies and international support measures*

Economic stagnation, including a chronic foreign-exchange shortage, which has characterized the economy throughout the decade, worsened in 1987, leading to the institution of emergency measures in November 1987. The emergency measures were aimed primarily at eliminating hoarding of foreign currency and smuggling and reversing the severe foreign-exchange crisis. The measures were extended for 12 months in February 1988, as there were no signs of improvement. Severe cutbacks in imports of machinery and essential inputs, as well as frequent power cuts, have caused production to fall in all sectors. The Government even had difficulties in meeting payments of public-sector salaries, which in some cases were in arrears by four months.

The cut-off of external flows represented a critical blow to the country, which is already facing an astronomically high debt burden. As of end-June 1987. The country's total disbursed external debt (including arrears) had risen by 15 per cent over the corresponding figure one year earlier. More immediately relevant was the fact that the ratio of debt-service accrual to exports of goods had risen to 94.7 per cent during FY 1986/87, as compared to 66.5 per cent during the preceeding fiscal year.

SOMALIA

1. *Improving the efficiency of resource allocation*

The Public Investment Programme (PIP) for the period 1987-1989, formulated within the framework of the Five-Year Development Plan (1987-1991), aims at increasing production, promoting exports and import-substituting industries, and improving the country's infrastructure, social and economic services. Strong emphasis is placed on investment in productive sectors.

(a) External sector policies

The exchange auction system, launched in June 1987 to strengthen the flexibility of the exchange rate, was abolished in September 1987. The official exchange rate of the Somali shilling was fixed at So.Sh. 100 per dollar, corresponding to a 60 per cent appreciation as compared to the last auction rate, but a series of devalutaions from June 1988 onwards brought about a cumulative cut of 60 per cent in the vaule of the shilling to a rate of So.Sh. 252 per dollar by the end of September 1988.[180] In order to support the fixed official exchange rate as the only legal rate, the authorities adopted several regulations on the use of foreign-currency accounts. The export earnings to be channelled through the official exchange market were reduced from 100 per cent to 60 per cent and the retained export proceeds were to be credited to export promotion accounts. External accounts could be replenished through foreign remittances and used for imports, but not for transfer to other accounts. However, despite these and other measures, the discrepancy between the official and the free market rates widened as the latter reached a level of So.Sh. 400 per dollar in September 1988.

(b) Demand-management measures

The disbursement level of the core PIP 1987-1989 was reduced from the planned outlay of $1.1 billion to $720 million over the three-year period. In 1987, the overall budgetary deficit (after account is taken of external grants) more than doubled to 14.6 per cent of GDP, but in 1988 this deficit was projected to decline to 4.3 per cent of GDP. Current expenditure is budgeted to decline to an estimated 6.3 per cent of GDP as compared to 16.0 per cent in 1987, while investment expenditure is expected to decline by 7.3 percentage points to 16.2 per cent of GDP. The decline in current expenditure was expected as a result of the major reorganization of the Government in 1988 and a sharp decline in budgeted outlays for goods and services. Domestic credit expansion was reduced to 14.5 per cent in 1987 compared to 20.7 per cent in 1986.

(c) Mobilization of domestic savings

According to the 1988 budget, domestic revenue is to increase by 24 per cent in nominal terms (led by a 30 per cent increase in import duties) and to cover 89 per cent of ordinary expenditure. Measures have been initiated to increase tax revenue through changes in tax rates, for example an increase in import taxes for luxury items, and the enhancement of the efficiency of tax administration.

(d) Expanded role for the private sector

The private sector is being encouraged to participate in economic activities through the facilities provided by the currency regulations referred to in section (a) above. A new law governing foreign investment, currently under consideration, is also expected to provide increased incentives for the foreign and domestic private sectors. According to the PIP, the de-

180 All conversions in this chapter are made on the basis of this rate.

velopment of the manufacturing sector is left largely to the private sector.

(e) *Improving the efficiency of public enterprises*

As part of the measures announced in September 1987, several parastatal organizations, which had been performing poorly, are to be eliminated. Public-sector enterprises are being granted more management autonomy and allowed to charge prices reflecting the full cost of production plus a profit margin.

2. *Sectoral policies*

(a) *Food and agriculture*

In February 1988, the Government introduced price controls for essential foodstuffs. Prices were fixed at three levels: the producer (or importer), the wholesaler and the retailer. To enhance its efforts to increase food crop production, the Government is encouraging the private sector to be more actively involved in agricultural production. A land area totalling 320,000 hectares, was prepared and distributed to applicants, and a sum of So.Sh. 500 million ($2.0 million), provided by the Government and multilateral organizations, was approved to this end. The construction of the Badhera Dam, costing $317 million, which represents 18 per cent of total investment outlays during the period 1987-1991, is the cornerstone of the Government's strategy to achieve food self-sufficiency by increasing the area under cultivation. In the livestock subsector, government policies aim at integrating pastoralists into a regional livestock production programme, increasing livestock production within the limits set by conservation measures, promoting domestic trade in livestock and livestock products, upgrading production-oriented skills and improving management institutions.

(b) *Industry and energy*

Government efforts are concentrated on the rehabilitation and reform of public-sector manufacturing enterprises. Private- sector investment in manufacturing activities is being encouraged through the provision of loans by the Somali Development Bank, protection of domestic production, promotion of joint ventures and fiscal incentives for new industrial units in disadvantaged areas. The overall objectives of the energy sector are to reduce the dependence on imported fuels, reduce the rate of deforestation, and ensure the delivery of sufficient supplies of energy to outlying areas. Several companies, including Shell, Chevron and Amoco, have been granted concessions for oil exploration in Somalia.

(c) *Mining*

Current production activities, carried out mainly by the private sector, consist of quarrying for marble, limestone and building materials. Work is continuing on surveying the country's mineral resource inventory through conventional ground methods and modern techniques.

(d) *Social development*

The Primary Health Care Programme (PHC) is being expanded through the gradual transformation of existing Maternity and Child Health Units' facilities and services into PHC systems. Steps are being taken to accelerate the implementation of the Expanded Programme for Immunization for the six immunizable childhood diseases. As budgetary allocations for health services declined from 4 per cent of total expenditures in 1980 to 1.3 per cent in 1986, development expenditures in the health sector are being financed mainly from external sources. The goal of achieving universal primary education, which was one of the objectives of the Five-Year Development Plan 1980-1986, was not realized. This was mainly due to the scarcity of resources available and the difficulty of providing educational opportunities to the nomads. Attempts by the Government to achieve this objective during the current Five-Year Development Plan are being supported by bilateral and multilateral donors.

3. *Measures to improve the physical infrastructure*

The PIP accords high priority to expanding and rehabilitating the physical infrastructure. The rehabilitation of Mogadishu, Kismayu and Berbera ports at a cost of So.Sh. 1.3 billion ($5.2 million) has started. The projects include roll-on and roll-off facilities, a quay and container terminals. A 450 km road to establish links between the north-eastern regions of Somalia is under construction. The building of six bridges over the Juba and Shabelle Rivers and the Kuntawarey-Alafuto road will be completed during the PIP period.

4. Measures to improve institutional capabilities in the field of development planning and policy

The Ministry of Planning and Juba Valley Development is responsible for overall economic planning and for establishing policy and project priorities. Measures are being implemented to strengthen the planning capabilities of other ministries and to enhance multisectoral planning. However, these efforts are constrained by the shortage of trained planners. Training of counterparts by foreign experts is being obstructed by the lack of formal training programmes and the low level of incentives.

5. International support measures

The World Bank Consultative Group Meeting in April 1987 endorsed the Public Investment Programme for the period 1987-1989, with a disbursement level for the core programme amounting to $720 million, including external financing of $635 million. Official transfers in support of the PIP increased to $343 million in 1987, compared to $196 million in 1986. In addition, the Paris Club agreement of July 1987 rescheduled $108 million worth of end-1986 arrears and 1987 maturities.

6. Impact of national policies and international support measures

The performance of the Somali economy is determined to a large extent by developments in livestock and agricultural production. Thus, as a result of the drought and the subsequent flooding, real GDP is estimated to have increased by only 3.3 per cent in 1987; livestock off-take is estimated to have declined by 4 per cent, while crop production increased by only 1 per cent.

In view of its narrow resource base and low saving capacity, external flows play an important role in enhancing Somalia's development efforts. In the 1988 budget, external flows were projected at about 48.8 per cent of total receipts. However, the difficulties with bilateral donors and multilateral financial institutions arising from the suspension of the foreign-currency auction system have led to a substantial reduction of projected receipts. Despite the Paris Club rescheduling agreement of July 1987, the debt-service ratio, on an accrual basis, was estimated at 116 per cent and on a cash basis at 40 per cent of exports of goods and services during that year.

SUDAN

1. Improving the efficiency of resource allocation

The implementation of the Four-Year Programme for Salvation, Recovery and Development (PSRD), 1988/89-1991/92, was adversely affected in its first year by the unprecedented floods and rains which struck the central and northern parts of the country. About two million people were displaced and the damage to the agricultural sector and physical infrastructure was estimated at over $400 million. The Government's immediate efforts and those of the international donor community in the second half of 1988 were thus focused on relief and rehabilitation. Pledges amounting to $357 million for rehabilitation programmes were announced at the conclusion of the meeting of the World Bank Consultative Group on 29 November 1988.

(a) External sector policies

The exchange-rate system and import and export regulations underwent major modifications in October 1988. A dual exchange-rate system including a free foreign-exchange market was established in order to improve competitiveness in the external sector and redirect remittances by Sudanese working abroad through official channels. A Committee composed of representatives of commercial banks is to fix the commercial exchange rate on a daily basis. This rate was initially fixed at LSd 11.40 per dollar, equivalent to the previous black-market rate. The official exchange rate of LSd 4.50 per dollar established after the devaluation of October 1987 remained unchanged. It will continue to apply to imports of about 28 essential commodities and intermediate goods and to 70 per cent of surrendered export earnings. The remaining 30 per cent are to be channelled through the free market rate and can be used for free market imports. In effect, this raises the LSd value of the dollar by 47 per cent, as compared to an estimated rate of inflation of 35 per cent since the last devaluation of October 1987. Export licences for all commodities were abolished. The monopoly of the Sudan Oilseeds Company was also abolished. In view of the expected production increase, exports of sesame, groundnuts and sorghum have been authorized. Trade protocols amounting to $200 million with Egypt and $100 million with Yugoslavia are currently in force.

(b) *Demand-management measures*

In the fiscal year 1987/88[181] governmental borrowing from the banking system amounted to LSd 1.6 billion (4.6 per cent of GDP), compared with budget estimates of LSd 800 million. In view of the serious implications of this high level of deficit financing for the national economy, policies in the 1988/89 budget are geared towards curbing current expenditures and reforming the parastatal sector. In order to reduce current expenditures, the Government is proposing to reduce the voluntary retirement age to 45 years, the duration of employment to 20 years and the compulsory retirement age to 55 years.

(c) *Mobilization of domestic savings*

In FY 1988/89 domestic revenue is projected to increase by 58 per cent over the previous year's level. This increase will result from increases in direct and indirect taxes, as well as non-tax revenue. Direct taxes are projected to increase by 95 per cent as a result of an intensive administrative effort to improve tax collection and broaden the tax base to cover more traders, self-employed professionals and farmers in the mechanized sector. Indirect taxes are projected to increase by 65 per cent, due to the increase of import and excise duties. The tariff structure is to be rationalized and simplified by reducing the number of tariff rates. Non-tax revenue will increase by 38 per cent, reflecting increased efficiency in collection of outstanding bills and the revision of fees to cover the real cost of services.

(d) *Expanded role for the private sector*

The 1980 Investment Act is being revised to improve incentives available both to potential domestic and foreign investors, to simplify procedures and gear them towards promotion rather than regulation. Private-sector participation in foreign trade is to be increased through imports financed from the 30 per cent retention of export earnings and the introduction of competition with parastatals in the marketing of sesame and groundnuts. The possibility of allowing the private sector to participate in the ginning and marketing of cotton is being examined.

(e) *Improving the efficiency of public enterprises*

A policy of rehabilitation, privatization and liquidation is being implemented. Policy reforms aim at achieving financial and economic viability of economic enterprises and improving the performance of social enterprises. Government policies include: revision of production relations in agriculture, particularly in the irrigated sub-sector, reduction of production costs and improvement of the administrative, financial and institutional framework of public enterprises. The Government has announced plans to dissolve four enterprises and divest itself of two others; the liquidation of one company has already begun.

---

181 The fiscal year (FY) ends on 30 June.

2. *Sectoral policies*

(a) Food and agriculture

The agricultural sector continues to get the largest allocation of budgeted resources in development budgets. In the irrigated sub-sector, emphasis is placed on the rehabilitation and modernization of viable existing schemes, crop diversification and alternative management structures. A comprehensive study has been prepared for the development of the rain-fed sub-sector, which foresees (a) the rehabilitation of certain projects, (b) credit expansion through the Agricultural Bank and commercial banks operating in rural areas, and (c) an improved infrastructure. The Government plans to achieve 87 per cent self-sufficiency in wheat by 1992. This would represent a sharp reversal of the recent trend, in view of the fact that the self-sufficiency ratio fell from 60 per cent to 24 per cent between 1980/81 and 1986/87, while production declined from 218,000 tons to 149,000 tons during the same period. Funds have been earmarked for the development of livestock farming through the improvement of transport routes and the provision of services on traditional routes.

(b) Industry and energy

In the manufacturing sector priority is accorded to raising the present low level of capacity utilization and encouraging the development of small-scale industries and handicrafts. To achieve this, several rehabilitation programmes covering the sugar, textile and food-processing subsectors are under implementation. In 1988, a new Act for Industrial Development and Co-ordination was approved and a new industrial policy document was issued. Projects in the energy sector emphasize the rehabilitation and reinforcement of transmission and distribution networks of electricity. Oil exploration, suspended since 1985, is to be resumed.

(c) Mining

The data base for the mineral potential of the country is to be upgraded, and a promotional campaign to attract investments starting with gold is to be launched. The mineral development legislation is to be amended to facilitate private-sector participation.

(d) Social development

The main projects to be implemented during FY 1988/89 include: the expansion and rehabilitation of educational institutions, improvement of both therapeutic and preventive health care, control of epidemic diseases and support of rural health services. The PRSD aims at increasing the primary-school enrolment ratio from 57 per cent at present to 72 per cent by 1991/92.

3. *Measures to improve the physical infrastructure*

Emphasis is laid on the maintenance of existing roads and the rehabilitation and modernization of the railways network. New airports are to be established in Port Sudan and the western regions. The Italian Government has provided a loan of $21.5 million to finance the extension of the railway line in the western part of the country.

4. *Measures to improve institutional capabilities in the field of development planning and policy*

The following organs have been established: an advisory National Planning Council, an External Finance Unit within the Ministry of Finance and Economic Planning to manage Sudan's external debt and a National Council for the Promotion of Exports.

5. *International support measures*

During FY 1987/88 the inflow of ODA amounted to $431 million. In FY 1988/89 commodity aid and project aid, excluding disaster relief (see introductory paragraph), are expected to reach $557 million and $302 million respectively against an "external resource gap" officially estimated before the 1988 floods at $1.8 billion, which is equivalent to 120 per cent of import requirements. With debt service excluded, the gap was estimated at about $850 million, equivalent to 57 per cent of import requirements.

6. *Impact of national policies and international support measures*

In FY 1987/88 real GDP is estimated to have increased by 4.2 per cent, compared to 2.9 per cent in FY 1986/87. Sectoral growth ranged from less than one per cent in the agricultural sector to 9.7 and 4.8 per cent in the manufacturing and construction sectors respectively. In the agricultural sector, cotton production declined by 11 per cent. The production of sorghum, the staple food crop, declined by 60 per cent, due mainly to the decline of market prices in the 1986/87 season, leading to a decline of the acreage cultivated.

TOGO

1. *Improving the efficiency of resource use and allocation*

The third phase of the Togolese structural adjustment programme was launched in the context of a three-year policy framework for 1988-1990. Its basic objectives are the following: (i) to achieve real GDP growth of 3-4 per cent annually by the early 1990s; (ii) to maintain the average annual rate of inflation at less than 4 per cent; (iii) to further reduce the external current account deficit, excluding grants, from 12 per cent of GDP in 1987 to about 6 per cent in 1990, and to reduce the budget deficit from 7 per cent of GDP in 1987 to 1 per cent in 1990.

(a) External sector policies

The Government has adopted a system of flexible pricing which links agricultural producer prices directly to world market prices and ensures maximum prices for farmers compatible with world market conditions. After allowing for the costs of processing and export marketing, surplus revenue will be shared between farmers, processors, traders and the Treasury.

Between the 1983/84 and the 1986/87 crop years, official producer prices for Togo's three principal export crops - coffee, cocoa and cotton - were raised by 29, 20 and 25 per cent respectively in real terms. For the 1987/88 crop year, the Government is maintaining producer prices for these crops at the level paid in 1986/87.

(b) Demand-management measures

The Public Investment Programme fell by 36 per cent in 1987 to CFAF 32 billion ($91.4 million) and was projected to fall by another 12 per cent to CFAF 28.30 billion ($88.4 million) in 1988. The Government's overall wage bill for 1988 was frozen at its 1987 level, following a 13 per cent increase in 1987. Between 1983 and 1986 there had been a wage freeze in the public sector, and reductions in the civil service were accomplished by allowing retirements to exceed new recruitment. As a result, there was a 17 per cent nominal cut in public payrolls.

The Government has started budget reforms to offset lower tax receipts from agricultural and phosphate exports, whose value in terms of GDP fell from 9.1 per cent in 1984 to 3.7 per cent in 1987: it raised its non-fiscal receipts from the Petroleum Stabilization Fund and the post and telecommunications monopoly, largely by way of price and rate increases. Other state enterprises' contributions to the budget rose from nothing in 1986 to $24 million in 1987.

The tax system has been liberalized to stimulate the private sector. Export duties and taxes have been abolished on industrial products and reduced for mining companies. Import duties were reduced by 75 per cent on raw materials and semi-finished products, and by 50 per cent on other finished products.

(c) Expanded role for the private sector

Since 1982 Togo has changed its policy towards the private sector, which has recently been encouraged to engage in trade generally and export agriculture in particular. In 1987, the state trading company, the Société Nationale de Commerce (Sonacom) lost its import monopolies over such items as sheet steel, salt, soap and some alcoholic beverages. Its remaining import monopolies over tobacco, rice, sugar, and milk were to be eliminated by the end of 1988.

The Government policy is aimed at the promotion of small and medium enterprises (SME). The establishment of an institutional support structure for SME development is being initiated in conjunction with the IDA-supported Private Enterprise Development Project (PEDP). It will be pursued by way of export promotion, investment incentives and a more liberal regulatory framework.

In order to improve the participation of private Togolese interests in the privatization process, the Government is examining the feasibility of a mutual investment fund, which would subscribe to shares in privatized companies and be financed by bonds issued to local investors.

(d) Improving the efficiency of public enterprises

At the end of 1987, 29 state-owned enterprises were already affected by the divestiture/privitization programme, and further privatizations are expected. The moratorium on the creation of new state enterprises will be maintained, and measures have been adopted to reduce or even terminate the operations of the national railway company (CFT).

The new framework for the parastatal sector and public enterprises has already resulted in reduced budgetary subsidies, and will be complemented by measures to grant greater financial and managerial autonomy to public enterprise managers.

2. *Sectoral policies*

(a) Food and agriculture

The Government plans to introduce measures to expand and improve agricultural research, extension services and credit, and to deregulate the marketing of outputs and the supply of inputs. It is reducing agricultural marketing costs by: (i) reforming the operations of OPAT, the export-crop marketing agency; (ii) cutting OPAT's costs through reductions in its personnel and its non-marketing activities; and (iii) examining appropriate measures to increase the operating efficiency of Togograin, the official food-grain security agency.

(b) Industry

Agro-based industry remains the most important industrial activity. The textile subsector, second in importance, is expected to grow substantially following the successful restructuring, merger and privatization of the two former state textile enterprises, ITT and TOGOTEX. The operation is expected to allow 5,000 new recruitments in the sector.

(c) Mining and energy

The Nangbeto Dam has been completed. It will raise Togo's self-sufficiency in energy from 30 to 50 per cent. A feasibility study is already underway for a second hydroelectric dam at Ajanala, which is 100 km downstream from Nangbeto. Like the Nangbeto Dam, construction of the Ajanala Dam would be undertaken in co-operation with Benin.

Phosphate exports are faced with problems over their cadmium content. Technical studies are presently under way to find economical means to resolve this problem, while the search for new exploitable mineral resources gains urgency.

3. *Measures to improve the physical infrastructure*

Togo is to launch a $310 million project to rehabilitate its transport infrastructure. The largest share - 70 per cent - is allocated to the road network, followed by the coastal infrastructure.

Early in 1988, a new terminal at the international airport of Lomé-Tokoin was opened. It enables the airport to handle 700,000 passengers a year, compared to 250,000 previously, and triples freight capacity.

4. Measures to improve institutional capabilities in the field of development planning and policy

Early in 1988, a programme aimed at the preparation of a population policy and sponsored by the World Bank, UNDP and the African Development Bank, was adopted.

The Government intends to protect the lowest income groups by (i) raising recurrent expenditure in basic social services, and (ii) expanding primary health and education services under IDA-supported projects.

5. International support measures

The Government launched the first and second phases of its structural adjustment programme in 1983 and 1985 respectively. In March 1988, within the context of the third phase, the IMF approved a 13-month stand-by agreement amounting to SDR 13 million, and a three-year structural adjustment arrangement amounting to SDR 24.38 million, of which the first annual tranche amounting to SDR 7.68 million was drawn immediately. Substantial debt relief has been obtained from Paris and London Club creditors, and new loans from bilateral sources, particularly France, have been received.

6. Impact of national policies and international support measures

During the first and second phases of the structural adjustment programme, i.e. between 1982 and 1986, incomes of coffee, cocoa and cotton farmers are estimated to have risen by 132 per cent in nominal terms or by 97 per cent in real terms. In 1988, cotton production soared and coffee output gained significantly, while the previously declining cocoa production was stabilized.

Stimulated by the enhanced incentives for the agricultural sector, successful privatizations of a number of public enterprises and a rise in directly productive investment, the economy enjoyed an average rate of growth of close to 4.0 per cent annually in 1985 and 1986, which was only slightly above that of population growth.

TUVALU

1. Improving the efficiency of resource allocation.

The principal objectives of the country's Third Development Plan (1984-1987) focused on (i) nation building; (ii) strengthening and diversification of the economy; and (iii) improving the standard of living to reasonable levels on all islands.

(a) External sector policies

The Government has encouraged the establishment of co-operatives for the production of export products, mainly handicrafts and copra. The Australian dollar continues to be legal tender. Stamp sales, a major foreign-exchange earner, experienced another setback in 1987. Only one-quarter of the planned sets could be issued due to factors beyond the Government's control, such as the collapse of the principal sales agent, customs problems in the United Kingdom and the military coup in Fiji, which prevented stocks reaching Tuvalu.

(b) Demand-management measures

As the majority of the population lives in a subsistence economy, the Government has realized that the application of conventional monetary and fiscal measures has only a very limited impact on the efficient use and allocation of resources at the present level of economic development. The country's use of Australian dollars precludes the pursuit of an independent monetary policy. Even if a national currency existed, the present lack of domestic investment opportunities would reduce the effectiveness of interest rate policy in stimulating domestic economic activity. Nevertheless, the Government's economic policies have aimed at limiting imports and increasing domestic production, as well as promoting exports and overseas employment to boost remittances.

(c) *Mobilization of domestic savings*

The principal constraints on the operation of the Bank of Tuvalu are the small size of the monetized economy and the communications problem between the islands. As Australia has announced its intention to withdraw its low-denomination notes from circulation, the Government has revised the country's currency ordinance regulating the issues of Tuvalu coins.

(d) *Mobilization of human resources*

Tuvalu has an excess of skilled manpower relative to job opportunities. It is estimated that only about 30 per cent of school leavers are able to find employment. This situation is worsening, since a number of Tuvaluans who were employed in mines abroad have returned in recent years. The Tuvalu Maritime School is expected to provide a continuing opportunity for young men to obtain overseas employment, thus helping to offset the very limited employment opportunities within the country.

(e) *Expanded role for the private sector*

Tuvalu encourages private investment through the Business Development Advisory Bureau. The Bureau assists entrepreneurs in conducting market research, compiling feasibility studies, and negotiating with the Government and the National Bank, as well as with overseas agencies and supplies. Furthermore, it provides assistance as regards credits, management and accounting.

2. *Sectoral policies*

(a) *Agriculture and fisheries*

The Government has placed considerable emphasis on the development of agriculture, and particularly on the increase of food production, with a view to reducing the import of staple foods. To this end, agricultural extension services have been strengthened and extended to all islands. Coconut replanting and rehabilitation has been hampered due to the constraints of the land tenure system and low export prices for copra. The concession of fishing licenses to foreign fleets earns the country an annual revenue of about $100,000.

(b) *Industry and energy*

The Government has promoted small-scale agro-industrial enterprises and the production of handicrafts articles for export.

(c) *Export development and diversification*

A grant extended by Japan is used for the purchase of machinery and equipment for fisheries and training vessels with a view to modernizing existing facilities and creating a base for exports.

(d) *Social development*

A population census, the first since 1979, is scheduled for 1989.

3. *Measures to improve the physical infrastructure*

The wide geographical dispersion of the islands makes internal transport and communication a very difficult and costly service. As the only ship that had provided inter-island service during the past 20 years was increasingly showing signs of wear and tear, the Government successfully approached donors for assistance in replacing the ship. A new ship is to take up service in 1988.

4. *International support measures*

As Tuvalu is handicapped by its poor endowment of natural resources, the low level of its population and the almost total lack of domestic sources of savings and investment, the country depends on foreign aid for financing both its recurrent and its development budgets. In order to diminish the uncertainty related to its extremely high external dependence and to free other aid funds for development projects, the Government invited its donors to contribute to a trust fund, the interest of which would then be used for covering recurrent expenditures of the Government. The Tuvalu Trust Fund was set up with a volume of $19 million in 1987. It is expected to yield up to $1.5 million annually, which would finance about 45 per cent of the country's recurrent budget.

5. *Impact of national policies and international support measures*

Tuvalu represents the smallest LDC economy in terms of area and population. Despite efforts undertaken within the framework of the Third Development Plan, the socio-economic development of the country towards self-sustained growth is hardly perceivable at present.

UGANDA

1. *Improving the efficiency of resource allocation*

In May 1987 the Ugandan Government launched a four-year Economic Rehabilitation and Development Plan (FY1987/88-1990/91).[182] The RDP seeks to achieve an economic growth rate of 5 per cent annually, reduce the rate of inflation to 10 per cent and achieve a sustainable balance-of-payments position during the next few years.

(a) *External sector policies*

The Government has replaced the current administrative system of foreign-exchange allocation with an Open General Licensing (OGL) system for imported inputs directed to five essential industries. Under this system importers automatically obtain import licences and foreign exchange up to a predetermined semi-annual ceiling, provided that neither the price nor the quantity requested is considered excessive by the central bank. Uganda announced a currency reform on 15 May 1987, in which one new Uganda shilling was issued for every 100 old Uganda shillings and a conversion tax of 30per cent was levied on all cash holdings. The new Uganda shilling, which was simultaneously devalued from USh 14 to USh 60 per US dollar, was further devalued in July 1988 to USh 150, but the rate of domestic price inflation was considerably higher, causing the margin between the official and parallel rates to widen further. The Government has put a stop to further countertrade deals.

(b) *Demand-management measures*

The Government will strengthen revenue collection and administration. Fiscal restraint will be more strictly enforced by streamlining the civil service through limiting of subsidies to public enterprises and prohibiting of unauthorized overspending by Ministries. The measures will be accompanied with a crackdown on corruption in the management of public funds and a planned reduction in defence expenditures as civil strife subsides.

(c) *Mobilization of domestic savings*

Negative real interest rates have in the past discouraged savings and biased the low savings flow towards short-term risk-free instruments. The Government's recent policy stance is to shift to positive real interest rates, so as to attract savings into medium and

182 The fiscal year (FY) ends on 30 June.

longer-term instruments. To mobilise savings, the Government is planning to initiate secondary trading of government paper by setting competitive rates of interest for Treasury bills.

(d) Expanded role for the private sector

The Government is pursuing its policy of returning expropriated properties to their former owners. In addition, the Government is working closely with the World Bank on plans for public-enterprise divestiture. The private sector is encouraged to participate in the exports of virtually all export items except coffee.

(e) Improving the efficiency of the public enterprises

Major initiatives under way to improve public enterprises include institutional reorganization, management training programmes, increased management autonomy and financial accountability of the enterprises. The Uganda Development Corporation is being restructured to enhance its role in the promotion and development of operating enterprises and to enable it to act as a catalyst for new investment opportunities.

2. Sectoral policies

(a) Food and agriculture

In the agricultural sector, crop expansion and diversification will be encouraged by substantial increases in real producer prices, improved access to credit, removal of transport bottlenecks and prompt payment to farmers through stricter monitoring and supervision of producers' co-operatives. Problems of inefficiencies in crop marketing will be addressed by measures to revamp management and crack down on corruption.

(b) Industry and energy

The Government is continuing to implement measures aimed at reactivating the manufacturing sector. Key industries (cement, tobacco, beverages, textiles and soap) have been given OGL privileges for imported inputs and spare parts (see 1(a) above). To this end, the Government has mobilized IDA and other external resources under a Special Credit Facility, which will provide the required foreign exchange, as well as ensure firms' ability to obtain local cover for the imports. Procedures for industrial licencing are being reviewed with a view to facilitating investment and encouraging competition.

During FY 1987/88 the Government was concerned with keeping electricity-generating plants operating and combating problems of overloaded lines and shortages of spare parts, rather than starting new projects.

(c) Mining

The Government, with the help of the Democratic People's Republic of Korea, will rehabilitate the copper mine. The Government is also willing to issue concessions for oil exploration in the Rift Valley area.

(d) Social development

The Government will concentrate on restoring and rehabilitating medical and educational facilities, especially in areas where such facilities were destroyed by war. Expansion of facilities for technical and commercial education will be given priority.

3. Measures to improve the physical infrastructure

As a land-locked country Uganda faces high transport costs for her exports. The country's vulnerability in this regard was highlighted when the common border with Kenya was closed for two weeks in December 1987. For these reasons the Government will pursue its policy of diverting part of its exports through the port of Dar-es-Salaam. Bulk shipments transiting through Kenya will use rail transport as a cost-saving measure, and the purchase of rolling stock and spare parts will be given high priority.

4. *Measures to improve institutional capabilities in the field of development planning and policy*

A Public Enterprise Secretariat has been set up in the Ministry of Industries to oversee the operations of industrial public enterprises and assist in divestiture.

5. *International support measures*

The RDP has been strongly endorsed by the international community. The Consultative Group for Uganda, which met in Paris on 11-12 June 1987, agreed that for its implementation, the Government required substantial levels of concessional assistance, including substantial balance-of-payments support over the next few years. The minimum level of these assistance requirements was estimated at about $250million per year over the planning cycle of the RDP. Aid indications made by members of the Group for the first year of the RDP exceeded this level; moreover, the Group assured Uganda of its continued support for future years.

6. *Impact of national policies and international support measures*

Policy measures introduced under the RDP have not yet had a significant impact: the economy continues to stagger under the weight of low productivity, acute foreign-exchange shortages, high defence spending and a growing clandestine economy. Coffee exports, which provide almost all of Uganda's official foreign-exchange earnings, were down to $20 million per month in 1987, as against $25 million in 1986, with the situation in 1988 expected to be only marginally better.

Aid disbursements at the beginning of the RDP were sluggish, as many donors made their aid conditional on an IMF-sponsored economic programme. Once agreement thereon was reached, external resource disbursements accelerated, reaching a total of $454million during FY 1987/88, as compared with $298million in the preceding fiscal year, an increase of 52 per cent.

The crucial impact of external flows on Uganda's economic performance is reflected in the very high share of imports financed by ODA (47 per cent in 1987). Despite the high aid-dependency ratio, an external financing gap subsists. With a projected debt-service-to-exports ratio of 35 percent in 1987, additional aid, including debt cancellation, would be required to help meet the country's import requirements, if equilibrated recovery is to be achieved.

UNITED REPUBLIC OF TANZANIA

1. *Improving the efficiency of resource allocation*

The fiscal year 1987/88[183] is the second year of the United Republic of Tanzania's three-year Economic Recovery Programme (ERP). The ERP seeks to increase the rate of growth of output, especially in agriculture and industry, to rehabilitate the infrastructure and to restore the external balance.

(a) External sector policies

The trade regime has been progressively liberalized. Producer prices for the country's principal export products have been substantially increased. The "own-funded imports" scheme, whereby the importer is authorized to use foreign exchange from unofficial sources to import a wide range of commodities, has been extended. Export retention schemes, under which exporters of non-traditional commodities are allowed to retain a percentage of sales in foreign exchange, have been improved. Starting from February 1988, the Government made a pre-determined portion of foreign exchange

[183] Fiscal year (FY) ends on 30 June.

receipts available on a non-administrative (automatic) basis for selected high-priority import categories through an Open General Licence (OGL) system. The United Republic of Tanzania has made use of countertrade, notably with Mozambique, in its effort to increase its external trade. Between early 1986 and May 1988, the Tanzanian shilling was depreciated from TSh 16 to TSh 96 per US dollar.

(b) Demand-management measures

The Public Investment Programme has been curtailed, placing emphasis on rehabilitation and the completion of ongoing projects. Quarterly targets have been established for domestic credit. During FY 1987/88, civil service salary increases were kept to a minimum, and during FY 1988/89 the Government will continue its policy of freezing employment in the civil service, except in the education, health and revenue departments.

(c) Mobilization of domestic savings

To enhance tax collection, the Government will simplify the structure of customs and sales taxes and reform personal and corporate taxes with the aim of broadening the tax base, while achieving a needed reduction in nominal rates to a range of 15 to 55percent. Deposit and lending rates are being adjusted in line with the prevailing inflation rate.

(d) Expanded role for the private sector

The private sector has also been encouraged to invest in export agriculture, and recently a number of Government-owned sisal estates have been offered for sale to private businesses.

(e) Improving the efficiency of public enterprises

The restructuring of the parastatal sector, initiated in FY1984/85, will be accelerated. Managers are being given more autonomy to set prices and salaries and to manage enterprises in a commercial manner. High productivity in public enterprises would be awarded with a variety of incentives such as bonuses. Budgetary subsidies have been reduced.

2. Sectoral policies

(a) Food and agriculture

Trade in grain for local consumption has been liberalized. The National Milling Corporation (NMC), which had hitherto monopolized this trade, will in future handle a much reduced market share. Improvements in the marketing of export crops include increases in real prices, relaxation of constraints on the exports of minor non-traditional crops and permits for some public and private sisal and tea estates to sell their products directly. The Government plans to undertake measures to reduce the economic cost of food distribution, provide adequate food security, increase the ginning capacity from 300,000 to 500,000 bales of cotton by the early 1990s and modernize equipment for tobacco curing.

(b) Industry and energy

Government policy is aimed at the improvement of industrial production capacity utilization for all manufacturing sectors over the 1989-1992 period. The first phase of the action programme prepared by the Government is aimed at the restructuring and rehabilitation of the leather, textiles and agroprocessing sectors.

(c) Mining

New licencing conditions for small gold and gemstone mining operations have been established, making it more attractive for them to operate through legal channels.

(d) Social development

The Government will concentrate on maintenance of hospitals and schools, provide text books and rehabilitate water pumps and machines for the provision of clean water, especially in rural areas.

3. Measures to improve the physical infrastructure

The Government has started on an overall review of transport policy and has already introduced changes in the way road and rail tariffs are set. The *Tanzanian Harbours Authority* has embarked on a rehabilitation programme. This programme should increase the Port of Dar-es-Salaam's annual capacity from 2.5million tonnes to 4.4million tonnes in 1991, at a cost of more than $100 million.

The first phase of the Emergency Programme (EP) for the *Tanzania Railways Corporation* is now nearing completion. A programme is also under way to strengthen the Tanzanian-Zambian Railway (TAZARA), which connects the Zambian copper belt with Dar-es-Salaam. This is a key element in the 10-year investment plan for the transport sector valued at $250million. In 1987, 14 of the 22 projects of this plan, representing a value of $145million, mainly for locomotives and wagons, were approved by multilateral and bilateral donors. Discussions are going on concerning other projects under this plan worth $49million, leaving the residual amount of $56million for a subsequent period. The capacity of the Railway will be increased to 2.5million tonnes per year, of which 1.4million tonnes will be available to neighbouring countries.

4. Measures to improve institutional capabilities in the field of development planning and policy

A Population Unit was established in the Ministry of Finance, Economic Affairs and Planning to co-ordinate the preparation of a population policy. The country needs to take measures to reduce - over time - its present high rate of population growth which at 3.5 per cent per annum imposes an intolerable strain on basic services.

5. International support measures

The ERP has been strongly endorsed by the international community. The third Consultative Group meeting, held in 1988, agreed to fully meet the United Republic of Tanzania's total financing requirements (including further debt relief), which amounted to about $1.5 billion and $1.3 billion for 1988 and 1989 respectively. A large portion of these resources would be in the form of balance-of-payments support.

6. Impact of national policies and international support measures

Economic recovery, which was already apparent during the first year of the ERP, was sustained during the second year. GDP in FY 1987/88 is estimated to have grown by about 4.O per cent, compared to 3.8 per cent in FY 1986/87. Although this performance falls short of the ERP's target of 4.5 per cent annual growth over the three-year period 1986- 1989, it marks a clear departure from the dismal average growth rate of 0.9 per cent attained during the period 1980-1985. In FY 1987/88 all sectors except mining registered some growth. The best-performing sectors were those which received priority resource allocations under the ERP, but even the agricultural sector, which led with a 4.5 percent growth rate, exhibited underlying structural weaknesses. Growth in this sector was mainly accounted for by substantial increases in grain and cotton production. Industrial growth, which lagged behind the economy's overall growth rate, was limited to a few products (cement, agricultural implements, tyres and paper). For the agricultural sector, transport and processing bottlenecks impeded conversion of increased production into exports, while non-availability of intermediate goods and spare parts continue to seriously inhibit faster growth in the industrial sector.

The crucial impact of external flows on the United Republic of Tanzania's performance is reflected in the very high share of imports financed by ODA, which is projected to be 45 per cent during the three-year period of the ERP. Despite this high aid-dependency ratio, a financing gap subsists, which is equivalent to 41 per cent of import requirements for FY 1988/89 (partly due to repayment of arrears accumulated in FY 1987/88) and over 22 per cent in FY 1989/90. The import financing gap could be filled in part by a further improvement of the ODA disbursement/commitment ratio, which was estimated at 60 per cent for FY1987/88 as against 55 per cent in the preceding year. However, even with such an improvement, additional aid, including debt cancellation, would still be required to help meet the country's import requirements for equilibrated growth.

VANUATU

1. Improving the efficiency of resource use and allocation

Within the framework of Vanuatu's Second National Development Plan (1987-1991), which foresees expenditures of VT 29.3 billion ($267 million), economic policies aim at achieving a greater degree of economic self-reliance. To this end, the Government emphasizes balanced regional and rural development, a more intensive utilization of the country's natural resources, accelerated human resource development and the promotion of the private sector. However, the cyclone Uma, which hit the country in February 1987 causing severe damage to productive capacity and infrastructure facilities, provided an inauspicious start to the implementation of the Plan. In early 1988, the economy received further shocks from cyclones Anne and Bola.

(a) External sector policies

Vanuatu has maintained an open-economy policy, with only a few restrictions on exports and imports. The exchange system is free of any restriction on payments, including remittances and capital transactions. The Government had pursued a flexible exchange-rate policy till October 1986, including several adjustments of the vatu-SDR parity. However, during 1987 and early 1988, the value of the vatu remained unchanged in terms of the SDR. The exchange-rate fluctuations of major currencies in 1987 led to a depreciation of the vatu against some currencies, e.g. the yen, the deutsche mark and the New Zealand dollar. Conversely, the weakness of the US dollar, in which about 85 per cent of the country's exports are denominated, resulted in a 15.6 per cent appreciation of the vatu *vis-à-vis* the US dollar during the same year. To reduce mounting speculative movements from the vatu into foreign currencies, the decision was taken on 5 February 1988 to delink the vatu from the SDR and to peg it to a basket of currencies, the components of which are not officially specified.

(b) Demand-management measures

The Government continued its austerity policy in 1987. Recurrent expenditures were lowered by a freeze in public-sector recruitment, resulting in a reduction in the public-sector payroll and restrictions on purchases of goods and services by government departments.

(c) Mobilization of domestic savings

In 1987, the setting up of a National Provident Fund was under way. The Government undertook measures to raise the tax revenue, including a reduction in the number of customs-exempt imports. The Government issued bonds worth VT 500.1 million ($4.6 million) in 1987.

(d) Mobilization of human resources

The Second National Development Plan cites among its major objectives the acceleration of human resource development in line with the country's developmental needs. As the size of the modern sector is small and prospects for employment creation are limited, only part of secondary-school leavers find adequate job opportunities. Aware of the various aspects of increasing youth unemployment, the Government is following policies aimed at limiting the number of educated unemployed.

(e) Expanded role for the private sector

The Second National Development Plan stresses the importance of both domestic and foreign investment for the country's development. Various incentives, including extensive tax holidays, are provided to foreign investors. The country's investment code contains provisions guaranteeing protection against expropriation. The Government plans to strengthen its services to support indigenous entrepreneurs.

2. Sectoral policies

(a) Food and agriculture

In order to overcome the strong export dependence on copra, the Government is promoting the cultivation of new export crops, such as spices, peanuts and kava. Furthermore, increased emphasis will be given to applied research into traditional food crops. The Government has continued to support the development of both the smallholder sub-sector and larger commercial plantation schemes. Individual projects initiated by the Government will continue to concentrate on smallholders, whereas increased funds will be provided to enable the Development Bank of Vanuatu to accommodate loan requests from the plantation sector. However, a major obstacle to a rapid rise in agricultural output and productivity is the large number of pending land tenure disputes.

(b) Industry

The Government promotes the investment of both domestic and foreign capital in non-agricultural activities. Efforts are made to stimulate investment that utilizes domestic resources for export production. The country's investment code contains provisions guaranteeing protection against expropriation.

(c) Services

New legislation concerning the activities of the Finance Centre came into effect in 1987. Companies previously registered under French law were required to re-register under Vanuatu law, thus swelling the total number of companies on the register to 1,244 by December 1987, including a record number of 247 fresh registrations. As regards the shipping register, it is estimated that there was a significant increase both in the number of ships on the register and in the fees collected. Tourism was adversely affected by a number of economic and non-economic developments. In addition to the cyclone damage to hotels and other facilities following hurricane Uma, the number of tourists declined considerably, mainly due to the high cost of living as compared to other Pacific island destinations and bottlenecks in international transport services.

(d) Export development

The exchange-rate policy followed from October 1986 to February 1988 brought about a discernible change in the destination of exports. In 1987, Japan's share in Vanuatu's total exports rose to the highest-ever level of 28.9 per cent from 17.5 per cent in the previous year. The Republic of Korea's share more than doubled to 4.4 per cent, whereas the shares of the United States and the Netherlands fell. In 1987, the trade deficit widened by about 25 per cent, reflecting mainly an increase in imports destined for repairing cyclone devastation.

(e) Social development

Almost one-quarter of development expenditure under the Second National Development Plan is allocated to social development. High priority will be accorded to improving the health service. The Central Hospital in the capital will be extended, but the Community and Rural Health Programme focuses on the building or rehabilitation of dispensaries in outlying islands.

3. Measures to improve the physical infrastructure

Infrastructural development figures prominantly in the Second National Development Plan. About four-fifths of the funds earmarked for *marine transport* will be used for the construction of port facilities. One of the biggest projects in this regard is the reconstruction of the Luganville wharf, at a total cost of about VT 717 million ($6.5 million), equivalent to about 8 per cent of the country's GDP. As for *air transport*, efforts are concentrated on the improvement and the expansion of international airports, particularly the Bauerfield Airport. In the *land transport* sector, funds will be allocated for the construction of new urban and rural roads, as well as for maintenance. Upon completion of the *rural telecommunications* programme, it is expected that about 98 per cent of the population will be within reasonable distance of telephone services.

4. *International support measures*

Excluding compensation payments for export earnings losses under the EEC's STABEX scheme and relief assistance of $6.4 million to cover cyclone damage, external grants recorded a decline of 34 per cent between 1981 and 1987. This decline has been primarily due to the phasing out of recurrent grants received from both France and the United Kingdom, which will terminate entirely after 1988. At the first Round Table Meeting for Vanuatu held on 28 October 1988, donors agreed to direct greater attention in the future to the problem of recurrent-cost financing. The United Kingdom announced its financing of a defined percentage of the recurrent costs of individual projects over a given time period. France confirmed its intention to maintain its programme for technical assistance, which focuses primarily on education and training.

5. *Impact of national policies and international support measures*

The country's effort to expedite economic development was dealt a heavy blow in February 1987 by cyclone Uma, which affected about 34 per cent of the total population. The total damage caused by the cyclone was estimated at VT 4 billion ($36.4 million). However, although the output of major crops was slashed and tourist arrivals slowed down immediately after the cyclone, favourable world copra prices, the revival of tourist traffic in the second half of 1987 and the commencement of rehabilitation and reconstruction work limited the decline in GDP to about one per cent. The crucial impact of external flows for the successful implementation of the Second National Development Plan is reflected in the fact that about 96 per cent of development expenditures are to be financed by external assistance during the Plan period.

YEMEN ARAB REPUBLIC

1. *Improving the efficiency of resource allocation*

The emphasis in the Third Five-Year Development Plan (1987-1991) is placed on self-reliance, with particular attention to agriculture and industries that use local raw materials. Incentives are offered for investments outside the main cities.

(a) External sector policies

In February 1988 the commercial and official exchange rates of the rial were unified at YRs 9.76 per dollar. Yemen joined the rank of oil exporters in December 1987. Production is estimated at about 200,000 b/d. Estimated oil exports for 1988 will boost the total merchandise export figures from $51 million in 1987 to $650 million. The Yemen Crude Oil Marketing Company was established in 1988 to market the Government's share of oil production. With the advent of an easier balance-of-payments situation, the Government began moves towards the relaxation of austerity measures (originally imposed in mid-1986) as part of the implementation of the 1988 budget. The cash deposits required to cover letters of credit were lowered from 40 to 25 per cent for imports of food, medicine and petrochemicals, and from 60 to 35 per cent for all other imports. As a result, imports in 1988 are projected to amount to $1.5 billion, 7 per cent higher than in 1987.

(b) Demand-management measures

With the inflow of oil revenue, the budget deficit is projected to decline by about 47 per cent in 1988. The limit on commercial banks' ability to extend overdrafts has been increased to 25 per cent. In order to mobilize the commercial banks' excess liquidity for economic activity, the Central Bank has reduced interest rates by one percentage point, bringing the highest rates for one-year deposits to 7.5 per cent. Public sector enterprises will be allowed to seek more credit. All these measures are expected to lead to a 14 per cent increase in money supply, compared to 10 per cent in 1987.

(c) Mobilization of domestic savings

Revenues are projected to increase by 70 per cent in 1988 (19 per cent excluding oil revenue). The increase in non-oil revenue is due mainly to the increase in indirect taxes and higher consumption taxes, particularly on cigarettes and real estate. Expenditure is budgeted to rise by 31 per cent. Nevertheless, the budget deficit will be little over one-half of the 1987 deficit. Of the total investment outlay of $3.75 billion projected for the Third Five-Year Development Plan, about 60 per cent will come from domestic sources, as against 40 per cent in the previous Plan.

(d) Expanded role for the private sector

The new policy directives of the Central Bank (see (b) above) are expected to further enhance the role of the private sector through the provision of increased resources for investment. Private-sector imports are to be increased substantially in 1988, so as to increase capacity utilization, which had declined in certain cases to a level of only 30 per cent.

(e) Improving the efficiency of public enterprises

The Government is assessing the performance of the parastatal trading organizations. A study is being prepared with the assistance of UNCTAD, which will contain recommendations for ensuring effective participation by these organizations in the procurement, stock management and distribution of commodities.

2. Sectoral policies

(a) Food and agriculture

The growth target for the agricultural sector in the Third Five-Year Development Plan has been set at an average annual rate of 7 per cent. This growth target, which is considerably higher than the 2.4 per cent growth rate actually achieved during the previous Plan, is believed to be attainable as a result of the completion of some important projects, notably the Marib Dam and the Wadi Mawr irrigation systems. The second stage for the Marib Dam, costing $22 million, has started. In this phase some 80 km of branch canals will be built, the irrigation network will be expanded, and a model farm and an agricultural laboratory will be established. The ban on the import of fruits and vegetables has been maintained and producer prices increased. As a result, domestic production increased and watermelons were exported in 1987. The first private agricultural marketing company has been established. Besides marketing activities, the company will also provide farmers with high-quality seeds and extension services.

(b) Industry and energy

Most large industrial enterprises are owned by the Government or are under mixed ownership. A new cement plant with an annual capacity of one million tons is to be built, and the capacity of another one is to be increased from 300,000 tons to 1 million tons annually. The increase in the production of cement is vital for the booming construction sector and for the implementation of the development projects included in the Development Plan. The milling capacity of the Red Sea Flour Mills Company in Hodeida is to be increased from 520 tons/d to 1920 tons/d at a total cost of $100 million. Grain storage capacity is to increase fourfold. The major priority in the energy sector is the expansion of electricity supply. A rural electricity supply project costing $22 million, to improve supply in the earthquake-affected Dhamar Governate, is under construction. The fourth national power project, at a cost of $60 million, aims at connecting 20,000 households to the national grid and improving services for another 18,000 consumers. The distribution networks of Sana'a, Hodeida and Taiz are being expanded. Geothermal energy exploration is under way, and four exploratory wells will be drilled in the Dhamar and Rada'a regions to assess potential.

(c) Mining

The Amman-based Arab Mining Company, a pan-Arab venture, has been awarded a contract to conduct technical and economic feasibility studies on the exploitation of Yemen's marble and granite resources.

(d) Social development

The immunization programme is entering the second year of its second (1987-1991) phase. The programme covers 3,500 vaccination sites involving a staff of 30,000. Finance is being provided by bilateral and multilateral donors. IDA is to provide a $17.6 million credit, to be matched by the Government in local currency, to finance equipment and infrastructure for the 1988-1993 rural extension programme.

3. Measures to improve the physical infrastructure

Projects to rehabilitate existing roads and construct new ones include: upgrading the 217 km Sana'a - Hodeida road ($38 million), construction of a 56.4 km road between Fardah and Al-Hazm ($11.9 million), construction of a 214 km road between Sa'adah and Haradh ($24.5 million), construction of a 127 km road east of Sana'a ($42 million), and a feeder road project north of Sana'a ($8.6 million). The new 60 km road between Marib and the oil installation at Safer is expected to be completed in mid-1988. A loan of $25 million, provided by France, will be utilized to expand the communications network and install a central electricity control system.

4. Measures to improve institutional capabilities in the field of development planning and policy

The Ministry of Economy, Supply and Trade is attempting to strengthen its technical and managerial capacities to improve the efficiency and performance of the trade sector with the help of a UNDP-financed project executed by UNCTAD. A Trade and Pricing Information Unit will be established to enhance the flow and quality of information required for the implementation of the control/supervision procedures. The Department of Statistics, Planning and Follow-up is to be strengthened through the provision of data-processing equipment and the upgrading of its technical capacities through a parallel project.

5. International support measures

Net disbursements of total financial flows, which amounted to about $302 million in 1986, were estimated at $333 million in 1987.

6. Impact of national policies and international support measures

The 1988 budget estimates indicate a reversal of the expansionary policy followed in the previous year. Estimates of expenditure are below actual expenditures in 1987, while revenue will increase by 65 per cent. In 1987, the Government adopted an expansionary fiscal policy. Expenditures increased by 20 per cent, leading to a 56 per cent increase in the budget deficit as compared to 1986. The deficit was financed by increased foreign borrowing and deficit financing from the banking system equivalent to 20 per cent of money supply. Real GDP is estimated to have increased by 5.0 per cent in 1987, but growth in 1988 is likely to accelerate due to the beginning of large-scale oil exports. Imports, which had been projected at $950 million in the budget estimates, recovered to their 1984 level of $1.4 billion, but were still well below the 1981-1983 average of $1.8 billion. This raised the current-account deficit to about $600 million, equivalent to 14 per cent of GDP, as compared to $125 million in 1986. The single most significant economic development registered during the year was the commencement of the export of petroleum, which already overshadows all other exports, even though these also doubled. Private remittances reached their highest level since 1985, amounting to $800 million. The growth of non-oil exports and of remittances was a reflection of the changes in the exchange rate of the rial.

Imports will increase by only about 8 per cent in 1988. In view of the fact that oil revenue will be offset by declining official and private transfers, even this moderate increase in imports would have to be financed by borrowing, mainly through the use of suppliers' credits. These increased significantly in 1987, a policy which the Government had avoided in the past.

Annex

BASIC DATA ON THE LEAST DEVELOPED COUNTRIES

Annexe

DONNÉES DE BASE RELATIVES AUX PAYS LES MOINS AVANCÉS

CONTENTS

TABLE DES MATIERES

Tables Page

Tableaux Pages

Tables Page

Tableaux Pages

EXPLANATORY NOTES

A. Definition of country groupings

Least developed countries

In this document, the 41 countries identified by the United Nations as least developed are: Afghanistan, Bangladesh, Benin, Bhutan, Botswana, Burkina Faso, Burma, Burundi, Cape Verde, Central African Republic, Chad, Comoros, Democratic Yemen, Djibouti, Equatorial Guinea, Ethiopia, Gambia, Guinea, Guinea-Bissau, Haiti, Kiribati, Lao People's Democratic Republic, Lesotho, Malawi, Maldives, Mali, Mauritania, Nepal, Niger, Rwanda, Samoa, Sao Tome and Principe, Sierra Leone, Somalia, Sudan, Togo, Tuvalu, Uganda, United Republic of Tanzania, Vanuatu and Yemen. Except where otherwise indicated, the totals and the tables for least developed countries as a group refer to these 41 countries. The United Nations General Assembly at its forty-third session in December 1988 has approved the inclusion of Mozambique which will be covered in the next issue of the *Basic Data*.

Major economic areas

The classification of countries and territories according to main economic areas used in this document has been adopted for purposes of statistical convenience only and follows that in the UNCTAD *Handbook of International Trade and Development Statistics, 1988*. Countries and territories are classified according to main economic areas as follows :

Developed market-economy countries : United States, Canada, EEC (Belgium, Denmark, France, Germany, Federal Republic of, Greece, Ireland, Italy, Luxembourg, Netherlands, Portugal, Spain, United Kingdom), EFTA (Austria, Finland, Iceland, Norway, Sweden, Switzerland), Faeroe Islands, Gibraltar, Israel, Japan, Australia, New Zealand, South Africa.

Socialist countries of Eastern Europe : Albania, Bulgaria, Czechoslovakia, German Democratic Republic, Hungary, Poland, Romania, USSR.

Socialist countries of Asia : China, Democratic People's Republic of Korea, Mongolia, Viet Nam.

Developing countries and territories : All other countries , territories and areas in Africa, Asia, America, Europe and Oceania not specified above.

In some tables the group of *all developing countries* excludes, as indicated, major petroleum exporters. *Major petroleum exporters* are defined as those countries for which petroleum and petroleum products accounted for more than 50 per cent of their total exports in 1978, namely, Algeria, Angola, Bahrain, Brunei, Congo, Ecuador, Gabon, Indonesia, Iran (Islamic Republic of), Iraq, Kuwait, Libyan Arab Jamahiriya, Mexico, Nigeria, Oman, Qatar, Saudi Arabia, Syrian Arab Republic, Trinidad and Tobago, United Arab Emirates and Venezuela.

Other country groupings

DAC member countries : In this document, the countries members of the OECD Development Assistance Committee are Australia, Austria, Belgium, Canada, Denmark, Finland, France, Germany, Federal Republic of, Ireland, Italy, Japan, Netherlands, New Zealand, Norway, Sweden, Switzerland, United Kingdom and United States.

OPEC member countries : The countries members of the Organization of the Petroleum Exporting Countries are Algeria, Ecuador, Gabon, Indonesia, Iran (Islamic Republic of), Iraq, Kuwait, Libyan Arab Jamahiriya, Nigeria, Qatar, Saudi Arabia, United Arab Emirates and Venezuela.

B. Terms, definitions and sources used

The estimates of *population* are for mid-year and are primarily based on data from the Population Division of the Department of International Economic and Social Affairs of the United Nations Secretariat.

National accounts data are mainly based on information from the United Nations Statistical Office, the United Nations Economic Commission for Africa, the World Bank and national sources.

The estimates relating to *agricultural production, food* and *nutrition*, are derived mainly from information provided by FAO.

Trade data are estimates by the UNCTAD secretariat mainly derived from the UNCTAD *Handbook of International Trade and Development Statistics, Supplement, 1988*. Unless otherwise indicated, trade data refer to merchandise trade. Exports are valued f.o.b. and imports c.i.f.

The figures concerning *aid flows* are mainly based on information provided by the OECD secretariat.

Following the DAC definitions[1] *concessional assistance* refers to flows which qualify as official development assistance (ODA), i.e., grants or loans undertaken by the official sector, with promotion of economic development and welfare as main objectives, and at concessional financial terms (if a loan, at least 25 per cent grant element). *Non-concessional flows* include grants from private agencies (private aid) and transactions at commercial terms : export credits, bilateral portfolio investment (including bank lending) by residents or institutions in donor countries; direct investment (including reinvested earnings); and purchases of securities of international organisations active in development. Figures for *commitments* reflect a firm obligation to furnish assistance specified as to volume, purpose, financial terms and conditions, while figures for *disbursements* represent the actual provision of funds. Unless otherwise specified, disbursement figures are shown net, i.e., less capital repayments on earlier loans. Grants, loans and credits for military purposes and loans and credits with a maturity of less than one year are excluded from aid flows.

The data for the years 1977-1986 concerning aid flows from OPEC member countries and multilateral agencies mainly financed by them have been supplied directly by the donors to the UNCTAD secretariat. In a few cases the figures represent estimates by the UNCTAD secretariat based on secondary sources.

Tables 29 and 35 present data for individual DAC and OPEC member countries respectively on the estimated amount of official development assistance provided to LDCs expressed as a percentage of the GNP of each donor. So as to give a clear picture of the total flow, an attempt has been made to estimate the share of multilateral flows to LDCs which is provided by each donor. In order to do so, the share of each agency's disbursements to LDCs, expressed as a percentage of its total disbursements to developing countries, was applied to the donor's contributions to the agency in question; the sum for all agencies thus calculated was then added to the donor's bilateral ODA and expressed as a percentage of its GNP.

Debt data are based on information provided by the OECD secretariat, except tables 47 and 48 which are derived from the World Bank Debt Reporting System.

With regard to other economic and social indicators, data on area are from the United Nations, *Demographic Yearbook* 1986[2] and the FAO, *Production Yearbook 1986*.

The estimates relating to *urban population* are not strictly comparable from country to country because of differences in definitions and coverage. They have been mainly derived from the United Nations, *World Population Chart 1985*[3] and the World Bank, *World Development Report 1988*.

The labour force participation rate refers to economically active population as a percentage of total population of sex(es) specified of all ages, as shown in ILO, *Economically active population 1950-2025*.

Crude birth rates and *crude death rates* indicate respectively the number of births and deaths per thousand of population. Together with *life expectancy at birth* and *infant mortality rates, crude birth* and *death rates* have been derived mainly from the *United Nations, Demographic Yearbook 1986;* United Nations, *World Population Prospects: estimates and projections as United Nations, World Population Prospect assessed in 1984.*[4]

Life expectancy at birth indicates the average number of years the newly born children would live, if subject to the same mortality conditions in the year(s) to which the life expectancy refers, while the *infant mortality rate* is the number of infants who die before reaching one year of age per thousand live births in the reference year.

Under the heading *health at birth, low birth weight* directly reflects the nutritional status of mothers and indirectly, mediated through the status of women, that of the population in general. The figures are drawn from WHO, *World Health Statistics Annual 1986* and UNICEF, *The State of the World's Children 1987.*

The *percentage of women attended during childbirth by trained personnel* is a good indicator of the availability of medical services. It reflects the geographical distribution of the facilities and hence their accessibility, and indeed whether the hospitals had the equipment and supplies to dispense effective medical care. The percentage of women attended during childbirth by trained personnel also to a degree reflects the status of women. Data are drawn from WHO, *World Health Statistics Annual 1986.*

The percentage of children immunized against DPT (3 doses) refers to the vaccination coverage of children under one year of age for the target diseases of the Expanded Programme of Immunization (diphtheria, tetanus, whooping-cough, measles, poliomyelitis and tuberculosis). Data are drawn from WHO, *World Health Statistics Annual 1986.*

The estimates of *average daily calorie intake per capita* was calculated by dividing the calorie equivalent of the food supplies in an economy by the population. Food supplies comprise domestic production, imports less exports, and changes in stocks; they exclude animal feed, seeds for use in agriculture, and food lost in processing and distribution. The data in this table are weighted by population and are taken from FAO, *Production Yearbook 1986* and FAO, *The State of Food and Agriculture 1985 and 1986.*

The percentage of population with access to safe water or adequate sanitation are estimates by WHO. The percentage with access to safe water refers to the share of people with "reasonable" access to treated surface waters or untreated but uncontaminated water, such as that from protected boreholes, springs and sanitary wells, as a percentage of their respective populations. In an urban area a public fountain or standpost located not more than 200 metres from a house is considered as being within "reasonable" access to that house; in rural areas, "reasonable" access would imply that the housewife or members of the household do not spend a disproportionate part of the day in fetching the family's water needs.

The *percentage of population with access to adequate sanitation* includes the share of urban population served by connexions to public sewers or by systems (pit privies, pour-flush latrines, septic tanks, communal toilets, etc.) and the share of rural population with adequate disposal such as pit privies, pour-flush latrines, etc.

With respect to both water and sanitation, the figures are derived from *The International drinking water supply and sanitation decade: review of national progress* (as at 31 December 1985).

1 See, OECD *Development Co-operation, 1983 Review,* (Paris, 1983) , p.176.

2 ST/ESA/STAT/SER.R/16, United Nations Publication, Sales No. E/F.87.XIII.1.

3 ST/ESA/SER.A/98/Add.1, United Nations Publication, Sales No. E.85.XIII.A.

4 ST/ESA/SER.A/98, United Nations Publication, Sales No. E.86.XIII.3.

Data relating to *education and literacy* are mainly derived from information provided by UNESCO. The *adult literacy rate* is the percentage of people aged 15 and over who can read and write. The data on *school enrolment ratios* refer to estimates of total, male, and female, enrolment of students of all ages in primary/secondary school, expressed as percentages of the total, male, and female, population of primary/secondary school age.

Data on *post offices open to the public per 100,000 inhabitants* are derived from Universal Postal Union, *Statistique des services postaux 1980-1986*.

Data on *telephones per 1000 inhabitants* are based on ITU, *Yearbook of Common Carrier Telecommunication Statistics* (15th edition).

Data on *radio receivers per 1000 inhabitants* are based on data from UNESCO, *Statistical Yearbook 1987*. The ratio uses the number of receivers in use and/or licenses issued, depending on the method of estimation used in each reporting country.

Data on *circulation of daily newspapers per 1000 inhabitants* refer to circulation of "daily general interest newspaper" and are based on data from UNESCO, *Statistical Yearbook 1987*.

As regards transport indicators, special problems of comparability arise in the case of *roads*, where the definition may vary widely from country to country. The main sources used are *The Far East and Australasia, The Middle East and North Africa, Africa South of the Sahara, South America, Central America and the Caribbean,* Europa Publications Limited 1988.

The figures for *railways* cover domestic and international traffic on all railway lines within each country shown, except railways entirely within an urban unit and plantation, industrial mining, funicular and cable railways. The figures relating to passenger-kilometres include all passengers except military, government and railway personnel when carried without revenue. Those relating to ton-kilometres are freight net ton-kilometres and include both fast and ordinary goods services but exclude service traffic, mail, baggage and non-revenue governmental stores. The data are mainly derived from *The Railway Directory and Yearbook 1987*.

The figures relating to *civil aviation* cover both domestic and international schedules services operated by airlines registered in each country. Schedules services include supplementary services occasioned by overflow traffic on regularly scheduled trips and preparatory flights for new scheduled services. Freight means all goods, except mail and excess baggage, carried for remuneration. The data are derived from *ICAO Digest of Statistics - Airport Traffic 1986*.

Data on *energy consumption per capita* refer, on the one hand, to forms of primary energy, including hard coal, lignite, peat and oil shale, crude petroleum and natural gas liquids, natural gas, and primary electricity (nuclear, geothermal, and hydroelectric power) - often called "commercial energy" - and, on the other hand, to the use of fuelwood, charcoal and bagasse. All data are converted into coal equivalent and are based on information from United Nations, *Energy Statistics Yearbook 1984*[5] and *1986*.[6]

The data on *installed electricity capacity* are also derived from United Nations, *Energy Statistics Yearbook 1984* and *1986*.

C. Calculation of annual average growth rates

In general, they are defined as the coefficient b in the exponential trend function $y' = ae^{bt}$, where t stands for time. This method takes all observations in a period into account. Therefore, the resulting growth rates reflect trends that are not unduly influenced by exceptional values.

D. Other notes

"Dollars" ($) refer to United States dollars, unless otherwise stated.

Details and percentages in tables do not necessarily add up to totals, because of rounding.

The following symbols have been used :

A dash (-) or a zero (0) indicates that the amount is nil or negligible.

Two dots (..) indicate that the data are not available or are not separately reported.

Use of a hyphen (-) between dates representing years, e.g. 1970-1980, signifies the full period involved, including the initial and final years.

5 ST/ESA/STAT/SER.J/28, United Nations Publication, Sales No. E/F.86.XVII.2.

6 ST/ESA/STAT/SER.J/30, United Nations Publication, Sales No. E/F.88.XVII.3.

E. Abbreviations used

AfDB	African Development Bank
AfDF	African Development Fund
AFESD	Arab Fund for Economic and Social Development
AsDB	Asian Development Bank
BADEA	Arab Bank for Economic Development in Africa
CMEA	Council for Mutual Economic Assistance
CRS	Creditor Reporting System (OECD)
DAC	Development Assistance Committee (of OECD)
DRS	Debtor Reporting System (World Bank)
EDF	European Development Fund
EEC	European Economic Community
EIB	European Investment Bank
FAO	Food and Agriculture Organization of the United Nations
IBRD	International Bank for Reconstruction and Development (World Bank)
ICAO	International Civil Aviation Organization
IDA	International Development Association
IDB	Inter-American Development Bank
IFAD	International Fund for Agricultural Development
IFC	International Finance Corporation
IMF	International Monetary Fund
LDCs	Least Developed Countries
mill.	Millions
OAPEC	Organization of Arab Petroleum Exporting Countries
ODA	Official development assistance
OECD	Organisation for Economic Co-operation and Development
OPEC	Organisation of Petroleum Exporting Countries
SAAFA	Special Arab Aid Fund for Africa
SITC	Standard International Trade Classification, Revision 1
SNPA	Substantial New Programme of Action for the 1980s for the Least Developed Countries
UN	United Nations
UNDP	United Nations Development Programme
UNHCR	Office of the United Nations High Commissioner for Refugees
UNICEF	United Nations Children's Fund
UNTA	United Nations Technical Assistance
WFP	World Food Programme

NOTES EXPLICATIVES

A. Définition des groupements de pays

Pays en développement les moins avancés

Les 41 pays ainsi identifiés par l'Organisation des Nations Unies qui figurent dans ce document sont les suivants : Afghanistan, Bangladesh, Bénin, Bhoutan, Birmanie, Botswana, Burkina Faso, Burundi, Cap-Vert, Comores, Djibouti, Ethiopie, Gambie, Guinée, Guinée-Bissau, Guinée équatoriale, Haïti, Kiribati, Lesotho, Malawi, Maldives, Mali, la Mauritanie, Népal, Niger, Ouganda, République centrafricaine, République démocratique populaire lao, République-Unie de Tanzanie, Rwanda, Samoa, Sao Tomé-et-Principe, Sierra Leone, Somalie, Soudan, Tchad, Togo, Tuvalu, Vanuatu, Yémen, et Yémen démocratique. Les totaux et les tableaux concernant l'ensemble des pays les moins avancés se rapportent à ces 41 pays. L'Assemblée générale des Nations Unies, au cours de sa quarante-troisième session en décembre 1988, a approuvé l'inclusion du Mozambique qui sera compris dans la prochaine édition des *Données de base*.

Grandes zones économiques

Le classement des pays et territoires par grandes zones économiques, utilisé dans ce document, n'a été adopté qu'aux fins de présentation des statistiques et il suit celui qui est utilisé dans le *Manuel de statistiques du commerce international et du développement, 1988*. Les pays et territoires sont classés en grandes zones économiques, constituées comme suit :

Les pays développés à économie de marché : Etats-Unis d'Amérique, Canada, Communauté économique européenne (Allemagne, République fédérale d', Belgique, Danemark, Espagne, France, Grèce, Irlande, Italie, Luxembourg, Pays-Bas, Portugal, Royaume-Uni), AELE (Autriche, Finlande, Islande, Norvège, Suède, Suisse), Gibraltar, iles Féroé, Israël, Japon, Australie, Nouvelle-Zélande, Afrique du Sud.

Les pays socialistes d'Europe orientale : Albanie, Bulgarie, Hongrie, Pologne, République démocratique allemande, Roumanie, Tchécoslovaquie, URSS.

Les pays socialistes d'Asie : Chine, Mongolie, République populaire démocratique de Corée, Viet Nam.

Les pays et territoires en développement : tous les autres pays, terrritoires et zones d'Afrique, d'Asie, d'Amérique, d'Europe et d'Océanie non mentionnés ci-dessus.

Dans certains tableaux, il est indiqué que *l'ensemble des pays en développement* ne comprend pas les principaux pays exportateurs de pétrole. Par *principaux pays exportateurs de pétrole*, on entend les pays pour lesquels les exportations de pétrole et de produits pétroliers ont représenté plus de 50 pour cent de leurs exportations totales en 1978, c'est-à-dire : Algérie, Angola, Arabie saoudite, Bahrein, Brunei, Congo, Emirats arabes unis, Equateur, Gabon, Indonésie, Iraq, Iran, République islamique d', Jamahiriya arabe libyenne, Koweit, Mexique, Nigeria, Oman, Qatar, République arabe syrienne, Trinité-et-Tobago et Venezuela.

Autres groupements de pays

Les pays membres du Comité d'aide au développement (CAD) qui figurent dans ce document sont les suivants : Allemagne, République fédérale d', Australie, Autriche, Belgique, Canada, Danemark, Etats-Unis, Finlande, France, Irlande, Italie, Japon, Norvège, Nouvelle-Zélande, Pays-Bas, Royaume-Uni, Suède et Suisse.

Les pays membres de l'Organisation des pays exportateurs de pétrole (OPEP) sont les suivants : Algérie, Arabie saoudite, Emirats arabes unis, Equateur, Gabon, Indonésie, Iraq, Iran, République islamique d', Koweit, Jamahiriya arabe libyenne, Nigéria, Qatar et Venezuela.

B. Définitions, terminologie et sources utilisées

Les estimations de la *population* sont des estimations de milieu d'année fondées essentiellement sur des données fournies par la Division de la population du Département des affaires économiques et sociales internationales de l'ONU.

Les données se rapportant aux *comptes nationaux* ont été établies principalement d'après des informations provenant du Bureau de statistique des Nations Unies, de la Commission économique pour l'Afrique et de la Banque mondiale, ainsi que de sources nationales.

Les estimations concernant la *production agricole, l'alimentation et la nutrition,* sont surtout tirées d'informations communiquées par la FAO.

Les données se rapportant au *commerce* sont des estimations du secrétariat de la CNUCED tirées en grande partie *du Manuel de statistiques du commerce international et du développement, 1988.* Sauf indication contraire, les données du commerce se rapportent au commerce de marchandises. Les exportations sont données en valeur f.o.b. et les importations en valeur c.a.f.

Les chiffres se rapportant aux *apports d'aide* sont principalement fondés sur des informations communiquées par le secrétariat de l'OCDE. Suivant les définitions du CAD[7], *l'aide concessionnelle* désigne les apports qui sont considérés comme une "aide publique au développement" (APD), c'est-à-dire les dons ou les prêts accordés par le secteur public, dans le but essentiel d'améliorer le développement économique et le niveau de vie, et assortis de conditions financières libérales (dans le cas des prêts, 25 pour cent au moins d'élément de don).

Les apports *non-concessionnels* comprennent les dons des organismes privés (aide privée) et les transactions assorties de conditions commerciales: crédits à l'exportation, investissements bilatéraux de portefeuille (prêts bancaires compris) effectués par des résidents ou des institutions des pays donneurs; investissements directs (bénéfices réinvestis compris) et achats de titres d'organisations internationales s'occupant du développement. Les données concernant les *engagements* se rapportent au moment où le donneur prend l'engagement ferme de fournir une aide déterminée quant à son volume, sa destination, ses conditions financières et ses modalités, tandis que les données concernant les *versements* correspondent à la fourniture effective des fonds. Sauf indication contraire, les chiffres des versements sont indiqués "nets", c'est-à-dire déduction faite des remboursements effectués au titre de prêts antérieurs. Les dons, les prêts et les crédits de caractère militaire, ainsi que les prêts et les crédits dont la durée de remboursement est inférieure à un an, sont exclus.

Les données pour les années 1977-1986, concernant l'aide en provenance des pays membres de l'OPEP et des institutions multilatérales essentiellement financées par ceux-ci, ont été généralement fournies directement par les donneurs eux-mêmes. Dans quelques cas, les chiffres sont des estimations du secrétariat de la CNUCED à partir de sources secondaires.

Les tableaux 29 et 35 présentent des estimations, pour les divers pays membres du CAD et de l'OPEP, sur le montant de l'aide publique au développement qui a été fourni aux PMA, exprimé en pourcentage du PNB de chaque donneur. Afin de donner un aperçu précis des apports totaux, on a essayé d'estimer la part des apports multilatéraux qui a été fournie par chaque donneur aux PMA. A cette fin, on a appliqué aux contributions du pays donneur à chacune des institutions multilatérales, la part respective des versements nets de chacune de ces institutions aux PMA exprimée en pourcentage des versements nets correspondant à l'ensemble des pays en développement. La somme ainsi obtenue pour l'ensemble des institutions est ajoutée à l'aide bilatérale du pays donneur et exprimée en pourcentage de son PNB.

Les données concernant la *dette* sont fondées sur des renseignements communiqués par le secrétariat de l'OCDE, à l'exception des tableaux 47 et 48 qui sont tirés du système de déclaration des débiteurs de la Banque Mondiale.

En ce qui concerne les autres indicateurs économiques et sociaux, les données relatives aux *superficies* sont tirées de l'*Annuaire démographique 1986* des Nations Unies[8] et de l'*Annuaire de la production 1986* de la FAO.

Les estimations concernant la *population urbaine* ne sont pas toujours comparables d'un pays à l'autre en raison des différences qui existent dans les définitions et la couverture. Elles sont principalement tirées du *World Population Chart 1985* des Nations Unies[9] et du *Rapport sur le développement dans le monde 1988* de la Banque Mondiale.

Le *taux d'activité* est le rapport (en pourcentage) entre la population active et la population du ou des sexes indiqués, tous âges confondus. Les chiffres sont tirés de la *Population active 1950-2025* du BIT.

Les *taux bruts de natalité et de mortalité* indiquent respectivement le nombre de naissances vivantes et de décès pour mille habitants. Ces taux, ainsi que *l'espérance de vie à la naissance* et les *taux de mortalité infantile*, sont principalement tirés de l'*Annuaire démographique 1986;* de *World Population Prospects: estimates and projections as assessed in 1984*[10], de *World Population Chart 1985* des Nations Unies, et *Social Indicators of Development 1988* de la Banque Mondiale.

L'espérance de vie à la naissance indique le nombre moyen d'années que vivrait un nouveau-né pour autant que les conditions de mortalité ne changent pas, alors que le *taux de mortalité infantile* exprime le nombre de décès d'enfants de moins d'un an pour mille naissances vivantes survenus pendant l'année de référence.

Sous la rubrique *santé à la naissance*, le *poids insuffisant à la naissance* reflète directement le statut nutritionnel des mères et indirectement, compte tenu du statut de la femme, celui de la population en général. Les chiffres sont tirés de l'*Annuaire de statistiques sanitaires mondiales 1986* de l'OMS.

Le *pourcentage de femmes ayant reçu des soins prodigués par du personnel qualifié pendant l'accouchement* constitue un indicateur de la disponibilité des services médicaux. Il reflète la distribution géographique de l'équipement et par conséquent leur accessibilité et dans quelle mesure les hôpitaux disposent du matériel et des fournitures qu'il faut pour offrir des soins médicaux efficaces. Le pourcentage de femmes ayant reçu des soins prodigués par du personnel qualifié pendant l'accouchement reflète aussi dans une certaine mesure le statut de la femme. Les données sont tirées de l'*Annuaire de statistiques sanitaires mondiales 1986* de l'OMS et de *La situation des enfants dans le monde* de la FISE.

Le *pourcentage d'enfants vaccinés DTC (3 doses)* se rapporte à la couverture vaccinale des enfants de moins d'un an pour les maladies cibles du programme élargi de vaccination (diphtérie, tétanos, coqueluche, rougeole, poliomyélite et tuberculose). Les données sont tirées de l'*Annuaire de statistiques sanitaires mondiales 1986* de l'OMS.

On a calculé les *disponibilités alimentaires* en divisant l'équivalent en calorie de l'offre de denrées alimentaires disponible dans un pays par sa population totale. Cette offre comprend la production intérieure, les importations diminuées des exportations et les variations de stocks; elle ne recouvre ni l'alimentation du bétail, ni les semences utilisées dans l'agriculture, ni les pertes en cours de traitement et de distribution. Les chiffres présentés sur ce tableau sont pondérés par la population. Les données sont tirées de l'*Annuaire de la production 1986* et de *La situation mondiale de l'alimentation et de l'agriculture 1985 et 1986* de la FAO.

Les *pourcentages de la population disposant d'eau saine ou de mesures suffisantes d'hygiène du milieu* sont des estimations de l'OMS. Le *pourcentage de la population disposant d'eau saine* indique la part en pourcentage de

7 Voir OCDE, *Coopération pour le développement, examen 1983* (Paris 1983), p. 200.

8 ST/ESA/STAT/SER/16, publication des Nations Unies, no. de vente E/F.87.XIII.1.

9 ST/ESA/SER.A/98/Add.1, publication des Nations Unies, no. de vente E.85.XIII.A.

10 ST/ESA/SER.A/98, publication des Nations Unies, no. de vente E.86.XIII.3.

personnes jouissant d'un accès "raisonnable" aux eaux superficielles traitées ou à une eau non traitée mais non contaminée, provenant par exemple de forages, de sources et de puits protégés, par rapport à la population en question. Dans une zone urbaine, une fontaine publique ou une borne-fontaine située dans un rayon de 200 mètres est considérée comme étant d'accès "raisonnable". Dans les zones rurales, pour que l'accès soit "raisonnable" il faut que la ménagère ou toute autre personne faisant partie du ménage ne passe pas une trop grande partie de la journée à se procurer l'eau nécessaire à la famille.

Le pourcentage de la population disposant de mesures suffisantes d'hygiène du milieu comprend la part de la population urbaine jouissant de raccordements aux égouts publics ou de systèmes ménagers (cabinets à fosse, latrines à entraînement par eau, fosses septiques, toilettes communales, etc.) et la part de la population rurale jouissant de moyens suffisants d'évacuation (cabinets à fosses, latrinements à entraînement par eau, etc.).

Tant pour l'eau que pour l'hygiène du milieu, les données se basent sur *The International drinking water supply and sanitation decade : review of national progress* (as at 31 December 1985).

Les données concernant *l'enseignement et l'alphabétisme* sont principalement tirées de renseignements fournis par l'UNESCO. Le *taux d'alphabétisation des adultes* est le pourcentage de la population âgée de 15 ans ou plus, sachant lire et écrire. Les données concernant les *taux d'inscription scolaire* sont des estimations du nombre total de garçons et du nombre de filles inscrits à l'école primaire et secondaire, de tous âges, exprimées en pourcentage de la population totale, masculine et féminine en âge de fréquenter l'école primaire ou secondaire.

Les données concernant *bureaux de poste ouverts au public* sont tirés de la *Statistique des services postaux 1980-1986* de l'Union Postale Universelle.

Les données sur les *téléphones pour mille habitants* se basent sur *l'Annuaire statistique des télécommunications du secteur public* (15ème édition) de l'UIT.

Les données sur les *postes récepteurs de radio pour 1000 habitants* sont établies d'après des données de *l'Annuaire statistique 1987* de l'UNESCO. Le rapport est calculé à partir du nombre de postes récepteurs en service et/ou de licenses délivrées selon la méthode d'estimation employée dans chaque pays qui fournit des données.

Les données sur la *circulation des journaux quotidiens pour 1 000 habitants* se rapportent à "la circulation des journaux quotidiens d'information générale" et sont établies d'après des données de *l'Annuaire statistique 1987* de l'UNESCO.

En ce qui concerne les indicateurs de transports, des problèmes spéciaux de comparabilité se posent dans le cas des *routes* dont la définition peut varier largement de pays à pays. Les principales sources utilisées sont *The Far East and Australasia, The Middle East and North Africa, Africa South of the Sahara, South America, Central America and the Caribbean,* Europa Publications Limited 1988.

Les données concernant les *chemins de fer* se rapportent au trafic intérieur et international de toutes les lignes du pays indiqué; en sont exclus, les lignes entièrement urbaines ou desservant une plantation, une entreprise industrielle ou minière, les téléfériques et les funiculaires. Les passagers (voyageurs-kilomètres) comprennent tous les voyageurs à l'exception des voyageurs transportés gratuitement (militaires, fonctionnaires et le personnel des chemins de fer). Le frêt se rapporte aux tonnes-kilomètres nettes en petite et grande vitesse à l'exception des transports pour les besoins du service, le courrier, les bagages et les transports gratuits du matériel du gouvernement. Les données sont tirées principalement de *The Railway Directory and Yearbook 1987.*

Les données concernant *l'aviation civile* se rapportent aux services réguliers, intérieurs ou internationaux, des compagnies de transport aérien enregistrées dans chaque pays. Les services réguliers comprennent aussi les vols supplémentaires nécessités par un surcroît d'activité des services réguliers et les vols préparatoires en vue de nouveaux services réguliers. Par frêt, on entend toutes les marchandises transportées contre paiement, mais non le courrier et les excédents de bagages. Les données sont tirées du *Recueil de statistiques - Trafic des entreprises de transport aérien, OACI.*

Les données concernant la *consommation d'énergie par habitant* se rapportent, d'une part, aux formes d'énergie primaire (houille, lignite, tourbe et schiste bitumineux, pétrole brut et liquides extraits du gaz naturel, et électricité primaire (nucléaire, géothermique et hydraulique) - souvent appelées "énergie commerciale" - et, d'autre part, à l'utilisation de bois de chauffage, de charbon de bois et de bagasse. Toutes les données sont converties en équivalent charbon et ont été établies d'après *l'Annuaire des statistiques de l'énergie 1984*[11] et *1986*[12] des Nations Unies.

Les données sur la *puissance électrique installée* sont également tirées de *l'Annuaire des statistiques de l'énergie 1984* des Nations Unies.

C. Calcul des taux moyens de croissance annuelle

En général, ces taux sont définis par le coefficient b de la fonction expotentielle de tendance $y' = ae^{bt}$, où t représente le temps. Cette méthode permet de prendre en compte toutes les observations concernant une période donnée. Les taux de croissance obtenus traduisent ainsi des tendances qui ne sont pas faussées par des valeurs exceptionnelles.

11 ST/ESA/STAT/SER.J./28, publication des Nations Unies, no. de vente E/F.86.XVII.2.

12 ST/ESA/STAT/SER.J./30, publication des Nations Unies, no. de vente E/F.88.XVII.3.

D. Autres notes

Sauf indication contraire, le terme "dollar" s'entend du dollar des Etats-Unis d'Amérique.

Les chiffres étant arrondis, les totaux indiqués ne correspondent pas toujours à la somme des composantes et des pourcentages portés dans les tableaux.

Les symboles suivants ont été utilisés :

Un tiret (-) ou un zéro (0) signifient que le montant est nul ou négligeable.

Deux points (..) signifient que les données ne sont pas disponibles ou ne sont pas montrées séparément.

Le trait d'union (-) entre deux millésimes, par exemple (1970-1980), indique qu'il s'agit de la période tout entière (y compris la première et la dernière année mentionnée).

E. Abréviations utilisées

AID Association internationale de développement

APD Aide publique au développement

ATNU Assistance technique des Nations Unies

BADEA Banque arabe pour le développement économique de l'Afrique

BAfD Banque africaine de développement

BAsD Banque asiatique de développement

BEI Banque européenne d'investissement

BID Banque interaméricaine de développement

BIRD Banque internationale pour la reconstruction et le développement (Banque mondiale)

CAD Comité d'aide au développement (de l'OCDE)

CAEM Conseil d'assistance économique mutuelle

CEE Communauté économique européenne

CTCI Classification type pour le commerce international (révision 1)

FADES Fonds arabe de développement économique et social

FAfD Fonds africain de développement

FAO Organisation des Nations Unies pour l'alimentation et l'agriculture

FED Fonds européen de développement

FIDA Fonds international pour le développement agricole

FMI Fonds monétaire international

FSAAA Fonds spécial d'aide arabe à l'Afrique

mill. millions

NPSA Nouveau Programme d'action pour les années 80 en faveur des pays les moins avancés

OACI Organisation de l'aviation civile internationale

OCDE Organisation de coopération et de développement économiques

ONU Organisation des Nations Unies

OPAEP Organisation des pays arabes exportateurs de pétrole

OPEP Organisation des pays exportateurs de pétrole

PAM Programme alimentaire mondial

PMA Les pays les moins avancés

PNUD Programme des Nations Unies pour le développement

SFI Société financière internationale

SNPC "Système de notification des pays créanciers" de l'OCDE

SNPD "Système de notification des pays débiteurs de la Banque mondiale

UNHCR Haut Commissariat des Nations Unies pour les réfugiés

UNICEF Fonds des Nations Unies pour l'enfance

TABLES
TABLEAUX

1. Per capita GDP and population : levels and growth

1. PIB par habitant et population : niveaux et croissance

Country	Per capita GDP in 1986 dollars / PIB par habitant en dollars de 1986: Actual / Réel 1970	1986	Projected 1990 / Projection 1990: A [a]	B [b]	Annual average growth rates of per capita real GDP (%) / Taux d'accroissement annuels moyens du PIB réel par habitant (%): 1970-1980	1980-1986	Population: Level / Niveau (mill.) 1986	Annual average growth rates (%) / Taux d'accroissement annuels moyens: 1970-1980	1980-1986	Pays
Afghanistan [c]	250	250 [d]	250	298	1.2 [e]	-0.6 [e]	18.6	2.5	2.6	Afghanistan [c]
Bangladesh [f]	122	153	162	182	1.0	1.5	100.6	2.7	2.2	Bangladesh [f]
Benin	308	334	341	398	-0.4	0.2	4.2	2.7	3.2	Bénin
Bhutan [g]	..	145	..	173	..	4.1	1.4	2.1	2.0	Bhoutan [g]
Botswana [f]	278	997	1372	1189	9.7	8.3	1.2	3.9	3.9	Botswana [f]
Burkina Faso	166	174	176	207	0.0	-0.7	7.1	2.0	2.5	Burkina Faso
Burma	131	210	236	250	2.3	3.0	37.9	2.2	2.0	Birmanie
Burundi	213	254	265	303	1.4	-0.2	4.9	1.7	2.9	Burundi
Cape Verde	223	353 [h]	396	421	0.7	3.9	0.3	0.9	2.5	Cap-Vert
Central African Rep.	447	381	366	454	0.0	-1.2	2.7	2.1	2.7	Rép. centrafricaine
Chad	315	178	154	212	-0.3	-5.3	5.1	2.1	2.2	Tchad
Comoros	456	341	317	407	-4.3	0.7	0.5	3.5	3.3	Comores
Democratic Yemen	470	420 [i]	408	501	-0.5	-3.2	2.4	3.1	3.1	Yémen démocratique
Djibouti	982	470 [j]	391	560	-3.8	-4.4	0.5	7.0	6.7	Djibouti
Equatorial Guinea	..	294	..	351	..	0.3	0.4	1.9	2.2	Guinée équatoriale
Ethiopia [k]	137	122	119	145	-0.1	-3.1	44.9	2.7	2.9	Ethiopie [k]
Gambia [f]	215	215	215	256	2.2	-2.2	0.8	3.2	3.3	Gambie [f]
Guinea	250	279	287	333	2.2	-1.6	6.2	2.1	2.4	Guinée
Guinea-Bissau	243	185	173	221	-2.4	1.9	0.9	4.4	1.9	Guinée-Bissau
Haiti [l]	335	419	443	500	3.0	-2.0	5.4	1.4	1.4	Haïti [l]
Kiribati	..	317 [h]	..	378	..	-1.1	0.1	2.0	2.0	Kiribati
Lao People's Dem. Rep.	165	179	183	213	-1.5	3.3	3.7	1.4	2.0	Rép. Dém. populaire lao
Lesotho [g]	111	181	205	216	6.1	-1.0	1.6	2.3	2.7	Lesotho [g]
Malawi	143	170	178	203	3.2	-0.8	7.2	2.8	3.2	Malawi
Maldives	..	462 [h]	..	551	10.2 [m]	6.6	0.2	3.1	3.0	Maldives
Mali	165	185	190	221	1.6	-1.5	8.3	2.1	2.9	Mali
Mauritania	485	413	397	493	-1.4	-1.0	2.0	2.7	3.0	Mauritanie
Nepal [n]	141	150	152	179	0.2	0.9	17.1	2.5	2.6	Népal [n]
Niger	399	329	313	392	-1.0	-4.9	6.3	2.5	2.9	Niger
Rwanda	..	296	..	353	..	-1.5	6.2	3.3	3.3	Rwanda
Samoa	..	548	..	653	..	-0.6	0.2	0.7	0.9	Samoa
Sao Tome and Principe	304	324 [h]	329	386	2.8	-4.1	0.1	2.5	2.7	Sao Tomé-et-Principe
Sierra Leone [f]	295	309	313	368	0.0	-0.7	3.7	1.5	1.8	Sierra Leone [f]
Somalia	500	454	443	541	-0.3	0.2	5.5	3.0	2.9	Somalie
Sudan [f]	384	384	384	458	2.2	-3.2	22.2	3.0	2.9	Soudan [f]
Togo	332	322	319	384	1.7	-3.8	3.1	2.4	3.0	Togo
Tuvalu	..	245 [hj]	..	292	..	..	0.0	2.0	1.2	Tuvalu
Uganda	416	220 [o]	188	262	-4.4	-2.0	16.0	2.9	3.4	Ouganda
United Rep. of Tanzania	203	193	191	230	1.1	-2.1	23.0	3.3	3.5	Rép.-Unie de Tanzanie
Vanuatu	..	499 [h]	..	595	..	-0.6	0.1	3.0	2.8	Vanuatu
Yemen [f]	254	529	636	631	6.5	1.8	8.2	3.0	2.5	Yémen [f]
All LDCs	**199**	**219**	**224**	**261**	**1.0**	**-0.4**	**380.9**	**2.6**	**2.6**	**Ensemble des PMA**
All developing countries	**675**	**884** [h]	**946**	**1054**	**3.0**	**-0.3** [p]	**2582.6**	**2.5**	**2.3**	**Ensemble des pays en développement**
Developed market economy countries	**8071**	**11080** [h]	**11993**	**n.a.**	**2.2**	**2.0** [p]	**797.2**	**0.9**	**0.6**	**Pays développés à economie de marché**
Socialist countries of Eastern Europe	..	..	..	..	**4.4** [e]	**2.7** [ep]	**397.2**	**0.8**	**0.8**	**Pays socialistes d'Europe orientale**

Source: UNCTAD secretariat calculations based on data from the United Nations Statistical Office, the Economic Commission for Africa, the World Bank and other international and national sources.

Source: Chiffres calculés par le secrétariat de la CNUCED d'après des données du Bureau de statistique des Nations Unies, de la Commission Economique pour l'Afrique, de la Banque mondiale et d'autres sources internationales et nationales.

a At 1970-1986 growth rate.
b Based on the target rate of 4.5 per cent as called for by the International Development Strategy for the third United Nations Development Decade.
c Years beginning 21 March. *d* GNP per capita in 1985.
e Net material product. *f* Years ending 30 June.
g Years beginning 1 April. *h* 1985. *i* 1984.
j Income accruing to indigenous population.
k Years ending 7 July. *l* Years ending 30 September.
m 1974-1980. *n* Years ending 15 July.
o GNP per capita in 1984. *p* Preliminary figures.

a D'après le taux d'accroissement 1970-1986.
b D'après l'objectif de 4,5 pour cent prévu dans la Stratégie Internationale du développement pour la Troisième Décennie de développement des Nations Unies.
c Années commençant le 21 Mars. *d* PNB par habitant en 1985.
e Produit matériel net. *f* Années finissant le 30 juin.
g Années commençant le 1er avril. *h* 1985. *i* 1984.
j Revenu afférent à la population locale.
k Années finissant le 7 juillet. *l* Années finissant le 30 septembre.
m 1974-1980. *n* Années finissant le 15 juillet.
o PNB par habitant en 1984. *p* Chiffres préliminaires.

2. Real GDP, total and per capita : annual average growth rates

In per cent

Country	Total real product / Produit réel total							
	1970-1980	1980-1986	1980-1981	1981-1982	1982-1983	1983-1984	1984-1985	1985-1986
Afghanistan [a] [b]	3.7	2.0	1.2	1.7	4.0	1.6	-0.3	4.1
Bangladesh [c]	3.7	3.7	6.8	0.8	3.6	4.2	3.6	4.9
Benin	2.3	3.3	9.0	6.8	-2.0	2.3	6.6	0.0
Bhutan [d]	..	6.3	9.0	10.8	6.1	2.6	3.3	9.2
Botswana [c]	14.0	12.5	8.7	-2.3	24.0	20.0	8.1	14.0
Burkina Faso	1.9	1.7	8.8	1.1	-4.2	-0.9	6.7	5.6
Burma	4.6	5.0	6.4	5.6	4.4	5.6	4.3	3.7
Burundi	3.1	2.7	10.3	-2.7	1.0	3.1	4.1	4.9
Cape Verde	1.5	6.5	5.2	14.6	5.7	3.5	4.0	6.6
Central African Rep.	2.2	1.5	1.5	1.8	-6.1	7.5	3.9	1.2
Chad	1.8	-3.2	-9.0	-7.3	-7.0	-4.6	6.9	5.2
Comoros	-0.9	4.0	3.2	6.8	3.8	4.2	2.7	2.1
Democratic Yemen	2.6	-0.2	6.6	-4.6	4.0	2.0	-1.0	-9.7
Djibouti	3.0	2.0	-8.0	13.6	0.9	0.5	0.6	1.8
Equatorial Guinea	..	2.5	2.3	3.8	-3.0	2.3	7.3	4.2
Ethiopia [e]	2.6	-0.3	2.5	1.1	5.1	-3.9	-6.5	2.4
Gambia [c]	5.4	1.1	-6.5	9.2	13.4	-6.9	-8.4	6.4
Guinea	4.3	0.8	0.6	1.8	1.3	-2.7	2.6	2.4
Guinea-Bissau	2.0	3.9	18.9	4.4	-3.2	5.6	4.6	-0.7
Haiti [f]	4.4	-0.6	-2.9	-3.4	0.8	0.3	0.2	0.6
Kiribati	..	0.9	-5.0	7.6	-3.4	11.4	-9.3	3.0
Lao People's Dem. Rep.	-0.1	5.4	6.3	2.0	3.0	6.4	9.1	7.0
Lesotho [d]	8.5	1.7	-1.4	1.0	-4.4	8.2	1.6	5.8
Malawi	6.1	2.4	-6.2	2.5	3.8	4.3	5.8	-1.1
Maldives	3.6 [g]	9.9	7.9	9.6	5.9	12.9	14.4	7.1
Mali	3.8	1.4	0.1	5.9	-4.3	1.0	-0.1	10.8
Mauritania	1.3	2.0	3.8	-2.1	6.5	0.3	-0.0	4.9
Nepal [h]	2.7	3.5	8.3	3.8	-3.0	7.8	3.0	4.0
Niger	1.5	-2.2	1.2	-1.2	-1.8	-14.7	5.9	6.5
Rwanda	8.8	1.8	8.8	1.7	0.3	-6.0	7.5	4.9
Samoa	..	0.3	-9.0	-1.0	0.5	1.3	6.0	0.5
Sao Tome and Principe	5.4	-1.5	-27.5	26.3	-8.7	-8.3	8.5	0.9
Sierra Leone [c]	1.6	1.1	5.5	4.9	-1.8	0.3	0.1	-0.3
Somalia	2.7	3.1	6.7	5.6	2.1	-1.4	7.6	-0.6
Sudan [c]	5.3	-0.4	2.2	7.6	3.3	-3.8	-14.4	9.3
Togo	4.1	-0.9	-3.4	-3.3	-5.7	0.7	5.0	3.1
Tuvalu	..	..	..	..	..	..	..	..
Uganda	-1.5	1.3	3.9	8.2	4.3	-5.4	-1.0	-0.2
United Rep.of Tanzania	4.5	1.3	-0.8	1.8	-2.0	3.2	2.3	3.8
Vanuatu	..	2.2	2.0	2.0	3.0	4.6	0.4	-1.0
Yemen [c]	9.7	4.4	7.5	8.1	1.3	2.2	4.2	6.0
All LDCs	**3.6**	**2.2**	**3.6**	**2.9**	**2.0**	**0.9**	**0.8**	**4.4**
All developing countries	**5.5**	**2.1** [i]	**1.6**	**1.4**	**1.8**	**3.0**	**1.9**	**3.3** [i]
Developed market economy countries	**3.1**	**2.6** [i]	**2.2**	**-0.3**	**2.6**	**4.6**	**3.1**	**2.7** [i]
Socialist countries of Eastern Europe [b]	**5.3**	**3.5** [i]	**2.4**	**3.1**	**4.1**	**3.5**	**3.6**	**4.2** [i]

Source: UNCTAD secretariat calculations based on data from the United Nations Statistical Office, the Economic Commission for Africa, the World Bank and other international and national sources.

a Years beginning 21 March.
b Net material product.
c Years ending 30 June.
d Years beginning 1 April.
e Years ending 7 July.
f Years ending 30 September.
g 1974-1980.
h Years ending 15 July.
i Preliminary figures.

2. Produit intérieur brut réel, total et par habitant : taux d'accroissement annuels moyens

En pourcentage

Per capita real product / Produit réel par habitant								
1970-1980	1980-1986	1980-1981	1981-1982	1982-1983	1983-1984	1984-1985	1985-1986	Pays
1.2	-0.6	-1.3	-0.8	1.4	-1.0	-2.9	1.4	Afghanistan [a,b]
1.0	1.5	4.7	-1.5	1.4	1.9	1.6	2.9	Bangladesh [c]
-0.4	0.2	5.7	3.5	-5.0	-0.8	3.3	-3.2	Bénin
..	4.1	6.7	8.5	3.9	0.6	1.3	6.9	Bhoutan [d]
9.7	8.3	4.4	-6.2	19.4	15.6	4.4	9.5	Botswana [c]
0.0	-0.7	6.1	-1.3	-6.5	-3.2	4.3	2.7	Burkina Faso
2.3	3.0	4.2	3.5	2.4	3.6	2.4	1.6	Birmanie
1.4	-0.2	7.0	-5.5	-1.8	0.3	1.4	1.7	Burundi
0.7	3.9	2.7	11.9	3.1	1.0	1.5	4.1	Cap-Vert
0.0	-1.2	-0.9	-0.6	-8.3	4.9	1.4	-3.7	Rép. centrafricaine
-0.3	-5.3	-11.0	-9.3	-9.0	-6.7	4.6	2.7	Tchad
-4.3	0.7	0.3	3.8	0.8	1.4	0.0	-4.8	Comores
-0.5	-3.2	3.4	-7.5	0.9	-1.1	-4.0	-12.5	Yémen démocratique
-3.8	-4.4	-11.9	-1.0	-2.0	-4.9	-5.3	-4.0	Djibouti
..	0.3	0.1	1.6	-5.1	0.2	5.1	1.7	Guinée équatoriale
-0.1	-3.1	-0.3	-1.7	2.2	-6.5	-9.0	-1.2	Ethiopie [e]
2.2	-2.2	-9.5	5.7	9.7	-9.9	-11.5	3.1	Gambie [c]
2.2	-1.6	-1.9	-0.6	-1.0	-4.9	0.4	-0.2	Guinée
-2.4	1.9	16.6	2.4	-5.0	3.6	2.7	-2.8	Guinée-Bissau
3.0	-2.0	-4.2	-4.8	-0.7	-1.1	-1.2	-1.0	Haïti [f]
..	-1.1	-6.8	5.5	-5.3	9.2	-11.1	1.0	Kiribati
-1.5	3.3	4.2	0.0	1.0	4.3	6.8	4.9	Rép. dém. pop. lao
6.1	-1.0	-3.6	-2.9	-7.0	7.8	-2.2	2.5	Lesotho [d]
3.2	-0.8	-9.2	-0.7	0.6	1.3	2.8	-4.6	Malawi
10.2 [g]	6.6	4.7	6.4	2.8	9.5	11.0	3.9	Maldives
1.6	-1.5	-2.8	2.9	-7.0	-1.8	-2.7	7.4	Mali
-1.4	-1.0	0.7	-5.0	3.5	-2.5	-2.7	1.5	Mauritanie
0.2	0.9	5.8	1.2	-5.4	5.1	0.4	1.0	Népal [h]
-1.0	-4.9	-1.8	-4.0	-4.5	-16.9	3.1	3.2	Niger
5.3	-1.5	5.5	-1.5	-2.8	-9.0	4.1	1.4	Rwanda
..	-0.6	-9.6	-1.9	-0.5	1.6	3.4	-0.1	Samoa
2.8	-4.1	-29.6	23.0	-11.3	-10.8	5.4	-0.9	Sao Tomé-et-Principe
0.0	-0.7	3.6	3.0	-3.5	-1.5	-1.6	-2.3	Sierra Leone [c]
-0.3	0.2	3.7	2.7	-0.8	-4.2	4.6	-3.3	Somalie
2.2	-3.2	-0.9	4.5	0.4	-6.4	-16.7	6.0	Soudan [c]
1.7	-3.8	-6.4	-6.2	-8.4	-2.2	2.1	-0.2	Togo
..	..	..	..	..	..	..	..	Tuvalu
-4.4	-2.0	0.5	4.7	0.9	-8.5	-4.3	-3.5	Ouganda
1.1	-2.1	-4.1	-1.6	-5.3	-0.3	-1.1	0.2	Rép.-Unie de Tanzanie
..	-0.6	-0.8	-0.8	0.2	1.8	-2.4	-3.7	Vanuatu
6.5	1.8	4.9	5.5	-1.1	-0.2	1.7	3.0	Yémen [c]
1.0	**-0.4**	**1.1**	**0.3**	**-0.5**	**-1.5**	**-1.6**	**1.6**	**Ensemble des PMA**
3.0	**-0.3** [i]	**-0.9**	**-1.0**	**-0.5**	**0.7**	**-0.3**	**1.0** [i]	**Ensemble des pays en développement**
2.2	**2.0** [i]	**1.5**	**-0.9**	**2.0**	**4.0**	**2.5**	**2.1** [i]	**Pays développés à economie de marché**
4.4	**2.7** [i]	**1.5**	**2.2**	**3.2**	**2.6**	**2.7**	**3.3** [i]	**Pays socialistes d'Europe orientale** [b]

Source: Chiffres calculés par le secrétariat de la CNUCED d'après des données du Bureau de statistique des Nations Unies, de la Commission économique pour l'Afrique, de la Banque mondiale et d'autres sources internationales et nationales.

a Années commençant le 21 mars.
b Produit matériel net.
c Années finissant le 30 juin.
d Années commençant le 1er avril.
e Années finissant le 7 juillet.
f Années finissant le 30 septembre.
g 1974-1980.
h Années finissant le 15 juillet.
i Chiffres préliminaires.

3. The agricultural sector

Country	Percentage share of: labour force in agriculture / Part en pourcentage de: la main d'oeuvre dans l'agriculture 1986	Percentage share of: agriculture in GDP / Part en pourcentage de: l'agriculture dans le PIB 1986	Annual average growth rates (%) / Taux d'accroissement annuels moyens (%) — Total agricultural production / Production agricole totale 1970-1980	1980-1987	1983-1984	1984-1985	1985-1986	1986-1987
Afghanistan	57	(64)	2.4	0.5	0.2	-0.7	0.8	0.4
Bangladesh	71	47	2.2	1.4	1.4	5.6	-2.1	-5.4
Benin	65	49	2.5	7.0	23.3	4.9	6.1	0.4
Bhutan	91	51	2.4	4.5	8.5	1.1	4.0	14.8
Botswana	66	4	-2.0	-0.2	-6.0	-3.0	6.1	5.2
Burkina Faso	85	47	1.1	6.1	-0.9	22.3	12.6	-5.9
Burma	49	48	2.6	5.7	5.6	5.4	3.3	4.8
Burundi	92	58	1.9	2.6	-5.2	9.5	4.7	1.6
Cape Verde	47	20 [a]	2.3	1.9	18.4	-9.3	32.8	8.6
Central African Rep.	67	44	2.1	1.2	-1.2	4.6	2.3	1.1
Chad	78	46	1.7	3.1	-12.1	23.2	1.4	-2.1
Comoros	81	42	2.6	2.2	-1.2	5.4	0.2	2.4
Democratic Yemen	35	10 [b]	2.4	1.1	0.7	1.6	2.7	-0.6
Djibouti	..	6	..	..	..	..	..	..
Equatorial Guinea	60	46	..	..	..	..	..	..
Ethiopia	77	43	1.6	0.2	-12.3	12.4	4.3	-2.4
Gambia	82	33 [a]	-2.6	4.7	10.3	22.7	12.6	-10.6
Guinea	77	44	1.5	0.6	1.8	1.0	4.8	0.9
Guinea-Bissau	80	45	2.6	6.2	15.8	3.8	9.3	2.2
Haiti	66	(31) [a]	1.4	1.9	1.8	1.8	1.4	2.7
Kiribati	..	29 [a]	..	..	..	..	..	..
Lao People's Dem.Rep.	73	(61)	2.1	5.3	11.4	6.6	6.2	-4.6
Lesotho	82	21	0.8	0.3	1.8	11.4	-6.8	4.8
Malawi	79	37	4.0	1.7	3.7	0.5	2.4	-0.9
Maldives	..	29 [b]	1.7	3.6	3.9	1.5	3.1	2.8
Mali	83	55	2.9	2.7	-8.1	5.0	5.8	-0.3
Mauritania	67	29	0.4	1.3	0.5	3.7	12.8	0.5
Nepal	92	62 [a]	1.3	1.9	-0.5	0.8	-3.4	2.4
Niger	89	46	4.2	0.0	-17.7	26.8	3.0	-9.0
Rwanda	92	40	4.2	0.7	-7.1	1.5	2.8	2.2
Samoa	..	51 [c]	1.6	-1.4	-5.3	5.7	-5.2	-10.7
Sao Tome and Principe	..	28 [a]	-3.5	-3.0	-13.0	1.2	0.1	1.2
Sierra Leone	65	43	1.6	1.3	-10.4	0.1	12.5	0.8
Somalia	72	58 [a]	0.8	3.2	3.3	9.0	6.4	2.2
Sudan	65	36	2.4	2.6	-6.2	19.4	3.2	-3.3
Togo	71	32	0.9	1.8	11.0	1.3	3.0	2.8
Tuvalu	..	11 [a]	..	..	..	..	..	..
Uganda	83	76	0.4	6.2	-23.0	52.6	3.6	-1.1
Un. Rep. of Tanzania	83	55	4.4	1.6	4.8	-2.1	3.9	3.5
Vanuatu	..	40 [a]	3.7	1.9	14.5	-9.5	5.0	-1.6
Yemen	65	34 [a]	3.2	5.4	10.1	8.0	16.6	1.2
All LDCs	**73**	**46**	**2.1**	**2.0**	**-2.0**	**7.6**	**2.9**	**-2.7**
All developing countries	**57**	**19**	**2.8**	**2.5**	**2.5**	**4.5**	**0.6**	**0.5**

Source: UNCTAD secretariat calculations based on data from FAO, the Economic Commission for Africa, the World Bank and other international and national sources.

a 1985.
b 1984.
c 1982.

3. Le secteur agricole

Annual average growth rates (%)
Taux d'accroissement annuels moyens (%)

Per capita agricultural production
Production agricole par habitant

1970-1980	*1980-1987*	*1983-1984*	*1984-1985*	*1985-1986*	*1986-1987*	*Pays*
-0.1	-2.0	-2.4	-3.2	-1.8	-2.1	Afghanistan
-0.5	-0.7	-0.8	3.5	-4.0	-7.3	Bangladesh
-0.1	3.8	19.6	1.7	2.7	-2.7	Bénin
0.4	2.4	6.4	-0.9	1.8	12.5	Bhoutan
-5.6	-3.9	-9.5	-6.3	1.9	1.3	Botswana
-0.9	3.5	-3.2	19.5	9.5	-8.4	Burkina Faso
0.4	3.6	3.6	3.5	1.3	2.8	Birmanie
0.1	-0.3	-7.7	6.7	1.6	-1.4	Burundi
1.4	-0.5	15.6	-11.5	29.6	6.1	Cap-Vert
0.0	-1.6	-3.5	2.2	-2.6	-1.7	Rép. centrafricaine
-0.4	0.9	-14.0	20.6	-1.0	-4.2	Tchad
-0.9	-1.3	-3.8	2.7	-6.5	-1.1	Comores
-0.6	-1.9	-2.4	-1.5	-0.4	-3.6	Yémen démocratique
..	..	..	..	..	..	Djibouti
..	..	..	..	..	..	Guineé équatoriale
-1.1	-2.7	-14.7	9.3	0.6	-5.2	Ethiopie
-5.6	1.4	6.8	18.6	9.1	-13.4	Gambie
-0.6	-1.7	-0.5	-1.2	2.1	-1.6	Guinée
-1.7	4.2	13.6	2.0	6.9	0.0	Guinée-Bissau
0.0	0.5	0.4	0.4	-0.2	1.2	Haïti
..	..	..	..	..	..	Kiribati
0.7	3.2	9.2	4.3	4.0	-6.5	Rép. dém. pop. lao
-1.5	-2.3	1.4	7.1	-9.7	2.0	Lesotho
1.2	-1.5	0.6	-2.4	-1.1	-4.3	Malawi
-1.3	0.5	0.9	-1.5	0.0	-0.2	Maldives
0.8	-0.2	-10.6	2.2	2.5	-3.3	Mali
-2.2	-1.7	-2.4	0.9	9.1	-2.6	Mauritanie
-1.2	-0.7	-3.0	-1.7	-6.3	-0.2	Népal
1.6	-2.9	-19.9	23.4	-0.2	-11.8	Niger
0.8	-2.5	-10.0	-1.7	-0.7	-1.0	Rwanda
0.9	-2.3	-5.0	3.1	-5.8	-11.5	Samoa
-5.9	-5.6	-15.4	-1.6	-1.7	-1.5	Sao Tomé-et-Principe
0.0	-0.5	-12.0	-1.6	10.3	-1.1	Sierra Leone
-2.1	0.3	0.4	6.0	3.4	-0.6	Somalie
-0.6	-0.3	-8.7	16.2	0.1	-6.2	Soudan
-1.5	-1.2	7.9	-1.4	-0.3	-0.4	Togo
..	..	..	..	..	..	Tuvalu
-2.4	2.7	-25.6	47.6	0.2	-4.3	Ouganda
1.0	-1.9	1.3	-5.4	0.2	0.0	Rép.-Un. de Tanzanie
0.7	-0.9	11.4	-12.0	2.2	-4.3	Vanuatu
0.3	2.8	7.5	5.4	13.3	-1.3	Yémen
-0.5	**-0.6**	**-4.4**	**5.0**	**0.1**	**-5.1**	**Ensemble des PMA**
0.3	**0.2**	**0.1**	**2.1**	**-1.6**	**-1.7**	**Ensemble des pays en developpement**

Source: Chiffres calculés par le secrétariat de la CNUCED, d'après des données de la FAO, de la Commission économique pour l'Afrique, de la Banque mondiale, et d'autres sources internationales et nationales.

a 1985.
b 1984.
c 1982.

4. Annual average growth rates of total and per capita food production

In per cent

Countries	*Total food production / Production alimentaire totale*								
	1970-1980	*1980-1987*	*1980-1981*	*1981-1982*	*1982-1983*	*1983-1984*	*1984-1985*	*1985-1986*	*1986-1987*
Afghanistan	2.4	0.5	2.5	0.6	0.9	0.2	-0.7	0.6	0.4
Bangladesh	2.3	1.4	0.0	3.6	2.3	1.7	3.1	0.5	-5.1
Benin	2.9	6.4	-0.8	2.0	3.8	21.5	5.1	5.1	-0.3
Bhutan	2.4	4.5	2.0	1.6	3.2	8.5	1.0	4.0	14.8
Botswana	-2.0	-0.2	19.0	-0.5	-6.2	-6.1	-3.0	6.1	5.3
Burkina Faso	0.9	5.8	10.0	0.6	1.6	-0.9	21.8	12.0	-6.1
Burma	2.6	5.8	8.1	10.1	4.2	5.6	5.3	3.4	5.4
Burundi	1.8	2.6	11.0	-0.2	-0.9	-2.9	11.5	3.2	0.7
Cape Verde	2.3	2.0	-23.8	-1.4	-9.8	18.5	-9.1	32.6	8.6
Central African Rep.	2.3	1.2	2.3	0.9	-0.8	-2.3	5.8	2.5	0.8
Chad	1.9	3.1	-5.5	3.6	5.6	-9.2	24.3	1.9	-3.0
Comoros	2.8	2.1	-7.2	5.0	6.5	-1.3	5.3	0.3	2.4
Democratic Yemen	2.8	0.9	2.0	-5.4	4.2	0.7	1.7	2.8	-0.6
Djibouti	..	..	..	..	..	..	..	..	..
Equatorial Guinea	..	..	..	..	..	..	..	..	..
Ethiopia	1.6	0.5	-1.0	9.3	-6.5	-9.6	11.9	4.2	-2.3
Gambia	-2.8	4.8	31.2	19.5	-30.1	9.9	22.9	12.8	-10.7
Guinea	1.5	0.6	1.9	2.0	-6.1	1.8	1.0	5.0	1.0
Guinea-Bissau	2.6	6.3	19.9	14.6	-12.0	15.8	3.8	9.3	2.2
Haiti	1.5	2.2	0.7	0.5	4.3	2.4	2.4	1.4	3.1
Kiribati	..	..	..	..	..	..	..	..	..
Lao People's Dem.Rep.	2.1	5.3	9.6	0.2	4.4	11.5	6.5	6.0	-5.1
Lesotho	1.5	0.1	0.2	-12.8	1.6	2.0	12.6	-7.4	5.0
Malawi	3.5	0.7	4.4	3.6	-2.9	1.0	0.0	1.7	-1.1
Maldives	1.7	3.6	0.7	4.2	7.1	3.9	1.5	3.1	2.8
Mali	2.6	2.5	10.6	8.4	4.2	-8.8	4.4	5.7	-1.0
Mauritania	0.4	1.3	5.9	-6.0	-4.2	0.5	3.7	12.8	0.5
Nepal	1.3	2.0	3.6	-5.9	17.0	-0.2	0.7	-3.9	2.5
Niger	4.2	0.0	-2.4	0.9	-0.7	-17.8	26.8	3.0	-9.0
Rwanda	3.9	0.4	8.0	5.6	-2.9	-6.0	0.2	3.2	2.1
Samoa	1.6	-1.5	-5.0	3.8	1.4	-5.5	6.0	-5.4	-11.1
Sao Tome and Principe	-3.5	-3.1	7.4	-7.6	-1.4	-13.1	1.3	0.1	1.2
Sierra Leone	1.5	1.1	1.0	10.5	3.0	-9.3	-3.6	10.7	0.7
Somalia	0.8	3.2	1.8	3.6	-4.2	3.3	9.0	6.4	2.2
Sudan	3.3	2.4	14.0	-11.2	2.4	-7.7	22.8	5.5	-4.5
Togo	0.9	1.5	1.6	-1.3	-5.4	12.0	-1.6	2.6	3.0
Tuvalu	..	..	..	..	..	..	..	..	..
Uganda	1.0	6.1	11.6	6.9	6.5	-24.6	55.1	4.0	-1.2
United Rep.of Tanzania	5.3	2.0	3.0	-2.4	3.5	4.8	-0.8	3.0	3.5
Vanuatu	3.8	1.9	25.1	-13.8	4.5	14.9	-9.7	5.0	-1.7
Yemen	3.3	5.5	6.5	2.5	-6.3	10.4	8.2	17.0	1.2
All LDCs	**2.4**	**1.9**	**3.8**	**1.7**	**1.2**	**-2.0**	**7.3**	**3.4**	**-2.7**
All developing countries	**3.0**	**2.6**	**4.6**	**1.7**	**3.1**	**2.3**	**4.1**	**1.6**	**0.1**

Source: UNCTAD secretariat calculations, based on data from FAO.

4. Taux d'accroissement annuels moyens de la production alimentaire totale et par habitant

En pourcentage

Per capita food production / Production alimentaire par habitant									
1970-1980	*1980-1987*	*1980-1981*	*1981-1982*	*1982-1983*	*1983-1984*	*1984-1985*	*1985-1986*	*1986-1987*	*Pays*
-0.1	-2.1	-0.1	-1.9	-1.6	-2.4	-3.3	-2.0	-2.1	Afghanistan
-0.4	-0.7	-2.0	1.2	0.0	-0.5	1.1	-1.4	-7.0	Bangladesh
0.2	3.1	-3.8	-1.1	0.6	17.8	1.9	1.7	-3.4	Bénin
0.3	2.4	-0.1	-0.5	1.0	6.4	-0.9	1.8	12.5	Bhoutan
-5.7	-3.9	14.3	-4.4	-9.6	-9.5	-6.3	2.0	1.3	Botswana
-1.1	3.2	7.2	-1.8	-0.8	-3.2	19.0	8.9	-8.6	Burkina Faso
0.4	3.8	6.0	7.9	2.2	3.6	3.4	1.4	3.4	Birmanie
0.1	-0.3	7.7	-3.0	-3.7	-5.6	8.6	0.2	-2.2	Burundi
1.4	-0.5	-25.6	-3.8	-11.9	15.7	-11.3	29.4	6.2	Cap-Vert
0.2	-1.6	0.0	-1.5	-3.1	-4.5	3.3	-2.5	-1.9	Rép. centrafricaine
-0.2	0.9	-7.5	1.3	3.3	-11.2	21.6	-0.5	-5.1	Tchad
-0.7	-1.3	-9.8	2.0	3.4	-3.9	2.6	-6.5	-1.1	Comores
-0.3	-2.1	-1.1	-8.2	1.0	-2.3	-1.4	-0.3	-3.6	Yémen démocratique
..	..	..	..	..	..	..	..	..	Djibouti
..	..	..	..	..	..	..	..	..	Guinée équatoriale
-1.1	-2.4	-3.7	6.3	-9.1	-12.0	8.8	0.5	-5.2	Ethiopie
-5.8	1.4	27.0	15.6	-32.4	6.4	18.8	9.3	-13.5	Gambie
-0.6	-1.7	-0.6	-0.4	-8.2	-0.5	-1.2	2.3	-1.6	Guinée
-1.7	4.2	17.6	12.4	-13.7	13.6	2.0	6.9	0.0	Guinée-Bissau
0.1	0.8	-0.7	-1.0	2.8	1.0	0.9	-0.2	1.6	Haïti
..	..	..	..	..	..	..	..	..	Kiribati
0.7	3.2	7.4	-1.8	2.4	9.3	4.3	3.9	-7.0	Rép. dém. pop. lao
-0.8	-2.5	-2.0	-16.1	-1.2	1.6	8.3	-10.3	2.2	Lesotho
0.7	-2.4	1.1	0.4	-5.8	-2.0	-2.8	-1.9	-4.4	Malawi
-1.3	0.5	-2.3	1.1	3.9	0.9	-1.5	0.0	-0.2	Maldives
0.5	-0.4	7.4	5.4	1.3	-11.2	1.7	2.5	-3.9	Mali
-2.2	-1.7	2.7	-8.9	-7.0	-2.4	0.9	9.1	-2.6	Mauritanie
-1.1	-0.7	1.2	-8.3	14.1	-2.7	-1.9	-6.8	-0.1	Népal
1.6	-2.9	-5.3	-2.0	-3.4	-20.0	23.5	-0.2	-11.8	Niger
0.6	-2.8	4.8	2.2	-6.0	-9.0	-3.0	-0.3	-1.1	Rwanda
1.0	-2.4	-5.6	2.8	0.3	-5.2	3.4	-6.0	-11.9	Samoa
-5.9	-5.6	4.3	-10.0	-4.2	-15.5	-1.6	-1.7	-1.5	Sao Tomé-et-Principe
0.0	-0.8	-0.8	8.6	1.2	-10.9	-5.2	8.5	-1.2	Sierra leone
-2.1	0.3	-1.1	0.7	-6.9	0.4	6.0	3.5	-0.6	Somalie
0.3	-0.5	10.6	-13.8	-0.5	-10.2	19.5	2.4	-7.3	Soudan
-1.5	-1.5	-1.5	-4.2	-8.1	8.9	-4.3	-0.7	-0.2	Togo
..	..	..	..	..	..	..	..	..	Tuvalu
-1.9	2.6	7.9	3.4	3.1	-27.0	50.0	0.6	-4.4	Ouganda
1.9	-1.5	-0.5	-5.7	0.0	1.2	-4.2	-0.6	0.0	Rép.-Unie de Tanzanie
0.8	-0.8	21.7	-16.2	1.6	11.8	-12.1	2.2	-4.3	Vanuatu
0.3	2.9	4.0	0.0	-8.6	7.7	5.6	13.6	-1.3	Yémen
-0.2	**-0.7**	**1.3**	**-1.0**	**-1.3**	**-4.4**	**4.7**	**0.6**	**-5.2**	**Ensemble des PMA**
0.5	**0.2**	**2.2**	**-0.6**	**0.7**	**0.0**	**1.7**	**-0.6**	**-2.2**	**Ensemble des pays en développement**

Source: Chiffres calculés par le secrétariat de la CNUCED, d'après des données de la FAO.

5. The manufacturing sector

5. Le secteur manufacturier

Country	Share in GDP / Part dans le PIB	Annual average growth rates [a] / Taux d'accroissement annuels moyens [a] (In per cent / En pourcentage)								Pays
	1986	1970-1980	1980-1986	1980-1981	1981-1982	1982-1983	1983-1984	1984-1985	1985-1986	
Afghanistan	..	..	..	..	..	..	..	..	..	Afghanistan
Bangladesh	8	11.8	2.1	5.4	1.6	-1.6	3.7	3.3	1.8	Bangladesh
Benin	4	-1.3	4.6	-6.1	63.0	-9.7	-12.1	17.5	-12.8	Bénin
Bhutan	4	..	6.3 [b]	..	-1.5	16.1	4.8	11.7	-5.8	Bhoutan
Botswana	6	16.0	4.0	26.7	23.8	-7.4	3.8	-18.6	22.1	Botswana
Burkina Faso	14	2.1	3.8	1.1	3.0	8.1	-1.2	3.9	10.0	Burkina Faso
Burma	10	4.2	5.8	7.6	5.3	3.3	8.2	4.5	6.9	Birmanie
Burundi	10	3.7	6.9	14.1	-2.9	6.6	10.2	11.1	4.1	Burundi
Cape Verde	..	..	..	..	..	..	..	..	..	Cap-Vert
Central African Rep.	7	-4.1	3.0	2.5	-1.5	7.8	3.1	2.6	1.7	Rép. centrafricaine
Chad	9	0.5	-4.1	-12.6	-6.8	-7.6	-5.2	5.4	3.9	Tchad
Comoros	4	-4.9	5.3	6.6	4.9	4.0	7.6	3.5	5.3	Comores
Democratic Yemen	11 [c]	..	..	22.6	-11.2	..	..	..	..	Yémen démocratique
Djibouti	10	6.3	0.8	-0.3	3.3	0.9	-1.6	0.9	1.8	Djibouti
Equatorial Guinea	5	..	2.1	3.7	3.3	-6.4	6.8	4.2	3.8	Guinée équatoriale
Ethiopia	12	2.3	4.2	2.8	-19.1	35.5	3.3	1.0	1.9	Ethiopie
Gambia	10 [d]	..	..	..	..	..	..	..	..	Gambie
Guinea	1	0.8	1.5 [e]	0.8	-2.0	3.0	5.6	-1.0	..	Guinée
Guinea-Bissau	4 [f]	2.1	0.4 [e]	-4.0	3.0	-1.7	1.0	3.4	..	Guinée-Bissau
Haiti	(17) [d]	7.4	-1.4 [e]	-12.4	-1.6	5.5	-5.9	6.0	..	Haïti
Kiribati	2 [d]	..	..	..	..	..	..	..	..	Kiribati
Lao People's Dem.Rep.	..	..	..	..	..	..	..	..	..	Rép. dém. pop. lao
Lesotho	11	17.2	12.8	7.9	15.3	14.5	23.7	-1.2	14.5	Lesotho
Malawi	12	6.0	2.4	3.4	-0.3	7.1	2.4	0.5	0.3	Malawi
Maldives	5 [c]	..	11.7	26.2	21.9	6.3	5.5	12.0	5.1	Maldives
Mali	8	..	8.9	0.8	8.0	5.5	28.9	-0.5	5.4	Mali
Mauritania	6 [c]	4.2	4.3	2.2	-0.8	3.4	5.0	5.5	14.2	Mauritanie
Nepal	5 [d]	..	..	..	..	..	..	..	..	Népal
Niger	4	..	..	..	..	..	..	..	..	Niger
Rwanda	16	4.9	4.1	5.9	-4.0	13.5	2.5	2.5	3.9	Rwanda
Samoa	6 [f]	..	8.8 [g]	7.2	3.6	17.7	..	..	..	Samoa
Sao Tome and Principe	9 [d]	2.3	-3.0 [e]	-26.4	13.6	2.5	-29.3	49.0	..	Sao Tomé-et-Principe
Sierra Leone	6	4.1	2.2	7.3	58.2	-10.8	-11.4	-4.9	-7.5	Sierra leone
Somalia	6 [d]	3.1	-1.5	-0.8	-0.7	-5.3	-15.5	16.0	8.0	Somalie
Sudan	7	3.9	-0.1	17.2	-18.9	10.1	-1.2	-2.8	6.0	Soudan
Togo	7	0.5 [h]	-2.6	9.1	4.2	-7.4	-18.2	7.1	3.7	Togo
Tuvalu	..	..	..	..	..	..	..	..	..	Tuvalu
Uganda	5	-9.1	-0.3	-5.4	14.2	2.8	3.4	-11.0	-12.0	Ouganda
United Rep.of Tanzania	7	6.0	-2.9	-10.7	-3.0	-3.4	-1.4	-2.2	1.8	Rép.-Unie de Tanzanie
Vanuatu	4 [d]	..	..	..	..	..	..	..	..	Vanuatu
Yemen	7 [d]	12.2	16.5 [e]	19.2	20.4	23.2	7.4	11.6	..	Yémen
All LDCs [i]	**8**	**(4.8)**	**2.1**	**4.1**	**-1.5**	**4.0**	**2.0**	**2.0**	**3.3**	**Ensemble des PMA [i]**

Source: UNCTAD secretariat calculations based on data from the United Nations Statistical Office, the Economic Commission for Africa World Bank and other international and national sources.

a Value added at constant prices.
b 1981-1986.
c 1984.
d 1985.
e 1980-1985.
f 1983.
g 1980-1983.
h 1976-1980.
i Growth rates relate to countries for which data are available for all the years 1980 to 1986.

Source: Chiffres calculés par le secrétariat de la CNUCED d'apr des données du Bureau de statistique des Nations Unies, de la Commission économique pour l'Afrique, de la Banq mondiale et d'autres sources internationales et nationale

a Valeur ajoutée aux prix constants.
b 1981-1986.
c 1984.
d 1985.
e 1980-1985.
f 1983.
g 1980-1983.
h 1976-1980.
i Les taux d'accroissement se rapportent à l'ensemble des pays pour lesquels les données sont disponibles pour toutes les années de 1980 à 1986.

6. Investment [a] / 6. Investissement [a]

Country	Share in GDP / Part dans le PIB: Average 1981-1983	Average 1984-1986	Annual average growth rates [b] / Taux d'accroissement annuels moyens [b] (In per cent / En pourcentage): 1970-1980	1980-1986	1980-1981	1981-1982	1982-1983	1983-1984	1984-1985	1985-1986	Pays
Afghanistan	..	..	..	..	..	..	..	..	..	..	Afghanistan
Bangladesh	15	12	4.8	2.4	3.1	-7.8	-0.4	7.7	15.0	-4.2	Bangladesh
Benin	22	12	11.4	-15.5	13.8	7.0	-53.4	-20.9	14.0	-3.3	Bénin
Bhutan	..	..	..	..	..	..	..	..	..	..	Bhoutan
Botswana	39	26	6.9	-1.5	1.9	-3.4	-30.6	-2.0	59.3	-9.8	Botswana
Burkina Faso	10	6	3.9	-15.3	-19.1	-1.4	-26.2	-26.5	34.4	-44.4	Burkina Faso
Burma	21	15	8.0	-3.2	14.1	0.6	-14.2	-9.4	2.5	1.6	Birmanie
Burundi	18	16	16.3	5.0	37.6	-27.0	87.9	-22.9	-14.5	19.1	Burundi
Cape Verde	59	50 [c]	13.3 [d]	7.5 [e]	56.7	4.3	5.9	-9.6	4.8	..	Cap-Vert
Central African Rep.	7	9	-9.7	4.8	5.0	-4.1	7.0	18.3	-4.7	7.5	Rép. centrafricaine
Chad	8	7	-0.8	-11.9	-39.8	-21.0	-13.6	-5.5	7.1	1.5	Tchad
Comoros	27	32	-1.0	3.2	-16.1	8.8	14.2	42.2	-22.3	-19.9	Comores
Democratic Yemen	..	..	..	..	..	..	..	..	..	..	Yémen démocratique
Djibouti	25	24	-1.4	2.9	27.8	10.1	1.8	-6.1	-3.8	1.8	Djibouti
Equatorial Guinea	18	15	..	1.1	5.2	3.6	-7.0	3.3	2.6	3.0	Guinée équatoriale
Ethiopia	11	11	-1.1	4.8	42.6	5.3	10.5	-6.7	-6.1	4.3	Ethiopie
Gambia	24	18	31.4	-8.4 [e]	-2.3	-17.6	7.6	-32.6	24.3	..	Gambie
Guinea	14	10	-1.4	-7.6 [e]	-9.1	-1.3	2.8	-23.1	-6.1	..	Guinée
Guinea-Bissau	25	31	-1.7	4.8	-16.5	28.1	-3.0	5.5	10.1	0.0	Guinée-Bissau
Haiti	17	14	12.8	-3.3	0.7	-6.8	5.4	4.6	-13.6	-14.5	Haïti
Kiribati	..	..	..	..	..	..	..	..	..	..	Kiribati
Lao People's Dem.Rep.	..	..	..	..	..	..	..	..	..	..	Rép. Dém. pop. lao
Lesotho	33	35	22.4	..	-0.3	0.8	-12.5	..	..	..	Lesotho
Malawi	21	14	3.5	-7.9	-29.4	22.6	10.7	-35.1	24.7	-37.3	Malawi
Maldives	30	32 [c]	..	..	..	0.9	62.4	-6.8	..	..	Maldives
Mali	18	21	..	6.4	-1.9	7.2	-1.0	6.4	20.0	7.6	Mali
Mauritania	35	24	19.5	-4.9	24.7	25.7	-52.4	16.5	2.8	5.8	Mauritanie
Nepal	18	21	17.5 [f]	7.0 [e]	4.3	-0.6	18.4	3.0	9.5	..	Népal
Niger	17	9	7.6	-44.9 [g]	3.6	-15.4	-5.7	-93.1	..	..	Niger
Rwanda	16	18	10.9	10.1	-0.1	41.5	-4.6	17.3	2.4	5.5	Rwanda
Samoa	31	28	..	-7.7	5.3	-33.7	-5.9	11.7	-6.6	-9.8	Samoa
Sao Tome and Principe	42	42 [c]	15.8	3.0 [e]	-6.7	36.6	-34.9	59.8	-18.2	..	Sao Tomé-et-Principe
Sierra Leone	14	9	-1.5	-11.4	-15.9	-13.9	-7.6	-10.3	-13.5	-8.3	Sierra Leone
Somalia	15	16 [c]	-4.7	21.5 [e]	261.1	-2.0	-4.0	8.6	5.3	..	Somalie
Sudan	20	14	8.4	-5.2	4.1	72.0	-19.4	-21.5	-23.9	-7.4	Soudan
Togo	27	25	11.9	-3.9	-3.9	-16.3	-18.9	-0.4	23.8	4.2	Togo
Tuvalu	..	..	..	..	..	..	..	..	..	..	Tuvalu
Uganda	16	..	-11.1	..	22.3	20.5	..	..	..	..	Ouganda
United Rep.of Tanzania	20	14	2.5	-1.6	9.3	-4.2	-20.4	-9.9	31.9	3.7	Rép.-Unie de Tanzanie
Vanuatu	..	29 [c]	..	..	..	..	..	..	..	..	Vanuatu
Yemen	35	22	25.5	-12.9 [e]	-15.9	-6.7	-32.9	3.0	-1.3	..	Yémen
All LDCs [h]	**19**	**14**	**(5.1)**	**-1.3**	**5.6**	**8.9**	**-12.0**	**-6.5**	**5.7**	**-2.3**	**Ensemble des PMA [h]**

Source: UNCTAD secretariat calculations based on data from the United Nations Statistical Office, the Economic Commission for Africa World Bank and other international and national sources.

a Gross fixed capital formation *plus* increase in stocks.
b Real investment.
c Average 1984-1985.
d 1973-1980.
e 1980-1985.
f 1975-1980.
g 1980-1984.
h Growth rates relate to countries for which data are available for all the years 1980 to 1986.

Source: Chiffres calculés par le secrétariat de la CNUCED d'après des données du Bureau de statistique des Nations Unies, de la Commission économique pour l'Afrique, de la Banque mondiale et d'autres sources internationales et nationales.

a Formation brute de capital fixe *plus* variation des stocks.
b Investissements réels.
c Moyenne 1984-1985.
d 1973-1980.
e 1980-1985.
f 1975-1980.
g 1980-1984.
h Les taux d'accroissement se rapportent à l'ensemble des pays pour lesquels les données sont disponibles pour toutes les années de 1980 à 1986.

7. Exports and imports : basic comparisons

7. Exportations et importations : comparaisons de base

Country	Exports in 1986 / Exportations en 1986: Total ($ million) / Totales (millions de dollars)	As % of GDP / En % du PIB	Per capita ($) / Par habitant (dollars)	Growth of purchasing power of exports per capita [a] / Accroissement du pouvoir d'achat des exportations par habitant [a]: 1970-1980	1980-1987	Imports in 1986 / Importations en 1986: Total ($ million) / Totales (millions de dollars)	As % of GDP / En % du PIB	Per capita ($) / Par habitant (dollars)	Growth of import volume per capita [a] / Accroissement du volume des importations par habitant [a]: 1970-1980	1980-1987	Pays
Afghanistan	525	11.3	28	5.3	-6.3	851	18.3	46	3.7	6.9	Afghanistan
Bangladesh	955	6.2	9	-8.6	6.8	2014	13.0	20	0.0	2.5	Bangladesh
Benin	40	2.9	10	-12.5	-3.8	370	26.5	89	2.7	-4.5	Bénin
Bhutan	..	..	..	..	..	..	..	..	..	..	Bhoutan
Botswana	858	74.7	745	14.1	9.1	684	59.6	594	8.9	-2.9	Botswana
Burkina Faso	70	5.6	10	3.1	-2.9	280	22.5	39	6.1	-4.9	Burkina Faso
Burma	265	3.3	7	-1.4	-12.0	304	3.8	8	-6.1	-5.7	Birmanie
Burundi	169	13.7	35	1.7	7.0	205	16.6	42	6.2	1.1	Burundi
Cape verde	5	4.1	15	-9.1	4.4	80	66.2	234	-2.2	-0.7	Cap-Vert
Central African Rep.	131	12.6	48	-1.1	-1.4	252	24.2	92	-5.0	6.5	Rép. centrafricaine
Chad	85	9.3	17	-0.7	1.7	190	20.8	37	-6.4	13.0	Tchad
Comoros	25	15.4	53	-3.6	3.0	40	24.6	84	-4.7	3.3	Comores
Democratic Yemen	500	50.3	211	0.5	-7.3	1150	115.7	486	-1.1	-1.1	Yémen démocratique
Djibouti	25	11.7	55	-19.6	3.6	115	53.6	252	-9.7	-5.9	Djibouti
Equatorial Guinea	20	17.0	50	-17.2	3.8	30	25.5	75	-19.3	0.0	Guinée équatoriale
Ethiopia	477	8.7	11	-3.5	0.5	1097	20.0	24	-1.5	4.1	Ethiopie
Gambia	35	21.1	45	-4.5	3.2	100	60.3	130	7.1	-5.3	Gambie
Guinea	450	25.8	72	11.0	0.0	430	24.7	69	2.6	6.6	Guinée
Guinea-Bissau	15	8.9	17	-1.7	2.4	60	35.7	66	-10.6	2.7	Guinée-Bissau
Haiti	170	7.6	32	4.1	-1.2	400	17.8	75	6.4	0.5	Haïti
Kiribati	22	105.4	334	..	..	15	71.9	228	-1.1	-1.8	Kiribati
Lao People's Dem. Rep.	30	4.5	8	3.7	-3.8	70	10.6	19	-10.8	-9.4	Rép. dém. pop. lao
Lesotho	21	7.4	13	8.8	-15.9	260	91.2	165	12.8	-12.1	Lesotho
Malawi	245	20.0	34	0.4	-2.9	258	21.1	36	1.0	-7.8	Malawi
Maldives	25	28.9	134	-7.8	18.8	55	63.6	294	7.3	11.2	Maldives
Mali	192	12.5	23	4.9	-0.5	466	30.3	56	6.7	0.6	Mali
Mauritania	349	43.3	179	-8.6	8.9	221	27.4	113	2.0	-0.6	Mauritanie
Nepal	142	5.5	8	-5.4	6.7	459	17.9	27	2.1	3.7	Népal
Niger	260	12.5	41	15.8	-12.1	370	17.8	59	10.4	-6.8	Niger
Rwanda	118	6.4	19	4.2	-1.1	352	19.0	56	8.6	2.7	Rwanda
Samoa	12	13.3	73	-0.6	-1.7	48	53.4	293	3.9	-1.0	Samoa
Sao Tome and Principe	5	14.0	45	-3.3	-19.1	15	42.0	136	-4.9	-3.5	Sao Tomé-et-Principe
Sierra Leone	145	12.8	39	-7.6	-2.0	132	11.6	36	-2.8	-15.2	Sierra leone
Somalia	85	3.4	15	-1.6	-12.4	125	5.0	23	3.5	-20.9	Somalie
Sudan	333	3.9	15	-8.7	-9.4	961	11.2	43	1.8	-10.9	Soudan
Togo	200	20.3	65	4.2	-5.9	200	20.3	65	9.2	-14.5	Togo
Tuvalu	..	..	..	..	..	..	..	..	..	..	Tuvalu
Uganda	420	11.9	26	-10.2	1.4	350	10.0	22	-11.7	-0.7	Ouganda
United Rep.of Tanzania	346	7.8	15	-8.5	-11.0	780	17.5	34	-2.8	-7.5	Rép.-Unie de Tanzanie
Vanuatu	17	25.2	126	-2.1	-9.0	57	84.6	422	0.3	-1.1	Vanuatu
Yemen	10	0.2	1		-21.2	1100	25.4	134	33.1	-10.7	Yémen
All LDCs	**7775**	**9.3**	**20**	**-2.9**	**-1.9**	**14946**	**17.9**	**39**	**1.7**	**-3.1**	**Ensemble des PMA**
All developing countries [b]	**280148**	**21.2**	**135**	**2.9**	**4.5**	**301338**	**22.8**	**145**	**3.3**	**0.4**	**Ensemble des pays en développement [b]**

Source: UNCTAD secretariat estimates mainly based on UNCTAD *Handbook of International Trade and Development Statistics 1988*, and table 8.

a Annual average growth rates in per cent.

b Excluding major petroleum exporters.

Source: Estimations du secrétariat de la CNUCED principalement d'après le *Manuel de statistiques du commerce international et du développement 1988*, de la CNUCED et le tableau 8.

a Taux annuels moyens en pourcentage.

b Non compris les principaux pays exportateurs de pétrole.

8. Unit value indices of imports

1980 = 100

8. Indices de valeur unitaire des importations

1980 = 100

Country	1970	1981	1982	1983	1984	1985	1986	1987	Pays
Afghanistan	31	93	90	87	87	88	90	93	Afghanistan
Bangladesh	29	94	90	89	88	88	90	94	Bangladesh
Benin	29	95	92	89	87	87	90	93	Bénin
Burkina faso	30	95	92	88	88	88	90	93	Burkina Faso
Burma	29	96	94	92	90	91	97	101	Birmanie
Central African Rep.	32	94	91	89	88	89	95	98	Rép. centrafricaine
Chad	30	95	92	89	89	90	92	96	Tchad
Ethiopia	26	99	96	92	90	90	87	92	Ethiopie
Gambia	28	93	89	86	85	85	89	90	Gambie
Malawi	30	96	94	91	90	91	93	97	Malawi
Mali	29	95	92	89	88	89	91	94	Mali
Mauritania	29	94	90	87	85	85	88	90	Mauritanie
Niger	30	97	94	90	89	89	87	92	Niger
Rwanda	30	94	91	89	89	89	92	96	Rwanda
Sierra leone	28	95	91	88	86	86	86	89	Sierra Leone
Somalia	29	93	88	87	86	86	91	93	Somalie
Sudan	28	95	91	88	86	86	88	90	Soudan
Togo	28	97	93	89	88	88	86	89	Togo
Uganda	30	95	93	91	90	91	98	102	Ouganda
United Rep.of Tanzania	27	98	95	91	90	90	88	92	Rép.-Unie de Tanzanie
All LDCs [a]	**29**	**95**	**92**	**89**	**88**	**89**	**90**	**94**	**Ensemble des PMA** [a]
All developing countries [b]	**25**	**98**	**94**	**91**	**90**	**89**	**86**	**90**	**Ensemble des pays en développement** [b]
All developing countries [c]	**26**	**96**	**93**	**90**	**89**	**89**	**88**	**92**	**Ensemble des pays en développement** [c]

Source: UNCTAD secretariat estimates.

a This index is based on the indices for individual countries shown above. It has been applied to obtain the data on import volume, export purchasing power and aid in constant prices in the case of individual LDCs for which such an index was not available.

b Excluding major petroleum exporters.

c Including major petroleum exporters.

Source: Estimations du secrétariat de la CNUCED.

a Cet indice est basé sur les indices pour les pays individuels qui figurent ci-dessus. On l'a utilisé pour obtenir les données concernant le volume des importations, le pouvoir d'achat des exportations et l'aide en prix constants dans les cas des PMA pour lesquels un tel indice n'était pas disponible.

b Non compris les principaux pays exportateurs de pétrole.

c Y compris les principaux pays exportateurs de pétrole.

9. Export value and purchasing power of exports : annual average growth rates

In per cent

Countries	Export value / Valeur des exportations								
	1970-1980	*1980-1987*	*1980-1981*	*1981-1982*	*1982-1983*	*1983-1984*	*1984-1985*	*1985-1986*	*1986-1987*
Afghanistan	21.2	-4.7	3.6	2.0	3.0	-13.2	-12.0	-5.7	-1.0
Bangladesh	6.3	8.0	-10.3	0.8	3.4	35.4	-0.7	3.0	25.0
Benin	1.8	-1.8	-46.0	-29.4	179.2	-50.7	21.2	0.0	0.0
Bhutan	..	..	..	..	..	..	..	..	..
Botswana	34.4	12.2	-20.5	14.2	39.2	6.0	10.4	15.3	8.4
Burkina Faso	18.4	-1.5	-16.7	-25.3	1.8	38.6	-11.4	0.0	-2.9
Burma	14.3	-10.2	1.1	-17.4	-3.8	-18.0	1.6	-15.9	-16.2
Burundi	17.2	8.9	9.2	23.9	-9.1	22.5	13.3	52.3	-49.1
Cape Verde	4.0	5.9	-25.0	33.3	-25.0	0.0	66.7	0.0	0.0
Central African Rep.	13.4	1.3	-31.3	38.0	-31.2	14.7	2.3	48.9	-23.7
Chad	14.0	3.4	16.9	-30.1	27.6	86.5	-42.0	6.3	-2.4
Comoros	13.0	5.5	-20.0	25.0	0.0	5.0	19.0	0.0	0.0
Democratic Yemen	17.5	-5.4	-22.1	31.0	-15.2	-4.3	7.0	-27.5	-2.0
Djibouti	-2.6	9.2	-52.6	44.4	-15.4	18.2	7.7	78.6	0.0
Equatorial Guinea	-4.4	5.0	14.3	6.2	17.6	0.0	0.0	0.0	0.0
Ethiopia	13.3	1.8	-8.5	3.9	-0.5	3.7	-20.1	43.2	2.7
Gambia	11.9	5.2	-12.9	63.0	9.1	-2.1	-8.5	-18.6	37.1
Guinea	28.5	1.3	25.6	-16.3	-2.4	17.5	2.1	-6.3	-2.2
Guinea-Bissau	16.3	3.3	27.3	-14.3	91.7	-21.7	-22.2	7.1	0.0
Haiti	19.6	-0.8	-33.2	7.9	-5.5	16.2	-2.8	-2.3	5.9
Kiribati	..	..	44.4	-46.2	57.1	224.2	-57.9	388.9	0.0
Lao People's Dem.Rep.	19.1	-2.9	6.5	21.2	-35.0	-53.8	141.7	3.4	0.0
Lesotho	26.1	-14.6	-13.8	-30.0	-45.7	10.5	0.0	0.0	-4.8
Malawi	16.4	-0.4	-5.3	-8.9	-6.9	34.9	-18.1	-3.2	12.7
Maldives	7.7	21.1	-10.0	11.1	30.0	38.5	27.8	8.7	28.0
Mali	21.1	1.4	-24.9	-5.2	13.0	18.2	-12.8	12.9	-1.0
Mauritania	5.9	10.5	34.5	-11.1	31.5	-2.6	25.9	-6.7	22.6
Nepal	9.8	8.3	75.0	-37.1	6.8	36.2	25.0	-11.3	7.7
Niger	33.8	-10.9	-19.6	-27.0	-9.9	-8.4	-18.6	16.6	-1.9
Rwanda	21.3	1.6	-1.8	-6.4	17.5	19.0	-9.0	-9.9	-4.2
Samoa	13.3	-1.9	-35.3	18.2	46.2	0.0	-21.1	-20.0	0.0
Sao Tome and Principe	12.4	-17.8	-30.0	-35.7	-33.3	16.7	-28.6	0.0	0.0
Sierra Leone	6.4	-2.0	-25.0	-41.8	3.4	60.9	-29.1	38.1	0.0
Somalia	15.0	-10.6	14.3	30.9	-48.2	-55.3	97.8	-6.6	-3.5
Sudan	7.0	-8.2	21.2	-24.2	25.1	0.8	-41.7	-9.3	8.1
Togo	21.1	-4.9	-37.0	-16.1	-8.5	17.9	-0.5	5.3	-10.0
Tuvalu	..	..	..	..	..	..	..	..	..
Uganda	4.6	5.0	-29.9	43.4	7.2	7.3	-4.8	10.5	-4.8
United Rep.of Tanzania	7.5	-9.3	20.7	-25.8	-19.6	3.3	-24.9	21.8	-16.2
Vanuatu	14.3	-7.5	-8.6	-28.1	26.1	51.7	-29.5	-45.2	5.9
Yemen	16.7	-20.0	104.3	-17.0	-30.8	-66.7	11.1	0.0	0.0
All LDCs	**12.9**	**-0.4**	**-5.9**	**-4.9**	**1.2**	**6.2**	**-6.1**	**2.4**	**2.6**
All developing countries	**20.7**	**4.9**	**5.3**	**-5.0**	**5.1**	**11.6**	**-1.5**	**5.2**	**22.5**

For sources and notes, see table 7.

9. Valeur et pouvoir d'achat des exportations : taux d'accroissement annuels moyens

En pourcentage

Purchasing power of exports / Pouvoir d'achat des exportations									
1970-1980	*1980-1987*	*1980-1981*	*1981-1982*	*1982-1983*	*1983-1984*	*1984-1985*	*1985-1986*	*1986-1987*	*Pays*
7.9	-3.9	10.9	6.3	6.2	-13.1	-12.8	-8.4	-4.2	Afghanistan
-6.1	9.0	-4.9	5.1	5.2	36.3	-0.3	0.7	20.0	Bangladesh
-10.2	-0.8	-43.0	-27.1	189.1	-49.7	20.7	-3.8	-3.0	Bénin
..	..	..	..	..	..	..	..	..	Bhoutan
18.6	13.4	-16.6	18.2	43.7	7.4	9.9	13.6	4.1	Botswana
5.2	-0.5	-12.1	-22.7	5.4	40.0	-11.9	-2.3	-6.1	Burkina Faso
0.8	-10.3	5.7	-16.2	-1.5	-16.5	0.8	-21.2	-19.7	Birmanie
3.5	10.1	14.6	28.2	-6.2	24.1	12.8	49.9	-51.1	Burundi
-8.3	7.0	-21.3	37.9	-22.6	1.3	66.0	-1.5	-3.9	Cap-Vert
1.0	1.4	-26.8	42.4	-29.5	15.1	1.3	39.1	-25.4	Rép. centrafricaine
1.4	4.0	23.0	-28.0	32.0	86.6	-42.7	3.5	-5.9	Tchad
-0.2	6.7	-16.1	29.3	3.2	6.4	18.5	-1.5	-3.9	Comores
3.7	-4.4	-18.3	35.5	-12.5	-3.0	6.5	-28.6	-5.9	Yémen démocratique
-14.0	10.4	-50.3	49.4	-12.7	19.8	7.2	75.8	-3.9	Djibouti
-15.6	6.1	19.9	9.9	21.4	1.3	-0.4	-1.5	-3.9	Guinée équatoriale
-0.9	3.5	-7.2	6.6	3.9	5.7	-20.3	48.4	-2.5	Ethiopie
-1.4	6.6	-6.4	70.6	12.4	0.0	-8.5	-22.3	34.3	Gambie
13.4	2.3	31.8	-13.4	0.7	19.1	1.7	-7.7	-6.1	Guinée
2.6	4.4	33.5	-11.3	97.8	-20.7	-22.6	5.5	-3.9	Guinée-Bissau
5.5	0.3	-29.9	11.7	-2.5	17.8	-3.2	-3.8	1.7	Haïti
..	..	51.5	-44.3	62.2	228.6	-58.1	381.4	..	Kiribati
5.1	-1.8	11.6	25.4	-32.9	-53.2	140.6	1.9	-3.9	Rép. dém. pop. lao
11.3	-13.6	-9.6	-27.6	-44.0	12.0	-0.4	-1.5	-8.5	Lesotho
3.2	0.2	-1.5	-6.9	-3.4	36.5	-18.9	-5.3	7.7	Malawi
-5.0	22.4	-5.6	14.9	34.2	40.3	27.2	7.0	23.0	Maldives
7.2	2.4	-21.1	-2.4	17.5	19.1	-13.7	11.0	-4.6	Mali
-6.2	12.2	43.1	-7.2	35.7	-0.5	26.4	-10.0	20.2	Mauritanie
-3.1	9.5	83.5	-35.0	10.3	38.0	24.5	-12.6	3.5	Népal
18.7	-9.5	-16.9	-24.6	-5.9	-7.8	-19.0	19.5	-6.6	Niger
7.7	2.1	4.4	-2.7	19.7	19.2	-9.2	-12.8	-8.1	Rwanda
0.0	-0.8	-32.1	22.2	50.9	1.3	-21.4	-21.2	-3.9	Samoa
-0.8	-16.9	-26.6	-33.5	-31.2	18.2	-28.9	-1.5	-3.9	Sao Tomé-et-Principe
-6.2	-0.3	-20.9	-39.3	7.2	64.5	-29.1	36.9	-2.9	Sierra leone
1.4	-9.9	23.4	37.1	-47.5	-54.8	98.6	-12.1	-5.8	Somalie
-5.9	-6.7	27.8	-21.0	29.6	3.0	-41.6	-11.1	5.5	Soudan
6.7	-3.0	-35.0	-13.0	-4.4	20.3	-0.6	8.1	-13.6	Togo
..	..	..	..	..	..	..	..	..	Tuvalu
-7.5	4.8	-26.1	45.7	10.1	8.3	-6.2	2.9	-8.2	Ouganda
-5.5	-7.9	23.3	-23.8	-16.1	5.4	-25.0	23.6	-19.9	Rép.-Unie de Tanzanie
0.9	-6.5	-4.1	-25.7	30.2	53.8	-29.8	-46.0	1.7	Vanuatu
3.0	-19.1	114.3	-14.2	-28.5	-66.2	10.6	-1.5	-3.9	Yémen
-0.4	**0.6**	**-1.3**	**-1.6**	**4.4**	**7.6**	**-6.5**	**0.8**	**-1.4**	**Ensemble des PMA**
5.3	**6.9**	**7.8**	**-1.6**	**9.1**	**13.2**	**-1.3**	**9.5**	**16.3**	**Ensemble des pays en développement**

Pour la source et les notes, se reporter au tableau 7.

10.Import value and volume : annual average growth rates

In per cent

Countries	Import value / Valeur des importations								
	1970-1980	*1980-1987*	*1980-1981*	*1981-1982*	*1982-1983*	*1983-1984*	*1984-1985*	*1985-1986*	*1986-1987*
Afghanistan	19.4	8.7	12.7	11.7	-24.5	120.2	-13.6	-14.8	8.1
Bangladesh	16.4	3.8	-8.1	-4.2	-8.6	28.7	6.3	-7.2	24.2
Benin	19.5	-2.5	64.4	-14.7	-36.6	5.4	29.0	-7.5	-8.1
Bhutan	..	..	..	..	..	..	..	..	..
Botswana	28.2	-0.2	15.6	-13.9	7.0	-3.9	-17.5	17.3	18.4
Burkina Faso	21.8	-3.5	-5.6	2.4	-16.8	-28.1	60.9	-15.9	1.8
Burma	8.8	-3.8	5.7	9.4	-34.3	-10.8	18.4	7.4	0.7
Burundi	22.4	2.9	-4.2	32.9	-14.5	1.6	0.0	10.2	3.4
Cape Verde	11.8	0.6	4.4	1.4	9.7	-10.1	14.1	-1.2	-18.8
Central African Rep.	8.9	9.3	17.3	33.7	-33.1	2.4	25.3	131.2	-50.4
Chad	7.5	14.8	45.9	0.9	7.3	38.5	17.3	0.0	2.6
Comoros	11.8	5.8	3.0	-5.9	0.0	-6.3	0.0	33.3	50.0
Democratic Yemen	15.6	0.9	117.6	12.7	-7.3	4.0	-16.4	-10.9	-20.0
Djibouti	9.4	-0.8	-4.0	-4.2	0.0	-4.3	0.0	4.5	4.3
Equatorial Guinea	-6.8	1.1	19.2	35.5	-28.6	0.0	0.0	0.0	16.7
Ethiopia	15.7	5.4	2.4	6.5	11.3	7.5	5.7	10.1	-16.1
Gambia	25.5	-3.5	-25.2	-20.5	18.6	-14.8	-5.1	7.5	28.0
Guinea	18.7	8.0	18.5	-3.1	-3.2	20.0	16.7	2.4	9.3
Guinea-Bissau	5.8	3.6	-9.1	0.0	10.0	-12.7	25.0	0.0	16.7
Haiti	22.3	0.9	26.6	-13.6	13.7	7.3	-6.4	-9.5	..
Kiribati	14.4	-0.9	-17.6	0.0	0.0	0.0	-7.1	15.4	..
Lao People's Dem.Rep.	2.4	-8.6	-4.6	4.0	-29.2	-47.8	35.4	7.7	42.9
Lesotho	30.8	-10.7	13.8	-0.2	11.4	-46.8	-19.9	4.0	15.4
Malawi	17.1	-5.4	-20.5	-11.1	0.0	-13.5	6.7	-10.1	14.7
Maldives	25.3	13.3	6.9	38.7	32.6	-7.0	0.0	3.8	45.5
Mali	23.2	2.6	-12.5	-13.8	3.9	8.7	9.3	13.7	0.9
Mauritania	18.2	0.9	-7.3	3.0	-16.8	8.4	-4.9	-5.6	72.9
Nepal	18.6	5.3	7.9	7.0	17.5	-10.3	8.9	1.3	13.3
Niger	27.5	-5.5	-14.1	-8.6	-30.5	-12.0	40.4	-7.5	10.8
Rwanda	26.4	5.5	5.3	7.8	-2.5	9.7	-0.3	19.7	0.3
Samoa	18.5	-1.1	-11.1	-10.7	12.0	-10.7	2.0	-5.9	29.2
Sao Tome and Principe	10.5	-1.9	-10.5	-11.8	-33.3	20.0	8.3	15.4	13.3
Sierra Leone	12.0	-15.2	-24.6	-23.1	-30.8	0.0	-6.0	-15.4	-3.0
Somalia	21.0	-19.3	47.1	-35.5	-45.5	-41.7	6.7	11.6	..
Sudan	19.2	-9.8	0.1	-18.6	5.4	-15.3	-34.0	26.9	-12.6
Togo	26.9	-13.6	-21.3	-9.7	-27.4	-4.6	6.3	-30.6	-5.0
Tuvalu	..	..	..	..	..	..	..	..	..
Uganda	2.9	2.9	17.7	9.3	0.0	-8.8	-4.9	7.0	25.7
United Rep.of Tanzania	14.2	-5.7	-1.1	-6.7	-27.3	8.2	16.0	-24.3	9.0
Vanuatu	17.1	0.5	-18.3	1.7	6.8	9.5	2.9	-19.7	22.8
Yemen	55.3	-9.4	-5.1	-13.5	4.7	-3.4	-16.2	-14.7	-22.7
All LDCs	**18.3**	**-1.6**	**5.3**	**-5.1**	**-7.6**	**3.3**	**-2.2**	**-2.7**	**2.9**
All developing countries	**21.2**	**0.8**	**6.0**	**-8.2**	**-2.0**	**3.7**	**-3.6**	**3.1**	**18.5**

For sources and notes, see table 7.

10. Valeur et volume des importations : taux d'accroissement annuels moyens

En pourcentage

Import volume / Volume des importations									
1970-1980	*1980-1987*	*1980-1981*	*1981-1982*	*1982-1983*	*1983-1984*	*1984-1985*	*1985-1986*	*1986-1987*	*Pays*
6.3	9.7	20.6	16.5	-22.1	120.3	-14.4	-17.2	4.5	Afghanistan
2.8	4.7	-2.6	0.0	-7.1	29.6	6.8	-9.3	19.2	Bangladesh
5.4	-1.5	73.5	-11.9	-34.4	7.7	28.5	-11.0	-10.9	Bénin
..	..	..	..	..	..	..	..	..	Bhoutan
13.2	0.8	21.3	-10.9	10.4	-2.7	-17.9	15.5	13.8	Botswana
8.2	-2.5	-0.4	6.0	-13.8	-27.4	60.0	-17.9	-1.6	Burkina Faso
-4.1	-3.8	10.6	11.0	-32.7	-9.2	17.5	0.7	-3.5	Birmanie
8.0	4.0	0.5	37.5	-11.7	3.0	-0.4	8.5	-0.7	Burundi
-1.4	1.7	9.5	4.9	13.3	-8.9	13.6	-2.7	-22.0	Cap-Vert
-3.0	9.5	25.0	38.0	-31.4	2.8	24.1	116.0	-51.5	Rép. centrafricaine
-4.4	15.5	53.6	4.0	11.1	38.6	15.9	-2.6	-1.1	Tchad
-1.3	6.9	8.1	-2.6	3.2	-5.0	-0.4	31.3	44.1	Comores
2.0	2.0	128.3	16.6	-4.3	5.4	-16.8	-12.2	-23.2	Yémen démocratique
-3.4	0.3	0.7	-0.9	3.2	-3.1	-0.4	3.0	0.2	Djibouti
-17.8	2.2	25.0	40.1	-26.3	1.3	-0.4	-1.5	12.1	Guinée équatoriale
1.2	7.2	3.8	9.4	16.2	9.6	5.5	14.1	-20.4	Ethiopie
10.5	-2.2	-19.6	-16.8	22.2	-13.0	-5.1	2.6	25.4	Gambie
4.7	9.1	24.3	0.2	-0.1	21.6	16.2	0.8	5.0	Guinée
-6.6	4.8	-4.7	3.4	13.5	-11.6	24.5	-1.5	12.1	Guinée-Bissau
7.9	2.0	32.7	-10.6	17.4	8.7	-6.8	-10.9	-3.9	Haïti
0.9	0.2	-13.6	3.4	3.2	1.3	-7.5	13.6	-3.9	Kiribati
-9.6	-7.6	0.0	7.6	-26.9	-47.1	34.8	6.1	37.2	Rép. dém. pop. lao
15.4	-9.7	19.3	3.2	15.0	-46.1	-20.2	2.4	10.8	Lesotho
3.8	-4.8	-17.3	-9.2	3.7	-12.5	5.7	-12.1	9.6	Malawi
10.6	14.6	12.1	43.5	36.8	-5.8	-0.4	2.2	39.7	Maldives
9.0	3.6	-8.1	-11.2	8.1	9.6	8.3	11.7	-2.8	Mali
4.7	2.4	-1.4	7.6	-14.2	10.7	-4.5	-8.9	69.4	Mauritanie
4.7	6.4	13.2	10.7	21.3	-9.1	8.4	-0.2	8.8	Népal
13.2	-4.1	-11.3	-5.6	-27.4	-11.5	39.7	-5.2	5.6	Niger
12.2	6.1	12.0	12.0	-0.7	9.8	-0.6	15.9	-3.8	Rwanda
4.6	0.0	-6.8	-7.6	15.6	-9.5	1.6	-7.3	24.1	Samoa
-2.5	-0.9	-6.2	-8.7	-31.2	21.6	7.9	13.6	8.9	Sao Tomé-et-Principe
-1.3	-13.7	-20.5	-19.7	-28.3	2.2	-6.1	-16.1	-5.8	Sierra leone
6.7	-18.6	58.9	-32.5	-44.7	-40.9	7.1	5.0	-2.3	Somalie
4.9	-8.3	5.6	-15.1	9.2	-13.4	-33.9	24.4	-14.7	Soudan
11.8	-11.9	-18.8	-6.3	-24.1	-2.7	6.2	-28.7	-8.8	Togo
..	..	..	..	..	..	..	..	..	Tuvalu
-9.1	2.6	24.1	11.0	2.7	-7.9	-6.3	-0.3	21.2	Ouganda
0.4	-4.3	1.0	-4.2	-24.2	10.4	15.8	-23.3	4.2	Rép.-Unie de Tanzanie
3.3	1.6	-14.3	5.2	10.2	11.0	2.5	-20.9	18.0	Vanuatu
37.1	-8.5	-0.5	-10.5	8.1	-2.1	-16.6	-16.0	-25.8	Yémen
4.4	**-0.6**	**10.4**	**-1.8**	**-4.6**	**4.7**	**-2.6**	**-4.2**	**-1.2**	**Ensemble des PMA**
5.8	**2.6**	**8.5**	**-4.9**	**1.7**	**5.1**	**-3.4**	**7.3**	**12.5**	**Ensemble des pays en développement**

Pour la source et les notes, se reporter au tableau 7.

11. Leading exports of individual LDCs, in 1980 and 1986

11. Principales exportations des PMA en 1980 et 1986, par pays individuels

Country/Pays		Value Valeur ($ million) (mill. de $)	% Share of the three major products [a] Parts en % des trois produits principaux [a]			Description of products [b] Description des produits [b]
Afghanistan	A	705.2	33.1	18.6	14.7	natural gas/gaz naturel, raisins/raisins secs, carpets/tapis
	B	551.9	47.0	11.8	7.2	natural gas/gaz naturel, raisins/raisins secs, carpets/tapis
Bangladesh	A	740.4	28.7	25.4	18.3	weaves of jute/tissus de jute, bags of jute/sacs de jute, raw jute/jute brut (10.2)
	B	951.5	19.7	12.3	11.6	bags of jute/sacs de jute, weaves of jute/tissus de jute, men's shirts/chemises d'hommes (0.0)
Benin/Bénin	A	63.3	22.5	18.4	13.8	cocoa beans/fèves de cacao, raw cotton/coton brut, palm kernel oil/huile de palmiste
Botswana	A	502.9	60.8	20.7	7.2	diamonds/diamants, copper and nickel matte/matte de cuivre et de nickel, meat/viande
	B	857.8	74.5	7.6	7.5	diamonds/diamants, copper and nickel matte/matte de cuivre et de nickel, meat/viande
Burkina Faso	A	90.2	43.9	11.5	8.5	cotton/coton, bovine cattle/espèce bovine, sheep and goats/espèces ovine et caprine (3.2)
	B	70.0	30.0	15.1	8.6	cotton/coton, edible nuts/noix comestibles (8.2), bovine cattle/espèce bovine
Burma/Birmanie	A	473.2	39.0	14.6	8.2	rice/riz, wood sawn, non-coniferous/bois sciés, non-conifères (15.4), sawlogs and veneerlogs, non-coniferous/non-conifères pour sciage et placage
	B	299.2	31.2	26.7	20.7	sawlogs and veneerlogs, non-coniferous/non-conifères pour sciage et placage, rice/riz, pulses/plantes légumineuses (4.2)
Burundi	A	65.4	78.4	1.9	1.7	coffee/café, tea/thé, raw cotton/coton brut (0.1)
	B	169.3	88.4	2.7	2.2	coffee/café, tea/thé, cotton fabrics/tissus de coton (0.0)
Cape Verde/Cap-Vert	A	4.2	22.0	19.0	11.7	fresh fish/poisson frais, fish products/produits de poisson, bananas/bananes
	B	5.2	38.5	18.3	9.6	fresh fish/poisson frais, bananas/bananes, fish products/produits de poisson
Central African Rep./	A	115.4	27.4	25.0	23.7	coffee/café, diamonds/diamants, sawlogs and veneerlogs, non-coniferous/non-conifères pour sciage et placage (NC)
Rép. centrafricaine	B	131.3	27.0	22.4	10.4	diamonds/diamants, coffee/café, sawlogs and veneerlogs, non-coniferous/non-conifères pour sciage et placage (NC)
Comoros/Comores	A	11.6	60.9	18.1	3.6	spices/épices, essential oils/huiles essentielles, copra/coprah
	B	20.4	88.6	9.0	0.4	spices/épices, essential oils/huiles essentielles, copra/coprah
Equatorial Guinea/	A	12.2	69.1	20.6	3.2	cocoa/cacao, sawlogs and veneerlogs, non-coniferous/ non-conifères pour sciage et placage, coffee/café
Guinée équatoriale [c]	B	23.5	68.8	23.9	5.6	cocoa/cacao, sawlogs and veneerlogs, non-coniferous/ non-conifères pour sciage et placage, coffee/café
Ethiopia/Ethiopie	A	424.7	64.1	7.4	6.8	coffee/café, fuel oils, sheep skins/peaux d'ovins
	B	454.9	77.1	7.8	7.3	coffee/café, fuel oils, sheep skins/peaux d'ovins
Guinea/Guinée	A	414.6	68.3	28.1	2.0	bauxite, alumina/alumine, coffee/café (3.5)
	B	531.0	70.2	16.4	6.8	bauxite, alumina/alumine, diamonds/diamants (0.2)
Guinea-Bissau/	A	11.4	29.5	25.0	17.1	shell fish/crustacés et mollusques, groundnuts/arachides (5.5), castor oil seed/graines de ricin (0.0)
Guinée-Bissau	B	9.6	53.6	10.1	8.5	edible nuts/noix comestibles (3.8), shell fish/crustacés et mollusques, palm kernel/amandes de palmiste (0.0)
Haiti/Haïti	A	226.1	43.6	8.7	7.9	coffee/café, alumina/alumine, sporting goods/articles de sport
Kiribati	A	2.7	90.5	7.8	0.8	copra/coprah, fresh fish/poisson frais, dried fish/poisson seché
	B	2.5	55.3	42.7	0.8	fresh fish/poisson frais, copra/coprah, dried fish/poisson seché
Lao People's Dem.Rep./	A	30.5	26.9	17.4	3.6	sawlogs and veneerlogs, non-coniferous/non-conifères pour sciage et placage, electricity/electricité, coffee/café
Rép. dém. pop. lao [c]	B	47.6	57.6	18.1	7.6	electricity/electricité, sawlogs and veneerlogs, non-coniferous/ non-conifères pour sciage et placage, coffee/café
Lesotho	A	58.2	54.6	9.1	7.5	diamonds/diamants, greasy wool/laine en suint, mohair
Malawi	A	285.1	44.3	14.6	11.0	tobacco/tabacs, raw sugar/sucre brut, tea/thé
	B	248.3	52.9	14.8	8.6	tobacco/tabacs, tea/thé, sugar/sucre

11. Leading exports of individual LDCs, in 1980 and 1986 *(continued)* / 11. Principales exportations des PMA en 1980 et 1986, par pays individuels *(suite)*

Country/Pays		*Value Valeur ($ million) (mill. de $)*	*% Share of the three major products [a] Parts en % des trois produits principaux [a]*			*Description of products [b] Description des produits [b]*
Maldives	A	7.8	61.8	26.2	5.7	fresh fish/poisson frais, dried fish/poisson seché (10.5), mica (0.0)
	B	24.9	39.8	34.6	10.5	fresh fish/poisson frais, garments/vêtements (0.0), frozen fish/poisson congelé (0.0)
Nepal/Népal [c]	A	93.7	25.0	15.3	10.5	goat and kid skins/peaux de chèvres (0.0), raw jute/ jute brut (1.8), vegetables/légumes (7.3)
	B	128.5	15.9	10.5	9.8	dresses/robes (0.0), wool carpets/tapis en laine (7.1), rice/riz (5.1)
Niger	A	579.7	84.7	4.9	4.7	uranium ore/minerais d'uranium, bovine cattle/espèce bovine, vegetables/légumes (0.0)
	B	330.0	76.7	16.5	3.1	uranium ore/minerais d'uranium, bovine cattle/espèce bovine, sheep and goats/espèces ovine et caprine (0.5)
Samoa	A	17.6	52.0	17.5	6.4	copra/coprah (4.5), cocoa/cacao, taro
	B	10.5	27.9	18.5	13.6	coconut oil/huile de coprah (0.6), taro, cocoa/cacao
Sao Tome & Principe/ Sao Tomé-et-Principe	A	18.5	94.5	4.3	0.8	cocoa/cacao, copra/coprah, palm kernel/amandes de palmiste (0.0)
	B	6.0	90.4	8.3	1.1	cocoa/cacao, copra/coprah, coffee/café (0.3)
Sierra Leone [c]	A	219.5	52.1	12.5	10.4	diamonds/diamants, coffee/café (9.0), cocoa/cacao (9.9)
	B	145.5	20.2	20.1	16.4	rutile (5.5), diamonds/diamants, bauxite (6.2)
Somalia /Somalie	A	132.6	31.8	26.0	18.8	live animals for food nes/animaux vivants destinés à l'alimentation humaine nda (n.a.), sheep and goats/espèces ovine et caprine, bovine cattle/espèce bovine
	B	89.4	67.1	14.9	5.6	sheep and goats/espèces ovine et caprine, bananas/bananes (8.2), bovine cattle/espèce bovine
Sudan/Soudan	A	594.0	39.7	14.2	11.0	raw cotton/coton brut, sorghum/sorgho, etc. (1.7), oilseeds/graines oléagineuses (7.1)
	B	333.3	44.0	17.0	7.4	raw cotton/coton brut, gum arabic/gomme arabique (5.3), sheep and goats/espèces ovine et caprine (6.8)
Togo [c]	A	334.9	40.3	11.5	8.8	phosphates, cocoa/cacao, gas oils (1.5)
	B	190.0	48.8	13.9	8.0	phosphates, coffee/café (7.0), cocoa/cacao
Tuvalu	A	0.1	78.4	17.5	5.2	copra/coprah, developed-cinema film/films cinématographiques développés, dried meat/viande sechée
Uganda/Ouganda	A	345.8	97.9	1.2	0.1	coffee/café, raw cotton/coton brut, tea/thé
	B	407.2	97.6	1.3	0.8	coffee/café, raw cotton/coton brut, tea/thé
Un. Rep. of Tanzania/ Rép.-Un. de Tanzanie	A	536.6	25.8	9.7	9.6	coffee/café, raw cotton/coton brut, spices/épices
	B	340.0	49.4	9.8	5.9	coffee/café, raw cotton/coton brut, spices/épices
Vanuatu	A	12.7	67.3	10.6	8.4	copra/coprah, cocoa/cacao, coconut oil/huile de coprah (9.0)
	B	14.4	30.3	12.9	9.6	copra/coprah, cocoa/cacao, bovine meat/viande de bovins (2.2)
Yemen/Yémen	A	22.6	18.2	9.7	6.0	bakery products/produits de boulangerie, sugar candy/sucreries, fruit juice/jus de fruits

Source: UNCTAD secretariat, based on data from the UN Statistical Office, FAO, IMF and national sources.

A = 1980
B = 1986

Note: There are no consistent data available for Bhutan, Chad, Democratic Yemen, Djibouti, Gambia, Mali, Mauritania and Rwanda.

a If one of the products did not belong to the three major ones in any of the two years, the comparable share for that year is indicated in brackets behind the description.

b The products are in general defined at the SITC Rev. 2 4-digit level, except tobacco, garments, vegetables, taro, copper and nickel matte and diamonds, which are defined at other levels.

c The second line is based on data for 1985.

Source: Secrétariat de la CNUCED, d'après des données du Bureau de statistique de l'ONU, de la FAO, du FMI et sources nationales.

A = 1980
B = 1986

Note: Il n'y a pas des données comparables disponibles pour le Bhoutan, le Tchad, le Yémen démocratique, le Djibouti, la Gambie, le Mali, la Mauritanie et le Rwanda.

a Lorsqu'un produit ne figure pas parmi les trois produits principaux dans une des deux années, la part comparable pour cette année est indiquée entre parenthèses après la description du produit.

b Les produits sont en général definis au niveau des sous-groupes (4-digit) de la CTCI Rev. 2, exceptés les tabacs, les vêtements, le taro, le matte de cuivre et de nickel, et les diamants, qui sont definis à des autres niveaux.

c La seconde ligne est fondée sur des données se réferant à 1985.

12. Commodity structure of imports of LDCs by main category 1986 (or latest year available)

12. Composition des importations des PMA, par principales catégories de produits 1986 (ou année la plus récente disponible)

Country	Main category of imports (in %) / Principales catégories de produits importés (en %)						Selected commodity groups (in %) / Quelques groupes de produits (en %)			Pays
	All food items	Agricultural raw materials	Fuels	Ores and metals	Manufactured goods	Un-allocated	Cereals	Crude and manufactured fertilizers	Transport equipment	
	Produits alimentaires	Matières premières d'origine agricole	Combus-tibles	Minerais et métaux	Produits manufac-turés	Non-distribués	Céréales	Engrais bruts et manufac-turés	Matériel de transport	
SITC	0+1+22+4	2-22-27-28	3	27+28+ 67+68	5+6+7+8 -67-68	9	04	271+56	73	CTCI
Afghanistan	12.1	-	21.4	-	56.3	10.2	-	0.5	(30.8)	Afghanistan
Bangladesh	19.4	3.8	18.8	9.9	47.8	0.3	5.5	1.7	4.6	Bangladesh
Benin	14.8	2.5	5.2	1.8	75.5	0.3	3.6	0.5	5.0	Bénin
Bhutan	15.3	-	23.0	3.1	48.2	10.4	6.5	0.0	16.2	Bhoutan
Botswana	17.5	3.2	11.5	9.1 a	46.9	11.7	..	..	12.8	Botswana
Burkina Faso	25.5	2.1	17.1	4.1	51.2	-	10.9	2.0	11.3	Burkina Faso
Burma	4.9	1.1	2.5	8.4	80.9	2.3	0.1	1.9	17.6	Birmanie
Burundi	11.9	2.2	14.4	12.2	55.8	3.5	5.5	2.1	10.3	Burundi
Cape Verde	32.6	0.8	13.9	2.2	50.3	0.2	8.5	0.0	8.4	Cap-Vert
Central African Rep.	(16.6)	..	(24.8)	..	(57.4)	(1.1)	..	..	15.0	Rép. centrafricaine
Chad	(18.1)	(1.0)	(1.2)	(1.5)	(77.9)	(0.3)	(9.7)	(4.3)	(21.4)	Tchad
Comoros	(22.2)	(1.0)	(7.2)	(3.1)	(61.8)	(4.7)	(14.7)	(0.0)	(13.4)	Comores
Democratic Yemen	(24.3)	(0.8)	(37.5)	(2.6)	(34.6)	(0.2)	(7.0)	(0.0)	(6.6)	Yémen démocratique
Djibouti	(38.4)	..	(9.8)	..	(41.4)	(10.4)	..	-	(8.0)	Djibouti
Equatorial Guinea	23.5	..	16.8	..	44.5	15.2	..	..	..	Guinée équatoriale
Ethiopia	29.8	3.0	14.8	3.2	49.3	-	18.9	1.4	14.2	Ethiopie
Gambia	36.6	1.4 b	10.7	..	50.6 c	0.6	12.8	0.1	5.9	Gambie
Guinea	12.8	0.7	29.2	2.9	53.9	0.5	5.3	0.3	7.8	Guinée
Guinea-Bissau	20.3	..	10.9	..	63.4	5.3	..	..	17.6	Guinée-Bissau
Haiti	28.1	2.7	14.2	-	54.1	0.9	..	..	18.4	Haïti
Kiribati	32.6	0.9 b	15.0	..	50.6 c	0.9	9.8	..	1.6	Kiribati
Lao People's Dem.Rep.	(20.8)	(0.1)	(18.9)	(3.6)	(53.5)	(3.1)	(16.2)	(3.3)	(14.1)	Rép. dém. pop. lao
Lesotho	26.9	1.2	7.6	1.7	61.7	1.0	7.8	1.2	5.4	Lesotho
Malawi	8.2	1.5	18.0	4.2	67.8	0.3	2.4	8.7	7.5	Malawi
Maldives	(28.6)	(0.0)	(15.5)	(5.9)	50.0	-	6.5	0.0	7.4	Maldives
Mali	15.4	0.7	17.6	2.6	63.1	0.4	5.4	7.0	10.0	Mali
Mauritania	36.3	..	13.9	-	(49.8)	-	..	..	9.7	Mauritanie
Nepal	14.0	2.2	11.6	7.5	64.7	0.0	0.8	4.7	5.2	Népal
Niger	(16.9)	(0.6)	(4.2)	(6.1)	(72.0)	(0.2)	(2.9)	(0.4)	(6.9)	Niger
Rwanda	(15.7)	..	(16.2)	..	(66.9)	(1.3)	(5.2)	(0.7)	(10.6)	Rwanda
Samoa	26.7	0.7 b	17.0	..	55.5 c	0.1	..	..	24.6 d	Samoa
Sao Tome and Principe	36.3	0.5	1.8	4.4	56.8	0.2	15.3	0.1	10.7	Sao Tomé-et-Principe
Sierra Leone	35.0	1.7 b	16.4	-	46.9 c	-	..	..	24.8 d	Sierra Leone
Somalia	(23.9)	(1.5)	(18.3)	(2.8)	(53.5)	(0.2)	(10.7)	(0.2)	(14.9)	Somalie
Sudan	19.7	..	18.7	..	61.6	-	..	..	10.3	Soudan
Togo	27.8	..	10.4	0.6	44.8	16.4	2.4	-	7.9	Togo
Tuvalu	29.0	1.4	11.7	0.5	55.5	1.9	9.4	..	6.3	Tuvalu
Uganda e	(10.8)	-	-	(1.9)	(71.8)	(15.5)	..	-	(9.0)	Ouganda e
United Rep.of Tanzania	(7.9)	-	(22.7)	(15.9)	(53.4)	(0.2)	..	(0.9)	(11.0)	Rép.-Unie de Tanzanie
Vanuatu	25.3 b	0.8	9.7	..	61.1 c	3.0	5.0	..	6.5	Vanuatu
Yemen	33.1	0.3	6.7	7.2	52.3	0.4	9.2	0.7	9.9	Yémen
All LDCs	**20.4**	**1.8**	**16.1**	**5.8**	**53.7**	**2.2**	**5.0**	**1.2**	**10.9**	**Ensemble des PMA**
All developing countries	**11.3**	**3.0**	**18.5**	**6.5**	**56.0**	**4.7**	..	..	..	**Ensemble des pays en développement**

Source: UNCTAD *Handbook of International Trade and Development Statistics 1988*, and other international and national sources.

a Including metal products. **b** SITC 2. **c** SITC 5+6+7+8. **d** SITC 7.
e The percentage distribution excludes imports financed through loans or grants.

Source: CNUCED, *Manuel de statistiques du commerce international et du développement 1988*, et autres sources internationales et nationales.

a Y compris les produits métalliques. **b** CTCI 2. **c** CTCI 5+6+7+8. **d** CTCI 7.
e La distribution en pourcentage ne comprend pas les importations financées par des prêts ou par des dons.

13. Main markets for exports and main sources of imports of LDCs: relative shares in 1986 (or latest year available)

13. Principaux marchés aux exportations et principales sources d'importation des PMA: parts relatives en 1986 (ou année la plus récente disponible)

	Developed market economy countries / Pays développés à économie de marché								Socialist countries of Eastern Europe / Pays socialistes d'Europe orientale		Socialist countries of Asia / Pays socialistes d'Asie		Developing countries / Pays en développement		
	Total		EEC / CEE		Japan / Japon		USA and Canada / Etats-Unis et Canada								
Country	X	M	X	M	X	M	X	M	X	M	X	M	X	M	Pays
Afghanistan	11.6	21.0	9.1	6.9	0.0	12.3	0.7	0.8	69.0	40.2	0.0	7.2	10.2	22.2	Afghanistan
Bangladesh	59.2	44.9	20.7	15.8	8.0	12.5	25.2	11.8	7.5	6.1	2.8	3.7	30.3	28.3	Bangladesh
Benin	70.6	(65.0)	58.4	(38.1)	12.3	(5.5)	-	(14.4)	-	(2.4)	-	(1.9)	28.8	(29.2)	Bénin
Bhutan	-	6.5	-	0.8	-	3.7	-	1.0	-	-	-	-	99.5	90.9	Bhoutan
Botswana	93.4	88.2	3.7	2.5	-	-	0.2	2.8	-	-	-	-	6.0	7.6	Botswana
Burkina Faso	62.6	55.3	57.1	42.3	3.8	2.6	1.2	9.4	-	0.3	0.0	0.5	16.5	43.2	Burkina Faso
Burma	19.9	76.0	11.4	26.7	7.5	43.6	0.9	2.2	1.0	2.2	6.2	3.7	70.4	18.1	Birmanie
Burundi	69.7	69.0	61.9	55.6	1.5	6.7	5.2	2.6	-	0.4	-	2.1	27.2	26.4	Burundi
Cape Verde	26.5	76.4	26.5	67.7	-	1.1	-	2.0	-	2.2	-	0.2	71.4	21.0	Cap-Vert
Central African Rep.	96.3	62.9	90.8	56.9	0.0	3.0	0.0	2.6	-	0.2	-	0.5	3.7	20.6	Rép. centrafricaine
Chad	..	(42.4)	..	(37.7)	..	(0.4)	..	(3.6)	..	-	..	0.3	..	(53.2)	Tchad
Comoros	95.9	63.3	2.7	63.2	-	-	53.2	0.1	-	-	-	-	4.1	36.7	Comores
Democratic Yemen	..	..	..	..	..	..	..	..	..	..	..	..	..	..	Yémen démocratique
Djibouti	(10.2)	..	(7.6)	..	-	..	(0.9)	..	-	..	-	..	(89.8)	..	Djibouti
Equatorial Guinea	95.7	88.6	94.6	87.9	-	0.3	0.5	-	-	-	0.0	0.3	4.2	10.9	Guinée équatoriale
Ethiopia	78.1	72.9	51.7	46.4	8.4	6.1	14.9	11.3	6.5	17.0	0.2	0.5	15.1	8.8	Ethiopie
Gambia	(33.4)	(67.2)	(19.5)	(50.3)	(1.8)	(4.7)	(0.3)	(10.1)	-	(4.3)	-	(9.5)	(65.8)	(15.2)	Gambie
Guinea	86.6	(85.7)	60.4	(73.8)	0.2	(0.5)	25.2	(8.5)	1.5	(1.2)	-	(1.4)	11.9	(11.0)	Guinée
Guinea-Bissau	51.9	63.1	51.4	55.2	-	1.0	-	-	36.0	3.0	9.4	1.0	2.6	30.0	Guinée-Bissau
Haiti	94.3	76.7	37.4	12.8	0.4	7.0	55.0	53.3	-	-	-	-	5.6	23.1	Haïti
Kiribati	56.7	75.7	20.5	6.2	1.6	21.2	8.2	2.6	-	-	-	3.6	43.3	20.6	Kiribati
Lao People's Dem.Rep.	(35.9)	(32.4)	(10.4)	(9.2)	(5.0)	(20.3)	(17.5)	(0.0)	-	-	(42.6)	(1.4)	(15.5)	(48.1)	Rép. dém. pop. lao
Lesotho	94.0	99.4	5.0	1.4	-	0.1	2.7	0.4	-	-	-	-	6.0	0.6	Lesotho
Malawi	87.3	87.5	58.4	41.7	6.7	9.6	10.0	3.9	-	-	-	-	12.4	11.5	Malawi
Maldives	41.9	(26.4)	3.5	(11.4)	3.6	(10.0)	34.6	-	-	-	-	(0.1)	58.1	(73.5)	Maldives
Mali	65.5	63.6	55.5	55.7	2.2	2.2	6.0	4.4	-	0.7	0.9	1.5	30.3	32.4	Mali
Mauritania	81.3	82.7	53.7	74.6	27.1	2.5	0.3	3.4	3.6	0.3	-	4.9	15.1	12.0	Mauritanie
Nepal	55.7	(41.2)	28.0	(13.6)	1.0	(22.7)	23.8	(2.9)	-	-	2.1	(7.2)	42.2	(51.4)	Népal
Niger	85.9	62.7	81.6	57.8	0.0	2.9	4.3	0.8	-	0.6	-	2.4	11.9	25.9	Niger
Rwanda	94.6	66.6	88.9	46.2	0.9	12.7	3.1	5.3	-	0.1	-	4.1	5.4	28.9	Rwanda
Samoa	83.7	71.5	22.9	7.7	0.2	9.5	9.7	4.8	-	0.1	-	1.6	16.3	25.0	Samoa
Sao Tome and Principe	100.0	82.3	98.4	57.4	-	19.9	-	-	-	-	-	-	-	17.7	Sao Tomé-et-Principe
Sierra Leone	(72.1)	(76.9)	(67.7)	(52.1)	(0.0)	(5.5)	(4.0)	(14.5)	-	(0.5)	-	(1.2)	(1.4)	(16.5)	Sierra Leone
Somalia	20.8	56.0	20.3	49.9	0.0	1.4	0.4	4.5	-	1.2	3.8	2.5	75.4	40.2	Somalie
Sudan	40.9	58.4	28.1	39.9	6.6	4.7	5.4	9.1	18.5	4.4	0.1	1.9	40.5	33.0	Soudan
Togo	71.2	77.0	57.7	63.3	0.2	5.3	8.0	6.0	3.5	0.9	0.1	2.0	16.9	18.2	Togo
Tuvalu	..	60.2	..	2.5	..	2.1	..	0.7	..	-	..	0.0	..	39.8	Tuvalu
Uganda	91.7	48.2	56.3	38.0	3.9	5.0	29.9	2.3	-	-	-	0.9	8.2	50.8	Ouganda
United Rep.of Tanzania	79.6	(60.9)	(64.5)	(35.1)	5.4	(10.9)	3.5	(5.8)	0.8	(1.2)	0.1	(1.4)	17.2	(35.9)	Rép.-Unie de Tanzanie
Vanuatu	57.3	74.8	39.5	31.2	10.8	11.7	-	-	-	-	-	1.5	8.3	12.4	Vanuatu
Yemen	23.1	56.7	22.8	31.0	-	18.5	-	4.5	-	1.5	0.4	3.6	70.1	30.4	Yémen
All LDCs	**68.8**	**60.6**	**39.2**	**33.2**	**4.5**	**9.1**	**11.5**	**7.7**	**7.8**	**5.6**	**0.9**	**2.5**	**20.1**	**26.0**	**Ensemble des PMA**
All developing countries	**61.8**	**58.3**	**19.7**	**22.2**	**12.9**	**12.9**	**23.5**	**16.4**	**4.7**	**6.9**	**2.4**	**3.2**	**30.0**	**31.6**	**Ensemble des pays en développement**

Source: UNCTAD *Handbook of International Trade and Development Statistics 1988*, and other international and national sources.

Note: X = exports.
M = imports.

Source: CNUCED, *Manuel de statistiques du commerce international et du développement 1988*, et autres sources internationales et nationales.

Note: X = exportations.
M = importations.

14. External assistance (net disbursements) , exports and imports, 1986

Country	*Technical assistance DAC* / *Assistance technique CAD*	*Concessional assistance*[a] / *Aide concessionnelle*[a] — *All sources* / *Toutes provenances*	*of which:/dont:* *DAC*[b] / *CAD*[b]	*OPEC*[c] / *OPEP*[c]	*Non-concessional assistance from all sources*[d] / *Aide non-concessionnelle de toutes provenances*[d]	*Trade balance*[e] / *Balance commerciale*[e]	*Concessional assistance from all sources as % of imports* / *Aide concessionnelle de toutes provenances en % des importations*
	In millions of dollars / En millions de dollars						
Afghanistan	13.0	268.4	6.0	-2.6	0.2	-326	31.5
Bangladesh	158.1	1504.3	1373.4	84.3	-25.7	-1059	74.7
Benin	38.4	145.7	135.2	4.3	39.2	-330	39.4
Bhutan	10.6	40.0	31.7	8.3	0.1	..	..
Botswana	43.4	105.2	105.3	-1.3	65.8	174	15.4
Burkina Faso	96.1	284.5	264.1	20.2	-0.1	-210	101.6
Burma	54.1	426.4	416.0	-0.4	-3.5	-39	140.3
Burundi	53.8	187.3	177.1	10.2	-2.7	-36	91.3
Cape Verde	24.5	108.4	105.1	0.8	2.9	-75	135.5
Central African Rep.	45.8	143.7	132.0	11.2	3.4	-121	57.0
Chad	46.0	165.6	162.9	2.7	-2.3	-105	87.2
Comoros	13.6	46.7	40.3	6.2	0.8	-15	116.7
Democratic Yemen	8.6	176.2	39.6	21.4	-17.0	-650	15.3
Djibouti	45.5	110.4	79.3	31.1	-36.1	-90	96.0
Equatorial Guinea	7.8	33.1	21.9	-0.2	9.8	-10	110.3
Ethiopia	115.5	721.1	642.6	0.0	48.3	-620	65.7
Gambia	32.5	101.1	101.8	-0.7	12.4	-65	101.1
Guinea	26.5	170.9	173.0	1.1	5.9	20	39.8
Guinea-Bissau	22.5	73.8	67.4	3.6	-0.1	-45	123.0
Haiti	51.5	175.3	173.9	1.4	-1.9	-230	43.8
Kiribati	5.0	13.4	13.4	-	0.3	7	89.3
Lao People's Dem. Rep.	17.9	133.1	46.6	1.5	0.2	-40	190.2
Lesotho	39.1	88.3	89.8	-1.7	4.3	-239	34.0
Malawi	44.8	202.9	202.8	0.1	26.2	-13	78.6
Maldives	4.4	16.4	16.0	0.4	0.8	-30	29.8
Mali	89.0	374.3	331.1	31.3	-8.0	-274	80.3
Mauritania	43.8	220.0	146.1	32.0	-11.2	128	99.6
Nepal	74.8	300.9	296.3	4.6	36.7	-317	65.6
Niger	92.0	316.3	300.2	8.8	-12.7	-110	85.5
Rwanda	66.4	212.7	203.4	9.3	6.6	-234	60.4
Samoa	8.2	24.6	23.1	1.5	-0.3	-36	51.4
Sao Tome and Principe	4.1	17.2	12.4	-	-	-10	114.7
Sierra Leone	29.6	87.2	79.6	7.5	4.9	13	66.0
Somalia	159.7	527.1	518.7	3.0	90.4	-40	421.7
Sudan	161.1	840.8	732.6	103.2	-62.2	-628	87.5
Togo	42.3	175.2	166.4	8.8	-40.2	0	87.6
Tuvalu	1.8	4.4	4.4	-	-	..	..
Uganda	49.9	198.9	194.1	3.8	1.3	70	56.8
Un. Rep. of Tanzania	163.4	685.5	675.7	5.3	-31.4	-434	87.9
Vanuatu	15.6	24.4	24.4	-	-53.0	-40	42.8
Yemen	75.7	311.8	161.8	151.9	-9.7	-1090	28.3
All LDCs	**2096.4**	**9763.8**	**8487.5**	**573.1**	**42.5**	**-7171**	**65.3**
All developing countries[f]	**8892.1**	**39075.0**	**30287.9**	**3385.7**	**20426.4**	**-21190**	**13.0**

Source: UNCTAD secretariat estimates mainly based on data from the OECD/DAC secretariat, the World Bank, and *UNCTAD Handbook of International Trade and Development Statistics 1988*.

a Including technical assistance.

b Including multilateral agencies mainly financed by DAC member countries.

c Including multilateral agencies mainly financed by OPEC member countries.

d Including private flows from DAC member countries.

e Exports (f.o.b.) *less* imports (c.i.f.).

f Excluding major petroleum exporters.

14. Aide extérieure (versements nets) , exportations et importations, 1986

Technical assistance DAC / Assistance technique CAD	Concessional assistance[a] / Aide concessionnelle[a] — All sources / Toutes provenances	of which:/dont: DAC[b] / CAD[b]	OPEC[c] / OPEP[c]	Non-concessional assistance from all sources[d] / Aide non-concessionnelle de toutes provenances[d]	Exports / Exportations (f.o.b.)	Imports / Importations (c.i.f.)	Pays
In dollars per capita / En dollars par habitant							
0.7	14.4	0.3	-0.1	0.0	28.2	45.7	Afghanistan
1.6	15.0	13.6	0.8	-0.3	9.5	20.0	Bangladesh
9.2	34.9	32.4	1.0	9.4	9.6	88.6	Bénin
7.3	27.6	21.9	5.7	0.0	..	..	Bhoutan
37.7	91.3	91.4	-1.2	57.1	744.7	593.7	Botswana
13.5	39.9	37.0	2.8	-0.0	9.8	39.2	Burkina Faso
1.4	11.3	11.0	-0.0	0.0	7.0	8.0	Birmanie
11.1	38.5	36.4	2.1	-0.6	34.7	42.1	Burundi
71.6	316.8	307.2	2.3	8.5	14.6	233.8	Cap-Vert
16.7	52.4	48.2	4.1	1.2	47.8	92.0	Rép. centrafricaine
9.0	32.2	31.7	0.5	-0.4	16.5	37.0	Tchad
28.6	98.1	84.7	13.0	1.7	52.5	84.0	Comores
3.6	74.5	16.7	9.1	-7.2	211.4	486.3	Yémen démocratique
99.8	242.1	173.9	68.2	-79.2	54.8	252.2	Djibouti
19.4	82.4	54.6	-0.4	24.5	49.8	74.7	Guineé équatoriale
2.6	16.1	14.3	0.0	1.1	10.6	24.4	Ethiopie
42.1	130.9	131.9	-1.0	16.1	45.3	129.5	Gambie
4.2	27.4	27.7	0.2	0.9	72.2	69.0	Guinée
24.8	81.2	74.1	4.0	-0.0	16.5	66.0	Guinée-Bissau
9.6	32.7	32.5	0.3	-0.4	31.7	74.7	Haïti
75.8	203.2	203.2	-	4.6	333.7	227.5	Kiribati
4.8	36.1	12.6	0.4	0.0	8.1	19.0	Rép. dém. pop. lao
24.8	56.0	56.9	-1.1	2.7	13.3	164.8	Lesotho
6.2	28.2	28.2	0.0	3.6	34.1	35.9	Malawi
23.5	87.7	85.5	2.2	4.3	133.6	293.8	Maldives
10.7	44.9	39.7	3.8	-1.0	23.0	55.9	Mali
22.5	112.8	74.9	16.4	-5.7	178.9	113.3	Mauritanie
4.4	17.6	17.3	0.3	2.1	8.3	26.8	Népal
14.6	50.1	47.5	1.4	-2.0	41.2	58.6	Niger
10.6	34.1	32.6	1.5	1.1	18.9	56.4	Rwanda
50.0	150.3	140.9	9.5	-1.8	73.2	292.7	Samoa
37.3	156.5	112.7	-	-	45.5	136.4	Sao Tomé-et-Principe
8.1	23.7	21.7	2.0	1.3	39.5	35.9	Sierra Leone
28.8	95.2	93.7	0.5	16.3	15.3	22.6	Somalie
7.3	37.8	33.0	4.6	-2.8	15.0	43.3	Soudan
13.8	57.3	54.4	2.9	-13.1	65.4	65.4	Togo
216.0	528.1	528.1	-	-	..	..	Tuvalu
3.1	12.4	12.1	0.2	0.0	26.3	21.9	Ouganda
7.1	29.7	29.3	0.2	-1.4	15.0	33.8	Rép.-Unie de Tanzanie
115.6	180.8	180.8	-	-392.7	125.9	422.3	Vanuatu
9.2	38.1	19.8	18.6	-1.2	1.2	134.4	Yémen
5.5	**25.6**	**22.3**	**1.5**	**0.1**	**20.5**	**39.4**	**Ensemble des PMA**
4.3	**18.8**	**14.6**	**1.6**	**9.8**	**134.8**	**145.0**	**Ensemble des pays en développement[f]**

Source: Estimations du secrétariat de la CNUCED principalement d'après des données du secrétariat de l'OCDE/CAD, de la Banque mondiale, et du *Manuel de statistiques du commerce international et du développement 1988*, de la CNUCED.

a Y compris l'assistance technique.

b Y compris les institutions multilatérales essentiellement financées par les pays membres du CAD.

c Y compris les institutions multilatérales essentiellement financées par les pays membres de l'OPEP.

d Y compris les apports privés en provenance des pays membres du CAD.

e Exportations (f.o.b.) *moins* importations (c.i.f.).

f Non compris les principaux pays exportateurs de pétrole.

15. Foreign exchange receipts [a] and import volume per capita

In constant 1980 dollars

Country	A. Purchasing power of exports / Pouvoir d'achat des exportations										
	1976	1977	1978	1979	1980	1981	1982	1983	1984	1985	1986
Afghanistan	35.5	33.1	29.8	36.5	42.0	45.4	47.1	48.7	41.2	35.0	31.3
Bangladesh	9.0	8.3	9.0	8.7	8.3	7.8	8.0	8.2	10.9	10.7	10.5
Benin	12.6	19.9	11.4	15.9	18.2	10.0	7.1	19.9	9.7	11.4	10.6
Bhutan	..	..	..	..	..	..	..	..	..	..	..
Botswana	377.1	338.2	359.6	571.8	549.7	440.2	499.8	691.5	715.5	759.4	828.7
Burkina Faso	16.1	14.6	10.0	14.6	14.6	12.5	9.5	9.7	13.3	11.5	10.9
Burma	10.0	10.5	9.4	13.0	14.0	14.5	11.9	11.5	9.4	9.3	7.2
Burundi	24.3	35.2	24.0	29.9	15.9	17.6	22.0	20.0	24.2	26.6	38.6
Cape Verde	11.8	16.0	9.5	7.9	13.5	10.4	14.0	10.6	10.4	16.9	16.3
Central African Rep.	44.6	56.2	42.6	38.8	49.7	35.5	49.4	34.0	38.3	37.8	50.1
Chad	24.8	40.1	32.6	23.1	15.8	19.0	13.4	17.3	31.6	17.7	17.9
Comoros	45.4	40.1	34.8	53.4	51.8	42.2	53.1	53.2	55.1	63.6	58.4
Democratic Yemen	171.2	155.0	143.6	283.2	395.6	313.6	412.1	349.7	329.0	339.9	235.2
Djibouti	261.7	232.1	90.9	43.5	61.3	29.1	37.9	32.2	36.4	36.8	61.0
Equatorial Guinea	51.9	64.9	69.1	97.3	39.8	46.6	50.1	59.6	59.1	57.7	55.4
Ethiopia	15.2	16.2	12.6	13.6	11.3	10.2	10.5	10.7	11.0	8.5	12.2
Gambia	107.7	130.2	91.2	110.3	48.9	44.3	73.1	79.5	76.9	68.0	51.2
Guinea	73.7	78.3	78.2	69.3	72.1	92.7	78.4	77.1	89.8	89.3	80.3
Guinea-Bissau	12.7	22.0	18.7	21.0	13.6	17.8	15.5	30.1	23.4	17.8	18.4
Haiti	45.4	46.7	45.9	35.4	46.0	31.8	35.0	33.6	39.1	37.3	35.3
Kiribati	..	..	..	..	46.2	68.5	37.4	59.5	191.7	78.7	371.3
Lao People's Dem.Rep.	6.5	4.9	5.2	12.6	9.5	10.4	12.7	8.4	3.8	9.1	9.0
Lesotho	23.5	17.3	34.6	39.9	43.3	38.3	26.6	14.5	16.2	15.5	14.8
Malawi	52.8	56.4	45.2	44.0	47.9	45.6	41.1	38.5	51.1	40.2	36.7
Maldives	48.7	53.9	37.5	45.8	64.0	58.6	65.4	85.1	115.9	143.1	148.6
Mali	22.6	29.6	23.4	24.6	29.2	22.4	21.2	24.2	28.1	23.6	25.4
Mauritania	206.7	161.7	109.9	108.3	118.9	165.1	148.6	195.9	189.4	232.9	202.9
Nepal	11.1	11.8	8.7	8.8	5.5	9.8	6.2	6.7	9.0	10.9	9.2
Niger	48.1	50.9	80.0	100.3	106.6	85.9	62.9	57.5	51.6	40.7	47.2
Rwanda	30.1	30.8	20.0	27.0	21.8	22.0	20.8	24.1	27.8	24.4	20.6
Samoa	77.7	151.1	98.7	134.9	109.3	73.7	89.3	133.4	135.6	104.0	81.4
Sao Tome and Principe	150.9	391.1	316.0	274.8	213.2	152.0	98.4	65.8	75.7	52.3	50.6
Sierra Leone	57.4	61.3	71.9	75.4	61.9	48.1	28.7	30.2	48.8	34.0	45.7
Somalia	37.6	22.2	32.8	28.3	28.5	34.1	45.5	23.2	10.2	19.7	16.8
Sudan	55.1	58.2	40.2	33.5	29.1	36.0	27.7	34.8	34.9	19.8	17.1
Togo	76.1	102.5	134.5	100.3	131.2	82.6	69.7	64.7	75.6	73.1	76.5
Tuvalu	..	..	..	..	..	..	..	..	..	..	..
Uganda	50.5	70.6	37.3	38.0	26.3	18.8	26.5	28.3	29.6	26.9	26.8
United Rep.of Tanzania	50.8	49.9	37.8	33.1	27.1	32.3	23.8	19.3	19.6	14.2	17.0
Vanuatu	248.6	528.6	536.3	489.3	306.0	285.5	206.4	261.4	390.9	266.8	140.1
Yemen	2.2	2.6	1.5	2.4	3.3	6.8	5.7	4.0	1.3	1.4	1.4
All LDCs	**27.3**	**28.9**	**24.7**	**26.3**	**25.8**	**24.9**	**23.8**	**24.3**	**25.5**	**23.2**	**22.8**
All developing countries [b]	**117.1**	**123.2**	**123.9**	**126.6**	**126.7**	**133.5**	**128.4**	**137.0**	**151.8**	**146.6**	**157.1**

For sources and notes, see end of table.

Pour les sources et les notes, se reporter à la fin du tableau.

15. Rentrées de devises [a] et volume des importations par habitant

En dollars constants de 1980

B. External assistance [c] / Aide extérieure [c]											
1976	*1977*	*1978*	*1979*	*1980*	*1981*	*1982*	*1983*	*1984*	*1985*	*1986*	*Pays*
14.2	13.3	12.6	12.4	21.0	19.0	11.9	24.2	15.3	14.6	16.0	Afghanistan
11.9	12.1	16.7	16.0	14.1	12.8	16.8	14.5	15.2	12.9	16.3	Bangladesh
29.4	31.6	32.6	34.4	113.5	35.1	58.3	33.1	50.4	49.9	48.9	Bénin
4.6	3.7	3.6	5.4	6.5	7.9	9.2	10.6	14.6	19.3	30.8	Bhoutan
115.9	75.0	34.6	184.1	58.4	121.8	129.6	141.4	193.4	165.4	165.1	Botswana
26.0	30.4	37.8	41.8	38.1	37.1	42.8	33.4	30.1	33.6	44.2	Burkina faso
3.9	5.2	14.5	17.8	12.5	10.7	14.1	10.0	10.2	10.9	11.5	Birmanie
20.6	24.3	26.3	29.9	32.9	34.3	40.3	46.4	37.8	37.8	42.2	Burundi
150.9	142.8	167.5	135.6	211.4	180.8	227.1	241.8	242.0	252.3	362.0	Cap-Vert
31.5	29.7	30.3	42.2	55.0	46.8	46.4	45.9	51.6	50.3	56.2	Rép. centrafricaine
26.8	33.5	45.6	22.2	7.5	12.3	13.8	22.0	25.8	40.4	34.4	Tchad
129.3	144.9	49.4	54.3	111.0	132.8	97.9	114.7	113.6	129.4	111.0	Comores
213.0	117.9	75.6	68.5	129.9	77.4	118.4	96.1	96.3	172.8	74.9	Yémen démocratique
206.4	334.2	482.2	86.6	229.5	212.6	171.6	200.5	404.5	261.3	181.3	Djibouti
-7.3	-13.4	5.4	6.4	28.4	33.8	36.3	36.2	52.8	59.9	119.0	Guinée équatoriale
7.5	5.5	5.9	8.0	7.2	9.1	9.6	11.1	15.4	23.0	19.6	Ethiopie
34.8	72.8	91.2	87.5	136.3	140.5	76.2	62.8	96.2	91.6	166.0	Gambie
7.1	13.9	24.8	15.2	28.4	23.5	15.7	15.9	26.0	26.2	31.6	Guinée
73.9	89.0	102.3	86.7	111.3	93.0	82.9	87.8	89.6	86.0	90.3	Guinée-Bissau
26.5	28.7	26.8	30.2	24.0	23.9	28.0	27.5	29.5	31.1	36.0	Haïti
126.7	175.7	260.4	184.4	327.7	405.4	270.9	301.1	204.9	209.8	231.2	Kiribati
27.4	28.9	44.2	34.0	26.8	28.9	42.4	40.3	33.4	48.6	40.2	Rép. dém. pop. lao
41.8	48.9	57.4	56.9	70.4	81.4	74.1	83.9	74.6	88.7	65.3	Lesotho
25.1	32.2	29.8	41.3	31.6	32.4	22.4	17.7	31.1	18.7	34.4	Malawi
66.9	54.9	91.9	51.9	146.1	112.9	12.8	62.2	47.3	63.8	102.3	Maldives
24.9	29.9	38.2	37.2	38.3	36.6	31.0	32.7	48.4	54.3	48.5	Mali
240.8	128.0	188.0	124.8	89.8	132.0	137.2	144.4	136.4	134.1	121.4	Mauritanie
6.3	13.1	7.7	11.3	11.0	12.6	14.3	14.1	14.1	16.8	21.9	Népal
59.9	44.2	62.2	59.5	47.4	70.1	55.5	40.3	27.1	55.1	55.1	Niger
32.4	32.3	35.9	37.0	30.3	30.8	31.0	32.7	31.3	34.7	38.3	Rwanda
129.9	245.8	209.0	250.2	160.4	165.8	163.3	222.4	100.4	142.7	165.2	Samoa
220.7	76.0	134.5	37.5	41.6	66.2	107.9	137.8	133.8	134.4	174.1	Sao Tomé-et-Principe
21.6	22.7	23.8	22.9	28.1	21.0	29.7	22.4	26.6	23.0	29.0	Sierra leone
50.1	146.2	73.0	65.8	113.5	83.5	141.6	71.9	93.5	82.5	122.3	Somalie
40.2	35.3	37.0	40.8	44.8	38.3	44.0	64.4	43.4	56.0	40.0	Soudan
51.6	77.7	150.3	97.5	70.8	19.7	37.8	44.2	46.2	37.6	51.7	Togo
696.2	504.7	532.2	627.8	634.9	712.3	793.0	574.9	755.5	466.9	587.6	Tuvalu
6.5	4.0	-14.7	3.4	10.4	11.9	13.1	11.4	12.3	15.9	12.8	Ouganda
35.7	40.0	40.9	47.6	44.7	44.3	39.2	30.9	31.5	28.3	32.1	Rép.-Unie de Tanzanie
681.1	243.7	302.6	449.7	369.9	263.2	289.0	311.9	403.4	332.2	-235.8	Vanuatu
71.2	86.3	66.6	59.3	77.9	61.8	75.0	70.7	49.9	42.0	41.1	Yémen
21.8	**23.1**	**25.0**	**25.7**	**26.9**	**24.5**	**27.1**	**26.0**	**26.1**	**27.9**	**28.7**	**Ensemble des PMA**
43.5	**38.0**	**46.6**	**44.0**	**37.7**	**42.4**	**38.9**	**33.6**	**33.1**	**24.9**	**33.4**	**Ensemble des pays en développement [b]**

For sources and notes, see end of table.

Pour les sources et les notes, se reporter à la fin du tableau.

15. Foreign exchange receipts [a] and import volume per capita

In constant 1980 dollars

Country	C. Foreign exchange receipts [a] / Total des rentrées de devises [a]										
	1976	*1977*	*1978*	*1979*	*1980*	*1981*	*1982*	*1983*	*1984*	*1985*	*1986*
Afghanistan	49.7	46.4	42.4	48.9	63.0	64.4	58.9	72.9	56.5	49.7	47.2
Bangladesh	20.8	20.4	25.7	24.7	22.5	20.6	24.7	22.7	26.1	23.6	26.9
Benin	42.0	51.5	43.9	50.3	131.7	45.1	65.4	53.0	60.1	61.2	59.5
Bhutan	..	..	..	..	..	..	..	..	..	..	..
Botswana	493.0	413.2	394.2	755.9	608.1	562.0	629.4	832.8	908.9	924.8	993.8
Burkina Faso	42.2	45.1	47.9	56.4	52.7	49.6	52.2	43.2	43.4	45.1	55.1
Burma	14.0	15.7	24.0	30.7	26.4	25.2	26.0	21.4	19.6	20.2	18.7
Burundi	44.9	59.5	50.4	59.8	48.7	51.9	62.2	66.5	62.0	64.4	80.9
Cape Verde	162.7	158.8	177.0	143.5	224.9	191.2	241.1	252.4	252.4	269.2	378.2
Central African Rep.	76.1	85.9	72.9	80.9	104.7	82.3	95.8	79.9	89.9	88.1	106.3
Chad	51.6	73.6	78.2	45.3	23.3	31.3	27.2	39.2	57.4	58.1	52.3
Comoros	174.7	185.1	84.1	107.7	162.8	175.1	151.0	167.9	168.7	193.0	169.5
Democratic Yemen	384.3	272.9	219.2	351.7	525.5	391.0	530.5	445.8	425.3	512.6	310.2
Djibouti	468.1	566.3	573.1	130.0	290.7	241.7	209.5	232.7	440.9	298.1	242.3
Equatorial Guinea	44.6	51.5	74.5	103.7	68.2	80.4	86.4	95.8	111.9	117.6	174.4
Ethiopia	22.6	21.7	18.4	21.6	18.4	19.3	20.2	21.8	26.3	31.5	31.8
Gambia	142.5	203.0	182.4	197.7	185.2	184.8	149.3	142.3	173.1	159.6	217.1
Guinea	80.9	92.1	103.0	84.5	100.6	116.3	94.1	93.0	115.8	115.5	111.9
Guinea-Bissau	86.6	111.0	121.0	107.6	124.9	110.7	98.3	117.8	113.0	103.8	108.6
Haiti	71.9	75.5	72.7	65.6	70.0	55.7	63.0	61.2	68.6	68.3	71.3
Kiribati	..	..	..	..	373.8	474.0	308.3	360.6	396.6	288.5	602.5
Lao People's Dem.Rep.	33.9	33.8	49.4	46.5	36.3	39.3	55.2	48.7	37.2	57.6	49.2
Lesotho	65.3	66.2	92.0	96.8	113.7	119.7	100.8	98.4	90.8	104.2	80.1
Malawi	77.9	88.6	75.0	85.3	79.5	78.1	63.6	56.2	82.1	58.9	71.1
Maldives	115.6	108.8	129.3	97.7	210.0	171.5	78.2	147.3	163.2	206.8	250.9
Mali	47.6	59.5	61.6	61.8	67.5	59.0	52.2	57.0	76.5	77.9	73.9
Mauritania	447.5	289.7	297.9	233.1	208.7	297.1	285.9	340.3	325.8	367.0	324.3
Nepal	17.5	24.9	16.3	20.2	16.5	22.4	20.5	20.7	23.1	27.7	31.2
Niger	108.0	95.1	142.2	159.8	154.0	156.1	118.4	97.8	78.7	95.8	102.3
Rwanda	62.5	63.1	55.9	64.0	52.1	52.8	51.8	56.8	59.1	59.1	58.8
Samoa	207.7	397.0	307.7	385.1	269.8	239.5	252.6	355.8	236.0	246.7	246.6
Sao Tome and Principe	371.6	467.1	450.6	312.3	254.8	218.2	206.4	203.6	209.5	186.8	224.7
Sierra Leone	79.0	84.0	95.6	98.3	90.0	69.1	58.4	52.6	75.4	57.0	74.7
Somalia	87.7	168.4	105.8	94.1	142.0	117.6	187.1	95.1	103.8	102.2	139.2
Sudan	95.3	93.6	77.2	74.3	73.9	74.3	71.6	99.3	78.3	75.8	57.2
Togo	127.7	180.2	284.8	197.7	202.0	102.3	107.6	108.9	121.8	110.7	128.1
Tuvalu	..	..	..	..	..	..	..	..	..	..	..
Uganda	57.0	74.6	22.6	41.4	36.7	30.8	39.6	39.7	41.9	42.7	39.5
United Rep.of Tanzania	86.5	89.9	78.7	80.7	71.8	76.5	62.9	50.2	51.2	42.5	49.1
Vanuatu	929.7	772.3	839.0	938.9	675.9	548.6	495.5	573.2	794.3	599.0	-95.6
Yemen	73.4	88.9	68.0	61.6	81.2	68.6	80.7	74.7	51.3	43.5	42.4
All LDCs	**49.0**	**51.9**	**49.6**	**52.0**	**52.6**	**49.3**	**50.9**	**50.1**	**51.4**	**51.0**	**51.4**
All developing countries [b]	**160.5**	**161.2**	**170.5**	**170.5**	**164.5**	**175.9**	**167.4**	**170.6**	**184.8**	**171.5**	**190.5**

For sources and notes, see end of table.

Pour les sources et les notes, se reporter à la fin du tableau.

15. Rentrées de devises [a] et volume des importations par habitant

En dollars constants de 1980

D. Import volume / Volume des importations											
1976	*1977*	*1978*	*1979*	*1980*	*1981*	*1982*	*1983*	*1984*	*1985*	*1986*	*Pays*
39.8	52.5	54.7	50.6	34.6	40.7	46.2	35.1	75.3	62.8	50.7	Afghanistan
16.4	21.9	22.0	20.8	22.2	21.2	20.7	18.9	23.9	25.0	22.2	Bangladesh
119.8	119.5	131.4	110.4	95.6	160.8	137.3	87.3	91.2	113.7	97.9	Bénin
..	..	..	..	..	..	..	..	..	..	..	Bhoutan
447.8	518.6	571.8	683.3	755.2	879.3	752.4	800.2	750.5	595.1	660.6	Botswana
43.0	55.6	52.3	57.3	58.1	56.5	58.4	49.1	34.9	54.5	43.5	Burkina faso
10.1	14.4	13.2	10.8	10.5	11.3	12.4	8.2	7.3	8.4	8.3	Birmanie
28.7	29.3	34.1	43.7	41.0	40.0	53.4	45.8	45.9	44.5	46.9	Burundi
176.9	235.1	203.7	162.1	230.0	245.8	251.6	278.1	247.2	274.0	260.2	Cap-Vert
41.5	43.9	32.6	34.4	35.0	42.7	57.5	38.6	38.7	46.9	96.4	Rép. centrafricaine
49.6	70.8	71.5	22.3	16.4	24.7	25.1	27.3	37.1	42.0	40.0	Tchad
65.6	80.3	73.4	87.9	85.5	89.8	84.9	85.1	78.7	76.3	93.5	Comores
398.6	465.9	427.8	238.3	331.1	733.1	828.8	769.6	787.0	635.4	541.1	Yémen démocratique
828.6	641.2	474.7	411.1	403.2	388.4	335.4	336.2	308.2	289.1	280.6	Djibouti
20.8	46.4	36.6	63.8	73.9	90.3	123.8	89.3	88.7	86.5	83.2	Guinée équatoriale
18.5	18.2	21.2	18.5	19.1	19.3	20.5	23.2	24.8	25.4	28.0	Ethiopie
227.8	211.7	233.9	268.0	257.1	200.2	161.2	190.5	160.4	147.1	146.3	Gambie
43.8	50.7	62.2	55.3	49.9	60.6	59.3	57.8	68.8	78.1	76.7	Guinée
94.0	68.2	78.7	91.4	68.0	63.6	64.5	71.9	62.4	76.3	73.4	Guinée-Bissau
75.2	68.0	63.8	63.6	72.1	94.3	83.1	96.1	103.0	94.7	83.1	Haïti
374.6	363.1	343.3	302.9	290.6	246.0	249.5	252.4	250.8	227.3	253.2	Kiribati
22.8	28.9	32.9	33.7	40.0	39.3	41.4	29.7	15.4	20.3	21.1	Rép. dém. pop. lao
286.6	283.3	295.2	319.2	346.5	404.2	401.2	448.7	240.9	184.9	183.4	Lesotho
65.6	65.7	82.5	78.5	73.9	59.2	52.0	52.3	44.5	45.6	38.7	Malawi
36.5	43.1	112.4	152.7	185.5	201.8	281.0	373.2	341.2	329.7	327.0	Maldives
40.0	37.7	59.7	60.1	62.7	55.9	48.2	50.7	54.0	57.0	61.7	Mali
209.1	214.2	161.8	190.9	175.4	167.6	174.9	145.8	156.9	145.7	128.5	Mauritanie
27.1	27.5	21.8	20.5	23.3	25.8	27.8	32.9	29.1	30.8	29.8	Népal
45.6	62.3	86.5	103.5	111.8	96.3	88.3	62.3	53.7	73.1	67.1	Niger
38.3	37.3	51.2	44.0	47.2	51.3	55.6	53.5	56.9	54.8	61.4	Rwanda
333.2	413.1	475.5	546.9	405.1	375.4	343.5	393.2	356.9	353.5	325.7	Samoa
169.8	238.1	331.1	249.9	202.6	184.6	164.0	109.7	129.7	136.0	151.7	Sao Tomé-et-Principe
87.2	91.7	116.1	108.7	125.6	98.0	77.3	54.5	54.8	50.5	41.6	Sierra leone
61.7	80.2	73.8	62.1	74.5	115.0	75.5	40.6	23.3	24.3	24.8	Somalie
97.5	95.2	90.2	69.5	84.4	86.4	71.2	75.6	63.7	40.9	49.4	Soudan
134.8	183.0	251.2	238.3	215.3	169.5	154.1	113.5	107.3	110.8	76.5	Togo
..	..	..	..	..	..	..	..	..	..	..	Tuvalu
23.9	23.7	27.2	17.2	22.4	26.8	28.8	28.6	25.5	23.1	22.3	Ouganda
66.9	68.7	90.6	69.8	65.4	63.8	59.1	43.3	46.2	51.7	38.3	Rép.-Unie de Tanzanie
497.2	763.5	791.7	759.9	620.8	517.4	529.6	567.8	613.1	611.0	469.9	Vanuatu
110.5	248.5	266.6	252.9	263.2	255.6	223.2	235.5	225.0	183.1	149.5	Yémen
43.0	**50.7**	**54.4**	**48.8**	**50.5**	**54.4**	**52.1**	**48.4**	**49.5**	**47.0**	**43.8**	**Ensemble des PMA**
145.2	**152.5**	**157.3**	**159.3**	**168.8**	**178.9**	**166.3**	**165.5**	**170.2**	**160.9**	**169.0**	**Ensemble des pays en développement [b]**

Source: UNCTAD secretariat estimates mainly based on *UNCTAD Handbook of International Trade and Development Statistics 1988.*

Note: The deflators used to express exports, external assistance and total foreign exchange receipts in all years in terms of their command over imports at 1980 prices are shown in table 8.

a Purchasing power of exports *plus* external assistance.

b Excluding major petroleum exporters.

c Total financial flows as in table 17C.

Source: Estimations du secrétariat de la CNUCED d'après le *Manuel de statistiques du commerce international et du développement 1988*, de la CNUCED.

Note: Les déflateurs utilisés pour exprimer les recettes d'exportations, les rentrées au titre de l'aide extérieure et le total des rentrées de devises pour toutes les années en pouvoir d'achat à l'importation au prix de 1980 figurent au tableau 8.

a Pouvoir d'achat des exportations *plus* aide extérieure.

b Non compris les principaux pays exportateurs de pétrole.

c Total des apports financiers comme au tableau 17C.

16. GDP growth and net external receipts of LDCs, average 1980-1986 / **16. Croissance du PIB et recettes extérieures nettes des PMA, moyenne 1980-1986**

LDCs classified according to population size	GDP annual growth / PIB croissance annuelle (%)	Net financial flows in $ per capita / Apports financiers nets en dollars par habitant: Total	ODA / APD	% shares in total flows / Parts en % dans le total des apports: ODA / APD	Other official flows / Autres apports publics	Private flows / Apports privés	Ratios / Rapports (%): ODA/GDP / APD/PIB	ODA/Domestic investment / APD/ Investissement intérieur	PMA classés d'après la taille de la population
Large [a]									***Grands*** [a]
Burma	5.0	10.7	9.6	89.3	0.2	10.3	5.3	29.1	Birmanie
Bangladesh	3.7	13.4	13.3	99.7	0.5	0.6	9.0	66.1	Bangladesh
Nepal	3.5	13.8	13.4	97.1	0.3	2.1	9.2	47.2	Népal
Afghanistan	2.0	15.8	15.8	100.5	-1.2	0.7	6.9	..	Afghanistan
Uganda	1.3	11.8	10.5	88.8	11.7	-0.4	4.9	(29.3)	Ouganda
United Rep.of Tanzania	1.3	33.2	30.2	90.9	3.9	5.9	11.2	62.8	Rép.-Unie de Tanzanie
Ethiopia	-0.3	12.7	11.9	93.7	0.9	5.3	10.5	96.3	Ethiopie
Sudan	-0.4	42.5	39.9	93.9	7.9	-1.7	9.3	56.5	Soudan
Medium [b]									***Moyens*** [b]
Botswana	12.5	128.5	99.1	77.1	26.7	-3.8	10.2	30.8	Botswana
Bhutan	6.3	13.1	13.0	99.9	-	0.1	10.5	..	Bhoutan
Lao People's Dem.Rep.	5.4	34.1	33.0	96.7	-	3.3	19.5	..	Rép. dém. pop. lao
Yemen	4.4	54.6	48.6	89.0	1.9	9.1	10.3	34.9	Yémen
Benin	3.3	50.7	25.7	50.7	0.9	48.5	9.0	53.8	Bénin
Somalia	3.1	91.4	81.8	89.5	3.1	7.4	16.5	(112.6)	Somalie
Burundi	2.7	35.6	31.9	89.6	3.1	7.2	13.6	81.2	Burundi
Malawi	2.4	25.2	21.6	86.0	8.1	6.1	11.7	63.8	Malawi
Mauritania	2.0	114.5	105.1	91.8	7.7	0.9	25.2	82.1	Mauritanie
Rwanda	1.8	30.1	29.6	98.1	0.1	1.7	11.3	67.9	Rwanda
Lesotho	1.7	70.5	67.2	95.4	4.1	0.5	30.6	90.6	Lesotho
Burkina Faso	1.7	33.9	32.3	95.4	3.2	1.4	20.6	233.5	Burkina faso
Central African Republic	1.5	46.6	43.8	94.0	3.6	3.1	14.0	178.7	Rép. centrafricaine
Mali	1.4	38.2	38.2	100.0	-0.1	0.4	22.9	121.8	Mali
Sierra Leone	1.1	23.1	22.2	95.8	4.1	1.5	6.5	52.2	Sierra leone
Guinea	0.8	22.0	19.3	87.8	1.4	11.1	6.0	48.2	Guinée
Democratic Yemen	-0.2	100.3	92.3	92.0	-0.4	9.6	23.9	..	Yémen démocratique
Haiti	-0.6	26.2	26.1	99.4	-0.7	2.0	7.7	51.2	Haïti
Togo	-0.9	40.2	37.8	94.1	25.1	-19.2	12.3	46.5	Togo
Niger	-2.2	46.2	39.3	85.2	8.6	6.2	11.9	66.3	Niger
Chad	-3.2	20.8	21.2	102.1	0.1	-2.0	13.6	163.1	Tchad
Small [c]									***Petits*** [c]
Maldives	9.9	72.1	72.0	99.8	4.0	-3.8	18.5	(45.2)	Maldives
Cape Verde	6.5	226.0	218.6	96.7	2.8	0.5	64.9	(112.4)	Cap-Vert
Comoros	4.0	106.1	101.6	95.8	3.3	1.0	34.5	116.3	Comores
Guinea-Bissau	3.9	84.1	78.8	93.7	5.3	1.0	37.9	134.4	Guinée-Bissau
Equatorial Guinea	2.5	48.5	44.2	91.2	8.6	0.1	20.7	123.9	Guinée équatoriale
Vanuatu	2.2	222.7	227.4	102.1	-17.5	15.4	47.9	..	Vanuatu
Djibouti	2.0	217.3	210.5	96.9	-0.1	3.2	40.3	172.6	Djibouti
Gambia	1.1	99.0	85.8	86.7	5.9	7.4	29.6	133.6	Gambie
Kiribati	0.9	255.8	238.7	93.3	7.1	-0.4	79.6	..	Kiribati
Samoa	0.3	147.2	149.8	101.8	-0.3	-1.3	24.0	80.2	Samoa
Sao Tome and Principe	-1.5	104.8	104.8	100.0	-	-	30.6	(68.4)	Sao Tomé-et-Principe
Tuvalu	..	593.8	599.1	100.9	-	-0.9	206.8	..	Tuvalu
ALL LDCs	**2.2**	**24.6**	**22.8**	**92.8**	**3.4**	**4.0**	**10.6**	**61.5**	**Ensemble des PMA**

Source: UNCTAD secretariat calculations based on data from the OECD secretariat, the World Bank, the Economic Commission for Africa, and other international and national sources.
a More than 10 million. ***b*** Between 1 and 10 million. ***c*** Less than 1 million.

Source: Chiffres calculés par le secrétariat de la CNUCED d'après des données du secrétariat de l'OCDE, de la Banque mondiale, de la Commission économique pour l'Afrique, et d'autres sources internationales et nationales.
a Plus de 10 millions. ***b*** Entre 1 et 10 millions. ***c*** Moins de 1 million.

17A. Composition of total financial flows to all LDCS in current dollars

17A. Composition des courants financiers à l'ensemble des PMA en dollars courants

Net disbursements in $ million / *Versements nets en millions de dollars*

	1976	1977	1978	1979	1980	1981	1982	1983	1984	1985	1986	
Concessional loans & grants	3406	4026	5211	6144	7517	7184	7679	7661	7727	8767	9764	Prêts concessionnels et dons
of which:												*dont:*
DAC	2439	2765	4131	5038	5816	5643	5863	5721	6205	7352	8487	CAD
- Bilateral	1504	1723	2537	3195	3722	3536	3767	3499	3627	4463	5278	- Apports bilatéraux
- Multilateral [a]	936	1042	1595	1843	2094	2107	2095	2222	2578	2889	3209	- Apports multilatéraux [a]
- Grants	1591	1807	3001	3637	4978	4344	4234	4120	4331	5441	6048	- Dons
- Loans	848	958	1131	1402	838	1299	1628	1601	1874	1911	2439	- Prêts
- Technical assistance	675	686	931	1196	1526	1608	1581	1614	1581	1818	2096	- Assistance technique
- Other	1764	2080	3201	3843	4290	4035	4282	4107	4625	5534	6391	- Autres
OPEC	755	1022	872	859	1095	963	1153	1027	803	562	573	OPEP
- Bilateral	656	903	759	760	955	742	963	863	698	480	480	- Apports bilatéraux
- Multilateral [b]	99	120	113	99	140	221	190	164	105	82	94	- Apports multilatéraux [b]
- Grants	396	742	386	243	440	257	574	633	481	332	316	- Dons
- Loans	359	280	486	616	655	706	579	394	321	230	257	- Prêts
Non-concessional flows	422	536	437	938	1275	656	928	525	579	387	42	Courants financiers non-concessionnels
of which:												*dont:*
DAC	374	533	478	912	1225	624	1005	483	559	409	98	CAD
- Bilateral official	37	32	18	124	233	162	188	216	270	141	132	- Apports publics bilatéraux
- Multilateral [a]	21	42	69	91	89	88	103	116	65	147	-5	- Apports multilatéraux [a]
- Export credits [c]	249	348	319	499	990	231	275	102	138	126	-72	- Crédits à l'exportation [c]
- Direct investment	45	117	50	34	52	102	168	30	66	31	26	- Investissements directs
- Other [d e]	22	-6	22	162	-140	42	271	20	20	-35	16	- Autres [d e]
Total financial flows	**3828**	**4562**	**5648**	**7082**	**8793**	**7840**	**8607**	**8185**	**8307**	**9154**	**9806**	**Total des apports financiers**

Source: UNCTAD secretariat calculations mainly based on OECD/DAC and UNCTAD data.

a From multilateral agencies mainly financed by DAC member countries.

b From multilateral agencies mainly financed by OPEC member countries.

c Guaranteed private.

d Bilateral financial flows originating in DAC countries and their capital markets in the form of bond lending and bank lending (either directly or through syndicated "Eurocurrency credits").

e Only flows allocated by individual recipient country.

Source: Chiffres calculés par le secrétariat de la CNUCED d'après des données de l'OCDE/CAD et de la CNUCED.

a En provenance des institutions multilatérales essentiellement financées par les pays membres du CAD.

b En provenance des institutions multilatérales essentiellement financées par les pays membres de l'OPEP.

c Privés garantis.

d Apports financiers bilatéraux provenant des pays membres du CAD ou passant par leurs marchés de capitaux, sous forme d'émissions d'obligations et de prêts bancaires (soit directement, soit comme crédits consortiaux en euromonnaies).

e Uniquement les apports alloués par pays bénéficiaires.

17B. Composition of total financial flows to all LDCS in constant dollars

17B. Composition des courants financiers à l'ensemble des PMA en dollars constants

Net disbursements in millions of 1980 dollars — *Versements nets en millions de dollars de 1980*

	1976	1977	1978	1979	1980	1981	1982	1983	1984	1985	1986	
Concessional loans & grants	5744	6196	7184	7116	7517	7534	8330	8579	8769	9906	10864	Prêts concessionnels et dons
of which:												*dont:*
DAC	4114	4256	5695	5835	5816	5919	6360	6407	7042	8307	9444	CAD
- Bilateral	2535	2652	3497	3700	3722	3709	4087	3919	4116	5043	5873	- Apports bilatéraux
- Multilateral [a]	1578	1604	2198	2135	2094	2210	2273	2488	2926	3264	3571	- Apports multilatéraux [a]
- Grants	2683	2781	4137	4212	4978	4556	4593	4614	4915	6148	6730	- Dons
- Loans	1431	1475	1559	1623	838	1362	1767	1793	2127	2159	2714	- Prêts
- Technical assistance	1139	1055	1283	1385	1526	1686	1715	1808	1794	2054	2333	- Assistance technique
- Other	2975	3200	4412	4450	4290	4232	4645	4599	5248	6253	7111	- Autres
OPEC	1273	1573	1202	995	1095	1010	1250	1150	911	635	638	OPEP
- Bilateral	1106	1389	1047	881	955	778	1045	966	792	542	534	- Apports bilatéraux
- Multilateral [b]	167	184	155	115	140	231	206	184	119	93	104	- Apports multilatéraux [b]
- Grants	668	1142	532	281	440	269	622	709	546	375	351	- Dons
- Loans	606	432	670	714	655	740	628	442	364	260	286	- Prêts
Non-concessional flows	712	825	603	1086	1275	688	1007	588	657	437	47	Courants financiers non-concessionnels
of which:												*dont:*
DAC	631	820	660	1056	1225	655	1090	541	635	462	108	CAD
- Bilateral official	62	49	24	144	233	170	204	242	307	159	147	- Apports publics bilatéraux
- Multilateral [a]	36	65	96	106	89	92	112	130	74	166	-5	- Apports multilatéraux [a]
- Export credits [c]	421	535	439	578	990	242	298	114	156	142	-80	- Crédits à l'exportation [c]
- Direct investment	76	180	69	40	52	107	182	33	75	34	29	- Investissements directs
- Other [d e]	37	-10	31	188	-140	44	294	22	23	-40	18	- Autres [d e]
Total financial flows	**6456**	**7021**	**7787**	**8202**	**8793**	**8222**	**9337**	**9166**	**9426**	**10344**	**10912**	**Total des apports financiers**

For sources and notes, see table 17A.

Pour les sources et les notes, se reporter au tableau 17A.

17C. Composition of total financial flows to all LDCS in constant dollars per capita

17C. Composition des courants financiers à l'ensemble des PMA en dollars constants par habitant

Net disbursements in 1980 dollars — *Versements nets en dollars de 1980*

	1976	1977	1978	1979	1980	1981	1982	1983	1984	1985	1986	
Concessional loans & grants	19.4	20.4	23.1	22.3	23.0	22.5	24.2	24.3	24.2	26.7	28.5	Prêts concessionnels et dons
of which:												*dont:*
DAC	13.9	14.0	18.3	18.3	17.8	17.7	18.5	18.2	19.5	22.4	24.8	CAD
- Bilateral	8.6	8.7	11.2	11.6	11.4	11.1	11.9	11.1	11.4	13.6	15.4	- Apports bilatéraux
- Multilateral [a]	5.3	5.3	7.1	6.7	6.4	6.6	6.6	7.1	8.1	8.8	9.4	- Apports multilatéraux [a]
- Grants	9.1	9.2	13.3	13.2	15.2	13.6	13.4	13.1	13.6	16.6	17.7	- Dons
- Loans	4.8	4.9	5.0	5.1	2.6	4.1	5.1	5.1	5.9	5.8	7.1	- Prêts
- Technical assistance	3.8	3.5	4.1	4.3	4.7	5.0	5.0	5.1	5.0	5.5	6.1	- Assistance technique
- Other	10.1	10.5	14.2	14.0	13.1	12.6	13.5	13.0	14.5	16.9	18.7	- Autres
OPEC	4.3	5.2	3.9	3.1	3.3	3.0	3.6	3.3	2.5	1.7	1.7	OPEP
- Bilateral	3.7	4.6	3.4	2.8	2.9	2.3	3.0	2.7	2.2	1.5	1.4	- Apports bilatéraux
- Multilateral [b]	0.6	0.6	0.5	0.4	0.4	0.7	0.6	0.5	0.3	0.2	0.3	- Apports multilatéraux [b]
- Grants	2.3	3.8	1.7	0.9	1.3	0.8	1.8	2.0	1.5	1.0	0.9	- Dons
- Loans	2.0	1.4	2.2	2.2	2.0	2.2	1.8	1.3	1.0	0.7	0.8	- Prêts
Non-concessional flows	2.4	2.7	1.9	3.4	3.9	2.1	2.9	1.7	1.8	1.2	0.1	Courants financiers non-concessionnels
of which:												*dont:*
DAC	2.1	2.7	2.1	3.3	3.7	2.0	3.2	1.5	1.8	1.2	0.3	CAD
- Bilateral official	0.2	0.2	0.1	0.5	0.7	0.5	0.6	0.7	0.8	0.4	0.4	- Apports publics bilatéraux
- Multilateral [a]	0.1	0.2	0.3	0.3	0.3	0.3	0.3	0.4	0.2	0.4	-	- Apports multilatéraux [a]
- Export credits [c]	1.4	1.8	1.4	1.8	3.0	0.7	0.9	0.3	0.4	0.4	-0.2	- Crédits à l'exportation [c]
- Direct investment	0.3	0.6	0.2	0.1	0.2	0.3	0.5	0.1	0.2	0.1	0.1	- Investissements directs
- Other [d e]	0.1	-	0.1	0.6	-0.4	0.1	0.9	0.1	0.1	-0.1	-	- Autres [d e]
Total financial flows	**21.8**	**23.1**	**25.0**	**25.7**	**26.9**	**24.5**	**27.1**	**26.0**	**26.1**	**27.9**	**28.7**	**Total des apports financiers**

For sources and notes, see table 17A.

Pour les sources et les notes, se reporter au tableau 17A.

18. Percentage distribution of financial flows to all LDCs and to all developing countries, by type of flow

18. Répartition en pourcentage des apports financiers à l'ensemble des PMA et à l'ensemble des pays en développement, par catégories d'apports

In per cent — *En pourcentage*

	Least developed countries Pays les moins avancés							*All developing countries Ensemble des pays en développement*							
	1980	1981	1982	1983	1984	1985	1986	1980	1981	1982	1983	1984	1985	1986	
Concessional loans & grants *of which:*	85.5	91.6	89.2	93.6	93.0	95.8	99.6	45.8	38.1	39.7	45.9	40.1	73.8	60.6	Prêts concessionnels et dons *dont:*
DAC	66.1	72.0	68.1	69.9	74.7	80.3	86.6	30.0	25.3	28.1	33.0	30.4	57.3	46.5	CAD
- Bilateral	42.3	45.1	43.8	42.8	43.7	48.8	53.8	20.9	18.0	19.9	23.2	21.5	40.6	33.8	- Apports bilatéraux
- Multilateral [a]	23.8	26.9	24.3	27.1	31.0	31.6	32.7	9.1	7.3	8.2	9.8	8.9	16.8	12.7	- Apports multilatéraux [a]
- Grants	56.6	55.4	49.2	50.3	52.1	59.4	61.7	20.5	16.9	18.7	22.7	21.6	42.0	33.4	- Dons
- Loans	9.5	16.6	18.9	19.6	22.6	20.9	24.9	9.6	8.4	9.4	10.3	8.8	15.3	13.1	- Prêts
- Technical assistance	17.4	20.5	18.4	19.7	19.0	19.9	21.4	9.0	7.8	8.6	10.7	9.4	17.3	13.8	- Assistance technique
- Other	48.8	51.5	49.7	50.2	55.7	60.5	65.2	21.1	17.6	19.5	22.3	21.0	40.0	32.6	- Autres
OPEC	12.5	12.3	13.4	12.6	9.7	6.1	5.8	11.3	8.6	6.8	7.2	4.8	7.0	6.1	OPEP
- Bilateral	10.9	9.5	11.2	10.5	8.4	5.2	4.9	11.0	8.2	6.5	6.8	4.6	6.6	6.0	- Apports bilatéraux
- Multilateral [b]	1.6	2.8	2.2	2.0	1.3	0.9	1.0	0.3	0.4	0.4	0.4	0.2	0.3	0.2	- Apports multilatéraux [b]
- Grants	5.0	3.3	6.7	7.7	5.8	3.6	3.2	5.0	3.6	3.5	3.4	4.1	5.4	5.4	- Dons
- Loans	7.4	9.0	6.7	4.8	3.9	2.5	2.6	6.4	5.0	3.3	3.8	0.7	1.5	0.7	- Prêts
Non-concessional flows	14.5	8.4	10.8	6.4	7.0	4.2	0.4	54.2	61.9	60.3	54.1	59.9	26.2	39.4	Courants financiers non-concessionnels
of which:															*dont:*
DAC	13.9	8.0	11.7	5.9	6.7	4.5	1.0	54.6	62.2	60.6	54.0	59.0	25.3	39.5	CAD
- Bilateral official	2.6	2.1	2.2	2.6	3.3	1.5	1.3	5.5	4.3	6.3	4.8	6.4	8.2	4.0	- Apports publics bilatéraux
- Multilateral [a]	1.0	1.1	1.2	1.4	0.8	1.6	-	5.7	5.7	7.5	9.8	9.6	15.0	11.0	- Apports multilatéraux [a]
- Export credits [c]	11.3	2.9	3.2	1.2	1.7	1.4	-0.7	13.8	9.2	7.6	6.7	5.3	3.5	-1.6	- Crédits à l'exportation [c]
- Direct investment	0.6	1.3	2.0	0.4	0.8	0.3	0.3	12.5	16.9	13.9	12.6	13.2	12.6	16.9	- Investissements directs
- Other [d e]	-1.6	0.5	3.1	0.2	0.2	-0.4	0.2	17.2	26.1	25.4	20.2	24.4	-14.1	9.2	- Autres [d e]
Total financial flows	**100.0**	**100.0**	**100.0**	**100.0**	**100.0**	**100.0**	**100.0**	**100.0**	**100.0**	**100.0**	**100.0**	**100.0**	**100.0**	**100.0**	**Total des apports financiers**

For sources and notes, see table 17A.

Pour les sources et les notes, se reporter au tableau 17A.

19. Share of LDCs in flows to all developing countries, by type of flow

19. Part des PMA dans les apports financiers à l'ensemble des pays en développement, par catégories d'apports

In per cent | *En pourcentage*

	1976	1977	1978	1979	1980	1981	1982	1983	1984	1985	1986	
Concessional loans & grants *of which:*	17.0	20.6	19.3	20.1	20.3	19.8	22.7	23.2	23.3	25.1	23.3	Prêts concessionnels et dons *dont:*
DAC	20.2	21.9	24.7	24.5	24.0	23.4	24.5	24.1	24.8	27.1	26.4	CAD
- Bilateral	17.4	19.2	21.4	21.6	22.0	20.6	22.2	21.0	20.4	23.3	22.6	- Apports bilatéraux
- Multilateral [a]	27.4	28.5	32.8	31.7	28.4	30.3	29.9	31.5	35.3	36.5	36.6	- Apports multilatéraux [a]
- Grants	21.1	22.0	27.5	26.4	30.1	27.0	26.5	25.2	24.4	27.4	26.2	- Dons
- Loans	18.7	21.7	19.4	20.5	10.9	16.2	20.4	21.7	25.8	26.4	27.0	- Prêts
- Technical assistance	17.7	16.8	18.6	19.1	21.0	21.8	21.5	21.0	20.4	22.2	21.9	- Assistance technique
- Other	21.3	24.3	27.3	26.8	25.2	24.1	25.8	25.7	26.7	29.3	28.3	- Autres
OPEC	13.5	22.5	11.3	12.0	11.9	11.8	19.8	19.9	20.4	17.1	13.5	OPEP
- Bilateral	12.7	21.0	10.2	11.0	10.7	9.5	17.5	17.7	18.4	15.3	11.6	- Apports bilatéraux
- Multilateral [b]	23.7	49.8	38.1	39.9	51.3	63.8	58.6	55.7	71.3	55.6	68.6	- Apports multilatéraux [b]
- Grants	15.2	24.6	15.7	6.5	10.9	7.5	19.0	25.7	14.2	13.0	8.4	- Dons
- Loans	12.1	18.5	9.2	18.1	12.8	14.9	20.6	14.6	59.2	31.7	52.1	- Prêts
Non-concessional flows	1.4	1.7	1.0	1.9	2.9	1.1	1.8	1.3	1.2	3.1	0.2	Courants financiers non-concessionnels
of which:												*dont:*
DAC	1.3	1.7	1.0	1.9	2.8	1.1	1.9	1.2	1.2	3.4	0.4	CAD
- Bilateral official	1.8	1.7	0.6	4.8	5.3	3.9	3.5	6.3	5.1	3.6	4.7	- Apports publics bilatéraux
- Multilateral [a]	0.9	1.6	2.4	2.4	2.0	1.6	1.6	1.6	0.8	2.1	-	- Apports multilatéraux [a]
- Export credits [c]	4.1	4.2	3.4	5.9	8.9	2.6	4.2	2.1	3.1	7.5	6.4	- Crédits à l'exportation [c]
- Direct investment	0.6	1.3	0.5	0.3	0.5	0.6	1.4	0.3	0.6	0.5	0.2	- Investissements directs
- Other [d e]	0.2	..	0.1	0.7	..	0.2	1.3	0.1	-	0.5	0.3	- Autres [d e]
Total financial flows	**7.6**	**8.9**	**7.8**	**9.0**	**10.9**	**8.2**	**10.1**	**11.4**	**10.1**	**19.4**	**14.2**	**Total des apports financiers**

Note: No percentage is shown when either the net flow to all LDCs or the net flow to all developing countries in a particular year is negative.
For other notes and sources, see table 17A.

Note: Aucune donnée n'est indiquée dans les cas où dans une année quelconque, les versements nets, soit aux PMA soit aux pays en développement dans leur ensemble, sont négatifs.
Pour les autres notes et sources, se reporter au tableau 17A.

20. ODA commitments from individual DAC member countries and individual multilateral agencies [a] to all LDCs

20. Engagements de l'APD de chaque pays membre du CAD et de chaque institution multilatérale [a] en faveur de l'ensemble des PMA

$ million — *Millions de dollars*

	1976	1977	1978	1979	1980	1981	1982	1983	1984	1985	1986	
Bilateral donors												***Donneurs bilatéraux***
Australia	13.2	84.9	50.2	40.6	58.7	101.9	67.3	62.3	64.0	52.4	43.9	Australie
Austria	0.9	0.3	2.4	0.3	0.9	1.1	6.3	5.7	4.9	7.4	10.7	Autriche
Belgium	68.4	76.1	101.0	105.9	112.9	89.8	72.1	32.2	34.4	41.8	84.5	Belgique
Canada	156.6	359.0	516.6	198.8	121.9	204.3	238.3	310.2	342.7	308.2	285.8	Canada
Denmark	46.2	50.0	223.3	134.6	114.8	63.8	132.4	88.7	153.8	135.4	191.5	Danemark
Finland	10.6	9.7	8.3	43.3	39.6	40.4	40.7	21.5	50.8	108.7	86.8	Finlande
France	307.5	240.1	233.5	364.2	615.6	615.1	538.9	574.9	653.6	635.7	636.6	France
Germany, Fed.Rep.of	378.5	366.1	553.3	1234.6	1868.1	807.6	515.2	546.1	554.8	725.0	676.8	Allemagne, Rép. Féd. d'
Ireland	0.4	0.7	2.0	3.2	5.1	5.6	6.2	6.8	6.8	8.0	10.0	Irlande
Italy	12.1	16.5	15.8	19.4	43.9	225.7	219.0	285.9	302.0	418.1	1207.6	Italie
Japan	126.0	392.6	444.9	504.3	440.4	550.4	776.2	401.3	669.6	571.0	962.7	Japon
Netherlands	148.2	269.7	419.6	329.4	370.8	317.5	211.4	254.4	204.0	206.9	353.4	Pays-Bas
New Zealand	2.1	3.7	8.6	5.3	9.9	9.8	4.4	3.7	5.4	11.4	9.6	Nouvelle-Zélande
Norway	34.9	57.0	71.5	69.3	76.3	121.0	102.0	86.2	109.1	128.5	209.4	Norvège
Sweden	130.0	265.3	224.8	285.7	164.3	193.0	167.6	145.2	145.5	146.7	220.0	Suède
Switzerland	7.8	34.6	41.5	24.5	56.7	106.9	36.1	80.9	51.3	105.1	108.0	Suisse
United Kingdom	253.2	127.5	442.5	505.5	454.4	240.4	161.4	195.3	236.4	198.3	328.0	Royaume-Uni
United States	387.4	387.4	448.9	524.4	650.8	664.7	725.9	808.0	1079.3	1091.6	925.8	Etats-Unis
Total bilateral	2084.0	2741.3	3808.7	4393.2	5205.1	4359.0	4021.3	3909.5	4668.4	4900.3	6351.1	Total bilatéraux
Multilateral donors												***Donneurs multilatéraux***
AfDB/AfDF	80.0	121.9	144.5	164.1	190.3	224.4	210.1	243.6	173.5	293.3	385.4	BAfD/FAfD
AsDB	173.3	153.3	196.6	215.7	254.8	300.7	312.9	457.8	400.8	382.8	198.9	BAsD
EEC/EDF	384.6	472.4	380.9	483.9	502.0	597.0	605.0	481.5	536.0	421.8	562.8	CEE/FED
IBRD	62.7	31.5	-	-	-	-	-	-	-	-	-	BIRD
IDA	570.7	642.2	803.6	760.8	1327.3	1055.7	1313.5	1398.2	1387.5	1190.9	1493.7	AID
IDB	5.0	15.7	43.5	4.1	9.1	-	32.6	17.4	-	24.7	56.0	BID
IFAD	-	-	62.3	120.1	144.6	154.8	60.5	82.8	89.7	83.1	57.6	FIDA
UN	319.3	302.4	421.5	512.4	630.1	772.8	722.2	764.7	846.4	1022.0	925.1	ONU
Total	1595.6	1739.4	2052.9	2261.0	3058.2	3105.4	3256.8	3446.0	3433.9	3418.6	3679.5	Total
Grand total	**3679.5**	**4480.7**	**5861.6**	**6654.2**	**8263.3**	**7464.4**	**7278.1**	**7355.4**	**8102.3**	**8318.9**	**10030.6**	**Total général**

Source: UNCTAD secretariat, based on information from the OECD/DAC secretariat.

a Multilateral agencies mainly financed by DAC member countries.

Source: Secrétariat de la CNUCED d'après des renseignements du sécretariat de l'OCDE/CAD.

a Institutions multilatérales essentiellement financées par les pays membres du CAD.

21A. Bilateral ODA from DAC member countries and total financial flows from multilateral agencies [a] to all LDCs

21A. APD bilatérale des pays membres du CAD et apports financiers totaux des institutions multilatérales [a] à l'ensemble des PMA

Net disbursements in $ million — *Versements nets en millions de dollars*

	1976	1977	1978	1979	1980	1981	1982	1983	1984	1985	1986	
A. Bilateral donors												***A. Donneurs bilatéraux***
Australia	18.0	21.5	39.9	63.0	52.5	69.0	106.1	63.2	80.2	46.7	48.4	Australie
Austria	1.5	2.4	3.1	3.0	5.8	9.1	7.1	7.1	5.5	7.2	7.7	Autriche
Belgium	54.6	59.7	76.0	102.6	96.6	85.6	69.8	56.0	55.3	91.4	84.4	Belgique
Canada	129.4	122.2	173.8	191.1 [b]	170.6 [b]	171.9	228.6	232.1	238.1	284.8	217.8	Canada
Denmark	47.4	60.9	82.9	104.4	127.7	80.1	85.8	99.1	81.3	114.3	141.4	Danemark
Finland	15.9	11.3	10.6	14.9	23.1	24.8	22.8	35.2	38.9	45.0	72.1	Finlande
France	254.6	232.7	276.9	387.7 [b]	453.0	532.0	441.8	414.4	528.3	545.2	619.9	France
Germany, Fed.Rep.of	245.3	271.5	415.7	587.0	618.6	566.4	614.3	533.8	445.5	515.6	592.8	Allemagne, Rép. Féd. d'
Ireland	0.4	0.7	2.0	3.2	5.1	5.6	6.2	6.8	6.8	8.0	10.0	Irlande
Italy	9.9	11.5	13.1	17.1	37.3	60.9	115.9	168.1	252.6	344.4	738.9	Italie
Japan	87.2	128.3	321.7	509.2	517.4	423.0	522.5	385.0	378.0	485.4	821.8	Japon
Netherlands	81.7	156.6	232.7	262.1	314.7	293.3	257.0	208.0	239.0	203.3	301.0	Pays-Bas
New Zealand	4.8	5.6	5.9	6.8	7.0	6.2	5.1	5.5	5.8	6.3	6.9	Nouvelle-Zélande
Norway	39.1	61.8	78.0	91.7	97.0	93.6	123.9	122.1	101.1	122.8	183.4	Norvège
Sweden	115.3	142.0	149.8	216.5	198.5	181.2	167.5	147.7	124.8	131.0	220.0	Suède
Switzerland	11.8	20.5	42.7	29.6	58.0	56.2	59.1	66.8	70.8	68.4	110.4	Suisse
United Kingdom	116.4	139.5	225.0	294.5	385.9	327.9	277.0	231.3	209.1	246.1	230.2	Royaume-Uni
United States	270.0	274.0	387.0	394.0	573.0	549.0	657.0	717.0	766.0	1197.0	871.0	Etats-Unis
Total bilateral concessional	1503.3	1722.8	2537.0	3278.3	3741.6	3535.9	3767.4	3499.3	3627.1	4462.8	5278.1	Total des apports bilatéraux concessionnels
B. Multilateral donors												***B. Donneurs multilatéraux***
1.Concessional												***1. Apports concessionnels***
AfDF	10.5	23.3	35.7	54.3	86.0	77.9	85.8	119.5	77.8	137.1	165.7	FAfD
AsDB	21.3	33.6	114.3	79.4	88.9	86.1	94.3	98.4	147.0	227.8	211.4	BAsD
EEC/EDF	193.7	225.1	321.7	424.3	452.1	508.2	406.5	385.7	474.2	447.5	524.1	CEE/FED
IBRD	0.1	6.1	13.3	19.5	18.7	9.8	3.0	2.5	0.5	0.4	-	BIRD
IDA	375.4	383.6	403.4	511.6	523.7	616.7	743.2	785.4	964.3	952.1	1278.4	AID
IDB	15.7	21.3	16.9	15.9	8.9	10.0	12.5	14.9	16.2	10.7	3.1	BID
IFAD	-	-	-	1.1	12.9	22.6	28.0	50.8	51.6	91.0	101.4	FIDA
IMF Trust fund	-	46.8	268.1	225.2	272.9	2.9	-	-	-	-	-	Fonds fiduciaire du FMI
UN	319.3	302.4	421.5	512.4	630.2	772.7	722.2	764.7	846.4	1022.1	925.2	ONU
of which: UNDP	100.9	96.3	119.7	150.8	188.9	280.7	244.8	210.9	214.7	243.7	268.5	*dont:* PNUD
UNHCR	10.0	7.6	18.0	35.8	96.9	100.9	88.6	111.1	133.2	183.1	160.2	UNHCR
UNICEF	25.9	34.4	53.5	77.1	79.5	71.2	65.9	85.7	86.0	108.1	113.6	UNICEF
UNTA	18.3	22.8	28.6	25.5	7.2	33.2	30.4	44.6	33.5	53.5	42.7	ATNU
WFP	98.1	118.0	153.6	179.4	174.4	221.5	220.8	236.9	298.9	340.7	239.9	PAM
Total	935.9	1042.2	1594.9	1843.7	2094.2	2106.9	2095.4	2221.8	2577.9	2888.7	3209.3	Total
2. Non-concessional												***2. Apports non-concessionnels***
AfDB	16.3	21.4	18.1	25.6	31.6	27.1	44.0	52.2	37.6	71.6	30.5	BAfD
AsDB	0.9	0.9	2.7	-0.5	0.9	-0.7	-1.1	-0.8	-0.9	-0.9	-0.9	BAsD
EEC/EDF	-	-0.1	12.5	15.2	18.9	17.3	14.4	17.2	5.2	5.8	-5.7	CEE/FED
IBRD	-1.7	13.4	19.8	37.7	31.8	41.7	38.2	39.5	5.7	52.2	-37.1	BIRD
IFC	5.6	6.6	16.2	13.2	6.4	2.5	7.7	7.5	17.1	17.9	8.5	SFI
Total	21.1	42.2	69.3	91.2	89.6	87.8	103.1	115.6	64.7	146.6	-4.7	Total
Total concessional (A+B.1)	***2439.2***	***2765.1***	***4131.9***	***5122.0***	***5835.9***	***5642.8***	***5862.8***	***5721.1***	***6205.0***	***7351.5***	***8487.4***	***Total des apports concessionnels (A+B.1)***
GRAND TOTAL	***2460.3***	***2807.3***	***4201.2***	***5213.2***	***5925.5***	***5730.6***	***5966.0***	***5836.7***	***6269.8***	***7498.1***	***8482.7***	***TOTAL GÉNÉRAL***

For sources and notes, see table 21C.

Pour les sources et les notes, se reporter au tableau 21C.

21B. Bilateral ODA from DAC member countries and total financial flows from multilateral agencies [a] to all LDCs

Net disbursements in millions of 1980 dollars

21B. APD bilatérale des pays membres du CAD et apports financiers totaux des institutions multilatérales [a] à l'ensemble des PMA

Versements nets en millions de dollars de 1980

	1976	1977	1978	1979	1980	1981	1982	1983	1984	1985	1986	
A. Bilateral donors												***A. Donneurs bilatéraux***
Australia	30.4	33.1	55.0	72.9	52.5	72.4	115.1	70.8	91.0	52.7	53.9	Australie
Austria	2.5	3.7	4.3	3.5	5.8	9.5	7.7	8.0	6.3	8.1	8.5	Autriche
Belgium	92.1	91.9	104.8	118.8	96.6	89.8	75.7	62.7	62.7	103.3	93.9	Belgique
Canada	218.2	188.1	239.6	221.3 [b]	170.6 [b]	180.3	248.0	260.0	270.2	321.8	242.4	Canada
Denmark	79.9	93.8	114.3	120.9	127.7	84.0	93.1	110.9	92.2	129.1	157.3	Danemark
Finland	26.8	17.3	14.6	17.2	23.1	26.0	24.7	39.4	44.1	50.9	80.2	Finlande
France	429.3	358.0	381.7	449.0 [b]	453.0	558.0	479.2	464.1	599.6	616.1	689.8	France
Germany, Fed.Rep.of	413.6	417.8	573.0	679.8	618.6	594.0	666.4	597.7	505.6	582.6	659.7	Allemagne, Rép. Féd. d'
Ireland	0.7	1.1	2.7	3.7	5.1	5.8	6.7	7.6	7.7	9.1	11.1	Irlande
Italy	16.7	17.7	18.1	19.7	37.3	63.8	125.8	188.3	286.7	389.2	822.2	Italie
Japan	147.1	197.5	443.5	589.6	517.4	443.7	566.8	431.2	428.9	548.5	914.4	Japon
Netherlands	137.7	241.0	320.8	303.6	314.7	307.6	278.8	232.9	271.3	229.7	334.9	Pays-Bas
New Zealand	8.2	8.6	8.2	7.9	7.0	6.5	5.6	6.1	6.6	7.2	7.7	Nouvelle-Zélande
Norway	65.9	95.2	107.5	106.2	97.0	98.2	134.4	136.8	114.8	138.7	204.1	Norvège
Sweden	194.4	218.5	206.5	250.8	198.5	190.1	181.7	165.4	141.6	148.0	244.8	Suède
Switzerland	19.9	31.5	58.8	34.3	58.0	59.0	64.1	74.8	80.3	77.2	122.8	Suisse
United Kingdom	196.3	214.7	310.2	341.1	385.9	343.9	300.5	259.0	237.3	278.0	256.2	Royaume-Uni
United States	455.3	421.7	533.5	456.3	573.0	575.8	712.7	802.9	869.3	1352.5	969.2	Etats-Unis
Total bilateral concessional	2535.0	2651.3	3497.3	3796.6	3741.6	3708.3	4087.0	3918.6	4116.1	5042.7	5873.0	Total des apports bilatéraux concessionnels
B. Multilateral donors												***B. Donneurs multilatéraux***
1.Concessional												***1. Apports concessionnels***
AfDF	17.7	35.9	49.2	62.9	86.0	81.7	93.1	133.8	88.3	154.9	184.4	FAfD
AsDB	35.9	51.7	157.6	92.0	88.9	90.3	102.3	110.2	166.8	257.4	235.2	BAsD
EEC/EDF	326.6	346.4	443.5	491.3	452.1	533.0	441.0	431.9	538.1	505.6	583.2	CEE/FED
IBRD	0.2	9.4	18.3	22.6	18.7	10.3	3.3	2.8	0.6	0.5	-	BIRD
IDA	633.1	590.3	556.1	592.5	523.7	646.8	806.2	879.5	1094.3	1075.8	1422.5	AID
IDB	26.4	32.7	23.3	18.4	8.9	10.5	13.5	16.7	18.3	12.1	3.4	BID
IFAD	-	-	-	1.3	12.9	23.7	30.3	56.8	58.5	102.8	112.8	FIDA
IMF Trust fund	-	72.0	369.6	260.8	272.9	3.0	-	-	-	-	-	Fonds fiduciaire du FMI
UN	538.5	465.4	581.1	593.4	630.2	810.4	783.5	856.3	960.5	1154.9	1029.5	ONU
of which: UNDP	170.2	148.2	165.0	174.6	188.9	294.4	265.6	236.2	243.6	275.4	298.8	*dont:* PNUD
UNHCR	16.9	11.6	24.8	41.4	96.9	105.9	96.2	124.4	151.1	206.9	178.3	UNHCR
UNICEF	43.7	52.9	73.8	89.3	79.5	74.7	71.5	96.0	97.6	122.1	126.4	UNICEF
UNTA	30.9	35.1	39.4	29.5	7.2	34.8	33.0	49.9	38.0	60.5	47.5	ATNU
WFP	165.4	181.5	211.8	207.8	174.4	232.3	239.5	265.3	339.2	385.0	266.9	PAM
Total	1578.3	1603.9	2198.7	2135.1	2094.2	2209.7	2273.2	2488.1	2925.5	3264.1	3571.0	Total
2. Non-concessional												***2. Apports non-concessionnels***
AfDB	27.4	32.9	25.0	29.7	31.6	28.4	47.7	58.4	42.7	80.9	33.9	BAfD
AsDB	1.5	1.4	3.7	-0.6	0.9	-0.7	-1.2	-0.9	-1.0	-1.0	-1.0	BAsD
EEC/EDF	-	-0.1	17.2	17.6	18.9	18.1	15.6	19.3	5.9	6.6	-6.3	CEE/FED
IBRD	-2.9	20.6	27.3	43.7	31.8	43.7	41.4	44.2	6.5	59.0	-41.3	BIRD
IFC	9.4	10.2	22.3	15.3	6.4	2.6	8.4	8.4	19.4	20.2	9.5	SFI
Total	35.5	65.0	95.5	105.7	89.6	92.1	111.9	129.4	73.4	165.6	-5.2	Total
Total concessional (A+B.1)	***4113.4***	***4255.3***	***5696.0***	***5931.7***	***5835.9***	***5918.0***	***6360.2***	***6406.7***	***7041.6***	***8306.8***	***9444.1***	***Total des apports concessionnels (A+B.1)***
GRAND TOTAL	***4148.9***	***4320.2***	***5791.5***	***6037.3***	***5925.5***	***6010.1***	***6472.1***	***6536.1***	***7115.0***	***8472.4***	***9438.8***	***TOTAL GÉNÉRAL***

21C. Bilateral ODA from DAC member countries and total financial flows from multilateral agencies [a] to all LDCs- main recipients in 1986 [d]

21C. APD bilatérale des pays membres du CAD et apports financiers totaux des institutions multilatérales [a] à l'ensemble des PMA- principaux bénéficiaires en 1986 [d]

	Main recipients in 1986 [d] / Principaux bénéficiaires en 1986 [d]	
A. Bilateral donors		*A. Donneurs bilatéraux*
Australia	Bangladesh, Ethiopia/Ethiopie, Burma/Birmanie, Vanuatu.	Australie
Austria	Rwanda, Cape Verde/Cap-Vert, Ethiopia/Ethiopie.	Autriche
Belgium	Rwanda, Burundi.	Belgique
Canada	Bangladesh, U.-R.of Tanzania/R.-U.de Tanzanie.	Canada
Denmark	U.-R. of Tanzania/R.-U. de Tanzanie, Bangladesh.	Danemark
Finland	U.-R. of Tanzania/R.-U. de Tanzanie, Somalia/Somalie, Ethiopia/Ethiopie.	Finlande
France	Mali.	France
Germany,Fed.Rep.of	Bangladesh.	Allemagne, Rép. Féd. d'
Ireland	Lesotho, U.-R. of Tanzania/R.-U. de Tanzanie, Sudan/Soudan.	Irlande
Italy	Somalia/Somalie, Ethiopia/Ethiopie, Sudan/Soudan.	Italie
Japan	Bangladesh, Burma/Birmanie.	Japon
Netherlands	U.-R. of Tanzania/R.-U. de Tanzanie, Sudan/Soudan, Bangladesh.	Pays-Bas
New Zealand	Samoa, Tuvalu, Vanuatu, Kiribati.	Nouvelle-Zélande
Norway	U.-R. of Tanzania/R.-U. de Tanzanie, Bangladesh.	Norvège
Sweden	U.-R. of Tanzania/R.-U. de Tanzanie, Ethiopia/Ethiopie, Bangladesh	Suède
Switzerland	U.-R. of Tanzania/R.-U. de Tanzanie.	Suisse
United Kingdom	Bangladesh, Sudan/Soudan.	Royaume-Uni
United States	Sudan/Soudan, Bangladesh, Ethiopia/Ethiopie.	Etats-Unis
B. Multilateral donors		*B. Donneurs multilatéraux*
1. Concessional		*1. Apports concessionnels*
AfDF	Niger, Mali.	FAfD
AsDB	Bangladesh, Nepal/Népal, Burma/Birmanie.	BAsD
EEC/EDF	Sudan/Soudan, Ethiopia/Ethiopie.	CEE/FED
IBRD	-	BIRD
IDA	Bangladesh.	AID
IDB	Haiti/Haïti.	BID
IFAD	Bangladesh.	FIDA
UN	Sudan/Soudan, Ethiopia/Ethiopie, Bangladesh, Somalia/Somalie.	ONU
of which:		*dont:*
UNDP	Bangladesh.	PNUD
UNHCR	Sudan/Soudan, Somalia/Somalie, Ethiopia/Ethiopie.	UNHCR
UNICEF	Ethiopia/Ethiopie, Bangladesh, U.-R. of Tanzania/R.-U. de Tanzanie, Sudan/Soudan.	UNICEF
UNTA	-	ATNU
WFP	Bangladesh, Ethiopia/Ethiopie, Somalia/Somalie.	PAM
2. Non-concessional		*2. Apports non-concessionnels*
AfDB	Botswana, Burkina Faso, Central African Rep./Rép. centraficaine, Uganda/Ouganda.	BAfd
AsDB	Bangladesh, Burma/Birmanie.	BAsD
EEC/EDF	Guinea/Guinée.	CEE/FED
IBRD	Mauritania/Mauritanie, Malawi.	BIRD
IFC	Yemen/Yémen, Bangladesh, Uganda/Ouganda.	SFI

Source: UNCTAD secretariat, based on information from the OECD/DAC secretariat.

a Multilateral agencies mainly financed by DAC countries.

b Including flows not allocated by recipient country.

c Actual disbursements were converted to 1980 prices using the index for LDCs in Table 8.

d Accounting each for 10 per cent or more of the total provided to all LDCs.

Source: Secrétariat de la CNUCED, d'après des renseignements du secrétariat de l'OCDE/CAD.

a Institutions multilatérales essentiellement financées par les pays du CAD.

b Y compris les apports aux PMA non alloués par pays bénéficiaires.

c Les versements effectifs ont été convertis aux prix de 1980 en utilisant l'indice pour les PMA qui figure au tableau 8.

d Recevant individuellement 10 pour cent ou davantage du total accordé à l'ensemble des PMA.

22. Concessional assistance to LDCs from individual DAC member countries and multilateral agencies mainly financed by them: percentage distribution by donor and shares allocated to LDCs in total ODA flows

22. Aide concessionnelle aux PMA en provenance des pays membres du CAD et des institutions multilatérales essentiellement financées par ceux-ci: répartition en pourcentage par donneur et parts allouées aux PMA dans le total des apports d'APD

In per cent | *En pourcentage*

	Percentage distribution by donor / *Répartition en pourcentage par donneur*							*Share of LDCs in ODA flows to all developing countries* / *Parts des PMA dans le total des apports concessionnels aux pays en développement*							
	1980	1981	1982	1983	1984	1985	1986	1980	1981	1982	1983	1984	1985	1986	
Bilateral donors															***Donneurs bilatéraux***
Australia	0.9	1.2	1.8	1.1	1.3	0.6	0.6	10.8	12.6	18.9	12.0	13.4	9.0	9.7	Australie
Austria	0.1	0.2	0.1	0.1	0.1	0.1	0.1	4.0	5.8	4.4	5.8	4.1	4.2	5.6	Autriche
Belgium	1.7	1.5	1.2	1.0	0.9	1.2	1.0	21.8	23.9	24.5	19.2	21.6	34.1	23.6	Belgique
Canada	2.9	3.0	3.9	4.1	3.8	3.9	2.6	26.0	23.1	27.8	27.5	23.1	29.0	21.0	Canada
Denmark	2.2	1.4	1.5	1.7	1.3	1.6	1.7	50.5	39.6	42.0	42.9	37.1	52.2	41.2	Danemark
Finland	0.4	0.4	0.4	0.6	0.6	0.6	0.8	41.8	37.2	29.5	41.5	37.4	37.6	40.6	Finlande
France	7.8	9.4	7.5	7.2	8.5	7.4	7.3	13.2	15.1	13.4	13.3	16.8	16.8	15.0	France
Germany, Fed.Rep.of	10.6	10.0	10.5	9.3	7.2	7.0	7.0	28.9	25.8	29.5	27.7	25.9	28.2	23.5	Allemagne, Rép. Féd. d'
Ireland	0.1	0.1	0.1	0.1	0.1	0.1	0.1	52.0	53.8	50.8	48.6	46.6	46.8	39.7	Irlande
Italy	0.6	1.1	2.0	2.9	4.1	4.7	8.7	44.8	36.8	38.8	38.5	41.1	45.0	50.9	Italie
Japan	8.9	7.5	8.9	6.7	6.1	6.6	9.7	25.9	19.0	26.2	18.6	18.6	22.4	24.6	Japon
Netherlands	5.4	5.2	4.4	3.6	3.9	2.8	3.5	25.9	26.2	24.5	25.9	27.6	27.0	25.7	Pays-Bas
New Zealand	0.1	0.1	0.1	0.1	0.1	0.1	0.1	13.4	12.3	10.3	11.6	13.2	14.7	11.4	Nouvelle-Zélande
Norway	1.7	1.7	2.1	2.1	1.6	1.7	2.2	35.9	37.4	39.0	38.1	35.0	37.9	38.7	Norvège
Sweden	3.4	3.2	2.9	2.6	2.0	1.8	2.6	32.0	34.4	32.6	31.0	27.0	24.7	31.1	Suède
Switzerland	1.0	1.0	1.0	1.2	1.1	0.9	1.3	33.0	34.6	32.3	30.8	32.6	30.3	34.3	Suisse
United Kingdom	6.6	5.8	4.7	4.0	3.4	3.3	2.7	29.4	24.8	28.9	26.9	26.9	29.7	23.1	Royaume-Uni
United States	9.8	9.7	11.2	12.5	12.3	16.3	10.3	16.3	15.6	16.1	16.8	14.7	19.4	15.5	Etats-Unis
Total bilateral	64.1	62.7	64.3	61.2	58.5	60.7	62.2	22.2	20.6	22.2	21.0	20.4	23.3	22.6	Total bilatéraux
Multilateral donors															***Donneurs multilatéraux***
AfDF	1.5	1.4	1.5	2.1	1.3	1.9	2.0	89.8	86.1	70.2	75.7	69.9	65.3	61.0	FAfD
AsDB	1.5	1.5	1.6	1.7	2.4	3.1	2.5	62.5	60.4	53.2	44.3	48.5	58.2	50.9	BAsD
EEC/EDF	7.7	9.0	6.9	6.7	7.6	6.1	6.2	43.5	35.6	35.8	32.1	37.3	31.9	32.1	CEE/FED
IBRD	0.3	0.2	0.1	0.0	0.0	0.0	-	17.5	11.1	5.2	5.3	1.2	1.2	-	BIRD
IDA	9.0	10.9	12.7	13.7	15.5	13.0	15.1	34.1	32.3	31.5	34.7	40.8	40.0	42.1	AID
IDB	0.2	0.2	0.2	0.3	0.3	0.1	0.0	2.7	2.3	3.4	4.1	3.7	3.0	1.1	BID
IFAD	0.2	0.4	0.5	0.9	0.8	1.2	1.2	24.0	30.3	27.8	36.1	32.3	36.3	38.5	FIDA
IMF Trust fund	4.7	0.1	-	-	-	-	-	16.7	10.6	-	-	-	-	-	Fonds fiduciaire du FMI
UN	10.8	13.7	12.3	13.4	13.6	13.9	10.9	26.5	28.4	27.2	29.3	32.4	35.5	32.6	ONU
Total multilateral	35.9	37.3	35.7	38.8	41.5	39.3	37.8	28.4	30.3	29.9	31.5	35.3	36.5	36.6	Total multilatéraux
Grand total	**100.0**	**100.0**	**100.0**	**100.0**	**100.0**	**100.0**	**100.0**	**24.1**	**23.4**	**24.5**	**24.1**	**24.8**	**27.1**	**26.4**	**Total général**

Source: UNCTAD secretariat, based on information from the OECD/DAC secretariat.

Source: Secrétariat de la CNUCED d'après des renseignements du sécretariat de l'OCDE/CAD.

23. Net ODA [a] as a percentage of donors' GNP and as a ratio to average ODA in 1976-1980 from individual DAC member countries to LDCs as a group

23. Apports nets au titre de l'APD [a] de chaque pays membre du CAD à l'ensemble des PMA, en pourcentage du PNB et par rapport à l'APD moyenne pour 1976-1980

In per cent / *En pourcentage*

Donor country [b]	% of GNP / En % du PNB						Ratio to average ODA in 1976-1980 / Rapport à l'APD moyenne pour 1976-1980						Pays donateur [b]
	1981	1982	1983	1984	1985	1986	1981	1982	1983	1984	1985	1986	
Norway	0.30	0.38	0.36	0.32	0.35	0.41	1.34	1.64	1.53	1.34	1.57	2.18	Norvège
Denmark	0.27	0.30	0.27	0.30	0.32	0.30	1.06	1.16	1.07	1.13	1.28	1.72	Danemark
Netherlands	0.30	0.30	0.24	0.30	0.26	0.28	1.36	1.32	1.03	1.20	1.05	1.56	Pays-Bas
Sweden	0.26	0.32	0.25	0.22	0.23	0.25	1.14	1.19	0.87	0.78	0.86	1.24	Suède
Italy	0.06	0.07	0.07	0.11	0.11	0.18	2.01	2.28	2.43	3.94	3.92	9.25	Italie
Finland	0.09	0.09	0.11	0.12	0.14	0.16	1.62	1.59	1.98	2.26	2.69	4.10	Finlande
France	0.13	0.13	0.12	0.15	0.16	0.13	1.66	1.52	1.36	1.60	1.75	2.04	France
Belgium	0.17	0.15	0.13	0.15	0.18	0.13	1.28	1.03	0.83	0.89	1.16	1.14	Belgique
Canada	0.12	0.12	0.13	0.13	0.16	0.13	1.12	1.15	1.45	1.49	1.76	1.52	Canada
Germany, Fed. Rep. of	0.13	0.13	0.14	0.13	0.14	0.11	1.24	1.21	1.24	1.08	1.19	1.33	Allemagne, Rép. Féd. d'
Switzerland	0.09	0.08	0.10	0.10	0.10	0.10	1.52	1.41	1.88	1.70	1.74	2.58	Suisse
Ireland [c]	0.03	0.04	0.08	0.09	0.09	0.10	2.44	2.72	5.50	6.08	6.47	9.82	Irlande [c]
United Kingdom	0.12	0.12	0.10	0.10	0.10	0.08	1.49	1.34	1.08	0.98	1.10	1.08	Royaume-Uni
Australia	0.07	0.12	0.09	0.08	0.08	0.08	1.24	2.27	1.59	1.67	1.51	1.56	Australie
Japan	0.07	0.07	0.07	0.08	0.07	0.08	1.25	1.19	1.44	1.59	1.66	2.54	Japon
New Zealand	0.04	0.04	0.04	0.04	0.04	0.04	1.08	0.99	0.85	0.86	0.97	1.08	Nouvelle-Zélande
United States	0.03	0.05	0.04	0.04	0.04	0.03	1.15	1.76	1.68	1.68	1.79	1.70	Etats-Unis
Austria	0.04	0.04	0.03	0.04	0.05	0.03	1.96	1.72	1.35	1.61	2.32	1.65	Autriche
Total DAC	0.08	0.09	0.08	0.08	0.08	0.08	1.31	1.41	1.36	1.42	1.52	1.89	Total CAD

Source: UNCTAD secretariat calculations, based on information from the OECD/DAC secretariat.

a Including imputed flows through multilateral channels.

b Ranked in descending order of the ODA/GNP ratio in 1986.

c Ireland became a member of DAC at the end of 1985.

Source: Chiffres calculés par le secrétariat de la CNUCED d'après des renseignements du sécretariat de l'OCDE/CAD.

a Y compris le montant imputé de l'APD fournie aux PMA à travers les voies multilatérales.

b Classés par ordre décroissant du rapport APD/PNB en 1986.

c L'Irlande est devenue membre du CAD à la fin de 1985.

24. ODA commitments from DAC member countries to individual LDCs

24. Engagements de l'APD à chacun des PMA en provenance des pays membres du CAD

$ million — Millions de dollars

Country	1976	1977	1978	1979	1980	1981	1982	1983	1984	1985	1986	Pays
Afghanistan	45	59	56	25	8	4	5	6	5	8	8	Afghanistan
Bangladesh	627	545	1012	758	1302	840	694	701	783	699	867	Bangladesh
Benin	32	13	79	43	58	60	58	42	74	42	72	Bénin
Bhutan	1	1	1	1	1	5	1	8	4	15	15	Bhoutan
Botswana	41	41	134	104	113	74	87	84	88	69	118	Botswana
Burkina Faso	68	102	146	201	170	189	146	135	159	127	202	Burkina faso
Burma	46	295	154	414	129	317	402	149	384	275	365	Birmanie
Burundi	33	44	44	69	90	93	69	70	74	77	78	Burundi
Cape Verde	13	26	32	52	40	46	47	54	48	43	62	Cap-Vert
Central African Rep.	25	34	26	51	99	73	79	80	77	75	102	Rép. centrafricaine
Chad	57	58	77	38	21	50	43	56	77	134	137	Tchad
Comoros	8	0	0	9	15	27	18	19	25	13	23	Comores
Democratic Yemen	3	8	14	4	5	5	51	8	23	27	3	Yémen démocratique
Djibouti	26	30	20	23	36	45	52	51	54	45	89	Djibouti
Equatorial Guinea	..	..	..	0	6	7	7	6	9	7	16	Guinée équatoriale
Ethiopia	54	51	70	64	80	92	96	107	285	373	455	Ethiopie
Gambia	17	9	16	38	36	36	24	29	45	23	56	Gambie
Guinea	11	13	16	49	57	49	46	65	63	108	154	Guinée
Guinea-Bissau	23	27	53	31	43	41	29	37	30	32	42	Guinée-Bissau
Haiti	64	65	45	53	47	83	86	91	100	111	136	Haïti
Kiribati	7	11	12	46	12	10	13	14	9	11	6	Kiribati
Lao People's Dem.Rep.	27	24	41	19	45	21	11	18	19	11	31	Rép. dém. pop. lao
Lesotho	33	41	30	92	83	65	42	62	60	53	71	Lesotho
Malawi	36	63	217	127	84	91	63	70	71	68	193	Malawi
Maldives	1	8	2	1	4	1	3	8	8	6	9	Maldives
Mali	89	91	97	187	109	167	82	152	297	242	209	Mali
Mauritania	37	34	36	68	64	76	60	61	107	91	112	Mauritanie
Nepal	61	59	65	130	113	115	139	110	106	198	159	Népal
Niger	81	84	118	191	124	169	131	189	197	169	249	Niger
Rwanda	66	80	112	126	145	113	105	80	110	110	113	Rwanda
Samoa	2	13	21	14	15	27	10	12	15	22	12	Samoa
Sao Tome and Principe	1	2	1	1	3	6	3	4	4	2	8	Sao Tomé-et-Principe
Sierra Leone	9	20	29	60	57	55	38	25	28	91	59	Sierra leone
Somalia	18	30	58	77	234	272	184	198	186	208	565	Somalie
Sudan	56	77	274	274	625	350	357	430	396	637	535	Soudan
Togo	35	102	32	43	104	40	45	82	76	159	109	Togo
Tuvalu	2	5	3	12	2	6	4	3	4	3	12	Tuvalu
Uganda	4	4	9	26	80	90	41	93	88	49	122	Ouganda
United Rep.of Tanzania	266	481	591	734	675	457	534	385	384	368	641	Rép.-Unie de Tanzanie
Vanuatu	26	12	22	39	71	25	26	25	22	21	19	Vanuatu
Yemen	31	81	47	99	201	66	92	93	76	80	117	Yémen
All LDCs	**2084**	**2741**	**3809**	**4393**	**5205**	**4359**	**4021**	**3909**	**4668**	**4900**	**6351**	**Ensemble des PMA**

Source: UNCTAD secretariat, based on information from the OECD/DAC secretariat.

Source: Secrétariat de la CNUCED, d'après des renseignements du secrétariat de l'OCDE/CAD.

25. Bilateral ODA from DAC member countries to individual LDCs

25. APD bilatérale reçue par chacun des PMA en provenance des pays membres du CAD

Net disbursements in millions of dollars / Versements nets en millions de dollars

Country	1976	1977	1978	1979	1980	1981	1982	1983	1984	1985	1986	Pays
Afghanistan	35	28	32	47	11	-8	0	5	-1	7	-2	Afghanistan
Bangladesh	320	384	667	775	850	672	822	583	674	622	761	Bangladesh
Benin	28	27	30	49	36	45	41	41	40	48	73	Bénin
Bhutan	1	1	1	1	2	3	3	3	5	7	14	Bhoutan
Botswana	41	38	55	74	84	76	83	75	65	59	82	Botswana
Burkina Faso	60	72	97	132	151	158	147	128	122	122	175	Burkina faso
Burma	39	55	157	259	231	203	208	216	149	253	308	Birmanie
Burundi	26	29	39	44	60	65	75	69	70	77	90	Burundi
Cape Verde	7	16	25	27	39	36	43	45	39	41	76	Cap-Vert
Central African Rep.	26	30	30	51	75	73	69	65	68	62	85	Rép. centrafricaine
Chad	43	50	71	49	20	31	35	51	59	96	102	Tchad
Comoros [a]	8	2	2	6	13	18	14	15	18	18	21	Comores [a]
Democratic Yemen	9	7	13	5	4	5	10	7	5	11	2	Yémen démocratique
Djibouti	28	33	29	19	32	36	45	41	49	46	65	Djibouti
Equatorial Guinea	..	..	..	0	1	4	5	4	8	7	11	Guinée équatoriale
Ethiopia	73	59	56	71	91	76	77	93	187	416	401	Ethiopie
Gambia	5	13	15	13	17	19	24	21	32	31	59	Gambie
Guinea	4	5	10	14	33	31	27	27	42	60	98	Guinée
Guinea-Bissau	12	26	37	34	34	41	34	32	31	24	41	Guinée-Bissau
Haiti	32	40	50	49	63	67	79	79	71	103	126	Haïti
Kiribati	4	6	10	9	19	14	14	14	10	11	12	Kiribati
Lao People's Dem.Rep.	24	27	43	26	17	17	21	13	14	16	19	Rép. dém. pop. lao
Lesotho	18	21	30	46	64	62	57	65	66	52	56	Lesotho
Malawi	46	54	56	92	76	82	65	56	52	53	90	Malawi
Maldives	1	1	4	1	2	3	1	3	3	7	11	Maldives
Mali	53	61	93	94	131	133	96	97	224	251	204	Mali
Mauritania	18	25	40	35	54	67	62	72	69	100	105	Mauritanie
Nepal	29	38	40	82	84	88	111	110	98	124	170	Népal
Niger	80	59	78	117	105	123	124	107	102	206	184	Niger
Rwanda	57	61	79	88	97	103	99	95	96	103	124	Rwanda
Samoa	7	11	11	21	14	14	15	17	11	13	18	Samoa
Sao Tome and Principe	1	2	2	1	1	2	4	3	4	3	7	Sao Tomé-et-Principe
Sierra Leone	8	12	14	29	57	34	56	36	23	30	51	Sierra leone
Somalia	20	25	47	50	139	140	142	151	193	163	354	Somalie
Sudan	54	56	113	150	272	296	358	439	309	647	464	Soudan
Togo	21	42	67	69	52	37	50	49	53	53	92	Togo
Tuvalu	3	2	3	4	5	4	5	4	5	3	4	Tuvalu
Uganda	10	4	8	16	42	79	53	44	47	42	77	Ouganda
United Rep.of Tanzania	212	257	333	458	524	486	485	429	410	373	514	Rép.-Unie de Tanzanie
Vanuatu	31	13	18	38	43	24	23	24	22	19	21	Vanuatu
Yemen	11	34	37	51	79	77	85	72	82	84	115	Yémen
All LDCs [b]	**1504**	**1723**	**2537**	**3195**	**3722**	**3536**	**3767**	**3499**	**3627**	**4463**	**5278**	**Ensemble des PMA [b]**
All developing countries	**8660**	**8980**	**11874**	**14788**	**16887**	**17154**	**16943**	**16662**	**17748**	**19168**	**23381**	**Ensemble des pays en développement**

Source: UNCTAD secretariat, based on information from the OECD/DAC secretariat.

a Excluding grants from France to Mayotte.

b Excluding $31.8 million and $69.7 million from Canada and France respectively in 1979, not allocated by recipient country. Excluding $19.5 million from Canada in 1980, not allocated by recipient country.

Source: Secrétariat de la CNUCED, d'après des renseignements du secrétariat de l'OCDE/CAD.

a Non compris l'aide versée au titre de dons par la France à Mayotte.

b Non compris 13,8 millions de dollars et 69,7 millions de dollars, en provenance du Canada et de la France respectivement en 1979, non alloués par pays bénéficiaires. Non compris 19,5 millions de dollars en provenance du Canada en 1980, non alloués par pays bénéficiaires.

26. Grant element of ODA commitments [a] individual DAC member countries to LDCs as a group

26. Elément de libéralité des engagements de l'APD [a] de chaque pays membre du CAD en faveur de l'ensemble des PMA

In per cent — *En pourcentage*

	1981	1982	1983	1984	1985	1986	
Australia	100	100	100	100	100	100	Australie
Austria	94	95	99	100	100	100	Autriche
Belgium	98	98	96	98	95	98	Belgique
Canada	100	100	100	100	100	100	Canada
Denmark	94	96	99	100	99	100	Danemark
Finland	95	95	100	100	100	98	Finlande
France	89	82	80	77	76	80	France
Germany, Fed.Rep.of	97	98	95	94	99	99	Allemagne, Rép. Féd. d'
Ireland	100	100	100	100	100	100	Irlande
Italy	55	70	90	81	96	98	Italie
Japan	81	77	88	79	84	82	Japon
Netherlands	98	99	100	100	100	100	Pays-Bas
New Zealand	100	100	100	100	100	100	Nouvelle-Zélande
Norway	100	100	100	100	100	100	Norvège
Sweden	100	100	100	100	100	100	Suède
Switzerland	100	100	100	100	100	100	Suisse
United Kingdom	100	100	100	100	100	100	Royaume-Uni
United States	96	98	96	98	97	96	Etats-Unis
Total DAC countries	92	91	94	91	94	94	Total des pays du CAD
of which: loans	61	61	58	57	59	61	*dont:* prêts
Multilateral agencies [b]	92	90	89	89	90	90	Institutions multilatérales [b]
of which: loans	82	82	82	82	82	82	*dont:* prêts

Source: UNCTAD secretariat estimates based on OECD/DAC data.

Note: The grant element, used as a standard measure of the concessionality of aid programmes, reflects the grant share of new commitments as well as the financial terms of loans (i.e. their interest rate, maturity and grace period).

a Excluding debt reorganisation.

b Mainly financed by DAC member countries.

Source: Estimations du secrétariat de la CNUCED, d'après des renseignement du sécretariat de l'OCDE/CAD.

Note: L'élément de libéralité, pris comme étalon de la libéralité des programmes d'aide, rend compte de la proportion de dons dan les engagements nouveaux ainsi que des conditions financières des prêts (c'est-à-dire taux d'intérêt, échéance, et delai de grâce).

a Non compris la réorganisation de la dette.

b Essentiellement financées par les pays membres du CAD.

27. Bilateral grants from DAC member countries to individual LDCs

27. Dons reçus par chacun des PMA en provenance des pays membres du CAD

Net disbursements in millions of dollars

Versements nets en millions de dollars

Country	*1976*	*1977*	*1978*	*1979*	*1980*	*1981*	*1982*	*1983*	*1984*	*1985*	*1986*	*Pays*
Afghanistan	19	28	32	43	18	2	7	12	5	8	9	Afghanistan
Bangladesh	148	222	531	538	1045	543	618	481	573	543	592	Bangladesh
Benin	16	17	36	33	42	41	36	33	37	39	58	Bénin
Bhutan	1	1	1	1	2	3	3	3	5	7	14	Bhoutan
Botswana	32	32	86	70	81	76	84	76	66	60	82	Botswana
Burkina Faso	48	62	92	166	133	161	126	106	110	114	161	Burkina faso
Burma	27	32	42	53	79	69	71	74	78	79	106	Birmanie
Burundi	26	28	37	43	57	65	61	59	62	60	78	Burundi
Cape Verde	7	16	25	27	39	36	43	45	39	38	75	Cap-Vert
Central African Rep.	24	31	29	53	72	59	61	51	65	48	68	Rép. centrafricaine
Chad	40	46	65	51	20	47	35	50	60	91	96	Tchad
Comoros [a]	8	1	1	8	14	23	12	14	15	14	17	Comores [a]
Democratic Yemen	9	6	7	5	8	5	6	5	4	9	3	Yémen démocratique
Djibouti	26	30	30	21	34	38	44	38	42	52	66	Djibouti
Equatorial Guinea	..	..	..	0	1	4	5	4	8	7	11	Guinée équatoriale
Ethiopia	47	55	61	66	88	78	72	95	158	402	386	Ethiopie
Gambia	4	10	11	11	24	18	21	22	30	28	55	Gambie
Guinea	0	3	9	13	15	22	17	14	30	44	52	Guinée
Guinea-Bissau	12	25	35	34	32	40	33	32	30	30	40	Guinée-Bissau
Haiti	25	27	33	36	48	54	64	67	58	87	131	Haïti
Kiribati	4	6	10	9	19	14	14	14	10	11	12	Kiribati
Lao People's Dem.Rep.	14	14	29	24	17	17	22	13	15	17	22	Rép. dém. pop. lao
Lesotho	18	21	30	43	64	62	57	65	66	52	58	Lesotho
Malawi	27	21	79	120	58	78	64	57	50	55	80	Malawi
Maldives	1	1	3	1	2	3	2	4	4	6	11	Maldives
Mali	42	49	75	146	120	133	91	91	122	156	172	Mali
Mauritania	20	22	30	35	53	56	51	61	63	89	84	Mauritanie
Nepal	28	39	41	70	95	84	109	104	91	113	150	Népal
Niger	59	41	92	126	87	105	117	102	88	187	175	Niger
Rwanda	50	57	76	101	92	93	94	92	94	96	111	Rwanda
Samoa	7	11	11	22	14	14	15	17	11	13	18	Samoa
Sao Tome and Principe	1	2	2	1	1	2	4	3	4	3	7	Sao Tomé-et-Principe
Sierra Leone	7	9	13	22	28	23	23	22	18	77	43	Sierra leone
Somalia	19	26	27	39	157	117	105	109	108	138	308	Somalie
Sudan	28	43	93	112	377	275	337	369	269	568	410	Soudan
Togo	20	25	25	32	31	33	32	36	39	161	68	Togo
Tuvalu	3	2	3	4	5	4	5	4	5	3	4	Tuvalu
Uganda	3	4	9	28	41	91	54	69	47	40	80	Ouganda
United Rep.of Tanzania	170	192	421	439	608	443	429	378	364	345	572	Rép.-Unie de Tanzanie
Vanuatu	29	12	18	36	44	25	24	25	22	19	21	Vanuatu
Yemen	8	22	30	44	151	55	60	78	70	66	97	Yémen
All LDCs	**1074**	**1290**	**2277**	**2725**	**3913**	**3109**	**3130**	**2992**	**3033**	**3975**	**4600**	**Ensemble des PMA**
All developing countries	**5896**	**6398**	**8581**	**10795**	**13192**	**12151**	**12351**	**12655**	**13973**	**15519**	**18665**	**Ensemble des pays en développement**

Source: UNCTAD secretariat, based on information from the OECD/DAC secretariat.

a Excluding grants from France to Mayotte.

Source: Secrétariat de la CNUCED, d'après des renseignements du secrétariat de l'OCDE/CAD.

a Non compris l'aide versée au titre de dons par la France à Mayotte.

28. ODA commitments from multilateral agencies mainly financed by DAC member countries to individual LDCs

28. Engagements de l'APD à chacun des PMA en provenance des institutions multilatérales essentiellement financées par les pays membres du CAD

$ million — Millions de dollars

Country	1976	1977	1978	1979	1980	1981	1982	1983	1984	1985	1986	Pays
Afghanistan	73	53	79	123	9	9	9	11	9	12	10	Afghanistan
Bangladesh	251	348	400	458	705	615	817	654	835	773	668	Bangladesh
Benin	26	61	42	36	41	65	96	20	77	47	50	Bénin
Bhutan	2	2	2	5	14	7	11	17	24	32	22	Bhoutan
Botswana	12	17	20	20	14	39	14	18	20	45	27	Botswana
Burkina Faso	66	37	56	54	74	133	122	60	43	122	46	Burkina faso
Burma	83	64	109	136	165	135	193	204	51	68	102	Birmanie
Burundi	36	32	34	59	81	129	29	87	36	114	77	Burundi
Cape Verde	7	11	16	7	17	26	13	20	46	19	29	Cap-Vert
Central African Rep.	8	28	36	34	31	13	67	62	20	30	62	Rép. centrafricaine
Chad	57	29	57	12	14	46	25	43	60	76	120	Tchad
Comoros	4	15	15	13	20	29	26	15	25	14	10	Comores
Democratic Yemen	14	17	32	27	51	51	63	48	30	40	23	Yémen démocratique
Djibouti	0	3	3	9	11	13	20	24	22	16	27	Djibouti
Equatorial Guinea	-2	0	1	3	14	12	7	11	16	34	26	Guinée équatoriale
Ethiopia	78	126	47	81	147	204	200	321	312	243	346	Ethiopie
Gambia	13	4	19	29	37	29	24	31	36	10	63	Gambie
Guinea	6	33	80	41	91	20	60	56	113	68	77	Guinée
Guinea-Bissau	18	20	13	33	21	19	29	54	45	17	21	Guinée-Bissau
Haiti	38	40	85	33	30	53	110	62	34	44	75	Haïti
Kiribati	2	1	0	0	1	1	3	2	1	3	1	Kiribati
Lao People's Dem.Rep.	4	12	28	47	36	26	8	36	19	15	30	Rép. dém. pop. lao
Lesotho	20	41	30	35	40	46	30	37	63	38	63	Lesotho
Malawi	33	83	50	58	59	120	21	200	73	154	73	Malawi
Maldives	1	1	1	5	2	3	4	8	6	3	3	Maldives
Mali	74	63	69	62	50	98	128	127	82	173	122	Mali
Mauritania	22	16	39	81	54	34	56	37	34	80	53	Mauritanie
Nepal	101	70	119	77	157	134	71	173	287	155	145	Népal
Niger	99	34	53	59	61	70	78	51	112	67	188	Niger
Rwanda	50	67	30	36	62	94	92	99	46	77	89	Rwanda
Samoa	6	9	11	15	10	19	4	5	6	9	13	Samoa
Sao Tome and Principe	1	1	13	2	2	2	5	6	10	12	33	Sao Tomé-et-Principe
Sierra Leone	8	32	14	48	10	60	36	34	39	12	26	Sierra leone
Somalia	82	50	52	107	132	186	123	116	155	164	207	Somalie
Sudan	73	79	140	155	343	186	158	231	223	309	291	Soudan
Togo	31	49	30	35	33	40	67	67	39	75	63	Togo
Tuvalu	0	0	0	0	1	1	1	0	1	0	0	Tuvalu
Uganda	14	13	8	49	130	105	159	202	206	92	94	Ouganda
United Rep.of Tanzania	138	145	166	114	216	181	174	126	117	97	245	Rép.-Unie de Tanzanie
Vanuatu	1	1	0	1	2	6	6	6	1	8	3	Vanuatu
Yemen	46	31	52	61	69	44	96	66	65	54	58	Yémen
All LDCs	**1596**	**1739**	**2053**	**2261**	**3058**	**3105**	**3257**	**3446**	**3434**	**3418**	**3679**	**Ensemble des PMA**

Source: UNCTAD secretariat, based on information from the OECD/DAC secretariat.

Source: Secrétariat de la CNUCED, d'après des renseignements du secrétariat de l'OCDE/CAD.

29. Concessional assistance from multilateral agencies mainly financed by DAC member countries to individual LDCs

29. Aide concessionnelle reçue par chacun des PMA en provenance des institutions multilatérales essentiellement financées par les pays membres du CAD

Net disbursements in millions of dollars

Versements nets en millions de dollars

Country	*1976*	*1977*	*1978*	*1979*	*1980*	*1981*	*1982*	*1983*	*1984*	*1985*	*1986*	*Pays*
Afghanistan	29	48	44	53	19	11	9	11	9	11	8	Afghanistan
Bangladesh	201	202	295	357	358	343	376	375	500	518	612	Bangladesh
Benin	23	18	27	33	51	33	35	39	38	44	63	Bénin
Bhutan	2	2	3	5	7	7	8	10	13	15	18	Bhoutan
Botswana	7	9	14	26	20	21	10	17	27	33	23	Botswana
Burkina Faso	23	36	61	61	54	50	54	53	56	69	89	Burkina faso
Burma	32	45	117	102	77	79	98	81	122	103	108	Birmanie
Burundi	19	18	33	45	49	53	45	63	58	59	87	Burundi
Cape Verde	6	9	8	5	21	13	11	15	21	23	29	Cap-Vert
Central African Rep.	12	10	22	31	34	29	20	28	43	42	47	Rép. centrafricaine
Chad	18	32	47	30	15	29	26	44	56	85	61	Tchad
Comoros	3	7	6	7	12	14	12	14	16	21	20	Comores
Democratic Yemen	14	25	34	35	35	31	48	51	41	38	38	Yémen démocratique
Djibouti	..	2	3	4	9	14	10	11	11	16	15	Djibouti
Equatorial Guinea	0	0	1	3	8	6	8	7	7	11	11	Guinée équatoriale
Ethiopia	68	53	81	104	120	151	123	176	176	290	241	Ethiopie
Gambia	4	5	12	17	24	26	19	20	19	18	43	Gambie
Guinea	7	12	38	34	52	48	33	41	47	52	75	Guinée
Guinea-Bissau	7	10	11	16	21	22	26	26	22	31	27	Guinée-Bissau
Haiti	40	45	43	44	42	39	47	54	63	49	48	Haïti
Kiribati	0	0	1	0	1	2	1	2	2	1	2	Kiribati
Lao People's Dem.Rep.	4	4	29	24	23	18	17	17	19	21	27	Rép. dém. pop. lao
Lesotho	12	16	21	20	31	41	33	35	29	38	34	Lesotho
Malawi	17	25	42	50	66	55	56	61	107	60	113	Malawi
Maldives	1	1	1	2	4	2	2	4	3	4	5	Maldives
Mali	33	36	58	86	93	77	63	72	86	98	127	Mali
Mauritania	20	24	47	74	33	44	31	35	41	43	41	Mauritanie
Nepal	21	34	36	51	72	81	84	91	101	114	126	Népal
Niger	45	32	57	51	57	42	44	51	54	97	116	Niger
Rwanda	22	29	42	57	52	43	50	54	63	73	80	Rwanda
Samoa	4	8	8	9	11	10	7	10	9	6	5	Samoa
Sao Tome and Principe	1	1	2	2	3	4	6	8	7	9	5	Sao Tomé-et-Principe
Sierra Leone	8	13	27	20	27	24	25	29	22	31	28	Sierra leone
Somalia	47	43	41	52	151	167	137	132	141	152	165	Somalie
Sudan	61	54	111	112	170	188	197	161	191	266	268	Soudan
Togo	20	22	36	41	35	26	23	58	53	51	75	Togo
Tuvalu	0	0	0	0	0	1	1	0	0	0	1	Tuvalu
Uganda	11	10	10	25	70	57	75	81	118	140	117	Ouganda
United Rep.of Tanzania	55	70	90	126	123	165	173	136	133	105	162	Rép.-Unie de Tanzanie
Vanuatu	1	2	0	1	1	6	3	3	2	3	4	Vanuatu
Yemen	36	30	36	31	43	38	52	52	53	52	47	Yémen
All LDCs	**936**	**1042**	**1595**	**1843**	**2094**	**2107**	**2095**	**2222**	**2578**	**2889**	**3209**	**Ensemble des PMA**
All developing countries	**3419**	**3655**	**4869**	**5817**	**7363**	**6963**	**7010**	**7044**	**7312**	**7919**	**8778**	**Ensemble des pays en développement**

Source: UNCTAD secretariat, based on information from the OECD/DAC secretariat.

Source: Secrétariat de la CNUCED, d'après des renseignements du secrétariat de l'OCDE/CAD.

30. Grants from multilateral agencies mainly financed by DAC member countries to individual LDCs

30. Dons reçus par chacun des PMA en provenance des institutions multilatérales essentiellement financées par les pays membres du CAD

Net disbursements in millions of dollars

Versements nets en millions de dollars

Country	*1976*	*1977*	*1978*	*1979*	*1980*	*1981*	*1982*	*1983*	*1984*	*1985*	*1986*	*Pays*
Afghanistan	14	20	22	34	9	10	9	11	9	12	9	Afghanistan
Bangladesh	82	87	108	105	96	131	153	123	170	85	115	Bangladesh
Benin	17	10	18	23	25	19	17	16	18	17	21	Bénin
Bhutan	2	2	3	5	7	7	7	9	12	11	15	Bhoutan
Botswana	6	7	11	21	17	17	10	16	21	30	23	Botswana
Burkina Faso	16	17	37	32	27	33	40	32	41	41	43	Burkina faso
Burma	8	9	11	23	19	19	21	22	18	28	38	Birmanie
Burundi	17	12	17	25	27	39	19	26	23	25	27	Burundi
Cape Verde	6	9	8	5	11	9	9	13	18	18	25	Cap-Vert
Central African Rep.	12	9	11	18	18	21	14	18	24	20	20	Rép. centrafricaine
Chad	13	14	22	19	13	27	25	43	50	76	51	Tchad
Comoros	3	7	5	5	7	11	10	10	7	11	11	Comores
Democratic Yemen	7	17	15	17	19	22	30	24	19	20	17	Yémen démocratique
Djibouti	..	2	3	4	8	13	9	10	9	10	8	Djibouti
Equatorial Guinea	0	0	1	3	2	6	8	6	7	6	5	Guinée équatoriale
Ethiopia	31	18	33	42	81	111	88	118	128	216	181	Ethiopie
Gambia	3	2	8	11	16	22	15	10	14	10	19	Gambie
Guinea	6	6	19	17	29	22	20	17	23	19	24	Guinée
Guinea-Bissau	7	10	11	14	17	13	13	11	16	14	15	Guinée-Bissau
Haiti	9	8	13	14	14	13	19	13	20	16	16	Haïti
Kiribati	0	0	0	0	1	2	1	2	2	1	1	Kiribati
Lao People's Dem.Rep.	4	4	20	17	13	12	8	8	10	12	15	Rép. dém. pop. lao
Lesotho	10	10	15	14	20	28	16	23	20	24	22	Lesotho
Malawi	5	9	14	17	27	26	22	18	25	18	25	Malawi
Maldives	1	1	1	2	2	2	2	3	3	3	3	Maldives
Mali	17	20	32	49	56	49	39	40	61	56	59	Mali
Mauritania	16	16	36	66	18	36	24	26	31	34	26	Mauritanie
Nepal	11	15	14	20	34	32	30	36	32	35	33	Népal
Niger	42	24	41	38	25	27	31	30	34	64	55	Niger
Rwanda	14	18	28	32	31	32	33	26	29	37	34	Rwanda
Samoa	3	4	2	4	5	5	4	5	4	4	4	Samoa
Sao Tome and Principe	1	1	2	2	3	2	3	6	7	8	4	Sao Tomé-et-Principe
Sierra Leone	6	8	7	8	14	18	14	18	12	17	15	Sierra leone
Somalia	39	33	31	44	126	146	112	105	109	104	105	Somalie
Sudan	22	28	35	57	105	105	102	96	108	224	197	Soudan
Togo	16	12	16	14	13	15	9	23	26	17	24	Togo
Tuvalu	0	0	0	0	0	1	1	0	0	0	1	Tuvalu
Uganda	8	9	8	24	40	43	31	41	51	44	51	Ouganda
United Rep.of Tanzania	26	24	36	48	50	66	61	52	66	63	75	Rép.-Unie de Tanzanie
Vanuatu	1	2	0	1	1	6	2	2	2	2	3	Vanuatu
Yemen	18	14	14	17	21	21	27	20	21	15	14	Yémen
All LDCs	**517**	**518**	**724**	**912**	**1065**	**1235**	**1105**	**1128**	**1298**	**1466**	**1448**	**Ensemble des PMA**
All developing countries	**1636**	**1815**	**2339**	**2975**	**3342**	**3949**	**3606**	**3666**	**3813**	**4324**	**4445**	**Ensemble des pays en développement**

Source: UNCTAD secretariat, based on information from the OECD/DAC secretariat.

Source: Secrétariat de la CNUCED, d'après des renseignements du secrétariat de l'OCDE/CAD.

31. Non-concessional assistance from multilateral agencies mainly financed by DAC member countries to individual LDCs

31. Aide non-concessionelle reçue par chacun des PMA en provenance des institutions multilatérales essentiellement financées par les pays membres du CAD

Net disbursements in millions of dollars

Versements nets en millions de dollars

Country	*1976*	*1977*	*1978*	*1979*	*1980*	*1981*	*1982*	*1983*	*1984*	*1985*	*1986*	*Pays*
Afghanistan	-	-	-	-	-	-	-	-	-	-	-	Afghanistan
Bangladesh	0	0	-1	-1	1	-0	0	-1	-1	-1	2	Bangladesh
Benin	1	4	3	1	3	3	-0	0	-0	-1	-2	Bénin
Bhutan	-	-	-	-	-	-	-	-	-	-	-	Bhoutan
Botswana	2	3	3	6	3	10	17	19	23	38	9	Botswana
Burkina Faso	1	-0	1	-1	0	-1	-0	3	2	2	6	Burkina faso
Burma	-1	0	3	0	1	-0	-0	-0	-0	-0	-0	Birmanie
Burundi	2	1	0	-0	0	0	1	10	11	5	3	Burundi
Cape Verde	..	..	..	..	..	..	7	4	1	1	..	Cap-Vert
Central African Rep.	0	..	0	-0	0	0	-0	1	2	3	6	Rép. centrafricaine
Chad	-	-	-	-	-	-	-	-	-	-	-	Tchad
Comoros	..	..	..	..	..	..	1	3	3	3	1	Comores
Democratic Yemen	-	-	-	-	-	-	-	-	-	-	-	Yémen démocratique
Djibouti	-	-	-	-	-	-	-	-	-	-	-	Djibouti
Equatorial Guinea	..	..	..	..	1	2	3	1	0	-0	0	Guinée équatoriale
Ethiopia	-2	-4	-4	-4	-2	-1	-2	-1	-2	-3	-2	Ethiopie
Gambia	..	0	0	1	6	2	1	1	4	2	..	Gambie
Guinea	-2	-0	-2	-1	-3	-2	1	2	13	-0	-6	Guinée
Guinea-Bissau	..	..	..	..	0	0	2	4	3	1	..	Guinée-Bissau
Haiti	..	..	..	..	..	..	..	1	..	..	-0	Haïti
Kiribati	..	..	..	..	..	8	..	..	..	..	..	Kiribati
Lao People's Dem.Rep.	-	-	-	-	-	-	-	-	-	-	-	Rép. dém. pop. lao
Lesotho	..	..	0	..	..	0	2	2	5	11	-1	Lesotho
Malawi	3	9	12	22	16	27	22	3	1	4	1	Malawi
Maldives	-	-	-	-	-	-	-	-	-	-	-	Maldives
Mali	-0	1	3	2	1	0	2	1	..	-1	-1	Mali
Mauritania	0	1	0	0	-1	16	39	34	-1	-6	2	Mauritanie
Nepal	-0	2	1	-0	-0	-0	-0	..	2	3	-0	Népal
Niger	-0	-0	1	7	7	4	1	15	1	-1	-3	Niger
Rwanda	..	0	0	..	0	0	1	1	-0	-0	-0	Rwanda
Samoa	-	-	-	-	-	-	-	-	-	-	-	Samoa
Sao Tome and Principe	-	-	-	-	-	-	-	-	-	-	-	Sao Tomé-et-Principe
Sierra Leone	1	1	-0	2	3	1	0	-1	-4	-1	-3	Sierra leone
Somalia	0	0	0	-0	..	0	-0	-0	1	2	2	Somalie
Sudan	0	-3	4	3	-2	-1	-3	-5	-9	-5	-4	Soudan
Togo	1	2	30	29	32	-3	-3	-1	-1	-3	-4	Togo
Tuvalu	-	-	-	-	-	-	-	-	-	-	-	Tuvalu
Uganda	3	3	1	3	2	5	6	7	5	49	4	Ouganda
United Rep.of Tanzania	12	24	16	20	21	18	7	17	8	34	-21	Rép.-Unie de Tanzanie
Vanuatu	-	-	-	-	-	-	-	-	-	-	-	Vanuatu
Yemen	..	..	..	2	..	..	..	-1	-1	11	6	Yémen
All LDCs	**21**	**42**	**69**	**91**	**89**	**88**	**103**	**116**	**65**	**147**	**-5**	**Ensemble des PMA**
All developing countries	**2468**	**2625**	**2878**	**3838**	**4574**	**5414**	**6381**	**7018**	**7913**	**7112**	**7591**	**Ensemble des pays en développement**

Source: UNCTAD secretariat, based on information from the OECD/DAC secretariat.

Source: Secrétariat de la CNUCED, d'après des renseignements du secrétariat de l'OCDE/CAD.

32. Concessional assistance from DAC member countries and multilateral agencies [a] to individual LDCs : net disbursements and leading donors in 1986 [b]

32. Aide concessionelle reçue par chacun des PMA en provenance des pays membres du CAD et des intitutions multilatérales [a] : versements nets et principaux donneurs en 1986 [b]

Country	Net disbursements Versements nets ($ mill./mill. de dollars)	Leading donors Principaux donneurs	Pays
Afghanistan	6	UNDP/PNUD, Sweden/Suède.	Afghanistan
Bangladesh	1373	IDA/AID, Japan/Japon, USA/Etats-Unis, AsDB/BAsD.	Bangladesh
Benin	135	Germany, Fed.Rep.of/Allemagne, Rép. féd. d', IDA/AID, France.	Bénin
Bhutan	32	UNDP/PNUD, Japan/Japon, Norway/Norvège, WFP/PAM.	Bhoutan
Botswana	105	Sweden/Suède, Germany, Fed.Rep. of/ Allemagne, Rép.Féd. d', Norway/Norvège.	Botswana
Burkina Faso	264	France, Italy/Italie, IDA/AID.	Burkina Faso
Burma	416	Japan/Japon, IDA/AID.	Birmanie
Burundi	177	IDA/AID, France, Belgium/Belgique.	Burundi
Cape Verde	105	Italy/Italie, EEC-EDF/CEE-FED.	Cap-Vert
Central African Rep.	132	France, IDA/AID.	Rép. centrafricaine
Chad	163	France, Italy/Italie, EEC-EDF/CEE-FED.	Tchad
Comoros	40	France, EEC-EDF/CEE-FED, IDA/AID.	Comores
Democratic Yemen	40	IDA/AID, WFP/PAM.	Yémen démocratique
Djibouti	79	France, Italy/Italie.	Djibouti
Equatorial Guinea	22	France, IDA/AID, AfDF/FAfD, UNDP/PNUD.	Guinée équatoriale
Ethiopia	643	Italy/Italie, USA/Etats-Unis, EEC-EDF/CEE-FED.	Ethiopie
Gambia	102	Italy/Italie, U.K./Royaume-Uni, IDA/AID, EEC-EDF/CEE-FED.	Gambie
Guinea	173	France, IDA/AID.	Guinée
Guinea-Bissau	67	Sweden/Suède, Italy/Italie, IDA/AID, Netherlands/Pays-Bas.	Guinée-Bissau
Haiti	174	USA/Etats-Unis, IDA/AID.	Haïti
Kiribati	13	Japan/Japon, U.K./Royaume-Uni, Australia/Australie.	Kiribati
Lao People's Dem.Rep.	47	UNDP/PNUD, Sweden/Suède, IDA/AID, AsDB/BAsD, Japan/Japon.	Rép. dém. pop. lao
Lesotho	90	USA/Etats-Unis, Germany, Fed. Rep. of/Allemagne, Rép. féd. d'	Lesotho
Malawi	203	IDA/AID, Germany, Fed. Rep. of/Allemagne, Rép.féd. d'	Malawi
Maldives	16	Japan/Japon, Norway/Norvège.	Maldives
Mali	331	France, IDA/AID.	Mali
Mauritania	146	France, Italy/Italie, USA/Etats-Unis, EEC-EDF/CEE-FED.	Mauritanie
Nepal	296	Japan/Japon, IDA/AID, AsDB/BAsD.	Népal
Niger	300	France, IDA/AID, USA/Etats-Unis.	Niger
Rwanda	203	IDA/AID, Belgium/Belgique, USA/Etats-Unis.	Rwanda
Samoa	23	Japan/Japon, Australia/Australie, New Zealand/Nouvelle-Zélande.	Samoa
Sao Tome and Principe	12	Japan/Japon, France, UNDP/PNUD.	Sao Tomé-et-Principe
Sierra Leone	80	USA/Etats-Unis, Italy/Italie, IDA/AID, Germany, Fed.Rep.of/Allemagne, Rép.féd.d'.	Sierra Leone
Somalia	519	Italy/Italie, USA/Etats-Unis, UNHCR.	Somalie
Sudan	733	USA/Etats-Unis, Italy/Italie, EEC-EDF/CEE-FED.	Soudan
Togo	166	IDA/AID, France, Japan/Japon.	Togo
Tuvalu	4	U.K./Royaume-Uni, New Zealand/Nouvelle-Zélande, Australia/Australie.	Tuvalu
Uganda	194	IDA/AID, Italy/Italie.	Ouganda
United Rep.of Tanzania	676	Sweden/Suède, IDA/AID, Norway/Norvège.	Rép.-Unie de Tanzanie
Vanuatu	24	France, U.K./Royaume-Uni, Australia/Australie.	Vanuatu
Yemen	162	USA/Etats-Unis, IDA/AID, Netherlands/Pays-Bas.	Yémen

Source: UNCTAD secretariat, based on information from the OECD/DAC secretariat.

a Multilateral agencies mainly financed by DAC countries.

b Accounting each for 10 per cent or more of the total concessional assistance received by the given LDC.

Source: Secrétariat de la CNUCED, d'après des renseignements du secrétariat de l'OCDE/CAD.

a Institutions multilatérales essentiellement financées par les pays du CAD.

b Donnant 10 pour cent ou davantage de l'aide concessionnelle totale reçue par le PMA en question.

33. Technical assistance disbursements [a]

33. Versements au titre de l'assistance technique [a]

Millions of dollars — Millions de dollars

Country	1976	1977	1978	1979	1980	1981	1982	1983	1984	1985	1986	Pays
Afghanistan	20	28	31	38	22	15	14	15	12	15	13	Afghanistan
Bangladesh	60	27	100	148	159	147	133	176	158	169	158	Bangladesh
Benin	16	14	17	20	26	25	28	26	28	30	38	Bénin
Bhutan	3	2	2	5	6	7	6	7	9	10	11	Bhoutan
Botswana	16	18	23	36	48	48	43	41	35	37	43	Botswana
Burkina Faso	38	38	49	61	73	72	74	65	71	70	96	Burkina faso
Burma	17	14	18	31	31	39	42	37	38	47	54	Birmanie
Burundi	23	26	30	36	45	44	47	43	43	46	54	Burundi
Cape Verde	2	3	6	6	12	11	21	17	17	19	25	Cap-Vert
Central African Rep.	19	21	25	33	34	34	31	29	39	34	46	Rép. centrafricaine
Chad	22	25	29	21	12	17	15	22	19	43	46	Tchad
Comoros	2	2	1	3	7	10	10	10	9	11	14	Comores
Democratic Yemen	11	11	11	8	12	13	15	14	10	13	9	Yémen démocratique
Djibouti	14	15	14	19	28	30	31	29	30	30	46	Djibouti
Equatorial Guinea	0	0	1	2	2	5	4	4	7	6	8	Guinée équatoriale
Ethiopia	32	30	27	29	44	64	53	64	81	104	116	Ethiopie
Gambia	4	3	7	10	13	14	17	16	15	18	33	Gambie
Guinea	6	6	10	11	19	21	21	14	18	20	27	Guinée
Guinea-Bissau	7	5	7	9	12	13	15	16	12	15	23	Guinée-Bissau
Haiti	14	14	21	24	32	33	34	31	33	42	52	Haïti
Kiribati	3	3	4	3	5	4	5	4	4	5	5	Kiribati
Lao People's Dem.Rep.	5	5	12	12	14	13	11	11	12	14	18	Rép. dém. pop. lao
Lesotho	12	13	17	21	32	33	35	35	34	31	39	Lesotho
Malawi	17	18	24	30	36	38	37	35	40	35	45	Malawi
Maldives	1	1	2	2	3	3	4	4	4	5	4	Maldives
Mali	23	26	35	50	77	63	55	53	60	61	89	Mali
Mauritania	13	14	19	24	29	38	34	33	31	36	44	Mauritanie
Nepal	20	26	31	38	51	53	64	68	68	70	75	Népal
Niger	28	31	38	47	62	59	68	61	61	76	92	Niger
Rwanda	32	41	43	51	55	53	50	54	50	61	66	Rwanda
Samoa	5	6	7	6	10	11	8	7	7	8	8	Samoa
Sao Tome and Principe	1	1	2	1	1	1	3	2	2	3	4	Sao Tomé-et-Principe
Sierra Leone	10	10	13	15	21	22	21	19	19	22	30	Sierra leone
Somalia	16	19	22	32	93	103	92	114	107	132	160	Somalie
Sudan	31	38	60	69	103	132	118	128	122	204	161	Soudan
Togo	17	19	22	25	29	30	30	28	30	30	42	Togo
Tuvalu	0	0	1	1	1	2	2	1	1	2	2	Tuvalu
Uganda	8	8	12	16	21	34	30	34	32	37	50	Ouganda
United Rep.of Tanzania	77	80	107	139	173	177	181	174	139	141	163	Rép.-Unie de Tanzanie
Vanuatu	15	2	3	22	25	17	16	16	13	12	16	Vanuatu
Yemen	16	25	33	40	50	61	65	60	62	56	76	Yémen
All LDCs	**675**	**686**	**931**	**1196**	**1526**	**1608**	**1581**	**1614**	**1581**	**1818**	**2096**	**Ensemble des PMA**
All developing countries	**3808**	**4077**	**5000**	**6252**	**7255**	**7383**	**7364**	**7696**	**7737**	**8173**	**9574**	**Ensemble des pays en développement**

Source: UNCTAD secretariat, based on information from the OECD/DAC secretariat.

a Bilateral contributions from DAC member countries plus contributions from multilateral agencies mainly financed by them.

Source: Secrétariat de la CNUCED, d'après des renseignements du secrétariat de l'OCDE/CAD.

a Somme des contributions bilatérales des pays membres du CAD et des contributions des institutions multilatérales essentiellement financées par ceux-ci.

34. ODA commitments from individual DAC member countries and individual multilateral agencies mainly financed by them, to LDCs as a group, by purpose

34. Engagements de l'APD de chaque pays membre du CAD et de chaque institution multilatérale essentiellement financée par ceux-ci, en faveur de l'ensemble des PMA, par objet

		Agriculture / *Agriculture*	Industry, mining, construction / *Industries manufacturières, extraction, construction*	Energy / *Energie*	Transport and communication / *Transports et communication*	Health / *Santé*	Education / *Enseignement*	Social Infrastructure / *Infrastructure sociale*	Trade, banking, tourism / *Commerce, banques, tourisme*	General economic support [a] / *Soutien économique général* [a]	Other [b] / *Autres* [b]	Total	
		As percentage of total / En pourcentage du total										*in $ million / en mill. de $*	
Bilateral donors													***Donneurs bilatéraux***
Australia	A	7.4	-	-	9.1	10.4	0.9	-	0.4	52.8	19.0	231	Australie
	B	10.0	1.3	3.1	6.9	10.6	3.1	-	-	36.3	28.7	160	
Austria	A	-	-	-	-	-	-	-	-	-	100.0	13	Autriche
	B	-	-	-	-	-	-	-	-	-	100.0	23	
Belgium	A	-	1.5	-	-	1.0	-	-	-	8.0	88.7	194	Belgique
	B	1.9	-	-	-	-	-	-	-	-	98.1	160	
Canada	A	25.5	13.2	5.9	7.4	2.9	4.3	0.1	0.5	2.1	38.0	752	Canada
	B	24.7	3.2	9.3	21.2	4.2	2.5	4.9	0.4	0.5	29.1	937	
Denmark	A	32.1	0.6	1.9	8.4	22.7	1.3	-	-	4.9	28.0	285	Danemark
	B	22.8	7.9	18.8	11.5	21.8	3.4	0.6	-	0.2	13.0	481	
Finland	A	11.6	5.8	1.0	-	1.0	-	-	-	16.5	64.1	103	Finlande
	B	-	-	-	-	-	-	-	-	-	100.0	247	
France	A	13.5	3.8	6.9	12.6	2.7	0.8	1.5	1.0	1.2	55.9	1729	France
	B	14.3	4.8	5.3	13.1	4.4	0.6	1.2	1.3	7.7	47.3	1927	
Germany, Fed.Rep.of	A	6.7	0.8	12.3	15.7	3.2	-	0.2	0.3	15.9	44.8	1869	Allemagne,Rép.féd.d'
	B	7.2	0.4	10.5	7.9	7.0	0.1	0.7	-	28.0	38.1	1957	
Italy	A	15.0	1.4	11.2	7.1	6.7	0.7	-	-	17.2	40.6	731	Italie
	B	6.6	3.6	3.3	2.9	1.2	-	0.3	-	16.2	65.9	1928	
Japan	A	17.7	3.1	17.7	10.4	8.4	0.4	0.8	-	32.8	8.7	1727	Japon
	B	21.3	3.3	7.6	18.5	6.0	1.8	0.5	-	34.0	7.0	2204	
Netherlands	A	18.6	1.4	3.8	7.2	7.2	1.1	1.8	0.4	27.7	30.8	783	Pays-Bas
	B	29.6	2.7	3.0	3.0	5.6	-	0.2	0.4	29.1	26.4	764	
New Zealand	A	38.9	-	-	5.6	5.6	-	-	-	-	49.9	18	Nouvelle-Zélande
	B	3.6	-	14.3	3.6	3.6	-	-	-	-	74.9	26	
Norway	A	9.4	5.5	1.3	7.8	9.4	3.2	7.4	0.3	8.7	46.9	309	Norvège
	B	12.0	4.7	8.5	21.2	19.2	6.0	3.6	2.0	11.4	11.4	446	
Sweden	A	19.6	8.3	1.9	2.3	7.6	11.2	1.5	0.3	25.2	22.1	506	Suède
	B	13.9	9.7	2.1	8.0	6.7	9.5	2.8	0.2	24.1	23.0	513	
Switzerland	A	34.4	1.2	1.2	12.0	11.2	10.4	2.4	2.4	0.4	24.4	224	Suisse
	B	22.6	0.4	0.4	8.7	9.0	9.4	6.8	2.3	6.4	34.0	264	
United Kingdom	A	0.5	-	7.8	9.0	-	1.1	-	-	35.4	46.2	596	Royaume-Uni
	B	5.8	-	13.6	10.4	1.9	-	0.3	0.1	33.8	34.1	762	
United States	A	17.0	0.1	2.2	1.7	7.0	2.5	0.4	0.3	36.8	32.0	2199	Etats-Unis
	B	13.3	-	1.3	3.3	6.1	2.5	2.0	1.0	40.2	30.3	3097	
Total [c]	A	15.0	2.6	7.2	8.2	6.0	1.9	0.8	0.4	21.9	35.9	12271	Total [c]
	B	14.2	2.5	5.6	9.3	5.9	1.8	1.4	0.5	24.3	34.5	15895	

34. ODA commitments from individual DAC member countries and individual multilateral agencies mainly financed by them, to LDCs as a group, by purpose *(continued)*

34. Engagements de l'APD de chaque pays membre du CAD et de chaque institution multilatérale essentiellement financée par ceux-ci, en faveur de l'ensemble des PMA, par objet *(suite)*

		Agriculture / *Agriculture*	*Industry, mining, construction* / *Industries manufacturières, extraction, construction*	*Energy* / *Energie*	*Transport and communication* / *Transports et communication*	*Health* / *Santé*	*Education* / *Enseignement*	*Social Infrastructure* / *Infrastructure sociale*	*Trade, banking, tourism* / *Commerce, banques, tourisme*	*General economic support* [a] / *Soutien économique général* [a]	*Other* [b] / *Autres* [b]	*Total*	
		As percentage of total / En pourcentage du total										*in $ million / en mill. de $*	
Multilateral donors													***Donneurs multilatéraux***
AfDF	A	22.4	1.2	7.7	17.7	21.7	9.1	2.2	-	-	18.0	678	FAfD
	B	27.9	4.4	7.2	21.9	15.7	9.1	-	0.5	-	13.3	851	
AsDB [d]	A	40.6	2.5	23.1	4.3	7.4	2.4	-	0.4	3.2	16.1	1072	BAsD [d]
	B	26.2	2.6	28.0	11.9	3.2	3.2	-	0.4	-	24.5	983	
EEC/EDF	A	38.7	3.1	3.8	13.3	10.4	2.7	0.5	0.3	21.0	6.2	1684	CEE/FED
	B	11.4	3.2	2.3	6.1	3.3	1.4	1.1	3.2	22.9	45.0	1521	
IDA	A	37.1	4.6	15.0	17.9	3.1	8.8	1.8	0.9	4.1	6.7	3768	AID
	B	22.3	3.2	17.1	13.5	5.7	8.4	6.0	-	16.8	7.0	4072	
IDB [d]	A	38.7	10.7	-	-	-	-	-	-	8.0	42.6	50	BID [d]
	B	21.4	-	-	-	9.2	12.2	-	-	-	57.1	81	
UN	A	-	-	-	-	-	-	-	-	-	100.0	2260	ONU
	B	-	-	-	-	-	-	-	-	-	100.0	2793	
IFAD	A	100.0	-	-	-	-	-	-	-	-	-	299	FIDA
	B	100.0	-	-	-	-	-	-	-	-	-	231	
Total	A	30.4	2.8	9.8	10.8	5.2	4.7	0.9	0.5	5.5	29.3	9808	Total
	B	18.5	2.3	10.2	9.1	4.4	4.6	2.4	0.5	9.5	38.5	10532	
Grand total [c]	**A**	**21.7**	**2.7**	**8.3**	**9.3**	**5.7**	**3.2**	**0.9**	**0.4**	**14.8**	**33.0**	**22079**	**Total général** [c]
	B	**15.9**	**2.4**	**7.4**	**9.2**	**5.3**	**2.9**	**1.8**	**0.5**	**18.4**	**36.1**	**26427**	

Source: OECD "Creditor Reporting System".

Note: For technical reasons the amounts to sectors may be understated.

A= 1981 to 1983.
B= 1984 to 1986.

a Including current imports financing, food aid and other emergency and disaster relief, budget support, balance of payments support and debt re-organisation.

b Technical cooperation not allocated by sector and other unallocated commitments.

c Excluding Ireland.

d Special funds.

Source: "Système de notification des pays créanciers" de l'OCDE.

Note: Pour des raisons techniques les données sectorielles peuvent être sous-estimées.

A= 1981 à 1983.
B= 1984 à 1986.

a Comprend les contributions destinées à financer des importations courantes, l'aide alimentaire et autres secours d'urgence, le soutien budgétaire, le soutien à la balance des paiements et le réaménagement de la dette.

b Coopération technique non-ventilée par secteur et autres engagements non-ventilés.

c Non compris l'Irlande.

d Fonds spéciaux.

35. ODA commitments from individual OPEC member countries and individual multilateral agencies mainly financed by them, to LDCs as a group

35. Engagements de l'APD de chaque pays membre de l'OPEP et de chaque institution multilatérale essentiellement financée par ceux-ci, en faveur de l'ensemble des PMA

$ million — *Millions de dollars*

	1977	1978	1979	1980	1981	1982	1983	1984	1985	1986	
Bilateral donors											***Donneurs bilatéraux***
Algeria	2.5	0.5	34.5	-	20.0	0.2	-	-	100.0	-	Algérie
Iran (Islamic Republic)	-	-	-	-	-	-	-	-	-	-	Iran (Rép. islamique)
Iraq	1.3	75.5	327.5	289.5	145.8	37.4	-	-	-	-	Iraq
Kuwait	158.7	116.8	175.8	214.9	272.7	295.5	165.6	142.0	189.4	171.7	Koweit
Libyan Arab Jamahiriya	0.9	25.4	6.0	42.8	24.5	-	-	10.0	-	-	Jamahiriya arabe libyenne
Nigeria	0.1	0.9	1.7	2.5	-	-	-	-	-	-	Nigéria
Qatar	4.7	10.8	4.8	40.5	22.6	7.6	7.4	2.0	5.1	27.9	Qatar
Saudi Arabia	842.5	912.1	463.8	407.0	432.9	896.9	1056.2	495.3	306.5	522.8	Arabie saoudite
United Arab Emirates	282.4	144.9	93.7	294.4	44.2	90.8	8.7	102.9	20.1	5.0	Emirats arabes unis
Total	1293.2	1286.9	1107.7	1291.6	962.7	1328.4	1237.9	752.3	621.0	727.5	Total
Multilateral donors											***Donneurs multilatéraux***
BADEA	29.9	22.6	8.2	44.8	10.0	32.0	20.5	0.3	11.0	26.2	BADEA
AFESD	95.1	0.5	50.7	43.6	68.6	76.5	172.6	137.2	79.6	118.2	FADES
Islamic Development Bank	31.1	13.6	18.3	17.9	19.0	45.1	23.5	92.9	65.4	28.6	Banque islamique de développement
OPEC Fund	98.0	65.4	95.5	119.4	180.2	178.4	81.1	74.7	35.9	46.5	Fonds de l'OPEP
Total	254.2	102.2	172.7	225.8	277.9	332.1	297.6	305.0	192.0	219.5	Total
Grand total	**1547.3**	**1389.1**	**1280.4**	**1517.3**	**1240.6**	**1660.5**	**1535.5**	**1057.3**	**813.0**	**946.9**	**Total général**

Source: UNCTAD secretariat estimates.

Source: Estimations du secrétariat de la CNUCED.

36A. Bilateral ODA from OPEC member countries and total financial flows from multilateral agencies mainly financed by them, to LDCs as a group

36A. APD bilatérale des pays membres de l'OPEP et apports financiers totaux des institutions multilatérales essentiellement financées par ceux-ci, en faveur de l'ensemble des PMA

Net disbursements in $ million — *Versements nets en millions de dollars*

	1977	1978	1979	1980	1981	1982	1983	1984	1985	1986	
A. Bilateral donors											***A. Donneurs bilatéraux***
Algeria	2.5	0.5	14.5	20.0	9.6	0.2	-	-	-	-	Algérie
Iran (Islamic Republic)	-	15.0	-	-	-	-	-	-	-	-0.4	Iran (Rép. islamique)
Iraq	25.0	42.5	47.5	53.8	-	-	-	-3.6	-19.6	-17.5	Iraq
Kuwait	136.0	118.4	137.8	190.9	180.1	138.5	158.8	153.9	209.2	122.0	Koweit
Libyan Arab Jamahiriya	0.9	10.4	0.0	8.2	24.5	-	-	-	10.0	-	Jamahiriya arabe libyenne
Nigeria	1.4	-	0.1	0.1	-	-	-	-	-	-	Nigéria
Qatar	5.0	8.5	5.7	41.5	23.3	7.7	7.4	1.8	5.1	27.1	Qatar
Saudi Arabia	608.7	405.5	441.9	487.5	417.9	741.6	645.6	513.0	233.4	293.9	Arabie saoudite
United Arab Emirates	123.2	158.3	113.1	152.8	86.7	75.1	51.0	32.9	41.9	54.5	Emirats arabes unis
Total bilateral concessional	902.6	759.2	760.5	954.7	742.0	963.1	862.9	698.0	480.0	479.6	Total des apports bilatéraux concessionnels
B. Multilateral donors											***B. Donneurs multilatéraux***
1. Concessional											***1. Apports concessionnels***
BADEA	4.6	19.7	15.9	18.5	15.1	15.6	20.6	12.1	9.2	10.1	BADEA
AFESD	32.4	69.8	34.4	45.7	58.5	43.8	48.1	33.1	24.1	52.1	FADES
Islamic Development Bank	-	4.9	11.3	5.4	18.3	10.5	15.8	24.1	28.3	23.4	Banque islamique de développement
OPEC Fund	82.8	18.1	37.3	70.4	128.8	119.7	79.9	35.3	20.4	7.9	Fonds de l'OPEP
Total	119.8	112.5	98.9	140.0	220.6	189.5	164.4	104.5	82.0	93.5	Total
2. Non-concessional											***2. Apports non-concessionnels***
BADEA	-	8.2	4.3	8.8	1.2	2.3	-0.4	0.5	9.6	6.3	BADEA
Islamic Development Bank	5.0	8.8	110.4	97.4	105.3	-56.3	10.8	16.8	-37.4	-65.8	Banque islamique de développement
OPEC Fund	-	-	-	0.5	-	-	0.4	-0.1	-0.1	-0.2	Fonds de l'OPEP
Total	5.0	17.0	114.7	106.7	106.5	-54.1	10.7	17.1	-27.9	-59.7	Total
Total concessional (A+B.1)	***1022.4***	***871.7***	***859.4***	***1094.7***	***962.7***	***1152.7***	***1027.3***	***802.5***	***562.0***	***573.1***	***Total des apports concessionnels (A+B.1)***
GRAND TOTAL [a]	***1029.6***	***888.7***	***974.1***	***1201.4***	***1069.2***	***1108.5***	***1068.0***	***822.1***	***538.6***	***513.4***	***TOTAL GÉNÉRAL [a]***

Source: UNCTAD secretariat estimates.

Note: The figures include only those amounts allocated to a specific country and therefore understate financial flows to the extent that certain donors have recorded disbursements in favour of groups of countries including some LDCs.

a Including bilateral non-concessional flows.

Source: Estimations du secrétariat de la CNUCED.

Note: Les données ne comprennent que les montants imputables à un pays bénéficiaire déterminé. Par conséquent, les apports financiers sont sous-estimés dans la mesure où certains donneurs ont alloué des versements à des groupes de pays comprenant des PMA.

a Y compris des apports bilatéraux non-concessionnels.

36B. Bilateral ODA from OPEC member countries and total financial flows from multilateral agencies mainly financed by them, to LDCs as a group

36B. APD bilatérale des pays membres de l'OPEP et apports financiers totaux des institutions multilatérales essentiellement financées par ceux-ci, en faveur de l'ensemble des PMA

Net disbursements in millions of 1980 dollars [a] — *Versements nets en millions de dollars de 1980* [a]

	1977	1978	1979	1980	1981	1982	1983	1984	1985	1986	
A. Bilateral donors											***A. Donneurs bilatéraux***
Algeria	3.9	0.7	16.7	20.0	10.1	0.3	-	-	-	-	Algérie
Iran (Islamic Republic)	-	20.7	-	-	-	-	-	-	-	-0.4	Iran (Rép. islamique)
Iraq	38.5	58.6	55.0	53.8	-	-	-	-4.1	-22.1	-19.5	Iraq
Kuwait	209.2	163.3	159.5	190.9	188.8	150.2	177.9	174.7	236.4	135.8	Koweit
Libyan Arab Jamahiriya	1.3	14.3	0.0	8.2	25.7	-	-	-	11.3	-	Jamahiriya arabe libyenne
Nigeria	2.1	-	0.1	0.1	-	-	-	-	-	-	Nigéria
Qatar	7.7	11.7	6.6	41.5	24.4	8.4	8.3	2.1	5.8	30.2	Qatar
Saudi Arabia	936.7	559.0	511.7	487.5	438.3	804.5	723.0	582.1	263.7	327.0	Arabie saoudite
United Arab Emirates	189.5	218.3	131.0	152.8	90.9	81.4	57.1	37.3	47.4	60.6	Emirats arabes unis
Total bilateral concessional	1389.1	1046.6	880.7	954.7	778.2	1044.9	966.3	792.1	542.4	533.7	Total des apports bilatéraux concessionnels
B. Multilateral donors											***B. Donneurs multilatéraux***
1. Concessional											***1. Apports concessionnels***
BADEA	7.1	27.2	18.5	18.5	15.8	16.9	23.0	13.7	10.4	11.3	BADEA
AFESD	49.8	96.3	39.8	45.7	61.3	47.5	53.8	37.6	27.2	58.0	FADES
Islamic Development Bank	-	6.8	13.1	5.4	19.2	11.4	17.7	27.3	32.0	26.0	Banque islamique de développement
OPEC Fund	127.5	24.9	43.1	70.4	135.1	129.8	89.5	40.0	23.0	8.7	Fonds de l'OPEP
Total	184.3	155.2	114.5	140.0	231.4	205.6	184.1	118.6	92.6	104.0	Total
2. Non-concessional											***2. Apports non-concessionnels***
BADEA	-	11.3	5.0	8.8	1.3	2.5	-0.5	0.6	10.9	7.0	BADEA
Islamic Development Bank	7.7	12.1	127.9	97.4	110.5	-61.1	12.1	19.0	-42.2	-73.2	Banque islamique de développement
OPEC Fund	-	-	-	0.5	-	-	0.5	-0.2	-0.2	-0.2	Fonds de l'OPEP
Total	7.7	23.4	132.8	106.7	111.7	-58.7	12.0	19.4	-31.5	-66.4	Total
Total concessional (A+B.1)	***1573.4***	***1201.7***	***995.2***	***1094.7***	***1009.6***	***1250.4***	***1150.4***	***910.7***	***635.0***	***637.7***	***Total des apports concessionnels (A+B.1)***
GRAND TOTAL [b]	***1584.4***	***1225.1***	***1128.1***	***1201.4***	***1121.4***	***1202.5***	***1196.0***	***933.0***	***608.6***	***571.3***	***TOTAL GÉNÉRAL*** [b]

Source: Table 36A.

a Actual disbursements were converted to 1980 prices using the index for LDCs in table 8.

b Including bilateral non-concessional flows.

Source: Tableau 36A.

a Les versements effectifs ont été convertis aux prix de 1980 en utilisant l'indice pour les PMA qui figure au tableau 8.

b Y compris des apports bilatéraux non-concessionnels.

37. Net ODA [a] as a percentage of donors' GNP and as ratio to average ODA in 1976-1980 from individual OPEC member countries to LDCs as a group

37. Apports nets au titre de l'APD [a] de chaque pays membre de l'OPEP à l'ensemble des PMA, en pourcentage du PNB et par rapport à l'APD moyenne pour 1976-1980

In per cent — *En pourcentage*

	% of GNP En % du PNB						Ratio to average ODA in 1976-1980 Rapport à l'APD moyenne pour 1976-1980						
Donor country [b]	1981	1982	1983	1984	1985	1986	1981	1982	1983	1984	1985	1986	Pays donateur [b]
Kuwait	0.77	0.96	1.04	1.06	1.25	0.76	1.24	1.30	1.42	1.42	1.50	0.94	Koweït
Qatar	0.44	0.34	0.31	0.12	0.12	0.68	1.42	0.96	0.71	0.31	0.28	1.31	Qatar
Saudi Arabia	0.33	0.61	0.70	0.73	0.44	0.61	0.96	1.68	1.49	1.26	0.67	0.80	Arabie saoudite
United Arab Emirates	0.35	0.39	0.28	0.14	0.18	0.29	0.74	0.77	0.50	0.24	0.29	0.40	Emirats arabes unis
Nigeria	0.12	0.04	0.02	0.04	0.03	0.04	3.61	1.03	0.72	1.13	0.78	0.63	Nigéria
Algeria	0.08	0.08	0.06	0.07	0.03	0.04	1.59	1.58	1.18	1.59	0.83	1.14	Algérie
Libyan Arab Jamahiriya	0.20	0.10	0.20	0.04	0.07	0.01 [c]	1.55	0.70	1.37	0.25	0.42	0.07	Jamahiriya arabe libyenne
Venezuela	0.05	0.05	0.07	0.01	0.01	0.01	1.94	2.01	2.83	0.33	0.17	0.26	Venezuela
Iran (Islamic Rep.of)	0.00	0.00	0.00	-	0.00	-0.00 [c]	0.01	0.00	0.29	-	0.01	-0.02	Iran (Rép. islamique)
Iraq	0.07	0.06	0.00	-0.01	-0.05	-0.04 [c]	0.29	0.32	0.02	-0.04	-0.34	-0.31	Iraq
Total OPEC	**0.20**	**0.25**	**0.23**	**0.20**	**0.14**	**0.15**	**1.05**	**1.33**	**1.22**	**1.00**	**0.68**	**0.68**	**Total OPEP**

Source: UNCTAD secretariat estimates.

a Including imputed flows through multilateral channels.

b Ranked in descending order of the ODA/GNP ratio in 1986.

c 1986 ODA as a percentage of GNP in 1985.

Source: Estimations du secrétariat de la CNUCED.

a Y compris le montant imputé de l'APD fournie aux PMA à travers les voies multilatérales.

b Classés par ordre décroissant du rapport APD/PNB en 1986.

c APD accordée en 1986 en pourcentage du PNB en 1985.

38. ODA commitments from OPEC member countries to individual LDCs

38. Engagements de l'APD à chacun des PMA en provenance des pays membres de l'OPEP

$ million | Millions de dollars

Country	1977	1978	1979	1980	1981	1982	1983	1984	1985	1986	Pays
Afghanistan	39	20	..	..	1	..	..	0	0	1	Afghanistan
Bangladesh	61	68	32	37	201	281	319	27	33	1	Bangladesh
Benin	1	8	..	..	..	..	0	10	0	0	Bénin
Bhutan	..	..	..	..	..	..	9	7	7	4	Bhoutan
Botswana	..	..	0	18	4	20	..	..	..	..	Botswana
Burkina Faso	0	1	13	1	2	..	14	21	0	3	Burkina faso
Burma	..	..	..	..	..	..	..	0	..	..	Birmanie
Burundi	6	..	..	4	12	9	15	9	7	6	Burundi
Cape Verde	..	..	0	14	..	..	4	..	..	..	Cap-Vert
Central African Rep.	..	..	4	2	2	..	6	..	5	5	Rép. centrafricaine
Chad	0	12	2	2	..	..	..	0	..	..	Tchad
Comoros	20	0	35	2	11	16	6	2	0	0	Comores
Democratic Yemen	76	22	38	90	32	48	21	22	105	16	Yémen démocratique
Djibouti	20	64	1	61	25	41	39	25	9	33	Djibouti
Equatorial Guinea	..	..	..	..	..	..	..	1	..	..	Guinée équatoriale
Ethiopia	1	0	1	0	10	..	..	..	100	0	Ethiopie
Gambia	25	..	..	22	4	1	0	0	0	0	Gambie
Guinea	7	2	7	181	..	..	11	55	..	..	Guinée
Guinea-Bissau	1	12	..	3	..	..	23	1	8	5	Guinée-Bissau
Haiti	-	-	-	-	-	-	-	-	-	-	Haïti
Kiribati	-	-	-	-	-	-	-	-	-	-	Kiribati
Lao People's Dem.Rep.	-	-	-	-	-	-	-	-	-	-	Rép. dém. pop. lao
Lesotho	..	5	..	6	..	..	..	..	..	..	Lesotho
Malawi	..	..	..	..	..	0	..	..	0	0	Malawi
Maldives	1	11	1	33	7	1	1	5	3	1	Maldives
Mali	20	15	11	31	8	126	0	1	10	8	Mali
Mauritania	41	156	232	99	134	112	2	21	36	2	Mauritanie
Nepal	33	..	7	..	..	..	0	24	20	8	Népal
Niger	3	16	0	38	91	40	..	22	8	6	Niger
Rwanda	1	..	0	..	8	..	19	0	13	10	Rwanda
Samoa	..	..	..	..	..	..	1	4	..	4	Samoa
Sao Tome and Principe	-	-	-	-	-	-	-	-	-	-	Sao Tomé-et-Principe
Sierra Leone	0	0	4	4	..	..	2	14	1	5	Sierra leone
Somalia	411	66	72	93	57	176	13	70	2	2	Somalie
Sudan	187	392	170	241	116	105	518	80	178	410	Soudan
Togo	0	..	5	8	..	..	17	10	0	1	Togo
Tuvalu	-	-	-	-	-	-	-	-	-	-	Tuvalu
Uganda	10	16	..	0	10	..	0	10	10	0	Ouganda
United Rep.of Tanzania	6	0	..	27	74	..	0	15	..	0	Rép.-Unie de Tanzanie
Vanuatu	-	-	-	-	-	-	-	-	-	-	Vanuatu
Yemen	325	400	474	274	154	352	199	295	65	194	Yémen
All LDCs	**1293**	**1287**	**1108**	**1292**	**963**	**1328**	**1238**	**752**	**621**	**727**	**Ensemble des PMA**

Source: UNCTAD secretariat estimates.

Source: Estimations du secrétariat de la CNUCED.

39. Concessional assistance from OPEC member countries [a] to individual LDCs

39. Aide concessionnelle reçue par chacun des PMA en provenance des pays membres de l'OPEP [a]

Net disbursements in millions of dollars

Versements nets en millions de dollars

Country	1976	1977	1978	1979	1980	1981	1982	1983	1984	1985	1986	Pays
Afghanistan	15	1	16	8	1	20	0	-2	-1	-1	-2	Afghanistan
Bangladesh	7	26	45	13	51	47	127	110	14	7	82	Bangladesh
Benin	0	1	..	2	2	1	0	2	-0	3	3	Bénin
Bhutan	..	..	..	..	..	..	..	..	0	3	8	Bhoutan
Botswana	..	..	..	..	0	..	6	8	10	4	-1	Botswana
Burkina Faso	0	0	1	1	1	2	..	0	1	14	11	Burkina faso
Burma	..	..	..	..	..	..	..	..	0	..	..	Birmanie
Burundi	0	0	2	2	3	2	6	3	9	3	8	Burundi
Cape Verde	1	1	..	..	..	..	..	0	1	2	1	Cap-Vert
Central African Rep.	1	..	..	1	2	0	1	0	1	1	8	Rép. centrafricaine
Chad	1	0	6	6	0	..	..	0	0	..	..	Tchad
Comoros	3	22	2	3	16	11	8	6	3	4	2	Comores
Democratic Yemen	142	89	29	24	53	44	57	23	39	45	14	Yémen démocratique
Djibouti	..	20	64	..	31	12	2	12	39	8	25	Djibouti
Equatorial Guinea	..	..	..	..	..	..	..	..	..	0	0	Guinée équatoriale
Ethiopia	..	1	0	1	0	10	..	..	..	..	0	Ethiopie
Gambia	1	1	8	4	7	14	2	1	1	-0	-1	Gambie
Guinea	0	13	9	9	0	-0	1	-1	30	2	3	Guinée
Guinea-Bissau	7	1	2	2	1	0	3	6	3	3	4	Guinée-Bissau
Haiti	-	-	-	-	-	-	-	-	-	-	-	Haïti
Kiribati	-	-	-	-	-	-	-	-	-	-	-	Kiribati
Lao People's Dem.Rep.	-	-	-	-	-	-	-	-	-	-	-	Rép. dém. pop. lao
Lesotho	..	..	0	0	0	0	..	3	3	3	-0	Lesotho
Malawi	..	..	..	..	..	..	0	..	..	0	0	Malawi
Maldives	3	1	3	4	17	6	2	4	0	-0	-0	Maldives
Mali	3	12	5	21	19	7	20	32	10	23	30	Mali
Mauritania	143	51	113	65	63	68	54	43	79	49	16	Mauritanie
Nepal	0	37	2	4	7	9	0	-1	-1	-1	4	Népal
Niger	4	6	16	1	2	24	82	18	12	0	6	Niger
Rwanda	0	5	1	1	1	1	0	2	6	6	8	Rwanda
Samoa	..	..	..	..	..	..	..	..	..	0	2	Samoa
Sao Tome and Principe	-	-	-	-	-	-	-	-	-	-	-	Sao Tomé-et-Principe
Sierra Leone	0	0	0	4	4	0	0	1	15	0	6	Sierra leone
Somalia	31	208	106	96	128	38	161	32	65	30	3	Somalie
Sudan	92	114	98	288	219	175	142	353	166	106	84	Soudan
Togo	3	0	..	..	0	0	3	2	2	9	8	Togo
Tuvalu	-	-	-	-	-	-	-	-	-	-	-	Tuvalu
Uganda	2	5	7	7	0	0	1	2	-2	1	3	Ouganda
United Rep.of Tanzania	1	7	1	4	16	15	14	18	11	10	5	Rép.-Unie de Tanzanie
Vanuatu	-	-	-	-	-	-	-	-	-	-	-	Vanuatu
Yemen	198	279	224	189	311	233	271	183	180	147	141	Yémen
All LDCs	**656**	**903**	**759**	**760**	**955**	**742**	**963**	**863**	**698**	**480**	**480**	**Ensemble des PMA**
All developing countries	**5160**	**4296**	**7446**	**6896**	**8890**	**7808**	**5503**	**4868**	**3793**	**3140**	**4117**	**Ensemble des pays en développement**

Source: UNCTAD secretariat estimates. For 1976, OECD secretariat estimates.

Note: The figures relating to LDCs include only those amounts allocated to a specific recipient country and therefore understate financial flows to the extent that certain donors have recorded disbursements in favour of groups of countries including some LDCs.

a The members of OPEC included here and providing assistance to LDCs are listed in table 36A.

Source: Estimations du secrétariat de la CNUCED. Pour 1976, estimations du secrétariat de l'OCDE.

Note: Les données se rapportant aux PMA ne commprennent que les montants imputables à un pays bénéficiaire déterminé. Par conséquent, les apports financiers sont sous-estimés dans la mesure où certains donneurs ont alloué des versements à des groupes de pays comprenant des PMA.

a La liste des membres de l'OPEP qui sont inclus ici et qui fournissent de l'aide aux PMA figure au tableau 36A.

40. Grant element of ODA commitments from individual OPEC member countries and individual multilateral agencies mainly financed by them, to LDCs as a group

40. Elément de libéralité des engagements de l'APD de chaque pays membre de l'OPEP et de chaque institution multilatérale essentiellement financée par ceux-ci, en faveur de l'ensemble des PMA

In per cent | *En pourcentage*

	1981	1982	1983	1984	1985	1986	
Bilateral donors							***Donneurs bilatéraux***
Algeria	54.8	100.0	-	-	50.0	-	Algérie
Iran (Islamic Republic)	-	-	-	-	-	-	Iran (Rép. islamique)
Iraq	47.0	42.1	-	-	-	-	Iraq
Kuwait	69.8	68.2	68.5	63.5	79.9	74.0	Koweït
Libyan Arab Jamahiriya	76.5	-	-	61.8	-	-	Jamahiriya arabe libyenne
Nigeria	-	-	-	-	-	-	Nigéria
Qatar	100.0	100.0	100.0	100.0	100.0	100.0	Qatar
Saudi Arabia	64.5	82.5	94.3	83.8	82.7	95.5	Arabie saoudite
United Arab Emirates	63.0	61.4	100.0	100.0	46.9	34.6	Emirats arabes unis
Total bilateral	64.2	76.9	91.0	81.9	75.6	90.2	Total bilaterale
of which: loans	54.1	56.1	54.0	54.0	50.8	61.0	*dont:* prêts
Multilateral donors							***Donneurs multilatéraux***
BADEA	31.3	32.3	33.3	100.0	47.3	31.1	BADEA
AFESD	39.5	37.5	36.7	37.7	41.0	38.5	FADES
Islamic Development Bank	53.2	61.8	59.8	70.7	64.3	69.1	Banque islamique de développement
OPEC Fund	53.2	57.5	51.4	55.4	53.8	48.5	Fonds de l'OPEP
Total multilateral	49.0	51.0	42.3	52.2	51.7	43.7	Total multilatérale
of which: loans	45.7	47.8	40.1	48.2	46.5	40.9	*dont:* prêts
Grand total	**60.8**	**71.7**	**81.5**	**73.3**	**69.9**	**79.4**	**Total général**

Source: UNCTAD secretariat estimates.

Source: Estimations du secrétariat de la CNUCED.

41. Grants from OPEC member countries to individual LDCs

41. Dons reçus par chacun des PMA en provenance des pays membres de l'OPEP

Net disbursements in millions of dollars

Versements nets en millions de dollars

Country	*1976*	*1977*	*1978*	*1979*	*1980*	*1981*	*1982*	*1983*	*1984*	*1985*	*1986*	*Pays*
Afghanistan	3	0	5	..	..	1	..	..	0	0	1	Afghanistan
Bangladesh	3	11	7	..	20	6	91	80	10	8	4	Bangladesh
Benin	..	1	..	..	..	..	..	0	0	0	0	Bénin
Bhutan	..	..	..	..	..	..	..	..	..	..	0	Bhoutan
Botswana	..	..	..	..	0	..	..	..	..	..	..	Botswana
Burkina Faso	1	0	1	1	1	2	..	0	0	0	3	Burkina faso
Burma	..	..	..	..	..	..	..	..	0	..	..	Birmanie
Burundi	0	0	..	..	..	..	..	0	0	0	0	Burundi
Cape Verde	1	1	..	..	..	..	..	0	..	0	..	Cap-Vert
Central African Rep.	-	-	-	-	-	-	-	-	-	-	-	Rép. centrafricaine
Chad	2	0	6	6	0	..	..	0	0	..	..	Tchad
Comoros	2	20	1	1	2	8	1	2	1	0	0	Comores
Democratic Yemen	129	77	9	18	34	20	31	13	21	47	16	Yémen démocratique
Djibouti	..	20	64	..	25	12	0	6	25	0	21	Djibouti
Equatorial Guinea	..	..	..	..	..	..	..	..	..	0	0	Guinée équatoriale
Ethiopia	..	1	0	1	..	..	..	..	..	..	0	Ethiopie
Gambia	2	0	0	0	0	3	1	0	0	0	0	Gambie
Guinea	0	1	2	0	0	0	..	1	25	..	..	Guinée
Guinea-Bissau	4	1	..	0	0	..	0	1	..	0	2	Guinée-Bissau
Haiti	-	-	-	-	-	-	-	-	-	-	-	Haïti
Kiribati	-	-	-	-	-	-	-	-	-	-	-	Kiribati
Lao People's Dem.Rep.	-	-	-	-	-	-	-	-	-	-	-	Rép. dém. pop. lao
Lesotho	-	-	-	-	-	-	-	-	-	-	-	Lesotho
Malawi	..	..	..	..	..	..	0	..	..	0	0	Malawi
Maldives	2	1	0	1	1	1	0	1	1	0	0	Maldives
Mali	3	5	1	12	5	0	0	1	1	0	2	Mali
Mauritania	..	37	5	9	11	10	17	9	16	36	3	Mauritanie
Nepal	0	33	..	..	..	..	..	0	0	0	0	Népal
Niger	3	3	16	0	2	2	2	1	4	0	0	Niger
Rwanda	0	1	..	..	..	0	..	0	0	0	0	Rwanda
Samoa	..	..	..	..	..	..	..	..	..	0	0	Samoa
Sao Tome and Principe	-	-	-	-	-	-	-	-	-	-	-	Sao Tomé-et-Principe
Sierra Leone	0	0	0	..	4	0	0	1	15	0	6	Sierra leone
Somalia	14	191	51	32	79	24	149	10	16	2	2	Somalie
Sudan	42	83	37	12	28	16	105	338	164	104	110	Soudan
Togo	3	0	..	..	0	..	..	0	0	0	0	Togo
Tuvalu	-	-	-	-	-	-	-	-	-	-	-	Tuvalu
Uganda	2	0	5	0	0	0	0	0	0	0	0	Ouganda
United Rep.of Tanzania	..	..	0	..	..	..	..	0	0	..	0	Rép.-Unie de Tanzanie
Vanuatu	-	-	-	-	-	-	-	-	-	-	-	Vanuatu
Yemen	180	256	176	148	227	150	175	166	177	121	140	Yémen
All LDCs	**396**	**742**	**386**	**243**	**440**	**256**	**572**	**630**	**478**	**322**	**310**	**Ensemble des PMA**
All developing countries	**2594**	**3015**	**2459**	**3743**	**4034**	**3401**	**3009**	**2451**	**3390**	**2531**	**3752**	**Ensemble des pays en développement**

Source: UNCTAD secretariat estimates. For 1976, OECD secretariat estimates.

Source: Estimations du secrétariat de la CNUCED. Pour 1976, estimations du secrétariat de l'OCDE.

42. ODA commitments from multilateral agencies mainly financed by OPEC member countries to individual LDCs

42. Engagements de l'APD à chacun des PMA en provenance des institutions multilatérales essentiellement financées par les pays membres de l'OPEP

$ million — Millions de dollars

Country	*1977*	*1978*	*1979*	*1980*	*1981*	*1982*	*1983*	*1984*	*1985*	*1986*	*Pays*
Afghanistan	4	..	4	..	..	..	..	..	..	..	Afghanistan
Bangladesh	24	7	19	41	26	20	15	12	20	5	Bangladesh
Benin	2	2	5	5	6	..	9	4	7	17	Bénin
Bhutan	..	..	..	..	..	..	1	..	..	..	Bhoutan
Botswana	1	..	4	7	..	4	..	2	..	0	Botswana
Burkina Faso	4	7	2	6	10	20	3	15	..	6	Burkina faso
Burma	7	6	2	4	..	14	7	..	..	2	Birmanie
Burundi	6	6	5	5	18	..	..	5	2	3	Burundi
Cape Verde	2	2	1	4	1	3	11	0	..	..	Cap-Vert
Central African Rep.	..	..	..	..	1	8	..	..	8	4	Rép. centrafricaine
Chad	2	8	..	..	..	..	0	8	6	..	Tchad
Comoros	1	2	..	3	1	19	..	0	..	2	Comores
Democratic Yemen	5	..	26	11	35	31	20	31	37	21	Yémen démocratique
Djibouti	..	..	..	2	5	12	14	11	6	3	Djibouti
Equatorial Guinea	1	..	1	..	1	..	5	1	..	..	Guinée équatoriale
Ethiopia	5	1	..	..	1	..	..	5	..	8	Ethiopie
Gambia	2	3	1	7	3	2	1	2	..	..	Gambie
Guinea	5	6	8	..	..	24	..	7	..	12	Guinée
Guinea-Bissau	2	2	1	2	3	2	2	1	1	1	Guinée-Bissau
Haiti	3	..	4	4	..	..	3	1	..	..	Haïti
Kiribati	-	-	-	-	-	-	-	-	-	-	Kiribati
Lao People's Dem.Rep.	2	5	..	2	4	..	..	3	..	..	Rép. dém. pop. lao
Lesotho	2	..	3	11	4	..	3	2	..	..	Lesotho
Malawi	2	..	..	..	1	..	..	..	..	..	Malawi
Maldives	1	1	1	1	1	3	1	..	..	1	Maldives
Mali	9	5	15	16	15	16	8	24	8	9	Mali
Mauritania	2	6	36	12	8	25	52	28	22	13	Mauritanie
Nepal	4	3	5	1	11	..	..	1	..	..	Népal
Niger	9	2	5	4	8	1	5	20	13	0	Niger
Rwanda	15	..	5	3	1	10	..	5	..	8	Rwanda
Samoa	..	1	..	1	1	2	..	1	..	..	Samoa
Sao Tome and Principe	0	..	..	..	1	..	1	1	..	..	Sao Tomé-et-Principe
Sierra Leone	7	..	2	10	7	8	1	6	6	0	Sierra leone
Somalia	38	3	9	13	33	30	21	21	..	5	Somalie
Sudan	29	10	..	28	15	14	67	50	14	69	Soudan
Togo	..	..	4	..	7	..	4	1	..	2	Togo
Tuvalu	-	-	-	-	-	-	-	-	-	-	Tuvalu
Uganda	5	11	..	5	0	16	0	5	..	..	Ouganda
United Rep.of Tanzania	5	5	..	10	11	22	5	..	..	3	Rép.-Unie de Tanzanie
Vanuatu	-	-	-	-	-	-	-	-	-	-	Vanuatu
Yemen	51	1	9	11	39	28	40	34	42	25	Yémen
All LDCs	**254**	**102**	**173**	**226**	**278**	**332**	**298**	**305**	**192**	**219**	**Ensemble des PMA**

Source: UNCTAD secretariat estimates.

Source: Estimations du secrétariat de la CNUCED.

43. Concessional assistance from multilateral agencies mainly financed by OPEC member countries [a] to individual LDCs

43. Aide concessionnelle reçue par chacun des PMA en provenance des institutions multilatérales [a] essentiellement financées par les pays membres de l'OPEP

Net disbursements in millions of dollars

Versements nets en millions de dollars

Country	*1976*	*1977*	*1978*	*1979*	*1980*	*1981*	*1982*	*1983*	*1984*	*1985*	*1986*	*Pays*
Afghanistan	..	4	..	..	..	..	-0	-0	-0	..	-0	Afghanistan
Bangladesh	..	14	1	10	4	31	22	13	12	3	2	Bangladesh
Benin	..	3	5	1	1	3	2	4	1	1	1	Bénin
Bhutan	-	-	-	-	-	-	-	-	-	-	-	Bhoutan
Botswana	..	..	0	1	2	0	2	4	1	1	-1	Botswana
Burkina Faso	..	3	2	5	7	9	9	2	-2	3	10	Burkina faso
Burma	..	2	..	2	0	2	13	5	4	-1	-0	Birmanie
Burundi	..	1	1	4	5	2	1	2	-0	1	2	Burundi
Cape Verde	11	2	1	1	2	1	0	-0	3	4	-1	Cap-Vert
Central African Rep.	..	2	..	..	..	..	-0	-0	2	1	4	Rép. centrafricaine
Chad	..	1	2	..	0	1	1	0	0	1	3	Tchad
Comoros	11	0	1	0	1	2	2	3	3	5	4	Comores
Democratic Yemen	7	5	14	9	12	18	12	17	12	19	8	Yémen démocratique
Djibouti	..	..	..	..	..	1	2	3	10	7	7	Djibouti
Equatorial Guinea	..	1	..	..	..	1	1	0	-0	-0	-0	Guinée équatoriale
Ethiopia	..	2	2	..	0	0	-0	-0	-0	-0	-0	Ethiopie
Gambia	..	2	1	2	7	2	1	1	1	0	0	Gambie
Guinea	..	2	5	3	4	3	2	1	5	6	-2	Guinée
Guinea-Bissau	..	2	1	1	3	2	1	1	0	0	..	Guinée-Bissau
Haiti	..	3	..	..	..	1	2	1	0	1	1	Haïti
Kiribati	-	-	-	-	-	-	-	-	-	-	-	Kiribati
Lao People's Dem.Rep.	..	2	..	4	1	0	0	0	1	0	2	Rép. dém. pop. lao
Lesotho	..	2	0	..	..	1	3	5	2	2	-1	Lesotho
Malawi	..	..	..	..	1	-0	-0	-0	-0	-0	-0	Malawi
Maldives	..	0	0	0	1	2	1	1	1	0	1	Maldives
Mali	..	4	7	3	10	15	12	16	5	5	2	Mali
Mauritania	16	10	22	0	3	7	17	24	18	6	16	Mauritanie
Nepal	..	4	..	..	..	3	5	2	0	-0	1	Népal
Niger	..	3	5	6	7	9	0	-1	-2	-0	3	Niger
Rwanda	..	1	3	2	6	8	2	-0	0	0	2	Rwanda
Samoa	..	2	1	1	1	1	1	-0	0	-0	-1	Samoa
Sao Tome and Principe	10	0	0	..	..	1	0	0	0	0	..	Sao Tomé-et-Principe
Sierra Leone	..	1	0	1	3	2	1	2	3	5	2	Sierra leone
Somalia	4	6	8	11	16	20	22	22	10	2	0	Somalie
Sudan	29	16	18	16	23	29	20	1	4	1	20	Soudan
Togo	..	..	..	..	4	..	..	3	2	0	1	Togo
Tuvalu	-	-	-	-	-	-	-	-	-	-	-	Tuvalu
Uganda	..	5	0	0	0	0	5	8	0	0	1	Ouganda
United Rep.of Tanzania	0	6	1	1	4	9	14	14	7	-1	..	Rép.-Unie de Tanzanie
Vanuatu	-	-	-	-	-	-	-	-	-	-	-	Vanuatu
Yemen	13	11	10	12	14	37	14	11	3	8	11	Yémen
All LDCs	**99**	**120**	**113**	**99**	**140**	**221**	**190**	**164**	**105**	**82**	**94**	**Ensemble des PMA**
All developing countries	**418**	**240**	**295**	**248**	**273**	**346**	**324**	**295**	**147**	**147**	**136**	**Ensemble des pays en développement**

Source: UNCTAD secretariat estimates. For 1976, OECD secretariat estimates.

a The multilateral agencies included here and providing assistance to LDCs are listed in table 36A.

Source: Estimations du secrétariat de la CNUCED. Pour 1976, estimations du secrétariat de l'OCDE.

a La liste des institutions multilatérales qui sont incluses ici et qui fournissent de l'aide aux PMA figure au tableau 36A.

44. Non-concessional assistance from multilateral agencies [a] mainly financed by OPEC member countries to individual LDCs

44. Aide non-concessionnelle reçue par chacun des PMA en provenance des institutions multilatérales [a] essentiellement financées par les pays membres de l'OPEP

Net disbursements in millions of dollars — Versements nets en millions de dollars

Country	*1977*	*1978*	*1979*	*1980*	*1981*	*1982*	*1983*	*1984*	*1985*	*1986*	*Pays*
Afghanistan	-	-	-	-	-	-	-	-	-	-	Afghanistan
Bangladesh	..	..	37	-15	34	-11	39	13	-32	-21	Bangladesh
Benin	..	0	2	2	1	2	-0	-0	1	0	Bénin
Bhutan	-	-	-	-	-	-	-	-	-	-	Bhoutan
Botswana	..	..	..	1	..	..	0	-0	2	-0	Botswana
Burkina Faso	..	..	..	3	3	0	0	-2	-0	..	Burkina faso
Burma	..	0	2	2	1	2	-0	-0	1	0	Birmanie
Burundi	..	..	..	..	..	..	..	..	1	2	Burundi
Cape Verde	-	-	-	-	-	-	-	-	-	-	Cap-Vert
Central African Rep.	..	..	..	..	..	..	..	..	0	0	Rép. centrafricaine
Chad	-	-	-	-	-	-	-	-	-	-	Tchad
Comoros	..	..	..	..	4	-0	-2	-1	-0	..	Comores
Democratic Yemen	..	..	..	13	1	5	-20	..	..	-2	Yémen démocratique
Djibouti	-	-	-	-	-	-	-	-	-	-	Djibouti
Equatorial Guinea	..	..	..	..	..	..	..	..	..	0	Guinée équatoriale
Ethiopia	..	0	2	2	1	2	-0	-0	1	0	Ethiopie
Gambia	..	..	..	..	7	-2	1	-1	..	..	Gambie
Guinea	..	2	11	18	4	-9	-2	-2	0	..	Guinée
Guinea-Bissau	..	..	..	8	5	..	..	1	2	-0	Guinée-Bissau
Haiti	-	-	-	-	-	-	-	-	-	-	Haïti
Kiribati	-	-	-	-	-	-	-	-	-	-	Kiribati
Lao People's Dem.Rep.	-	-	-	-	-	-	-	-	-	-	Rép. dém. pop. lao
Lesotho	-	-	-	-	-	-	-	-	-	-	Lesotho
Malawi	-	-	-	-	-	-	-	-	-	-	Malawi
Maldives	..	..	..	..	3	..	..	..	..	..	Maldives
Mali	..	..	3	-0	-2	..	..	..	..	-1	Mali
Mauritania	..	..	6	2	10	-1	-8	..	10	-10	Mauritanie
Nepal	-	-	-	-	-	-	-	-	-	-	Népal
Niger	..	5	10	7	15	-15	-4	-0	1	4	Niger
Rwanda	-	-	-	-	-	-	-	-	-	-	Rwanda
Samoa	-	-	-	-	-	-	-	-	-	-	Samoa
Sao Tome and Principe	-	-	-	-	-	-	-	-	-	-	Sao Tomé-et-Principe
Sierra Leone	-	-	-	-	-	-	-	-	-	-	Sierra leone
Somalia	..	..	4	15	13	-6	-5	..	-10	-8	Somalie
Sudan	5	2	39	33	7	-3	-7	-8	..	-24	Soudan
Togo	..	2	1	0	..	-0	-0	-0	1	1	Togo
Tuvalu	-	-	-	-	-	-	-	-	-	-	Tuvalu
Uganda	..	..	..	..	..	0	2	-0	1	1	Ouganda
United Rep.of Tanzania	..	6	1	1	0	0	-0	0	..	..	Rép.-Unie de Tanzanie
Vanuatu	-	-	-	-	-	-	-	-	-	-	Vanuatu
Yemen	..	..	0	20	3	-15	17	17	-6	-1	Yémen
All LDCs	**5**	**17**	**115**	**107**	**107**	**-54**	**11**	**17**	**-28**	**-60**	**Ensemble des PMA**
All developing countries	**41**	**163**	**258**	**120**	**369**	**9**	**141**	**255**	**262**	**-107**	**Ensemble des pays en développement**

Source: UNCTAD secretariat estimates.

a The multilateral agencies included here and providing assistance to LDCs are listed in table 36A.

Source: Estimations du secrétariat de la CNUCED.

a La liste des institutions multilatérales qui sont inclues ici et qui fournissent de l'aide aux PMA figure au tableau 36A.

45. ODA commitments from individual OPEC member countries and individual multilateral agencies mainly financed by them, to LDCs as a group, by purpose, 1982 to 1986

45. Engagements de l'APD de chaque pays membre de l'OPEP et de chaque institution multilatérale essentiellement financée par ceux-ci, en faveur de l'ensemble des PMA, par objet, 1982 à 1986

	Agriculture / *Agriculture*	*Mining* / *Industries extractives*	*Manufacturing* / *Industries manufacturières*	*Electricity, gas and water* / *Electricité, gaz et eau*	*Transport and storage* / *Transports et entrepôts*	*Other services* / *Autres services*	*Multi-purpose* / *Objet multiple*	*Balance of payments* / *Soutien à la balance des paiements*	*Distress relief* / *Secours d'urgence*	*Other and unallocated* [a] / *Autres et non-ventilés* [a]	*Total*	
	As percentage of total / En pourcentage du total										*in $ million / en mill. de $*	
Bilateral donors												***Donneurs bilatéraux***
Algeria	-	-	-	-		0.2	-	-	99.8	-	100	Algérie
Iraq	-	-	-	-	94.9	5.1	-	-	-	-	37	Iraq
Kuwait	6.9	-	5.3	28.6	19.8	-	5.9	-	1.0	32.4	964	Koweit
Libyan Arab Jamahiriya	-	-	-	-	-	-	-	-	-	100.0	10	Jamahiriya arabe libyenne
Qatar	-	-	-	-	-	-	-	-	-	100.0	50	Qatar
Saudi Arabia	2.3	1.6	3.4	2.5	6.5	1.3	3.3	23.4	7.8	47.9	3277	Arabie saoudite
United Arab Emirates	-	-	- 12.6	-	6.7	-	-	-	1.7	79.0	227	Emirats arabes unis
Total	3.0	1.2	4.1	7.7	9.8	0.9	3.5	16.4	8.0	45.4	4667	Total
Multilateral donors												***Donneurs multilatéraux***
BADEA	9.8	-	-	10.8	73.8	-	-	-	-	5.7	90	BADEA
AFESD	25.6	-	9.9	22.9	31.7	5.0	3.4	-	-	1.5	584	FADES
Islamic Development Bank	14.6	-	-	18.9	20.9	6.3	13.6	-	-	25.6	255	Banque islamique de développement
OPEC Fund	6.7	6.2	2.5	23.4	15.8	7.0	-	20.9	-	17.4	417	Fonds de l'OPEP
Total	16.5	2.0	5.1	21.5	27.4	5.6	4.0	6.6	-	11.3	1346	Total
GRAND TOTAL	**6.0**	**1.3**	**4.3**	**10.8**	**13.7**	**2.0**	**3.7**	**14.2**	**6.2**	**37.7**	**6013**	**TOTAL GÉNÉRAL**

Source: UNCTAD secretariat estimates.

a Mainly budget support in the case of bilateral flows. Mainly Technical assistance in the case of multilateral flows.

Source: Estimations du secrétariat de la CNUCED.

a Principalement soutien budgétaire dans les cas des apports bilatéraux. Principalement assistance technique dans les cas des apports multilatéraux.

46. LDCs' external debt (at year end) and debt service, by source of lending

46. Dette extérieure (en fin d'année) et service de la dette des PMA, par catégorie de prêteur

	External debt / Dette extérieure							Debt service / Service de la dette							
	Millions of dollars / En millions de dollars					% of total / En % de total		Millions of dollars / En millions de dollars					% of total / En % de total		
	1982	1983	1984	1985	1986	1982	1986	1982	1983	1984	1985	1986	1982	1986	
I. Long-term	30639	33327	35357	40977	46985	88.1	87.8	1458	1577	1876	2148	2665	72.3	75.0	I. Dette à long terme
A. Concessional	21024	22921	25001	29210	33685	60.4	63.0	491	508	743	928	1158	24.3	32.6	A. Concessionnel
(a) OECD countries	4814	4971	5664	7209	8974	13.8	16.8	140	144	205	240	284	7.0	8.0	(a) Pays de l'OCDE
(b) Other countries	8424	9000	9210	9982	10442	24.2	19.5	217	210	319	321	427	10.8	12.0	(b) Autres pays
(c) Multilateral agencies	7786	8950	10127	12019	14269	22.4	26.7	134	154	219	367	447	6.7	12.6	(c) Institutions multilatérales
B. Non-concessional	9614	10409	10352	11765	13300	27.6	24.9	967	1068	1133	1220	1507	48.0	42.4	B. Non-concessionnel
(a) OECD countries	6688	7222	7196	8356	9944	19.2	18.6	693	825	848	935	1188	34.4	33.4	(a) Pays de l'OCDE
(i) official/ officially supported	4599	5263	4784	5917	7596	13.2	14.2	464	545	601	632	855	23.0	24.1	(i) Prêts de l'Etat et garantis par l'Etat
(ii) financial markets	2029	1902	2351	2376	2277	5.8	4.3	226	277	239	296	326	11.2	9.2	(ii) Marchés financiers
(iii) Other private	60	57	61	63	71	0.2	0.1	3	3	8	7	7	0.2	0.2	(iii) Autres prêts privés
(b) Other countries	1788	1977	1878	1957	1720	5.1	3.2	133	94	99	95	77	6.6	2.2	(b) Autres pays
(c) Multilateral agencies	1138	1210	1278	1452	1636	3.3	3.1	141	149	186	190	242	7.0	6.8	(c) Institutions multilatérales
II. Short-term	2172	2749	2763	3686	4057	6.2	7.6	236	202	218	261	264	11.7	7.4	II. Dette à court terme
III. Use of IMF credit	1982	2332	2078	2266	2439	5.7	4.6	322	345	475	466	629	16.0	17.7	III. Crédits du FMI
GRAND TOTAL [a]	**34793**	**38407**	**40199**	**46926**	**53484**	**100.0**	**100.0**	**2016**	**2124**	**2569**	**2879**	**3555**	**100.0**	**100.0**	**TOTAL GÉNÉRAL** [a]

Source: UNCTAD secretariat calculations, based on information from the OECD secretariat.

a Total external debt includes long-term and short-term debt as well as use of IMF credit. Total external debt service includes debt service on long-term debt, interest on short-term debt and repurchases and charges from IMF.

Source: Secrétariat de la CNUCED, d'après des données du secrétariat de l'OCDE.

a Le total de la dette extérieure comprend la dette à long terme, la dette à court terme et les crédits du FMI. Le total du service de la dette comprend les paiements au titre de la dette à long terme, les intérêts sur la dette à court terme et les rachats et les frais au FMI.

47. LDCs' bilateral concessional debt and debt service by main creditor country [a] and group of countries

47. Dette des PMA au titre de l'APD bilatérale et service de cette dette, par principal pays créancier [a] et groupe de pays créanciers

Creditor	Outstanding debt disbursed at year-end / Encours de la dette en fin d'année (montants versés)				ODA debt-service [b] / Service de la dette de l'APD [b]					Créancier
	$ billion / En milliards de $		% distribution / Répartition en %		$ million / En millions de $			% distibution / Répartition en %		
	1982	1986	1982	1986	1982	1986	Average / Moyenne 1987-1990	1982	1986	
DAC countries	4.64	8.60	39.1	48.0	103.8	224.9	420.8	33.1	36.5	Pays membres du CAD
of which:										*dont:*
Japan	1.84	4.16	15.6	23.3	40.8	110.4	184.0	13.0	17.9	Japon
United States	1.68	2.01	14.2	11.2	37.4	49.0	88.0	11.9	8.0	Etats-Unis
France	0.29	1.18	2.4	6.6	11.8	31.5	87.9	3.8	5.1	France
Germany, Fed. Rep. of	0.44	0.59	3.7	3.3	9.1	20.4	26.8	2.9	3.3	Allemagne, Féd. Rép. d'
Italy	0.06	0.20	0.5	1.1	1.0	8.7	19.7	0.3	1.4	Italie
Denmark	0.17	0.15	1.5	0.9	-	0.2	1.9	-	0.0	Danemark
Socialist countries of Eastern Europe	2.16	3.32	18.2	18.5	113.0	197.7	356.0	36.0	32.1	Pays socialistes d'Europe orientale
of which:										*dont:*
USSR	1.76	2.86	14.9	16.0	78.9	147.3	290.4	25.2	23.9	URSS
Czechoslovakia	0.19	0.22	1.6	1.3	13.1	22.5	32.5	4.2	3.7	Tchécoslovaquie
German Dem. Rep.	0.08	0.12	0.7	0.7	6.5	14.7	15.3	2.1	2.4	Rép. dém. allemande
Other developed countries	0.08	0.09	0.7	0.5	0.4	0.9	10.2	0.1	0.1	Autres pays développés
China	1.24	1.11	10.5	6.2	12.1	31.5	80.7	3.9	5.1	Chine
OPEC countries	3.36	4.27	28.4	23.8	63.0	142.2	438.8	20.1	23.1	Pays membres de l'OPEP
of which:										*dont:*
Saudi Arabia	1.45	1.84	12.3	10.3	14.5	53.3	205.1	4.6	8.7	Arabie saoudite
Kuwait	0.62	1.01	5.3	5.6	20.0	37.9	81.1	6.4	6.2	Koweït
United Arab Emirates	0.36	0.49	3.1	2.8	6.0	24.7	65.9	1.9	4.0	Emirats arabes unis
Iraq	0.50	0.37	4.2	2.1	15.7	20.5	55.1	5.0	3.3	Iraq
Libyan Arab Jamahiriya	0.29	0.36	2.5	2.0	6.1	4.5	18.2	2.0	0.7	Jamahiriya arabe libyenne
Algeria	0.09	0.16	0.8	0.9	0.3	0.8	11.3	0.1	0.1	Algérie
Other developing countries	0.37	0.26	3.1	1.4	21.2	14.6	46.9	6.8	2.4	Autres pays en développement
Total bilateral concessional debt	**11.84**	**17.89**	**100.0**	**100.0**	**313.6**	**615.5**	**1369.6**	**100.0**	**100.0**	**Dette de l'APD bilatérale totale**

Source: The data in this table are derived from the World Bank Debtor Reporting System (DRS). They cover 36 LDCs only (Afghanistan, Bhutan, Kiribati, Lao People's Democratic Republic, and Tuvalu are not covered by the DRS). Hence they are not comparable with data shown in table 46.

a Countries with outstanding ODA loans to LDCs exceeding $100 million in 1986.

b Data for 1982 and 1986 refer to debt service paid whereas data for 1987-1990 refer to projected debt service payments falling due in that period, based upon debt outstanding (including undisbursed debt) as of end-1986.

Source: Les données du présent tableau sont tirées du système de déclaration des débiteurs de la Banque mondiale. Elles ne visent que 36 PMA (l'Afghanistan, le Bhoutan, Kiribati, la République démocratique populaire lao, et Tuvalu n'étant pas couverts par le système de déclaration des débiteurs). Elles ne peuvent donc pas être comparées avec les données du tableau 46.

a Pays envers lesquels les PMA avaient une dette de l'APD depassant 100 millions de dollars en 1986.

b Les données pour 1982 et 1986 concernent les sommes payées au titre du service de la dette, tandis que pour 1987-1990 il s'agit des paiements exigibles cette période là au titre du service de la dette d'après des projections fondées sur l'encours de la dette (y compris au titre de prêts non encore versés) à la fin de 1986.

48. LDCs' multilateral debt and debt service by main creditor agency [a]

48. Dette multilatérale des PMA et service de cette dette, par principale institution créancière [a]

	Outstanding debt disbursed at year-end / Encours de la dette en fin d'année (montants versés)				*Debt-service [b] / Service de la dette [b]*					
	$ billion / En milliards de $		*% of total / En % du total*		*$ million / En millions de $*			*% of total / En % du total*		
	1982	1986	1982	1986	1982	1986	*Average / Moyenne* 1987-1990	1982	1986	
Concessional	7.61	14.06	87.1	89.6	118.4	442.7	598.8	48.2	64.8	Concessionnel
of which:										*dont:*
IDA	4.31	8.71	49.3	55.5	38.7	103.7	146.0	15.8	15.2	AID
AsDB	0.51	1.18	5.8	7.6	7.4	20.0	43.6	3.0	2.9	BAsD
AfDF	0.34	0.93	3.9	6.0	3.0	7.6	22.9	1.2	1.1	FAfD
OPEC Special Fund	0.45	0.57	5.1	3.7	6.4	47.6	74.3	2.6	7.0	Fonds spécial de l'OPEP
AFESD	0.40	0.52	4.5	3.3	22.9	38.5	80.3	9.3	5.6	FADES
IFAD	0.06	0.32	0.7	2.0	0.3	2.0	6.4	0.1	0.3	FIDA
EEC	0.13	0.19	1.5	1.2	0.5	1.0	5.0	0.2	0.1	CEE
BADEA	0.12	0.18	1.4	1.1	3.8	11.4	22.8	1.5	1.7	BADEA
Islamic Dev. Bank	0.09	0.18	1.0	1.1	2.8	13.5	19.7	1.1	2.0	Banque islamique de dév.
IBRD	0.19	0.16	2.2	1.0	18.4	25.5	20.6	7.5	3.7	BIRD
European Dev. Fund	0.08	0.14	1.0	0.9	1.1	2.4	5.2	0.4	0.4	Fonds européen de dév.
IDB	0.08	0.12	0.9	0.8	1.1	2.8	5.0	0.4	0.4	BID
European Investment Bank	0.05	0.10	0.6	0.7	1.3	2.2	9.7	0.5	0.3	Banque européene d'inv.
Non-concessional	1.12	1.63	12.9	10.4	127.1	240.2	353.3	51.8	35.2	Non-concessionnel
of which:										*dont:*
IBRD	0.41	0.51	4.7	3.3	48.1	101.8	90.4	19.6	14.9	BIRD
African Development Bank	0.19	0.44	2.2	2.8	19.1	57.7	96.3	7.8	8.4	Banque africaine de dév.
Arab Monetary Fund	0.25	0.27	2.9	1.7	12.6	14.9	68.9	5.1	2.2	Fonds monétaire arabe
Total multilateral debt	**8.73**	**15.69**	**100.0**	**100.0**	**245.5**	**682.9**	**952.1**	**100.0**	**100.0**	**Total de dette multilatérale**

Source: The data in this table are derived from the World Bank Debtor Reporting System (DRS). They cover 36 LDCs only (Afghanistan, Bhutan, Kiribati, Lao People's Democratic Republic, and Tuvalu are not covered by the DRS). Hence they are not comparable with data shown in table 46.

a Agencies with outstanding ODA loans to LDCs exceeding $100 million in 1986.

b Data for 1982 and 1986 refer to debt service paid whereas data for 1987-1990 refer to projected debt service payments falling due in that period, based upon debt outstanding (including undisbursed debt) as of end-1986.

Source: Les données du présent tableau sont tirées du système de déclaration des débiteurs de la Banque mondiale. Elles ne visent que 36 PMA (l'Afghanistan, le Bhoutan, Kiribati, la République démocratique populaire lao, et Tuvalu n'étant pas couverts par le système de déclaration des débiteurs). Elles ne peuvent donc pas être comparées avec les données du tableau 46.

a Institutions envers lesquelles les PMA avaient une dette de l'APD depassant 100 millions de dollars en 1986.

b Les données pour 1982 et 1986 concernent les sommes payées au titre du service de la dette, tandis que pour 1987-1990 il s'agit des paiements exigibles cette période là au titre du service de la dette d'après des projections fondées sur l'encours de la dette (y compris au titre de prêts non encore versés) à la fin de 1986.

49A. Total external debt [a]

49A. Encours de la dette extérieure totale [a]

$ million — Millions de dollars

Country	1976	1977	1978	1979	1980	1981	1982	1983	1984	1985	1986	Pays
Afghanistan	930	1073	1221	1285	1195	1242	1410	817	872	1123	1288	Afghanistan
Bangladesh	1934	2307	2793	3348	3614	3938	4942	5605	5864	6855	8227	Bangladesh
Benin	115	149	186	237	484	574	623	749	700	897	1073	Bénin
Bhutan	-	-	-	-	-	-	9	2	5	6	17	Bhoutan
Botswana	294	304	286	295	283	286	340	360	352	419	574	Botswana
Burkina Faso	84	131	197	260	295	312	390	438	441	550	664	Burkina faso
Burma	336	540	876	1201	1524	1737	2095	2337	2300	3057	3753	Birmanie
Burundi	20	44	68	112	151	175	252	316	352	459	555	Burundi
Cape Verde	12	14	15	18	20	40	57	76	78	108	115	Cap-Vert
Central African Rep.	89	112	127	132	164	188	262	275	265	346	436	Rép. centrafricaine
Chad	96	115	162	172	156	126	157	171	158	177	179	Tchad
Comoros	18	23	28	39	50	53	81	86	105	135	161	Comores
Democratic Yemen	158	257	354	427	549	798	843	1080	1201	1626	2023	Yémen démocratique
Djibouti	26	27	31	51	28	22	47	64	141	239	250	Djibouti
Equatorial Guinea	29	32	34	36	57	67	124	120	101	146	165	Guinée équatoriale
Ethiopia	430	473	543	616	704	963	1239	1439	1651	1920	2196	Ethiopie
Gambia	15	30	50	81	118	145	212	217	247	245	314	Gambie
Guinea	897	885	985	1064	1111	1301	1440	1361	1275	1386	1529	Guinée
Guinea-Bissau	19	24	42	66	104	111	152	168	181	294	318	Guinée-Bissau
Haiti	86	136	185	227	269	356	667	715	725	784	765	Haïti
Kiribati	-	-	-	-	-	-	8	9	10	11	11	Kiribati
Lao People's Dem.Rep.	35	48	77	77	75	65	321	458	433	528	564	Rép. dém. pop. lao
Lesotho	16	24	32	54	76	91	117	131	134	170	193	Lesotho
Malawi	310	408	492	567	746	767	882	903	903	1021	1115	Malawi
Maldives	1	3	7	10	28	39	48	71	80	83	85	Maldives
Mali	351	433	518	533	692	739	855	1018	1277	1511	1772	Mali
Mauritania	392	458	585	633	754	894	1201	1317	1329	1478	1807	Mauritanie
Nepal	45	73	106	155	185	243	352	455	480	600	764	Népal
Niger	158	207	310	406	608	703	891	974	1014	1203	1493	Niger
Rwanda	49	74	101	127	161	180	221	262	305	372	456	Rwanda
Samoa	22	30	34	49	57	56	64	69	73	75	74	Samoa
Sao Tome and Principe	-	-	-	-	-	-	22	35	32	68	83	Sao Tomé-et-Principe
Sierra Leone	167	212	299	360	389	392	615	686	681	694	645	Sierra leone
Somalia	293	409	549	679	749	906	1266	1537	1669	1750	1815	Somalie
Sudan	1821	2260	2760	3396	3953	4731	6367	6936	7505	8333	8615	Soudan
Togo	177	328	656	858	916	871	1046	952	841	994	1184	Togo
Tuvalu	-	-	-	-	-	-	0	0	0	0	0	Tuvalu
Uganda	252	281	355	492	609	593	879	1050	1057	1166	1191	Ouganda
United Rep.of Tanzania	975	1202	1366	1592	1734	1951	2740	3083	3169	3578	4223	Rép.-Unie de Tanzanie
Vanuatu	7	7	10	12	10	7	14	78	93	128	176	Vanuatu
Yemen	271	342	500	627	984	1223	1541	1988	2100	2395	2613	Yémen
All LDCs	**10925**	**13473**	**16938**	**20293**	**23602**	**26885**	**34793**	**38408**	**40198**	**46929**	**53481**	**Ensemble des PMA**

Source: UNCTAD secretariat, based on information from the OECD secretariat.

a Disbursed outstanding at year-end including short-term debt and use of IMF credit. Data for the years 1982-1986 are not strictly comparable with those for the years 1976-1981.

Source: Secrétariat de la CNUCED, d'après des renseignements du secrétariat de l'OCDE.

a Encours en fin d'année (montants versés) y compris la dette à court terme et les crédits du FMI. Les données pour les années 1982-1986 ne sont pas strictement comparables à celles qui se rapportent aux années 1976-1981.

49B. Total debt service payments [a]

49B. Paiements totaux au titre du service de la dette [a]

$ million | Millions de dollars

Country	1976	1977	1978	1979	1980	1981	1982	1983	1984	1985	1986	Pays
Afghanistan	26	38	55	13	180	140	40	41	43	47	46	Afghanistan
Bangladesh	86	84	102	99	109	151	233	225	342	395	521	Bangladesh
Benin	7	11	14	16	24	55	30	71	47	52	82	Bénin
Bhutan	-	-	-	-	-	-	2	2	0	9	0	Bhoutan
Botswana	19	41	67	46	40	36	62	31	49	56	52	Botswana
Burkina Faso	6	7	9	10	17	15	27	23	26	31	35	Burkina faso
Burma	36	34	54	106	113	151	208	237	181	210	267	Birmanie
Burundi	2	3	5	4	7	6	19	24	26	26	37	Burundi
Cape Verde	0	0	0	0	0	0	2	3	7	5	5	Cap-Vert
Central African Rep.	5	7	7	3	2	4	10	17	38	30	32	Rép. centrafricaine
Chad	6	9	13	15	12	8	3	2	11	13	8	Tchad
Comoros	1	1	1	2	2	1	2	2	3	3	3	Comores
Democratic Yemen	3	6	6	13	23	68	39	48	102	149	138	Yémen démocratique
Djibouti	4	4	3	11	6	5	4	7	17	35	62	Djibouti
Equatorial Guinea	2	2	0	1	2	4	7	11	10	13	11	Guinée équatoriale
Ethiopia	26	32	32	28	35	55	84	116	156	162	213	Ethiopie
Gambia	0	1	1	1	2	7	18	16	14	15	33	Gambie
Guinea	56	98	97	117	128	118	107	101	122	82	135	Guinée
Guinea-Bissau	0	0	1	4	4	4	4	4	7	15	15	Guinée-Bissau
Haiti	10	19	19	12	22	16	32	35	43	54	73	Haïti
Kiribati	-	-	-	-	-	-	0	0	0	1	1	Kiribati
Lao People's Dem.Rep.	2	3	2	3	2	2	4	5	12	33	18	Rép. dém. pop. lao
Lesotho	0	0	1	2	6	7	14	13	15	19	15	Lesotho
Malawi	26	28	37	46	70	91	99	91	110	115	134	Malawi
Maldives	-	0	0	0	0	1	2	6	26	13	19	Maldives
Mali	7	13	18	21	17	13	35	20	31	63	68	Mali
Mauritania	38	52	51	51	41	59	63	63	68	109	107	Mauritanie
Nepal	2	2	3	5	13	8	21	25	23	24	32	Népal
Niger	11	18	28	46	87	116	172	128	108	129	165	Niger
Rwanda	1	2	3	2	3	4	10	8	21	24	28	Rwanda
Samoa	1	2	2	4	5	4	4	4	5	7	7	Samoa
Sao Tome and Principe	-	-	-	-	-	-	0	1	2	3	4	Sao Tomé-et-Principe
Sierra Leone	20	28	38	54	43	55	49	62	56	49	62	Sierra leone
Somalia	5	6	8	9	20	31	33	41	62	100	132	Somalie
Sudan	159	146	119	96	100	135	231	194	221	234	287	Soudan
Togo	31	40	50	52	78	58	61	71	108	104	124	Togo
Tuvalu	-	-	-	-	-	-	-	-	0	0	0	Tuvalu
Uganda	16	32	14	17	15	61	87	120	178	167	143	Ouganda
United Rep.of Tanzania	36	48	53	108	115	93	115	172	130	121	161	Rép.-Unie de Tanzanie
Vanuatu	1	0	1	3	3	1	2	4	16	20	67	Vanuatu
Yemen	8	13	18	23	47	110	82	79	134	147	213	Yémen
All LDCs	**658**	**829**	**931**	**1045**	**1395**	**1694**	**2016**	**2124**	**2569**	**2882**	**3555**	**Ensemble des PMA**

Source: UNCTAD secretariat, based on information from the OECD secretariat.

a Total external including short-term and use of IMF credit. Data for the years 1982-1986 are not strictly comparable with those for the years 1976-1981.

Source: Secrétariat de la CNUCED, d'après des renseignements du secrétariat de l'OCDE.

a Dette extérieure totale y compris la dette à court terme et les crédits du FMI. Les données pour les années 1982-1986 ne sont pas strictement comparables à celles qui se rapportent aux années 1976-1981.

49C. Ratios: debt/GDP and debt service/exports

49C. Rapports: dette/PIB et service de la dette/exportations

In per cent — En pourcentage

Country	Debt/GDP Dette/PIB 1982	1983	1984	1985	1986	Debt service/exports [a] Service de la dette/exportations [a] 1982	1983	1984	1985	1986	Pays
Afghanistan	(40)	(23)	(20)	(25)	(28)	5	5	5	7	8	Afghanistan
Bangladesh	37	46	42	43	53	23	23	28	31	46	Bangladesh
Benin	60	76	73	88	77	16	38	21	21	30	Bénin
Bhutan	6	1	3	3	8	6	6	1	24	..	Bhoutan
Botswana	40	37	31	41	50	10	4	6	6	5	Botswana
Burkina Faso	38	48	53	59	53	15	15	15	19	15	Burkina Faso
Burma	35	38	36	46	47	40	53	42	55	61	Birmanie
Burundi	25	29	35	43	45	17	24	23	20	26	Burundi
Cape Verde	53	68	70	92	(95)	6	10	18	14	12	Cap-Vert
Central African Rep.	35	42	42	49	42	6	10	25	16	17	Rép. centrafricaine
Chad	23	26	27	27	20	5	2	8	13	5	Tchad
Comoros	71	78	97	118	99	9	11	27	12	10	Comores
Democratic Yemen	111	127	128	(169	(204)	20	27	62	89	102	Yémen démocratique
Djibouti	23	32	69	116	117	2	4	11	23	40	Djibouti
Equatorial Guinea	179	173	123	194	139	41	50	42	54	41	Guinée équatoriale
Ethiopia	28	30	34	40	40	14	20	25	25	26	Ethiopie
Gambia	102	102	120	156	189	22	19	13	17	33	Gambie
Guinea	82	71	64	65	88	24	20	24	16	24	Guinée
Guinea-Bissau	75	73	114	186	189	23	25	28	83	86	Guinée-Bissau
Haiti	45	44	40	39	34	12	12	13	15	24	Haïti
Kiribati	47	51	52	52	(53)	0	-	1	3	6	Kiribati
Lao People's Dem.Rep.	87	89	58	57	85	7	11	20	43	22	Rép. dém. pop. lao
Lesotho	35	38	47	67	68	3	3	4	7	5	Lesotho
Malawi	75	74	76	87	91	36	32	31	40	48	Malawi
Maldives	80	107	105	99	(98)	3	8	31	14	19	Maldives
Mali	70	94	120	143	115	19	10	13	27	25	Mali
Mauritania	160	168	184	214	224	21	18	21	27	24	Mauritanie
Nepal	15	19	22	26	30	8	9	8	7	10	Népal
Niger	45	55	73	81	72	39	33	31	51	50	Niger
Rwanda	15	18	20	22	25	6	5	12	14	12	Rwanda
Samoa	59	70	75	88	83	18	14	19	26	28	Samoa
Sao Tome and Principe	63	102	98	194	(233)	4	8	11	33	29	Sao Tomé-et-Principe
Sierra Leone	46	46	63	66	57	32	43	32	31	40	Sierra Leone
Somalia	55	71	51	72	72	13	23	58	78	113	Somalie
Sudan	72	85	85	95	101	25	24	28	28	52	Soudan
Togo	127	129	125	141	120	14	20	28	30	31	Togo
Tuvalu	-	2	4	5	-	-	-	-	..	..	Tuvalu
Uganda	(27)	(34)	(32)	(34)	(34)	25	33	42	45	35	Ouganda
United Rep.of Tanzania	44	52	59	58	95	22	35	27	28	35	Rép.-Unie de Tanzanie
Vanuatu	26	139	139	195	(261)	4	7	19	24	83	Vanuatu
Yemen	43	51	52	63	60	24	26	53	73	128	Yémen
All LDCs	**47**	**53**	**53**	**59**	**64**	**19**	**20**	**23**	**27**	**32**	**Ensemble des PMA**

Source: UNCTAD secretariat, mainly based on information from the OECD secretariat, the World Bank and IMF.

Note: Debt and debt service are defined as in tables 49A and 49B.

a Exports of goods and all (factor and non-factor) services.

Source: Secrétariat de la CNUCED, principalement d'après des renseignements du secrétariat de l'OCDE, de la Banque mondiale et du FMI.

Note: La dette et le service de la dette sont definis comme aux tableaux 49A et 49B.

a Exportations de biens et de tous les services (facteurs et non-facteurs).

50A. Long- and medium-term and total concessional debt

50A. Dette à long et moyen terme et dette concessionnelle

$ million — Millions de dollars

Country	*Long- and medium-term debt / Dette à long et moyen terme*					*of which: concessional / dont: dette concessionnelle*					Pays
	1982	*1983*	*1984*	*1985*	*1986*	*1982*	*1983*	*1984*	*1985*	*1986*	
Afghanistan	1400	809	866	1118	1270	1375	785	843	1112	1269	Afghanistan
Bangladesh	4479	5059	5414	6373	7593	4090	4378	4992	5963	7153	Bangladesh
Benin	577	626	590	685	770	204	255	263	314	390	Bénin
Bhutan	8	2	3	5	17	1	2	2	5	17	Bhoutan
Botswana	299	311	342	417	547	102	106	115	128	129	Botswana
Burkina Faso	357	406	409	503	608	256	286	306	382	481	Burkina faso
Burma	2005	2231	2261	2964	3693	1509	1774	1876	2420	3108	Birmanie
Burundi	226	300	340	433	522	193	260	286	355	449	Burundi
Cape Verde	57	75	78	106	109	30	37	46	66	76	Cap-Vert
Central African Rep.	226	235	226	300	393	123	136	150	211	278	Rép. centrafricaine
Chad	146	146	136	145	140	84	88	84	99	119	Tchad
Comoros	70	84	102	132	156	66	80	96	122	142	Comores
Democratic Yemen	814	1001	1143	1485	1956	759	917	1039	1344	1773	Yêmen démocratique
Djibouti	27	51	117	209	219	16	26	60	85	105	Djibouti
Equatorial Guinea	90	94	86	121	141	31	33	27	31	47	Guinée équatoriale
Ethiopia	1090	1292	1515	1795	2038	878	1059	1163	1388	1625	Ethiopie
Gambia	163	166	177	192	245	116	119	121	137	169	Gambie
Guinea	1339	1249	1169	1222	1334	928	923	860	901	913	Guinée
Guinea-Bissau	148	159	162	259	292	106	113	121	143	170	Guinée-Bissau
Haiti	454	527	552	610	626	297	344	401	458	492	Haïti
Kiribati	8	9	8	10	11	1	1	1	1	1	Kiribati
Lao People's Dem.Rep.	307	437	396	454	558	306	435	396	453	556	Rép. dém. pop. lao
Lesotho	117	131	133	170	188	77	93	108	134	148	Lesotho
Malawi	722	729	744	804	915	394	408	476	529	660	Malawi
Maldives	44	54	59	68	71	35	40	36	38	50	Maldives
Mali	816	943	1153	1342	1597	769	857	991	1241	1430	Mali
Mauritania	1045	1177	1209	1374	1641	665	741	780	858	1057	Mauritanie
Nepal	306	365	452	566	726	299	360	430	536	673	Népal
Niger	785	826	844	1032	1242	295	332	355	453	573	Niger
Rwanda	200	245	268	345	429	189	218	241	313	398	Rwanda
Samoa	59	60	65	66	65	45	49	55	57	58	Samoa
Sao Tome and Principe	18	31	30	67	82	16	20	22	57	72	Sao Tomé-et-Principe
Sierra Leone	446	410	425	430	473	244	254	247	242	267	Sierra leone
Somalia	1189	1384	1518	1581	1646	870	938	1063	1121	1255	Somalie
Sudan	5153	5658	6222	6676	6841	2160	2470	2853	3026	2848	Soudan
Togo	924	814	703	797	901	289	336	353	317	421	Togo
Tuvalu	-	0	0	0	0		0	0	0	0	Tuvalu
Uganda	609	683	708	843	916	393	395	441	565	651	Ouganda
United Rep.of Tanzania	2482	2741	2823	3056	3617	1554	1712	1689	1875	1922	Rép.-Unie de Tanzanie
Vanuatu	11	46	82	106	134	4	3	3	5	6	Vanuatu
Yemen	1420	1760	1826	2115	2263	1253	1537	1609	1727	1734	Yémen
All LDCs	**30639**	**33327**	**35357**	**40977**	**46985**	**21024**	**22921**	**25001**	**29210**	**33685**	**Ensemble des PMA**

Source: UNCTAD secretariat, based on information from the OECD secretariat.

Source: Secrétariat de la CNUCED, d'après des renseignements du secrétariat de l'OCDE.

50B. Long- and medium-term and concessional debt service payments

50B. Paiements au titre du service de la dette à long et moyen terme et de la dette concessionnelle

$ million — Millions de dollars

Country	*Long- and medium-term debt service / Service de la dette à long et moyen terme* 1982	1983	1984	1985	1986	*of which: concessional / dont: service de la dette concessionnelle* 1982	1983	1984	1985	1986	Pays
Afghanistan	39	40	42	46	45	37	37	39	24	44	Afghanistan
Bangladesh	155	161	235	291	361	101	101	131	172	227	Bangladesh
Benin	18	64	40	39	65	4	5	5	8	12	Bénin
Bhutan	1	2	0	9	0	0	0	0	9	0	Bhoutan
Botswana	60	27	46	54	51	2	2	5	9	8	Botswana
Burkina Faso	26	20	23	28	32	4	4	8	7	12	Burkina faso
Burma	143	195	165	191	230	41	49	66	77	102	Birmanie
Burundi	16	17	20	24	35	2	5	11	12	15	Burundi
Cape Verde	2	3	7	5	5	0	1	1	1	1	Cap-Vert
Central African Rep.	7	13	27	17	23	1	2	18	9	13	Rép. centrafricaine
Chad	1	1	8	8	4	0	0	5	3	2	Tchad
Comoros	2	2	3	2	3	1	1	2	1	2	Comores
Democratic Yemen	34	42	94	139	121	21	25	70	100	97	Yémen démocratique
Djibouti	4	5	15	33	60	2	2	2	13	8	Djibouti
Equatorial Guinea	4	8	1	4	8	0	0	0	0	2	Guinée équatoriale
Ethiopia	67	83	116	119	174	21	27	35	43	68	Ethiopie
Gambia	12	8	7	7	13	2	2	5	3	6	Gambie
Guinea	95	92	114	71	116	49	44	68	44	82	Guinée
Guinea-Bissau	3	3	6	12	12	1	1	0	10	6	Guinée-Bissau
Haiti	18	17	25	29	39	4	5	7	9	24	Haïti
Kiribati	0	0	0	0	1	-	-	0	0	-	Kiribati
Lao People's Dem.Rep.	2	4	4	22	13	2	2	2	20	13	Rép. dém. pop. lao
Lesotho	12	13	15	19	15	1	2	3	5	6	Lesotho
Malawi	68	65	74	84	95	8	7	12	18	16	Malawi
Maldives	2	5	24	11	18	2	3	5	4	5	Maldives
Mali	8	14	19	47	40	5	10	13	32	30	Mali
Mauritania	48	44	47	88	87	19	15	16	38	41	Mauritanie
Nepal	10	13	11	16	30	5	8	10	13	18	Népal
Niger	163	117	94	116	150	12	13	14	21	25	Niger
Rwanda	7	6	18	21	26	6	4	6	9	11	Rwanda
Samoa	3	2	4	5	5	1	1	1	2	2	Samoa
Sao Tome and Principe	0	0	1	2	4	0	0	-	2	0	Sao Tomé-et-Principe
Sierra Leone	21	39	22	23	23	3	2	5	7	15	Sierra leone
Somalia	22	33	45	79	87	9	11	28	51	56	Somalie
Sudan	121	89	106	109	172	37	27	24	26	35	Soudan
Togo	52	61	92	82	105	3	12	20	34	19	Togo
Tuvalu	-	0	0	0	0	-	-	-	0	0	Tuvalu
Uganda	63	84	106	73	39	21	29	30	15	19	Ouganda
United Rep.of Tanzania	71	119	80	80	105	17	19	26	23	37	Rép.-Unie de Tanzanie
Vanuatu	2	2	12	18	65	1	1	0	1	1	Vanuatu
Yemen	74	61	108	124	188	46	30	47	54	78	Yémen
All LDCs	**1458**	**1577**	**1876**	**2148**	**2665**	**491**	**508**	**743**	**928**	**1158**	**Ensemble des PMA**

Source: UNCTAD secretariat, based on information from the OECD secretariat.

Source: Secrétariat de la CNUCED, d'après des renseignements du secrétariat de l'OCDE.

51A. Non-concessional long- and medium-term debt

51A. Dette non-concessionnelle à long et moyen terme

$ million — Millions de dollars

Country	Non-concessional debt / Dette non-concessionnelle					of which: official and off. guaranteed / dont: dette publique et dette garantie par l'Etat					Pays
	1982	1983	1984	1985	1986	1982	1983	1984	1985	1986	
Afghanistan	25	24	22	6	1	24	24	22	0	-	Afghanistan
Bangladesh	389	680	421	411	440	269	455	143	139	120	Bangladesh
Benin	373	371	327	372	380	164	198	157	151	158	Bénin
Bhutan	7	0	1	0	-	-	0	0	0	-	Bhoutan
Botswana	197	205	227	289	418	81	81	101	129	223	Botswana
Burkina Faso	101	120	103	121	127	44	53	43	58	62	Burkina faso
Burma	496	456	385	544	585	279	296	263	438	455	Birmanie
Burundi	33	40	54	78	73	28	6	12	11	21	Burundi
Cape Verde	27	38	31	40	33	13	18	11	9	6	Cap-Vert
Central African Rep.	103	99	76	89	114	74	67	47	56	64	Rép. centrafricaine
Chad	61	58	51	46	20	24	18	17	7	6	Tchad
Comoros	4	4	6	10	13	1	1		1	2	Comores
Democratic Yemen	54	84	104	141	183	44	34	30	129	176	Yémen démocratique
Djibouti	11	26	57	124	114	4	19	24	34	67	Djibouti
Equatorial Guinea	59	61	60	90	94	45	39	39	69	69	Guinée équatoriale
Ethiopia	212	233	352	407	413	118	157	268	302	303	Ethiopie
Gambia	47	47	56	55	76	22	23	22	28	61	Gambie
Guinea	412	326	308	321	421	236	198	183	179	313	Guinée
Guinea-Bissau	42	46	40	116	123	15	8	6	22	17	Guinée-Bissau
Haiti	157	184	151	152	134	49	42	26	30	22	Haïti
Kiribati	8	8	8	10	10	0	0	0	-	0	Kiribati
Lao People's Dem.Rep.	2	2	0	2	2	1	0	0	2	-	Rép. dém. pop. lao
Lesotho	40	38	25	36	40	25	13	7	13	13	Lesotho
Malawi	329	321	268	275	255	88	94	63	96	104	Malawi
Maldives	9	15	23	30	21	1	1	1	2	2	Maldives
Mali	47	86	162	101	167	31	55	119	47	79	Mali
Mauritania	380	436	429	515	584	133	175	153	203	285	Mauritanie
Nepal	7	5	22	30	53	7	1	2	5	20	Népal
Niger	490	494	489	579	670	209	205	227	246	236	Niger
Rwanda	11	27	28	32	31	4	5	13	15	14	Rwanda
Samoa	14	12	10	9	7	5	4	3	4	4	Samoa
Sao Tome and Principe	2	11	8	10	11	2	11	8	7	4	Sao Tomé-et-Principe
Sierra Leone	201	156	178	188	206	154	116	105	102	135	Sierra leone
Somalia	320	446	454	459	391	137	167	193	214	128	Somalie
Sudan	2993	3189	3368	3650	3993	1176	1662	1683	2157	2768	Soudan
Togo	635	478	350	479	480	452	363	237	364	392	Togo
Tuvalu	-	0	0	0	0	-	-	-	-	-	Tuvalu
Uganda	216	288	267	278	265	101	170	136	127	91	Ouganda
United Rep.of Tanzania	928	1029	1135	1181	1695	453	328	290	335	960	Rép.-Unie de Tanzanie
Vanuatu	7	43	79	101	128	2	4	20	61	48	Vanuatu
Yemen	168	223	216	388	529	87	152	108	123	168	Yémen
All LDCs	**9614**	**10409**	**10352**	**11765**	**13300**	**4599**	**5263**	**4784**	**5917**	**7596**	**Ensemble des PMA**

Source: UNCTAD secretariat, based on information from the OECD secretariat.

Source: Secrétariat de la CNUCED, d'après des renseignements du secrétariat de l'OCDE.

51B. Non-concessional long- and medium-term debt service payments

51B. Paiements au titre du service de la dette non-concessionnelle à long et moyen terme

$ million | Millions de dollars

Country	*Non-concessional debt service / Service de la dette non-concessionnelle*					*of which: official and off. guaranteed / dont: service de la dette publique et de la dette garantie par l'Etat*					Pays
	1982	*1983*	*1984*	*1985*	*1986*	*1982*	*1983*	*1984*	*1985*	*1986*	
Afghanistan	2	3	3	22	1	1	2	3	22	-	Afghanistan
Bangladesh	55	60	104	119	134	29	32	46	69	73	Bangladesh
Benin	14	59	35	31	53	10	34	26	7	21	Bénin
Bhutan	1	2	0	0	0	-	0	0	0	-	Bhoutan
Botswana	58	24	41	45	43	2	7	11	16	15	Botswana
Burkina Faso	22	16	14	21	20	12	11	8	11	9	Burkina faso
Burma	102	146	99	114	128	75	84	68	87	109	Birmanie
Burundi	14	12	8	12	20	3	4	3	2	8	Burundi
Cape Verde	2	3	6	4	4	1	1	2	1	1	Cap-Vert
Central African Rep.	5	11	9	8	10	5	9	8	4	6	Rép. centrafricaine
Chad	1	1	3	5	2	0	0	0	0	0	Tchad
Comoros	1	1	1	1	1	0	0	0	0	0	Comores
Democratic Yemen	13	17	23	39	24	10	15	12	13	23	Yémen démocratique
Djibouti	2	3	12	19	52	1	1	10	3	14	Djibouti
Equatorial Guinea	4	8	1	4	6	2	6	1	2	5	Guinée équatoriale
Ethiopia	46	56	81	77	106	23	36	53	51	59	Ethiopie
Gambia	10	6	1	4	7	2	1	0	2	1	Gambie
Guinea	46	48	47	27	34	25	26	25	13	10	Guinée
Guinea-Bissau	2	2	5	2	6	2	1	1	2	1	Guinée-Bissau
Haiti	14	13	18	20	15	7	6	6	6	2	Haïti
Kiribati	0	-	-	-	1	-	-	-	-	1	Kiribati
Lao People's Dem.Rep.	0	1	2	2	0	-	1	2	2	0	Rép. dém. pop. lao
Lesotho	11	12	12	14	9	2	3	9	6	3	Lesotho
Malawi	61	58	62	66	79	24	24	26	16	23	Malawi
Maldives	1	3	19	7	13	0	1	1	1	1	Maldives
Mali	3	4	6	15	10	2	2	5	10	6	Mali
Mauritania	29	29	31	50	46	17	10	13	11	17	Mauritanie
Nepal	4	5	1	4	12	4	5	0	2	7	Népal
Niger	151	104	80	95	125	86	68	55	61	85	Niger
Rwanda	1	2	12	12	15	1	1	4	6	2	Rwanda
Samoa	2	1	2	3	3	1	1	1	0	1	Samoa
Sao Tome and Principe	0	0	1	0	4	0	0	1	1	0	Sao Tomé-et-Principe
Sierra Leone	18	37	17	16	8	12	30	8	10	2	Sierra leone
Somalia	13	22	17	28	31	1	5	13	9	14	Somalie
Sudan	85	62	82	83	137	27	0	23	69	129	Soudan
Togo	50	49	72	48	86	32	34	57	29	67	Togo
Tuvalu	-	-	-	-	-	-	-	-	-	-	Tuvalu
Uganda	42	55	76	58	20	4	14	33	17	6	Ouganda
United Rep.of Tanzania	53	100	54	57	68	21	55	12	11	11	Rép.-Unie de Tanzanie
Vanuatu	1	2	12	17	64	0	1	7	10	57	Vanuatu
Yemen	28	30	61	70	110	20	14	47	50	66	Yémen
All LDCs	**967**	**1068**	**1133**	**1220**	**1507**	**464**	**545**	**601**	**632**	**855**	**Ensemble des PMA**

Source: UNCTAD secretariat, based on information from the OECD secretariat.

Source: Secrétariat de la CNUCED, d'après des renseignements du secrétariat de l'OCDE.

52A. Multilateral debt

52A. Dette multilatérale

$ million — Millions de dollars

Country	*Total multilateral debt / Dette multilatérale totale* 1982	1983	1984	1985	1986	*of which: non-concessional / dont: dette non-concessionnelle* 1982	1983	1984	1985	1986	Pays
Afghanistan	110	109	109	119	129	-	-	-	-	-	Afghanistan
Bangladesh	1878	2114	2413	2916	3535	31	14	14	3	45	Bangladesh
Benin	159	187	201	239	296	27	26	23	27	32	Bénin
Bhutan	1	2	2	5	8	-	-	-	-	-	Bhoutan
Botswana	116	135	158	200	216	77	92	112	148	164	Botswana
Burkina Faso	222	244	255	308	395	17	17	18	25	37	Burkina faso
Burma	497	569	674	744	850	6	6	6	5	5	Birmanie
Burundi	122	170	209	258	341	4	14	24	32	40	Burundi
Cape Verde	29	34	40	54	63	7	11	11	13	15	Cap-Vert
Central African Rep.	74	88	103	137	190	3	10	9	13	22	Rép. centrafricaine
Chad	72	75	73	80	96	1	1	1	1	2	Tchad
Comoros	31	39	51	68	89	1	3	4	7	12	Comores
Democratic Yemen	160	212	258	329	384	-	-	-	-	-	Yémen démocratique
Djibouti	6	12	23	39	54	-	-	-	-	-	Djibouti
Equatorial Guinea	13	14	14	19	27	6	6	5	6	7	Guinée équatoriale
Ethiopia	442	490	522	609	694	34	35	36	37	40	Ethiopie
Gambia	68	72	77	90	121	12	10	10	13	15	Gambie
Guinea	194	208	227	263	303	58	59	59	59	58	Guinée
Guinea-Bissau	48	58	71	100	123	0	0	8	13	16	Guinée-Bissau
Haiti	209	245	284	319	355	-	-	-	-	-	Haïti
Kiribati	8	9	8	9	10	8	8	8	9	10	Kiribati
Lao People's Dem.Rep.	54	63	71	88	111	-	-	-	-	-	Rép. dém. pop. lao
Lesotho	75	90	107	142	161	1	3	8	21	23	Lesotho
Malawi	341	371	447	517	631	85	85	90	100	108	Malawi
Maldives	13	14	15	16	22	7	6	6	6	0	Maldives
Mali	289	340	365	418	515	7	6	8	9	10	Mali
Mauritania	253	314	329	341	396	94	127	122	111	123	Mauritanie
Nepal	251	311	378	466	567	0	3	4	6	7	Népal
Niger	192	226	241	284	365	31	43	43	49	52	Niger
Rwanda	134	161	188	242	305	1	2	2	2	2	Rwanda
Samoa	44	47	53	55	56	-	-	-	-	-	Samoa
Sao Tome and Principe	16	20	20	21	25	-	-	-	-	-	Sao Tomé-et-Principe
Sierra Leone	113	117	122	146	155	22	20	16	17	16	Sierra leone
Somalia	383	432	439	507	602	131	145	133	129	146	Somalie
Sudan	869	903	963	1044	1116	187	156	130	146	164	Soudan
Togo	159	223	240	291	359	21	31	31	32	31	Togo
Tuvalu	-	0	0	0	0	-	-	-	-	-	Tuvalu
Uganda	191	242	336	473	570	22	29	64	86	96	Ouganda
United Rep.of Tanzania	807	887	945	1060	1152	213	222	234	262	258	Rép.-Unie de Tanzanie
Vanuatu	-	0	1	1	2	-	-	-	-	-	Vanuatu
Yemen	279	316	369	453	515	24	20	39	66	80	Yémen
All LDCs	**8923**	**10162**	**11400**	**13473**	**15904**	**1138**	**1210**	**1278**	**1452**	**1636**	**Ensemble des PMA**

Source: UNCTAD secretariat, based on information from the OECD secretariat.

Source: Secrétariat de la CNUCED, d'après des renseignements du secrétariat de l'OCDE.

52B. Multilateral debt service payments

52B. Paiements au titre du service de la dette multilatérale

$ million

Millions de dollars

	Multilateral debt service Service de la dette multilatérale					*of which: non-concessional dont: service de la dette non-concessionnelle*					
Country	*1982*	*1983*	*1984*	*1985*	*1986*	*1982*	*1983*	*1984*	*1985*	*1986*	*Pays*
Afghanistan	2	2	1	12	3	-	-	-	-	-	Afghanistan
Bangladesh	28	41	63	75	107	10	18	25	12	20	Bangladesh
Benin	5	7	7	12	15	3	4	3	6	6	Bénin
Bhutan	-	-	0	9	0	-	-	-	-	-	Bhoutan
Botswana	10	12	15	20	30	9	10	13	17	27	Botswana
Burkina Faso	6	4	9	8	15	2	1	1	3	5	Burkina faso
Burma	5	7	14	20	28	1	0	1	1	1	Birmanie
Burundi	2	3	9	12	14	1	1	3	3	5	Burundi
Cape Verde	0	1	2	2	1	0	1	1	1	0	Cap-Vert
Central African Rep.	1	2	3	5	8	0	1	0	2	3	Rép. centrafricaine
Chad	1	0	0	2	3	1	-	0	0	1	Tchad
Comoros	0	1	1	1	1	0	0	0	0	0	Comores
Democratic Yemen	5	7	10	39	32	-	-	-	-	-	Yémen démocratique
Djibouti	0	0	1	1	3	-	-	-	-	-	Djibouti
Equatorial Guinea	0	0	0	2	2	-	0	-	1	0	Guinée équatoriale
Ethiopia	13	13	17	22	28	5	5	5	5	7	Ethiopie
Gambia	1	5	3	2	8	0	4	1	0	4	Gambie
Guinea	12	14	15	15	26	10	10	11	8	13	Guinée
Guinea-Bissau	1	0	0	1	1	-	-	-	-	-	Guinée-Bissau
Haiti	2	3	5	7	10	-	-	-	-	-	Haïti
Kiribati	0	-	0	0	-	0	-	-	-	-	Kiribati
Lao People's Dem.Rep.	1	1	0	11	1	-	-	-	-	-	Rép. dém. pop. lao
Lesotho	1	2	3	7	9	0	0	1	3	4	Lesotho
Malawi	13	18	19	18	29	9	12	12	9	18	Malawi
Maldives	0	1	0	1	7	-	1	-	1	6	Maldives
Mali	4	5	9	19	18	1	1	0	2	1	Mali
Mauritania	11	17	20	45	33	6	11	15	33	19	Mauritanie
Nepal	4	6	7	10	16	0	-	-	-	2	Népal
Niger	32	11	12	18	21	27	5	7	9	12	Niger
Rwanda	4	3	4	6	8	0	0	1	0	1	Rwanda
Samoa	1	1	1	2	2	-	-	-	-	-	Samoa
Sao Tome and Principe	0	0	-	0	0	-	-	-	-	-	Sao Tomé-et-Principe
Sierra Leone	3	4	10	3	13	2	2	7	1	3	Sierra leone
Somalia	14	17	13	19	20	10	11	4	5	1	Somalie
Sudan	25	32	34	17	31	7	18	19	3	9	Soudan
Togo	11	7	10	15	17	10	4	3	7	8	Togo
Tuvalu	-	-	0	0	0	-	-	-	-	-	Tuvalu
Uganda	17	9	12	19	29	3	2	7	9	14	Ouganda
United Rep.of Tanzania	31	34	50	53	69	23	23	34	38	40	Rép.-Unie de Tanzanie
Vanuatu	-	-	-	0	0	-	-	-	-	-	Vanuatu
Yemen	9	15	26	26	31	0	5	13	11	12	Yémen
All LDCs	**275**	**303**	**405**	**557**	**689**	**141**	**149**	**186**	**190**	**242**	**Ensemble des PMA**

Source: UNCTAD secretariat, based on information from the OECD secretariat.

Source: Secrétariat de la CNUCED, d'après des renseignements du secrétariat de l'OCDE.

53. ODA debt and debt service payments to OECD countries

53. Dette d'APD et paiements au titre du service de cette dette aux pays de l'OCDE

$ million — Millions de dollars

Country	Debt / *Dette* 1982	1983	1984	1985	1986	Debt service / *Service de la dette* 1982	1983	1984	1985	1986	Pays
Afghanistan	157	145	133	141	142	10	10	10	5	8	Afghanistan
Bangladesh	1783	1755	2093	2559	3107	39	39	49	50	84	Bangladesh
Benin	45	47	46	63	83	2	1	1	1	2	Bénin
Bhutan	-	-	-	-	-	-	-	-	-	-	Bhoutan
Botswana	56	49	45	46	46	1	1	2	2	3	Botswana
Burkina Faso	34	44	49	71	95	1	1	1	2	2	Burkina faso
Burma	855	1011	1005	1463	2047	30	35	48	50	62	Birmanie
Burundi	19	24	29	57	77	0	1	1	2	2	Burundi
Cape Verde	1	0	0	4	5	-	-	0	-	0	Cap-Vert
Central African Rep.	37	42	39	67	91	0	1	16	5	6	Rép. centrafricaine
Chad	5	6	5	11	19	-	0	4	0	0	Tchad
Comoros	2	3	6	12	16	1	1	1	1	2	Comores
Democratic Yemen	15	15	16	19	20	1	1	1	1	2	Yémen démocratique
Djibouti	10	10	15	12	12	2	2	2	12	4	Djibouti
Equatorial Guinea	-	-	-	-	0	-	-	-	-	-	Guinée équatoriale
Ethiopia	183	175	187	223	263	9	11	11	11	10	Ethiopie
Gambia	14	11	14	20	24	0	0	1	1	1	Gambie
Guinea	123	127	132	165	222	9	4	4	6	4	Guinée
Guinea-Bissau	6	6	6	1	1	0	0	0	6	1	Guinée-Bissau
Haiti	88	99	117	139	138	2	2	2	1	15	Haïti
Kiribati	-	-	-	-	-	-	-	-	-	-	Kiribati
Lao People's Dem.Rep.	54	51	44	55	66	2	1	2	2	2	Rép. dém. pop. lao
Lesotho	3	2	2	3	1	0	0	0	0	0	Lesotho
Malawi	137	123	119	113	137	4	2	5	9	6	Malawi
Maldives	2	2	1	1	2	1	0	0	0	1	Maldives
Mali	26	24	117	261	319	1	1	1	4	6	Mali
Mauritania	41	46	46	70	107	3	2	1	2	3	Mauritanie
Nepal	20	25	31	51	84	1	1	1	1	2	Népal
Niger	77	75	80	123	153	6	6	6	8	10	Niger
Rwanda	23	22	20	34	52	1	1	1	2	2	Rwanda
Samoa	0	0	0	0	0	-	-	0	0	0	Samoa
Sao Tome and Principe	-	-	-	-	-	-	-	-	-	-	Sao Tomé-et-Principe
Sierra Leone	119	123	117	82	101	2	0	1	5	4	Sierra leone
Somalia	120	150	220	267	331	4	4	6	10	3	Somalie
Sudan	164	169	320	427	504	5	2	5	4	13	Soudan
Togo	149	141	137	43	70	1	8	13	26	8	Togo
Tuvalu	-	-	-	-	-	-	-	-	-	-	Tuvalu
Uganda	60	31	29	32	32	1	1	2	2	4	Ouganda
United Rep.of Tanzania	310	351	369	465	460	3	4	4	8	9	Rép.-Unie de Tanzanie
Vanuatu	4	3	2	3	4	1	1	0	1	1	Vanuatu
Yemen	70	64	73	106	143	1	1	2	2	4	Yémen
All LDCs	**4814**	**4971**	**5664**	**7209**	**8974**	**140**	**144**	**205**	**240**	**284**	**Ensemble des PMA**

Source: UNCTAD secretariat, based on information from the OECD secretariat.

Source: Secrétariat de la CNUCED, d'après des renseignements du secrétariat de l'OCDE.

54A. Area and population : economic characteristics

54A. Superficie et population : caractéristiques économiques

Country	Area / Superficie: Total / Totale (000 km²)	Area / Superficie: % of arable land and land under permanent crops / % de terres arables et sous cultures permanentes 1985	Population: Density / Densité Pop./km² 1987	Population: Total / Totale (mill.) 1987	Population: Urban / Urbaine % 1985	Activity rate [a] / Taux d'activité [a] 1985: M	F	T	Pays
Afghanistan	652.1	12.4	29	19.1	19	54	5	30	Afghanistan
Bangladesh	144.0	63.4	713	102.7	18	52	4	29	Bangladesh
Benin	112.6	16.3	38	4.3	35	51	46	49	Bénin
Bhutan	47.0	2.2	31	1.5	4	58	30	45	Bhoutan
Botswana	581.7	2.3	2	1.2	20	45	24	34	Botswana
Burkina Faso	274.2	9.6	27	7.3	8	58	51	54	Burkina Faso
Burma	676.6	14.9	57	38.6	24	56	34	45	Birmanie
Burundi	27.8	47.6	180	5.0	2	57	50	53	Burundi
Cape Verde	4.0	9.9	87	0.4	5	57	20	37	Cap-Vert
Central African Rep.	623.0	3.2	5	2.8	45	55	45	50	Rép. Centrafricaine
Chad	1284.0	2.5	4	5.3	27	57	15	36	Tchad
Comoros	2.2	44.7	221	0.5	25	54	38	46	Comores
Democratic Yemen	333.0	0.5	7	2.4	37	47	6	26	Yémen démocratique
Djibouti	23.2	..	21	0.5	77	..	..	..	Djibouti
Equatorial Guinea	28.1	8.2	15	0.4	60	52	34	43	Guinée équatoriale
Ethiopia	1221.9	11.4	38	46.3	15	55	34	44	Ethiopie
Gambia	11.3	14.6	71	0.8	20	57	39	48	Gambie
Guinea	245.9	6.4	26	6.4	22	56	38	47	Guinée
Guinea Bissau	36.1	8.9	26	0.9	27	58	39	48	Guinée-Bissau
Haiti	27.8	32.6	196	5.4	27	50	36	43	Haïti
Kiribati	0.7	52.1	92	0.1	34	..	..	..	Kiribati
Lao People's Dem.Rep.	236.8	3.8	16	3.8	15	53	45	49	Rép.dém.populaire lao
Lesotho	30.4	9.9	53	1.6	17	55	41	48	Lesotho
Malawi	118.5	20.1	63	7.4	12	52	37	44	Malawi
Maldives	0.3	10.0	648	0.2	20	..	..	..	Maldives
Mali	1240.2	1.7	7	8.6	20	55	10	32	Mali
Mauritania	1025.5	0.2	2	2.0	31	50	13	31	Mauritanie
Nepal	140.8	16.5	125	17.6	7	53	29	42	Népal
Niger	1267.0	3.0	5	6.5	15	56	49	52	Niger
Rwanda	26.3	38.4	245	6.4	5	53	48	50	Rwanda
Samoa	2.8	43.0	58	0.2	22	41 [b]	9 [b]	25 [b]	Samoa
Sao Tome & Principe	1.0	38.5	117	0.1	38	..	..	30 [b]	Sao Tomé-et-Principe
Sierra Leone	71.7	24.8	52	3.7	25	51	25	38	Sierra Leone
Somalia	637.7	1.7	9	5.7	34	52	34	43	Somalie
Sudan	2505.8	5.0	9	22.9	21	51	14	32	Soudan
Togo	56.8	25.1	56	3.2	23	53	31	42	Togo
Tuvalu	0.2	..	51	0.0	..	..	..	..	Tuvalu
Uganda	235.9	28.0	70	16.5	7	53	38	46	Ouganda
Un. Rep. of Tanzania	945.1	5.5	25	23.9	14	50	47	49	Rép. Unie de Tanzanie
Vanuatu	12.2	6.4	11	0.1	25	..	..	45 [b]	Vanuatu
Yemen	195.0	6.9	43	8.4	19	45	6	25	Yémen
ALL LDCs	**15107.2**	**6.6**	**26**	**390.8**	**18**	**53**	**24**	**39**	**Ensemble des PMA**
All developing countries	**66344.3**	**10.5**	**40**	**2643.6**	**34**	**53**	**22**	**37**	**Ensemble des pays en développement**

Source: United Nations, *Demographic Yearbook, 1986*; United Nations, *World Population Chart 1985*; FAO, *Production Yearbook 1986*; World Bank, *World Development Report 1988*; World Bank, *Social Indicators of Development 1987*; ILO, *Economically active population 1950-2025.*

a Economically active population as a percentage of total population of sex(es) specified of all ages.

b Year other than 1985.

Source: Nations Unies, *Annuaire démographique 1986*; Nations Unies, *World Population Chart 1985*; FAO, *Annuaire de la production 1986*; Banque Mondiale, *Rapport sur le développement dans le monde 1988*; Banque Mondiale *Social Indicators of Development 1987*; BIT, *Population active 1950-2025.*

a Population active en pourcentage de la population totale de tous âges du sexe ou des sexes précisés.

b Année autre que 1985.

54B. Birth and death rates, life expectancy

54B. Taux de natalité et de mortalité, espérance de vie

Country	*Infant mortality rate (per 1000 live births)* / *Taux de mortalité infantile (pour 1000 naissance (vivantes)*		*Average life expectancy at birth (years)* / *Espérance de vie moyenne à la naissance (années)*						*Crude bith rate (per 1000)* / *Taux brut de natalité (pour 1000)*		*Crude death rate (per 1000)* / *Taux brut de mortalité (pour 1000)*		Pays
	1975-80	*1980-85*	*1975-80*			*1980-85*			*1975-80*	*1980-85*	*1975-80*	*1980-85*	
			M	*F*	*T*	*M*	*F*	*T*					
Afghanistan	194	194	37	37	37	37	37	37	48.6	48.9	27.2	27.3	Afghanistan
Bangladesh	137	128	47	46	47	48	47	48	47.2	44.8	19.0	17.5	Bangladesh
Benin	130	120	40	44	42	42	46	44	51.1	50.7	24.6	21.2	Bénin
Bhutan	147	139	45	43	44	47	45	46	40.0	38.4	19.8	18.1	Bhoutan
Botswana	82	76	51	54	53	53	56	55	50.6	49.9	14.0	12.6	Botswana
Burkina Faso	157	150	42	45	43	44	47	45	48.1	47.8	24.0	20.1	Burkina Faso
Burma	75	70	53	57	55	56	59	58	32.9	30.5	12.4	11.0	Birmanie
Burundi	130	124	43	47	45	45	48	47	48.2	47.2	20.5	19.0	Burundi
Cape Verde	87	75	55	58	57	57	61	59	32.9	30.9	9.7	11.4	Cap-Vert
Central African Rep.	145	142	40	44	42	41	45	43	44.9	44.6	23.5	21.8	Rép. centrafricaine
Chad	154	143	39	43	41	41	45	43	44.1	44.2	23.1	21.4	Tchad
Comoros	97	88	46	50	48	48	52	50	46.6	46.4	17.2	15.9	Comores
Democratic Yemen	150	135	45	47	46	47	50	48	47.6	47.0	20.9	17.4	Yémen démocratique
Djibouti	..	115 [a]	..	..	..	..	..	47 [a]	..	47.0 [a]	..	18.0 [a]	Djibouti
Equatorial Guinea	149	137	40	44	42	42	46	44	42.5	42.5	22.7	21.0	Guinée équatoriale
Ethiopia	155	155	39	43	41	39	43	41	48.3	49.7	23.0	23.2	Ethiopie
Gambia	185	174	32	35	34	34	37	35	48.3	48.4	30.4	29.0	Gambie
Guinea	171	159	37	40	38	39	42	40	46.9	46.8	25.3	23.5	Guinée
Guinea-Bissau	154	143	39	43	41	41	45	43	40.9	40.7	21.9	21.7	Guinée-Bissau
Haiti	139	128	49	52	51	51	54	53	41.8	41.3	15.7	14.2	Haïti
Kiribati	..	65 [a]	..	..	..	..	..	52 [a]	..	34.0 [a]	..	13.0 [a]	Kiribati
Lao People's Dem.Rep.	135	123	46	49	48	48	51	50	43.1	40.8	17.3	15.7	Rép.dém.populaire lao
Lesotho	123	111	44	50	47	46	52	49	41.9	41.8	17.9	16.5	Lesotho
Malawi	177	163	42	44	43	44	46	45	53.0	53.2	23.1	21.5	Malawi
Maldives	..	58 [b]	..	..	..	53	50	53	..	45.3 [b]	..	8.1 [b]	Maldives
Mali	191	180	39	42	40	40	44	42	50.9	50.6	24.5	22.5	Mali
Mauritania	149	137	40	44	42	42	46	44	50.0	50.1	22.5	20.9	Mauritanie
Nepal	147	139	45	43	44	47	45	46	44.6	41.7	20.5	18.4	Népal
Niger	157	146	39	42	41	41	44	43	50.9	51.0	25.0	22.9	Niger
Rwanda	140	132	43	47	45	45	48	47	51.1	51.9	18.1	18.9	Rwanda
Samoa	..	51 [a]	..	..	..	..	..	65 [a]	..	34.0 [a]	..	7.0 [a]	Samoa
Sao Tome & Principe	..	62 [c]	..	..	..	..	..	65 [a]	..	36.3 [c]	..	8.8 [c]	Sao Tomé-et-Principe
Sierra Leone	191	180	31	33	32	33	36	34	47.8	47.4	31.9	29.7	Sierra Leone
Somalia	155	155	39	43	41	39	43	41	48.5	47.9	22.8	23.3	Somalie
Sudan	131	118	44	46	45	47	49	48	47.1	45.9	19.4	17.4	Soudan
Togo	111	102	46	50	48	49	52	51	45.5	45.2	18.6	15.7	Togo
Tuvalu	..	..	..	..	..	..	..	..	..	..	..	..	Tuvalu
Uganda	114	112	46	50	48	47	51	49	50.3	50.3	17.6	16.8	Ouganda
Un.Rep. of Tanzania	125	115	47	51	49	49	53	51	50.9	50.4	16.8	15.3	Rép.-Unie de Tanzanie
Vanuatu	..	46 [a]	..	..	..	..	..	61 [a]	..	34.0 [a]	..	6.0 [a]	Vanuatu
Yemen	150	135	45	47	46	47	50	48	48.6	48.6	24.1	18.4	Yémen
ALL LDCs	**138**	**131**	**44**	**46**	**45**	**46**	**48**	**47**	**46.3**	**45.3**	**20.0**	**18.6**	**Ensemble des PMA**
All developing countries	**121**	**109**	**50**	**52**	**51**	**52**	**54**	**53**	**37.6**	**35.8**	**13.8**	**12.5**	**Ensemble des pays en développement**

Source: United Nations, *Demographic Indicators by Countries as Assessed in 1984*; United Nations, *Demographic Yearbook 1986*; World Bank, *Social Indicators of Development 1988.*

a Most recent year available between 1980 and 1986.

b 1986.

c 1985.

Source: Nations Unies, *Indicateurs démographiques par pays estimés en 1984*; Nations Unies, *Annuaire démographique 1986*; Banque mondiale, *Social Indicators of Development 1988.*

a Année la plus récente disponible entre 1980 et 1986.

b 1986.

c 1985.

54C. Health at birth

54C. Santé à la naissance

Country	Low-birth-weight infants (in per cent) / Enfants de poids insuffisant à la naissance (en pourcentage) 1982-1983	Percentage of women attended during child-birth by trained personnel / Pourcentage des femmes ayant reçu des soins prodigués par du personnel qualifié pendant l'accouchement 1984	Percentage of children immunized against DPT (3 doses) / Pourcentage d'enfants vaccinés DTC (3 doses) 1984	Pays
Afghanistan	20.0	5.0	16.0	Afghanistan
Bangladesh	50.0	..	1.5 [g]	Bangladesh
Benin	9.6	34.3 [d]	15.8	Bénin
Bhutan	..	3.4	8.7	Bhoutan
Botswana	12.0	..	82.0 [d]	Botswana
Burkina Faso	21.0	..	2.0 [d]	Burkina Faso
Burma	7.0 [b]	97.0	8.4	Birmanie
Burundi	14.0	12.0	38.0 [d]	Burundi
Cape Verde	..	10.0 [e]	..	Cap-Vert
Central African Rep.	23.0	..	21.0 [d]	République centrafricaine
Chad	11.0	..	1.1	Tchad
Comoros	..	24.0 [f]	31.0	Comores
Democratic Yemen	12.0 [b]	10.0 [d]	7.0	Yémen démocratique
Djibouti	11.0 [c]	73.0	20.0 [c]	Djibouti
Equatorial Guinea	..	..	..	Guinée équatoriale
Ethiopia	10.4 [b]	58.0	6.0 [d]	Ethiopie
Gambia	14.0	80.0 [e]	87.8 [e]	Gambie
Guinea	18.0	..	4.0 [e]	Guinée
Guinea Bissau	15.0 [b]	..	24.0 [e]	Guinée-Bissau
Haiti	17.0	20.0 [e]	12.0	Haiti
Kiribati	..	..	..	Kiribati
Lao People's Dem. Rep.	35.0 [b]	..	..	Rép. dém. pop. lao
Lesotho	10.5	28.0	69.0	Lesotho
Malawi	20.0 [b]	58.6	66.0	Malawi
Maldives	26.0	..	23.0	Maldives
Mali	13.0	..	17.5 [h]	Mali
Mauritania	10.0 [b]	22.6	21.4	Mauritanie
Nepal	..	10.0 [c]	26.4 [g]	Népal
Niger	20.0	46.5 [e]	5.0 [e]	Niger
Rwanda	17.0	..	32.0 [e]	Rwanda
Samoa	2.4	52.0 [d]	84.3 [e]	Samoa
Sao Tome and Principe	5.9	..	28.0 [e]	Sao Tomé-et-Principe
Sierra Leone	17.0	25.0	28.6	Sierra Leone
Somalia	..	2.0 [d]	10.0	Somalie
Sudan	15.0 [b]	20.0	4.0	Soudan
Togo	16.9	..	9.0 [f]	Togo
Tuvalu	..	..	72.0 [d]	Tuvalu
Uganda	10.0	..	2.0 [e]	Ouganda
Un. Rep. of Tanzania	12.0	74.0 [e]	58.0 [d]	Rép. Unie de Tanzanie
Vanuatu	4.7	72.0 [e]	22.0	Vanuatu
Yemen	9.0	12.0 [d]	10.0	Yémen
All LDCs [a]	**23.7**	**46.0**	**13.6**	**Ensemble des PMA [a]**
All developing countries [a]	**20.8**	**41.1**	**41.4**	**Ensemble des pays en développpement [a]**

Source: WHO, *World Health Statistics Annual 1986* and UNICEF, *The State of the World's Children 1987*.

a Average of countries for which data are available.

b 1984.

c 1985.

d 1982.

e 1983.

f 1981.

g 1983-1984.

h 1980.

Source: OMS, *Annuaire de statistiques sanitaires mondiales 1986* et FISE, *La situation des enfants dans le monde 1987*.

a Moyenne des pays pour lesquels les données sont disponibles.

b 1984.

c 1985.

d 1982.

e 1983.

f 1981.

g 1983-1984.

h 1980.

54D. Food and water / 54D. Alimentation et eau

Country	*Average daily calorie intake per capita / Disponibilités alimentaires (calories par personne par jour)* Average/Moyenne 1979-1981	1983-1985	*Percentage of population with access to safe water or adequate sanitation / Pourcentage de la population disposant d'eau saine ou de mesures suffisantes d'hygiène du milieu* Urban/Urbaine Water/Eau 1980	1985	Urban/Urbaine Sanitation/Hygiène du milieu 1980	1985	Rural/Rurale Water/Eau 1980	1985	Rural/Rurale Sanitation/Hygiène du milieu 1980	1985	Pays
Afghanistan	2244 [c]	2196	28	38	..	5	8	17	..	..	Afghanistan
Bangladesh	1850	1859	26	24	21	24	40	49	1	3	Bangladesh
Benin	2140	2136	26	80	48	60	15	34	4	20	Bénin
Bhutan	..	..	50	..	..	..	5	19	..	1	Bhoutan
Botswana	2139	2164	..	84	..	93	..	46	..	28	Botswana
Burkina Faso	2033	1961	27	43	38	44	31	69	5	6	Burkina Faso
Burma	2375	2518	38	36	38	33	15	24	15	21	Birmanie
Burundi	2344	2217	90	98	40	84	20	21	35	56	Burundi
Cape Verde	2545	2614	100	83	34	32	21	50	10	9	Cap-Vert
Central African Rep.	2115	2045	..	13	..	..	..	..	..	..	Rép. Centrafricaine
Chad	1789 [c]	1575	..	..	..	..	..	..	..	..	Tchad
Comoros	2074	2090	..	..	..	..	..	..	..	..	Comores
Democratic Yemen	2211	2293	85	73 [a]	70	69 [a]	25	39 [a]	15	33 [a]	Yémen démocratique
Djibouti	..	..	50	50	43	78	20	20	20	17	Djibouti
Equatorial Guinea	..	..	..	47 [a]	..	99 [a]	..	..	..	..	Guinée équatoriale
Ethiopia	2104 [c]	1692	..	69	..	96	..	9	..	..	Ethiopie
Gambia	2176	2229	85	97	..	..	..	50	..	..	Gambie
Guinea	1768	1724	69	41	54	..	2	12	1	..	Guinée
Guinea-Bissau	1748 [c]	1979	18	17	21	29	8	22	13	18	Guinée-Bissau
Haiti	1904	1843	48	59	39	42	8	30	10	13	Haïti
Kiribati	2672	2616	93	..	87	..	25	..	80	..	Kiribati
Lao People's Dem.Rep.	1889 [c]	2242	21	28 [a]	..	13 [a]	12	20 [a]	..	4 [a]	Rép.dém.populaire lao
Lesotho	2347	2346	37	65	13	22	11	30	14	14	Lesotho
Malawi	2472	2429	77	97	100	75 [a]	37	50	81	..	Malawi
Maldives	1990 [c]	1992	11	59	60	100	3	12	1	1	Maldives
Mali	1752	1793	37	46	79	90	0	10	0	3	Mali
Mauritania	1998	2076	80	73	5	8	85	..	..	..	Mauritanie
Nepal	1974	2048	83	70	16	17	7	25	1	1	Népal
Niger	2363	2265	41	35	36	36 [a]	32	49	3	3	Niger
Rwanda	2073	2013	48	79	60	77	55	48	50	55	Rwanda
Samoa	2403	2373	97	75	86	88	94	67	83	83	Samoa
Sao Tome & Principe	2353	2435	..	33	..	2	..	45	..	2	Sao Tomé-et-Principe
Sierra Leone	2049	1834	50	68	31	60	2	7	6	10	Sierra Leone
Somalia	2054	2059	60	58	45	44	20	22	5	5	Somalie
Sudan	2319	2003	100	100 [a]	63	73 [a]	31	31 [a]	0	..	Soudan
Togo	2217	2202	70	100	24	31	31	41	10	9	Togo
Tuvalu	..	..	..	100	100	81	..	100	80	73	Tuvalu
Uganda	2169	2291	45	37	40	32	8	18	10	30	Ouganda
Un. Rep. of Tanzania	2427	2314	..	90	..	93	..	42	..	58	Rép. Unie de Tanzanie
Vanuatu	2403	2331	65	99	95	99	53	99	68	40	Vanuatu
Yemen	2197	2254	100	100	60	83	18	25	..	..	Yémen
All LDCs [b]	**2091**	**2035**	**47**	**50**	**36**	**44**	**27**	**32**	**9**	**16**	**Ensemble des PMA [b]**
All developing countries [b]	**2350**	**2375**	**72**	**74**	**50**	**57**	**32**	**42**	**11**	**15**	**Ensemble des pays en développement [b]**

Source: FAO, *Production Yearbook 1986 (Vol.40)*; FAO, *The State of Food and Agriculture 1985 and 1986*; WHO, *The International Drinking Water Supply and Sanitation Decade: Review of National Progress* (as at December 1985).

a Year other than 1985.

b Average of countries for which data are available.

c 1978-1980.

Source: FAO, *Annuaire de la production 1986 (vol.40)*; FAO, *La situation mondiale de l'alimentation et de l'agriculture 1985 et 1986*; OMS, *The International Drinking Water Supply and Sanitation Decade: Review of National Progress* (as at December 1985).

a Année autre que 1985.

b Moyenne des pays pour lesquels les données sont disponibles.

c 1978-1980.

54E. Education and literacy

54E. Enseignement et alphabétisme

Country	*Adult literacy rate / Taux d'alphabétisme (adultes) (%)*			*School enrolment ratio (% of relevant age group) / Taux d'inscription scolaire (en % du groupe d'âge pertinent)* — *Primary / Primaire*						*Secondary / Secondaire*						Pays
	1985			*1980*			*1985*			*1980*			*1985*			
	M	*F*	*T*	*M*	*F*	*T*	*M*	*F*	*T*	*M*	*F*	*T*	*M*	*F*	*T*	
Afghanistan	39	8	24	54	12	34	24	11	18	16	4	10	10	5	8	Afghanistan
Bangladesh	43	22	33	76	46	62	70	50	60	26	9	18	26	10	18	Bangladesh
Benin	37	16	26	88	40	64	87	43	65	24	9	16	29 [b]	12 [b]	20 [b]	Bénin
Bhutan	..	..	..	..	..	15	32	18	25	..	..	..	6	1	4	Bhoutan
Botswana	73	69	71	82	100	91	98	109	104	18	21	19	7	1	9	Botswana
Burkina Faso	21	6	13	26	15	21	41	24	32	4	2	3	7	3	5	Burkina Faso
Burma	..	..	..	..	..	91	..	..	102 [c]	..	..	22	..	..	24 [c]	Birmanie
Burundi	43 [d]	26 [d]	34 [d]	35	22	29	61	44	53	5	2	3	5	3	4	Burundi
Cape Verde	61	39	47	117	108	112	111	105	118	9	7	8	14	11	13	Cap-Vert
Central African Rep.	53	29	40	93	51	71	..	..	73	21	7	14	..	..	13	Rép. centrafricaine
Chad	(40)	(11)	(25)	..	..	..	55 [b]	21 [b]	38 [b]	..	..	..	11 [b]	2 [b]	6 [b]	Tchad
Comoros	56 [f]	40 [f]	45 [f]	109	78	93	..	..	..	31	16	24	..	..	..	Comores
Democratic Yemen	59	25	41	93	36	65	96 [c]	35 [c]	66 [c]	25	11	18	26 [c]	11 [c]	19 [c]	Yémen démocratique
Djibouti	..	..	..	..	..	..	..	..	..	..	..	..	..	..	..	Djibouti
Equatorial Guinea	..	..	37 [f]	..	..	84	..	..	108 [c]	..	..	..	..	..	..	Guinée équatoriale
Ethiopia	..	..	55 [c]	46	25	35	44	28	36	11	6	9	14	9	12	Ethiopie
Gambia	(36)	(15)	(25)	68	36	52	92	58	75	19	8	13	29	12	20	Gambie
Guinea	(40)	(17)	(28)	42	21	31	42	19	30	21	8	14	18	6	12	Guinée
Guinea-Bissau	46	17	31	95	41	67	81 [b]	40 [b]	60 [b]	10	2	6	18 [b]	4 [b]	11 [b]	Guinée-Bissau
Haiti	40	35	38	72	62	67	83 [b]	72 [b]	78 [b]	13	12	12	19 [b]	17 [b]	18 [b]	Haïti
Kiribati	..	..	..	..	..	..	..	..	..	..	..	..	..	..	..	Kiribati
Lao People's Dem. Rep.	92 [g]	76 [g]	84 [g]	102	86	94	101 [b]	79 [b]	91 [b]	21	14	18	23 [b]	15 [b]	19 [b]	Rép.dém.populaire lao
Lesotho	(62)	(84)	(74)	85	120	102	102	127	116	14	20	17	18 [b]	26 [b]	22 [b]	Lesotho
Malawi	(52)	(31)	(41)	74	49	61	71 [b]	53 [b]	62 [b]	5	2	4	6 [b]	2 [b]	4 [b]	Malawi
Maldives	..	..	..	..	..	..	..	..	..	..	..	..	..	..	..	Maldives
Mali	23	11	17	32	18	25	29 [c]	17 [c]	23 [c]	12	5	8	10 [c]	4 [c]	7 [c]	Mali
Mauritania	..	..	..	44	24	34	45 [d]	29 [d]	37 [d]	16	4	10	19 [d]	6 [d]	12 [d]	Mauritanie
Nepal	39	12	26	115	48	83	104 [b]	47 [b]	79	33	9	21	35 [b]	11 [b]	25	Népal
Niger	(19)	(9)	(14)	35	19	27	37 [e]	20 [e]	29 [e]	7	3	5	9	3	6	Niger
Rwanda	61	33	47	66	60	63	66	63	64	2	1	2	3	2	2	Rwanda
Samoa	..	..	..	..	..	..	..	..	..	..	..	..	..	..	..	Samoa
Sao Tome & Principe	73 [h]	42 [h]	57 [h]	..	..	..	..	..	..	..	..	..	..	..	..	Sao Tomé-et-Principe
Sierra Leone	(38)	(21)	(29)	64	45	54	68 [d]	48 [d]	58 [d]	20	8	14	23 [d]	11 [d]	17 [d]	Sierra Leone
Somalia	(18)	(6)	(12)	43	24	34	32 [c]	18 [c]	25 [c]	19	7	13	23 [c]	12 [c]	17 [c]	Somalie
Sudan	..	..	..	59	41	50	58 [b]	41 [b]	49 [b]	20	12	16	22 [b]	17 [b]	19 [b]	Soudan
Togo	53	28	41	150	93	122	118	73	95	..	..	34	33	10	21	Togo
Tuvalu	..	..	..	..	..	..	..	..	..	..	..	..	..	..	..	Tuvalu
Uganda	(70)	(45)	(57)	56	43	50	66 [d]	50 [d]	58 [d]	7	3	5	11 [d]	5 [d]	8 [d]	Ouganda
Un. Rep. of Tanzania	..	..	..	100	86	93	..	..	72	4	2	3	..	..	3	Rép.-Unie de Tanzanie
Vanuatu	..	..	..	..	..	..	..	..	..	..	..	..	..	..	..	Vanuatu
Yemen	(27)	(3)	(14)	80	12	46	112 [c]	22 [c]	67 [c]	8	1	5	17 [c]	3 [c]	10 [c]	Yémen
All LDCs [a]	**43**	**21**	**32**	**69**	**42**	**56**	**68**	**48**	**58**	**18**	**7**	**13**	**19**	**10**	**15**	**Ensemble des PMA [a]**
All developing countries [a]	**67**	**49**	**58**	**93**	**74**	**84**	**97**	**77**	**87**	**38**	**25**	**31**	**44**	**30**	**37**	**Ensemble des pays en développement [a]**

Source: UNESCO, Office of Statistics and *Statistical Yearbook 1987*; World Bank, *Social Indicators of Development 1988.*

a Average of countries for which data are available.

b 1984.

c 1983.

d 1982.

e 1986.

f 1980.

g Age group 15-45.

h 1981.

Source: UNESCO, Office des Statistiques et *Annuaire statistique 1987*; Banque Mondiale, *Social Indicators of Development 1988.*

a Moyenne des pays pour lesquels les données sont disponibles.

b 1984.

c 1983.

d 1982.

e 1986.

f 1980.

g Groupe d'âge 15-45.

h 1981.

54F. Communications and media / 54F. Communications et médias

Country	*Post offices open to the public per 100,000 inhabitants / Bureaux de poste ouverts au public pour 100,000 habitants* — *Total* 1980	1986	*of which: urban / dont: urbains* 1980	1986	*Telephones per 1000 inhabitants / Téléphones pour 1000 habitants* 1980	1986	*Radio receivers per 1000 inhabitants / Postes récepteurs de radio pour 1000 habitants* 1980	1985	*Circulation of daily newspapers per 1000 inhabitants / Tirage de journaux quotidiens pour 1000 habitants* 1979	1984	Pays
Afghanistan	..	..	..	..	2.0	2.0 [j]	75	83	4.4	3.7	Afghanistan
Bangladesh	8.2	7.6	0.7	0.7	1.1	1.4 [e]	8	41	4.7	5.6	Bangladesh
Benin	..	4.3	..	1.5	4.9 [g]	3.7	66	74	0.3	0.3	Bénin
Bhutan	6.3	..	..	..	..	1.3 [b]	5	14	..	..	Bhoutan
Botswana	6.3	13.0	1.3	1.1	13.3 [h]	18.6	94	126	19.3	16.8	Botswana
Burkina Faso	1.2	3.1 [b]	0.6	1.0 [b]	1.5 [g]	2.3	18	21	0.3	0.3	Burkina Faso
Burma	3.3	3.0 [b]	1.8	1.7 [b]	1.1 [h]	1.4 [e]	23	81	10.0	14.0	Birmanie
Burundi	0.4 [c]	0.4 [b]	0.0 [c]	0.1 [b]	1.3 [d]	1.6	37	53	..	..	Burundi
Cape Verde	18.7 [c]	17.2	7.1 [c]	6.4	5.7 [f]	7.3 [e]	139	150	..	..	Cap-Vert
Central African Rep.	3.0 [d]	2.8	0.2 [d]	0.3	2.1 [f]	2.7 [b]	52	58	..	..	Rép. Centrafricaine
Chad	0.5 [d]	0.6	0.1 [d]	0.5	1.5 [i]	0.9	167	219	..	0.2	Tchad
Comoros	..	..	..	..	5.0 [g]	5.8 [e]	101	113	..	..	Comores
Democratic Yemen	4.6	4.7	1.5	2.0	..	10.9 [e]	60	65	6.3	5.4	Yémen démocratique
Djibouti	1.6	1.5 [e]	0.3	0.5 [e]	16.8	18.1	68	70	..	..	Djibouti
Equatorial Guinea	4.6 [c]	4.7	4.1 [c]	4.5	..	3.7 [e]	284	255	..	2.7 [c]	Guinée équatoriale
Ethiopia	1.1 [f]	1.1	0.1 [f]	0.3	2.3	2.9 [j]	80	185	1.4	0.9	Ethiopie
Gambia	..	..	..	..	5.4 [h]	4.7 [b]	115	140	..	2.8	Gambie
Guinea	..	1.1 [e]	..	0.7 [e]	1.9 [i]	1.8 [e]	25	30	3.8	2.2	Guinée
Guinea-Bissau	..	..	..	..	..	5.9 [e]	31	34	7.8	6.9	Guinée-Bissau
Haiti	..	..	..	..	..	7.9 [j]	21	27	6.6	7.5	Haïti
Kiribati	42.4	..	6.8	..	12.3	17.4 [b]	203	200	..	..	Kiribati
Lao People's Dem. Rep.	2.1	..	2.0	..	2.1 [i]	2.2 [b]	107	119	..	..	Rép.dém.populaire lao
Lesotho	9.2	8.2	0.8	1.1	..	10.3	22	28	24.5	29.9	Lesotho
Malawi	3.9	3.8 [b]	0.6	0.5 [b]	5.2	6.2	46	245	..	5.5	Malawi
Maldives	5.8	14.3 [b]	1.3	1.7 [b]	6.8	14.2 [j]	45	104	..	5.7	Maldives
Mali	1.8 [c]	1.5	1.1 [c]	1.1	..	1.4 [j]	15	16	..	0.5	Mali
Mauritania	3.7	..	1.3	..	2.5 [c]	2.7 [e]	92	132	..	..	Mauritanie
Nepal	9.6	11.7 [b]	..	..	1.0 [g]	1.2 [e]	20	30	..	3.0	Népal
Niger	2.6	4.0	0.4	0.7	1.6	1.8 [j]	47	49	..	0.8	Niger
Rwanda	..	0.4	..	0.2	0.9	1.5	29	58	..	0.1	Rwanda
Samoa	..	28.8 [b]	..	2.4 [b]	36.9	38.0 [e]	205	429	..	..	Samoa
Sao Tome and Principe	55.9 [d]	52.8 [b]	14.7 [d]	14.8 [b]	15.1 [f]	24.8 [j]	245	241	..	..	Sao Tomé-et-Principe
Sierra Leone	3.3 [c]	2.7 [b]	1.7 [c]	0.5 [b]	..	4.0 [j]	140	222	3.1	2.8	Sierra Leone
Somalia	..	..	..	..	..	1.1 [e]	24	37	..	..	Somalie
Sudan	4.0	3.6	1.4	1.2	3.4	3.6 [b]	187	251	..	5.0	Soudan
Togo	15.2	12.7	..	0.8	3.8	4.2 [e]	215	206	2.8	3.5	Togo
Tuvalu	..	112.5	..	12.5	..	18.0	..	250	..	..	Tuvalu
Uganda	..	2.3	..	..	3.6	3.7 [e]	23	22	1.6	1.7	Ouganda
Un. Rep. of Tanzania	3.2	3.2	..	..	5.0	4.9 [j]	27	90	10.4	4.7	Rép. Unie de Tanzanie
Vanuatu	5.3	..	1.8	..	23.2 [g]	24.0	202	229	..	..	Vanuatu
Yemen	1.8	1.7	1.5	1.1	..	6.4 [e]	16	19	..	..	Yémen
All LDCs [a]	**5.0**	**4.6**	**0.7**	**0.7**	**2.1**	**2.7**	**44**	**88**	**5.2**	**4.9**	**Ensemble des PMA** [a]
All developing countries [a]	**13.1**	**13.0**	**1.9**	**2.1**	**20.8**	**29.4**	**109**	**154**	**34.9**	**32.9**	**Ensemble des pays en développement** [a]

Source: UNESCO, *Statistical Yearbook 1987*; Universal Postal Union, *Statistique des services postaux 1980-1986*; ITU, *Yearbook of Common Carrier Telecommunication Statistics* (15th edition) and other international and national sources.

a Average of countries for which data are available.

b 1985. *c* 1982. *d* 1983.

e 1984. *f* 1981. *g* 1978.

h 1979. *i* 1977. *j* 1987.

Source: UNESCO, *Annuaire statistique 1987*; Union postale universelle, *Statistique des services postaux 1980-1986*; UIT, *Annuaire statistique des télécommunications du secteur public* (15e édition) et autres sources internationales et nationales.

a Moyenne des pays pour lesquels les données sont disponibles.

b 1985. *c* 1982. *d* 1983.

e 1984. *f* 1981. *g* 1978.

h 1979. *i* 1977. *j* 1987.

54G. Transport indicators 1986 (or latest year available)

54G. Indicateurs des transports 1986 (ou année disponible la plus récente)

Country	Road network/Réseau routier			Railways/Chemins de fer				Civil aviation/Aviation civile				Pays
	Total	Paved Pavé	Density Densité	Network Réseau	Density Densité	Freight Frêt	Passenger Passagers	Freight Frêt Total	Freight Frêt International	Passenger Passagers Total	Passenger Passagers International	
	km	%	km/1000 km^2	km	km/1000 km^2	mio.ton-km	mio.pass-km	thousand tons / milliers de tonnes	thousand tons / milliers de tonnes	thousands / milliers	thousands / milliers	
Afghanistan	18,752	15.0	28.8	..	..	..	..	9.9	9.5	174	65	Afghanistan
Bangladesh	8,516	63.5	59.1	2,888	20.1	813	6,031	24.5	..	1,205	820	Bangladesh
Benin	8,645	8.1	76.8	635	5.6	184	137	..	..	..	..	Bénin
Botswana	8,006	25.5	13.8	724	1.2	1,325 [f]	..	..	..	62	47	Botswana
Burkina Faso	11,150	11.7	40.7	517	1.9	..	..	7.6	7.5	112	85	Burkina Faso
Burma	23,067	17.1 [a]	34.1	3,137	4.6	561	3,739	..	..	422	47	Birmanie
Burundi	5,400	13.8	194.0	..	..	..	..	8.8	8.8	44	44	Burundi
Cape Verde	2,250	29.3	557.9	..	..	..	..	1.3	0.7	132	61	Cap-Vert
Central African Rep.	22,260	2.1	35.7	..	..	..	..	13.3	13.3	84	82	Rép. centrafricaine
Chad	31,000 [b]	0.8	24.1	..	..	..	..	..	..	..	..	Tchad
Comoros	302 [c]	17.9	135.1	..	..	..	..	..	..	..	..	Comores
Democratic Yemen	6,851	15.5	20.6	..	..	..	..	..	..	..	..	Yémen démocratique
Djibouti	2,895	10.4	124.8	106	4.6	..	..	8.4	8.4	126	112	Djibouti
Equatorial Guinea	1,326 [d]	38.3	47.3	..	..	..	..	..	..	..	..	Guinée équatoriale
Ethiopia	37,871	33.9 [a]	31.0	681	0.6	122	360	49.7	15.5	365	171	Ethiopie
Gambia	2,358	21.0	208.8	..	..	..	..	..	..	..	..	Gambie
Guinea	28,000	3.6	113.9	622	2.7	7	42	..	..	..	..	Guinée
Guinea-Bissau	2,500	16.0	69.2	..	..	..	..	0.3	0.3	21	21	Guinée-Bissau
Haiti	3,000	20.0	108.1	135	4.9	..	..	29.6	29.6	487	484	Haïti
Kiribati	640	..	879.1	..	..	..	..	..	..	..	..	Kiribati
Lao People's Dem.Rep.	12,983	17.3	54.8	..	..	..	..	..	..	..	..	Rép.dém.populaire lao
Lesotho	2,775	17.1	91.4	..	..	..	..	..	..	80	23	Lesotho
Malawi	12,192	21.9 [a]	102.9	763	6.4	99	121	6.2	4.7	301	158	Malawi
Mali	18,000	8.3	14.5	641	0.5	251	173	10.2	9.7	176	164	Mali
Mauritania	7,335	21.0	7.2	689	0.7	6,142	7	1.7	1.6	212	68	Mauritanie
Nepal	6,134	45.0	43.6	52	0.4	..	..	9.0	8.7	721	526	Népal
Niger	19,000	17.0	15.0	..	..	..	..	5.6	5.5	97	83	Niger
Rwanda	8,000	5.5 [e]	303.7	..	..	..	..	21.1	21.1	62	53	Rwanda
Samoa	1,800	14.4	635.8	..	..	..	..	..	..	..	..	Samoa
Sao Tome & Principe	380	65.8	394.2	..	..	..	..	..	..	..	..	Sao Tomé-et-Principe
Sierra Leone	7,800	16.7	108.7	84	1.2	..	..	2.0	2.0	98	98	Sierra Leone
Somalia	21,311	11.7	33.4	..	..	..	..	..	..	..	..	Somalie
Sudan	9,018	33.0	3.6	4,784	1.9	3,190	1,031	..	..	..	..	Soudan
Togo	7,850	19.1	138.2	570	10.0	16	105	4.1	4.1	256	255	Togo
Uganda	27,000	6.7	114.5	1,240	5.3	67	191	4.3	..	84	65	Ouganda
Un.Rep. of Tanzania	50,000	5.3	52.9	2,600	2.8	770	1,186	7.8	5.7	625	183	Rép.-Unie de Tanzanie
Vanuatu	900	..	73.8	..	..	..	..	..	..	..	..	Vanuatu
Yemen	3,354	68.4	17.2	..	..	..	..	14.2	13.7	590	431	Yémen

Source: ESCAP, *Statistical Yearbook for Asia and the Pacific 1986*; ECA, *African Statistical Yearbook 1984*; Economist Intelligence Unit, *Country Profile; The Far East and Australasia, The Middle East and North Africa, Africa South of the Sahara, South America, Central America and the Caribbean*, EUROPA Publications Limited 1988; *Railway Directory and Yearbook 1987; Jane's World Railway 1987/88*; ICAO, *Airport Traffic 1986*; and national sources.

a Percentage of main roads.

b There are 7000 km of laterite roads and 24000 km of dirt tracks.

c Secondary roads only.

d In addition there are 1356 km of dirt roads in the forestry areas of the mainland.

e Percentage of all weather roads.

f 1077 million ton-km in transit.

Source: ESCAP, *Annuaire statistique pour l'Asie et le Pacifique 1986*; CEA, *Annuaire statistique pour l'Afrique 1984*; Economist Intelligence Unit, Country Profile; *The Far East and Australasia, The Middle East and North Africa, Africa South of the Sahara, South America, Central America and the Caribbean*, EUROPA Publications Limited 1988; *Railway Directory and Yearbook 1987; Jane's World Railway 1987/88*; OACI, *Trafic d'aéroport 1986*; et sources nationales.

a Pourcentage de routes principales.

b Dont 7000 km de routes en terre battue et 24000 km de pistes cendrées.

c Routes secondaires seulement.

d De plus, on compte 1356 km dé chemins de terre dans les régions forestières du continent.

e Pourcentage de routes "toutes saisons".

f 1077 million de tonnes-km en transit.

54H. Energy / 54H. Energie

Country	Coal, oil, gas and electricity / Charbon, pétrole, gaz et électricité		Fuelwood, charcoal and bagasse / Bois de chauffage, charbon de bois et bagasse		Installed electricity capacity / Puissance électrique installée		Pays
	Consummption per capita in kg. of coal equivalent / Consommation par habitant en kg. équivalant en charbon				(kw./1000 inhabitants) / (kw./1000 habitants)		
	1981	*1986*	*1981*	*1986*	*1981*	*1986*	
Afghanistan	49	89	88	92	23	25	Afghanistan
Bangladesh	45	64	91	88	11	13	Bangladesh
Benin	50	50	343	345	4	4	Bénin
Bhutan	11	12	750	678	12	13	Bhoutan
Botswana	..	..	333	332	..	..	Botswana
Burkina Faso	31	29	313	310	8	8	Burkina Faso
Burma	68	85	142	144	20	15	Birmanie
Burundi	16	17	253	253	2	2	Burundi
Cape Verde	53	41	..	..	10	15	Cap-Vert
Central African Rep.	29	31	358	364	18	16	République centrafricaine
Chad	22	19	206	206	7	6	Tchad
Comoros	45	40	..	..	8	6	Comores
Democratic Yemen	572	651	42	41	64	68	Yémen démocratique
Djibouti	284	228	..	..	108	88	Djibouti
Equatorial Guinea	83	95	397	372	14	12	Guinée équatoriale
Ethiopia	18	19	237	279	9	7	Ethiopie
Gambia	113	97	455	360	17	14	Gambie
Guinea	75	77	189	200	30	28	Guinée
Guinea-Bissau	42	44	171	155	8	8	Guinée-Bissau
Haiti	67	62	351	368	25	27	Haïti
Kiribati	167	136	..	..	33	30	Kiribati
Lao People's Dem. Rep.	38	35	348	351	52	61	Rép. dém. pop. lao
Lesotho	..	..	115	114	..	..	Lesotho
Malawi	52	41	301	299	24	22	Malawi
Maldives	112	203	..	..	19	21	Maldives
Mali	25	24	190	191	11	10	Mali
Mauritania	169	142	1	1	31	27	Mauritanie
Nepal	17	26	309	304	5	11	Népal
Niger	70	52	200	200	7	10	Niger
Rwanda	33	32	295	300	11	10	Rwanda
Samoa	327	348	167	152	109	104	Samoa
Sao Tome & Principe	175	155	..	..	52	55	Sao Tomé-et-Principe
Sierra Leone	95	69	706	707	32	30	Sierra Leone
Somalia	103	92	278	273	10	11	Somalie
Sudan	85	67	284	294	16	21	Soudan
Togo	64	57	68	68	12	11	Togo
Tuvalu	..	..	..	..	..	..	Tuvalu
Uganda	24	27	234	235	12	10	Ouganda
Un. Rep. of Tanzania	46	38	327	328	22	19	Rép. Unie de Tanzanie
Vanuatu	212	207	68	59	85	81	Vanuatu
Yemen	87	147	..	..	14	15	Yémen
All LDCs	**51**	**59**	**202**	**206**	**14**	**16**	**Ensemble des PMA**
All developing countries	**493**	**533**	**178**	**177**	**119**	**147**	**Ensemble des pays en développpement**

Source: United Nations, *Energy Statistics Yearbook 1984* and *1986*.

Source: Nations Unies, *Annuaire des statistiques de l'énergie 1984* et *1986*.